HANDBOOK ON GOVERNANCE AND DATA SCIENCE

ELGAR HANDBOOKS IN PUBLIC ADMINISTRATION AND MANAGEMENT

This series provides a comprehensive overview of recent research in all matters relating to public administration and management, serving as a definitive guide to the field. Covering a wide range of research areas including national and international methods of public administration, theories of public administration and management, and technological developments in public administration and management, the series produces influential works of lasting significance. Each *Handbook* will consist of original contributions by preeminent authors, selected by an esteemed editor internationally recognized as a leading scholar within the field. Taking an international approach, these *Handbooks* serve as an essential reference point for all students of public administration and management, emphasizing both the expansion of current debates, and an indication of the likely research agendas for the future.

For a full list of Edward Elgar published titles, including the titles in this series, visit our website at www.e-elgar.com.

Handbook on Governance and Data Science

Edited by

Sarah Giest

Professor of Public Policy, Innovation, and Sustainability, Institute of Public Administration, Leiden University, the Netherlands

Bram Klievink

Professor of Public Policy and Digitization, Institute of Public Administration, Leiden University, the Netherlands

Alex Ingrams

Assistant Professor of Public Administration, Institute of Public Administration, Leiden University, the Netherlands

Matthew M. Young

Assistant Professor of Public Administration, Institute of Public Administration, Leiden University, the Netherlands

ELGAR HANDBOOKS IN PUBLIC ADMINISTRATION AND MANAGEMENT

Edward Elgar
PUBLISHING

Cheltenham, UK • Northampton, MA, USA

© The Editors and Contributors Severally 2025

All rights reserved. No part of this publication may be reproduced, stored in a retrieval system or transmitted in any form or by any means, electronic, mechanical or photocopying, recording, or otherwise without the prior permission of the publisher.

Published by
Edward Elgar Publishing Limited
The Lypiatts
15 Lansdown Road
Cheltenham
Glos GL50 2JA
UK

Edward Elgar Publishing, Inc.
William Pratt House
9 Dewey Court
Northampton
Massachusetts 01060
USA

A catalogue record for this book
is available from the British Library

Library of Congress Control Number: 2024950680

This book is available electronically in the Elgaronline
Political Science and Public Policy subject collection
https://doi.org/10.4337/9781035301348

ISBN 978 1 0353 0133 1 (cased)
ISBN 978 1 0353 0134 8 (eBook)

Printed and bound by CPI Group (UK) Ltd, Croydon, CR0 4YY

Contents

List of contributors   vii

1   Introduction to the *Handbook on Governance and Data Science*   1
    Sarah Giest, Bram Klievink, Alex Ingrams and Matthew M. Young

PART I   DATA APPLICATIONS FOR POLICY CHALLENGES

2   Does it hold up? Testing big data's promise of novel information on labour market policymaking   14
    Simon Vydra

3   Data science meets political economy: applications to legislative favouritism around the world   41
    Cyril Benoît, Dominik Brenner and Mihály Fazekas

4   Data science from a national statistics institute perspective: limits and challenges illustrated by historical events   59
    Koen van 't Boveneind, Darius Keijdener, Pedro Lemlijn, Jolien Oomens and Eveline Vandewal

5   Soft OR, Big Data: use and limitations in policy-making   75
    Michael Howlett, Leong Ching and Tay Swee Kiat

6   Data and digitalization in energy efficiency policy design: the case of Singapore   93
    Ishani Mukherjee and Diandrea Ho

7   Examining the cost of living crisis: insights from e-petitions and constituency groupings   109
    Stephen D. Clark and Nik Lomax

8   Platform-based coordination for cross-agency collaboration in public service production   124
    Yiwei Gong and Marijn Janssen

9   Implementing social media monitoring in the public sector: a four-model approach   141
    Julián Villodre

10   Towards a framework for data science governance in the post-pandemic context: an analysis of three initiatives   158
    Rodrigo Sandoval-Almazan and David Valle-Cruz

PART II AI GOVERNANCE AND INNOVATION

11 Key challenges for the participatory governance of AI in public administration 179
Janis Wong, Deborah Morgan, Vincent J. Straub, Youmna Hashem and Jonathan Bright

12 Artificial intelligence and governance challenges in Latin America – the game between decolonization and dependence 198
Fernando Filgueiras

13 Proactive algorithmic transparency in government: the case of the Colombian repositories of public algorithms 222
Juan David Gutiérrez and Sarah Muñoz-Cadena

14 Decoding the privacy puzzle: a study on AI deployment in public governance 239
Jose Ramon Saura, Belem Barbosa and Sudhir Rana

PART III RESPONSIBLE AND PARTICIPATORY DATA USE BY GOVERNMENT

15 Intersecting digital governance and data science: preparing for communication to strengthen citizen-government partnerships 265
Jae-Seong Lee

16 Delivering on transparency's good governance promise? The state of government data against political corruption 282
Kristen Rose and Joseph Foti

17 System update: emerging transparency and oversight functions for responsible data use 298
Joseph Foti, Tara Davis and Divij Joshi

18 Classificatory versus transformative data regimes: towards a positive right to data production and analysis 316
Willie Gin

19 The Janus face of personal data agency in public and private use applications 332
Dale Mineshima-Lowe, Roxana Bratu and Sarah Giest

20 A social capital perspective to building sustainable data centers for science 346
Federica Fusi and Eric W. Welch

21 Public sector innovation labs as an approach to data-driven innovation 365
Francesco Leoni

22 Conclusion, research agenda, and policy recommendations for governance and data science 379
Bram Klievink and Sarah Giest

Index 385

Contributors

Belem Barbosa received her PhD in Business and Management Studies – Specialization in Marketing and Strategy from the University of Porto, Portugal. She is Assistant Professor at the School of Economics and Management of the University of Porto, full researcher at the Center for Economics and Finance at U.Porto (CEF.UP), and collaborator researcher at the Institute for Systems and Computer Engineering, Technology and Science (INESC TEC/LIAAD). Her main research interests include digital marketing and sustainability marketing.

Cyril Benoît is a CNRS researcher (Associate Research Professor) at the Centre for European Studies and Comparative Politics, Sciences Po, France. His research interests lie broadly in comparative political economy, with a focus on regulatory politics, business power, and distributive politics in and through legislative institutions. His ongoing research projects address the transformation of coordinated capitalism, the political control of regulatory agencies, and the political economy of legislative favouritism. He received his PhD in Political Science from Sciences Po Bordeaux.

Roxana Bratu is Senior Lecturer in Public Policy at the International School for Government, King's College London, UK. She holds a PhD in Sociology from the London School of Economics and Political Sciences. Her research interests and publications focus on anti-corruption public policies and practices, narratives of corruption and development, digitalization and its impact on (anti-)corruption, and artificial intelligence public policies and regulations.

Dominik Brenner is a Postdoctoral Fellow at Central European University (CEU), Department of Public Policy, Vienna, Austria. He received his PhD in Political Economy from CEU and is currently supporting the Global Corruption Observatory in the collection of novel legislative data and the development of legislative favouritism indicators. Dominik's research interests include legislative politics, the political economy of finance, and text-as-data methods

Jonathan Bright is a Fellow at the Turing Institute, UK, where he leads teams researching the use of artificial intelligence (AI) for Public Services and understanding Online Safety. Before joining the Turing Institute, he was Associate Professor at the Oxford Internet Institute. He is a widely published author in the area of government digitalization, artificial intelligence and online harms and safety. He is a former editor of the journal Policy & Internet.

Leong Ching is Vice Provost (Student Life) at the National University of Singapore and Associate Professor at its Lee Kuan Yew School of Public Policy. She works on water institutions and environmental collective action problems. Her research explores institutional change dynamics, and has investigated policies such as water privatization, recycled drinking water, and, more recently, willingness to accept vaccines and honesty in public behaviours.

Stephen D. Clark is a Research Fellow in the Consumer Data Research Centre at the University of Leeds, UK. Whilst having a background in transport planning, he has recently conducted research in the fields of health, consumption, housing, and politics.

Tara Davis is a researcher and practising attorney based in South Africa. She holds a BA degree from Rhodes University, an LLB from the University of Cape Town and an LLM (Information and Communications Law) from the University of the Witswatersrand. Her practice focuses on information rights – with a particular interest in data protection and the rights to privacy and access to information.

Mihály Fazekas is Associate Professor at the Central European University, Department of Public Policy, Vienna, Austria, with a focus on using Big Data methods to understand the quality of government globally. He is also the scientific director of an innovative think-tank, the Government Transparency Institute. He has a PhD from the University of Cambridge where he pioneered Big Data methods to measure and understand high-level corruption in Central and Eastern Europe. His research and policy interests revolve around corruption, favouritism, private sector collusion, and government spending efficiency. Mihály regularly consults international organizations such as the Organisation for Economic Co-operation and Development (OECD) and a range of national governments and non-governmental organizations (NGOs) across the globe. He led a team of FCDO UK, GTI, and the International Monetary Fund (IMF) which won the 1st prize at the IMF Anti-Corruption Challenge for measuring corruption and its costs globally.

Fernando Filgueiras is Associate Professor at the Federal University of Goiás (UFG), Brazil, Professor of the PhD in Public Policy at the National School of Public Administration (ENAP), a researcher at the National Council for Scientific and Technological Development (CNPq) and at the National Institute of Science and Technology – Quality of Government.

Joseph Foti is Principal Advisor for Emerging Issues at the Open Government Partnership (OGP). Prior to this role, he served as the Chief Research Officer and the Director of OGP's Independent Reporting Mechanism. He has published on a variety of topics including emerging technology, sustainable development, and fiscal policy.

Federica Fusi is Assistant Professor at the Department of Public Policy, Management, and Analytics at the University of Illinois Chicago, USA. Her research focuses on how public organizations leverage digital and data analytical tools to enhance their performance and improve outcomes for their communities. She also investigates the managerial challenges associated with the implementation of government and science open data portals. Federica's current research examines open government data, data sharing during COVID-19, and digital equity plans in US cities.

Sarah Giest is Professor and Chair of Public Policy with a focus on Innovation and Sustainability at the Public Administration Institute, Leiden University, the Netherlands. She has been developing an interdisciplinary research agenda on technical, environmental, and social solutions that shape sustainable societies through a policy lens. With expertise in Public Policy and Science, Technology, and Society (STS) Studies, Sarah has extensively published and is recognized as an expert by international organizations. She authored *The Capacity to Innovate* (University of Toronto Press, 2021), contributing to the discourse around innovation policy.

Willie Gin is Associate Professor of Political Science at Sonoma State University, USA. He specializes in racial and ethnic politics and is the author of a comparative study of minorities, *Minorities and Reconstructive Coalitions: The Catholic Question* (Routledge, 2017). He has devoted attention to technology and politics issues to see how they intersect with issues of identity and inequality in data analytics, and is the author of *Big Data and Labor: What Baseball Can Tell Us about Information and Inequality* (2018).

Yiwei Gong is Full Professor at the School of Information Management at Wuhan University, China. He serves as an editorial board member of *Government Information Quarterly* (GIQ), *International Journal of Information Management* (IJIM), and *Journal of Theoretical and Applied Electronic Commerce* (JTAER). His research interests include digital transformation, enterprise architecture, digital government, digital strategy, and data management. Personal Homepage: http://jszy.whu.edu.cn/yiweigong/en/index.htm.

Juan David Gutiérrez is Associate Professor at the School of Government of Universidad de los Andes, Colombia. He teaches and investigates public policy, public management, and artificial intelligence. He holds a PhD in Public Policy and an MSc in Public Policy from the University of Oxford. Juan David is a member of the Group of Experts of the Global Partnership on Artificial Intelligence (GPAI), where he leads the Algorithmic Transparency in Public Sector Project.

Youmna Hashem is a researcher at The Alan Turing Institute, UK, where she is working across the AI for Public Services team and Ethics and Responsible Innovation team to help shape the robust and responsible adoption of artificial intelligence in the public sector. At the Turing Institute, her research explores how and where the public sector engages with emerging technologies, with the aim of developing governance and policy strategies that are responsive to the differential impacts artificial intelligence is having across domains.

Diandrea Ho is an expert consultant on data analytics in the sustainability, infrastructure, and green finance sectors.

Michael Howlett is Burnaby Mountain Professor and Canada Research Chair (Tier 1) in the Department of Political Science at Simon Fraser University, Canada. He specializes in public policy analysis, political economy, and resource and environmental policy. His articles have been published in many professional journals in Canada, the United States, Europe, Latin America, Asia, and Australia and New Zealand. Michael currently edits the *Annual Review of Policy Design*, *Policy Sciences*, *Policy Design and Practice*, *Journal of Comparative Policy Analysis,* and *Policy & Society*, as well as the University of Toronto Press Series in Comparative Political Economy and Public Policy, the Policy Press International Library of Policy Analysis, Cambridge Studies in Comparative Public Policy, and Cambridge Elements of Public Policy. He is the founder of Research Committee 30 (Comparative Public Policy) of the International Political Science Association and sits on the Executive Committee of the International Public Policy Association. His most recent book is *Designing Public Policies: Principles and Instruments* (Routledge, 2024).

Alex Ingrams is Assistant Professor at the Institute of Public Administration, Leiden University, the Netherlands. His research addresses the impact of technology on public organizations, government transparency and good governance. In recent work on data science and governance, he addresses citizen perception of artificial intelligence for decision making in public services. He is the author of *Public Management in an Information Age* with Albert Meijer and Stavros Zouridis.

Marijn Janssen is Full Professor in ICT & Governance in the Technology, Policy and Management Faculty of Delft University of Technology, the Netherlands, and Head of the Engineering Systems & Services (ESS) department. Marijn's research is in the field of the governance of smart and open digital government, open data, and emerging technologies, like artificial intelligence, quantum computing and blockchain, which fundamentally change the organizational landscape and influence governance. More information: www.tbm.tudelft.nl/marijnj.

Divij Joshi is a lawyer and researcher studying the intersections of technology and society. He is a Doctoral researcher at the Faculty of Laws, University College London, UK, where his research examines the legal and political implications of emerging information technologies.

Darius Keijdener (PhD, Utrecht University in the field of Physics) is a statistical researcher at Statistics Netherlands, working on, amongst other things, on the Business Survey and several data science projects.

Tay Swee Kiat (SK) is a Research Fellow with the Lee Kuan Yew School of Public Policy at the National University of Singapore. His research focuses mainly on media psychology and media effects, such as motivated reasoning, selective exposure, and the impact of media exposure on individual attitudes and behaviours. His recent work is on behavioural public policy, examining the behavioural impact of public policy design and implementation.

Bram Klievink is Professor and Chair of Digitalisation and Public Policy at the Public Administration Institute at Leiden University, the Netherlands. He has a multi-disciplinary background with degrees in Information Technology, Political Science, and Technology and Public Administration. His research focuses on understanding the complexities of digital technologies in public policy and policy implementation.

Jae-Seong Lee completed his PhD in Science and Technology Policy at the University of Science and Technology in Korea. At the Korea Institute of Science and Technology Information (KISTI), a national research institute, he conducted research on artificial intelligence (AI)-based public service models using government information. Currently, he is associated in the Electronics and Telecommunications Research Institute (ETRI), a national research institute contributing to Korea's information and communications technology (ICT) strategy. His main research interests include digital governance, AI ethics, decision-support systems, and cybersecurity policy.

Pedro Lemlijn, holder of a Master's Degree in Information Management and Business Intelligence from Maastricht University, the Netherlands, currently serves as data analyst at Statistics Netherlands.

Francesco Leoni is a Postdoctoral Research Fellow in Politecnico di Milano's Design Department, Italy. He is a permanent research staff at the Design Policy Lab, a policy lab and research unit focused on "design for policy" (www.designpolicy.eu), and Polifactory, Politecnico's official makerspace and fab lab. He contributes to "design for policy", a subset of design research, by studying data-centric innovations in the public sector, their design, and their impact on policymaking. He is part of the Designing Policy Network.

Nik Lomax is Professor of Population Geography at the University of Leeds, UK, and a Fellow of the Alan Turing Institute, the UK's national institute for data science and artificial intelligence. His research interests and expertise include spatial demographic modelling and projection in applied contexts such as health and infrastructure development. Nik is Co-director of the ESRC-funded Consumer Data Research Centre which interfaces academia with business to provide insight from novel Smart Data.

Dale Mineshima-Lowe is currently Academic Co-Director for Environmental Education Projects, and Associate Lecturer in the School of Social Sciences at Birkbeck, University of London, UK. She is Visiting Faculty at Parami University (Myanmar), serves as Managing Editor for the Center of International Relations (USA), and was an OSUN-CLASP Fellow (2021– 23). Dale's current research examines the role and agency of bottom-up initiatives and their use in digital technologies for citizen engagement, in the areas of anti-corruption and in climate justice/environmentalism.

Deborah Morgan is a researcher in the AI for Public Services team at the Alan Turing Institute, UK. At the Turing Institute, her research is focused upon understanding the dimensions of responsible and effective adoption of artificial intelligence (AI) by government. She is also currently a PhD researcher within the Accountable, Responsible and Transparent AI CDT at the University of Bath with interests in AI regulation, governance, and digital policy.

Ishani Mukherjee is Associate Professor of Public Policy, Director of the Master of Sustainability (MST) at Singapore Management University (SMU). Her expertises include policy design for sustainable energy and natural resource management in Asia. Funding for this publication was generously supported by the Lee Kong Chian Fellowship.

Sarah Muñoz-Cadena holds a BSc in Political Science with a minor in Journalism, a BSc in Government and Public Affairs (both from Universidad de los Andes, Colombia), and a Master's in Economics of Public Policy (Universidad del Rosario, Colombia). Her research focuses on artificial intelligence implementation in the Colombian public sector, algorithmic transparency in the public sector, and design thinking. She is from Nariño, Colombia.

Jolien Oomens graduated cum laude at the University of Amsterdam, the Netherlands, with a Master's degree in Mathematics and worked as a data scientist at Statistics Netherlands for six years. She currently works at the Erasmus University Medical Center as a research software engineer.

Sudhir Rana is Associate Professor of Marketing and Strategy at the College of Healthcare Management and Economics, Gulf Medical University, UAE. His research papers are published in the *Journal of Knowledge Management*, *Journal of Business Research*, *Journal of Consumer Behaviour*, and *Journal of Strategic Marketing*, among others. He is the Editor-in-Chief of *FIIB Business Review* and Co-Editor-in-Chief of the *South Asian Journal of Marketing*. He is series editor of *Review of Management Literature*.

Kristen Rose is a research associate with the data & analytics team at the Open Government Partnership. She holds a Bachelor's degree in Public Policy from the University of Virginia's Frank Batten School of Leadership & Public Policy, USA, and she is currently pursuing a Master's degree in Data Science from the University of Virginia's School of Data Science. Kristen's professional interests lie at the intersection of anti-corruption, open data, and data science.

Rodrigo Sandoval-Almazan (PhD) is Associate Professor at the Political Sciences and Social Sciences Department in the Autonomous University of the State of Mexico. He holds the National Research Level II position in the Mexican National Research Science Ministry. He became a member of the Mexican Academy of Science in 2018. Rodrigo has authored or co-authored articles in top scholarly journals on the field of information technology and government. Since 2020, he has been leading the i-Lab Mexico. His research focuses on artificial intelligence in government, social media platforms for government, metrics for digital government, and open government.

Jose Ramon Saura is Vice-Dean of Research, Internationalization and Prof. Partnership in the Faculty of Business Economics (FCEE) at Rey Juan Carlos University, Spain. He is Associated Professor (Tenured) of Data Analytics and Digital Marketing in the Business Economics Department, Madrid. His research has primarily centred on the theoretical and practical implications of various dimensions of user-generated data and artificial intelligence. He has emphasized two pivotal research methodologies applied to government artificial intelligence (AI) deployment: privacy concerns and AI adoption.

Vincent Straub is a researcher and PhD student in the Leverhulme Centre for Demographic Science at the University of Oxford, UK, with interests in computational social science, artificial intelligence (AI) in government, and population health. Previously, he was a researcher in the AI for Public Services team at the Alan Turing Institute where his research is focused on the implications of bringing AI and machine learning into government and public service delivery.

David Valle-Cruz is Professor at the Unidad Académica Profesional Tianguistenco at the Universidad Autónoma del Estado de México. He holds a Bachelor's degree in Computer Engineering, a Master's degree in Computer Science, and a PhD in Economic-Administrative Sciences. David has undertaken research stays at the Center for Technology in Government (CTG), SUNY Albany, NY, and at the Computer Science and Multi-Agent Systems Laboratory of CINVESTAV, Guadalajara, Mexico. His publications appear in top journals such as *Government Information Quarterly*, *Cognitive Computation*, *International Review of Administrative Sciences*, and *Public Policy and Administration*. His research is related to artificial intelligence and data science for strategic decision making.

Koen van 't Boveneind, holder of a Master's degree in Economics and a Master's degree in Finance, both from VU University Amsterdam, the Netherlands, currently serves as a Researcher Business Cycles at Statistics Netherlands.

Eveline Vandewal (PhD, Maastricht University) is a statistical researcher at Statistics Netherlands, working predominantly on poverty statistics.

Julián Villodre is Assistant Professor at The Institute of Public Administration, Leiden University, the Netherlands. He is part of the The Hague Centre for Digital Governance. He is also a member of the Lab Research Group Innovation, Technology and Public Management (ITGesPub), Universidad Autónoma de Madrid (UAM). He holds a PhD in Law, Government and Public Policies from UAM. His research interests include digital government, open government, algorithmic governance, public sector transparency, and public communication.

Simon Vydra holds a PhD in Public Administration from TU Delft and Leiden, the Netherlands, and has previously worked at The Hague Centre for Digital Governance. His primary research interests are the (lack of) use of big data and artificial intelligence tools in public administrations and policymaking. Currently, Simon is Head of the Government Analytical Unit at the Office of the Government of the Czech Republic, working at the interface between research, data science, and policymaking.

Eric W. Welch is Professor at the School of Public Affairs at Arizona State University (ASU), USA, where he directs the Center for Science, Technology and Environmental Policy Studies (C-STEPS) and is a Senior Global Futures Scientist in ASU's Julie Ann Wrigley Global Futures Laboratory. He received his doctorate from the Syracuse University's Maxwell School of Citizenship and Public Affairs. His primary research interests include science and technology policy, data governance, climate adaptation, and advances in communication and information technologies.

Janis Wong is an independent researcher examining data governance through legal, sociotechnical, and policy lenses. She holds a Computer Science PhD from the University of St Andrews, UK, awarded best data protection thesis by the Council of Europe, and an LLB in Law from the London School of Economics. Currently, Janis is a Data and Technology Law Policy Advisor at the Law Society of England and Wales, leading on data, artificial intelligence, and technology to support the legal profession and justice.

Matthew M. Young is Assistant Professor of Public Administration at Leiden University, the Netherlands, and a fellow at Syracuse University's Autonomous Systems Policy Institute (ASPI) and the USC Civic Leadership Education and Research (CLEAR) Initiative. He studies technology and innovation, decision making, and service delivery in the public sector. He has given invited talks on his research to academic and practitioner audiences worldwide, including the United Nations, European Parliament, Korean Development Institute (KDI), and the US Association for Federal Enterprise Management.

1. Introduction to the *Handbook on Governance and Data Science*

Sarah Giest, Bram Klievink, Alex Ingrams and Matthew M. Young

OVERVIEW

This book is based on the idea that there are quite a few overlaps and connections between the field of governance studies and data science. Data science, with its focus on extracting insights from large datasets through sophisticated algorithms and analytics (Provost and Fawcett 2013), provides government with tools to potentially make more informed decisions, enhance service delivery, and foster transparency and accountability. Governance studies, concerned with the processes and structures through which public policy and services are formulated and delivered (Osborne 2006), increasingly rely on data-driven insights to address complex societal challenges, optimize resource allocation, and engage citizens more effectively (Meijer and Bolívar 2016). However, research insights in journals or at conferences remain quite separate, and thus there are limited spaces for having interconnected conversations. In addition, unprecedented societal challenges demand not only innovative solutions but new approaches to problem-solving.

In this context, data science techniques emerge as a crucial element in crafting a modern governance paradigm, offering predictive insights, revealing hidden patterns, and enabling real-time monitoring of public sentiment and service effectiveness, which are invaluable for public administrators (Kitchin 2014). However, the integration of data science into public governance also raises important considerations regarding data privacy, ethical use of data, and the need for transparency in algorithmic decision-making processes (Zuiderwijk and Janssen 2014). In short, this book is a space where governance and data science studies intersect and highlight relevant opportunities and challenges in this space at the intersection of both fields. Contributors to this book discuss *the types of data science techniques applied in a governance context and the implications these have for government decisions and services*. This also includes questions around *the types of data that are used in government and how certain processes and challenges are measured*.

GOVERNANCE AND DATA SCIENCE STUDIES

Data science, as defined by van der Aalst (2016), is "an interdisciplinary field aiming to turn data into real value." This data may be "structured or unstructured, big or small, static or streaming." It seeks to deliver value through a variety of outputs, including forecasts, autonomous decision-making, data-derived models, or insightful visualizations. The discipline encompasses a wide range of activities, such as gathering data, preparing and exploring it, transforming and storing it, as well as managing the computing infrastructure required for these tasks. It involves diverse methods of analysis and learning, presenting findings and forecasts, and leveraging these outcomes while considering ethical, societal, legal, and commercial implications (van der Aalst 2016). Thus, as Mannhardt (2022, 374) notes, "data science techniques are not limited to giving decision support to human decision makers but increasingly Artificial Intelligence (AI) is used to automate decisions based on predictive models."

Researchers in the field increasingly recognize that the growing reliance on data also escalates the chances of adverse outcomes resulting from its misuse, whether unintentional or deliberate. Misuse can vary widely, from violating individual privacy, conducting erroneous analyses due to low-quality data or unsuitable methods, to biased automated decisions made by systems trained on data that favor dominant groups. This possibility of misuse underscores the need for a conscientious approach to data handling, which includes fostering understanding and awareness of the potential harmful effects, as well as exploring both technical and socio-technical measures to avert such negative impacts (Mannhardt 2022).

Governance studies, on the other hand, refer to "a new process of governing; or a changed condition of ordered rule; or the new method by which society is governed" (Rhodes 2007, 1246). Scholars make a distinction between "governance in public administration and public policy, governance in international relations, European Union governance, governance in comparative politics, and good governance" (Rhodes 2007, 1246; Kjær 2004). In short, governance refers to governing with and through networks. This implies a focus on inter-organizational relationships and the governance of processes, as well as service effectiveness and outcomes (Osborne 2006).

Overall, governance studies aim to enhance the understanding of governance processes and institutions, inform policy and practice, and contribute to the promotion of good governance principles and outcomes. Under this conceptualization, public administrations serve as the operational units of governments, operating within a broader governance framework. This framework, which includes decision-making processes, prioritization of issues, and civic engagement, directs the actions of public administrations. The challenge for states lies in understanding how this governance structure might evolve with the integration of more data science techniques, since their adoption does not follow a universal blueprint, as evidenced by numerous unsuccessful endeavors highlighted by, for example, Bannister and Connolly (2012).

At the intersection of data science and governance studies is a dynamic field that leverages data science techniques to inform and enhance governance practices. Data science, with its collection of statistical, machine learning, and computational techniques, excels at dissecting large, complex datasets to reveal underlying patterns, trends, and insights. Governance studies delve into the mechanics of decision-making and policy implementation across various governance structures, aiming to improve accountability, efficiency, and public engagement. This nexus offers a powerful framework for governments to harness data-driven insights for more informed policymaking and efficient service delivery. It enables the exploration of vast governmental data to decipher decision-making processes, optimize resource distribution, and gauge policy impacts. Moreover, applying data science in governance can illuminate public sentiments through the analysis of digital footprints, enhancing responsiveness to citizen needs. However, this integration is not without its challenges. The deployment of advanced data analytics and artificial intelligence (AI) in governance raises critical ethical and accountability questions, necessitating a careful balance between innovation and the protection of public values. Thus, the intersection of data science and governance studies is not merely a technical endeavor but a collaborative pursuit that requires careful consideration of ethical standards, privacy concerns, and equitable access to the benefits of technology.

These aspects have especially been highlighted in the context of AI applications. AI refers to machines or computer systems performing tasks that typically need human intelligence, such as learning, problem-solving, and language comprehension. AI systems analyze data, adapt to new inputs, and refine their operations over time, enhancing decision-making and problem-solving capacities (Vogl et al. 2019; Young et al. 2019). In public administration, AI is recognized for its significant impact on socio-technical systems, potentially increasing the capacity for addressing social issues and improving the explainability of algorithmic decisions, thus enhancing bureaucratic and individual competencies. However, the integration of AI in public sectors prompts a debate on whether it represents an extension of e-government or introduces new challenges, with considerations about its potential to speed up tasks but also introduce new costs and complexities (Veale and Brass 2019). The digital transformation, influenced by AI, is seen as both potentially disruptive and a continuation of existing practices, with varied responses from citizens and institutions and differential impacts on social and economic disparities. The effectiveness and transformational impact of AI in public administration remain subjects of ongoing debate, with empirical studies often focusing on isolated instances and varying significantly across different national contexts.

Several of these concerns raised at the nexus of data science and governance studies are not new and have been highlighted in the context of evidence-based policymaking (EBP). This discussion links to the need for efficient and effective governance, which has resulted in a high demand for performance-related information, bolstering the role of data-based applications. However, as Head (2008) argues, there exists a significant gap between a narrowly focused, technical approach to knowledge and a more expansive, relational, and systemic knowledge approach that operates within networks involving multiple stakeholders. Head (2008) points towards the diversity of stakeholder evidence available to policymakers in different forms (political judgement, professional practices, scientific research) and the multitude of policy-relevant knowledge. In short, the idea that there are "several evidentiary bases" is combined with the fact that problems that policymakers face are increasingly complex, interlinked, and cutting across domains.

Relatedly, Wesselink et al. (2014) raise that point the "rhetoric of EBP implies that the nature and dimensions of the problem being addressed are known, measurable and unambiguous, and that appropriate monitoring will show the success of policy measures. However, … that this is rarely the case" (ibid., 340). They also raise an additional point, which is that evidence is presented or introduced by participants who add their own framing of the policy problem and thus "what is policy-relevant evidence is determined by context" (Wesselink et al. 2014, 342). These arguments all apply to the stakeholders in the decision-making process and those introducing evidence in the discourse on certain issues. Beyond this, there are also arguments that apply to individuals looking at the evidence. Studies in psychology suggest that there are also individual-level factors at play that are often summarized under the term "confirmation bias" when it comes to using evidence in policymaking. Confirmation bias is the tendency to cherry-pick information that confirms our existing beliefs or ideas. This means that individuals tend to take in data that confirms prior convictions and disregard data that does not conform to what they already believe. It is difficult to change people's beliefs, since this depends on (1) the old belief; (2) the confidence in that old belief; (3) the new piece of data; and (4) the confidence in that new piece of data. And the further away that piece of data is from what a person already believes, the less likely it is that the person changes their belief (Sunstein et al. 2017).

Questions have also been asked around the policy capacity of government to integrate data into policy processes at individual, organizational, and systemic levels and the types of capacities needed to do this effectively. This discussion has led to the development of a layered understanding of policy capacity, which is conceptualized as the essential skills and resources within the government required for executing policy-related tasks, as described by Wu et al. (2015). To dissect the various facets of policy capacity, it is categorized into analytical, operational, and political dimensions, each applicable at the individual, organizational, and systemic levels. Within this framework, capacities manifest in diverse forms such as the analytical capacity at the individual level, represented by technical expertise; operational capacity through entrepreneurial abilities; and political capacity via political savvy. At an organizational level, capacities are characterized by the ability to leverage external knowledge and data (analytical), the creation of cooperative frameworks (operational), and the garnering of support from political entities and stakeholders (political). At the systemic level, capacities extend to include the infrastructure for data gathering and analysis (analytical), the coordination and strategic planning across different government tiers (operational), and the cultivation of trust, legitimacy, and accountability within the political sphere (political).

In the wake of evolving policy capacity frameworks, discussions have increasingly emphasized the integration of big data analytics and the behavioral aspects of policymaking. Mukherjee et al. (2021) underscore the critical need for advanced competencies in leveraging software and models for generating policy-relevant insights, driven by the complexities introduced by big data. This has led to a call for enhancing big data readiness across the analytical, operational, and political dimensions of policy capacity (Clarke and Craft, 2017; Giest, 2017; Giest and Mukherjee, 2018; Klievink et al., 2017). A notable strategy in this context is to consider the accessibility of high-quality data as an indicator of capacity. This perspective has manifested in approaches that define capacity through the lens of "data availability," such as Riddell's (2007) emphasis on the "ready availability of quality data" or the concept of "statistical capacity," which encompasses the scope of statistical practices, data acquisition, and the availability of indicators, as highlighted by the World Bank (2020).

Building on these discussions, Verhulst et al. (2019) highlight challenges and considerations in the integration of data and data science within policymaking. A primary concern is the limited understanding among policymakers of the potential and value proposition of data, compounded by a general lack of trust in data handling, largely due to negative perceptions formed from private sector mismanagement. Moreover, a substantial amount of potentially useful governance data remains inaccessible, locked in private holdings or silos, and the technical capacities of officials to leverage data effectively are often lacking. Complicating these technical challenges is a deep conceptual and value gap between policy and technical communities, further hindered by infrequent interactions. The scarcity of evidence on the impact and utility of data in governance weakens the argument for increased data initiatives, while the debate between theory- and data-driven methods in policy and scientific knowledge generation continues, raising concerns about research traceability, the reliance on correlation over causation, and the amplification of biases. In essence, data science acts as a catalyst for innovation within public governance, driving advancements in policy analysis, urban planning, health care, and beyond. Yet, this relationship also necessitates ongoing dialogue between data scientists and public administrators to navigate the ethical and practical implications of deploying data-driven solutions in the public sector (Mergel et al. 2019).

These themes that emerge from those discussions are addressed from different perspectives in this book and set out in three different thematic parts. The first of these is "Data Applications for Policy Challenges." This part delves into the innovative interplay between governance and data science, highlighting the opportunities and challenges this fusion presents for institutions and policy areas. It emphasizes the potential of big data to illuminate complex societal issues and improve decision-making across various governance fields while also stressing the importance of institutional preparedness, methodological integrity, and ethical considerations. Contributors explore the role of digitalization and open data in enriching political research and enhancing policy effectiveness, advocating for an integrated approach that marries Soft Operational Research with big data for deeper stakeholder analysis. Moreover, it acknowledges the critical role of digital platforms in addressing contemporary challenges like the post-COVID-19 cost of living crisis and emphasizes the need for cohesive digital government platforms to support collaborative public services. Overall, contributors highlight the transformative promise of data science in governance, tempered by a call for careful navigation of its complexities.

The second theme that emerges is that of "AI Governance and Innovation." In this section, contributors explore how data-driven technologies, particularly AI, are being integrated into public sector governance across various global contexts, presenting both prospects and hurdles. The chapters address the broader implications of digital transformation, including its potential to improve public sector efficiency and innovation, while cautioning against issues like socio-economic disparities and misinformation. Special attention is given to the challenges faced by Latin America in leveraging AI for governance without compromising autonomy. Furthermore, the importance of ethical data governance and the need for transparency and privacy safeguards in AI applications are emphasized, advocating for legislative measures to ensure the responsible use of AI in government operations.

The third part, "Responsible and Participatory Data Use by Government," delves into the critical role of open and transparent data usage by governments and the essential participation of citizens in these processes. It highlights the intricate interplay between AI, data governance, and democratic oversight in public administration, stressing the importance of inclusive governance to maintain democratic control over AI technologies. The need for fairness, accountability, and transparency in integrating digital technologies into public services is emphasized, alongside the significance of open data in fostering transparent governance. The chapters also address the challenges posed by the misuse of data, advocating for regulatory frameworks that ensure both innovation and the protection of fundamental rights. Furthermore, scholars explore the concept of data agency, emphasizing citizens' control over their data, and discuss the sustainability of data centers, highlighting the role of community engagement in supporting data-driven innovation. This part calls for a balanced approach to the adoption of AI and digital technologies in governance, ensuring transparency, accountability, and equitable benefits. The book concludes with a research agenda for governance and data science that builds on the findings of each theme.

SYNOPSIS OF PART I: DATA APPLICATIONS FOR POLICY CHALLENGES

This part builds on the question of *where new insights at the intersection of governance and data science come from and what this means for institutions and different policy domains.* Its chapters explore the transformative potential of big data and data science in governance, policymaking, and public administration, while acknowledging challenges and limitations. A key theme is the capacity of big data to provide novel insights into complex societal issues, enhancing decision-making in domains like labor market governance and political accountability. Despite the enthusiasm, there is a cautionary note on the need for institutional readiness, methodological rigor, and ethical considerations in applying these technologies.

Simon Vydra explores and empirically tests if and how big data can provide novel information to policymaking in Chapter 2, "Does It Hold up? Testing Big Data's Promise of Novel Information on Labor Market Policymaking." Focusing on labor market policies, it is an empirically honest account of the differences that exist between data sources and their use for governance. The chapter makes four main contributions. First, it demonstrates how big data might enable new policy perspectives by providing the type and level of insight needed to make a shift to a new paradigm. Second, it develops an analytical instrument for this new paradigm by leveraging social media data to identify, interpret, and present topics that meet the analytical needs of the policy paradigm. Third, it reflects on why this does not generate policy-relevant insights, even though it is a likely-to-succeed case. This "non-finding" is an important caution against overly optimistic hopes for big data to solve analytical problems in policymaking. And fourth, by documenting the entire process so well, the chapter demonstrates that big data analysts unavoidably and perhaps unwittingly make many decisions and value trade-offs that may be consequential for the policies they mean to support.

In Chapter 3, "Data Science Meets Political Economy: Applications to Legislative Favouritism around the World," Cyril Benoît, Dominik Brenner, and Mihály Fazekas similarly provide a rich account of the potential role of data science. They focus on using large-scale legislative data in the study of political institutions. They employ this to illustrate how data science can be used as a tool for good governance. For a case, they look at legislative favoritism, which refers to legislation that disproportionally advantage specific private interests over others. This is a particularly challenging case as many of the stakeholders involved have an interest in hiding such behavior. One of the conclusions, therefore, speaks to making data science tools available to policy actors, journalists, and other actors that seek to identify and address corruption.

In Chapter 4, "Data Science from a National Statistics Institute Perspective: Limits and Challenges Illustrated by Historical Events," Koen van 't Boveneind, Darius Keijdener, Pedro Lemlijn, Jolien Oomens, Eveline Vandewal reflect on the current statistics agencies' paradigm based on sample surveys and population-wide censuses, the more recent increase in data availability, and the current opportunities that big data and machine learning offer to explore new sources and ways to produce official statistics. The chapter draws on the extensive experience of the authors, leading them to discuss a series of challenges that statisticians face when using big data for official statistics. They identify three categories of challenges (legal, technological, and societal) that may conflict and for which statistics agencies must find a balance. These limits and challenges are then illustrated through several key historical cases of official statistics. Using advances in data science in official statistics is not an easy process, and the chapter concludes by looking at how friction between 'traditional' statistics and data science occurs and what current and next steps are (to be) taken to further the integration between the two.

In Chapter 5, "Soft OR, Big Data: Use and Limitations in Policy-Making," Michael Howlett, Leong Ching, and Tay Swee Kiat study the intersection of big data and Soft Operational Research (OR). Their chapter shows how Soft OR can benefit greatly from more "data" in a big data sense, while big data can also be enhanced by fitting it better into Soft OR's stakeholder-driven problem structuring techniques. In their argument, they discuss the emergence of Soft OR as approaches that are better able to deal with complex or wicked problems and decision-making in comparison to "Hard OR," while still offering to structure problems. Based on this, they consider the data requirements of such structuring methods and seek to link them to the methods developed to analyze big data. Then they move on to discuss the relationship from the other end and assess not only the promises but also the problems of using big data in policymaking, and go on to argue for Soft OR techniques as remedies for the problems and limitations that the use of big data introduces. By having both angles meet eye-to-eye, they provide an intelligent account of a promising combination to better aid policymaking.

Ishani Mukherjee and Diandrea Ho are the authors of Chapter 6: "Data and Digitalization in Energy Efficiency Policy Design: The Case of Singapore." They focus on energy efficiency policy instruments and consider how digital tools and technologies play a key role therein. Digital tools help articulate policy goals and targets, but also aid in the formulation, implementation, and monitoring of energy efficiency policies' impacts. The chapter unpacks energy efficiency policy mixes and provides overviews of opportunities for and examples of the role and use of digital tools therein. The authors then discuss Singapore as a case, particularly of a land-scarce economy, which presents specific cases for utilizing digital data and tools to bridge the gaps between different energy policy goals that aren't easily reconciled. Illustrated by this case, the chapter identifies lessons about the role of data and digitalization for energy efficiency policy design.

In Chapter 7, "Examining the Cost of Living Crisis: Insights from E-Petitions and Constituency Groupings," Stephen Clark and Nik Lomax use topic models to analyze e-petitions in the context of a cost of living crisis. Governments have responded to the cost of living crisis and its effects on citizens in a reactive manner. To assess the effectiveness and impacts of these responses, e-petitions provide a mechanism for understanding public sentiments. The data gathered through such petitions can be analyzed and potentially put to use through topic modeling. The chapter presents such an analysis and reflects on the results this yields. The authors conclude by arguing that similar methodological approaches can be used to understand other concerns of the public and explore potential other uses for their methods.

Yiwei Gong and Marijn Janssen cover coordination mechanisms for digital platforms in Chapter 8, "Platform-Based Coordination for Cross-Agency Collaboration in Public Service Production." Platforms can support digital government services by enhancing access to data and data analytics. Yet, particularly in collaborative arrangements, digital platforms affect how actors work together and therefore present coordination challenges. The chapter conceptualizes both digital platforms and the coordination thereof. They present a theoretical framework, which they then illustrate by applying it in a demonstrative case study on a collaborative platform for service innovation in China. Ultimately, their framework speaks to platform transformation, and they identify three tensions that come with data and digital platform-based collaboration and that need to be addressed through coordination.

8   *Handbook on governance and data science*

In Chapter 9, "Implementing Social Media Monitoring in the Public Aector: A Four-Model Approach," Julián Villodre proposes four distinct but non-exclusive models of how governments can monitor social media activity. The performance-based model uses social media metrics as benchmarks for performance measurement and management of government communications and public relations activities. His opinion model envisions social media monitoring as a way for governments to dynamically assess citizen perspectives, satisfaction, and/or grievances in real time. A collaboration model frames social media monitoring to receive and solicit feedback on service provision, potentially enabling subsequent co-creation or co-productive activities. Finally, and perhaps most recognized in terms of government monitoring of online activities, his behavioral model captures governments' use of social media-based data to predict and/or "nudge" individual or group behaviors. The value of each model may differ across governments or over time, but may also overlap; multiple models can be employed simultaneously by the same public organization. The chapter also identifies critical challenges associated with each model: goal displacement for the performance model; non-representativeness for the opinion model; reliability and information quality for the collaboration model; and abuse of power and privacy violations for the behavioral model.

Rodrigo Sandoval-Almazan and David Valle-Cruz provide a multiple case study in Chapter 10, "Towards a Framework for Data Science Governance in the Post-Pandemic Context: An Analysis of Three Initiatives." They use the global COVID-19 pandemic spread by SARS-CoV-2 that began in 2020 as an inflection point for data governance across three initiatives: data-driven governance, strategies/initiatives for government data (e.g., the open data initiative), and public sector data ecosystems. Examples of each initiative are drawn from cases throughout the world. They find that the pandemic has made public sector underinvestment in data infrastructure – generation, storage, collection, and analysis – an obvious policy problem. They similarly identify critical shortcomings with respect to data literacy and analysis on the part of public sector labor forces, as well as governments' ability to design, deploy, and manage systems for generating and analyzing data in real time. This latter deficiency was particularly acute when governments were actively intervening to try to control disease spread, but remains relevant for monitoring both SARS-CoV-2 and the eventual next pandemic.

SYNOPSIS OF PART II: AI GOVERNANCE AND INNOVATION

In the part on AI governance and innovation, the chapters focus on *the challenges and opportunities of data-driven innovations and what these look like in different countries and contexts*. The chapters delve into the integration of digital tools and AI in public sector innovation and governance, highlighting both the opportunities and challenges this presents. Contributors also touch upon the digital transformation in the public sector, driven by rapid technological advances, and its implications for efficiency, service enhancement, and economic innovation while simultaneously underscoring the importance of robust data governance, ethical considerations, and international collaboration in managing and securing vast data volumes. Overall, contributors in this part highlight the transformative potential of AI technologies in public governance while emphasizing the need for careful consideration of ethical, transparency, and privacy issues to fully leverage these technologies for public benefit.

Chapter 11, "Key Challenges for the Participatory Governance of AI in Public Administration," by Janis Wong, Deborah Morgan, Vincent J. Straub, Youmna Hashem, and

Jonathan Bright, applies an institutional analysis and development (IAD)-based participatory governance framework to the study of how the process of public sector AI adoption can directly address issues of transparency, trust, and bias minimization. They draw upon prior applications of the IAD approach for modeling participatory processes for public sector data governance and identify five key elements for successful participatory AI governance: rules and frameworks; openness and access; actors; preference aggregation and elicitation; and intersections with more formal governance structures.

Fernando Filgueiras studies the tensions between decolonialism and dependence that arise from Latin American governments' use of AI in Chapter 12, "Artificial Intelligence and Governance Challenges in Latin America – the Game between Decolonization and dependence." He identifies structural imbalances in property rights for and access to system inputs (data), infrastructure and human capital for system design and development, and system maintenance and operations as risks for continuing or exacerbating Latin American dependency on the global north. At the same time, he argues that AI capabilities can be strategically utilized to help Latin American countries redesign existing and build new public sector capabilities that explicitly break with the colonialist logics embedded in the current status quo. For the latter possibility to manifest, he argues that focused investments in human capital and national regulatory frameworks are particularly essential.

Juan David Gutiérrez and Sarah Muñoz-Cadena leverage a unique empirical case in Chapter 13, "Proactive Algorithmic Transparency in Government: The Case of the Colombian Repositories of Public Algorithms." They study Colombia's national algorithm repository to examine how proactive, institutional approaches to transparency and accountability for data-intensive automated decision-making systems perform in practice. They find that the largest share of observed automated decision-making system adoptions are for economic affairs, followed by "general public services" and education. Their findings also center on the gaps in Colombia's repository, including under-registration of systems by ministries, bureaus, and other units; and incomplete information about the systems that are registered – particularly with respect to data inputs, performance audits, and purchase and operational costs.

Finally in this part, Chapter 14, "Decoding the Privacy Puzzle: A Study on AI Deployment in Public Governance," by Jose Ramon Saura, Belem Barbosa and Sudhir Rana, uses bibliometric analysis of published research in computer science and law to identify the most consistent and commonly identified privacy concerns associated with government use of AI. They find decision transparency, biases, trust, and ethics to be the dominant areas of concern and use their findings to develop a set of research questions to inform and guide future work.

SYNOPSIS OF PART III: RESPONSIBLE AND PARTICIPATORY DATA USE BY GOVERNMENT

In the third part, the authors reflect on *the open, transparent, and accessible use of data by the government and the role of citizens in these processes*. The chapters collectively address the evolving relationship between AI, data governance, and democratic control within public administrations, highlighting the opportunities and challenges this interplay presents. A central theme is the need for participatory governance to ensure democratic engagement and control over AI technologies, emphasizing deliberative practices and the importance of citizen involvement in the AI deployment process. The discussion also covers the strategic integration of digital technologies and AI in public services, focusing on ensuring fairness, accountability, and transparency. The chapters underscore the complexity of integrating AI and digital technologies into public governance, advocating for a balanced approach that ensures democratic control, transparency, accountability, and equitable access to the benefits of data-driven innovations.

In Chapter 15, "Intersecting Digital Governance and Data Science: Preparing for Communication to Strengthen Citizen-Government Partnerships," Jae-Seong Lee brings into question the scholarly and practitioner paradigm of digital transformation and cites as evidence the problems with a transformation perspective: the ongoing issues of data ownership, digital inequalities, and transparency. Lee argues that citizen-government partnerships should be integral to our understanding of digital transformation, but in practice, governments find this difficult to do. Lee explores the existing models of government engagement of stakeholders in citizen-government partnerships, including types of co-creation and co-production and considers how governments can better facilitate such partnerships. The case of South Korea illustrates these challenges, and Lee sums up the main policy points that need focus: fairness, accountability, and transparency.

Kristen Rose and Joseph Foti explore the good governance narrative of open and big data in Chapter 16, "Delivering on Transparency's Good Governance Promise? The State of Government Data against Political Corruption." They argue that data made available by governments that can be used by third parties for data science needs to be managed and prepared in ways that make it accessible and effective. They map the range of relevant data sources from public official assets, political finance, beneficial ownership, lobbying, and right to information performance metrics. Using data from the Global Data Barometer from 109 countries, Rose and Foti identify five critical kinds of gaps in global performance in the provision of critical data for public accountability: collection, publication, high-value data, usability, and use gaps. They argue that the effective use of data – in a public sector context – will depend on how effectively countries can address these gaps and make data readily available to data science experts, researchers, and citizens.

Joseph Foti, Tara Davis, and Divij Joshi discuss responsible data use in Chapter 17, "System Update: Emerging Transparency and Oversight Functions for Responsible Data Use." They consider two main types of societal harms that can result from irresponsible data use by governments: individual harms and collective harms. Having examined ethical and political aspects of these harms, such as privacy, bias, discrimination, public goods, and competition, the authors carry out a detailed mapping and analysis of the existing repertoire of open government regulatory solutions that have been considered by policymakers, including ethical guidelines and frameworks, data protection authorities, whistleblower protections, impact assessments, data registers, audits, and dispute resolution mechanisms.

Willie Gin considers dominant trends in data analytics and compares two ideal kinds of macro-level data regimes: classificatory and transformative in Chapter 18, "Classificatory versus Transformative Data Regimes: Towards a Positive Right to Data Production and Analysis." Using the cases of criminal justice and social welfare, Gin considers what kinds of affordances are associated with each kind of regime; the first being based on classification and economization, while the second is focused on human subjects as the beneficiaries of experimental, transformative approaches to data governance. Gin argues that classificatory data regimes are far more typical in existing social systems and suggests that one of the chief aspects of unfairness is that classification tends to exclude members of society from the benefits of iterative trial and experimentation that allow data subjects to transcend their classificatory status. If governments wish to move beyond classificatory regimes, Gin reasons, a focus on data transparency and privacy will need to be reconsidered. Instead, data subjects will need to be more actively involved in experimentation with data production, analysis, and use.

In Chapter 19, "The Janus Face of Personal Data Agency in Public and Private Use Applications," Dale Mineshima-Lowe, Roxana Bratu, and Sarah Giest examine the cases of four digital platforms, considering how individual agency and structural power differentials can be seen in their design. The potential for data agency is seen particularly in the way the platforms conceive the terms and processes as a basis for the exchange of data between users and providers. By considering data as an asset comparable to labor, the authors argue that the distinction between public and private spheres of agency becomes contestable and demands a rethink in the way that existing policies and legislation on privacy and data rights are structured. They argue that user awareness of data use, control thereof, the ability to update or withdraw data, and the ability to meaningfully manage data should be critical features of the concept of data agency.

Federica Fusi and Eric Welch explore forms of governance that contribute to the sustainability of data centers for scientific communities in Chapter 20, "A Social Capital Perspective to Building Sustainable Data Centers for Science." The authors posit that scientific data centers are critical infrastructure for the application and development of data science in science. Scientists can contribute and use different kinds of resources in data science centers. However, the open and community-driven aspect of data centers makes them challenging to sustain. They argue that social capital, with its stores of structural, human, and cognitive resources, is essential to the long-term sustainability of such centers. However, social capital works differently in open, diverse, and geographically dispersed communities, and these differences are critical to understanding how data centers can leverage social capital to maximize their effectiveness and longevity. Fusi and Welch generate nine propositions for how social capital concepts can be effectively knitted together with the open community characteristics of data centers.

Chapter 21, "Public Sector Innovation Labs as an Approach to Data-Driven Innovation," by Francesco Leoni traces the origins of innovation labs from the quintessential laboratory through the "living lab" concept to the present day. Leoni identifies how these innovation labs reflect and in turn inform conceptions of public sector privatization and atomization, as well as adaptive experimentation and public outreach and engagement. His findings include several implications for practitioners, including: the value of innovation labs as critical infrastructure for promoting public trust in government; examples of inclusive practices for data governance; the importance of interoperability; and how human-centered and data-centric design principles can be synthesized to improve user experience and increase public value.

The *Handbook* closes with Chapter 22, "Conclusion, Research Agenda and Policy Recommendations for Governance and Data Science." Bram Klievink and Sarah Giest sketch a future research agenda based on the preceding chapters. They acknowledge the potential of data science to offer novel insights and enhance decision-making but also question what data science genuinely fixes or improves in the public sector and highlight the ethical and technical challenges that come with its integration. They suggest that responsible data science should add real value and call for careful consideration of contextual factors that affect this value. Klievink and Giest also emphasize understanding the patterns that indicate successful data science applications, aiming to bridge the gap between technology and responsible governance.

An action-oriented approach is recommended to make data science tools accessible to a broader range of users, promoting accountability and transparency in public administration.

REFERENCES

Bannister, F. and R. Connolly. 2012. Forward to the past: Lessons for the future of e-government from the story so far. *Information Polity* 17, 211–26.

Clarke, A. and J. Craft. 2017. The vestiges and vanguards of policy design in a digital context. *Canadian Public Administration* 60(4), 476–97.

Giest, S. 2017. Big data for policymaking: Fad or fast track? *Policy Sciences* 50(3), 367–82.

Giest, S. and I. Mukherjee. 2018. Behavioral instruments in renewable energy and the role of big data: A policy perspective. *Energy Policy* 123, 360–6.

Head, B. 2008. Three lenses of evidence-based policy. *Australian Journal of Public Administration* 67(1), 1–11.

Kitchin, R. 2014. Big Data, new epistemologies and paradigm shifts. *Big Data & Society*, 1–12.

Kjær, A.M. 2004. *Governance*. Cambridge: Wiley.

Klievink, B, B.J. Romijn, S. Cunningham and H. de Bruijn. 2017. Big data in the public sector: Uncertainties and readiness. *Information Systems Frontiers* 19, 267–83.

Mannhardt, F. 2022. Responsible process mining. In: W.M.P. van der Aalst and J. Carmona (eds.), *Process Mining Handbook. Lecture Notes in Business Information Processing*, vol 448, 373–401. Cham: Springer.

Meijer, A. and M.P.R. Bolívar. 2016. Governing the smart city: A review of the literature on smart urban governance. *International Review of Administrative Sciences* 82(2), 392–408.

Mergel, I., N. Edelmann and N. Haug. 2019. Defining digital transformation: Results from expert interviews. *Government Information Quarterly* 36(4), 101385.

Mukherjee, I., M.K. Coban and A.S. Bali. 2021. Policy capacities and effective policy design: A review. *Policy Sciences* 54, 243–68.

Osborne, S.P. 2006. The new public governance? *Public Management Review* 8(3), 377–87.

Provost, F. and T. Fawcett. 2013. Data science and its relationship to Big Data and data-driven decision making. *Big Data* 1, 51–9.

Rhodes, R. 2007. Understanding governance: Ten years on. *Organization Studies* 28(8), 1243–64.

Riddell, N. 2007. *Policy Research Capacity in the Federal Government*. Ottawa: Policy Research Initiative.

Sunstein, C.R., S. Bobadilla-Suarez, S.C. Lazzaro and T. Sharot. 2017. How people update beliefs about climate change: Good news and bad news. 102 *Cornell Law Review* 1431.

van der Aalst, W. 2016. *Process Mining, Data Science in Action*. Berlin: Springer.

Veale, M. and Brass. 2019. Administration by algorithm? Public management meets public sector machine learning. In: K. Yeung and M. Lodge (eds.), *Algorithmic Regulation*. Oxford University Press. Available at SSRN: https://ssrn.com/abstract=3375391.

Verhulst, S.G., Z. Engin and J. Crowcroft. 2019. Data & Policy: A new venue to study and explore policy–data interaction. *Data & Policy* 1(e1). doi:10.1017/dap.2019.2.

Vogl, T,M., C. Seidelin, B. Ganesh and J. Bright. 2019. Algorithmic bureaucracy. In: *Proceedings of the 20th Annual International Conference on Digital Government Research*, 148–53. Dubai, United Arab Emirates: ACM, New York.

Wesselink, A., H. Colebatch and W. Pearce. 2014. Evidence and policy: Discourses, meanings and practices. *Policy Science* 47, 339–44.

World Bank. 2020. Statistical capacity indicators. Available at: https://datatopics.worldbank.org/statisticalcapacity.Last accessed: November 15, 2024.

Wu, X., M. Ramesh and M. Howlett. 2015. Policy capacity: A conceptual framework for understanding policy competences and capabilities. *Policy and Society* 34(3–4), 165–71.

Young, M.M., J.B. Bullock and J.D. Lecy. 2019. Artificial discretion as a tool of governance: A framework for understanding the impact of artificial intelligence on public administration. *Perspectives on Public Management and Governance* 2(4), 301–13.

Zuiderwijk, A. and Janssen, M. (2014). Barriers and development directions for the publication and usage of open data: A socio-technical view. In: M. Gascó-Hernández (ed.), *Open Government: Opportunities and Challenges for Governance*, (pp. 115–135). New York, NY: Springer.

PART I

DATA APPLICATIONS FOR POLICY CHALLENGES

2. Does it hold up? Testing big data's promise of novel information on labour market policymaking
Simon Vydra

INTRODUCTION

In the academic literature 'big data', and the requisite 'data science' tools to analyse big data, are argued to have a strong transformative potential (Brynjolfsson & McAfee, 2014) and the study of governance and policymaking is no exception. However, the extent of this transformative potential for governance is still debated. Accounts of big data in public administration range from those seeing it as profoundly transformative (Höchtl et al., 2016; Maciejewski, 2016) to those highlighting the issues with big data and the difficulty of changing policymaking practice (Iacus, 2015; Lavertu, 2016). Situated between these two positions are accounts seeing the transformative potential of big data as contingent on factors such as institutional readiness and capacity (Klievink et al., 2017) or the specific alignment between data source, method, and policy question (Vydra & Klievink, 2019). Even though the debate is not settled, it illustrates the complex, multifaceted, and context-dependent nature of the 'big data promise'.

This chapter focuses on a part of that promise: that of 'novel information'. This refers to the claim that because big data quantifies human interaction with 'higher resolution' and quantifies previously unquantified aspects of human interaction it can provide novel information for governance and policymaking. This has been articulated at multiple levels: At the level of general research efforts, Boyd & Crawford (2012) identify, somewhat critically, a mythological element of big data resting on 'the widespread belief that large data sets offer a higher form of intelligence and knowledge that can generate insights that were previously impossible' (Boyd & Crawford, 2012: 663). At the level of public administrations, one can argue that 'big data methods can uncover knowledge that was previously impossible to reveal. In turn, this new knowledge allows new tasks (previously impossible or even unimaginable) to be successfully carried out' (Maciejewski, 2016: 123). At the level of economic and sociological analysis, one can argue that big data will 'allow economic researchers to test theories of behaviour that were previously untestable, creating a new set of metrics for issues of economic interest which were previously in the realm of theory' (Taylor, Schroeder, & Meyer, 2014: 5), or that 'Big Data have a number of relevant pros that make them very interesting also for the definition of new social indicators' (Di Bella et al., 2018: 871).

Despite the fact that this 'novel information' promise is articulated in the literature, it remains empirically under-explored, creating a mismatch between the theoretical promise and empirical testing. Even though the nature of many big data sources, combined with a more 'unsupervised' approach often used to analyse them, do allow for the extraction of novel information, the promise needs to be empirically tested to better illustrate how this novel information interacts with governance and policymaking. This chapter works towards filling this gap in our understanding, but it can do so only very partially – terms like 'big data' and 'policymaking' are too sprawling and trying to understand their interaction at such aggregate level is bound to be misleading (Vydra & Klievink, 2019). This chapter thus selects a particular data source, policy puzzle, and analytical approach, which limits its external validity but allows it to remain empirically honest about the differences that exist between data sources and their use for governance.

To meet this goal, it is important to select a data source and a relevant policy puzzle that 'match' one another and where one can reasonably expect to find novel information. In the next section, the chapter outlines its scope of labour market governance, focus on social investment as a policy-relevant theoretical framework in need of novel empirical information, and the selection of social media data as a fitting data source. In the third section, the chapter elaborates on the data and the adopted topic modelling method. The fourth section then answers whether this empirical test has been successful – whether the selected data source and method is capable of providing policy-relevant 'novel information'. Given the limited external validity of this test, as well as the rapidly evolving data science toolkit, the fifth section extracts governance and policymaking implications that go beyond the empirical specification of the test itself and are relevant to other data science tools and approaches for analysing text. The final section provides concluding remarks.

LABOUR MARKETS, SOCIAL INVESTMENT, AND SOCIAL MEDIA AS TESTING GROUNDS

This chapter studies the promise of 'novel information' in the context of labour markets. One of the reasons for this is that labour market flows are a data-rich and methodologically developed field of study, but also the most studied area of economics when it comes to big data research (Taylor et al., 2014). The other (and more important) reason is that it is also illustrative of the mismatch between the conceptual promise and empirical testing: despite a wealth of research, most contributions attempt to predict or 'nowcast' key economic indicators or to substitute existing data sources with big data in order to produce cheaper and/or more accurate indicators (Taylor et al., 2014). Nowcasting unemployment is the prime example of replicating an existing indicator and can be done using Google search query data (Anvik & Gjelstad, 2010; Askitas & Zimmermann, 2009; Choi & Varian, 2009, 2012; D'Amuri, 2009; D'Amuri & Marcucci, 2010; Fondeur & Karamé, 2013; McLaren & Shanbhogue, 2011; Naccarato et al., 2018; Vicente et al., 2015) or micro-blogging and social media data (Antenucci et al., 2014; Biorci et al., 2017; Proserpio et al., 2016). Other relevant research utilises job listing data (Colace et al., 2019; Turrell et al., 2019) or mobile phone geo-location data (Dong et al., 2017; Toole et al., 2015). As much as some of the existing research provides additional 'depth' by looking at drivers of job search (Baker & Fradkin, 2011) or at psychological variables as leading indicators for a change in conventional economic indicators (Proserpio et al., 2016), the overarching ambition remains to replicate 'traditional' economic indicators, rather than provide novel information.

Social Investment as an Analytical Perspective

Contrary to the 'nowcasting' ambition of the literature, this chapter approaches labour markets and individuals' position in them from an analytically novel perspective – the social investment perspective. Social investment is a school of thought concerned with re-thinking welfare state and social policy analysis, highlighting the change of social risks and welfare states and arguing, that this change is a manifestation of a new paradigm, complete with normative commitments and political objectives as well as policy theory and instrumentation (Hemerijck, 2013, 2018). The political objectives of social investment are generally to reduce the inter-generational transfer of disadvantage through investment in children and to sustain the welfare state by increasing employment and productivity of those employed through investing in/protecting human capital (Hemerijck, 2018). This perspective has a few analytical implications that are worth highlighting. Firstly, it has a strong focus on life course transitions, motivated by the understanding that individuals experience more erratic life courses in terms of employment and family dynamics and that these transitions are a crucial determinant of labour market outcomes: in transitions individuals can get re-training and enter the labour market in a more productive sector (Nelson & Stephens, 2011) or, at the other extreme, their skills can atrophy to the point that they might never enter the labour market again (Leoni, 2015). Secondly, it is the importance of policy complementarities (Hemerijck et al., 2016), referring to the fact that sometimes a specific policy crucially influences the returns available from another policy (Peter & Gingerich, 2009). It can be that it is the interactions with other policies rather than features of a policy itself that make it perform well or poorly, which requires a more holistic approach to various policy interventions, rather than a 'silo' analytical approach. Thirdly, it is the emphasis on 'preparing' the policy mix to aid in transitions rather than 'repairing' the damage of unsuccessful transitions, meaning that intervention is provided before transition can become unsuccessful, after which point repairing the damage becomes difficult.

This more holistic approach to welfare state interventions, including labour market policies, has also garnered substantial political attention in Europe: its long-term goals are anchored in the Lisbon Treaty (Hemerijck, 2013) and in multiple Organisation for Economic Co-operation and Development (OECD) reports (OECD, 2007, 2011, 2015). 'Social investment' as a guiding principle to social policy was later endorsed in the European Union's (EU) Social Investment Package (SIP) (European Commission, 2013). Even though the SIP was arguably weakly institutionalised (de la Porte & Natali, 2018), social investment has not dissapeared from European policymaking, as evidenced by the 2019 report on Employment and Social Developments in Europe, which specifically mentions social investment but also its logic of improving well-being by 'enabling citizens to acquire new skills and become or remain active in the labour market and by providing them with support during critical life course transitions' (European Commission, 2019: 21). Even though social investment received such an endorsement, the importance of providing novel information for this approach is also evident. Following the SIP, the European Commission launched a methodological inquiry into social investment, which fell short in its core task of identifying quantitative indicators for social investment (de la Porte & Natali, 2018). Such indicators are unavailable to this day. A report produced as a part of the methodological inquiry also acknowledges that 'we continue to know surprisingly little about how to identify and empirically track particular policy mixes and reforms that manifest a social investment approach as distinct from other features of (social) policy efforts'

(Hemerijck, Burgoon, Di Pietro, & Vydra, 2016: 2–3), showing the difficulties with analytically grasping the complexity a social investment approach can introduce.

Social investment is thus a perspective situated in empirically rich literature sometimes utilising big data, but one that needs more detailed, faster, and more holistic information about individuals and their transitions. It is also a perspective that is salient for governance and policymaking. This makes it a fitting 'testing ground' for the novel information promise associated with big data and data science, since the type of micro-level data specific to individuals and their experience is often what big data is argued to provide.

Social Media Data as a Potential Solution

With the perspective clear and its need for additional novel information established, the question becomes from which data can such information potentially be extracted? Existing research points to social media data as a potential candidate: On Twitter (now X) posting updates about one's life is the most common use of the platform (Java et al., 2007), likely driven by the gratification individuals get from satisfying the need to belong and the need for self-presentation (Java et al., 2007). By the very definition of life course transitions, they have to do with important events in one's life, likely making them something worthy of sharing. Here the chapter focuses on perhaps the most important complementarity of social investment – the 'parenthood to employment' transition (including remaining in employment while becoming a parent). This is a 'flagship' complementarity between labour market and early childhood education and care (ECEC) policies both because of its importance for the goals of social investment reform but also because the complementarity involved here is conceptually clear (without ECEC provisions both parents are unlikely to utilise labour market policies, because they have to care for their children rather than be active in the labour market).

This specifies the cohort of interest to new parents and people of peak childrearing age, which is a good fit for social media: For new mothers specifically, blogging and social media can improve various wellbeing indicators, as they feel more connected to the world outside of their home and they receive social support from friends and extended family (McDaniel et al., 2012). New mothers experience increased Facebook use when transitioning into parenthood (Bartholomew et al., 2012) and it is even possible to identify new mothers on Twitter and observe changes in their behaviour (De Choudhury et al., 2013). Statistically Twitter penetration is also high in the specified national context of the Netherlands at the time of collecting data – with approximately 14.5 per cent of the total population being a Twitter user in 2019 (Statista, 2019), but a 2018 poll reporting 26 per cent of 20 to 39 year olds in the Netherlands using Twitter (Statista, 2018).

The focus on Twitter as a social media platform is a more pragmatic choice here: the ideal platform would likely be Facebook, be it due to its extremely high usage in European countries or due to the symmetry in the friendship relationship that Facebook is built on. In the Netherlands specifically, the internet penetration is around 96 per cent with close to 60 per cent of those users having a Facebook account (Internet World Stats, 2017). However, utilising data from this platform was not feasible for this test. Twitter is very much a 'second-best' option at the time of data collection. Selecting the Netherlands as a national context is motivated by the aforementioned high internet penetration and relatively high percentage of users between 20 and 39 years of age, but also because of its policies: the Netherlands is one of the earlier adopters of social investment policies (Nikolai, 2011) and boasts a relatively well-developed social investment agenda, but one that has faced some challenge in the form of substantial budget cuts, especially following the 2008 financial crisis (Soentken et al., 2017). This means that the Netherlands does have the main policy elements that together support individuals in their transition from parenthood to employment, but also that those elements are not perfect and are changing, which is likely to generate some issues for those experiencing this transition.

DATA AND METHODS

With the specific perspective, life course transition, national context, and platform established, it is necessary to operationalise what is meant by 'relevant' information given all these constraints. For the purposes of this chapter relevant information is:

1. *Concerned with a specific life course transition and the policies related to it.* This is primarily achieved with data collection, as tweets are collected based on a set of keywords capturing concepts specific to ECEC and labour market legislation, but also all commonly available childcare options, types of employment, and phrases related to employment status and job search (Appendix A).
2. *Personal to an individual's experience.* Social media is generally a good fit to gather personal experiences. Bot removal is used to remove accounts that likely do not correspond to individuals or are not used as a 'personal' account.

This is a relatively loose definition that minimises information loss, but it might introduce some unwanted information into the dataset. This is appropriate for this more exploratory task of finding novel information: *ex ante* defining all relevant information based on the risk of current literature missing information that is relevant, just not yet identified as such. In a more focused subset of this data further restrictions are applied to also make the data:

3. *Personal to an individual's experience.* This is now restricted further by necessitating that tweets include the pronouns 'I' and 'we' or their possessive forms.
4. *Explicit about what factors are making that transition difficult or easy.* This is an additional restriction and can be enforced by necessitating that tweets include some of the commonly understood factors restricting access to policies.

This more focused version of the data is much more supervised and concentrated on extracting predefined information and it constraints the data enough to allow for meaningful manual inspection, which is very difficult with the full data.

Data

The dataset of tweets spans a year from August 2018 to (and including) July 2019. The tweets have been collected using Twitters Streaming API based on being written in the Dutch language (to control for national context) and containing a word or a phrase from a set of keywords (Appendix A). The set of relevant keywords includes 139 keywords, many of which refer to the same concept but are spelled with and without a space or using English terms that have become popularly used in Dutch. The total number of tweets collected throughout this period is just over 4.15 million. As part of pre-processing all re-tweets were removed (1.36 million) followed by removing duplicate tweets (91,000 tweets). Quoted tweets have been pre-processed by joining the text of the tweet at hand and the text of the tweet it was responding to (222,000 tweets).

Another part of pre-processing – bot removal – is more conceptually challenging since the distinction between 'bots' and 'humans' is fuzzy. Some accounts are 'cyborg accounts' subjected to automation but also human intervention (Nimmo, 2019), some only going as far as scheduling the dissemination of human-created posts (Radziwill & Benton, 2016). Technically, this is a challenge often tackled as a supervised learning problem (Andriotis & Takasu, 2019; Inuwa-Dutse et al., 2018; Kantepe & Ganiz, 2017; Lee et al., 2011; Lundberg et al., 2019; Mazza et al., 2019), but such an approach necessitates ground truth about which accounts are bot accounts and which are not. Since this information is not available and approaches such as those proposed by Kantepe and Ganiz (2017) do not validate for this dataset, this chapter adopts a simple approach: removing tweets that are authored by an account with a very high tweet frequency that a human is unlikely to exhibit. This is judged based on the overall number of monthly tweets and on the monthly number of tweets captured in the dataset. Even though this approach is likely not as accurate as training a machine learning algorithm on a manually annotated dataset, it is parsimonious, cost-effective, language independent, and very easily interpretable. The thresholds adopted are 1,500 for all tweets and 450 for specific tweets (captured for this chapter) per month. This removes an additional 1.01 million tweets from the dataset, resulting in a baseline dataset of 1.69 million tweets.

When moving from the baseline dataset to a more focused version, the chapter concentrates on two specific areas: one focusing on affordability of childcare and the other on (in)sufficiency of unemployment insurance, both of which are important features of these respective policies. Here, all three criteria for potential relevant information are restricted as mentioned above: the focus on *specific life course transition and policies* is restricted by needing to include keywords specifically on ECEC (by including one of the keywords listed in Table 2.A1 in the Appendix) or unemployment support (by including one of the following keywords: 'uwv' unemployment insurance agency, 'payment', 'assistance', 'unemployment insurance', 'joblesness'). A specific focus on *factors making transition difficult or easy* is enforced by including one of the following keywords: 'cheap', 'expensive', 'costly', 'cost', 'price', 'affordable', 'unaffordable' for the ECEC subset. Or by including one of the following keywords: 'little', 'less', 'low', 'lower', 'sufficient', 'enough' for the (in)sufficiency of unemployment assistance subset. Being *personal to individual experience* is assured by the aforementioned use of pronouns. This results in high information loss, leaving a subset of only 501 tweets for ECEC affordability and 2,077 tweets for unemployment insurance sufficiency. As such, it is more appropriate for testing whether the already understood factors can be found in social media data rather than for providing truly 'novel' information.

Method

The method adopted here is iterative topic modelling and associated (pre-)processing steps, as it allows one to summarise a large corpus of texts in a rather unsupervised way. The unsupervised approach eliminates an important risk inherent in more supervised methods: it is impossible to a priori identify all the potential factors that can genuinely a transition. Because of this, a topic could be relevant if inspected, but would not be searched for based on the existing state of the literature. The topic modelling approach itself rests on the intuition that, when talking about a particular topic, individuals will use words reflecting that choice – some words are more related to some topics than others. This intuition is formalised into statistical models that are capable of describing which topics are contained in a document, as well as which terms are contained in each topic. With the pre-processing steps such as bot removal covered, the section turns to the other major steps identified in Figure 2.1.

In terms of processing, the most substantial step is lemmatisation, which tackles the problem that words often have inflectional and derivationally related forms that can make what is effectively the same word appear in many different forms (e.g., 'to work', 'works', 'working'). The Frog advanced natural language processing suite (Van Den Bosch et al., 2007) is used to lemmatise the corpus. The lemmatised tweets are then converted into a format that models can easily be trained on, which is a simple 'bag of words' representation (each tweet is represented as a count of all the words it contains).

For the modelling step, this chapter makes use of four popular topic models: Latent Dirichlet Allocation (LDA), Non-negative Matrix Factorization (NMF), Correlated Topic Model (CTM), and Structural Topic Model (STM). NMF is deterministic (and likely the most straightforward) model following the simple notion that a term-document matrix (bag of words representation) can be decomposed into two matrices – a term-topic matrix and topic-document matrix. LDA for topic modelling was proposed by Blei, Ng, and Jordan (2003) and it is a generative probabilistic model of a corpus that assumes the topic distribution to have a Dirichlet prior. The model here is trained using the online variational Bayes algorithm (Hoffman et al., 2010) implemented in the gensim library. CTM models assume logistic normal distribution, but primarily capture covariance amongst components, allowing for the assumption that the presence of a topic in a document is correlated with the presence or absence of other topics in that document (Blei & Lafferty, 2007). STM models incorporate document-level metadata and account for its relationship with topics (Roberts et al., 2019). Use of multiple models is motivated by the fact that different topic models, despite capturing generally similar information, can produce different topics or capture the 'same' topics differently (Contreras-Piña & Ríos, 2016). Given the popularity, interpretability, and relatively low computational requirements of the LDA model, it is used as a baseline model for much of the iterative process. Other models are primarily used to assess stability of topics (in the sense of appearing in multiple models) and add detail.

There are multiple (hyper-)parameters in topic models, but the most important one is likely the number of topics. To aid with selecting the number of topics, this chapter draws on the topic coherence approach of Röder, Both, and Hinneburg (2015), which aims at approximating human interpretability and the various coherence metrics are plotted in Figure 2.2 for LDA models from 5 to 150 topics. It is worth noting that other metrics can be adopted here, but were not available for all models and are thus not reported. The downward trend in coherence

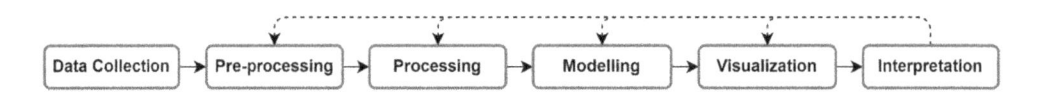

Data Collection → Pre-processing → Processing → Modelling → Visualization → Interpretation

Source: Author's own.

Figure 2.1   Method summary

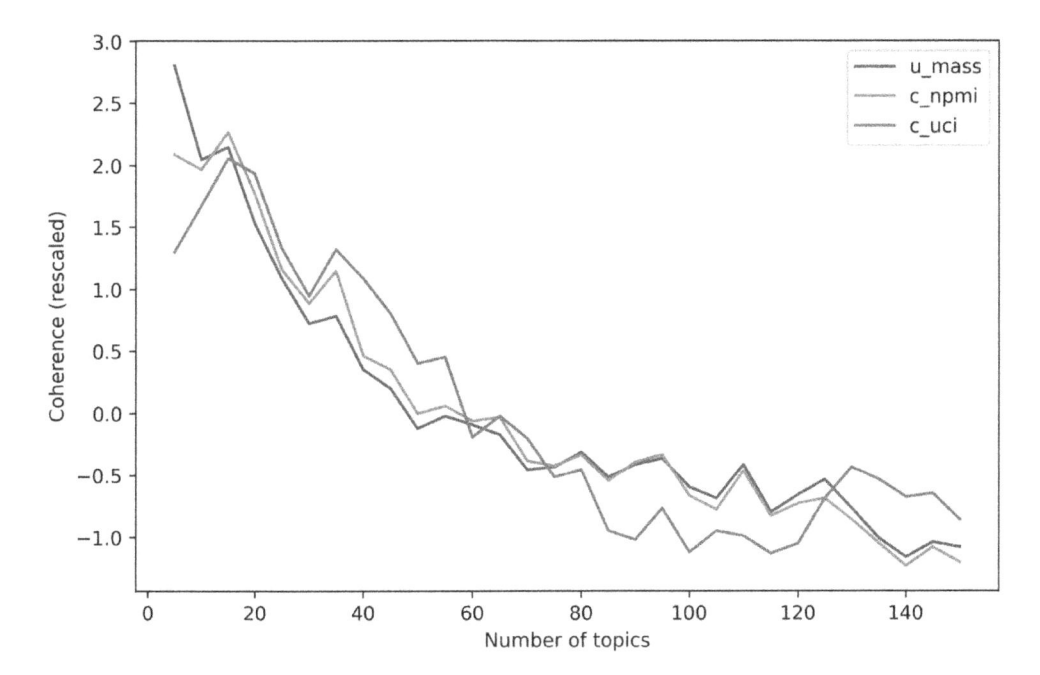

[Figure: line chart showing coherence (rescaled) on y-axis from -1.0 to 3.0 versus Number of topics on x-axis from 0 to 140, with three lines: u_mass, c_npmi, c_uci. All three metrics generally decrease as number of topics increases.]

Note: The three metrics are described by Röder et al. (2015) and implemented in gensim. There are multiple differences between them but fundamentally u_mass uses document co-occurrence counts to estimate coherence and c_uci and c_npmi use sliding windows and pointwise mutual information (which is normalised in c_npmi).
Source: Author's own.

Figure 2.2   Coherence metrics for LDA topic models based on number of topics

with the increase in topic number is unsurprising due to the fact that topics containing very general words tend to score well on coherence metrics (Roberts et al., 2014). The aim here is to strike a good balance between how detailed a topic is (increases with topic number) and how interpretable and exclusive a topic is (human interpretable and exclusive in the sense of words being used in very few topics rather than dispersed across multiple topics – both start decreasing with a high number of topics).

Models with 20, 35, and 65 topics form a baseline due to their relatively good performance in terms of balancing topic detail and coherence of the overall model (Figure 2.2 confirms this observation, with these models often having better coherence than their 'neighbours'). Models with less than 20 topics tend to provide an overly crude summarisation and models with more than 65 topics tend to start losing too much interpretability and present no additional insight that would be interpretable. The model with 35 topics seems to strike the best balance, and the 20- and 65-topic models provide extremes in either direction (while maintaining interpretability). Given that different models can provide different topics, or different versions of a topic, the most rigorous approach is to focus on topics that are robust across various models (in the sense of being identifiable in those models), to ensure they are not just a product of the specific model and parametrisation.

For visualising and interpreting the results, all models are visualised using primarily the LDAvis (for R) and pyLDAvis (for Python) libraries to produce comparable visualisations across different models (Sievert & Shirley, 2014) since some models are trained in Python and some in R. Besides this practical concern, this visualisation also provides a high level of customisation and interactivity, such as tuning the 'relevance' metric (frequency of words in topics versus their exclusivity) (Sievert & Shirley, 2014), which allows for a deeper insight than non-interactive approaches. Since interpretation is at the heart of the iterative process of topic modelling (illustrated in Figure 2.1), it is important to minimise the information loss here and gain as detailed understandings of topics as possible.

EMPIRICAL FINDINGS

The six topics that are robust across the majority of inspected models are the following. The first topic (Table 2.B1 in Appendix B) is concerned with employment openings advertised by employers and generally contains tokens like 'you', 'we', 'search', 'job offer', 'colleague', 'new', or 'team'. In some models, this topic also includes the qualities a prospective employee should have (e.g., 'enthusiastic'), seniority of the position (e.g., 'manager' or 'assistant'), or location. The second topic (Table 2.B2 in Appendix B) is about training and education and includes tokens like 'training', 'day', 'education', 'internship', 'year', 'school', or 'teaching'. The topics are generally about education and following various programmes, with the exception of the 20-topic LDA model which combines education and athletic training, making the topic more generic (35 topic models are detailed enough to disaggregate these two topics). The third topic (Table 2.B3 in Appendix B) is about unemployment and general social assistance, often concerned about who is contributing to the welfare system and who receives the benefits. It includes tokens like 'unemployment', 'employee insurance agency', 'payment', 'euro', 'assistance', 'to get', 'year', or 'right'. This topic is rather consistent across models but in the 65-topic LDA model it is less interpretable. The fourth topic (Table 2.B4 in Appendix B) is focused on the number of hours worked per month including tokens like 'hour', 'per', 'week', '24', '32', '36', '40'. This topic is focused mainly on job offers (and often co-occurs with topics concerned with job offers), but sometimes also includes education level and integers for years. The fifth topic (Table 2.B5 in Appendix B) is concerned with self-employment and freelance work including tokens like 'self-employment', 'the self-employed', 'entrepreneur', 'freelance', and 'interim' and the topic is both a commentary on the situation of the self-employed as well as offers for freelance contracts. In some models, the topic is more concerned with offers of contracts (mentioning the location, for example) and in some more with the commentary (mentioning issues such as 'pension', 'obliged', or 'economy'). The sixth topic (Table 2.B6 in Appendix B) is concerned with childcare and includes tokens like 'childcare', 'daycare', 'kindergarden', 'pedagogical', or 'out of school care (bso)'. In some models, this topic is more focused on the practicalities (including tokens like 'job application', 'company', or 'industry'). Appendix B reports this information in tables containing 15 of the most occurring words for a topic, for the three sizes of LDA models and the 35-topic CTM and NMF models. That said, there are numerous other interpretable topics, but some of these are not substantively relevant, extremely general, or not robust across enough models.

The number of topics modelled makes a difference in expected ways – as the topic number increases, the topics get more detailed but the fraction of uninterpretable topics increases. For example, the topic concerned with training and education also bundles in athletic training in the 20-topic model, is focused just on formal education in the 35-topic model, and gets disaggregated in the 65-topic model into a formal education topic and an internship topic. The type of model also influences the resulting insight. NMF models generally capture similar insight but highlight different topics and topics are generally less exclusive (words appear in multiple topics, making many topics have 'mixed' content). The CTM models are a bit more similar to the baseline LDA models, but sometimes capture novel topics such as topics about the general economic situation or about pensions. The STM models are very similar to CTM models, which is understandable since this chapter assumes metadata to change topic prevalence rather than topic content. The main benefit of CTM and STM models is that they generate additional information with regards to correlations (co-occurrence in one tweet) between topics and correlation between topic prevalence and metadata (such as tweeting behaviour). However, these features hold limited value here.

Each of the six topics (and their various versions across models) have been manually inspected by reading tweets that 'contain' this topic. For this particular dataset, it seems that it is impossible to identify a single topic that would satisfy the criteria for the relevance this chapter adopts – information that is (a) personal to an individual's experience, (b) concerned with a specific life course transition and the policies of interest related to it, and (c) explicit about what factors are making that transition difficult or easy. Multiple topics are concerned with relevant policies or aspects of transition, but the specificity to an individual's experience is something that cannot be identified at topic level and that seems to not be met for any of the topics following a manual inspection. However, especially with topic modelling, the absence of evidence is not evidence of absence – relevant information could still exist but simply not be picked up as a topic in any of the models.

This shortcoming of the more unsupervised approach motivates the more restrictive filtering of data already described in the third section: given that the data is still too large for thorough manual inspection, even when focusing on specific topics, a more specific subset is selected so that it focuses more on individual experience and factors affecting transition (what the previous approach was unable to find). These subsets of the corpus should be densely filled with relevant tweets – one focusing on affordability of childcare and the other on the (in)sufficiency of unemployment insurance. Since manually inspecting a large percentage of tweets is possible here, it is stronger evidence for the absence of relevant information.

The two corpus subsets are then topic modelled using LDA and after iterating through a few versions a 6-topic model and an 8-topic model are selected for the childcare affordability subset and the unemployment insurance subset, respectively. Here the topics become more general (given the more specific data) and do not provide a useful summary in and of themselves, but they are capable of identifying the more relevant tweets that can be manually inspected in each subset: for ECEC affordability it is topic 2 (consisting of tokens like 'daycare', 'cost', 'want', 'we', 'expensive', 'child benefits') and a relatively similar topic 3 (consisting of similar tokens but also including 'cheap', 'really', or 'money'). For unemployment insurance sufficiency, it is topic 1 (consisting of tokens like '@', 'payment', 'less', 'assistance', 'enough', 'should', 'to work', 'to get') and topic 6 (consisting of tokens like 'low', 'little', 'unemployment', 'we', 'uwv' – unemployment insurance agency, 'income'). For each of these topics, 50 of the most representative tweets are inspected, which should be the most relevant tweets in the entire dataset.

In terms of childcare affordability, the majority of tweets are about things (childcare being just one of them) getting more expensive and what policymakers are (not) doing about it, about the distributive aspects of policies like child benefits, or even news reports about childcare costs (including phrases like 'our correspondent' or 'we talked to parents' and thus meeting the personal criteria). These tweets offer a personal opinion about a political issue rather than personal anecdotes or requests for assistance. Only three inspected tweets included meaningful personal commentary mentioning that an individual relies on grandparents due to costs of childcare, that childcare feels too expensive, and that one cannot make ends meet without utilising childcare and the associated benefits. However, some of these tweets appear to be highly politicised (by @ mentioning various political parties, for example), which brings into question whether, even though they are personal commentary, their content is influenced by the political nature of the communication. In terms of sufficiency of unemployment insurance, tweets mainly include political statements about the welfare state, especially with regards to migrants receiving unemployment benefits. Much like with the affordability of childcare, the tweets express a personal opinion but about broader social issues and not about an individual situation – in the inspected tweets, there is no instance of personal (rather than political) statements. Iterating through different models, topics, or tweets does not meaningfully alter the findings for either subset.

This finding suggests that Twitter data does in fact not contain what is considered 'relevant information' in this chapter. There is a very small amount of identifiably personal commentary relevant to the parenthood to employment transition – so small that it holds no policy relevance when talking about relevant population sub-groups. Even though politicisation is the most obvious culprit here, the volumes of relevant data are seemingly so small that it is impossible to attribute this 'non-finding' to it: even if the identified personal content would not be political, the volume is still too small to generate any policy-relevant insight. The validity of this finding of course remains constrained to Twitter as a platform, to the specific policy features searched for, and the method used. Even though the results suggest that the proposed method is capable of tweets that were hypothesised to be relevant, more modern approaches using word vector representations of our text could be capable of better classification of text when it comes to distinguishing between sharing personal experience or personal political opinion.

IMPLICATIONS FOR GOVERNANCE AND POLICYMAKING

As much as the empirical finding has relevance in and of itself when it comes to tempering the optimism about the potential of some big data sources, the external validity limits are painfully apparent and fully acknowledged in this chapter. That said, there are important observations to be made about the process itself and how it applies to governance and policymaking specifically – a context that comes with an additional set of expectations and challenges: in governance, it is not just the model performance that makes a model 'fit for the job', but also its adherence to relevant public values and standards. Individual analytical steps can reflect assumptions about how systems in question work and what ought to be included or excluded from the analysis, which can be relevant to these public values. There is no such thing as 'raw' data (Gitelman, 2013) 'value-free' analysis (Kettl, 2018) in this context.

To provide some insights on how this analytical process interacts with public values and standards, this chapter utilises the iterative nature of its method and focuses on decisions made along the way that do not have an analytically 'right' or 'wrong' answer. Some of these decisions are presented in Figure 2.3 (which expands on Figure 2.1). These decisions reflect

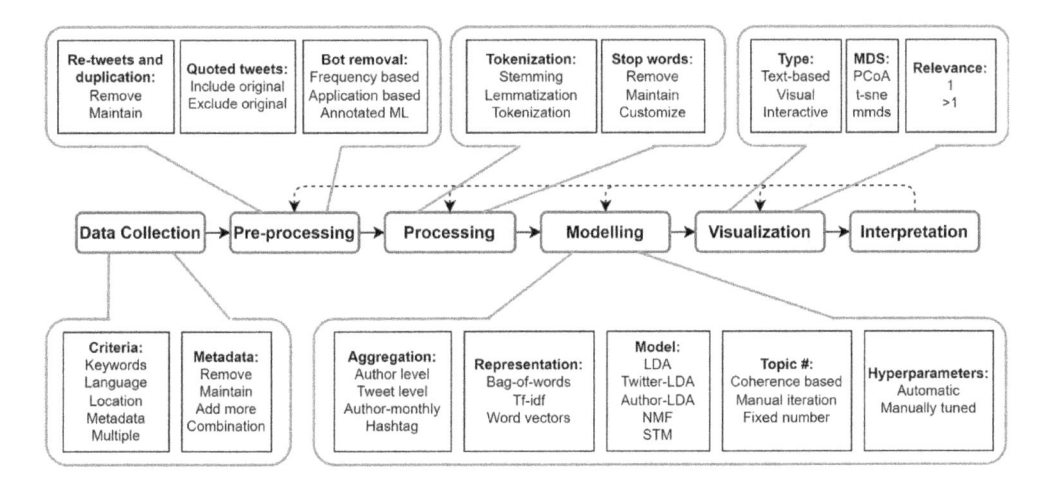

Figure 2.3 '*Subjective' decisions consequential for analytical output*

Source: Author's own.

assumptions about how individuals utilise social media and which content is of interest (which is also something that needs to be negotiated with the policymaker). As much as the author may believe these decision points to be informed and not arbitrary, they do involve trade-offs that different analysts or policymakers might make differently. Furthermore, what may seem as the best decision often results in longer and more iterative analysis, which is something often unavailable in the policymaking process. In such a context, one has to balance which 'good enough' decision best converts resources expended into improvements in the overall analysis, especially when the analytical question can adapt to changing context or the answers it yields, which can often happen in governance. Furthermore, and perhaps most importantly, what is 'better' analysis or even how 'interpretable' a topic is are all subjective metrics, the importance of which can hardly be understated as interpretation is key to iteration. Some analytical decisions might not even be a reflection of any assumptions but still need to be made and are potentially consequential for the outcome (such as dimensionality reduction).

At the stage of data collection and pre-processing, many of the decisions are necessarily subjective and politically informed, such as deciding on keywords and additional criteria to filter by. In the case of this chapter, this applies to constraining the data to the country of study: Using the language of the tweet to do that is relatively straightforward, but it also includes Dutch speakers living abroad and excludes English (or other) speakers living in the Netherlands. An alternative approach is using the geo-tags of tweets, which runs into the problem of the vast majority of tweets not being geo-tagged, resulting in large information loss. Some more advanced pre-processing approaches could be adopted, either utilising named entity recognition, account metadata, or more advanced processing using word vectors. However, regardless of which approach one adopts, there are trade-offs to be made between removing 'noise' from the data and information loss due to the fact that 'data' and 'noise' cannot be perfectly distinguished. This is true for many other steps at this stage of the analytical process. For example, in terms of bot removal, the selected thresholds are essentially a reflection of what is considered to be 'normal' tweeting behaviour and what deviation from this 'normal' is significant enough. Such decisions also reflect a preference for minimising information loss versus removing 'noise' from the data. This dilemma is the same for how quoted tweets are processed, which, despite being reasoned, is ultimately subjective. Technological progress can certainly help with optimising this trade-off, but the better technology gets here, the better it gets at identifying the truly 'edge cases' between data and noise; however, the decision on these 'edge cases' is ultimately up to the analyst.

In the modelling stage, many decisions are even more explicit, starting with the one already addressed in the previous section – the number of topics. The topic coherence measure used has an important caveat: since topic coherence aggregates the coherence of all topics in a given topic model, a low coherence score doesn't necessarily mean that *all* the topics are uninterpretable. This presents a trade-off between models that present simplistic and aggregate topics and models that contain more detailed topics but do so at the expense of also containing less interpretable topics. This trade-off can be made even more explicit by computing various metrics on a per-topic basis, but since the 'value' of these topics cannot be computed, the important decision on which topics are more 'valuable' is still left to the analyst. In general, there is no 'right' or 'wrong' when it comes to the number of topics and there is no substitute for careful validation of the actual topic models by making sense of individual topics (Grimmer & Stewart, 2013). Even though this chapter leans on robustness of topics across multiple models in order to minimise the effect of model (hyper-)parameters, it is possible that the topics that are not 'stable' across models capture unique information that is of interest.

Another explicit trade-off in the modelling stage are model hyper-parameters. For the 'baseline' LDA models, those hyper-parameters reflect expectations with regards to sparsity of words per topic and topics per documents (very simply put). These hyper-parameters can be left to the model to 'learn' from the data at hand (which is what this chapter does for most models), but especially for short micro-blogging data concerned with multiple policy areas there can be value in tweaking these hyper-parameters to reflect the assumption that a tweet likely contains relatively few topics. Similar decisions that require an analyst to make assumptions about the corpus and topics within it are also present for other models like STM: the relationship between the metadata and prevalence is up to the researcher to explicitly define. This chapter opts for a rather simple function $prevalence = frequency + followers + spline(days)$. This function assumes a linear relationship of topic prevalence with frequency and followers and a non-linear relationship with the date a tweet was posted on, but can be defined in other ways.

There are also decisions that are consequential for model output but are more arbitrary, such as the randomness involved in training models. Different libraries offer different solutions to initialising the training of a topic model (in the case of the gensim library, which this chapter utilises for some topic models, a 'seed' can be controlled). Sufficient training of the models helps with convergence across different seeds, but some differences still remain. The visualisation step contains a similarly arbitrary decision due to the necessity for dimensionality reduction: To visualise the 'semantic space', the models need to be reduced from 20+ dimensions (number of dimensions corresponds to the number of topics) down to two or three. As a result, the two axes used to visualise a topics model in this chapter do not have an inherent meaning – they simply try to maintain the distance that exists between topics in the high-dimensional space. This is impossible without some information loss and different algorithms discard different information. Principle coordinates analysis is utilised in this chapter as it seemingly provides the most informative 'clustering' of topics, but that judgement is subjective and there are other algorithms that generate a substantially different visualisation.

Utilising some of these analytical steps as illustrative examples reveals an important implication of this method: Many of the decisions that have to be made in topic modelling are consequential for the insight a model provides but also based on a subjective understanding of user behaviour and the broader social system, or even made arbitrarily and then iterated over in order to obtain the most interpretable (or desirable) outcome. This has some important implications for policymaking practice. Firstly, it highlights our lack of understanding of how some of these choices influence the result. Unfortunately, sensitivity analysis is difficult in this case because of the difficulty of objectively measuring 'interpretability' or 'value' different topic models provide. Secondly, there is the practical issue of politicians generally not being analytical experts and having to outsource this type of analysis to experts, which risks toutsourcing important subjective/normative decisions. Such experts are not democratically accountable and they might be unaware of the normative importance of the assumptions they are making and present their work as purely technical. Perhaps even worse, they might be aware of the importance but present those assumptions selectively, which can result in some important subjective or normative decisions being hidden from those who were elected to make them.

CONCLUSIONS AND DISCUSSION

The goal of this chapter is to start addressing the lack of empirical work with regards to the potential of big data to provide novel information in policymaking. It proposes a 'likely-to-succeed' scenario combining social investment as a framework and social media data as the data source. The test itself results in finding only a few individual tweets that would meet the criteria for relevant information, but even those tweets can be politicised, which likely diminishes their value as genuine reports of personal experience. For the governance and policymaking context, this is a 'non-finding': there is not enough information to generate any policy-relevant insight, even for the much more specific subset focused on the affordability of childcare and on sufficiency of unemployment insurance. However, these results are specific to Twitter as a platform, specific to the Netherlands, specific to parenthood to employment as a life course transitions, and specific to certain factors within that transition. These findings could be different when using Facebook data and looking at school to work transitions, for example. Even though this makes the external validity of this finding highly limited, the extent to which relevant information was absent should still temper some of the expectations when it comes to social media data.

The more important finding – and one that is far more applicable for multiple data sources – is illustrating how some of the decisions made along the way can be subjective but consequential for the model output. This brings to the forefront some important questions about deploying this type of analysis in governance practice (such as the interaction between domain experts and modelling experts). Many of these analytical choices are not dependent on the corpus used in this chapter or even Twitter as a platform – some choices will have to be made in modelling discussion board posts, Facebook updates, or Instagram posts using similar unsupervised methods. More supervised approaches have a distinct set of advantages, but in this case unsupervised models are a good fit due to the difficulty of a priori defining all potentially important factors as well as the practical concern that policymakers are not analytical experts and might lack the understanding of what questions a particular method can answer (unsupervised topic modelling approaches can start with an extremely broad question).

Even though cautionary, these findings should not be interpreted as topic models being arbitrary statistical artefacts – they do capture underlying structures in a corpus of text, but those structures are so multifaceted that they can be constructed in multiple ways. For example, should a topic model of the corpus differentiate between a childcare topic and a self-employment topic each of which mentions multiple regions, or should it differentiate between regional topics each including both childcare and self-employment mentions? Neither is wrong or less interpretable, but selecting one representation of the corpus over another is consequential for the insights a model carries. This of course does not need to be a conscious or deliberate choice, as the more normative impacts of various analytical decisions are not immediately obvious or quantifiable.

There are further methodological and theoretical limitations that are important to mention. Methodologically, there are other possible topic models and approaches that are likely to illuminate different aspects of the information contained in our corpus. Some of these approaches have become popular more recently with the advent of BERT language models (that are now easily available and even pre-trained for specific languages), or involve large language models (LLMs) that can be used on demand and provide a much more detailed understanding of text than bag of words representations do. That said, they are still iterative and even the presented method could effectively be iterated over endlessly to discover different information. The theoretical limitations stem from the simplistic use of the concepts like life course transition and policy complementarity. This chapter uses these concepts in a simplistic way to (a) provide an intuitive rather than rigorous sense of what information is needed, and (b) expand the scope from a single policy intervention to multiple interventions and general context. However, these concepts Could be done justice if the chapter was able to look at, for example, what users who are seeking ECEC are also saying about labour markets. However, since so little relevant information was discovered, developing such inquiries, further research seems of limited value.

There are other issues that this chapter doesn't address that stem from the unique context of governance and policymaking. One such concern being the ethical implications of collecting, analysing, and using data containing very personal information about likely vulnerable population sub-groups. Here, balancing ethical and privacy concerns with the quality of insight would be ineffective: different groups experience different life course transitions differently, meaning that the insight should come in relatively disaggregated form, but the more disaggregated the insight is, the more threats to privacy it poses for individuals whose data is being analysed. Such potential threats need to always be balanced with how much a given analysis can really improve policymaking practice and who is likely to benefit from such an 'improvement'. Making this trade-off requires accurate information from analysts, policymakers, and politicians, all of whom have to communicate with one another.

REFERENCES

Andriotis, P., & Takasu, A. (2019). Emotional bots: Content-based spammer detection on social media. In *10th IEEE International Workshop on Information Forensics and Security, WIFS 2018*, 1–8. Retrieved November 14, 2024, from https://doi.org/10.1109/WIFS.2018.8630760

Antenucci, D., Cafarellab, M., Levensteinc, M., Red, C., & Shapiro, M. (2014). *Using Social Media to Measure Labor Market Flows.* NBER Working Chapter No. 20010). Retrieved November 14, 2024, from https://www.nber.org/papers/w20010

Anvik, C., & Gjelstad, K. (2010, November). *'Just Google It': Forecasting Norwegian Unemployment Figures with Web Queries.* CREAM Publications. Retrieved November 14, 2024, from https://biopen.bi.no/bi-xmlui/handle/11250/95460

Askitas, N., & Zimmermann, K. (2009). *Google econometrics and unemployment forecasting.* IZA Discussion Chapters No. 4201.

Baker, S., & Fradkin, A. (2011). *What Drives Job Search? Evidence from Google Search Data.* SIEPR Working Chapter No. 10-020. Retrieved November 14, 2024, from https://siepr.stanford.edu/publications/working-paper/what-drives-job-search-evidence-google-search-data

Bartholomew, M.K., Schoppe-Sullivan, S.J., Glassman, M., Kamp Dush, C.M., & Sullivan, J.M. (2012). New Parents' Facebook Use at the Transition to Parenthood. *Family Relations*, *61*(3), 455–69. Retrieved November 14, 2024, from https://doi.org/10.1111/j.1741-3729.2012.00708.x

Biorci, G., Emina, A., Puliga, M., Sella, L., & Vivaldo, G. (2017). Tweet-Tales: Moods of Socio-Economic Crisis? *Data Science and Social Research*, 205–13. Retrieved November 14, 2024, from https://ideas.repec.org/p/ial/wpaper/04-2016.html

Blei, D.M., & Lafferty, J.D. (2007). A Correlated Topic Model of Science. *The Annals of Applied Statistics*, *1*(1), 17–35. Retrieved November 14, 2024, from https://doi.org/10.1214/07-AOAS114

Blei, D.M., Ng, A.Y., & Jordan, M.I. (2003). Latent Dirichlet Allocation. *Journal of Machine Learning Research*, *3*, 993–1022. Retrieved November 14, 2024, from https://dl.acm.org/doi/10.5555/944919.944937

Bonoli, G. (2013). *The Origins of Active Social Policy: Labour Market and Childcare Policies in a Comparative Perspective.* Oxford University Press.

Boyd, D., & Crawford, K. (2012). Critical Questions for Big Data: Provocations for a Cultural, Technological, and Scholarly Phenomenon. *Information Communication and Society*, *15*(5), 662–79. Retrieved November 14, 2024, from https://doi.org/10.1080/1369118X.2012.678878

Brynjolfsson, E., & McAfee, A. (2014). *The Second Machine Age : Work, Progress, and rosperity in a Time of Brilliant Technologies.* W.W. Norton & Company.

Choi, H., & Varian, H. (2009). *Predicting Initial Claims for Unemployment Benefits.* Retrieved November 14, 2024, from https://research.google.com/archive/papers/initialclaimsUS.pdf

Choi, H., & Varian, H. (2012). Predicting the Present with Google Trends. *Economic Record*, *88*(1), 2–9.

Clasen, J., & Clegg, D. (2011). *Regulating the Risk of Unemployment: National Adaptations to Post-Industrial Labour Markets in Europe.* Oxford University Press.

Colace, F., De Santo, M., Lombardi, M., Mercorio, F., Mezzanzanica, M., & Pascale, F. (2019). Towards Labour Market Intelligence through Topic Modelling. In *Proceedings of the 52nd Hawaii International Conference on System Sciences* (pp. 5256–65). Retrieved November 14, 2024, from https://hdl.handle.net/10125/59962

Contreras-Piña, C., & Ríos, S.A. (2016). An Empirical Comparison of Latent Sematic Models for Applications in Industry. *Neurocomputing*, *179*, 176–85. Retrieved November 14, 2024, from https://doi.org/10.1016/j.neucom.2015.11.080

D'Amuri, F. (2009). *Predicting Unemployment in Short Samples with Internet Job Search Query Data.* MPRA Chapter No. 18403. Retrieved November 14, 2024, from https://ideas.repec.org/p/pra/mprapa/18403.html

D'Amuri, F., & Marcucci, J. (2010). 'Google It!' Forecasting the US Unemployment Rate with a Google Job Search Index. *FEEM Working Chapter No. 31*. Retrieved November 14, 2024, from https://doi.org/http://dx.doi.org/10.2139/ssrn.1594132

De Choudhury, M., Counts, S., & Horvitz, E. (2013). Major Life Changes and Behavioral Markers in Social Media: Case of Childbirth. In *Proceedings of the 2013 Conference on Computer Supported*

Cooperative Work – CSCW '13 (pp. 1431–42). Retrieved November 14, 2024, from https://doi.org/10.1145/2441776.2441937

de la Porte, C., & Natali, D. (2018). Agents of Institutional Change in EU Policy : The Social Investment Moment. *Journal of European Public Policy*, 25(6), 828–43. Retrieved November 14, 2024, from https://doi.org/10.1080/13501763.2017.1401110

Di Bella, E., Leporatti, L., & Maggino, F. (2018). Big Data and Social Indicators: Actual Trends and New Perspectives. *Social Indicators Research*, 135, 869–78. Retrieved November 14, 2024, from https://link.springer.com/article/10.1007/s11205-016-1495-y

Dong, L., Chen, S., Cheng, Y., Wu, Z., Li, C., & Wu, H. (2017). Measuring Economic Activity in China with Mobile Big Data. *EPJ Data Science*, 6(1), 6–29. Retrieved November 14, 2024, from https://doi.org/10.1140/epjds/s13688-017-0125-5

Ebbinghaus, B. (2011). *The Varieties of Pension Governance: Pension Privatization in Europe*. Oxford University Press.

Esping-Andersen, G. (2015). Investing in Early Childhood. *Revue Belge de Sécurité Sociale*, 1, 99–112. Retrieved November 14, 2024, from https://socialsecurity.belgium.be/sites/default/files/rbss-1-2015-espingandersen-fr.pdf

Esping-Andersen, G., Gallie, D., Myles, J., & Hemerijck, A. (eds) (2002). *Why We Need a New Welfare State*. Oxford University Press.

European Commission. (2013). Towards Social Investment for Growth and Cohesion – including implementing the European Social Fund 2014-2020. COM(2013)83.

European Commission. (2019). Employment and Social Developments in Europe 2019. In *Employment and Social Developments in Europe*. Retrieved November 14, 2024, from https://ec.europa.eu/commission/presscorner/detail/en/IP_19_3412

Fondeur, Y., & Karamé, F. (2013). Can Google Data Help Predict French Youth Unemployment? *Economic Modelling*, 30, 117–25. Retrieved November 14, 2024, from https://doi.org/10.1016/J.ECONMOD.2012.07.017

Gitelman, L. (ed.). (2013). *'Raw Data'; Is an Oxymoron*. MIT Press.

Grimmer, J., & Stewart, B.M. (2013). Text as Data: The Promise and Pitfalls of Automatic Content Analysis Methods for Political Texts. *Political Analysis*, 21(3), 1–31. Retrieved November 14, 2024, from https://doi.org/10.1093/pan/mps028

Hemerijck, A. (2013). *Changing Welfare States*. Oxford University Press.

Hemerijck, A. (2018). Social Investment as a Policy Paradigm. *Journal of European Public Policy*, 25(6), 810–27. Retrieved November 14, 2024, from https://doi.org/10.1080/13501763.2017.1401111

Hemerijck, A., Burgoon, B., Di Pietro, A., & Vydra, S. (2016). *Assessing Social Investment Synergies*. Publications Office of the European Union.

Höchtl, J., Parycek, P., & Schöllhammer, R. (2016). Big Data in the Policy Cycle: Policy Decision Making in the Digital Era. *Journal of Organizational Computing and Electronic Commerce*, 26(1–2), 147–69. Retrieved November 14, 2024, from https://doi.org/10.1080/10919392.2015.1125187

Hoffman, M.D., Blei, D.M., & Bach, F. (2010). Online Learning for Latent Dirichlet Allocation. In J.D. Lafferty, C.K.I. Williams, J. Shawe-Taylor, R.S. Zemel, & A. Culotta (eds), *Proceedings of the 23rd International Conference on Neural Information Processing Systems, Volume 1 (NIPS'10)* (pp. 856–64). Curran Associates. Retrieved November 14, 2024, from https://dl.acm.org/doi/10.5555/2997189.2997285

Iacus, S.M. (2015). Big Data or Big Fail? The Good, the Bad and the Ugly and the Missing Role of Statistics. *Electronic Journal of Applied Statistical Analysis*, 5(1), 4–11. Retrieved November 14, 2024, from https://hdl.handle.net/2434/254508

Internet World Stats. (2017). *Europe Internet Usage Stats Facebook Subscribers and Population Statistics*. Retrieved January 15, 2021, from http://www.internetworldstats.com/stats4.htm

Inuwa-Dutse, I., Liptrott, M., & Korkontzelos, I. (2018). Detection of Spam-Posting Accounts on Twitter. *Neurocomputing*, 315, 496–511. Retrieved November 14, 2024, from https://doi.org/10.1016/j.neucom.2018.07.044

Java, A., Song, X., Finin, T., & Tseng, B. (2007). Why We Twitter: Understanding Microblogging Usage and Communities. In *Proceedings of the Joint 9th WEBKDD and 1st SNA-KDD Workshop 2007*. Retrieved November 14, 2024, from https://dl.acm.org/doi/10.1145/1348549.1348556

Kantepe, M., & Ganiz, M.C. (2017). Preprocessing Framework for Twitter Bot Detection. In *2017 International Conference on Computer Science and Engineering (UBMK)* (pp. 630–4). Retrieved November 14, 2024, from https://doi.org/10.1109/UBMK.2017.8093483

Kettl, D.F. (2018). *Little Bites of Big Data for Public Policy*. CQ Press.

Klievink, B., Romijn, B.J., Cunningham, S., & de Bruijn, H. (2017). Big Data in the Public Sector: Uncertainties and Readiness. *Information Systems Frontiers*, *19*(2), 267–83. Retrieved November 14, 2024, from https://doi.org/10.1007/s10796-016-9686-2

Lavertu, S. (2016). We All Need Help: 'Big Data' and the Mismeasure of Public Administration. *Public Administration Review*, *76*(6), 864–72. Retrieved November 14, 2024, from https://doi.org/10.1111/puar.12436

Lee, K., Eoff, B., & Caverlee, J. (2011). Seven Months with the Devils: A Long-Term Study of Content Polluters on Twitter. *ICWSM*. Retrieved November 14, 2024, from https://doi.org/10.1609/icwsm.v5i1.14106

Leoni, T. (2015). Welfare State Adjustment to New Social Risks in the Post-Crisis Scenario. A Review with Focus on the Social Investment Perspective. *WWWforEurope Working Chapters Series*. Retrieved November 14, 2024, from https://ideas.repec.org/b/wfo/wstudy/57899.html

Lundberg, J., Nordqvist, J., & Laitinen, M. (2019). Towards a Language Independent Twitter Bot Detector. In *Proceedings of 4th Conference of The Association Digital Humanities in the Nordic Countries*. Retrieved November 14, 2024, from https://api.semanticscholar.org/CorpusID:162183523

Maciejewski, M. (2016). To Do More, Better, Faster and More Cheaply: Using Big Data in Public Administration. *International Review of Administrative Sciences*, *83*(1), 120–35. Retrieved November 14, 2024, from https://doi.org/10.1177/0020852316640058

Mazza, M., Cresci, S., Avvenuti, M., Quattrociocchi, W., & Tesconi, M. (2019). *RTbust: Exploiting Temporal Patterns for Botnet Detection on Twitter*. Retrieved November 14, 2024, from http://arxiv.org/abs/1902.04506

McDaniel, B.T., Coyne, S.M., & Holmes, E.K. (2012). New Mothers and Media Use: Associations between Blogging, Social Networking, and Maternal Well-being. *Maternal and Child Health Journal*, *16*(7), 1509–17. Retrieved November 14, 2024, from https://doi.org/10.1007/s10995-011-0918-2

McLaren, N., & Shanbhogue, R. (2011). *Using Internet Search Data as Economic Indicators*. Bank of England. Retrieved November 14, 2024, from https://www.bankofengland.co.uk/quarterly-bulletin/2011/q2/using-internet-search-data-as-economic-indicators

Naccarato, A., Falorsi, S., Loriga, S., & Pierini, A. (2018). Combining Official and Google Trends Data to Forecast the Italian Youth Unemployment Rate. *Technological Forecasting and Social Change*, *130*, 114–22. Retrieved November 14, 2024, from https://doi.org/10.1016/J.TECHFORE.2017.11.022

Nelson, M., & Stephens, J. (2011). Do Social Investment Policies Produce More and Better Jobs? In N. Morel, B. Palier, & J. Palme (eds), *Towards a Social Investment Welfare State?: Ideas, Policies and Challenges* (pp. 205–234). Bristol Policy Press.

Nikolai, R. (2011). Towards Social Investment? Patterns of Public Policy in the OECD World. In N. Morel, B. Palier, & J. Palme (eds), *Towards a Social Investment Welfare State?: Ideas, Policies and Challenges* (pp. 91–116). The Policy Press.

Nimmo, B. (2019). *Measuring Traffic Manipulation on Twitter*. Retrieved November 14, 2024, from https://demtech.oii.ox.ac.uk/research/posts/measuring-traffic-manipulation-on-twitter/

OECD. (2007). *Babies and Bosses – Reconciling Work and Family Life*. OECD Publishing. Retrieved November 14, 2024, from https://doi.org/10.1787/9789264032477-en

OECD. (2011). *Doing Better for Families*. OECD Publishing. https://doi.org/10.1787/9789264098732-en

OECD. (2015). *In It Together – Why Less Inequality Benefits All*. OECD Publishing. Retrieved November 14, 2024, from https://doi.org/10.1787/9789264235120-en

Orloff, A. (2010). Gender. In F. Castles, S. Leibfried, J. Lewis, H. Obinger, & C. Pierson (eds), *The Oxford Handbook of the Welfare State* (pp. 252–64). Oxford University Press.

Peter, H., & Gingerich, D. (2009). Varieties of Capitalism and Institutional Complementarities in the Political Economy. *British Journal of Political Science*, *39*(3), 449–82. Retrieved November 14, 2024, from https://doi.org/10.1017/S0007123409000672

Proserpio, D., Counts, S., & Jain, A. (2016). The Psychology of Job Loss: Using Social Media Data to Characterize and Predict Unemployment. In *Proceedings of the 8th ACM Conference on Web Science* (pp. 223–32). Retrieved November 14, 2024, from https://doi.org/10.1145/2908131.2913008

Radziwill, N.M., & Benton, M.C. (2016). *Bot or Not? Deciphering Time Maps for Tweet Interarrivals*. Retrieved November 14, 2024, from http://arxiv.org/abs/1605.06555

Roberts, M.E., Stewart, B.M., & Tingley, D. (2019). Journal of Statistical Software stm: R Package for Structural Topic Models. *Journal of Statistical Software*, *91*(2). Retrieved November 14, 2024, from https://doi.org/10.18637/jss.v091.i02

Roberts, M.E., Stewart, B.M., Tingley, D., Lucas, C., Leder-Luis, J., Gadarian, S.K., Albertson, B., & Rand, D.G. (2014). Structural Topic Models for Open-Ended Survey Responses. *American Journal of Political Science*, *58*(4), 1064–82. Retrieved November 14, 2024, from https://doi.org/10.1111/ajps.12103

Röder, M., Both, A., & Hinneburg, A. (2015). Exploring the Space of Topic Coherence Measures. In *Proceedings of the Eighth ACM International Conference on Web Search and Data Mining – WSDM '15* (pp. 399–408). Retrieved November 14, 2024, from https://doi.org/10.1145/2684822.2685324

Schmid, G. (2008). *Full Employment In Europe: Managing Labour Market Transitions and Risks*. Edward Elgar.

Sievert, C., & Shirley, K. (2014). LDAvis: A Method for Visualizing and Interpreting Topics. In *Proceedings of the Workshop on Interactive Language Learning, Visualization, and Interfaces* (pp. 63–70).

Simonsen, M. (2010). Price of High-Quality Daycare and Female Employment. *Scandinavian Journal of Economics*, *112*(3), 570–94. Retrieved November 14, 2024, from https://doi.org/10.1111/j.1467-9442.2010.01617.x

Soentken, M., van Hooren, F., & Rice, D. (2017). The Impact of Social Investment Reforms on Income and Activation in the Netherlands. In A. Hemerijck (ed.), *The Uses of Social Investment* (pp. 235–43). Oxford University Press.

Statista. (2018). *Netherlands: Twitter Users, by Age Group 2017–2018*. Retrieved November 14, 2024, from https://www.statista.com/statistics/828876/twitter-penetration-rate-in-the-netherlands-by-age-group/

Statista. (2019). *Netherlands: Number of Twitter Users 2013–2019*. Retrieved November 14, 2024, from https://www.statista.com/statistics/880865/number-of-twitter-users-in-the-netherlands/

Taylor, L., Schroeder, R., & Meyer, E. (2014). Emerging Practices and Perspectives on Big Data Analysis in Economics: Bigger and Better or More of the Same? *Big Data & Society*, 1(2), 1–10. Retrieved November 14, 2024, from https://doi.org/10.1177/2053951714536877

Toole, J.L., Lin, Y.-R., Muehlegger, E., Shoag, D., González, M.C., & Lazer, D. (2015). Tracking Employment Shocks Using Mobile Phone Data. Journal of Royal Society Interface, 12. Retrieved November 14, 2024, from https://doi.org/10.1098/rsif.2015.0185

Turrell, A., Speigner, B.J., Djumalieva, J., Copple, D., & Thurgood, J. (2019). Transforming Naturally Occurring Text Data into Economic Statistics: The Case of Online Job Vacancy Postings. NBER Working Chapter Series, No. 25837. Retrieved November 14, 2024, from https://www.nber.org/papers/w25837

Van Den Bosch, A., Busser, B., Canisius, S., & Daelemans, W. (2007). An Efficient Memory-Based Morphosyntactic Tagger and Parser for Dutch. In F. van Eynde, P. Dirix, I. Schuurman, & V. Vandeghinste (eds), Selected Chapters of the 17th Computational Linguistics in the Netherlands Meeting (pp. 99–114). Leuven, BE: CLIN.

Verbist, G. (2017). Measuring Social Investment Returns: Do Publicly Provided Services Enhance Social Inclusion? In A. Hemerijck (ed.), The Uses of Social Investment (pp. 194–207). Oxford University Press.

Vicente, M., Lopez-Menendez, A., & Perez, R. (2015). Forecasting Unemployment with Internet Search Data: Does It Help to Improve Predictions When Job Destruction Is Skyrocketing? Technological Forecasting and Social Change, 92, 132–9.

Vydra, S., & Klievink, B. (2019). Techno-Optimism and Policy-Pessimism in the Public Sector Big Data Debate. Government Information Quarterly, 36(4). Retrieved November 14, 2024, from https://doi.org/10.1016/j.giq.2019.05.010

APPENDIX A

Table 2.A1   ECEC keywords

kinderopvang, kinder opvang	General childcare term
kinderdagverblijf, kdv	Refers to daycare centres that cover children up to 4 years old and provide care for 10 hours a day during working hours.
gastouder, gastouders, gastouderopvang, gastouder opvang, gastouderbureau	Available for toddlers up to pre-school by parents caring for up to 6 children in locations approved by the national childcare register. Often administered by agencies.
peuterspeelzalen, peuterspeelzaal, peuterspeelplaats	Pre-schools, these are usually part of a primary school and are a preparatory programme for children between 2 and 4. These do not cover the whole week or full days.
peutergroep, peutergroepen	A more informal playgroup setting for young children.
buitenschoolseopvang, buitenschoolse opvang, naschoolseopvang, naschoolse opvang, naschoolse, BSO, voorschoolse opvang, voorschoolse, voorschoolseopvang	Afterschool and outdoor school care. However, this is connected to primary schools and thus generally available to children from 4 years of age.
oppas, oppassers, babysitter, babysitters, nanny, nannies	Babysitter options.
kinderopvangtoeslag	Childcare subsidy in the Netherlands.
kindgebonden budget	Automatic child benefit if your child is under 18 and your income is not high.
kinderbijslag	Covers part of the cost of raising children and depends on their number and residence.

Source: Author's own.

Table 2.A2   LM keywords referring to policy

Participatiewet, Participatiewet, Gesubsidieerde arbeid	Overarching legislation is in place to support people who can work but need some sort of assistance in order to work.
opleiding, scholing, heropleiding, omscholing, training, retraining, re-training, studie, studeren	Training and re-training.
praktijktraining, werkervaringsplek, stage, stage lopen	On the job training.
werkervaringsplek, werkervaring plek, studeer en werkplek, studeer- en werkplek, traineeship	Apprenticeship.
Werkbedrijf, werk.nl, werkplein, werkpleinen, arbeidsadviseur, uwv, arbeidsbemiddelaar, arbeidsbemiddeling, loopbaan coach, werk coach	Employment services.
WW-uitkering, uitkering, bijstand, bijstandsuitkering	Unemployment (benefits).
meewerkaftrek	Subsidy for when your partner works in your business without pay.

Source: Author's own.

Table 2.A3   LM keywords referring to types of employment

full-time werk, full time work, full-time work, full-time baan, full time baan, fulltime baan, voltijd baan, voltijd werk, voltijdwerk, 1 fte, 1 wtf	Full-time work
deeltijd werk, part-time werk, part time werk, deeltijd baan, part-time baan, part time baan	Part-time work
vast contract, vaste baan, vaste aanstelling	Permanent contract
tijdelijk contract, tijdelijke baan, tijdelijke aanstelling	Temporary contract
uitzendcontract.	Contract with recruitment agency
nul uren contract, 0 uren contract	Zero-hour contract
zelfstandige zonder personeel, zzp, zzp.ers, zzp.er, zzper, zzpers, DBA modelovereenkomst	Freelancers
schijnzelfstandigheid	Sham independence
loondienst, in loondienst	Salaried employment
eigen baas, eigen baas zijn	Self-employment

Source: Author's own.

Table 2.A4   LM keywords referring to general job search

werkloosheid, werkeloosheid, werkloos, zonder baan, jobless, in between jobs, between jobs, in between two jobs, between two jobs	Unemployment
onderbezetting, onderbezet	Underemployment
zoek naar werk, kijken voor werk, een baan zoeken, zoeken naar een baan, banen zoeken	Job search
passend werk, passende arbeid, passende baan, passende job	Correct or fitting job
goed werk, slecht werk, beter werk, betere kansen op werk, beter arbeidscontract, goed arbeidscontract, slecht arbeidscontract	A good job
vacature, vacatures, openstaande baan	Job vacancies
vaardigheidseisen, ervaringseisen, werkervaring, werkervaringseisen, competenties	Skill/experience requirements

Source: Author's own.

APPENDIX B

Table 2.B1   Employment openings topic

LDA 20 - topic 5		LDA 35 - topic 6		LDA 35 - topic 23		LDA 65 - topic 60		CTM 35 - topic 17		NMF 35 - 27	
Dutch	English	Dutch	English	Dutch	English	Dutch	English	Dutch	English	Dutch	English
vacature	job offer	jij	you	vacature	job offer	jij	you	jij	you	wij	we
jij	you	wij	we	#	#	wij	we	wij	we	op_zoek	looking
zoeken	search	op_zoek	looking	nieuw	new	op_zoek	looking	op_zoek	looking	team	team
#	#	jou	you	zoeken	to search	jou	you	zoeken	to search	enthousiast	enthusiastic
wij	we	zoeken	to search	medewerker	employee	collega	colleague	vacature	job offer	!	!
op_zoek	looking	willen	want	baan	job	technisch	technical	collega	colleague	collega	colleague
nieuw	new	leuk	fun	amsterdam	Amsterdam	limburg	limburg	team	team	opdrachtgever	client
jou	you	collega	colleague	amp	amp	arnhem	arnhem	we	we	kijken	look
medewerker	employee	team	team	via	through	checken	check	jou	you	graag	gladly
bekijken	see	we	we	utrecht	utrecht	uitdaging	challenge	reageren	comment	direct	straight away
willen	want	werken	to work	werk	work	senior	senior	komen	come	snel	fast
collega	colleague	snel	fast	manager	manager	!	!	snel	fast	leuk	fun
amp	amp	graag	gladly	bekijken	see	assistent	assistant	communicatie	communication	informatie	information
werken	to work	komen	come	v	v	tijdelijk	temporarily	enthousiast	enthusiastic	bekijken	see
team	team	functie	position	m	m	ervaren	to experience	bekijken	to look	interesse	interest

Source: Author's own.

Table 2.B2 Training and education

LDA 20 - topic 18		LDA 35 - topic 21		LDA 65 - topic 18		CTM 35 - topic 4		NMF 35 - topic 13	
Dutch	English	Dutch	English	Dutch	English	Dutch	English	Dutch	English
training	training	opleiding	education	opleiding	education	@	@	opleiding	education
opleiding	education	leren	to learn	staan	stand	studie	study	volgen	to follow
#	#	onderwijs	teaching	leren	to learn	opleiding	education	starten	start
1	1	student	student	vaak	often	zullen	will	leren	to learn
jaar	year	volgen	to follow	halen	fetch	wel	well	student	student
vandaag	today	school	school	professional	professional	moeten	should	maken	to make
nieuw	new	groep	group	brengen	bring	gaan	to go	vandaag	today
2	2	tijdens	while	niveau	level	studeren	to study	2019	2019
2019	2019	jong	young	soort	kind	denken	to think	geven	to give
dag	day	starten	start	helaas	unfortunately	maken	to make	hbo	HBO education
week	week	leerling	pupil	geleden	ago	jaar	year	tijdens	while
3	3	docent	teacher	vorig	last	ander	other	onderwijs	teaching
volgen	to follow	geven	to give	elkaar	each other	weten	know	mbo	MBO education
stage	internship	kind	child	waarin	in which	eigen	own	dag	day
amp	amp	kennis	knowledge	mnd	month	zeggen	say	mooi	beautiful

Source: Author's own.

Table 2.B3 Unemployment and social assistance

LDA 20 - topic 20		LDA 35 - topic 20		LDA 65 - topic 9		CTM 35 - topic 11		NMF 35 - topic 2	
Dutch	English	Dutch	English	Dutch	English	Dutch	English	Dutch	English
@	@	uitkering	payment	uwv	unemployment insurance agency	@	@	@	@
uitkering	payment	uwv	unemployment insurance agency	bedrijf	company	uitkering	payment	uitkering	payment
		bijstand	assistance	gemeente	municipality	uwv	unemployment insurance agency	uwv	unemployment insurance agency
uwv	unemployment insurance agency	@	@	(	(	mens	person	krijgen	to get
krijgen	to get	krijgen	to get	werkgever	employer	krijgen	to get	zullen	will
mens	person	betalen	To pay	bieden	offer	bijstand	assistance	eigen	own
jaar	year	geld	money	mogelijkheid	possibility	betalen	To pay	bijstand	assistance
moeten	should	via	through	kwaliteit	quality	moeten	should	gewoon	just
zzp	self-employed	recht	right	oplossing	solution	jaar	year	ander	other
bijstand	assistance	moeten	should	ruim	spacious	werken	to work	zitten	to sit
via	via	euro	euro	cursus	class	geld	money	kind	child
betalen	to pay	land	country	enorm	huge	via	through	nl	NL
werken	to work	huis	House	branche	industry	land	country	betalen	To pay
eigen	own	telegraaf	News outlet	bestuur	governance	nederland	The Netherlands	alleen	only
nederland	The Netherlands	kind	child	lokaal	local	gaan	to go	denken	to think

Source: Author's own.

38 *Handbook on governance and data science*

Table 2.B4   Hours per week worked

LDA 20 - topic 16		LDA 35 - topic 27		LDA 65 - topic 21		CTM 35 - topic 29		NMF 35 - topic 23	
Dutch	English	Dutch	English	Dutch	English	Dutch	English	Dutch	English
uur	hour	uur	hour	week	week	uur	hour	uur	hour
zorg	care	1	1	per	per	week	week	per	per
per	per	per	per	uur	hour	per	per	week	week
vacature	job offer	week	week	€	€	maand	month	1	1
week	week	2	2	maand	month	hbo	HBO education	32	32
nijmegen	Nijmegen	2019	2019	10	10	1	1	dag	day
chauffeur	driver	3	3	aantal	number	2	2	maand	month
24	24	4	4	euro	euro	3	3	24	24
40	40	2018	2018	20	20	mbo	MBO education	2	2
welzijn	wellbeing	januari	January	extra	additional	4	4	36	36
32	32	5	5	16	16	40	40	aantal	number
verpleegkundig	nursing	maand	month	12	12	plaats	place	40	40
c	c	jaar	year	30	30	24	24	functie	position
36	36	€	€	lid	member	20	20	€	€
begeleider	mentor	plaats	place	organiseren	to organize	vacature	job offer	3	3

Source: Author's own.

Table 2.B5   Self-employment

LDA 20 - topic 13		LDA 35 - topic 7		LDA 65 - topic 62		CTM 35 - topic 1		CTM 35 - topic 15		NMF 35 - topic 17	
Dutch	English	Dutch	English	Dutch	English	Dutch	English	Dutch	English	Dutch	English
zzp	self-employed	zzp	self-employed	zzp	self-employed	‐	‐	vacature	job offer	zzp	self-employed
#	#	opdracht	order/contract	via	via	zzp	self-employed	#	#	freelance	freelance
opdracht	order/contract	interim	interim	opdracht	order/contract	‐	‐	amsterdam	Amsterdam	opdracht	order/contract
interim	interim	freelance	freelance	interim	interim	ondernemer	entrepreneur	zzp	self-employed	interim	interim
freelance	freelance	ondernemer	entrepreneur	freelance	freelance	verplichten	oblige	opdracht	order/contract	info	info
gen	gen	#	#	slag	battle	economie	economy	freelance	freelance	ondernemer	entrepreneur
vacature	job offer	info	info	sturen	send	zzp-er	self-employed person	interim	interim	lezen	read
parttime	part-time	mkb	SMEs	specialist	specialist	willen	want	info	info	maken	to make
€	€	lezen	read	manier	way	werknemer	employee	rotterdam	Rotterdam	mkb	SMEs
lezen	read	freelancer	freelancer	.	.	pensioen	retirement	project	project	loggen	logging
info	info	professional	professional	verzorgen	take care of	mkb	SMEs	locatie	Location	planetinterim	planetinterim
postbezorger	mail deliverer	ondernemen	to undertake	half	half	loondienst	salaried service	werk	work	project	project
nieuw	new	tip	tip	volkskrant	Volkskrant	zzper	zzper	zwolle	Zwolle	professional	professional
planetinterim	planetinterim	verplichten	oblige	veilig	safe	<emoji>	<emoji>	senior	senior	€	€
freelancer	freelancer	blog	blog	basis	base	petitie	petition	adviseur	adviser	verplichten	oblige

Source: Author's own.

Table 2.B6 Childcare

| LDA 20 - topic 14 || LDA 35 - topic 14 || LDA 35 - topic 17 || LDA 65 - topic 65 || LDA 65 - topic 59 || CTM 35 - topic 30 ||
Dutch	English	Dutch	English	Dutch	English	Dutch	English	Dutch	English	Dutch	English
kinderopvang	childcare	kinderopvang	childcare	kinderdagverblijf	daycare	kind	child	sector	sector	kind	child
the	the	the	the	agent	agent	kinderopvang	childcare	kdv	daycare	kinderopvang	childcare
thanks	thanks	to	to	oss	oss	onderwijs	Education	verwachten	expect	ouder	older
to	to	thanks	thanks	lelystad	lelystad	school	school	kids	kids	media	media
latest	latest	latest	latest	kunst	art	bso	out-of-school care	onzin	nonsense	bso	out-of-school care
pedagogisch	pedagogical	pedagogisch	pedagogical	peuterspeelzaal	kindergarten	passen	to fit	tonen	show	kinderdagverblijf	daycare
aantal	number	<emoji>	<emoji>	den_helder	den Helder	leerling	pupil	effect	effect	pedagogisch	pedagogical
dienstverband	employment	sollicitatie	job application	hogeschool	University	gelukkig	happy	lachen	laugh	open	Open
branche	industry	bso	out-of-school care	vdab	vdab	leerkracht	teacher	rtlnieuws	rtlnews	social	social
status	status	branche	industry	sa	sa	gebruik	use	meestal	mostly	kdv	daycare
medewerker	employee	dienstverband	employment	basisonderwijs	primary education	vier	four	behandelen	to treat	aantal	number
sollicitatie	job application	open	Open	psychiater	psychiatrist	samenwerking	cooperation	nauwelijks	barely	bedrijf	company
open	open	status	status	ko	ko	betreffen	concern	oor	ear	opvang	day care
bso	out-of-school care	bedrijf	company	lg	lg	durven	to dare	collectief	collective	1	1
bedrijf	company	kdv	daycare	lelystad	Lelystad	wo	Wed	verband	bandage	branche	industry

Source: Author's own.

3. Data science meets political economy: applications to legislative favouritism around the world

Cyril Benoît, Dominik Brenner and Mihály Fazekas

INTRODUCTION

In recent years, legislative institutions across the world have experienced a "transparency rush" that has led to the opening of large and extremely diversified deposits of data (see De Fine Licht et al., 2014; Matheus & Janssen, 2020). This trend has been paralleled by easier access to these deposits due to their increasing digitalisation – for example, many parliaments across the world have built their own 'open government' or "open data" infrastructures, such as Canada's House of Commons,[1] France's National Assembly,[2] Germany's Bundestag,[3] and Israel's Knesset.[4] While the motives behind these policy developments are diverse, the resulting programmes and facilities commonly aim at opening up government operations to a large audience of (non-) academic experts, practitioners, journalists, and, above all, citizens.

In the literature, whether the move towards the opening of (and the easier access to) large-scale legislative data effectively improved political accountability or was broadly unsuccessful is still a matter of debate (see notably Clarke & Margetts, 2014; Worthy, 2015). That it resulted in perceptible implications for the approaches and methods of a broad range of academics and policy experts is more widely recognised. Such implications have been, in effect, largely amplified by the simultaneous rise of data science and data analytics in political research – and this twofold "push" has eventually resulted in a more systematic use of large-scale micro-level datasets to tackle both academic and more policy-orientated questions in the field. In this context, novel answers were provided to a number of long-standing debates, and new avenues for future research have been delineated (see Monroe, 2013).

Grounded in recent advances in political science and political economy, this chapter provides a series of reflections on these developments. It more broadly shows how data science can improve our understanding of issues that, given their positive and normative implications, are central both for the expansion of knowledge in the field and for present-day governance. Beyond illuminating the kind of insights large-scale data and data science can bring to the study of political institutions, our goal in this chapter is thus also to expose some of its diverse functions – and to identify the challenges that result, notably for the connection of data science and good governance.

Throughout the chapter, we more specifically demonstrate our points by using legislative favouritism as a case study. This notion refers to legislations that, based on their design or features, disproportionately advantage specific private interests over others. As a research topic, legislative favouritism is located at the intersection of various domains of inquiry for political economists – including empirical research on lobbying or special interest influence in politics (de Figueiredo & Richter, 2014), the relation between other forms of particularistic legislation and electoral accountability (e.g., see Motolinia, 2021), and the role played by elected representatives in economic governance more broadly. But legislative favouritism has also been precociously identified as a major issue for policymaking by a number of international organisations like the Organisation for Economic Co-operation and Development (OECD), the United Nations, and the World Bank. That legislative favouritism constitutes a serious issue for scholars and practitioners alike is thus well established – but so far, both have faced a number of difficulties in their attempts at systematically detecting and measuring economic favouritism in law-making. We argue in this chapter that tools and methods drawn from data science applied to large-scale, now publicly available micro-data can offer a range of solutions to these issues. As discussed in greater detail below, they indeed provide the basis for an in-depth analysis of laws, of legislative processes (including voting shares, size and scope of debates) as well as of outcomes of legislation (such as laws passed and amended). Various additional features of law-making, including information on public consultation and impact assessments, can also be considered. On this basis, the chapter provides a series of tentative reflections about what data science can bring from two different standpoints (the academic and the governance ones).

The chapter is organised as follows. The next section briefly describes the trends towards greater availability of data sources and deposits of political institutions (with a more specific focus on legislatures) and presents some of the main applications of data science they have stimulated in political research. We then introduce legislative favouritism as a particularly instructive case study, especially given its broader resonance with both long-standing debates in political science and political economy and with more policy-orientated concerns. This topic serves as an example of the application of data science to the study of political institutions outlined in the following section. Here we introduce an original dataset as well as a range of indicators that allow for the detection and the measurement of favouritism in law-making (and outputs) of the legislative process based on descriptive statistics that contribute to the debates raised in the previous section. In the concluding section of this chapter, we more broadly reflect on our findings, both from a positive and a more normative perspective.

OPEN DATA, DATA SCIENCE, AND THE STUDY OF POLITICAL INSTITUTIONS

Data Availability and Accessibility of Political Institutions: An Overview

Recent years have seen a significant increase in the data that political institutions make publicly available. Usually, this movement has been paralleled with an improvement in the accessibility of such large-scale databases through dedicated websites and open-data interfaces. While other governmental entities or public services have also played a role in these transformations (as demonstrated by Pencheva et al., 2020), legislative institutions typically take centre stage. This is arguably attributed to their pivotal position at the intersection of the political and policy dimensions within the law-making process, coupled with the substantial volume of data generated by their activities.

Across countries, legislative institutions have thus "vastly enhanced their internet-based information to the public covering both history, rules of procedure and current developments"; "made available numerous legislative databases through their websites providing online access to important documents" while improving access to these data through dedicated platforms (Saalfeld, 2022). A comparative survey conducted by the Open Data Hub of the Interparliamentary Union has recently revealed the depth and magnitude of this trend. Among the 29 legislative institutions in Asia, Africa, Europe, and Latin America included in the survey, 86.2 per cent had an open data policy and about 80 per cent were already having or currently planned to develop a formal data governance plan. The dataset types that are made available disclose information about members of parliaments (in all cases included in the study); bills, voting results, and laws in the vast majority of the cases; and data about political parties, leaders, and members' financial records in less than half of these.[5]

The reasons behind these converging initiatives are diverse, even if a series of salient factors – that are not mutually exclusive – can be identified. Besides some obvious technological preconditions, the trend towards greater availability and accessibility to legislative data has been commonly attributed to the congruent demands of different groups of actors. Governments, notably in advanced liberal democracies, have faced growing pressures from international organisations (like the OECD[6]), civil society organisations, and non-governmental organisations (NGOs) to be more "transparent" and "open" in their approach to policymaking. Most of these actors typically emphasised in their demands the importance of transparency for the quality of democracy, fighting against corruption, or mitigating special interest influence in politics.[7] As this suggests, an overall concern for biased or unfair law-making has thus been a recurrent theme in these mobilisations. Another (though related) argument that they put forward was that greater transparency and data availability could provide citizens with more exhaustive information about their representatives, their votes, and their activities – and thus, better opportunities to hold elected officials to account.[8] For all of these demands, the online diffusion of legislative data sources may have appeared to policymakers of various countries as an appealing solution.

Other important factors are more internal – as they typically emanate from legislatures and their internal rules or codes of conduct. In newer democracies, for instance, similar initiatives towards greater availability and accessibility of legislative data have been the result of the adoption of more transparent legislative procedures. Large-n studies suggest that such adoption was, however, subject to substantial variation across countries. These variations are notably explicable by the characteristics of electoral systems and the resulting incentives they impose on legislators when deciding whether to promote or hinder greater transparency (Hug et al., 2015). More recent evidence indicates that the Covid-19 pandemic, as it forced legislators to rely more extensively on digital tools, has been an important driver of accelerated digitalisation of political institutions (notably in partially free countries, see Waismel-Manor et al., 2022). In turn, such greater reliance on digital devices has been conducive to a greater publicisation of legislatures' daily operations, like meetings, debates, and votes. Regardless of the importance of these factors, however, the endeavour to construct, publish, and disseminate extensive legislative datasets is contingent upon the capacities of legislatures, notably in terms of professionalism and resources (see Copeland & Patterson, 1994). This is clearly underscored by the survey conducted by the Interparliamentary Union mentioned above.

This brief review of the main factors that pushed for the development of large-scale legislative data availability and accessibility thus reveals different sources and motivations. Their consequences for students of legislative institutions, however, are largely similar: while they were accustomed to relying on "painstakingly collected information from the printed versions of the official records and minute, more recent studies can now rely on information easily available online" (Hug, 2013). This has arguably generated, in turn, an "enthusiasm" (in Hug's terms) for the collection and analysis of large-scale micro-level datasets among students of political institutions and beyond. Below we succinctly describe how the parallel emergence of data science and data analytics in political research has largely fuelled such enthusiasm.

The Rise of Data Science and Their Implications for the Study of Political Institutions

The notable expansion of open data in various legislative institutions across the world has resulted in large-scale databases that are usually made easily accessible online. More accurately, the discussion above suggests a mutually reinforcing (yet partly contingent) co-development of networked data infrastructures within legislative institutions; of rising "open data movements that seek to make as much data as possible openly available for all to use"; and, as suggested by the evidence gathered by the Interparliamentary Union, of the formation of "new institutional structures that seek to secure common guidelines and policies with respect to data formats structures, meta-data … and sharing protocols" (Kitchin, 2014). While the amount of available information may substantially vary, it is clear, though, that legislative institutions now generate and diffuse an increasingly large volume of data, characterised by their important variety (ranging from lobby registers to voting records) and by the digital formats through which they are made available.

This overall process is hardly specific to the case of legislative institutions. Similar developments have been noticed in many areas of social life, thus well beyond the realm of government and politics. Overall, such developments have stimulated lots of reflections and controversies about the so-called "data revolution" commonly attributed to four notable trends, namely, "extensive digital datafication, widespread connectedness, networking, and computer authoring" (Brady, 2019). What is also widely acknowledged is that at the same time, the greater availability of large quantities of data has enabled the application of data science and data analytics approaches and frameworks. By this, we more specifically refer to "a range of mathematical and computational methods" that notably "include machine learning (based on methods from engineering, computer science and statistics) to develop algorithms that describe patterns in large-scale data, simulate variables that are unknown from the associations between those that are known and developing predictive capacity" (Margetts, 2017).

Political research was not immune to these developments – data science significantly expanded in this field as well over the last two decades. The swift and extensive growth of new data sources, coupled with advanced analytical capabilities, has sparked focused discussions on the potential benefits and challenges of applying "big data" and "data science" to research tasks. In the areas usually covered by the social and political sciences, these debates have mostly related to the need for studying "societal and political change from big data and data science" per se; to the corresponding implications for social scientists faced with increasing amounts of data available; to the "new kinds of questions" they offer them to ask; to the "new ways" social and political scientists organise their work; and to the "ethical issues" in research they pose (Brady, 2019). Other more methodologically orientated debates have focused on the links (and have discussed the potential incompatibilities) between these developments and other important trends in political methodology, like formal theory and causal inference (e.g., see Clark & Golder, 2015; Monroe et al., 2015). Reviewing these debates goes well beyond the scope of the present chapter, and we will not attempt such a review. In what follows, we offer instead some applications of these approaches to the study of political institutions to illustrate what seems to be the least controversial claim in these discussions – namely, that the greater availability of large-scale data combined with the analytical capacities of data science can facilitate answering hard-to-tackle questions, sometimes with wide-ranging implications (Fazekas, 2014).

Although it is not without raising some important challenges, this is arguably the most obvious and conventionally accepted benefit accompanying the above trends. This is largely due to the fact that over recent years, political scientists, through relying on large-scale, recently opened and digitalised data sources (including administrative, legislative, and textual data), have been able to provide meaningful answers to long-standing research questions. Prominent examples in this regard include Kim's (2017) analysis of firm-level lobbying for trade liberalisation and Grimmer et al.'s (2012) study of the personal vote – which occurs when legislators direct projects and programmes to their districts and constituents, in turn, reward their legislator for the level of federal spending in the district. In the former study, Kim (2017) linked a dataset on lobbying by all publicly traded manufacturing firms from reports filed under the US Lobbying Disclosure Act of 1995 to all bills in Congress that had been lobbied. Through this analysis, he brought to light significant within-industry cleavages, showing the limitations of the common focus of existing scholarship on industry-level lobbying. In the latter study, Grimmer et al. (2012) analysed around 170,000 US House of Representatives press releases issued between 2005 and 2010 and revealed "how legislators' credit claiming messages – and not just expenditures in the district – affect constituents' credit allocation and the cultivation of a personal vote for incumbents". Here, constituents were notably shown to be more responsive to the total number of messages sent rather than to the amount claimed.

Among many notable others, the two above-mentioned contributions illustrate the impactful synergy of large-scale data and data science. They provide valuable insights into enduring questions in political science that relate to the politics of trade policy for the former, and legislative particularistic spending for the latter. But the very same approaches, as we emphasise here, can equally contribute to solving more directly policy-orientated questions. This is evidenced by an abundant literature that has discussed the intimate connection that exists between data science and data-driven decision-making (e.g., see Provost & Fawcett, 2013). When we are able to retrieve and cluster large-scale data according to certain characteristics, data science can indeed detect some problematic behaviours, trends, or patterns that may explain some unintended outcomes from the policy process – and that can, in turn, be central to improving its overall efficiency or transparency. It can also precisely document the frequency and magnitude of phenomena, like political corruption, that have been identified as important challenges for the quality of governance but that have typically proven to be hard to quantify in a systematic manner. To substantiate these arguments, we reflect in the rest of this chapter on the case of legislative favouritism, an important research topic that has also been identified as an important governance challenge by a number of governmental and non-governmental institutions in recent years. We thus see it as a relevant case study to illustrate and discuss further the implications of the trends described in this section, and to show both the promises and challenges of the application of data science to the study of political institutions for different purposes.

A Case Study on Legislative Favouritism

Legislative favouritism – that manifests through the passage of legislation that disproportionally advantage a specific firm or group of firms over others in a given economic sector[9] – has been the subject of sustained attention in widely different fields. In the area of political research, the topic has been studied in the broader context of the redistributive implications of legislation, and the ability of political decision-making to shape economic outputs. A long tradition has also studied it from the perspective of firms' political activism, under the general observation that business actors, while being "the most vigorous breast beaters against government regulation and interference are at the same time the most persistent seekers of government favour and protection" (Dykstra, 1951). But legislative favouritism, and a number of related terms such as policy capture, has also been an important matter of concern for a sizeable array of non-governmental and governmental organisations like the OECD, the World Bank, and the United Nations (OECD, 2017). Here, the notion has been typically linked to cronyism, unjust or unfair law-making, deliberate governmental avoidance of legislative reform, and unethical practices in politics – and the struggle against legislative favouritism was explicitly presented as an important challenge to achieve a broad range of quality governance and Sustainable Development Goals.[10]

While legislative favouritism thus constitutes a serious issue for academics and practitioners alike, its variation as well as its magnitude from one country to another are less firmly established. One of the main reasons for this situation has been a general lack of solid or thorough cross-country evidence of legislative favouritism, in large part due to limited data availability. Thus, students of legislative favouritism have tended to rely on aggregate-level data, typically derived from surveys of business or elite perceptions. Hence, favouritism was usually inferred on the basis of mere correlational evidence between the perceived interests of private actors and the outcomes associated with some specific legislations. Consequently, and as powerfully argued by Dan Carpenter and David Moss in their discussion of the related notion of regulatory capture, "what special interest influence actually looks like in practice, what mechanisms already exist for limiting such influence", and the circumstances under which these actors' pressures "work well or poorly" have been typically missing in both academic and more policy-orientated discussions on these issues (Carpenter & Moss, 2014). It is not difficult to imagine how, in this context, a greater availability of large-scale micro-data combined with more advanced analytical tools could help solve these pitfalls.

Before that, however, some clarifications about the concept of legislative favouritism as we understand it are needed. A critical corollary of our acceptance of the term is that legislative favouritism is the result of an implicit contract between legislator(s) and firm(s) amounting to a corrupt exchange that thus requires intent and action both from the firm(s) and legislator(s). On usually rare occasions, such a corrupt exchange might involve direct bribe payments from the firm(s) to legislator(s) in exchange for passing legislation, tabling an amendment, or any other legislative activity demanded by the firm to achieve the desired (and predetermined) outcome. However, it can also take the form of more indirect exchanges of favours, such as through campaign donations for a legislator or her own party; or when the favoured firm promises to hire a legislator (or some members of her circle) as a reward for her activities. As such, legislative favouritism is susceptible to interacting with the different goals traditionally pursued by elected representatives (such as re-election and office seeking, see Strøm, 1997) as well as with their various career prospects – both inside and outside the legislature.

Overall and more broadly, all of this suggests that legislative favouritism can have numerous implications both within (e.g., on legislative stability and on the law-making process per se) and outside the legislative domain (as it can significantly reshape sectoral dynamics or affect firms' performances and strategies).

Consequently, legislative favouritism shares obvious similarities, but also critical differences with other related concepts typically found in the literature interested in the politics of (re)distribution through legislation. Like pork-barrel politics, it is a subset of distributive policy; but while the former mostly applies to situations where legislators seek to maximise their re-election prospects through targeting states and congressional districts (see Evans, 2011), legislative favouritism might be driven by a broader range of motives, while targeting at the same time a more specific category of individual actors, namely, firms. The concept is also distinct from lobbying as it usually appears in pure models of interest-group politics, which do not imply a direct transfer of money to politicians (de Figueiredo, 2002) and, more importantly, which are usually expected to benefit a (sub)sector that interest groups are deemed to represent – while individual firms are, *ex ante*, the main drivers and targets of legislative favouritism. To some extent, the outcomes of legislative favouritism are similar to those of regulatory or policy capture; but unlike capture, it does not require a *repeated* or *consistent* redirection of a law away from the public interest to be inferred (Carpenter & Moss, 2014). It can be, in other terms, both a one-off event and less consistent than the cases of capture as defined by Carpenter and Moss. As it is driven by an explicit intent and action from the firm, legislative favouritism is also different from a strict ideological bias towards a specific company – that could, for instance, respond to explicit and publicly expressed beliefs and values of a firm's decision-makers (Goll & Zeitz, 1991). While corporate ideology may ease legislative favouritism, it can never be considered a necessary condition for it. This also distinguishes legislative favouritism from a sudden shift in legislators' policy preferences that may entail similar consequences (some firms suddenly benefiting from the law-making process at the expense of others), as such a shift is assumed not to be driven by direct actions from the firm.

USING LARGE-SCALE MICRO-DATA TO STUDY POLITICAL INSTITUTIONS: AN APPLICATION TO LEGISLATIVE FAVOURITISM

A Comprehensive Mapping of Legislative Processes and Outputs

We devote this section to illustrating some of the key promises and challenges associated with the greater availability of legislative data worldwide, paralleled with increased capacities to collect and analyse them. To do so, we use the case of legislative favouritism as defined in the previous section as a particularly relevant and instructive matter of inquiry. Rather than providing a fully-fledged analysis of the determinants and implications of legislative favouritism (a task that would arguably extend well beyond the scope of the present chapter), we here introduce some large-scale datasets as well as a range of original indicators, and provide descriptive data to substantiate two related arguments evoked in the previous section: first, that using large-scale micro-data can provide a solid empirical basis to address previously hard-to-tackle questions; and, second, that the application of data science techniques can help to detect patterns and trends in these data that can offer meaningful and robust answers to these questions. Overall, such an approach has a series of important implications for a range of questions of interest for academics and practitioners alike – an important point to which we return at the end of the present section.

Throughout this section, we rely on the large-scale datasets of the Global Corruption Observatory project (http://globalcorruptionobservatory.com/). In the context of this project, we have thus far collected legislative data from more than ten countries.[11] All data were scraped from national parliamentary websites, benefiting both from data collection techniques described above that have become common in political research and from the greater availability of large amounts of data that many political institutions across the world now make available online. The data collection process is based on a variable guide, a data collection handbook, and a tested validation process, not shown here due to space constraints. Overall, the current dataset consists of 258,168 bills (ongoing or rejected) and 58,629 enacted laws (see Table 3.1).

Over the course of this process, and in an attempt at overcoming empirical gaps in both academic and more applied debates on legislative favouritism, we collected fine-grained data about the different operations and stages of the legislative process. Our 65 variables reflect the number of stages through which a bill has passed, as well as information about these stages like their duration (including first and second reading, upper and lower chamber deliberations and votes); statistics and results for votes and tabled amendments; properties of the law (like its size) as well as additional information about the law-making process (such as whether or not impact assessments were conducted for the law in question). Table 3.2 showcases a few selected core variables from our encompassing variable list. We developed on this basis a range of indicators to allow for a more systematic detection of legislative favouritism that are introduced in the next section.

Table 3.1   *Data overview*

Country	Coverage (Years)	n (bills)		n (total)
Brazil	1946–2022	58,613	7,934	66,547
Bulgaria	2001–2022	3,432	1,659	5,091
Chile	1990–2022	11,004	15,019	26,023
Colombia	1998–2022	9,059	1,598	10,657
Germany	1972–2023	3,473	6,011	9,484
France	2012–2022	1,227	473	1,700
Hungary	1998–2022	2,527	3,225	5,752
India	1952–2022	5,589	3,433	9,022
Portugal	1976–2022	8,310	4,664	12,974
Russia	1995–2022	21,808	9,630	31,438
United Kingdom	2006–2022	2,582	541	3,123
United States	1995–2022	130,544	4,442	134,986
Total	-	**258,168**	**58,629**	**316,797**

Source: Authors' own.

Table 3.2   Core variables of the Global Corruption Observatory (subset of the full variable list)

Variable name	Description	Type
record_id	Assigned unique ID of the bill by the research team	string
bill_title	Short title of the passed bill/law	string
origin_type	Originator of a law: government, non-government	categorical
originator_name	names of the MPs or names government body/bodies	list
bill_status	Passed/rejected by the parliament or ongoing	categorical
affecting_laws_count	Count of laws which modify the enacted law	numeric
affecting_laws_first_date	Date when the enacted law was first modified	date
date_introduction	Date of introduction to parliament as	date
date_passing	Date of passing the law/enactment of the law	date
time_in_parl_days	The number of days a law spent in parliament	numeric
law_size	Size of the enacted law	numeric
law_text	Full text of the enacted law	string
economic_sector	NACE/ISIC classification for a given law	categorical
final_vote_in_favour	Number of votes in parliament in favor of a bill	numeric
final_vote_against	Number of votes in parliament against of a bill	numeric
final_vote_abst	Number of final absentee votes	numeric

Source: Authors' own.

Detecting and Measuring Legislative Favouritism

Favouritism indicators

Pure instances of private-sector actors' interventions on individual legislators are particularly hard to observe in the real world, especially when they take the form of informal bribes or a promise from the firm to hire a legislator after her term in office. More indirect forms of intervention, like campaign donations, are more easily found in countries like the US (where their importance in explaining some aspects of legislators' activities, such as votes, is however still debated; see Wright, 2014). But in many other countries, scholars have to rely on scant, sometimes aggregate-level data that can hardly serve as a rigorous basis to infer favouritism. Due to these limitations (which could more fundamentally impede cross-country comparisons), we believe that it is from within the law-making process itself that legislative favouritism shall be first identified – before being formally inferred with a range of covariates. Stated differently, our key assumption is that "favouristic" legislations should exhibit a range of generic properties that would allow for their identification. In accordance with a rich literature on governance transparency and political accountability (Bauhr et al.,

2020), we more specifically think that (at least) four main indicators have to be retained in this regard. They respectively concern the profile of the initiator of a bill, the features of the bill or the law effectively passed, the kind of legislative procedures that have been followed, and legislative behaviour once a law is enacted. Simply stated, we argue that for each of these generic steps of the legislative process, there are some outputs or developments that raise the risk of a law serving favouritistic ends. We discuss these as well as our arguments in greater detail below.

Chronologically, how – and more precisely, by whom – a bill enters the legislative stage constitutes, in our eyes, the first indicator of favouritism. Our assumption here is that bills initiated by legislators bear greater chances of being favouristic than those initiated by the government. The rationale for this assumption is rather intuitive. A government-initiated bill constitutes the standard path for a text to become law and involves a range of checks and debates in parliament with legislators from other parties. However, bills initiated by legislators do not necessarily need to go through the usual set of checks (like public consultation) and procedures (such as the committee stage). In turn, this could facilitate the passage of favouristic legislation, as this procedure would reduce other legislators' capacity to properly scrutinise a bill – and potentially, to detect its favouristic orientation. Theoretically, this scenario embodies a typical Kingdonian agenda-setting case, where a legislator takes on the role of a policy entrepreneur, purposefully connecting political, policy, or problem contexts to advocate for their favoured proposal (Kingdon, 2003). However, in this instance, it aligns not only with the legislator's preference but also corresponds to the favoured proposal of a specific firm. The argument here, of course, is not that all bills initiated by legislators are favouristic in essence but that they clearly entail a risk of favouritism that deserves more careful consideration.

We think that the features of a bill, and more particularly its size, constitute a second indicator of favouritism. Here the argument is that very large (and usually heterogeneous) bills or laws – often referred to in the literature as "monster bills", "omnibus legislation" or "big laws" – are more conducive to legislative favouritism.[12] As established by a now increasingly important literature, such laws are indeed associated with legislative work-(over)load, a decrease in the effective influence of non-(highly) specialised legislators in law-making, and create strong pressures on the legislative agenda (Rozenberg, 2021). While the adoption of such big and heterogeneous laws might be the result of different motives (like signalling or credit-claiming), they crucially provide a conducive context for corrupt legislators to exercise their influence over the course of the legislative process. Especially in institutional settings lacking clear rules restricting amendments to the matter at hand (e.g., see Alámán, 2009), interest groups can more easily pressure legislators to introduce favouristic amendments since they don't have to buy an entire piece of legislation. As bills become more complex and address a variety of different issues, the capacity of legislators to fully analyse every detail or article decreases. Consequently, omnibus legislation provides fertile ground for favouritism to be more easily concealed within amendments or other kinds of legislative texts.

A third and more widely used indicator of favouritism is the use of extraordinary or emergency procedures by the parliament to pass a bill. Bills that are notably "fast-tracked" in parliament in this context (typically passed within ten days, according to the OECD integrity indicator threshold) grant little opportunity for legislators to engage in a thorough evaluation of a bill, limit the space for deliberations, and prevent amendments during floor consideration

(Magar et al., 2021). In this context, and just as for our first indicator, such procedures are more conducive to legislative favouritism – as they allow the government to target specific firms without taking the risk that this would be revealed over the course of the legislative process. More generally, the simple fact of selecting this type of procedure instead of a regular one could in itself indicate that the government wants to act under the radar of legislative scrutiny – something which is usually associated with backdoor politics and greater business influence in the policy process.

Lastly, we consider the ex post career of laws (after their enactment) through the shape of their modifications as an additional indicator of favouritism. While laws should be modified if external circumstances change or the original goal of a law couldn't be obtained, frequent modifications shortly after enactment (and over time) cannot be justified merely based on efficiency grounds (Brenner & Fazekas, 2023). Instead, such legislative instability might indicate the undue influence of private interests on national legislators to receive favouristic legislative changes in a context where parliamentary scrutiny is less severe. Again, our point here is not to suggest that such modifications should lead us to automatically infer legislative favouritism – rather, that they require special attention as they *could* indicate that these kinds of modifications are driven by legislators' attempts at favouring specific actors, more than by a genuine concern for *ex post* scrutiny.

Descriptive results for favouritism indicators across countries

Now that we have described how we measure favouristic legislation, let us turn to an examination of the distribution of our four indicators in selected countries. Figure 3.1 plots the originators of legislation based on our categorical origin_type variable (Table 3.1) with data collected directly from the law pages of national parliamentary websites. The pie charts display the percentage of laws and bills grouped by the initiator of legislation and show strong variation in the success rate of bills between the UK, Portugal, and Hungary. While only 17 per cent of bills became law in the UK, the number increased to roughly one-quarter in Portugal and more than two-thirds in Hungary.

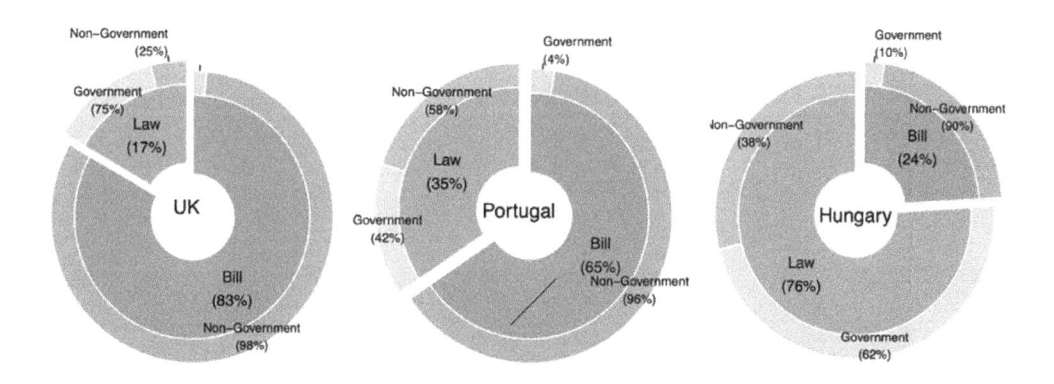

Source: Authors' own.

Figure 3.1   Originators of legislation in the United Kingdom, Portugal, and Hungary

52   *Handbook on governance and data science*

While all three cases offer interesting variation, we would like to draw the attention of the reader to the UK. Given that our argument about originators is more obvious in legislative systems with well-established structures that allow legislators to actively influence and shape the law-making process, the UK serves as a hard test for our first indicator. This is due to the UK government's dominance over the legislative process. Indeed, it is often claimed that the "parliament's legislative agenda is the government's agenda" and very few Private Members' bills become laws ((Bowler, 2010). At the same time, our data show that 25 per cent of laws were not initiated by the government, which supports the argument that, even in the UK, governments and legislators tend to cooperate rather than compete (Russell & Gover, 2018). This seems particularly true for intra-party cooperation between the government and government backbenchers (Russell & Cowley, 2018). Governments might then cooperate with government backbenchers to pass favouristic legislation that will not receive the degree of scrutiny typically demanded for government-initiated bills. Thus, stricter control mechanisms during the law-making process for government initiatives could encourage delegation early on and provide one potential justification for the relatively large share of non-government laws, even in the case of the Westminster model.

Figures 3.2 and 3.3 showcase the distribution of our second and third indicators, namely, omnibus legislation and extraordinary procedures. Both are important indicators of favouritism *during* the law-making process given the lack of parliamentary and/or public scrutiny to which they are usually associated, as well as the greater opportunities they confer to firms to exercise direct pressures on legislators.

Figure 3.2 shows the distribution of emergency procedures as a percentage of all laws passed in a given year in Bulgaria, India, and the UK. The indicator is based on the time_in_parl_days

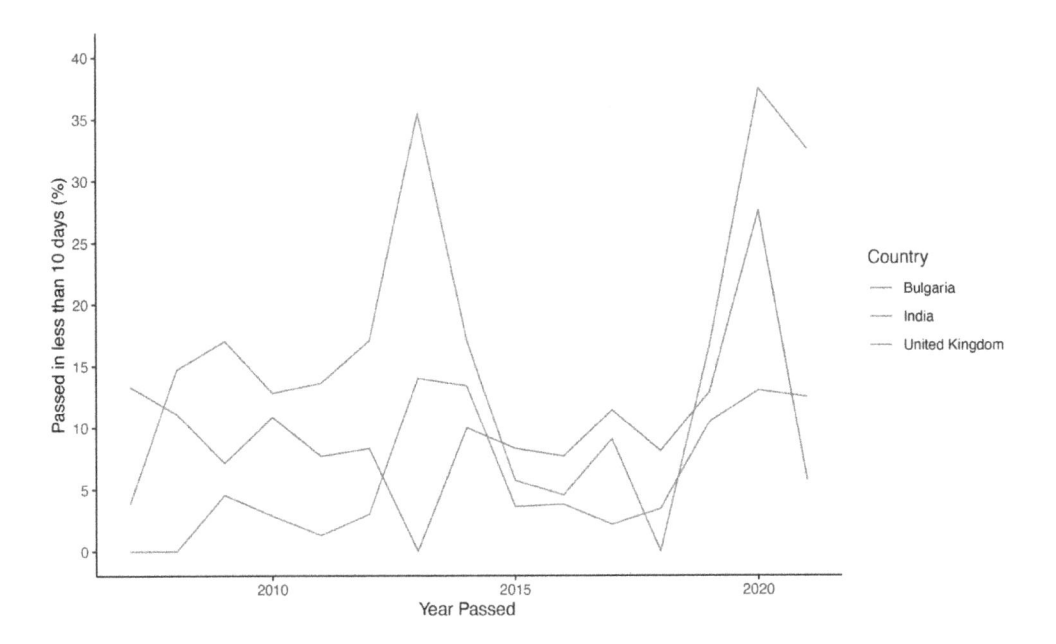

Source: Authors' own.

Figure 3.2   Laws passed through an extraordinary procedure as a percentage of all laws passed in a given year

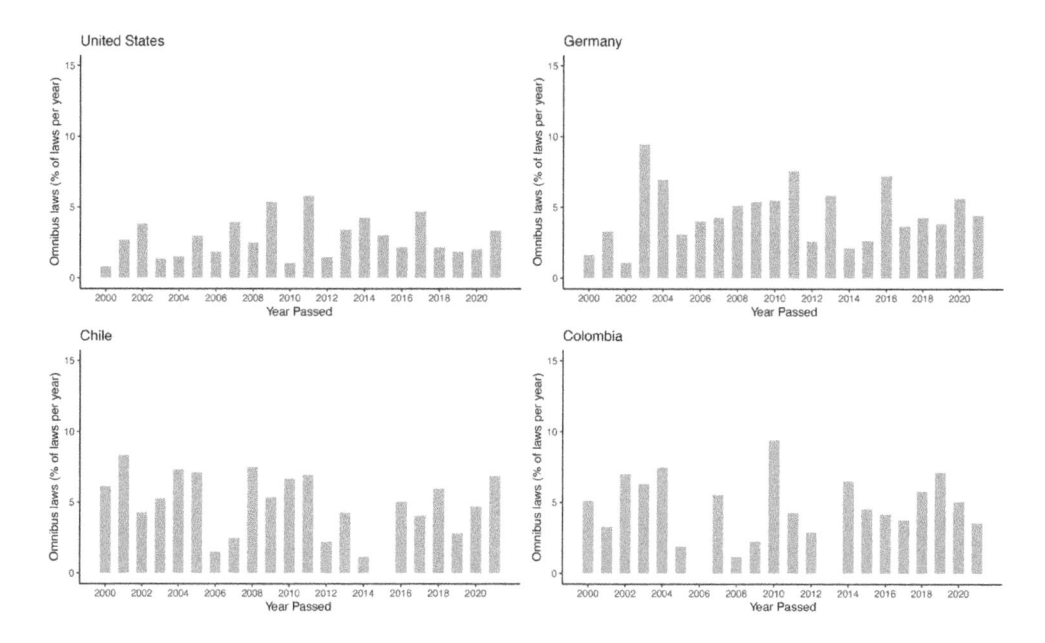

Figure 3.3   Omnibus laws as a percentage of all laws passed in a given year (until 2021)

variable (Table 3.1) which, in turn, is calculated as the difference between date_passing and date_introduction. Any law with ten or fewer days is thereby classified as an extraordinary procedure law. While the Covid-19 crisis explains the spike in extraordinary procedures in 2020, previous spikes and the evident cross-country variation across years require further detailed investigation. While short periods between the date of introduction and date_passing might be justified on efficiency grounds (Riedl, 2019), limited time for parliamentary scrutiny can also increase the chances of favouristic legislation passing.

Yet, extraordinary procedures are highly controversial and politically risky exactly because they diminish ordinary control mechanisms during the law-making stages. Governments in countries with generally strong democratic control mechanisms might therefore hesitate to rely on emergency procedures and resort to omnibus legislation instead. Omnibus legislation can be seen as an alternative to potentially corrupt legislative practices by minimising political resistance and limiting issue salience among the broader public. Figure 3.3 showcases the distribution of omnibus legislation as a percentage of all laws passed in a given year across four selected countries. Based on the size of the law text, we calculated the mean law size per year and labelled all laws as omnibus legislation that are at least two standard deviations from the mean.

Across our four-country sample, Germany shows the most consistent use of omnibus legislation. While these types of legislation are commonly used as a tool for political compromise and coalition-building, they also increase the chances for favouristic law-making since "one faction or interest group may swallow the toad in return for getting its favourite regulation and vice versa" (Meßerschmidt, 2021). The observable variation in both figures offers a first

54 *Handbook on governance and data science*

glimpse into cross-country differences worthy of further in-depth elaboration by researchers interested in legislative favouritism and beyond.

Lastly, Figure 3.4 shows the results for *ex post* modifications of legislation, our fourth indicator. Frequent modifications of laws after their enactment increase legislative instability and can constitute a potential tool of legislative favouritism *after* the law-making process – under the general assumption that frequent and rapid modifications could indicate a desire from legislators to protect some actors disadvantaged by a given legislation, instead of being driven by genuine *ex post* scrutiny. The latter is a sign of good legislative practice and tends to result in a small number of legislative modifications once a law does not achieve its intended goal. Yet, repeated changes over a short period of time can be considered a proxy of undue influence rather than *ex post* scrutiny. To capture this, we focus on the average annual number of modifications of laws by dividing the overall count of modifications by the months since enactment multiplied by 12. A value equal to or above 1 indicates that a law was, on average, modified (more than) once a year. Such repeated and frequent modifications increase legislative instability and potentially indicate legislative favouritism.

Focusing once more on the UK, the relatively high level of legislative instability, compared to Colombia and Chile, could likely be a consequence of Brexit. Yet, at the same time, the need for modifications due to Brexit increases the chances of favouritism occuring. This is further amplified by the presence of strong parliamentary scrutiny in the UK, which reduces the possibility of favouristic behaviour *during* the law-making stage. Lower levels of legislative

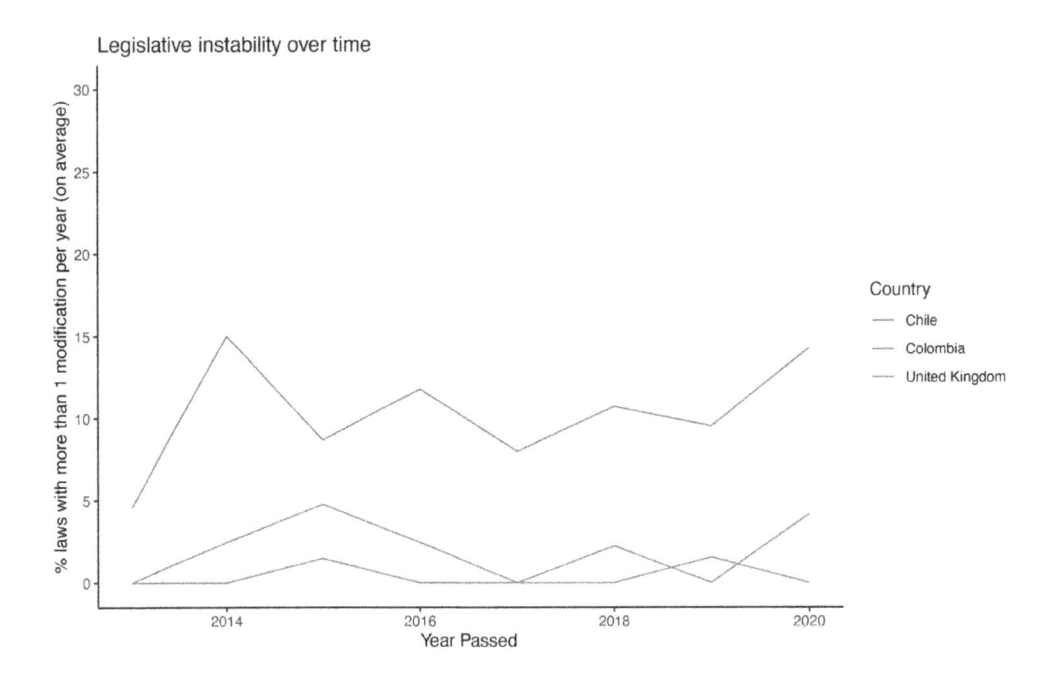

Source: Authors own.

Figure 3.4   *Percentage of laws with an average yearly modification count of 1 or more from all laws passed in a given year*

instability, on the other hand, do not imply less favouritism per se. Depending on the strength of legislative scrutiny in a country, favouristic patterns might have already occurred through any of the previous indicators.

DISCUSSION AND BROADER IMPLICATIONS

Recent trends towards greater availability of data sources and deposits of political institutions in machine-readable formats provide a unique opportunity for political researchers to combine data science methods with substantive area knowledge to test theoretical propositions that remain difficult to untangle. As a case at hand, this chapter introduced the concept of legislative favouritism which refers to the passage of legislation that disproportionally advantages a specific firm or group of firms over others. As a manifestation of political corruption, it is imperative that such actions remain unnoticed by both the political control mechanisms and the broader public. This secretive nature of legislative favouritism poses severe constraints on researchers since neither the recipient nor the provider of a favouristic law has an interest in disclosing any information that could potentially incriminate these actors.

The increasing reliance on data science methods can – to some extent – overcome this issue and offer a variety of advantages. To showcase this, our chapter relied on more than 316,797 legislative observations in 12 countries around the world and introduced four quantitative indicators of legislative favouritism. We showed that our indicators can be applied both over longer time periods and across highly diverse countries. In spite of the geographical, political, and economic differences of our country cases, our preliminary descriptive results offered interesting patterns that should encourage future research. The Global Corruption Observatory, for example, extends the analysis by differentiating laws into NACE economic sectors using state-of-the-art text-as-data methods, which allows for a more fine-grained analysis of favouristic patterns across our selected countries.

The broader, arguably key question that remains is the ability of data availability and data science to actually fix or offer scalable and viable solutions to corruption and favouritism in practice. While incorporating data sciences into the examination of political institutions can certainly establish a foundation for heightened accountability, progressing to the next phase and bringing about tangible changes in law-making and legislation requires purposeful policy action. This emphasises the pivotal role of political agency in the process. We believe that researchers can positively impact this endeavour in two essential ways. First, by utilising data science not only to generate insightful results but also to construct actionable indicators that enhance accountability and transparency in public administrations. We hope that the indicators presented in this chapter offer a compelling illustration of this point. Second, by making data and technologies more accessible by developing training tools that simplify the application of research insights. This effort is exemplified in our provision of various training tools through the Global Corruption Observatory website, catering to a diverse audience of practitioners, journalists, and citizens alike.[13] We are hopeful that the increasing interest across a diverse range of stakeholders in employing these technologies to combat corruption and favouritism will foster the potential for further expanding such synergies.[14]

NOTES

1. See https://www.ourcommons.ca/en/open-data. Accessed 5 December 2022.
2. See https://data.assemblee-nationale.fr. Accessed 5 December 2022.
3. See https://www.bundestag.de/services/opendata. Accessed 5 December 2022.
4. See https://www.hasadna.org.il/en/projects/open-knesset/. Accessed 5 December 2022.
5. Interparliamentary Union (2022) "Transforming Parliaments: Open Data in Parliaments 2022 Survey Results". Available at: https://www.ipu.org/event/transforming-parliaments-open-data-in-parliaments-2022-survey-results. Accessed 5 December 2022.
6. OECD (2016) Open Government: The Global Context and the Way Forward, Paris, December. Available at: https://www.oecd-ilibrary.org/governance/open-government_9789264268104-en. Accessed 5 December 2022.
7. See, for instance, Involve (2016). "UK Open Government National Action Plan 2016–2018: Launched!" Available at: https://involve.org.uk/resources/blog/opinion/uk-open-government-national-action-plan-2016-18-launched. Accessed 5 December 2022.
8. See, for instance, Regards citoyens (2022) NosDéputés.fr: Observatoire de l'activité des députés à l'Assemblée Nationale. Available at: https://www.regardscitoyens.org/nosdeputes-fr/. Accessed 5 December 2022.
9. Our definition of legislative favouritism thus involves firms taken in the neoclassical sense, namely, as the owners of the residual rights of production or investment. We thus exclude from our inquiry other types of favouritism (like ethnic favouritism, e.g., see Khalil et al., 2021) even if the main properties of economic favouritism as we define it could be easily applied to these other cases.
10. See Union of International Associations (2022) "Legislative Favouritism", *The Encyclopaedia of World Problems & Human Potential*. Available at: http://encyclopedia.uia.org/en/problems. Accessed 5 December 2022.
11. The data collection process is yet to be concluded, and we expect to gather data on additional countries in the coming years.
12. Empirically, we consider a bill or a law as "big" if it has significantly longer text compared to the average bill or law, namely, two standard deviations from the mean.
13. See https://globalcorruptionobservatory.com/trainings. Accessed 23 November 2023.
14. See, for instance. European Parliament (2021) Proceedings of the Workshop on Use of Big Data and AI in Fighting Corruption and Misuse of Public Funds, Department for budgetary affairs. Available at: https://www.europarl.europa.eu/RegData/etudes/STUD/2021/691722/IPOL_STU(2021)691722_EN.pdf. Accessed 23 November 2023.

REFERENCES

Alemán, E. (2009) "Institutions, Political Conflict and the Cohesion of Policy Networks in the Chilean Congress, 1961–2006", *Journal of Latin American Studies*, 41:467–91.

Bauhr, M., Czibik, A., Fazekas, M. & de Fine Licht, J. (2020) "Lights on the Shadows of Public Procurement. Transparency as an Antidote to Corruption", *Governance,* 33(3): 495–523.

Berntzen, L., Johannessen, M., Andersen, K. & Crusoe, J. (2019) "Parliamentary Open Data in Scandinavia", *Computers*, 8(3): 65.

Bowler, S. (2010) "Private Members' Bills in the UK Parliament: Is There an 'Electoral Connection'?", *The Journal of Legislative Studies*, 16(4): 476–94.

Brady, H. (2019) "The Challenge of Big Data and Data Science", *Annual Review of Political Science*, 22: 297–323.

Brenner, D. & Fazekas, M. (2023) "Can Impact Assessments Tame Legislative Drift? Event History Analysis of Modifications of Laws across Europe", *Governance*, 36(1): 141–65.
Carpenter, D. & Moss, D. (eds) (2014) *Preventing Regulatory Capture: Special Interest Influence and How to Limit It*. New York: Cambridge University Press.
Clark, W. & Golder, M. (2015) "Big Data, Causal Inference and Formal Theory: Contradictory Trends in Political Science?", *PS: Political Science & Politics*, 48(1): 65–70.
Clarke, A. & Margetts, H. (2014) "Governments and Citizens Getting to Know Each Other? Open, Closed and Big Data in Public Management Reform", *Policy & Internet*, 6(4): 393–417.
Copeland, G.W. & Patterson, S.C. (1994) *Parliaments in the Modern World: Changing Institutions*. Ann Arbor, MI: University of Michigan Press.
De Figueiredo, J.M. (2002) "Lobbying and Information in Politics", *Business & Politics*, 4(2): 125–9.
De Figueiredo, J.M. & Richter, B. (2014) "Advancing the Empirical Research on Lobbying", *Annual Review of Political Science*, 17: 163–85.
De Fine Licht, J., Naurin, D., Esaiasson, P. & Gilljam, M. (2014) "When Does Transparency Generate Legitimacy? Experimenting on a Context-Bound Relationship", *Governance*, 27(1): 111–34.
Dykstra, D. (1951) "Legislative Favouritism before the Court", *Indiana Law Journal*, 27(1): 38–57.
Evans, D. (2011) "Pork Barrel Politics", in Edwards III G., Lee, F. & Schickler, E. (eds), *The Oxford Handbook of the American Congress*. Oxford: Oxford University Press, pp. 315–339.
Fazekas, M., (2014) "The Use of 'Big Data' for Social Sciences Research: An Application to Corruption Research", in *Sage Research Methods Cases Part 1*. Sage. https://doi.org/10.4135/978144627305014528642
Goll, I. & Zeitz, G. (1991) "Conceptualizing and Measuring Corporate Ideology", *Organization Studies*, 12(2): 191–207.
Grimmer, J., Messing, S. & Westwood, S. (2012) "How Words and Money Cultivate a Personal Vote: The Effect of Legislator Credit Claiming on Constituent Credit Allocations", *American Political Science Review*, 106(4): 703–19.
Hug, S. (2013) "Parliamentary Voting", in Müller, W. & Narud, H. (eds), *Party Governance and Party Democracy*. New York: Springer, pp. 137–57.
Hug, S., Wegmann, S. & Wüest, R. (2015) "Parliamentary Voting Procedures in Comparison", *West European Politics*, 38(5): 940–68.
Khalil, U., Oak, M. & Ponnusamy, S. (2021) "Political Favouritism by Powerful Politicians: Evidence from India", *European Journal of Political Economy*, 66: 1019–49.
Kim, I.S. (2017) "Political Cleavages within Industry: Firm-Level Lobbying for Trade Liberalization", *American Political Science Review*, 111(1): 1–20.
Kingdon, J. (2003) *Agendas, Alternatives and Public Policies*. London: Longman.
Kitchin, R. (2014) *The Data Revolution: Big Data, Open Data, Data Infrastructures & Their Consequences*. London: Sage.
Magar, E., Palanza, V. & Sin, G. (2021) "Presidents on the Fast Track: Fighting Floor Amendments with Restrictive Rules", *The Journal of Politics*, 83(2): 633–46.
Margetts, H. (2017) "The Data Science of Politics", *Political Studies Review*, 15(2): 201–9.
Matheus, R. & Janssen, M. (2020) "A Systematic Literature Study to Unravel Transparency Enabled by Open Government Data: The Window Theory", *Public Performance & Management Review*, 43(3): 503–34.
Meßerschmidt, K. (2021) "Omnibus Legislation in Germany: A Widespread Yet Understudied Lawmaking Practice", in Bar-Siman-Tov, I. (ed.), *Comparative Multidisciplinary Perspectives on Omnibus Legislation*. New York: Springer, pp. 115–137.
Monroe, B. (2013) "The Five Vs of Big Data Political Science: Introduction to the Special Issue on Big Data in Political Science", Political Analysis, 21(V5): 1–9.
Monroe, B., Pan, J., Roberts, M., Sen, M. & Sinclair, B. (2015) "No! Formal Theory, Causal Inference and Big Data Are Not Contradictory Trends in Political Science", *PS: Political Science & Politics*, 48(1): 65–70.
Motolinia, L. (2021) "Electoral Accountability and Particularistic Legislation: Evidence from Mexico", *American Political Science Review*, 115(1): 97–113.
OECD (2017) *Preventing Policy Capture: Integrity in Public Decision Making. OECD Public Governance Reviews*. Paris: OECD Publishing. https://doi.org/10.1787/9789264065239-en

Pencheva, I., Esteve, M. & Mikhaylov, S. (2020) "Big Data and AI – a Transformational Shift for Government: So, What Next for Research?", *Public Policy and Administration*, 35(1): 24–44.

Provost, F. & Fawcett, T. (2013) "Data Science and Its Relationship to Big Data and Data-Driven Decision-Making", *Big Data*, 1(1): 51–9.

Riedl, J. (2019) "Uncovering Legislative Pace in Germany: A Methodical and Computational Application to Answer Temporal Questions of Law-making", *Government Information Quarterly*, 36(4): 1–12.

Rozenberg, O. (2021) "When Rationalization of Bureaucracy De-rationalizes Laws and Legislatures", in Bar-Siman-Tov, I (ed.). *Comparative Multidisciplinary Perspectives on Omnibus Legislation*. New York: Springer, pp. 95–114.

Russell, M. & Cowley, P. (2018) "Models of UK Executive-Legislative Relations Revisited", *The Political Quarterly*, 89(1): 18–28.

Saalfeld, T., Lutsenko, D. & Eklund, M. (2022) "The Digital Transformation of Parliaments and Implications for Democratic Representation", *European Liberal Forum Techno-Politics Series*, 4: 71–9.

Strøm, K. (1997) "Rules, Reasons and Routines: Legislative Roles in Parliamentary Democracies", *The Journal of Legislative Studies*, 3(1): 155–74.

Waismel-Manor, I., Bar-Siman-Tov, I., Rozenberg, O., Levanon, A., Benoît, C. & Ifergane, G. (2022) "Should I Stay (Open) or Should I Close? World Legislatures during the First Wave of Covid-19", *Political Studies*, 72(1): 200–226.

Worthy, B. (2015) "The Impact of Open Data in the UK: Complex, Unpredictable, and Political", *Public Administration*, 93(3): 788–905.

Wright, J. (2014) "Contributors, Lobbying, and Committee Voting in the U.S. House of Representatives", *American Political Science Review*, 84(2): 417–38.

4. Data science from a national statistics institute perspective: limits and challenges illustrated by historical events

Koen van 't Boveneind, Darius Keijdener, Pedro Lemlijn, Jolien Oomens and Eveline Vandewal

INTRODUCTION

Since Statistics Netherlands (in Dutch: Centraal Bureau voor de Statistiek, CBS) was founded in 1899, its primary purpose has been to compile statistics on a wide range of topics and to make the results publicly available. While the mission of official statistics has always been the same, the context in which these statistics are created and published is continuously developing. That also applies to collecting the necessary data to produce these statistics. CBS was founded at a time when it was challenging to collect and process large amounts of data. However, statistics based on sample data were frowned upon by experts (Bethlehem, 2009). Therefore, the first statistics produced were based on census data. It took another 30 years or so for sample data to be trusted enough to be used to create official statistics. Eventually, this led to a statistical paradigm based on sample surveys, with the occasional population-wide census.

Since then, data availability has improved – for example, following the increase in administrative sources – and collecting and processing data has become easier with technological innovation. Samples could be supplemented or replaced by register data. The significant advantage of using registers is that CBS does not have to approach individuals and companies as often. This reduces the survey burden. Nowadays, among other things, big data and artificial intelligence (AI), specifically Machine Learning (ML), make it possible to explore new sources and ways to produce official statistics. In this chapter, "data science" will be used as an umbrella term for the techniques and methods used to gather and analyse large amounts of data. This definition is broad on purpose due to the ongoing developments in this field.

Using data science as a government organisation has its limits and challenges. The first aim of this chapter is to illustrate these limits and challenges using historical events. Through past experiences, a set of challenges has been established. These challenges are the starting point and must be successfully addressed to proceed with a project. A good description of the challenges in every domain helps researchers at CBS leverage the advantages of lessons learned through past experiences. Every project starts with answering the following three questions:

- Is it legally allowed? (**Legal challenge**);
- Is it technically feasible? (**Technological challenge**);
- Is it socially acceptable and ethical? (**Societal challenge**).

Only when all three questions are answered affirmatively can a new technology, data source, or statistical output be implemented. In the following, these three challenges will be explained in more detail.

Legal challenge. Being a governmental organisation comes with strict boundaries. The law explicitly prescribes what the government is allowed to do, whereas private organisations are mainly limited by what is explicitly forbidden, a secondary effect of the principle of legality (Andenas, 2000). National statistical legislation is based on the United Nations (UN) Fundamental Principles of Official Statistics, first formulated in 1991, which describe the professional and scientific standards for official statistics. The majority of CBS's statistical production follows from European directives that are translated into Dutch law. Although both the budgetary and legislative frameworks of CBS are ultimately the responsibility of the Minister of Economic Affairs, its relationship with the Ministry was made non-hierarchical in 2004 as a means of protecting its autonomy. An independent body, the Commission for Advice, verifies the operations of CBS, which monitors the quality, relevance, and impartiality of studies and projects. This naturally leads to strict boundaries.

Technological challenge. The second challenge is the availability of mature technology. The advent of, on the one hand, new and an increasing number of data sources that are available and, on the other hand, increasing and cheaper computing power and sophisticated modern data science possibilities make it possible to explore new ways to produce official statistics faster and more accurately. However, to use these sources and methods in official statistics requires a certain level of maturity. By the time these reach the necessary level of maturity, they are often already succeeded by newer technology.

Societal challenge. Last are the societal challenges. On the one hand, there is an increasing demand for (more) timely, detailed, and coherent statistical information. On the other hand, there is more concern about the impact of increased data gathering by CBS on the personal lives of citizens. CBS has to continuously balance these two extremes to produce reliable statistics that minimise the burden on society.

The challenges described above often conflict, and CBS continuously has to find a balance between them. Table 4.1 briefly introduces the different historical events used to illustrate

Table 4.1   Historical events illustrating legal, technological, and social challenges

Historical event	Short description	Legal	Technological	Societal
Census of 1971	Social unrest triggers the move to register data	x	x	x
Household Budget Survey	Low response rates create a need for innovation	-	x	x
Railroad transportation statistics	Travelcard data enhances railroad transportation statistics	-	-	x
Consumer Price Index	Rising energy prices urge method change in a statistic that is a legal fact	x	x	x

Source: Authors' own.

these three main areas of limits and challenges. Although each historical event has been classified based on the area(s) it represents most, all events have faced limits and challenges in the legal, technological, and societal domains.

Events from the past have shown that the position of a national statistics institute (NSI), or a governmental organisation in a broader sense, is not set in stone. Sometimes, technological opportunities lead to changes in methods or processes. At other times, the changing attitude of society causes a need for adjustment. Therefore, this chapter ends with an outlook on the future by touching on new mechanisms being used and explored to integrate data science and all available data sources into day-to-day practice.

LIMITS AND CHALLENGES ILLUSTRATED BY EXAMPLES

Society Demanding Innovation: The Census of 1971

The first two examples will illustrate the opportunities technology can provide in response to societal changes. The first of these examples takes a closer look at the census of 1971. The European Statistical Office, Eurostat, imposes mandatory statistics on member states, including the decennial census. Every ten years, each country counts its entire population and gathers data about geographic, social, and economic factors, as well as household and family characteristics (Regulation (EC) No 763/2008 on population and housing censuses, 2008). In the Netherlands, the last traditional census – with interviewers going door to door – was held more than 50 years ago, in 1971. Since the 1980s, the census has been done digitally using registries.

History of registries

Since 1850, Dutch municipalities have been required by law to keep track of their inhabitants in a local population registry. These registries contained the addresses, names, dates of birth, marital status, and, most notably, religion. During the Second World War, the German occupiers used this high-quality data source to identify Jewish citizens quickly. The registries also made it harder for the resistance to falsify identity cards because the data could be checked for authenticity (Verzetsmuseum Amsterdam, 2009). The Dutch resistance asked municipal officials in the registries to mix up cards to hinder searching. They even organised physical attacks on registries, the most famous example being the attack on the registry of Amsterdam in 1943 when a fire was started. The local fire brigade was informed about its purpose, extinguished the fire inefficiently, and flooded the office afterward. In 1944, the British precision bombed Villa Kleykamp, where the registry of The Hague was housed (Gemeente Amsterdam, 2023). The legacy of registries in the Second World War made the Dutch suspicious about the government storing data, eventually leading to the end of the traditional census.

Privacy concerns

In 1970, a year before the fourteenth census, a public debate ensued about the necessity of the nationwide survey. The two main objections were that the study was not anonymous and that participation was mandatory. Not participating carried a fine of 500 Dutch guilders (approximately one month's median income) or 14 days imprisonment. Around 200 action groups, such as "Comité Waakzaamheid Volkstelling" (census vigilance committee), were formed, criticising CBS and the Dutch government.

One could wonder why the fourteenth census in 1971 received public backlash, whereas this was not the case for earlier editions in 1947 and 1961. A significant difference with the previous ones was that, for the first time, a computer now processed the data. The idea of automatic processing fuelled the privacy concerns about centralised storage lingering since the war. Two weeks before the 1971 census, the Minister of Economic Affairs declared that children of Jews and resistance fighters would not be prosecuted for refusing to participate (De burger in kaart , 2011; Sabel, 2021).

Outcomes
Although the census caused a wave of societal indignation, it was still executed. It turned out that only 23,000 people actively refused to participate, which was around 0.2 per cent of the population. The refusers were not prosecuted for monetary reasons and were granted amnesty. The cost would have been higher than the benefits for the government.

An additional 300,000 people (around 2.3 per cent) did not participate simply because no one from their household was home during the counting. In the previous census, this was not a problem because, until the 1960s, it was common for working women to be fired when they got married (Boef, 2019). Ten years later, a trial census showed that non-response would increase to 26 per cent if the census of 1981 would similarly take place. After the turbulent and costly 1971 census, CBS considered switching from the census to registries (Daas, Nordholt, Tennekes, & Ossen, 2021). During these years, computers emerged in a business context, and municipalities started using them to manage their registries. As a result of the increased use of computers, the registries grew in size and quality, enabling CBS to use them as a suitable replacement for a paper census questionnaire. So, from 1981 onwards, the census switched to digital registries, significantly reducing the society's burden. Hence, in this example, technological progress made it possible to alleviate societal concerns. However, technological development never stops, and new challenges must always be addressed. These new challenges can arise from all three domains discussed above. In the case of the Dutch census, technological development continuously creates new possibilities.

Figure 4.1

Publishing on an even more detailed level
CBS keeps improving the census statistics, thereby following global developments in statistical methods. In 2023, mathematicians from CBS and six other NSIs developed new statistical disclosure methods and tools to facilitate publishing even more detailed information. The census data will be published for 1 km^2 cells instead of seemingly arbitrary (municipal) boundaries. This allows users of the data to compare different areas more easily.

Two methods are combined to publish data on such a detailed level without revealing information about individual people and households: targeted record swapping and the cell key method (Statistics Netherlands, 2023c). In targeted record swapping, households get assigned a similarity profile which describes features like the number of household members and marital status, if applicable. Households sharing the same similarity profile get swapped: their locations are exchanged to ensure privacy. Suppose, for example, a square in a rural area contains only a single household. In that case, there is no way for users of the data to know whether the data for this square actually belongs to this household or a similar household

Translation note: "Census: no!"
Source: 1970–1971 by Lucebert, Willem Sandberg, Peter van Straaten.

Figure 4.1   *"Volkstelling Nee!"* Before you know it, it is that time again; one carries a whip and the other a Jewish badge (Star of David). (De burger in kaart, 2011)

somewhere else. This process continues until a predetermined percentage of swaps, the *swap rate*, is reached.

The cell key method adds small perturbations to aggregated results based on its underlying microdata records. Each cell of 1 km^2 consisting of several households is assigned a cell key. A perturbation table is then created, which contains a slight deviation for each combination of cell key and possible cell value. This method guarantees consistency between different statistics about the same population cells. Unfortunately, this method does not preserve the consistency of subtotals. This means that because of the noise, the sum of the parts does not necessarily equal the total value.

Combining these new methods makes it highly unlikely that users can reconstruct household information from the data. This way, CBS can publish census data from 2021 in more detail than ever before.

Maintaining Quality Standards: Response Rates and the Household Budget Survey

A more recent example of how technology can provide opportunities in response to societal changes is the Household Budget Survey ("Budgetonderzoek"). First conducted in 1978, the Household Budget Survey aims to collect data on household expenditures. Throughout the year, multiple waves of respondents record their household expenditures on goods and services for four weeks. Expenditures below €20 are only recorded for one of those weeks to reduce the administrative burden of the survey. Additionally, respondents complete multiple related questionnaires on their household's infrequent purchases (e.g., car, washing machine), fixed expenses, and holiday expenditures.

Unlike transaction data, the data obtained from the Household Budget Survey can be used to examine the expenditures of households with different socioeconomic backgrounds. Moreover, the Household Budget Survey results are used to calculate the so-called "household equivalence scales", which are necessary to compare different household types to each other.

In 2012, the Household Budget Survey moved entirely to online data collection, with expenditures being recorded through a web diary, supported by instructional videos, monitoring aspects, coding tools, and automated checks for common mistakes (To & McBride, 2013). Nonetheless, response rates remained very low, reaching a low point in 2020. This may have partially been due to the restrictions in place to combat the coronavirus (Rothbaum & Bee, 2021). However, this is also a more general problem that falls within the "societal challenges" driver that the Official Statistics community faces. To increase the response rate while at the same time keeping the costs in check, two types of improvements have been proposed for the Household Budget Survey in 2026.

First, the actual and perceived burden for the respondents should decrease. To achieve this, a smartphone application has been developed to record expenditures conveniently. This application can scan supermarket receipts; only missing information has to be added manually. Moreover, it is planned to shorten the related questionnaires (to decrease the actual burden), and to invite potential respondents differently (to decrease the perceived burden). Second, the survey design should be adjusted. More specifically, researchers plan to form a respondent panel, thereby participating multiple times and receiving higher incentives for participating in the Household Budget Survey.

Low response rates are not only a problem in and of themselves; they can also lead to biased results when the non-response is not random. In particular, households with a migration background and that are impoverished as well as wealthy households have become more challenging to reach. In the case of the Household Budget Survey, administrative data is used for non-response adjustment, and the National Accounts statistics are used as plausibility checks. However, these measures do not absolve NSIs from having to try to increase participation in surveys.

Starting in 2025, the Household Budget Survey will become obligatory by European Union (EU) regulation. The standardisation that comes with this will likely increase the comparability across different EU countries. However, it remains essential to improve such extensive and costly surveys. In this case, the "societal challenge" driver of low response rates makes innovation necessary; technology – a smartphone application to facilitate data entry – makes it possible. Like the census of 1971 described earlier, this example illustrates how technological progress can provide opportunities to combat societal challenges.

Social Licence to Operate: A New Data Source for Railroad Transport Statistics

As mentioned in the Introduction, using data science as a governmental agency has limits and challenges. To illustrate these challenges, especially the societal challenge, the following case is presented.

CBS regularly provides statistics on the use of public rail transportation (Regulation (EU) 2018/643 on rail transport statistics (recast), 2018), the European Harmonised Price Index (HICP) (Regulation (EU) 2016/792 on harmonised indices of consumer prices and the house price index, 2016), and the Services Producer Price Index (SPPI) (Regulation (EU) 2019/2152 on European business statistics, 2019). For a long time, Statistics Netherlands used data from paper ticket sales to provide figures on public rail transportation. In the 2000s, a new system called "OV-chipkaart" was developed. This system uses an RFID (Radio Frequency Identification) chip inside a personal card to replace paper tickets and could be used with all public transportation companies in the Netherlands. In 2012, the remaining regions switched to using the new card (NOS, 2011). Transportation companies could still sell their paper tickets, but the travel card was the only one accepted countrywide.

During the following years, it became increasingly difficult for CBS to produce reliable statistics about public rail transport as paper ticket sales dwindled. So, a process was started to initiate access to travel card data that could be used to supplement or substitute the existing data. The usefulness and need for access to travel card data were presented at the national public transport consultation chaired by the Dutch Department of Public Transport. Persuaded by the legal mission of CBS, working groups were set up to examine the practical and legal aspects of data access.

On a technical front, the project was deemed feasible, as the new data enabled Statistics Netherlands to match the accuracy of the given statistic and increase the quality (also encompassing, for example, timeliness and relevance). Because travellers have to check in and out when entering the vehicle or station, as well as when switching from a transporter, it was possible to translate single rides into travelling behaviour in public transport.

A legal check ensured that Statistics Netherlands had the right to access the data. After all, as previously mentioned, a key difference between a government organisation and private parties is that the government cannot perform activities that are not explicitly allowed by law. For CBS, this is defined in the "Wet op het Centraal bureau voor de Statistiek" (2022). Attention was also given to the General Data Protection Regulation (GDPR) (Uitvoeringswet Algemene verordening gegevensbescherming, 2021), as the data source included location data, which is considered personal data. Statistics Netherlands was deemed to have a legal basis for accessing the data, so the judicial challenge was also taken care of.

Special care was given to the social implications of the process. When accessing new data sources or technologies, CBS takes an approach that explicitly considers the social implications. Even if there is a legal basis for access to new data sources, there is an explicit consideration of whether Statistics Netherlands wants access or not. This involves proportionality, subsidiarity, and mitigating risks to an acceptable level. As Hurst and Johnston (2021, p. 2) mention, while businesses have traditionally assumed permission and approval to operate, increasingly public approval and subsequent SLO (social licence to operate) need to be earned and maintained. Gaining and retaining these licences is no easy task, as they may exist at multiple "scales" – local, regional, national, and international (Hurst, Johnston, & Lane, 2020; Parsons & Moffat, 2014) and various licences can be at "odds with one another" (Dare, Schirmer, & Vanclay, 2014, p. 190; Hurst et al., 2020).

The social licence is part of Statistics Netherlands' reputation. As mentioned in an article in the *Statistical Journal of the United Nations Economic Commission for Europe*, the reputation is of great importance to an NSI and critical to the willingness of the public to trust statistics (Rafalowska, 2005). It is of even greater importance when trying to maintain the willingness to both participate in government surveys and follow policy recommendations based on official statistics. As the general public determines the boundaries of ethics and this social licence, they had to be actively informed about the project and, if possible, participate.

In the spirit of the four main ELSA (ethical, legal, and social aspects) features, proximity, anticipation, interactivity, and interdisciplinarity (Zwart & Nelis, 2009) were given extra attention. The first two features were addressed by a press release that informed society of the intention to use the travel data for statistical purposes. This approach increased transparency and cooperation. The last two features were met by organising an ethics workshop in which all stakeholders from public transport organisations and citizens' representatives participated. Among these representatives was, for example, the director of Rover, a Dutch independent advisory body representing public transportation users. Additionally, the first question was to ask all participants to identify all the parties concerned and, if not present, to try to think from their perspective. During this workshop, Statistics Netherlands explained why they needed that specific data, and all parties discussed the possible benefits, limits, and mitigations of these limits that would be caused by sharing this data with Statistics Netherlands.

While this workshop and its subsequent meetings took an unexpected amount of time to complete, it also had benefits. If executed correctly, actively involving the general public in an NSI's work has several significant advantages. For the public, it creates a direct influence on the process. It prevents the image of a distant government agency with a never-ending urge to gather more data, and they get to deliver input themselves and have the opportunity to understand better why Statistics Netherlands needs it and to even influence its use. For the NSI, proactive communication and citizens' participation lead to higher research participation. It creates goodwill to have renowned authorities (representing the citizens) supporting the research. Also, these parties frequently employ experts who give valuable input to improve the method the institute is deploying. In this case, involving all parties in this way ensured swift cooperation, clear communication, and broad support. Next to project-specific benefits, this approach also proved its value in a broader context. Statistics Netherlands now considers the ethics workshop to be included in the standard process for new data source acquisition.

In short, this case highlights the importance of the social aspect of data science. Engaging early with the general public through representatives makes it possible to gather new, better data and strengthen public support simultaneously. This leads to a decreased chance of crossing the boundaries of the social licence, which could hamper the project's outcome. It also shows that the three aspects (technical, judicial, and societal) are intertwined and influence each other. For example, privacy concerns (societal) are related to complying with privacy laws (judicial), which can be met by using specific techniques like anonymising or pseudonymising (technical).

The Consumer Price Index: A Legal Fact

Another example of the entanglement of the three challenges discussed in this chapter is the following case about improving the Consumer Price Index (CPI). To accurately reflect the consumption patterns of the entire population, it is crucial to have a representative sample basket of goods and services. With the advent of new products and changes in consumer preferences, selecting a relevant and representative sample has become more challenging. CBS has to continuously update the CPI basket to incorporate emerging goods and services and adjust the sample weights accordingly.

In the past, price data was collected through traditional surveys, where enumerators manually recorded prices at stores and other points of sale. This method was labour-intensive and time-consuming. Now, CBS increasingly relies on automated web-scraping techniques to collect price information. Web scraping involves extracting data from websites using specialised software programs. CBS has developed systems that regularly scan various online stores, web pages, and other sources to gather price information. This results in more efficient data collection, reducing reliance on manual surveys. CBS also collaborates with large retailers to access their scanner data. These data provide detailed information on individual product prices and help in more accurate and timely measurement of price changes.

Although these technical innovations were successfully implemented in the production process, while modernising data collection methods for calculating CPI, CBS faces several issues. Ensuring the quality and accuracy of the collected data is a significant challenge. Maintaining data integrity and minimising errors in the collected data requires extensive validation and quality control processes. Data privacy and access issues emerge with the increasing reliance on scanner data and online sources. CBS has to navigate the complexities of data-sharing agreements with retailers and other data providers to ensure compliance with privacy regulations. Balancing the need for detailed data with individual privacy protection presents ongoing challenges.

Moreover, statistical methods used in calculating the CPI must also be reviewed regularly. Sometimes, extreme events can lead to questionable outcomes. Such a situation occurred with the rising energy prices throughout 2021–22. Up to the reporting month of May 2023, pricing data was obtained from the Netherlands Authority for Consumers and Markets (ACM) every month to calculate the CPI for energy. The data was collected through monthly sample surveys of only newly concluded energy contracts. For a long time, this method provided a good picture of price trends in the energy market.

However, with the significant price increases for energy products from mid-2021, the price development of new contracts was less representative of the broader market, as about half of all consumers had long-term, fixed-rate contracts when the price hikes started. In addition, many consumers with existing older, variable-rate contracts paid lower rates than consumers with new contracts. As the method described above does not provide a complete picture of all transactions in a volatile market, additional data was sought. Several energy companies agreed to submit overviews of consumer contract data to CBS. This data provides a comprehensive insight into the rates paid by all customers of the companies concerned, which significantly broadened CBS's view of price trends in the energy market. The availability of these new data sources also made it possible to apply new methods specifically designed for more detailed data. From June 2023, the new methodology for measuring energy prices is being used in calculating the CPI, replacing the old method (Statistics Netherlands, 2023a).

Typically, historical data is adjusted to a new method for as long as possible. However, the CPI is not a standard statistic. It is one of the most consulted statistics of CBS and is widely used for indexation purposes, premiums, and other rates and prices. Therefore, the monthly CPI is treated as a legal fact and cannot be revised unless it is evidently wrong. This poses a severe legal challenge and explains why historical figures are not adjusted for the new method. After all, the historic CPI can only be adjusted if the figure is wrong. In this case, the old method of energy prices was not flawed; Eurostat approved it. The method was only adjusted to reflect the economy's current status better.

As CBS is not allowed to revise previously published CPI figures, the new methodology for energy prices was not applied to previous CPI figures. Parties that use the CPI can continue to do so beyond May 2023. There is still a difference, however, between the inflation figures that have been published and what these would have been if the new methodology had been introduced earlier. As mentioned above, the inflation rate of the research series is lower than that of the CPI until November 2022. After November 2022, it is the other way around. Over a more extended period, this difference disappears. Since the CPI and the research series virtually coincide at the beginning and end of the study, there is no significant difference between the two inflation figures measured over the entire period.

To conclude, this case underlines the entanglement of technical, legal, and societal challenges for CBS. CBS aims to enhance the CPI calculation methodology to reflect changes in consumption behaviour and address quality adjustments. This demands technical expertise and collaboration with data providers. However, as the CPI is considered a legal fact, adjusting the method or the source data must be done with great care. Maintaining consistency in the CPI calculation over time while introducing necessary updates requires careful planning and stakeholder engagement.

FUTURE

Integrating Data Science and Official Statistics

Introducing data science into official statistics was and is no smooth process. Not all methods used are familiar to a "traditional" statistician, and it takes time for these methods to be accepted as valid statistical methods, just as when surveys were introduced (Bethlehem, 2009). Data science starts with the data and expects researchers to work "data-driven": to start with an analysis of the data and to use that as a basis to determine what to measure (Daas, 2023). This is a significant change in thinking for a "traditional" statistician as they have historically started working from a proper and transparent definition (i.e., "what to measure"), after which data is collected and moulded until it fits the definition. These approaches are the opposite, which can cause friction when introducing data science at an NSI. The transition to a data-driven approach poses a challenge that should not be underestimated and requires adaptation of both the workflow of data science and the classical statistical way of working. It is possible to discuss many examples and directions here, given the thin line between data science and other innovations within statistics. For the sake of brevity, the discussion in the rest of this section is mainly limited to machine learning (ML) models.

Currently, many ML projects at CBS try to merge data science techniques with solid, usable, proven statistical methods. This section introduces the following exciting examples of contemporary research areas (Daas, 2023; Puts & Daas, 2021a):

- Explainable models
- The extension of the "internal validity" of a model into "external validity"
- Rare occurrences
- Concept drift.

Explainable models
Contrary to data science, traditional statistics always start with strict definitions of the object of study. This is not always the case when using ML algorithms, especially not for exploratory data analysis and neural network-based methods like deep learning. Here, the neural network, with one or more "hidden" layers, is essentially a "black box". It has been trained by studying many examples, looking for various surface similarities rather than the central (abstract) property usually at the heart of definitions drawn up by humans.

This poses a challenge since the data-driven way of working could result in ML models that do not precisely measure the concept defined by official statistics. It requires validating the findings produced by ML models to ensure comparability between different measurements within an NSI and between NSIs in different countries. It is also crucial that policymakers can understand what the statistic describes. Explainable artificial intelligence is an example of a field of study that tries to create such an understanding.

The extension of the "internal validity" of a model into "external validity"
The internal validity of a model is the type of validity typical to data science: usually, 80 per cent of the available dataset is used to train the model while 20 per cent of the dataset is used to test, that is, determine the accuracy – or any other quality measure – of the model. When, for instance, a model is developed to determine whether a firm develops innovative technologies based on website texts, usually a training set with roughly 50 per cent innovative technology companies and 50 per cent other companies is chosen. The advantage of using 50 per cent positive and 50 per cent negative examples in the training set enables the researcher to verify precisely how well the model performs; a model with an accuracy above 50 per cent proves the model is extracting information from the data source used. Suppose such a hypothetical model can determine its objective with 99 per cent accuracy. This only means it can achieve that for a dataset composed of 50 per cent positives and 50 per cent negatives. However, these performance measures may not represent those in real-world data. In addition, the training (and test) data used might not even be a representative sample of the target population: they might contain multiple selection biases besides the boost in positive or negative examples. This means that it is unclear how well the model can detect innovative companies in data other

than the training and test set. For official statistics, it is essential to know the performance on the target population, that is, all companies listed in our business register. This is known as external validity. The accuracy of this dataset might be significantly lower than the 99 per cent suggested by the internal validity. However, this does not necessarily mean that the model cannot be applied to the broader population, but it does mean that care needs to be taken in its interpretation.

There are methods available to provide corrections for these cases. A second population sample can be inspected manually to overcome these differences. With this new sample, a correction for bias and an estimation of the uncertainty of the results can be achieved (Meertens, Diks, van den Herik, & Takes, 2019). Alternatively, this data could be used to (re) train the model on a random sample of positive and negative cases from the target population when their classification is known or by carefully calibrating the trained model (Puts & Daas, 2021a).

Rare occurrences

Data science methods can run into problems when studying rare occurrences in the data. Requests for "needle in a haystack" problems reach Statistics Netherlands from time to time. For instance, requests for finding companies working in new sectors are not yet adequately captured in the standardised NACE codes for business activity. Typically, these new industries are not yet widely established, and just a few companies occur, scattered across some NACE codes, in the large population of companies. For training models, one has to boost the training sample with more positive cases; otherwise, because there are only a few examples, the model cannot detect them. This poses the risk, however, that the model structurally overestimates the number of positive cases (Puts & Daas, 2021b). The solution from the previous chapter, where a training set is used that includes large numbers of positive cases, can, in theory, be applied. However, because the training set has to be selected with a proper sample design while finding a lot of positive cases, this method will take considerable effort. In the latter case, it is better to choose the parameters in the model so that it tends to have very few false negatives. It is then possible to counter the problem by manually confirming the predictions of a set of cases marked positive by the model. This has been applied in several research projects at Statistics Netherlands (Daas, Hassink, & Klijs, 2023; Statistics Netherlands, 2020). The result can be considered a reasonable estimate for the lower limit for the number of positive cases. Unfortunately, giving a proper estimate for an upper limit is impossible because of the lack of a check on the false negatives.

Concept drift

Even for nearly perfect working ML models, errors may increasingly occur over time. This is, for instance, observed for text-based ML models where textual data changes over time, especially with the presence of buzzwords. Words that initially were good indicators for Web 3.0, for instance, at the time of writing might be out of date by the time of printing. These textual changes affect the efficiency and validity of the model (internal and external), and both usually decrease over time. Here, the association between particular words (and their combination) evolves over time, making it challenging for the model to identify the concept with the original accuracy obtained. This is known as concept drift and poses a significant challenge for repeating measurements (Gama, Žliobaitė, Bifet, Pechenizkiy, & Bouchachia, 2014). In some instances, this can be fixed by retraining the algorithm with additional data added, but in other cases, this does not suffice (Daas & Jansen, 2020).

A diametrically opposed option is to use ungauged models, where no outside information is used (often because it is not available) to compare the definition provided by the algorithm with a human-defined quantity. These measurements are not strictly defined and are not meant to give an objective measurement but merely to provide a time series that has comparative qualities when compared to itself. In this case, usually, some index is established. For example, the number of times people Googled "symptoms of flu" correlates with typical flu seasons, but it is not a hard measurement of the number of ill people.

The main challenge for these algorithms is to prove they are comparable over time and, hence, not subject to concept drift. Ranging the same model on different parts of time series data can determine comparability over time. The downside is that this can only be used in retrospect. There are some examples of ungauged measurements, for instance, the index "intention to move house" and the Social Tension Indicator, both composed with X (formerly Twitter) data (Statistics Netherlands, 2023b). Both studies have not progressed further than the experimental stage, among others, due to discussions on the quality of the findings when they would be published as official statistics. Another example outside Statistics Netherlands can be found in the Geopolitical Risk Index (Caldara & Iacoviello, 2022).

Practical Considerations

Of course, there are also more practical challenges with applying data science in an NSI. It takes time and effort to be able to use the necessary tools and IT infrastructure within an airtight, secure environment. It also requires that many people change their way of working and learn new skills, in addition to dealing with the challenges the new data sources provide. Furthermore, effort will be put into finding the best ways to reuse already gathered data.

Another practical consideration is that an NSI typically prefers to have a long time series to study trends. Sometimes, changes occur in statistical sources such as government registries, which can disturb these long-term measurements. Much effort is spent identifying and mitigating the effects of these changes as much as possible in the end product. Most sources used for data science are usually a lot more volatile, as they are not created and maintained with the production of statistics in mind. Moreover, where an NSI is sometimes warned and/or consulted for changes in registries, this is not necessarily the case for sources not in governmental hands. In this respect, statistics based on data science usually demand more attention in upkeep and analysis.

This also leads to the production of new statistics, such as using satellite images to detect land use or sentiments on social media. These new statistics may not be bleeding-edge regarding newly developed theories, but they are entirely new for official statistics, policymakers, and the general public. Here, it also takes time for all involved to figure out how these new products can be used and how their quality needs to be interpreted.

CONCLUSION

This chapter explores the role of data science from a government perspective, focusing on its application within an NSI. Three key areas of interest are examined: technological advancements, and judicial and societal changes. By highlighting historical events, it is demonstrated how these drivers influence each other and influence the capabilities and impact of data science within an NSI.

Technological advancements play a transformative role in data science, enabling NSIs to harness the power of big data, advanced analytics, and automation. These institutes extract valuable insights from vast datasets using sophisticated algorithms, machine learning, and artificial intelligence, leading to more accurate, timely, and comprehensive statistical information. Simultaneously, social changes profoundly impact the role of data science within NSIs. As societies become more data-driven and information-savvy, there is an increasing demand for transparency, accessibility, and relevance in statistical information. People have quicker and more access to information and are more demanding towards government agencies, like an NSI, in these matters. On the other hand, privacy, security, and ethical considerations have become more urgent in the past decades. The historical events described in this chapter show how these drivers create challenges during data science projects. Sometimes, innovation is technologically feasible but lacks proper communication, increasing societal resistance. In other situations, social changes cause acceleration in adopting new techniques to decrease the burden on respondents.

The future of data science in NSIs holds immense promise and presents intriguing challenges. Technological advancements will continue to evolve, with emerging technologies offering new opportunities and complexities. NSIs must adapt to these developments, attending to data privacy, security, and ethical considerations. Moreover, the ever-growing demand for real-time, granular, and integrated data will necessitate further collaboration with other government agencies, international organisations, and private entities to access and leverage data from a plethora of sources. The evolving field demands professionals skilled in statistics, computer science, data engineering, and domain expertise. Partnerships with academia, research institutions, and industry will foster innovation, knowledge exchange, and cross-pollination of ideas, enabling NSIs to stay at the forefront of data science advancements.

Disclaimer: The opinions expressed in this chapter are those of the authors. They do not purport to reflect the opinions or views of Statistics Netherlands (CBS) or its members.

REFERENCES

Andenas, M. (2000). Judicial review in international perspective. *Judicial Review in International Perspective*, 1–544.

Bethlehem, J. (2009). The rise of survey sampling. Accessed 10-08-2023. Retrieved from https://www.cbs.nl/-/media/imported/documents/2009/07/2009–15-x10-pub.pdf

Boef, J. (2019). Werken na je huwelijk mocht vroeger niet, maar deze vrouwen deden het toch. EenVandaag. Retrieved from https://eenvandaag.avrotros.nl/item/werken-na-je-huwelijk-mocht-vroeger-niet-maar-deze-vrouwen-deden-het-toch/

Caldara, D., & Iacoviello, M. (2022). Measuring geopolitical risk. *American Economic Review*, 112(4), 1194–225. doi:10.1257/aer.20191823

Daas, P. (2023). *Big data in official statistics*. Eindhoven: Technische Universiteit Eindhoven.

Daas, P., & Jansen, J. (1 July 2020). Model degradation in web derived text-based models. Paper presented at the 3rd International Conference on Advanced Research Methods and Analytics.

Daas, P., Schulte Nordholt, E., Tennekes, M., & Ossen, S. (2021). Evaluation of the quality of administrative data used in the Dutch virtual census. In *Administrative Records for Survey Methodology* (pp. 61–83). (Wiley Series in Survey Methodology). Wiley.

Daas, P., Hassink, W., & Klijs, B. (2024). On the validity of using webpage texts to identify the target population of a survey: An application to detect online platforms. In *Journal of Official Statistics*, 40(1), 190-211. SAGE Publications.

Dare, M., Schirmer, J., & Vanclay, F. (2014). Community engagement and social licence to operate. *Impact Assessment and Project Appraisal*, 32(3), 188–97. doi:10.1080/14615517.2014.927108

De burger in kaart. (2011). [Television series episode]. Andere Tijden (Executive producer).

Gama, J., Žliobaitė, I., Bifet, A., Pechenizkiy, M., & Bouchachia, A. (2014). A survey on concept drift adaptation. *ACM Computing Surveys (CSUR)*, 46(4), 1–37.

Gemeente Amsterdam. (2023). Bevolkingsregister 1851–1853. Retrieved from https://archief.amsterdam/uitleg/indexen/69-bevolkingsregister-1851–1853?utm_source=OpenArchieven&utm_medium=browser&utm_campaign=OpenData#:~:text=In%201849%20werd%20door%20de,vanaf%201850%20verplicht%20werd%20gesteld

Hurst, B., & Johnston, K.A. (2021). The social imperative in public relations: Utilities of social impact, social license and engagement. *Public Relations Review*, 47(2), 102039. doi:https://doi.org/10.1016/j.pubrev.2021.102039

Hurst, B., Johnston, K.A., & Lane, A.B. (2020). Engaging for a social licence to operate (SLO). *Public Relations Review*, 46(4), 101931. doi:https://doi.org/10.1016/j.pubrev.2020.101931

Meertens, Q., Diks, C., van den Herik, H.J., & Takes, F.W. (2019). A Bayesian approach for accurate classification-based aggregates. Paper presented at the Proceedings of the 2019 SIAM International Conference on Data Mining.

NOS. (2011). Strippenkaart is geschiedenis. Accessed 09-08-2023. Retrieved from https://nos.nl/artikel/309776-strippenkaart-is-geschiedenis

Parsons, R., & Moffat, K. (2014). Constructing the meaning of social licence. *Social Epistemology*, 28(3–4), 340–63. doi:10.1080/02691728.2014.922645

Puts, M., & Daas, P. (2021a). Machine learning from the perspective of official statistic. *The Survey Statistician*, 84, 12–17.

Puts, M.J., & Daas, P.J. (2021b). Unbiased estimations based on binary classifiers: A maximum likelihood approach. arXiv preprint arXiv:2102.08659

Rafalowska, H. (2005). Building the reputation of a statistical office through effective communication. *Statistical Journal of the United Nations Economic Commission for Europe*, 22, 147–56. doi:10.3233/SJU-2005-22204

Regulation (EC) No 763/2008 on population and housing censuses, 763/2008 C.F.R. (2008).

Regulation (EU) 2016/792 on harmonised indices of consumer prices and the house price index, 2016/792 C.F.R. (2016).

Regulation (EU) 2018/643 on rail transport statistics (recast), 2018/643 C.F.R. (2018).

Regulation (EU) 2019/2152 on European business statistics, 2019/2152 C.F.R. (2019).

Rothbaum, J., & Bee, A. (2021). *Coronavirus infects surveys, too: Survey nonresponse bias and the coronavirus pandemic.* US Census Bureau.

Sabel, P. (2021). Met de volkstelling van vijftig jaar geleden begon in Nederland de discussie over privacy. Volkskrant. Accessed 10-08-2023. Retrieved from https://www.volkskrant.nl/wetenschap/met-de-volkstelling-van-vijftig-jaar-geleden-begon-in-nederland-de-discussie-over-privacy~b5852861/

Statistics Netherlands. (2020). Cybersecuritybedrijven in Nederland. Accessed 08-08-2023. Retrieved from https://www.cbs.nl/-/media/_pdf/2020/22/cybersecuritybedrijven-in-nederland.pdf

Statistics Netherlands. (2023a). CBS stapt over op nieuwe methode voor energieprijzen in de CPI [Press release]. Accessed 08-08-2023. Retrieved from https://www.cbs.nl/nl-nl/achtergrond/2023/26/cbs-stapt-over-op-nieuwe-methode-voor-energieprijzen-in-de-cpi

Statistics Netherlands. (2023b). Verhuiswens afleiden uit sociale media. Accessed 08-08-2023. Retrieved from https://www.cbs.nl/nl-nl/over-ons/onderzoek-en-innovatie/project/verhuiswens-afleiden-uit-sociale-media

Statistics Netherlands. (2023c). Volkstelling 2021: Nederland in vierkanten. Accessed 08-08-2023. Retrieved from https://www.cbs.nl/nl-nl/longread/statistische-trends/2023/volkstelling-2021-nederland-in-vierkanten/3-de-gebruikte-beveiligingsmethoden

To, N., & McBride, B. (2013). A comparison of consumer expenditure surveys. Paper presented at the Proceedings of the 2013 Federal Committee on Statistical Methodology (FCSM) Research Conference, Division of Consumer Expenditure Survey, US Bureau of Labor Statistics. Retrieved from https://fcsm. sites. usa. gov/files/2014/05/D2_To_2013FCSM. pdf

Uitvoeringswet Algemene verordening gegevensbescherming, BWBR0040940 C.F.R. (2021).

Verzetsmuseum Amsterdam. (2009). De aanslag op het Amsterdamse bevolkingsregister. Accessed 09-08-2023. Retrieved from https://web.archive.org/web/20090322080236/http://www.verzetsmuseum.org/tweede-wereldoorlog/nl/achtergrond/achtergrond,aanslag/amsterdamse_bevolkingsregister

Wet op het Centraal bureau voor de statistiek, BWBR0015926 C.F.R. (2022).

Zwart, H., & Nelis, A. (2009). What is ELSA genomics? Science & society series on convergence research. *EMBO Reports*, 10(6), 540–4. doi:10.1038/embor.2009.115

5. Soft OR, Big Data: use and limitations in policy-making
Michael Howlett, Leong Ching and Tay Swee Kiat

INTRODUCTION: OPERATIONAL RESEARCH (SOFT & HARD) AND PUBLIC POLICY-MAKING

Contemporary policy study is experiencing the unfolding of two key dynamics, one external – the increasing complexity of policy-making in general with problems and crises such as COVID-19 (Cairney, 2012; El-Taliawi & Hartley, 2020) – and the other internal – with a new focus from the "behavioural turn" in the policy sciences on how better to effect individual decision-making to help resolve these issues (Cairney & Weible, 2017; Howlett & Leong, 2022b; Leong & Howlett, 2022b).

Together, these two dynamics have given rise to new methods intended to deal with complexity through a more structured analysis and organisation of decision-making behaviour. The emergence of "Soft OR" or "Soft" Operational Research is one such method, with its strengths in helping to define (and redefine) the problem at hand through analysis of complex situations and input from a myriad of different stakeholders (Mingers, 2011). The effort to incorporate more and different kinds of data ("Big Data") is another, helping to widen the range and depth of available data, as well as the integration of hitherto distinct datasets (El-Taliawi et al., 2020; Goyal et al., 2021). Together, these new methods can help better model the subjective and qualitative understanding of human biases and policy-maker and policy-taker behaviour and inform decision-making practices accordingly (Howlett et al., 2020).

Both Big Data and Soft OR have been used in policy sciences before, but the intersection of the two methods remains both underutilised and understudied and few studies have explored the relationship between the two.

"Harder" OR techniques, with their focus on quantitative techniques and mathematical models for guiding decision-making processes, are a natural bedfellow with Big Data, which can supply them with the kinds of data needed for various techniques – like linear programming – to "work", thus forming a natural partnership. As argued below, the partnership between Soft OR and Big Data can be equally fruitful. In this chapter, we show how Soft OR can also benefit greatly from more "data" in a Big Data sense, while Big Data can also be enhanced by fitting it better into more of the stakeholder-driven problem structuring techniques which are a feature of Soft OR (Leong & Howlett, 2022a).

BACKGROUND: OPERATIONAL RESEARCH AND POLICY ANALYSIS

Operational Research (OR) is an interdisciplinary branch of mathematics that typically deals with the application of advanced analytical and statistical methods to support decision-making in complex real-world problems. OR, in its traditional form ("Hard OR"), combines mathematical modelling, computational techniques, and expert knowledge to provide insight into complex systems and helps organisations make informed decisions in fields such as transportation, logistics, supply chain management, healthcare, finance, and more.

Originally developed in the 1940s to help organise industrial production, OR was intended to bring the scientific method to problem-solving in a way that would ensure objectivity and improve decision-making and efficiency when problems arise (Trefethen, 1995; Keys, 1997; Mingers, 2000; Jackson, 2006). As the approach became more established, it started to lean more heavily into the use of mathematical models and techniques as the means to ensure this objectivity, especially in the US (Kirby, 2000, 2003).

However, the limitations of this "Hard OR" approach soon became apparent in many areas related to management and decision-making behaviours, culminating in a sustained period of criticism of such a "pure" approach when addressing problems with a human or social component (Ackoff, 1977; Mingers, 2000, 2003). With its emphasis on quantification, as Ackoff (1979) noted, Hard OR is "mathematically sophisticated but contextually naïve" (p. 94). The Hard OR approach was found to be especially ill-suited to addressing what Horst Rittel described as "wicked problems", that is, those where, as the originator of the term put it, decision-makers must deal with "social system problems which are ill-formulated, where information is confusing, where there are many clients and decision makers with conflicting values, and where the ramifications in the whole system are thoroughly confusing" (Churchman, 1967, p. B141; see also Rittel & Webber, 1973; Mingers, 2011).

Emergence of Soft OR

Critiques of the application of Hard OR in the realm of policy-relevant problems centred around two main issues (White, 2016). First, its emphasis on maintaining objectivity was said to lead to an overly narrow reliance on mathematical modelling (Ackoff, 1979), creating an illusion of objectivity that is ill-suited to the social world (Mingers, 2000, 2003; White, 2016). And second, the rigid adherence of most Hard OR models to a utility-maximising logic of human behaviour was said to simply assume that people would behave rationally in maximising their utility and allows the achievement of an optimal solution (White, 2016) while, of course, this is highly problematic in the social realm. Hard OR techniques were argued to fail to consider key decision-making factors such as emotions, social influences, norms, and contextual cues while other problems in the policy realm caused by uncertain futures, malicious behaviour, and non-compliance were also neglected, despite the significant impact they and other similar factors have in preventing any optimal outcome from being achieved (Leong & Howlett, 2022a).

These questions about the assumptions and pre-suppositions of traditional OR, mainly driven by UK scholars, led to a growth in interest in how to better incorporate more subjective and qualitative elements into OR thinking, resulting in the emergence of what came to be known as the "Soft OR" approach (Reisman & Oral, 2005; Ackermann, 2012).

At the foundational level, Soft OR is an effort to derive standardised problem structuring methods (PSMs) capable of making some sense out of otherwise wicked problem situations and thus able to aid deliberations in the social and policy, realms (White, 2016). Unlike Hard OR techniques, Soft OR assumes from the start that problems are perceived differently by different stakeholders according to their social, cultural, and psychological constructs and that these differences cannot simply be ignored or glossed over (Baumgartner & Jones, 1991;

Jenkins-Smith et al., 1991). It focuses on understanding multiple perspectives, structuring problems, and involving stakeholders in a flexible, iterative manner, thereby hoping to produce a logical framework to help resolve such problems by more carefully defining and redefining (or "structuring") a problem prior to the application of any more traditional problem-solving and policy design techniques (Leong & Howlett, 2022a).

THE POTENTIAL OF SOFT OR AS AN AID TO POLICY-MAKING

It has already been noted in many quarters that Soft OR approaches, with their ability to help structure problems to highlight and deal with the volatility of decision-making behaviour neglected by Hard OR, can be a useful addition to the policy sciences (Pluchinotta et al., 2019; Leong & Howlett, 2022a).

Most policies suffer from risks of uncertainty, maliciousness, and non-compliance (inherent vices) (Howlett & Leong, 2022a), for example, and Soft OR practices can help deal with these (Leong & Howlett, 2022a). Often, these risks are a product of human aspects of policy processes, such as when target populations fail to comply with policies. Soft OR methods, with their ability to work with ambiguity, can serve as useful methods to identify and correct the sources of these problems and make their appearance more transparent (Leong & Howlett, 2022a; see Table 5.1).

In particular, it has been argued that Soft OR techniques help formalise what has often been undertaken in a less than systematic, experiential way, such as through open-ended public

Table 5.1 Policy risk or failure modes and Soft OR solutions to them

		Design Problems & Solutions			
		Formulation Problems	Solution	Implementation Problems	Solution
Policy Volatility Sources in Inherent Vices	Uncertainty	Knowledge Gaps	SSM, Cognitive mapping, Journey making	Lack of incentives	Hypergames, Interactive planning
		Poor Learning	SCA, SAST, Interactive planning	Lack of enforcement and Disincentives	Cognitive mapping, SSM, SAST
		Institutional Complexity	SSM, Cognitive mapping, Journey making	Lack of Legitimacy in Decision-making	SCA, SSM, SAST, Hypergames
	Maliciousness	Self-interests of Policy Makers	SSM, SAST, Interactive planning	Policy-Taker Gaming and Evasion	Hypergames, Robustness analysis, Interactive planning
	Compliance	Divergence of Values and Government Intentions	SSM, Journey making, SAST, CSH, Interactive planning	Maladaptiveness to Changes in Policy Systems	SSM, SCA, SAST, CSH, Hypergames, Robustness analysis, Interactive planning
		Misalignment of Target Behaviour	SSM, SAST, CSH, Interactive planning	Policy Incompatibility with Cultural Practices or Market Incentives	SSM, SCA, SAST, CSH, Hypergames, Robustness analysis, Interactive planning

Source: Authors' own.

consultation exercises. Soft OR techniques allow people's perspectives and experiences with policy problems and potential solutions to be brought together to bear on problematic situations in ways that may lead to distinctly new solutions (Eden & Ackermann, 1998; White, 2002; Pluchinotta et al., 2020). In these instances, what to think of as the problem and how to think of it is a product of a collective process (White, 2016) and "solving" the problem may not always be a necessity – simply having the problem better structured and "bounded" can often enable decision-makers to move forward on some aspects of the issue – complete analysis and development being not necessary in order to act (Ackermann et al., 2020).

Ackermann (2012) has summarised the benefits of using the Soft OR approach in policy-making as follows (pp. 654–5):

1. Managing complexity, developing a comprehensive appreciation of the situation, and what the "problem" is;
2. Attending to multiple perspectives enables multiple stakeholders' ownership and commitment, and allows them to appreciate that there is not a single right point of view; and
3. Managing process and content helps in supporting a group's negotiation towards an agreed outcome.

Typical Soft OR Problem Structuring Methods (PSMs) and Their Data Requirements

Some of the more common Soft OR methods (or PSMs) that have been developed and used over the past several decades include the Strategic Choice Approach, the Soft Systems Methodology (SSM), and the cognitive mapping/Strategic Options Development and Analysis (SODA) (see Leong & Howlett, 2022a for a review of the methods). These and other Soft OR models require data of different kinds and most can potentially benefit from the developments and analytical methods developed to analyse "Big Data".

The Strategic Choice Approach, developed initially by Friend and Jessop (1977) and later by Friend and Hickling (1987), for example, promotes a four-phased or "mode" set of activities that can help decision-makers select, discuss, compare, and commit to proposed solutions for identified problems (Friend & Hickling, 1998; Lami & Todella, 2019). Its emphasis on comparing and evaluating proposed solutions makes the approach especially suited to tackling uncertainties in policy formulation and/or compliance, granting legitimacy, and providing incentives for the solutions implemented. But in doing so, it requires a great deal of data.

This can also be seen in SSM, which uses varying forms of non-mathematical data, and flexibly draws from historical to contemporary data sources, in order to promote better understanding of problem parameters. For instance, Hanafizadeh and Ghamkhari (2019) argue that SSM is particularly useful in elucidating specialised tacit knowledge, or "knowledge as discrete or digital existing in the libraries, archives, and databases" (p. 522).

Others have applied SSM methods to the analysis of ongoing social discourse, drawing from the fluid, empirical data of the social world. Tavella and Lami (2019), for example, applied SSM to situations that required fragile negotiations around competing perspectives and values and argue that "exploring how such negotiations evolve at the micro-level of real-time interactions can help grasp communicative behaviours and workshop structures that influence negotiation processes, and the achievement of outcomes" (p. 136). Avison et al. (1992) note that many "problem situations are difficult to model and tools are considered inappropriate by many traditional OR proponents" (p. 397) but that SSM is capable of forming a toolkit "to make sense of complex problem situations which involve human activity" (Avison et al., 1992, p. 397).

In this regard, the data needs of SSM practitioners are ever-evolving, pushing the limits of the method which, like the Strategic Choice Approach, could benefit from Big Data techniques tied to, for example, the more rapid and accurate analysis of the large corpus of documents and text.

BIG DATA IN POLICY-MAKING: POTENTIAL AND PROBLEMS

Like Soft OR, Big Data has also been seen as a potential game changer for modern public administration (Maciejewski, 2017; El-Taliawi et al., 2021; Goyal et al., 2021). Big Data has been defined as a "cultural, technological, and scholarly phenomenon that rests on the interplay of: technology… analysis … and mythology" (Boyd & Crawford, 2012, p. 663). Despite the nomenclature, it is not only about size and computation power, but also, like Operational Research, involves a belief in its ability to offer a "higher form intelligence … and the aura of truth, objectivity, and accuracy" (Boyd & Crawford, 2012, p. 663).

There is no doubt that digitisation, Web 2.0 services and technologies, as well as other recent cyber and technological developments, are producing an enormous and unprecedented amount of data that are rich in detail concerning human and societal behaviour and related contextual factors and dynamics, including the attitudes, preferences, and sentiment of different individuals and groups (see. e.g., Bollen, Mao, & Pepe, 2011; Gundecha & Liu, 2012). There is increasing belief that Big Data can transform society and be the source of new energy for social transformation and decision-making, and for better private and public services (Schintler & Kulkarni, 2014; White et al., 2016a).

Not surprisingly, Big Data has been seen to have great potential as a resource for helping to inform many different points in the policy process "from problem conceptualization to ongoing evaluation of existing policies, and even empowering and engaging citizens and stakeholders in the process" (Schintler & Kulkarni, 2014, p. 343).

Characteristic Features of Big Data

The power of Big Data can be concisely captured as a matter of scale, which can sometimes result in a real difference in kind: "Big Data allows users to do things at a large scale that cannot be done at a smaller one … by changing the amount we can change the essence" (Mayer-Schönberger & Cukier, 2013, p. 10).

But scale refers to more than just the size of the database. Big Data was initially characterized as defined by three main attributes: size (volume), speed (velocity), and shape (variety) (Laney, 2001). Subsequent formulations of Big Data have at times added a fourth characterisation: quality (veracity), leading to the 4 Vs of Big Data (Chen et al., 2014; Höchtl et al., 2016; Poel et al, 2018).

1. Volume: refers to the volume of data available, especially with the shift from macro-level data to personalised data, and partly as a result of the velocity of data generated;
2. Velocity: refers to the speed at which data is available, with the use of algorithms and modern hardware;

3. Variety: refers to the heterogeneity of data available – a central feature of Big Data is its ability to merge different formats and sources of data that were previously unavailable or impractical to analyse;
4. Veracity: refers to the quality of the data, with Big Data being characterised by incomplete and inaccurate data.

Together, these characteristics describe how Big Data-based analysis may be used in policy-making. While the volume of data available makes sampling less of a requirement (as a census data might be available and feasible to use), the use of algorithms and hardware for Big Data caters to a greater velocity of data analysis, and the ability to combine different sources of data allows for a greater variety of data (including meta-data), although there remains the concern of the quality of the data that is being used for analysis.

HOW SOFT OR TECHNIQUES CAN HELP OVERCOME THE LIMITS OF BIG DATA IN THE ANALYSIS OF POLICY-MAKING & VICE VERSA

Several of the most prominent limits in the application of Soft OR and Big Data techniques in government are listed below. As the analysis, shows, the strengths of each approach play directly to the weaknesses of the other, suggesting a fertile area for future research in exploring the linkages and complementarities between the two.

Problems with the Application of Soft OR to Policy Problems

Perceived lack of rigour

First, it has to be recognised that the label "Problem Structuring Methods" or PSMs is somewhat of a misnomer because the method is not just about "restructuring" problems. As such, its impact is often undervalued or not being credited with the label, diminishing its contribution in driving action. Soft OR isn't a much better name either as it continues to be seen by many "as having negative connotations within OR generally, implying imprecision and lack of rigor" (Mingers, 2011, p. 730). Furthermore, there is debate concerning what actually constitutes a PSM (Ackermann, 2012), making an appropriate label even harder to come up with.

More to the point, the subjective nature of Soft OR analysis tends to yield insights rather than testable results (Ackermann, 2012), which implies that its effectiveness can seldom be *proven* with empirical evidence. And the idiosyncrasies of each problem situation suggest that results also can't always be replicated (Mingers & Rosenhead, 2004).

For proponents of hard OR and traditionalists, this subjective component and lack of certainty is uncomfortable (Ackermann et al., 2020), and lead to concerns about the validity of the outcomes of Soft OR applications and the robustness of their findings (Mingers, 2011; Paucar-Caceres, 2011).

Some soft OR methods have become widely adapted across a broad range of industries, but not always with the proper understanding of the underlying theories and concepts (Ackermann, 2019), such as the use of cognitive maps by consultants. This further compounds the perception of a problem with the rigour and robustness of Soft OR methods and findings in any field, including public policy-making.

Training issues
Even for those convinced of the legitimacy and value of Soft OR, developing competence in the use of Soft OR techniques is still not a straightforward matter (Ackermann et al., 2020). First, there is a paucity of Soft OR/PSM courses, and training is mainly centred in the United Kingdom or Australia (Ackermann, 2019). And even when offered, the coverage of the methods is often fleeting or short, and not enough time is allocated to cover the approach and all its nuances (Ackermann, 2019).

A further difficulty with training is that a large proportion of students typically come into training without any direct experience of the *real world* and all its complexities (Ackermann et al., 2020). However, this experience is vital in Soft OR in order for users to facilitate the process of inquiry, negotiation, and accommodations between the various actors involved (Checkland & Poulter, 2010).

Students who encounter the Soft OR approach soon realise there is a steep learning curve involved, as they need to develop expertise in not only the modelling methods but also the process aspects of managing their application, such as intervention design and group facilitation (Ackermann, 2012). Soft OR requires its users to be proficient in the different OR methods (which are sophisticated and complex individually) so as to adopt the best method through their interactions with the participants of the study (Ackermann et al., 2020), and adding familiarity with Big Data techniques exacerbates these challenges. Most of the nuances involved in the approaches can also only be learned through experience, rather than from textbooks, so the lack of opportunities and qualified mentors can make the learning curve even steeper (Ackermann et al., 2020).

Problems with the Application of Big Data to Policy Analysis

While the expectations for Big Data in policy-making are high, there are still relatively few examples of Big Data being used to shape public policy (Schintler & Kulkarni, 2014; Poel et al., 2018; El-Taliawi et al., 2021; Goyal et al., 2021; but see White et al., 2016a, 2016b for an example based on smart ities). Concerns exist regarding whether or not its theoretical potential can be achieved in practice (Giest, 2017; Giest & Samuels, 2020). These Big Data limitations include:

1. Making "sense" of what the problem actually is;
2. The lack of ability to account for values;
3. Dealing with qualitative "truths" such as narratives;
4. Emotions, interactions between difficult emotions;
5. Cognitive biases in training datasets are implicitly picked up by Big Data analytics (Giest, 2017).

Making "sense" of what the problem actually is
A common criticism of Big Data is that its users are susceptible to apophenia; inferring patterns where there is actually nothing (White & Breckenridge, 2014). Instead of trying to understand a problem by building on what has been learned so far (i.e., theoretically grounded approach), it is easy to abuse the huge statistical power of Big Data to conveniently identify statistically significant relations that fit one's personal narratives. That is, Big Data separates its users from the issue at hand. By removing the need to engage in the research design and

data collection process, users of Big Data have limited opportunities to understand the contextual nuances of what is being researched (Daniel, 2019), reducing the complexity of their research problem to the data given.

The lack of ability to account for values
As Big Data users are typically working with data that is already collected, there are limited ways for users to control the quality of the dataset. This is because measures intended for preserving data integrity such as randomisation and counterbalancing can only be performed prior to the data collection process, not after (Boyd & Crawford, 2012). Large datasets obtained online also tend to be unreliable, prone to missing data and errors (Boyd & Crawford, 2012; Northcutt et al., 2021) and these issues can be magnified when error-prone datasets are used alongside other questionable datasets.

Dealing with qualitative "truths" such as narratives
Big Data is usually "exhaust data"; a by-product of other services (e.g., a customer relationship database intended for client management). Consequently, it is unlikely that Big Data can "establish a "ground truth" (i.e., whether the data measures what was assumed), provide a "thick description" (understanding of the social context and mechanisms at play) of situations that the data represent, and measure otherwise hidden dimensions" (Bjerre-Nielsen et al., 2022).

Big Data analytics, the methodologies used in qualitative analyses (e.g., case study, ethnography) are highly suited for producing context-specific analyses, "to trace and probe the complex interactions between the social context and social action, as well as the subjectivity of human actors" (Mills, 2018). Rather than blindly follow Big Data trends, issues of context-specificity in Big Data analytics have encouraged academics to adopt mixed method techniques that integrate both Big Data analytics and qualitative research approaches (e.g., Man et al., 2020).

Emotions, interactions between difficult emotions
It is often assumed that with enough data on various measures of emotions (facial expressions, heart rates, neuroimaging, surveys, etc.), Big Data analytics can "understand" how we feel. This assumption is inaccurate (Barrett et al., 2019). Big Data's difficulties with analysing emotions is not a technical issue but rather, emotions remain too subjective to quantify objectively. For example, there is no specific set of facial muscles that are reliably associated with each emotion (Keltner & Cordaro, 2017). Even in neuroscience where emotions are inferred directly from brain activations, there is still much debate on how emotions should be defined (Adolphs, 2017).

Cognitive biases in training datasets are implicitly picked up by Big Data analytics
Big Data analytics is also vulnerable to the cognitive biases of people whose inputs served as the source data. For example, facial recognition software tends to consider faces of Black NBA players as displaying more negative emotions than their white counterparts (Rhue, 2018). Machine learning models can also reflect racial and gender biases when trained using human texts (Caliskan et al., 2017).

THE ADVANTAGES OF COMBINING SOFT OR & BIG DATA

As the descriptions of these problems show, Soft OR and Big Data techniques can be seen to be complementary in the sense of helping each other overcome the problems each exhibits individually. Many of the limitations of Big Data cited above, for example, can be offset through the application of Soft OR techniques and vice versa.

Three relationships between Big Data and Soft OR techniques in particular show promise in improving the capacity of policy-makers and policy analysts to address complex current problems. These are "channelling" when Soft OR techniques help organise Big Data collection; "complementing" when Big Data is used to inform Soft OR methods; and "competing" when Big Data potentially replaces the use of public forums as a means of problem structuring.

Channelling

Channelling is using Soft OR as a method to explore the use of Big Data – for example, to understand how open data platforms may be developed and sustained (White et al., 2016b, p. 314), regardless of project or field.

That is, the belief in the growing significance of Big Data for policy-making is coupled with the recognition that its use comes with its own risks and problems (McNeely & Hahm, 2014; Schintler & Kulkarni, 2014; White et al., 2016a). The progress of Big Data being used for public policy is still not really encouraging (Giest 2017; Poel et al., 2018). Big Data collection is frequently not well structured (White et al., 2016a); it carries with it issues regarding privacy and security; is often collected as a by-product of other purposes and it carries the same "inherent vices" commonly associated with policy-making (Leong & Howlett, 2022a). To unlock the full potential of Big Data, it needs to be complemented with knowledge of economic, social, and political values in order to be able to translate the information from Big Data into actionable policies and impact (White et al., 2016a).

In contrast to customised research where the parameters of a study are tightly controlled, using Big Data often requires an adjustment to data that is frequently unorganized and incomplete. For some, Big Data datasets have limited use because of their irregularity and heterogeneity (Chen et al., 2012; White et al., 2016a). The potential for use exists, but a means to make sense of it is still required in order to properly tap into the potential of Big Data.

Public organisations need to better assess what the use of Big Data will require and what specific added value it could bring (Klievink et al., 2017, pp. 275–7) and this is where Soft OR can be useful. Soft OR techniques for problem structuring can serve as a useful approach in order to explore the best approaches in utilising Big Data in order to facilitate its more effective use (White et al., 2016b).

For example, White and colleagues (2016b) conducted workshops with various stakeholders from the public, private, and third (non-governmental and non-profit-making organisations) sectors, in order to develop an approach to Big Data management that puts it to more effective use by tapping into available information technology and citizen input.

These reciprocal interactions between the behaviour of organisations that interpret Big Data and the behaviour of users who generate it are often not sufficiently considered in Big Data analysis (White et al., 2016b).

For instance, White, Burger, and Yearworth (2016a, 2016b) coined the term "SMART OR" as the creative use of Big Data with Hard and Soft OR to enhance behaviour and positive results for decision-makers. They applied this concept to the planning and design of smart cities, where Soft OR methods are used to identify key areas in the city data repositories to focus on, and Hard OR approaches were then used for the planning of hardware and software solutions at a later stage (White et al., 2016b).

Complementing
Soft OR can also be employed in the traditional sense to identify key areas of focus, before using existing Big Data to generate evidence and inform policy-making in a complementary form of interaction (Ackermann, 2012; Mingers & Rosenhead, 2004; White et al., 2016a; Feitosa & Carpinetti, 2022).

Combining Soft OR and Big Data as complements can occur in three ways: (i) as a problem structuring guide to explore and examine existing Big Data repositories for a project, rather than Big Data in general (during policy-making); (ii) as a way to inform the design and implementation of Big Data collection (pre-policy-making); and (iii) as a way to visualise the results of Big Data analysis.

With existing Big Data during policy-making, Soft OR processes can provide the "procedural scaffolds" needed to guide data exploration (White et al., 2016b). Faced with more data than one may know what to do with it, Soft OR can be employed to identify key areas to focus on when presented with large and complicated Big Data datasets. This serves to improve the effectiveness of analysis using the Big Data at later stages of policy-making, implementation, or evaluation. In this sense, Soft OR helps fulfil the traditional role of problem identification, structuring, and exploration which is needed for successful Big Data application.

Pre-policy-making, complementing Big Data by making use of Soft OR methods to decide how to design and collect Big Data, can also lead to more productive results. For example, in policy innovation studies, crowdsourcing can be used as a way to gather Big Data feedback from the public during various milestones of a public policy project (Ghezzi et al., 2018). But the logistical issues of implementing this crowdsourcing need to be carefully considered.

For example, a challenge is to find an appropriate way to define the structure of the problem as presented to the public from the multitude of concerns and needs of its stakeholders in the study. The problem must also be carefully restructured and reframed to be easily understood, making it easier for the crowd to solve (Sieg et al., 2010; Natalicchio et al., 2014). The dissemination of the problem needs to provide sufficient information to the public (Afuah & Tucci, 2012), but also ensure that the framing is not loaded or biased, leading to constraints or restricting creativity (Sieg et al., 2010), while also avoiding disclosure of any confidential and sensitive information (Barbier et al., 2012; Nevo et al., 2014). Finally, innovation problems should, naturally, be relevant for the seeker, but they also have to be affordable, challenging, and of interest to the solvers, to ensure that solutions are submitted (Sieg et al., 2010). These are all challenges where the proper use of Soft OR may help to crystallise the solutions to maximise the effectiveness of the use of crowdsourcing (Ghezzi et al., 2018).

Finally, Soft OR can function as a way to present the results of Big Data analyses. The visualisation and presentation of Big Data is itself a challenge if it is expected to lead to meaningful action – Soft OR can serve as the subjective input to improve the odds of success. For instance, White and colleagues (2016b) found SMART OR to work well in supporting the process of co-designing visual interfaces and analytics reporting tools for decision-makers to effectively solicit support from the stakeholders and public. Combining PSMs to prompt critical (disruptive) learning moments, for example, with videotaped episodes and participant interaction data logging, improves the interpretation and understanding of the results (Engeström et al., 1996; White et al., 2016b) and helps bridge processes amongst data, insight, and action.

Competing

Big Data can also be used as an alternative means of data collection to the traditional workshops used in Soft OR. Instead of being used in conjunction with Soft OR, Big Data becomes the data source for problem structuring during the Soft OR process, such as through the use of online collaborative stakeholder engagement platforms (White et al., 2016a, 2016b), tapping intp the extensive subjective data collected through social media, or examination of experiences with distributed interaction (over email, internet) in place of workshops (Morton et al., 2007), or over online collaborative workspaces such as Slack or Discord.

A characteristic of Soft OR methods is their extensive use of workshops, where participants jointly create a model in situ through their interactions. While workshops continue to deliver significant value to the organisation that uses it, this (over-)reliance on workshops can make Soft OR very costly in terms of participant time, as well as in financial terms if the organisation is not physically colocated. Moreover, because involvement is restricted to workshop participants, what is often a key goal of Soft OR – to involve a broad constituency of opinion in organisational and policy decision-making – may be compromised (Morton et al., 2007). Townhalls and public consultation sessions can serve as the equivalent of workshops in Soft OR, but outreach is limited.

The ability to involve a wider audience is especially critical for policy-making, because the general public is also an important stakeholder for public policies, if not the most important at times. The search for an alternative to workshops in carrying out Soft OR methods then becomes essential, driven by the need to reach the public for feedback (which is impossible to do when using traditional Soft OR methods). In comparison, Big Data holds potential in reaching out to a lot of people in a short period of time. Big Data, whether through existing platforms or newly created platforms, helps to extend the reach to more people without being prohibitively time-consuming or costly, and even holds the potential of collating and merging data collected through different sources and platforms, and both self-reported data and "surveillance"-type data such as metadata (e.g., customer shopping patterns).

Therefore, a third option of pairing Big Data with Soft OR is by using the latter as the platform to analyse the former. In contrast to the complementing option, where Soft OR is still conducted in the traditional sense using familiar Soft OR methods and the extensive use of workshops to collect the subjective data required to complement Big Data sources, in the competing option, Soft OR methods are used with Big Data sources. Especially important in this option is the capability to collate the subjective and qualitative opinions that are emblematic of Soft OR, but on a much larger scale. This usually involves the use of "distributed" platforms, where the term refers to "distributed in space and asynchronous" (Morton et al., 2007). Examples of such platforms include emails and the internet, and more contemporaneously, social media, online discussion platforms, and Discord/Slack. And since workshops constrained by time and space are no longer the norm, which allows for wider participation.

The benefits of using Big Data to *replace* traditional workshops, for example, can be summarised as follows:

1. It is more timely, that is, velocity (conducting multiple workshops can be time-consuming) (White et al., 2016b);

2. It encourages wider participation without excessive time/logistics constraint, which is especially crucial for policy-making as the stakeholders often involve the general public, so public outreach is a priority (White et al., 2016b);
3. There is no need for a facilitator/facilitation through platform and structure rather than a person (thereby potentially getting around the problem of a lack of trained facilitators – in terms of both numbers and training) (Ackermann et al., 2020). Data management involves a shift from facilitation to curation (existing platforms) or moderation (newly created platforms); and
4. Asynchronicity, which gets around the logistical need for colocation of participants/stakeholders that is typical of more traditional workshops. For instance, online bulletin board systems and similar applications enable users to post commentary and ideas to a virtual "location" at one point in time, and other users can engage those thoughts at much later points in time. Much like the leaving and taking of notes on a bulletin board in a town square, the Web can foster a sense of ongoing dialogue between members of a community without those members having to be present at the same time (Ostwald, 1997 [2000], 2000). This capability for the Web is already being realised in some urban planning projects, as posting podcasts and meeting minutes on planning project websites is an exploitation of the Web's asynchrony and virtual permanence, particularly if these kinds of project websites are coexistent with online bulletin board systems (Brabham, 2009).

Another example of a Big Data technique that fits this purpose is macro-task crowdsourcing, which leverages the collective intelligence of a crowd through facilitated collaboration on a digital platform to address complex or wicked problems (Gimpel et al., 2023). Macro-task crowdsourcing aims to use the wisdom of a crowd to tackle non-trivial tasks such as wicked problems (Gimpel et al., 2023, p. 75). For macro-task crowdsourcing to realise its potential and tackle such complex problems, however, structure, guidance, and support are needed to coordinate the collaborating crowd workers (Gimpel et al., 2023, p. 76; see also Adla et al., 2011; Azadegan & Kolfschoten, 2014; Shafiei Gol et al., 2019), which is where Soft OR methods can be adapted for use.

The use of social media platforms to collect Big Data for Soft OR analysis is another example. Through the use of social media, any audience member can easily initiate new discussions, and responses to existing discussions can take various forms, such as text, audio, video, or images (Studinka & Guenduez, 2018). Therefore, one way for governments to identify emergent topics early and to create relevant agenda points is "to collect data from social networks with high degrees of participation and try to identify citizens' policy preferences, which can then be taken into account by the government in setting the agenda" (Höchtl et al., 2016, p. 159).

Sentiment analysis and opinion mining can also be used to identify opinion streams linked to any topic of interest in public policy, mentioned in textual messages (Alfaro et al., 2016, p. 198). For instance, new measures to track public opinion of US space policy over Google Trends and social media sources allowed for a more accurate gauge of public interest (Whitman Cobb, 2015). Panagiotopoulos et al. (2017) examined the value of Twitter data to explore how collective input by farmers on Twitter could be suitable as input in policy activities. A cluster mapping technique was used to summarise and visualise the large exploratory Twitter dataset and discover how conversations evolve, resulting in the discovery of two separate farming-relevant branches, dairy farming and arable farming. Terms clustering around dairy farming were often connected to topics concerning renewable energy, showing a mutually connected relevance, which provided interesting insights for policy-makers.

CONCLUSION: SOFT OR AND BIG DATA BETTER TOGETHER?

Soft OR has "come of age" over the 50 years of its existence (Mingers, 2011; also see Lowe & Yearworth, 2019; Gomes Júnior & Schramm, 2022 for a bibliometric analysis of Soft OR's progress) and has consistently been found to provide useful results for policy-makers when used by academics and other non-governmental actors.

However, there is little evidence to suggest that *governments* are leveraging on the approach effectively to improve their policy-making (Leong et al., 2023). Part of the reason for this is that many governments remain uninformed about specific Soft OR techniques and wedded to other more traditional consultation processes (Leong et al., 2023). However, a second barrier stems from the extensive informational and data needs of Soft OR cited above. It is here that the intersection of Soft OR and Big Data developments can help rectify these issues.

Big Data serves as the next frontier in this search for bigger, and better, data for Soft OR purposes, by enabling the large-scale incorporation and interpretation of public opinion (which is so crucial for public policy), and the incorporation of dispersed knowledge and innovative power into policy-making (Höchtl et al., 2016). Big Data techniques can extend the benefits of Soft OR through their characteristics of volume, velocity, and variety, resulting in the consideration of a greater multitude of opinions so essential for public policy analysis.

But Soft OR, with its strengths in managing complexity, attending to multiple perspectives, and managing process and content, helps to overcome the shortcomings of Big Data, including providing the problem structuring framework for making sense of the problem, accounting for more subjective input such as values, narratives, and emotions, and serving as a check and balance on the potential cognitive biases picked up through Big Data training datasets.

ACKNOWLEDGEMENT

We thank the support of Damien Soon and Theodore Lai (National University of Singapore, Lee Kuan Yew School of Public Policy) for their work in conducting literature reviews, particularly for the sections on Soft OR methods and Big Data limitations.

REFERENCES

Ackermann, F. (2012). Problem structuring methods "in the dock": Arguing the case for Soft OR. *European Journal of Operational Research, 219*(3), 652–8. https://doi.org/10.1016/j.ejor.2011.11.014.

Ackermann, F. (2019). PSMs are dead; long live PSMs. *Journal of the Operational Research Society, 70*(8), 1396-–397. https://doi.org/10.1080/01605682.2018.1502630.

Ackermann, F., Alexander, J., Stephens, A., & Pincombe, B. (2020). In defence of Soft OR: Reflections on teaching Soft OR. *Journal of the Operational Research Society, 71*(1), 1–15. https://doi.org/10.1080/01605682.2018.1542960.

Ackoff, R. (1977). Optimization + objectivity = opt out. *European Journal of Operational Research, 1*, 1–7. https://doi.org/10.1016/S0377–2217(77)81003–5.

Ackoff, R. (1979). The future of operational research is past. *Journal of the Operational Research Society, 30(2),* 93–104. http://www.jstor.org/stable/3009290.

Adla, A., Zarate, P., & Soubie, J.-L. (2011). A proposal of toolkit for GDSS facilitators. *Group Decision and Negotiation, 20*(1), 57–77. https://doi.org/10.1007/s10726-010-9204-8.

Adolphs, R. (2017). How should neuroscience study emotions? By distinguishing emotion states, concepts, and experiences. *Social Cognitive and Affective Neuroscience, 12*(1), 24–31. https://doi.org/10.1093/scan/nsw153.

Afuah, A., &Tucci, C.L. (2012). Crowdsourcing as a solution to distant search. *Academy of Management Review, 37*(3), 355–75. https://www.jstor.org/stable/23218093 [last accessed 11 Nov, 2024].

Alfaro, C., Cano-Montero, J., Gómez, J., Moguerza, J.M., & Ortega, F. (2016). A multi-stage method for content classification and opinion mining on weblog comments. *Annals of Operations Research, 236*(1), 197–213. https://doi.org/10.1007/s10479-013-1449-6.

Avison, D.E., Golder, P.A., & Shah, H.U. (1992). Towards an SSM toolkit: Rich picture diagramming. *European Journal of Information Systems, 1,* 397–408. https://doi.org/10.1057/ejis.1992.17.

Azadegan, A., & Kolfschoten, G. (2014). An assessment framework for practicing facilitator. *Group Decision and Negotiation, 23*(5), 1013–45. https://doi.org/10.1007/s10726-012-9332-4.

Barbier, G., Zafarani, R., Gao, H., Fung, G., & Liu, H. (2012). Maximizing benefits from crowdsourced data. *Computational and Mathematical Organization Theory, 18,* 257–79. https://doi.org/10.1007/s10588-012-9121-2.

Barrett, L.F., Adolphs, R., Marsella, S., Martinez, A.M., & Pollak, S.D. (2019). Emotional expressions reconsidered: Challenges to inferring emotion from human facial movements. *Psychological Science in the Public Interest, 20*(1), 1–68. https://doi.org/10.1177/1529100619832930.

Baumgartner, F.R., & Jones, B.D. (1991). Agenda dynamics and policy subsystems. *The Journal of Politics, 53*(4), 1044–74. https://doi.org/10.2307/2131866.

Bjerre-Nielsen, A., & Glavind, K.L. (2022). Ethnographic data in the age of big data: How to compare and combine. *Big Data & Society, 9*(1), 20539517211069893. https://doi.org/10.1177/20539517211069893.

Bollen, J., Mao, H., & Pepe, A. (2011). Modeling public mood and emotion: Twitter sentiment and socio-economic phenomena. *Proceedings of the International AAAI Conference on Web and Social Media, 5*(1), 450–3. https://doi.org/10.1609/icwsm.v5i1.14171.

Boudreau, K.J., & Lakhani, K.R. (2013). Using the crowd as an innovation partner. *Harvard Business Review, 91*(4), 60–9. https://hbr.org/2013/04/using-the-crowd-as-an-innovation-partner [last accessed 11 Nov, 2024].

Boyd, D., & Crawford, K. (2012). Critical questions for big data: Provocations for a cultural, technological, and scholarly phenomenon. *Information, Communication & Society, 15*(5), 662–79. https://doi.org/10.1080/1369118X.2012.678878.

Brabham, D.C. (2009). Crowdsourcing the Public participation process for planning projects. *Planning Theory, 8*(3), 242–62. https://www.jstor.org/stable/26166219 [last accessed 11 Nov, 2024].

Cairney, P. (2012). Complexity theory in political science and public policy. *Political Studies Review, 10*(3), 346–58. https://doi.org/10.1111/j.1478-9302.2012.00270.x.

Cairney, P., & Weible, C.M. (2017). The new policy sciences: combining the cognitive science of choice, multiple theories of context, and basic and applied analysis. *Policy Sciences, 50*(4), 619–27. https://doi.org/10.1007/s11077-017-9304-2.

Caliskan, A., Bryson, J.J., & Narayanan, A. (2017). Semantics derived automatically from language corpora contain human-like biases. *Science, 356*(6334), 183–6. https://doi.org/10.1126/science.aal4230.

Checkland, P., & Poulter, J. (2010). Soft systems methodology. In M. Reynolds & S. Holwell (Eds.), *Systems Approaches to Managing Change: A Practical Guide,* 191–242. London: Springer.

Chen, H., Chiang, R., & Storey, V. (2012). Business intelligence and analytics: From big data to big impact. *MIS Quarterly, 36,* 1165–88. https://doi.org/10.2307/41703503.

Chen, M., Mao, S., & Liu, Y. (2014). Big data: A survey. *Mobile Networks and Applications 19*(2), 171–209. https://doi.org/10.1007/s11036-013-0489-0.

Churchman, C.W. (1967). Guest editorial: Wicked problems. *Management Science, 14*(4), B141–B142. http://www.jstor.org/stable/2628678 [last accessed 11 Nov, 2024].

Daniel, B.K. (2019). Big Data and data science: A critical review of issues for educational research. *British Journal of Educational Technology, 50*(1), 101–13. https://doi.org/10.1111/bjet.12595.

Eden, C., & Ackermann, F. (1998). *Making Strategy: The Journey of Strategic Management*. London: Sage.

El-Taliawi, O.G., & Hartley, K. (2020). The COVID-19 crisis and complexity: A soft systems approach. *Journal of Contingencies and Crisis Management, 29*, 104–7. https://doi.org/10.1111/1468–5973.12337.

El-Taliawi, O.G., Goyal, N., & Howlett, M. (2021). Holding out the promise of Lasswell's dream: Big data analytics in public policy research and teaching. *Review of Policy Research*, 38(6), 640–60. https://doi.org/10.1111/ropr.12448.

Engeström, Y., Virkkunen, J., Helle, M., Pihlaja, J., & Poikela, R. (1996). The change laboratory as a tool for transforming work. *Lifelong Learning in Europe, 1*, 10–17.

Feitosa, I.S.C.S., & Ribeiro Carpinetti, L.C. (2022). Problem structuring combined with sentiment analysis to product-service system performance management. In K. Arai (Ed.), *Intelligent Computing*. SAI 2022. Lecture Notes in Networks and Systems, vol 507. Cham: Springer. https://doi.org/10.1007/978-3-031-10464-0_21.

Franco, L.A., & Lord, E. (2011). Understanding multi-methodology: Evaluating the perceived impact of mixing methods for group budgetary decisions. *Omega, 39*(3), 362–72. https://doi.org/10.1016/j.omega.2010.06.008.

Friend, J.K., & Hickling, A. (1987). *Planning under Pressure: The Strategic Choice Approach* (1st edn). New York: Pergamon.

Friend, J.K., & Hickling, A. (1998). *Planning under Pressure: The Strategic Choice Approach* (2nd edn). Oxford: Butterworth-Heinemann.

Friend, J.K., & Jessop, W.N. (1977). *Local Government and Strategic Choice* (2nd edn). New York: Pergamon.

Ghezzi, A., Gabelloni, D., Martini, A., & Natalicchio, A. (2018). Crowdsourcing: A review and suggestions for future research. *International Journal of Management Reviews, 20*(2), 343–63. https://doi.org/10.1111/ijmr.12135.

Giest, S. (2017, September). Big Data for policymaking: Fad or fasttrack? *Policy Sciences, 50*(3), 367–82. https://doi.org/10.1007/s11077–017–9293–1.

Giest, S., & Samuels, A. (2020, September). "For good measure": Data gaps in a Big Data world. *Policy Sciences, 53*(3), 559–69. https://doi.org/10.1007/s11077–020–09384–1.

Gimpel, H., Graf-Seyfried, V., Laubacher, R., & Meindl, O. (2023). Towards artificial intelligence augmenting facilitation: AI affordances in macro-task crowdsourcing. *Group Decision and Negotiation, 32*, 75–124. https://doi.org/10.1007/s10726–022–09801–1.

Gomes Júnior, A. de A., & Schramm, V.B. (2022). Problem structuring methods: A review of advances over the last decade. *Systemic Practice and Action Research, 35*(1), 55–88. https://doi.org/10.1007/s11213–021–09560–1.

Goyal, N., El-Taliawi, O.G., & Howlett, M. (2021). Embracing the future of the policy sciences: Big data in pedagogy and practice. In A.B. Brik & L.A. Pal (Eds), *The Future of the Policy Sciences*, 9–27. Cheltenham, UK and Northampton, MA, USA: Edward Elgar Publishing. https://doi.org/10.4337/9781800376489.

Gundecha, P., & Liu, H. (2012). Mining social media: A brief introduction. INFORMS 2012. https://doi.org/10.1287/educ.1120.0105.

Hanafizadeh, P., & Aliehyaei, R. (2011). The application of fuzzy cognitive map in Soft System Methodology. *Systemic Practice and Action Research, 24*(4), 325–54. https://doi.org/10.1007/s11213–011–9190-z.

Hanafizadeh, P., & Ghamkhari, F. (2019). Elicitation of tacit knowledge using Soft Systems Methodology. *Systemic Practice and Action Research, 32*(5), 521–55. https://doi.org/10.1007/s11213–018–9472–9.

Höchtl, J., Parycek, P., & Schöllhammer, R. (2016). Big data in the policy cycle: Policy decision making in the digital era. *Journal of Organizational Computing and Electronic Commerce, 26*(1–2), 147–69. https://doi.org/10.1080/10919392.2015.1125187.

Howlett, M., & Leong, C. (2022a). The "inherent vices" of policy design: Uncertainty, maliciousness, and noncompliance. *Risk Analysis, 42*(5), 920–30. https://doi.org/10.1111/risa.13834.

Howlett, M., & Leong, C. (2022b). What is behavioral in policy studies?: How far has the discipline moved beyond traditional utilitarianism? *Journal of Behavioral Public Administration, 5*(1). https://doi.org/10.30636/jbpa.51.292

Howlett, M., Ramesh, M., & Capano, G. (2020). Policy-makers, Policy-takers and policy tools: Dealing with behaviourial issues in policy design. *Journal of Comparative Policy Analysis: Research and Practice, 22*(6), 487–97. https://doi.org/10.1080/13876988.2020.1774367.

Jackson, M.C. (2006). Beyond problem structuring methods: Reinventing the future of OR/MS. *Journal of the Operational Research Society, 57*(7), 868–78. https://doi.org/10.1057/palgrave.jors.2602093.

Jenkins-Smith, H.C., St. Clair, G.K., & Woods, B. (1991). Explaining change in policy subsystems: Analysis of coalition stability and defection over time. *American Journal of Political Science, 35*(4), 851–80. https://doi.org/10.2307/2111497.

Keltner, D., & Cordaro, D.T. (2017). Understanding multimodal emotional expressions: Recent advances in basic emotion theory. In J.-M. Fernandez-Dols & J.A. Russell (Eds), *The Science of Facial Expression*, 57–76. New York: Oxford University Press.

Keys, P. (1997). Approaches to understanding the process of OR: Review, critique and extension. *Omega, 25*, 1–13. https://doi.org/10.1016/S0305–0483(96)00049–7.

Kirby, M. (2000). Operations research trajectories: The Anglo-American experience from the 1940s to the 1990s. *Operations Research, 48*(5), 661–70. https://doi.org/10.1287/opre.48.5.661.12402.

Kirby, M. (2003). The intellectual journey of Russell Ackoff: From OR apostle to OR apostate. *Journal of the Operational Research Society, 54*(11), 1127–40. https://doi.org/10.1057/palgrave.jors.2601627.

Klievink, B., Romijn, B.-J., Cunningham, S., & de Bruijn, H. (2017). Big data in the public sector: Uncertainties and readiness. *Information Systems Frontiers, 19*(2), 267–83. https://doi.org/10.1007/s10796–016–9686–2.

Lami, I.M., & Todella, E. (2019). Facing urban uncertainty with the strategic choice approach: The introduction of disruptive events. *Rivista di estetica, 71*, 222–40. https://doi.org/10.4000/estetica.5769.

Lazarus, R.J. (2009). Super wicked problems and climate change: Restraining the present to liberate the future. *Cornell Law Review, 94*, 1153–234. https://scholarship.law.cornell.edu/clr/vol94/iss5/8 [last accessed 11 Nov, 2024].

Leong, C., & Howlett, M. (2022a). Soft OR as a response to inherent vices: Problem structuring to offset policy volatility. *EURO Journal on Decision Processes, 10*, 100019. https://doi.org/10.1016/j.ejdp.2022.100019.

Leong, C., & Howlett, M. (2022b). Theorizing the behavioral state: Resolving the theory-practice paradox of policy sciences. *Public Policy and Administration, 37*(2), 203–25. https://doi.org/10.1177/0952076720977588.

Leong, C., Soon, D.W.X., Ong, C., & Howlett, M. (2023). Problems in applying Soft OR method to climate actions: Lessons from two cases of governmental use. *NPJ Climate Action, 2*(1). https://doi.org/10.1038/s44168–023–00037–6.

Lowe, D., & Yearworth, M. (2019). Response to viewpoint: Whither problem structuring methods (PSMs)? *Journal of the Operational Research Society, 70*(8), 1393–5. https://doi.org/10.1080/01605682.2018.1502629.

Maciejewski, M. (2017). To do more, better, faster and more cheaply: Using big data in public administration. *International Review of Administrative Sciences, 83*(1_suppl), 120–35. https://doi.org/10.1177/0020852316640058.

Man, Y., Sturm, T., Lundh, M., & MacKinnon, S.N. (2020). From ethnographic research to big data analytics – a case of maritime energy-efficiency optimization. *Applied Sciences, 10*(6), 2134. https://doi.org/10.3390/app10062134.

Mayer-Schönberger, V., & Cukier, K. (2013). *Big Data: A Revolution that Will Transform How We Live, Work, and Think*. New York: Houghton Mifflin Harcourt.

McNeely, C.L., & Hahm, J. (2014). The Big (Data) bang: Policy, prospects, and challenges. *Review of Policy Research, 31*(4), 304–10. https://doi.org/10.1111/ropr.12082.

Mills, K.A. (2018). What are the threats and potentials of big data for qualitative research? *Qualitative Research, 18*(6), 591–603. https://doi.org/10.1177/1468794117743465.

Mingers, J. (2000). The contribution of critical realism as an underpinning philosophy for OR/MS and systems. *Journal of the Operational Research Society, 51*, 1256–70. https://doi.org/10.1057/palgrave.jors.2601033.

Mingers, J. (2003). A classification of the philosophical assumptions of management science methods. *Journal of the Operational Research Society, 54*(6), 559–70. https://doi.org/10.1057/palgrave.jors.2601436.

Mingers, J. (2011). Soft OR comes of age – but not everywhere! *Omega, 39*, 729–41. https://doi.org/10.1016/j.omega.2011.01.005.

Mingers, J., & Brocklesby, J. (1997). Multimethodology: Towards a framework for mixing methodologies. *Omega, 25*, 489–509. https://doi.org/10.1016/S0305-0483(97)00018-2.

Mingers, J., & Rosenhead, J. (2004). Problem structuring methods in action. *European Journal of Operational Research, 152*(3), 530–54. https://doi.org/10.1016/S0377-2217(03)00056-0.

Morton, A., Ackermann, F., & Belton, V. (2007). Problem structuring without workshops? Experiences with distributed interaction within a PSM process. *Journal of the Operational Research Society, 58*(5), 547–56. https://doi.org/10.1057/palgrave.jors.2602210.

Natalicchio, A., Messeni Petruzzelli, A., & Garavelli, A.C. (2014). A literature review on markets for ideas: Emerging characteristics and unanswered questions. *Technovation, 34*(2), 65–76. https://doi.org/10.1016/j.technovation.2013.11.005.

Nevo, D., Kotlarsky, J., & Nevo, S. (2014). New capabilities: Can IT vendors leverage crowdsourcing? In R. Hirschheim, A. Heinzl, & J. Dibbern (Eds), *Information Systems Outsourcing. Progress in IS*. Berlin, Heidelberg: Springer. https://doi.org/10.1007/978-3-662-43820-6_19.

Northcutt, C.G., Athalye, A., & Mueller, J. (2021). Pervasive label errors in test sets destabilize machine learning benchmarks. *arXiv* preprint arXiv:2103.14749.

Ostwald, M. (2000). Virtual urban futures. In D. Bell & B.M. Kennedy (Eds), *The Cybercultures Reader*, 658–75. New York: Routledge. Originally published 1997.

Panagiotopoulos, P., Bowen, F., & Brooker, P. (2017). The value of social media data: Integrating crowd capabilities in evidence-based policy. *Government Information Quarterly, 34*(4), 601–12. https://doi.org/10.1016/j.giq.2017.10.009.

Paucar-Caceres, A. (2011). The development of management sciences/operational research discourses: Surveying the trends in the US and the UK. *Journal of the Operational Research Society, 62*(8), 1452–1470. https://doi.org/10.1057/jors.2010.109.

Pluchinotta, I., Kazakçi, A.O., Giordano, R., & Tsoukiàs, A. (2019). Design theory for generating alternatives in public decision making processes. *Group Decision and Negotiation, 28*, 341–75. https://doi.org/10.1007/s10726-018-09610-5.

Pluchinotta, I., Giordano, R., Zikos, D., Krueger, T., & Tsoukiàs, A. (2020). Integrating problem structuring methods and concept-knowledge theory for an advanced policy design: Lessons from a case study in Cyprus. *Journal of Comparative Policy Analysis: Research and Practice, 22*(6), 626–47. https://doi.org/10.1080/13876988.2020.1753512.

Poel, M., Meyer, E.T., & Schroeder, R. (2018). Big Data for policymaking: Great expectations, but with limited progress? *Policy & Internet, 10*(3), 347–67. https://doi.org/10.1002/poi3.176.

Poetz, M.K., & Schreier, M. (2012). The value of crowdsourcing: Can users really compete with professionals in generating new product ideas? *Journal of Product Innovation Management, 29*(2), 245–56. https://doi.org/10.1111/j.1540-5885.2011.00893.x.

Reisman, A., & Oral, M. (2005). Soft Systems Methodology: A context within a 50-year retrospective of OR/MS. *Interfaces, 35*(2), 164–78. https://doi.org/10.1287/inte.1050.0129.

Rhue, L. (2018). *Racial influence on automated perceptions of emotions*. Available at SSRN: http://dx.doi.org/10.2139/ssrn.3281765.

Rittel, H.W.J., & Webber, M.M. (1973). Dilemmas in a general theory of planning. *Policy Sciences, 4*, 155–69. https://doi.org/10.1007/BF01405730.

Schintler, L.A., & Kulkarni, R. (2014). Big Data for policy analysis: The Good, The Bad, and The Ugly. *Review of Policy Research, 31*(4), 343–8. https://doi.org/10.1111/ropr.12079.

Shafiei Gol, E., Stein, M.-K., & Avital, M. (2019). Crowdwork platform governance toward organizational value creation. *The Journal of Strategic Information Systems, 28*(2), 175–95. https://doi.org/10.1016/j.jsis.2019.01.001.

Sieg, J.H., Wallin, M.W., & Von Krogh, G. (2010). Managerial challenges in open innovation: A study of innovation intermediation in the chemical industry. *R&D Management, 40*(3), 281–91. https://doi.org/10.1111/j.1467-9310.2010.00596.x.

Studinka, J., & Guenduez, A.A. (2018). *The Use of Big Data in the Public Policy Process: Paving the Way for Evidence-Based Governance*. Smart Government Lab, Institute for Public Management and Governance, University of St. Gallen. https://www.alexandria.unisg.ch/handle/20.500.14171/100064 [last accessed 11 Nov, 2024].

Tavella, E., & Lami I. (2019). Negotiating perspectives and values through soft OR in the context of urban renewal. *Journal of the Operational Research Society, 70*(1), 136–61. https://doi.org/10.1080/01605682.2018.1427433.

Terwiesch, C., & Xu, Y. (2008). Innovation contests, open innovation, and multiagent problem solving. *Management Science, 54*(9), 1529–43. https://doi.org/10.1287/mnsc.1080.0884.

Trefethen F. (1995). A history of operations research. In P. Keys (Ed.), *Understanding the Process of Operational Research*, 47–76. Chichester: Wiley.

White, L. (2002). Size matters: Large group methods and the process of operational research. *Journal of the Operational Research Society, 53*(2), 149–60. https://doi.org/10.1057/palgrave.jors.2601298.

White, L. (2016). Behavioural operational research: Towards a framework for understanding behaviour in OR interventions. *European Journal of Operational Research, 249*(3), 827–41. https://doi.org/10.1016/j.ejor.2015.07.032.

White, L., Burger, K., & Yearworth, M. (2016a). Big Data and behavior in Operational Research: Towards a "Smart OR". In M. Kunc, J. Malpass, & L. White (Eds), *Behavioral Operational Research: Theory, Methodology and Practice*, 177–93. London: Palgrave Macmillan. https://doi.org/10.1057/978-1-137-53551-1_9.

White, L., Burger, K., & Yearworth, M. (2016b). Smart Cities: Big Data and behavioral Operational Research. In M. Kunc, J. Malpass, & L. White (Eds), *Behavioral Operational Research: Theory, Methodology and Practice*, 303–18. London: Palgrave Macmillan. https://doi.org/10.1057/978-1-137-53551-1_15.

White, P., & Breckenridge, R.S. (2014). Trade-offs, limitations, and promises of big data in social science research. *Review of Policy Research, 31*(4), 331–8. https://doi.org/10.1111/ropr.12078.

Whitman Cobb, W.N. (2015). Trending now: Using big data to examine public opinion of space policy. *Space Policy, 32*, 11–16. https://doi.org/10.1016/j.spacepol.2015.02.008.

Yearworth, M., & White, L. (2018). Spontaneous emergence of Community OR: Self-initiating, self-organising problem-structuring mediated by social media. *European Journal of Operational Research, 268*(2018), 809–24. https://doi.org/10.1016/j.ejor.2018.01.024.

6. Data and digitalization in energy efficiency policy design: the case of Singapore

Ishani Mukherjee and Diandrea Ho

INTRODUCTION

Overarching and broad policy goals for enhancing energy efficiency have existed globally over the last 50 years as a response to rising energy demands, heightening costs, and construction levels of residential and commercial buildings, and the associated rises in greenhouse gas emissions from energy use (Levine et al., 2007; World Bank, 2010). Buildings, in particular, have been widely recognized as offering the greatest potential for reducing energy use and related greenhouse gas emissions, followed by reduced energy consumption in manufacturing, appliances, electronic goods, and end-users of electricity (Levine, 2007; IEA, 2010). And while significant technological strides have been made globally to deliver major energy savings, barriers in the form of inadequate investments in data coordination and weakly supported policy signals have given rise to a perceived energy efficiency "gap" (IEA, 2007).

These conditions have invigorated a globally relevant drive on the part of governments to formulate comprehensive policy frameworks for energy efficiency in buildings as part of decarbonization and digital transitions at the national level. Additionally, in sub-national jurisdictions, the adoption of policy instruments targeted specifically for energy efficiency has been driven by and nested within regional, provincial, and city governments' broad policy goals towards reducing energy intensity across multiple sectors such as electricity, urban development, and transportation. For land-scarce economies, in particular, keeping sustainable energy policy ambitions in step with national climate mitigation commitments presents a unique set of opportunities to reconcile energy economy and renewable energy policy ambitions, but also a set of challenges stemming from the administration and coordination of these two policy goals. The reliance on digital tools and data has grown in step with ambitions to bridge this gap between evolving policy goals and rapidly evolving means to reconcile them.

Critically analyzing such "gaps" or the perceivable dissonance between evolving policy goals and means is the central inspiration of the last ten years of policy design research (Howlett, 2023). The new policy design orientation in the policy sciences has perpetuated a lengthy discussion on how to effectively integrate policy mixes so that multiple instruments are arranged together in complex portfolios of policy goals and means (Howlett, 2011; Jordan et al., 2014; Peters et al., 2018), often with a multi-level governance component (Howlett and del Rio, 2015). Effectively optimizing the choice of instruments in such mixes requires an additional level of knowledge of instrument-goal interactions and considerations of how mixes evolve over the long run. This requires an understanding of both long- and short-term processes of policy change. For example, a major concern of those working in the new orientation of policy design studies is whether combinations of different policy instruments, which have evolved independently and incrementally, as is the case of renewable energy and energy efficiency policy development, can accomplish complex policy goals as effectively as more deliberately customized portfolios (Peters et al., 2018).

In order to investigate such combinations of policy instruments, the first step is to break down the framework of policy design into its constituent parts and focus on how they interact. That is, the various components (goals, instruments, and calibrations) of a policy should be seen as parts of an overall mix of policy instruments. These elements of policies which are combined in the design process include those related to general goals and means, those linked to tools, and those linked to the settings or calibrations of those tools. Table 6.1 highlights these elements in the context of energy efficiency policy.

The components of such mixes include policy goals and policy means at various levels of generality (Cashore & Howlett, 2007Howlett, 2009; Kern & Howlett, 2009). Design and instrument selection in these contexts "are all about constrained efforts to match goals and expectations both within and across categories of policy elements" (Howlett, 2009, p. 74). Achieving effectiveness with respect to deploying such policy portfolios relies upon ensuring that mechanisms, calibrations, objectives, and settings display "coherence," "consistency," and "congruence" with each other (Howlett & Rayner, 2013). In the case of energy efficiency policy design, these ambitions are decidedly data-driven.

Concerns regarding how to make the most of policy synergies while curtailing contradictions in the formulation of new policy packages are a major topic of investigation within the new design orientation, and are also reflected significantly in policy practice (Lecuyer & Quirion, 2013). For example, evidence from the world concerning renewable energy and

Table 6.1 *Situating energy efficiency policy elements in the policy design framework*

Policy Content	High-Level Abstraction (Policy Level)	Operationalization (Program Level)	On-the-Ground Specification (Measures Level)
Policy Ends or Aims	**POLICY GOALS** **What General Types of Ideas Govern Policy Development?** (e.g. climate resilience and mitigation, national decarbonization frameworks)	**PROGRAM OBJECTIVES** **What Does Policy Formally Aim to Address?** (e.g., vehicle fuel economy standards, grid/energy demand flexibility)	**OPERATIONAL SETTINGS** **What Are the Specific On-the-ground Requirements of Policy** (e.g., considerations for building codes, energy performance certificates)
Policy Means or Tools	**INSTRUMENT LOGIC** **What General Norms Guide Implementation Preferences?** (e.g., preferences for the use of market-based vs. regulatory instruments)	**PROGRAM MECHANISMS** **What Specific Types of Instruments Are Utilized?** (e.g., the use of different tools such as tax incentives, technology standards, or public enterprises)	**TOOL CALIBRATIONS** **What Are the Specific Ways in Which the Instrument Is Used?** (e.g., designations of higher levels of targeted subsidies, adjustment of demand incentive schemes)

Source: Adapted from Cashore and Howlett (2007), and various iterations since then.

energy efficiency policy, due to climate change mitigation and energy security concerns, has revealed that policy packages combining voluntary compliance with command and control regulation can be inherently inconsistent, resulting in contradictory responses from the targets of these policy combinations where the demand for consolidating data across multiple sectors such as transport, buildings and power is high and progressively unmet, particularly in certain economic development and geographical contexts (Del Rio, Silvosa & Gomez, 2011).

The digitalization "turn" for meeting energy efficiency ambitions is particularly important in small island nations with resource constraints. Especially those that are developing nations and have traditionally been net energy importers, with limited scope for energy diversification domestically despite global technological developments that have reduced the costs of mainstream renewable energy technologies surrounding solar and wind. In the context of geographical limitations and challenges, policy tools designed to support energy resilience, by reducing energy demands and building energy efficiency in existing and planned infrastructure and working alongside renewable energy development, has resulted in a deliberate package of policy goals. The consolidated success of these interlinked policy priorities of energy efficiency, energy security, and renewable energy is a fundamental part of national sustainable energy policy targets. The design of such a mix of policy tools today rests heavily on advancements in data and digital technologies to facilitate coordination and coherence across relevant sectors (Giest and Mukherjee, 2022; Rogge, Kern & Howlett, 2009).

Inspired by these broad questions of policy design, this chapter will distill broad lessons emerging about the role of data and digitalization for energy efficiency policy design and explore the illustrative example of Singapore in how digital technologies and tools are being adopted to improve policy signals for energy efficiency. The chapter proceeds in three main sections. The next section briefly reviews the literature on the role of data in energy efficiency policy design along the lines of regulatory frameworks, policy capacity, and public awareness. The following section highlights the case of energy efficiency policy in Singapore. The final section discusses and concludes by highlighting the broad lessons learned about policy design through this sector.

ENERGY EFFICIENCY DATA AND DATA-POLICY IMPLICATIONS

Energy efficiency policy instruments and digitalization in the public sector are generally considered a "perfect match" (IEA, 2023). The International Energy Agency (IEA) outlines ten broad groupings of digital technologies and tools that have been central to global shifts towards low-carbon energy pathways (Table 6.2). The evolution of energy efficiency policies through such digitalization tools has involved a successive transformation of processes of data collection (e.g., through the deployment of sensors, smart meters, distributed ledgers and interfaces), data analysis (such as algorithms, the use of artificial intelligence (AI), and digital twin simulations), and data infrastructure (e.g., the development of infrastructure and retrofitting targets that are responsive to data analysis, automation, and controls) (Marinakis, 2020). While these tools are generally considered at the outset while articulating national energy efficiency policy goals and targets, their function permeates the entire policy cycle of energy efficiency from policy formulation, implementation to evaluation and monitoring of impacts (IEA, 2023).

Table 6.2   *Digital tools for energy efficiency policy design: a glossary*

Digital Tools	Description
Databases and big data	Energy data collected from "smart" devices, grids and other IT infrastructure and systems enables real-time monitoring and management of energy consumption and efficiency and provide a valuable resource for policy makers looking to deliver on energy and climate policy goals.
Non-intrusive load monitoring	Smart meter technologies allow policy makers to obtain information on appliance energy use to assess technology performance and raise awareness among residents, while guaranteeing complete anonymity.
Geographic information system (GIS) mapping and remote sensing	Digital technologies help to identify energy efficiency potential in buildings at a lower cost and drive government policy intervention, for example, prioritizing geographical areas for energy efficiency upgrades and retrofit programs, and ensuring buildings adhere to minimum performance standards.
Virtual buildings/digital twin cities	Virtual models of a city's systems allow policy makers to efficiently test how urban planning decisions may affect the city's infrastructure, people, and resource use.
Virtual audits	Virtual building code inspections conducted with the help of digital tools, such as Internet of Things (IoT) sensors, and digital twin and 3D modeling, offer the potential to provide expertise in remote areas and in areas where capacity to conduct audits may be constrained, at a much lower cost.
Digital certification and compliance	Electronic labels of energy efficiency performance on appliances and equipment (e.g., QR codes) provide a more effective certification system. Consumers can easily obtain information and compare energy efficiency across appliances, manufacturers benefit by being able to update product information and receive consumer feedback, officials can gain easier access to product registration databases, and policy makers can more accurately and efficiently monitor product quality.
Digital communication and networking	Digital communication and engagement tools allow policy makers and regulators to provide information on the energy efficiency performance of appliances, vehicles, and buildings. Digital tools for viewing and exploring datasets enable third-party access to data, potentially encouraging private energy efficiency investments and increasing transparency.
Smartphones and apps	Smartphone applications and the data have various uses in support of energy efficiency initiatives, for example, improving efficiency of transportation systems in cities, and providing insights and suggestions on how citizens can make more energy-efficient choices in their homes.
Natural language processing	Natural language processing, machine learning, and artificial intelligence provide an important source of information for policy makers to track progress of innovation in clean energy and energy efficiency across industry.

Digital Tools	Description
Web search and analytics	Analytics of web search data inform policy makers about markets for energy-using technologies at a lower cost and allow comparison of trends across markets. Web scraping allows regulators to scan through appliances being sold on the market and assess if they meet minimum energy performance standards.

Source: IEA (2023).

Through the main categories of policy instruments identified above, data digitalization has been shown to enable the key contributions that energy efficiency can make in policy portfolios and mixes with renewable energy production, energy security, and resilience policy goals, as well as energy access and equity objectives. Furthermore, the adoption of digital data tools in the energy efficiency sector plays a coordinating role for a diverse range of stakeholders including end-user communities and households, energy service companies (ESCOs), utilities, businesses, information technology (IT) companies and data providers (Table 6.3).

Examples such as these indicate that while the contribution of digital technologies and big data towards energy efficiency is indisputable, several questions remain to refine the lessons learned about policy design. For example, does the relationship between the use of digital tools and energy efficiency instruments reflect a hermeneutic cycle or a situation of "chasing its own tail" as dilemmas emerge due to the circularity of data use for the regulation of renewable energy and energy efficiency policy design? Secondly, what kind of data and databases lead to their own use legacies and work to ossify or entrench some energy efficiency targets over others? Similarly, what kind of databases do governments generate and/or use and to what granularity? These emerging questions are especially pertinent to generalize the role of digital tools for the design of effective energy efficiency programs that need to constantly reconcile the data demands for regulatory, market, and financial institutions with technical capacities in order to be sustainable.

Setting national targets or goals for energy efficiency not only sets the direction for a country's energy future but also informs how subsequently governments build political and public consensus around that future. Energy efficiency goal setting can therefore be multi-jurisdictional and not just limited to national aspirations, but also lead to articulating targets at the sub-national and sectoral levels of government. At these multiple levels, energy efficiency indicators may vary significantly enough in terms of relying on different streams of data. For example, nationally, energy efficiency targets may be expressed most frequently in terms of a rate of decrease in overall energy intensity of different sectors, while sub-nationally targets may specify a rate of energy savings over a period of time or specify a set volume of target savings. While the measures or objectives for energy efficiency may vary by jurisdiction or sector, sustainable energy policies are generally formulated to either regulate either demand-side or supply-side energy use.

Demand-side energy efficiency policy ecosystems tend to be complex and digital transformations have been shown to address multiple design and implementation barriers. These barriers can arise due to the structural considerations of energy efficiency networks that tend to be small and dispersed and implicate multiple stakeholders and

Table 6.3   *Energy efficiency stakeholders and interaction with digital tools (illustrative examples)*

EE Stakeholders	Examples
ESCOs	Sembcorp Industries, a Singaporean energy and urban development company developed a collaborative digital platform, GoNetZero, using blockchain technology. The platform provides analytics, reporting, and tracking tools, with the capability to verify renewable energy from source in real time, allowing corporate customers to execute their climate action plans.[a]
Utilities	Southern Company, an American utility company, partnered with mPrest, a provider of monitoring, control, and big data analytics software, to develop a product for monitoring and predictive analytics to enhance the resiliency, efficiency, and flexibility of its distribution grid.[b]
Businesses	Swire Properties, a property developer and operator invested in digitally efficient measurement tools, in partnership with Schneider Electric to model the energy efficiency of its buildings and was able to reduce GHG emissions by 19% across its portfolio (Schneider Electric, 2022).[c]
IT companies	MyHEAT, a Canadian digital platform, uses remote sensing data from thermal imaging sensors and advanced machine learning algorithms to identify buildings where heat losses are prevalent to create a comparative model. The platform also engages with users to recommend energy efficiency incentive programs, rebate information, online marketplaces, and energy audit resources.[d]
Data Providers	India's Building Energy Efficiency Program Dashboard is a digital tool which provides policy makers and other players with transparent and accessible data, helping them to understand the energy system better and develop well-informed energy policies that drive the ecosystem (IEA, 2023).

[a] https://www.sembcorp.com/en/media/media-releases/corporate/2022/november/sembcorp-launches-new-carbon-management-solutions-corporate-venture-gonetzero/
[b] https://www.southerncompany.com/newsroom/innovation/southern-company-mprest-partners.html
[c] https://www.eco-business.com/press-releases/companies-reduce-emissions-by-up-to-19-through-digital-tools-schneider-electric-and-cnbc-report/
[d] https://www.iea.org/articles/better-energy-efficiency-policy-with-digital-tools

users. Furthermore, there are generally no "one size fits all" solutions as diverse energy efficiency technologies often occupy the same data space. Relatedly, energy efficiency networks are also linked to heterogeneous markets and in developing countries; in particular, the financing for these markets are based on "savings" and not directly tradable assets. Digitalization of energy efficiency markets, then, aids in reducing the data/information transaction costs linked with measuring, analyzing, and communicating energy efficiency targets and outputs. In the supply side of energy policy, digital tools have been shown to have a significant contribution towards several of the policy instrument areas – regulatory, financial, and informational – identified as necessary for designing policies to support energy efficiency market transformations (Stuggins et al., 2013). These instruments face several administrative and strategy overlaps as they occupy the energy regulatory space concurrently. Table 6.4, for example, showcases examples of energy efficiency policy instruments from a variety of national energy efficiency policy portfolios. These policy "toolkits" for capturing greater energy efficiency gains in buildings are generally comprised of a mix of building codes, labels, incentive schemes, and regulations for new buildings to be "zero-energy." As Table 6.4 indicates, however, although working with similar types of instruments, the experience of different countries with policy formulation for building energy efficiency has shown some commonalities but has also been somewhat unique to each jurisdiction. This begs the question of the nature of the formulation process followed in each jurisdiction and how digital tools have differently affected policy decisions and outcomes.

In terms of regulations and authority-based tools of policy, data and digital tools have been fundamental in supporting overarching legal frameworks governing energy efficiency laws. These frameworks rely on real-time cost-reflective energy pricing, alongside, for example, use data generated to create and thereafter update standards and codes for the energy intensity of appliances and buildings. Enabling policy environments for successful energy efficiency programs further rely on digital tools in the design of energy efficiency incentive schemes earmarked for specific funding sources, as well as for support in public budgeting/procurement processes encouraging energy economy. The creation of dedicated institutions within government that have clearly defined energy efficiency mandates relies heavily on digitalization of process functions. Digital tools are important for inter-ministerial coordination, the establishment of monitoring and compliance enforcement mechanisms, and overall tracking of the progress of energy efficiency targets.

At the same time, governments are playing an important advisory role in the rollout of smart technologies linked with energy use, signaling public sector support for their commercial development and uptake. For example, the United States Environmental Protection Agency (EPA) endorses devices that demonstrate verified minimum energy savings for heating and cooling through their Energy Star program. Governments also play a key role in developing standards and verification principles for data use for aligning energy efficiency goals that encourage common regulatory frameworks across jurisdictions and businesses. The G20 Networked Devices Task Group is the largest alliance of its kind, bringing together government and industry representatives to implement voluntary design principles on the part of manufacturers (e.g., stakeholders dealing with energy-efficient connected devices, networks, and communication protocols) and policy makers (looking for a common global framework to use as a reference of best practices during policy formulation).

In terms of the financial viability of energy efficiency programs, digital tools are now fundamental for accessing bank lending (including credit lines and guarantees). These include financial solutions such as "Pay as You Save" schemes, public sector as well as commercial ESCO financing. At the level of designing incentives across sectors (such as energy, manufacturing, and transport) and at the household level (such as energy-efficient residential home/appliance credits) and urban development (in the form of green infrastructure and energy-efficient building incentives), management of data and the knowledge of digital tools have also increasingly become central to energy efficiency auditor/manager training and certification programs offered through both the private sector (i.e., private banks, ESCOs, end-users) and the public sector.

A cornerstone of successful energy efficiency policy program design concerns information gathering and dissemination to the citizenry regarding energy consumption and use, an area

Table 6.4 Policy instruments in national policy mixes for energy efficiency in buildings*

Country	Building Codes	Labels	Incentive Schemes	Zero-Energy Buildings
Australia	•	•	•	•
Austria	•	•	•	•
Belgium		•	•	•
Brazil		•		
Canada	•	•	•	•
China	•	•		
Czech Republic	•	•	•	•
Denmark	•	•	•	•
Finland	•	•	•	•
France	•	•	•	
Germany	•	•	•	•
Greece	•	•	•	•
Hungary	•	•	•	•
India	•	•		
Ireland	•	•	•	•
Italy	•	•	•	•
Japan	•	•	•	•
Korea	•	•	•	
Luxembourg	•	•	•	•
Netherlands	•	•	•	•
New Zealand	•	•	•	•
Norway	•	•	•	•
Poland	•	•	•	•
Portugal	•	•	•	
Russia	•	•		•
Singapore	•	•	•	
Slovak Republic	•	•	•	•
South Africa	•	•	•	
Spain	•	•	•	•
Sweden	•	•	•	•
Switzerland	•	•	•	•
Tunisia	•			
Turkey	•	•		•
United Kingdom		•	•	•
United States		•	•	•

Note: *National-level policies.
Source: International Energy Agency (IEA) Building Energy Efficiency Policy (BEEP) database.

that is today heavily dominated by data technologies. In addition to data centers, technologies supporting end-user efficiency are no longer limited to eco-labels and certification standards for appliances, but with the concurrent rise of decentralized renewable energy systems and the need to gauge the net energy use of households, information technologies have become critical for "prosumers" (or those individuals and households that both produce energy to feed back to electricity grids, as well as consume energy) (IEA, 2023).

To this end, the digitalization of the energy and electricity value chain enables a more seamless integration of energy use and production – to work towards sustainable energy policy priorities that integrate both renewable energy and energy efficiency (Table 6.5). Broadly, digitization tools at the operational level provide households and energy consumers with the essential information needed to make choices about their own use, choosing a supplier in an energy market (where available), and in the case of more decentralized electricity systems, these tools have also been shown to support peer-to-peer energy trading between customers (Papadaskalopoulous et al., 2015; Cao et al., 2023) in new policy design contexts.

As the ultimate policy goal for energy efficiency policy emphasizes energy savings, the policy design space for energy efficiency in certain contexts (such as the European Union (EU)) is favorable to this strategic layering of new policy elements in order to close the observed gap between present and potential energy efficiency gains (Levine et al., 2007). For example, recognizing that energy use in EU buildings makes up approximately 40 percent of total energy consumption, with large efficiency gains that are still untapped with existing instruments,

Table 6.5   Digital tools and the electricity/utilities value chain

Energy Generation	• Carbon capture and storage
	• Optimization of generation and equipment
	• Renewable energy market integration
	• Fuel switching.
	• Sensors and IoT monitoring (e.g., sensors in gas/oil reservoirs)
Electricity Transmission & Distribution	• Automation of distribution
	• Grid sensors and analytics
	• Substation modernization and security infrastructure
	• Monitoring and inspection drones
Residential and Commercial Buildings	• Aggregate smart meter analytics
	• Commercial energy storage
	• Demand/Load management
	• Grid-building integration
Households and "Prosumers"	• Smart meter and energy use analytics
	• Smart appliances
	• Feed-in, onsite renewables generation and storage
	• EV charging
	• Load shifting – usage regulation

policy recommendations from scholars of the field have indicated additional policies that "require high energy efficiency standards when roofs or windows have to be replaced and measures that accelerate the replacement of building elements" which, if added to the present policy mix, would provide opportunities for greater energy efficiency improvements than the present policy mix allows (Tommerup & Svendsen, 2006; Uihlein & Eder, 2010), Others have indicated the use of new financial instruments within EU states, such as tax rebates, clearer requirements for energy calculations, and targeted subsidy programs to encourage higher investment in accelerated refurbishments to existing buildings, and complementing the existing policy mix (Casales, 2006; Lechtenböhmer & Schüring, 2011).

An interesting example of the more problematic situation undermining such policy design efforts is evident in the Norwegian experience with energy efficiency policy in the buildings sector until the end of the last decade, which featured a set of poorly defined goals making policy formulation efforts less rational than they might otherwise have been. The energy efficiency policy of Norway ("Energiøkonomisering," or "ENØK"), as described by Ryghaug and Sorenson (2009), "was based on the premise that to save energy was not an end in itself; rather the aim was to improve the profitability of the production and use of energy. The result was that policymakers framed the energy efficiency issue to emphasize economic features rather than energy conservation: energy efficiency measures should be profitable" (Ryghaug & Sorenson, 2009, p. 985). The inconsistency of these definitions lent itself to ambiguity in terms of determining exactly which kinds of policy instruments encouraging economic savings versus actual energy savings could be employed in an effective policy mix for building energy efficiency. Building codes and standards in the late 1990s based on the ENØK did not provide standardized measurements of energy efficiency and only specified minimum and maximum baselines (Ryghaug, 2005). When new building codes were added in 2007 and 2008 to include greater R&D for building energy efficiency and stricter energy criteria, again no standardized measures of building energy efficiency were articulated, and the building industry actors still autonomously interpreted and responded to the broad goals of the ENØK (Ryghaug & Sorensen, 2009).

Therefore, where there has been evidence of new digital tools being added successfully to existing energy efficiency policy mixes, other evidence also points to the kind of barriers that can emerge for policy makers related to past tool choices. For example, while the Energy Efficiency Directive (EED) has provided a major impetus for EU member countries to intensify their energy efficiency efforts, regulatory policy instruments chosen to operate within national policy mixes have not always been consistent. In a study of EU energy efficiency in buildings presenting the feedback from policy professionals including policy makers and relevant ministry directors, data from Portugal, the Netherlands, and Latvia indicated that poorly crafted incentives and insufficient regulations linked with labeling represent "some ill-devised policy instruments [that] can themselves act as barriers" to attaining improved efficiency outcomes (Tuominen et al., 2012, p. 50; see also Golubchikov & Deda, 2012).

THE EXAMPLE OF SINGAPORE

Singapore's energy sector has evolved drastically in the past 50 years. Total final consumption of energy has risen steadily in the past two decades, reaching a high of 223.7 million megawatt hours in 2019 (Figure 6.1). Greenhouse gas emissions have also increased and were recorded to be 48 million tons in 2019 (Figure 6.2). Under the "Energy Reset" pillar in the Singapore Green Plan 2030, the Singapore government committed to becoming more sustainable in the way it

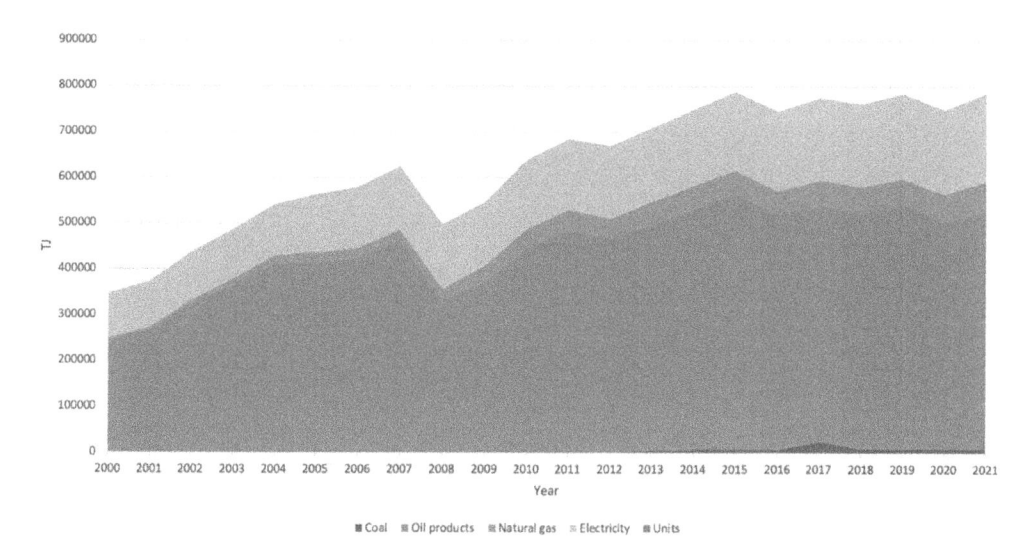

Source: International Energy Agency.

Figure 6.1   Total final consumption by source in Singapore from 2000 to 2019

uses and produces energy through tapping into clean energy sources across all sectors, while maintaining energy security. It aims to reduce energy consumption by more than 8 million megawatt hours per year and reduce greenhouse gas emissions by at least 3 million tons per year by 2030 (NCCS, 2021). Singapore will harness energy from from key sources, termed the "4 Switches," comprising natural gas, solar energy, regional power grids, and low-carbon alternatives (NCCS, 2021). Being a country which lacks conventional energy sources and land area for large-scale renewable energy projects, oil and natural gas remain the two largest sources of energy (Figure 6.3). As such, the Singapore government strongly emphasizes increasing energy efficiency as a key strategy for achieving its climate ambitions. For example, the government aims to achieve 80 percent improvement in energy efficiency for best-in-class green buildings by 2030 and for 80 percent of new developments to be Super Low Energy (SLE) buildings from 2030 (Ministry of National Development, 2019). In addition, the government also aims to enhance energy efficiency of airport operations by upgrading lighting and chilling systems, as well as optimizing flight operations through developing next-generation air navigation systems that support new concepts of managing air traffic (Ministry of National Development, 2019). These initiatives are coordinated and driven by the Energy Efficiency Programme Office (E2PO), a multi-agency committee led by the National Environment Agency (NEA) and the Energy Market Authority (EMA). The mandate of E2PO is to coordinate a whole-of-government effort in implementing measures to improve energy efficiency and reduce the energy use of three key sectors: the Household Sector, the Industry Sector, and the Public Sector. The government is also working closely with industry and academia partners to drive research and innovation initiatives. For example, in 2019, EMA embarked on a S$20 million partnership with Sembcorp and awarded Nanyang Technological University (NTU) a grant to develop Singapore's first Virtual Power Plant, which aims to integrate and coordinate distributed energy resources at various locations, thus optimizing energy usage and ensuring grid stability.

104 *Handbook on governance and data science*

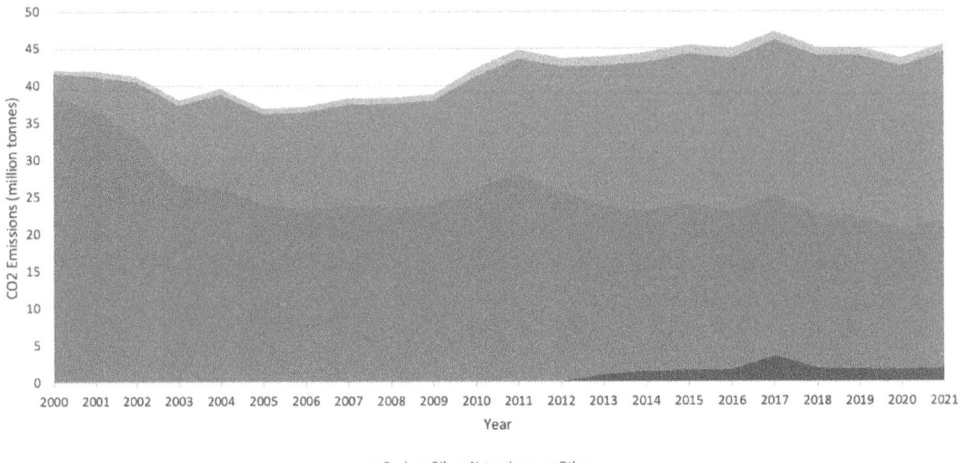

Source: International Energy Agency.

Figure 6.2   Carbon dioxide emissions in Singapore by source from 2000 to 2019

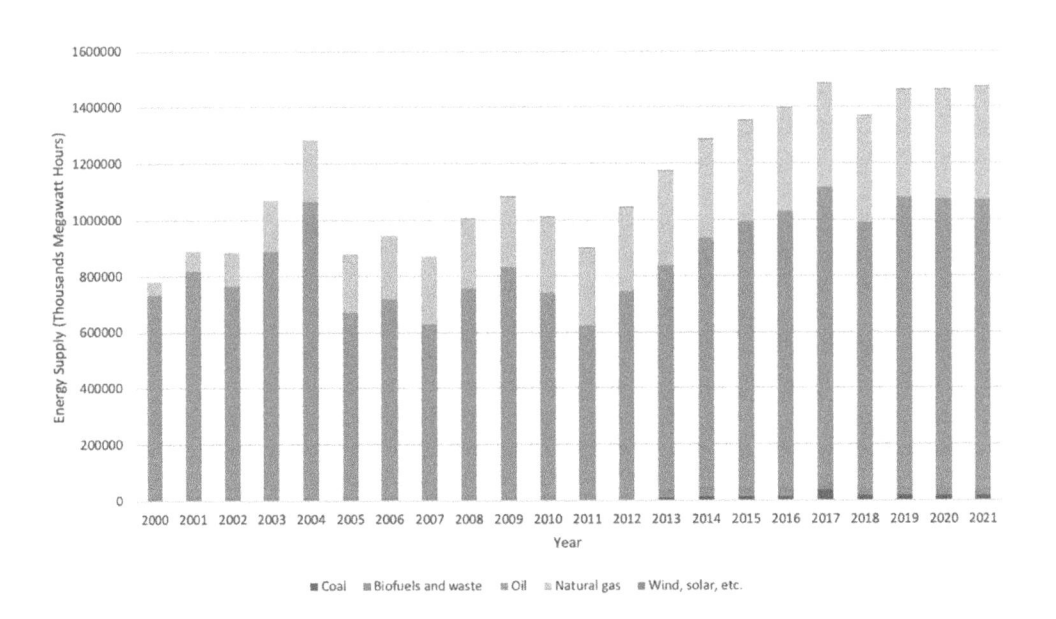

Source: International Energy Agency.

Figure 6.3   Total energy supply by source in Singapore from 2000 to 2019

The benefits and importance of improving energy efficiency are clear. According to the International Energy Agency (IEA), to achieve net-zero carbon emissions by 2050, global energy demand will have to be 8 percent lower than it is today but will be servicing an economy twice as large. To achieve this, annual improvements in energy intensity will need to triple over the next decade to deliver 13 gigatons of carbon reductions by 2030 (IEA, 2023). However, it has always been difficult and costly for policy makers to manage energy efficiency investments because of the complexity of aggregating potential energy savings from energy users across the country. Moreover, energy efficiency requires policy makers to interact with a diverse set of stakeholders, including end-users, businesses, utilities companies, and ESCOs. In order to overcome these challenges, digitalization has been identified as a tool that governments can adopt to drive energy efficiency improvements. Digital tools and big data provide policy makers with greater access to information on distributed energy resources, thereby allowing them to better engage with and target stakeholders, overcome barriers to scaling up energy efficiency implementation, and improve monitoring of energy efficiency policies.

The Singapore government has highlighted the need for catalyzing digitalization in the energy sector and has made strides to equip policy makers with digital tools in all stages of the policy cycle. Firstly, digital tools are key to providing access to real-time energy efficiency data, and advanced analytics and modeling capabilities can help predict the impact and cost-effectiveness of programs (IEA, 2023). EMA has commissioned an Information Management Hub to manage and integrate complex datasets that can drive analytics for policy formulation and decision making (EMA, 2018). Secondly, digital tools can also allow policy makers to better manage Singapore's various energy sources and align energy efficiency with renewable energy production. EMA has committed $55 million over five years to implement a next-generation grid system to transform management of energy supply and demand, by consolidating gas, solar, thermal, and other sources of energy into a single intelligent network (NCCS, 2021). More recently, EMA announced Singapore's first digital twin for the power grid to enhance grid resilience and support cleaner energy sources through asset optimization and network planning analysis (EMA, 2023). Thirdly, digitalization can improve the implementation of more user-centered energy efficiency policies by establishing communication lines between policy makers and end-users. EMA has also embarked on a partnership with Singapore Power (SP) Group to roll out advanced meters to all households by 2024 to empower consumers to better manage electricity consumption and nudge them towards the adoption of energy-efficient practices (Sandys et al., 2019).

CONCLUDING COMMENTS: FIRST- VS. SECOND-BEST POLICY DESIGN?

Effective energy efficiency policy design necessitates integration with renewable energy development, and quite often this integration has to be a policy-led one (Koronen, Åhman & Nilsson, 2020). Most ideal forms of policy design are thought to emerge out of propitious scenarios where all relevant policy-making capacities, resources, and government intention are present and aligned. In dealing with new policy issue areas, such as those defining the digitalization of energy efficiency, such "first-best" scenarios can also be characterized by a lack of historical policy tool legacies and relative flexibility for innovation, thus presenting policy makers with a formulation *tabula rasa* embedded within broader, more traditional policy sectors such as energy. The effective use of such ideal policy design spaces has additional prerequisites, as shown in the case of Singapore, for example, high technical capacity for policy analysis on the part of key policy actors, especially government, which is required to facilitate the effective matching of policy means to goals (Howlett, 2009, 2011). Without such preconditions, despite the best government intentions, poor designs can result either from incomplete knowledge or via less technical and more overtly political forms of policy formation that substitute different goals or criteria for optimality.

In the energy sector more broadly, global experience suggests that these include "technological lock-ins; path dependence in decision making, information asymmetries; poor enforcement of standards; corruption" and "split incentives or principal-agent problems (e.g., manufacturers vs. users)" (Golubchikov & Deda. 2012, p. 735). To some extent, these challenges represent common hindrances in the path of data governance in the energy sector experience across the globe (e.g., see Frerk, 2019; Sandys et al., 2019; Judson et al., 2020, among others).

In sum, these realizations about ideal policy design processes related to the deliberate dependence on digital tools for energy efficiency underscore the point made earlier on in the chapter. That is, at the heart of policy formulation processes with a design orientation lies the application of instrumental knowledge about various policy tools, but must also include an understanding of the constraints, complementarities, and interactions which exist within existing structures of governance. Sound policy design necessitates, firstly, encouraging better matching of broad policy goals with on-the-ground governance modes and policy capacities. Secondly, it calls for optimizing the available policy design space for greater energy efficiency by understanding the tractability and embeddedness of existing and related policy choices. As articulated succinctly by Golubchikov and Deda (2012 p. 734), "the deployment of technical 'fixes" alone is insufficient in the context of the comprehensive social relations that are essentially embedded in the built environment and must be supplemented by, and coordinated with, social policies." Thirdly, it advocates maximizing complementarity and reflexivity between the different policy elements that make up the energy efficiency policy mix while actively seeking out mutually beneficial synergies with related policy arenas such as renewable energy and household energy solutions (Klessmann et al., 2011).

FUNDING

This research work was supported by the Lee Kong Chian Fellowship at Singapore Management University.

REFERENCES

Cao, Liwei, Peiyu Hu, Xiang Li, Hui Sun, Jinrui Zhang, & Chuan Zhang (2023). Digital technologies for net-zero energy transition: A preliminary study. *Carbon Neutrality* 2, no. 1: 7.

Casales, Xavier Garcia (2006). Analysis of building energy regulation and certification in Europe: Their role, limitations and differences. *Energy and Buildings* 38, no. 5; 381–92

Cashore, B., & Howlett, M. (2007). Punctuating which equilibrium? Understanding thermostatic policy dynamics in Pacific Northwest forestry. *American Journal of Political Science* 51(3): 532–51.

Del Río, P., Silvosa, A. C., & Gómez, G.I. (2011). Policies and design elements for the repowering of wind farms: A qualitative analysis of different options. *Energy Policy* 39(4): 1897–908.

EMA. (2023). Leveraging Digital Solutions to Future-Proof Singapore's Energy Grid. Energy Market Authority – Government of Singapore. Media Factsheet. 24 October 2023.

Frerk, M. (2019). Smart meter energy data: Public Interest Advisory Group Final Report – Phase 1. Available at: https://docs.wixstatic.com/ugd/ea9deb_244fa0e7997b43ceb453762d930bab93.pdf, accessed November 14th, 2024.

Giest, S., & Mukherjee, I. (2022). Evidence integration for coherent nexus policy design: A Mediterranean perspective on managing water-energy interactions. *Journal of Environmental Policy & Planning* 24(5): 553–67.

Golubchikov, Oleg, Deda, P. (2012). Governance, technology, and equity: An integrated policy framework for energy efficient housing. *Energy Policy* 41: 733–41

Howlett, M. (2009). Governance modes, policy regimes and operational plans: A multi-level nested model of policy instrument choice and policy design. *Policy Sciences* 42: 73–89.

Howlett, M. (2011). *Designing Public Policies: Principles and Instruments*. New York: Routledge.

Howlett, M. (Ed.). (2023). *The Routledge Handbook of Policy Tools*. Abingdon: Routledge.

Howlett, M., & Del Rio, P. (2015). The parameters of policy portfolios: Verticality and horizontality in design spaces and their consequences for policy mix formulation. *Environment and Planning C: Government and Policy* 33(5): 1233–45.

Howlett, M., & Rayner, J. (2013). Patching vs packaging in policy formulation: Assessing policy portfolio design. *Politics and Governance* 1, no. 2: 170–82. doi:10.12924/pag2013.01020170.

IEA (2007). *Mind the Gap: Quantifying Principal-Agent Problems in Energy Efficiency*. Paris: International Energy Agency.

IEA (2023). *Energy Efficiency 2023*, Paris: International Energy Agency. https://www.iea.org/reports/energy-efficiency-2023, Licence: CC BY 4.0

Jordan, A., & Huitema, D. (2014). Innovations in climate policy: The politics of invention, diffusion, and evaluation. *Environmental Politics* 23(5): 715–34.

Judson, E., Soutar, I., & Mitchell, C. (2020). Governance challenges emerging from energy digitalisation. Exeter: University of Exeter Press.

Kern, F., & Howlett, M. (2009). Implementing transition management as policy reforms: A case study of the Dutch energy sector. *Policy Sciences* 42, no. 4 (November 1, 200): 391–408. doi:10.1007/s11077–009–9099-x.

Klessmann, C., Held, A., Rathmann, M., & Ragwitz, M. (2011). Status and perspectives of renewable energy policy and deployment in the European Union – what is needed to reach the 2020 targets? *Energy Policy* 39: 7637–57.

Koronen, C., Åhman, M., & Nilsson, L.J. (2020). Data centres in future European energy systems – energy efficiency, integration and policy. *Energy Efficiency* 13, no. 1: 129–44.

Lechtenböhmer, S., & Schüring, A. (2011). The potential for large-scale savings from insulating residential buildings in the EU. *Energy Efficiency* 4: 257–70.

Lecuyer, O., & Quirion, P. (2013). Can uncertainty justify overlapping policy instruments to mitigate emissions? *Ecological Economics* 93: 177–91.

Levine, M. et al. (2007). Residential and commercial buildings. In Climate Change 2007: Mitigation. Contribution of Working Group III to the Fourth Assessment Report of the Intergovernmental Panel on Climate Change. Cambridge and New York: Cambridge University Press.

Marinakis, V. (2020). Big data for energy management and energy-efficient buildings. *Energies* 13(7): 1555.

Ministry of National Development (2019). Going a Deeper Shade of Green with Super Low Energy Buildings. MND-LINK, Jul/Aug 2019.

NCCS (2021), Charting Singapore's Low-carbon and Climate Resilient Future, National Climate Change Secretariat – Government of Singapore.

Papadaskalopoulos, D., Fatouros, P., & Strbac, G. (2015). Addressing demand response concentration under dynamic pricing. In *2015 IEEE Eindhoven PowerTech*, pp. 1–6. IEEE.

Peters, B.G., Capano, G., Howlett, M., Mukherjee, I., Chou, M.H., & Ravinet, P. (2018). *Designing for Policy Effectiveness: Defining and Understanding a Concept*. Cambridge, UK: Cambridge University Press.

Rogge, K.S., Kern, F., & Howlett, M. (2017). Conceptual and empirical advances in analysing policy mixes for energy transitions. *Energy Research & Social Science* 33: 1–10.

Ryghaug, M. (2005). Policing sustainability. Strategies towards a sustainable architecture.. In *Sustainable Architectures. Cultures and Natures in Europe and North America*. Edited by S. Guy & S.A. Moore, pp. 145–62. New York, Spon Press.

Ryghaug, M., & Sorensen, K.H. (2009). How energy efficiency fails in the building industry. *Energy Policy* 37: 984–91.

Sandys, L. et al. (2019). A strategy for a modern digitalized energy system. Energy Data Taskforce report chaired by Laura Sandys. Available at: https://es.catapult.org.uk/wpcontent/uploads/2019/06/EDTF-A-Strategy-for-a-Modern-Digitalised-Energy-System-FINALREPORT-1.pdf, accessed November 14th, 2024.

Stuggins, G., Sharabaroff, A., & Semikolenova, Y. (2013). *Energy Efficiency: Lessons Learned from Success Stories*. Washington, DC: World Bank Publications.

Tommerup, H., & Svendsen, S. (2006). Energy savings in Danish residential building stock. *Energy and Buildings* 38, no. 6: 618–26.

Tuominen, P., Klobut, K., Tolman, A., Adjei, A., & de Best-Waldhober, M. (2012). Energy savings potential in buildings and overcoming market barriers in member states of the European Union. *Energy and Buildings*, 51, 48–55.

Uihlein, A., & Eder, P. (2010). Policy options towards an energy efficient residential building stock in the EU-27. *Energy and Buildings* 42: 791–8.

World Bank (2010). *Cities and Climate Change: An Urgent Agenda*. Washington, DC: The International Bank for Reconstruction and Development. World Bank.

7. Examining the cost of living crisis: insights from e-petitions and constituency groupings

Stephen D. Clark and Nik Lomax

INTRODUCTION

The 2020s have presented numerous challenges to governments and societies. The decade commenced with a global pandemic and further escalated into land wars in Europe and the Middle East, all accompanied by a cost of living crisis (Harari et al., 2022). In the United Kingdom (UK), this crisis was characterised by soaring prices for essential goods like food (Francis-Devine et al., 2022; Irvine et al., 2022), energy (Bolton & Stewart, 2023), transportation (Robinson & Mattioli, 2020; Sovacool et al., 2023), and housing (Wilson & Barton, 2022), along with stagnating wage growth (Cominetti et al., 2022). By the end of spring 2023, UK annual inflation had skyrocketed to 8.9 per cent, far exceeding the target level of 2 per cent. Inflation for specific expenditures, such as food, was even higher, as depicted in Figure 7.1 (Office for National Statistics, 2023).

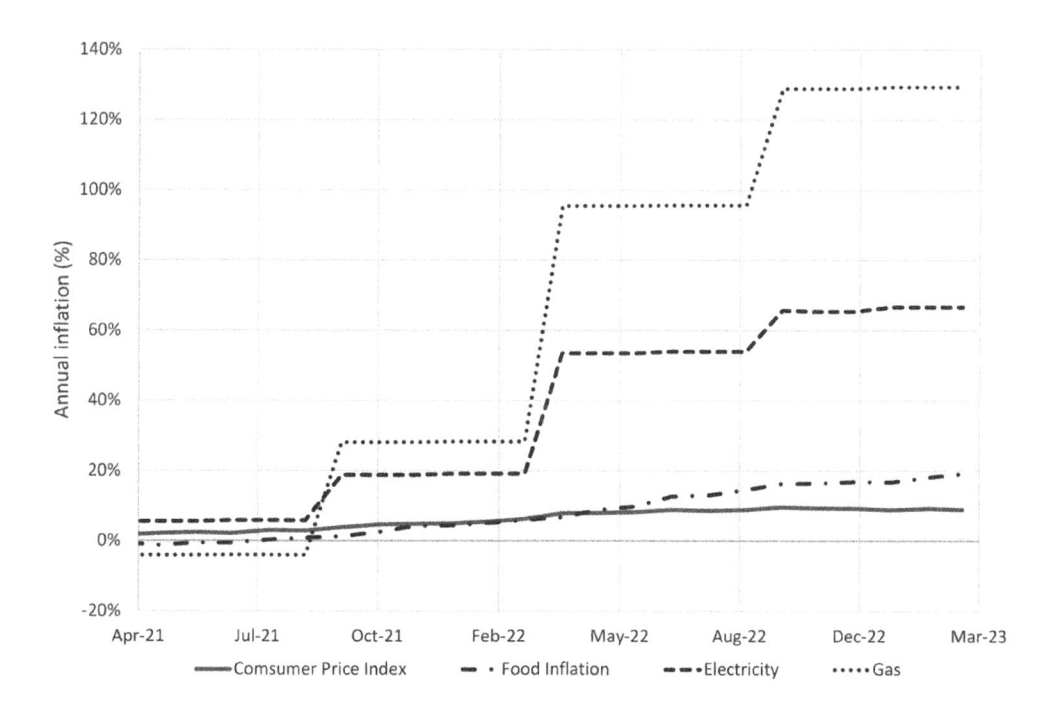

Source: Authors' own.

Figure 7.1   Annual rates of inflation for all goods, food, domestic gas, and electricity

The combination of high living costs and stagnant wages has a significant impact on individuals' well-being, both physically and mentally (Broadbent et al., 2023; Khan, 2022), with children being particularly vulnerable (Iacobucci, 2023). This situation can also contribute to adverse health effects, such as obesity (Robinson, 2023). These negative consequences are often exacerbated by the widening inequality resulting from prolonged periods of high living costs and low wages. This is evident when examining regional and city-specific inflation measures, with some locations experiencing a headline rate that can be as much as 3 per cent higher than in other locations (Rodrigues & Quinio, 2022).

While citizens rely on their government for support during a crisis, they also desire to influence the nature of that support. Much of the policy response during times of crisis is necessarily reactive, so mechanisms for scrutiny, both during and after, are important for maintaining trust between citizens and decision makers. Policy response to the COVID-19 pandemic has been scrutinised and criticised for its non-targeted approach (Milne, 2020) and unequal societal effects (Johnson, 2020). Similarly, responses to the cost of living crisis have been criticised as lacking in nuance, with the most vulnerable being hardest hit (Centre for Social Justice, 2022; National Energy Action, 2022). Given that policy is politically, socially, and economically motivated, having a strong view of public sentiment during and soon after periods of rapid decision making has the advantage of informing the government about both the effectiveness and perception of those policies. This evidence base for assessing effectiveness is essential for improving decision making in the future, while understanding perceptions helps with political messaging and communication. It is also important to have a holistic view of the impacts that policy has in multiple domains, given criticism that government decision making is often undertaken in policy silos (Sasse and Thomas, 2022). Understanding how policy impacts people's lives contributes to this multi-domain view.

One effective method for citizens to share their views is the creation and signing of e-petitions hosted on government platforms (Briassoulis, 2010), which provides a rich and current dataset for the assessment of sentiment. This chapter uses these e-petition data, with a focus on the period covering the latest cost of living crisis, to present a case study of the UK which will be of great interest to scholars examining e-petitions as an indicator of public opinion during times of upheaval worldwide. Drawing on established methods, we seek to accomplish three things in this chapter. First, we identify the topics in the e-petition data that are related to the most recent cost of living crisis in the UK. Second, we determine the level of support for each topic within each constituency, which could be seen as a proxy for public sentiment during a time of crisis. Third, we group together parliamentary constituencies based on their support for the topics identified which allows us to better understand how voter priorities vary by political representation and other spatial identifiers (e.g., deprivation). We contend that e-petitions offer a valuable mechanism for comprehending public sentiment, thus serving as a means to enhance democracy and democratic institutions. The methods presented can be adapted and applied to other research questions or contexts where similar data are available. As such, this chapter provides a guide to researchers wishing to capitalise on the rich information present in e-petition data.

PETITIONS

Petitioning has a long-standing tradition in most countries, dating back to the Middle Ages in Europe (Almbjär, 2019) and England (Dodd, 2007). Petitions serve multiple purposes

(Leston-Bandeira, 2019). They allow citizens to express their opinions on matters of concern, enable lobbying for policy changes, hold governments accountable for their actions or inaction, and provide feedback on policies, programmes, and services. The introduction of electronic platforms for hosting and signing petitions has further enhanced these roles. The use of such platforms reduces the cost and effort required to create an e-petition, as the platform handles the tasks of establishing and collating signatures. Once created, these platforms facilitate mobilising collective action, which can be easily accomplished through electronic means to promote e-petitions. This enables organisations and individuals to reach a larger audience and potentially attract the attention of sympathetic media.

The UK Parliament established its own e-petitioning platform in 2015 (UK Government and Parliament, 2022). Any citizen or resident of the United Kingdom is entitled to submit an e-petition to the platform. The text of the e-petition undergoes a verification process, during which duplicates of existing petitions or those on matters unrelated to the UK Parliament are rejected (approximately two-thirds of e-petitions are rejected). Once deemed suitable, an e-petition remains open for signatures for six months or until the end of the current Parliament. UK citizens or residents can sign an e-petition by providing their name, home postcode, and email address. A link is then sent to the email address, which, when clicked, completes the signature process. There is no requirement to register with the platform, the signatories do not have their name published, and they do not have an opportunity to leave a comment. E-petitions that accumulate more than 10,000 signatures are guaranteed a response from the government, and those with 100,000 or more signatures are considered for debate in Parliament. Additionally, the Pensions Committee of the Parliament can conduct its own inquiries in response to e-petitions that raise neglected concerns (Matthews, 2023). The Pension Committee provides real-time updates which are the three most popular e-petitions in the last hour, along with the current number of signatures for each petition in every parliamentary constituency.

According to Bochel (2016), the available evidence on the effectiveness of e-petitions in influencing politicians and government policy is limited. Blumenau (2020) found that a Member of Parliament's likelihood of advocating for the subject matter of an e-petition was influenced by factors such as party loyalty or electoral competition, even if the petition received significant support from their constituencies. Leston-Bandeira (2017) suggests that e-petitions can raise awareness of issues among politicians and in the media, serving as a vehicle for expressing discontent or protest. An e-petition that garners widespread support is likely to receive coverage in both mainstream and social media, with overlaps between the two (Asher et al., 2019). However, Matthews (2021) reports that e-petitions can present a biased view, as immediate and popular concerns may be prioritised over other more important matters. This, along with unreasonable expectations, can lead to misunderstandings about the work of government and Parliament, resulting in frustration for both petition signatories and initiators (Wright, 2015). Moreover, there is an ongoing debate regarding the effectiveness of e-participation, often referred to as 'slacktivism' or 'clicktivism' (Christensen, 2011), and how this form of activism may displace or galvanise other forms of support (Heley et al., 2022; Skoric, 2012).

Numerous studies in the literature have utilised data from the e-petition platform to gain insights into its functioning (Hale et al., 2018; Yasseri et al., 2013). They have identified the textual features of e-petitions that are likely to attract potential signers (Clark & Lomax, 2020), examined political outcomes through modelling (Clark et al., 2018), and characterised constituencies based on e-petition data (Anthony & Haworth, 2020; Clark et al., 2017). Moreover, there have been studies focusing on specific thematic e-petitions to monitor public concerns, such as the UK's energy sector (Kolosok et al., 2021), the promotion of animal welfare initiatives (Chaney et al., 2021), and the concerns of the British expatriate population (Clark & Lomax, 2022).

DATA

In this chapter, e-petition data from the UK Parliament's e-petition platform, specifically focusing on petitions related to the cost of living, is utilised. The phrases used to identify whether an e-petition is concerned with the cost of living are presented in Table 7.1 (see below). Regarding the timeframe of the e-petitions considered, only those opened between 1 September 2021 and 27 February 2023 are included. The choice of the earlier date is based on the suggestion by the Institute for Government (2022) that the UK has been facing a cost of living crisis since late 2021, triggered by prices rises, low income growth, and world events. Since e-petitions close after six months, many of these e-petitions will have been closed and cannot gain any more signatures. However some e-petitions will still be open and actively gaining signatures

Table 7.1   Cost of living phrases and their occurrence in e-petitions

Phrases	All e-petitions	Remove false positives e-petitions	signatures	signatures per e-petition
child care	35	30	301,508	10,050
cost of living	183	165	1,426,034	8,643
pensions	30	24	202,705	8,446
food price	13	12	97,786	8,149
energy companies	20	18	132,689	7,372
minimum wage	40	37	255,756	6,912
fuel price	34	34	234,072	6,884
poverty	48	40	240,430	6,011
inflation	90	84	252,940	3,011
interest rate	14	13	33,134	2,549
heating	31	27	68,480	2,536
salary	51	36	90,997	2,528
afford	163	127	271,839	2,141
energy bill	81	72	56,742	788
utility companies	6	5	1,715	343
economic crisis	8	8	1,095	137
Total	847	732	3,667,922	5,011
Total (excl. duplicate phrases)		482	2,422,016	5,025

Source: Authors' own.

so a cut-off date of 27 February 2023 is applied, which allows sufficient time for an e-petition to realise its full potential by 1 May 2023. This May date is when the number of signatures and text for each e-petition is captured for this study, which is exactly 63 days or 1,512 hours after 27 February 2023. According to Yasseri et al. (2017), it is estimated that an e-petition can expect to achieve at least 90 per cent of its eventual support after 1,500 hours. Signature count data is collected for each of the 650 UK parliamentary constituencies, along with the short title of the e-petition and the more extensive background text provided by the e-petition initiator.

METHODS

In this chapter, we employ the methods described by Vidgen and Yasseri (2020) to accomplish several tasks. First, we use these methods to identify the topics present in the e-petitions related to the cost of living. Next, we determine the level of support for each topic within each constituency. Finally, we create groupings of constituencies that exhibit similar levels of support for the identified topics.

A latent Dirichlet allocation (LDA) topic model (Blei et al., 2003) is employed in this chapter to identify topics based on the assumption that each e-petition's text can be considered as a 'bag of words' associated with various topics. The LDA model probabilistically estimates the proportion of each e-petition's text that is linked to each topic. Consequently, the model does not consider the order of words or the grammar of the text when identifying topics, and the number of topics needs to be specified externally (metrics such as Cao et al., 2009; Griffiths & Steyvers, 2004 can assist in making this choice). Once the topic proportions are determined for each e-petition, the number of signatures gained by each e-petition in each constituency can be reallocated to each topic using these proportions. By summing across all e-petitions, the number of signatures for each topic can be calculated. Essentially, this process serves as a dimensionality reduction exercise, summarising the support for a smaller number of topics from the signatures received for hundreds of e-petitions.

The subsequent step involves determining whether there are any shared patterns of support for different topics among the constituencies. To achieve this, an unsupervised classification algorithm is employed to cluster the constituencies together (Everitt et al., 2001), utilising the Ward technique (Ward, 1963) to create hierarchical groupings. Once these groupings are established, the strength of the identified topics among the group members is described. Additionally, it is possible to generate maps illustrating these groupings and compare them with the political affiliation of the constituency's Member of Parliament (MP), as well as the level of deprivation in the constituency.

RESULTS

From 3 March 2020 to 1 May 2023, a total of 10,880 e-petitions were hosted by the UK Parliament's e-petition platform. Among them, 9,711 e-petitions were closed, and 1,169 were open, accumulating a total of 51,010,140 signatures. For the purpose of this study, we focus on the e-petitions that were open between 1 September 2021 and 27 February 2023, resulting in 3,687 relevant e-petitions (34 per cent of all e-petitions) with 11,962,029 signatures (24 per cent of all signatures). Table 7.1 provides a list of the 16 base phrases used to identify cost of

114 *Handbook on governance and data science*

living e-petitions and indicates the number of signatures gained by such e-petitions. However, it should be noted that this text matching approach may include some e-petitions that are not directly related to the cost of living and are therefore irrelevant. Therefore, both authors independently identified and removed these false positives. Considering that multiple phrases can appear in the same e-petition, the total number of e-petitions included in this study is 482 (12 per cent of all e-petitions between 1 September 2020 and 27 February 2023), with a combined total of 2,422,016 signatures (20 per cent of all signatures).

Before establishing the topics within the 482 e-petitions, it is necessary to determine the number of topics. By modelling the Title, Background, and Additional text content of all e-petitions and exploring a range of possible topics, it becomes possible to make an informed decision regarding the optimal number of topics. In this study, three metrics are utilised: maximum likelihood, maximum Griffiths, and minimum Cao. Figure 7.2 illustrates these metrics across a range of topic numbers. Based on the graph, the range of topics appears to be between 30 and 40, and ultimately, we have chosen the most parsimonious option of 30 topics.

Analysing the most common words found in each topic, along with the titles of e-petitions that predominantly feature those topics, enables the labelling of each topic. The frequent words and corresponding topic labels can be observed in Figure 7.3. Several noteworthy topics emerge, such as 'period poverty' which pertains to the affordability and accessibility of sanitary products for women. Another topic relates to increasing the mileage allowance eligible for taxation deductions, while a separate topic focuses on the transition to more environmentally

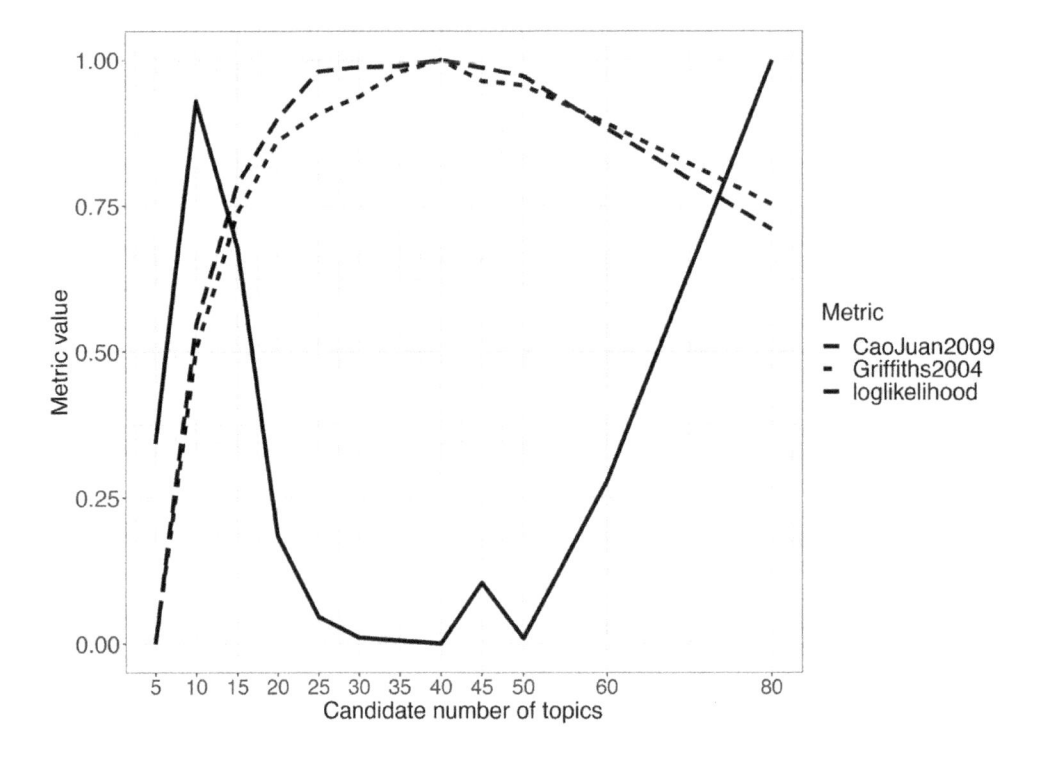

Source: Authors' own.

Figure 7.2   Values of three suitability metrics for a range of topic numbers

Examining the cost of living crisis 115

Source: Authors' own.

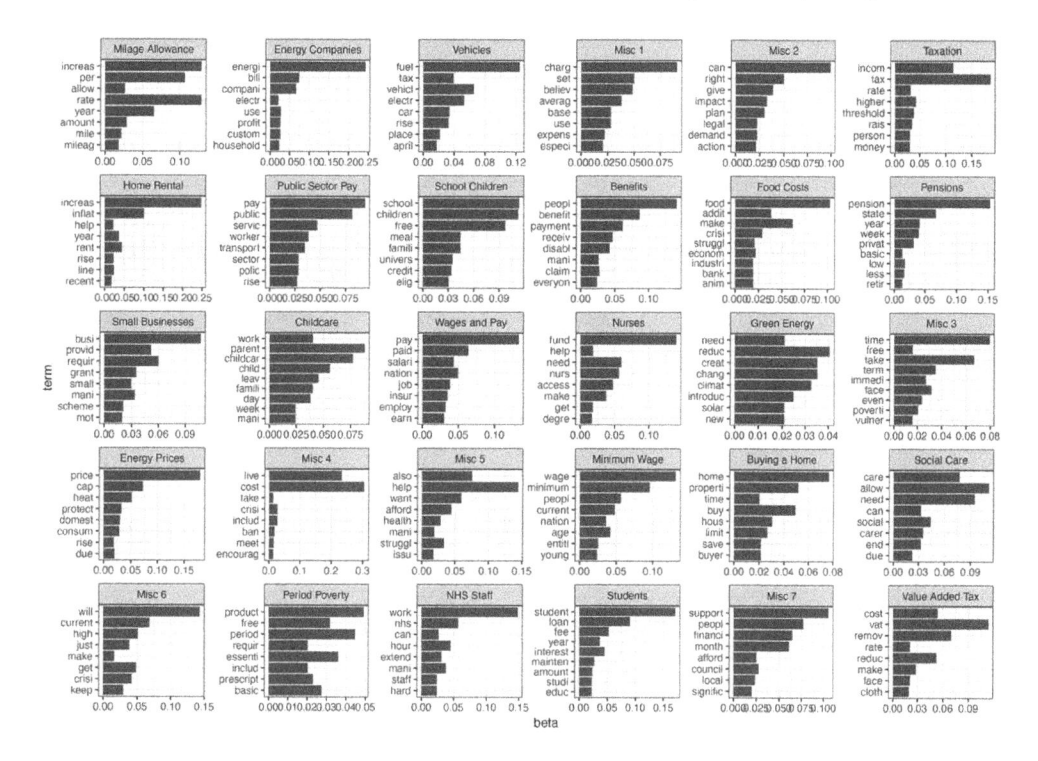

Figure 7.3   Most frequent words with each topic and the labels given to these topics

friendly energy sources. Additionally, there are seven 'miscellaneous' outlying topics that are challenging to categorise distinctly (resembling the concept of incoherent topics discussed by Hagen et al., 2016).

By employing the methodologies detailed in Vidgen and Yasseri (2020), it becomes feasible to allocate the signatures of each e-petition to their respective topics within each constituency. Aggregating these allocations across all e-petitions provides an overview of the strength and distribution of support for each topic across the parliamentary constituencies. The resulting analysis is depicted in Figure 7.4.

Topics related to the high price of food garner a substantial number of signatures across numerous constituencies. Following closely are topics concerning the minimum wage, which set the foundation for people's expected earnings, and social care. In comparison, the miscellaneous topics tend to receive fewer signatures compared to the more cohesive topics.

To establish groups of constituencies, a Ward's D hierarchical classification is applied after standardisation (Murtagh & Legendre, 2014). The dendrogram illustrating this classification process is presented in Figure 7.5. Here we identify four groupings.

The level of support for each topic within the four groups is depicted by the average percentage of signatures allocated to each topic, as shown in Table 7.2. Group 1 exhibits significant support for NHS staff, recognising and rewarding their contributions during the COVID-19 pandemic (Willan et al., 2020). Group 2 displays notably high support for the cost of food and various aspects of social care. In contrast, Group 3 does not demonstrate strong support

116 *Handbook on governance and data science*

Source: Authors' own.

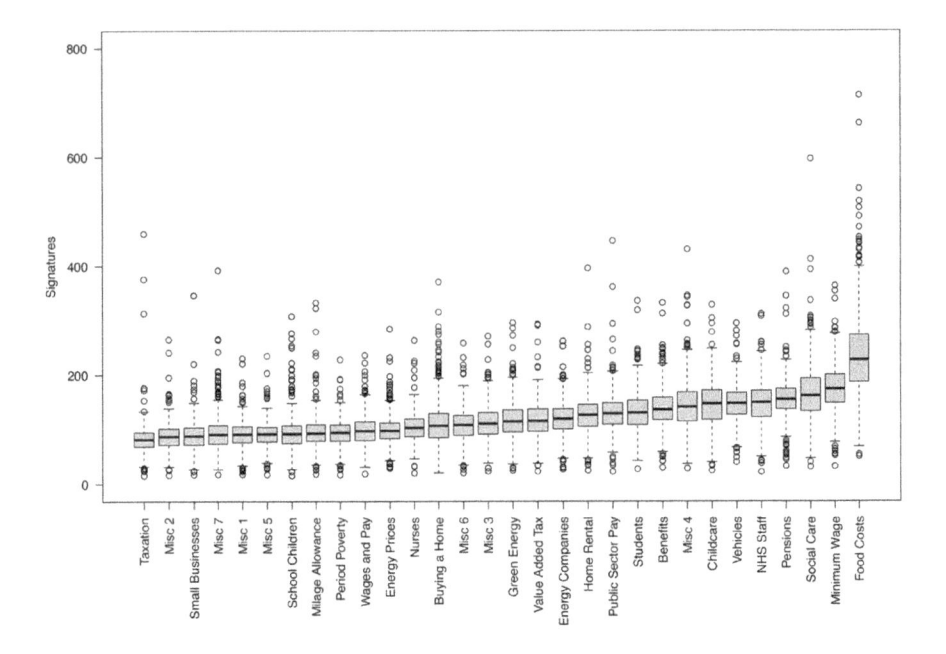

Figure 7.4   Distribution of support for each topic amongst all constituencies

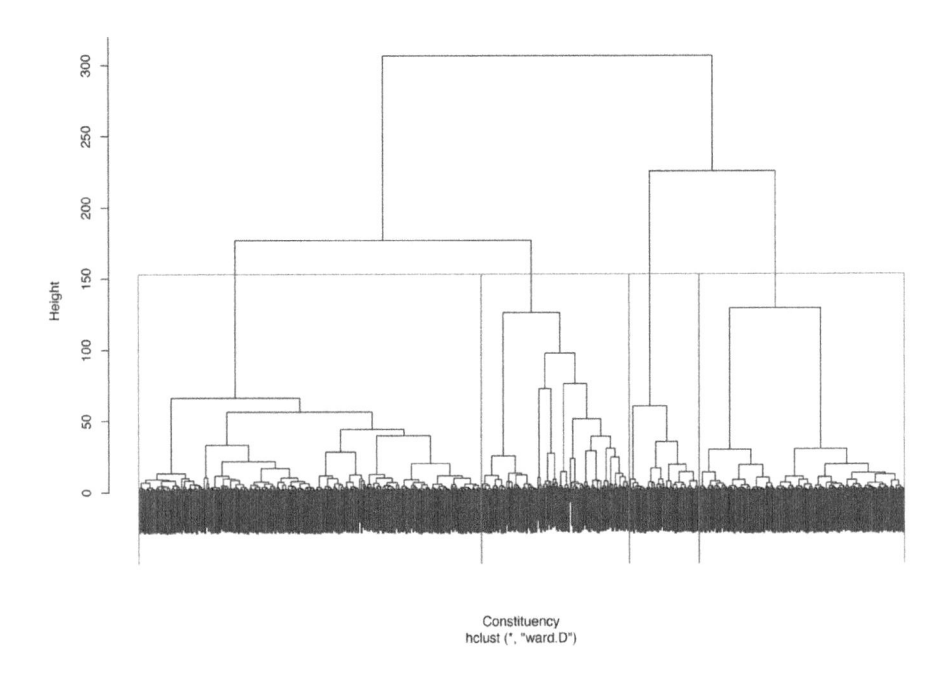

Source: Authors' own.

Figure 7.5   Dendrogram on the formation of groups of constituencies, with the group of four illustrated

Table 7.2 Percentage of signature support for each topic within each group (unusual values boxed in bold grey)

Topic	Topic category	NHS	Social Costs and Care	Celtic Fringe	Housing
Energy Companies	Expenditure	3.3%	3.3%	3.3%	3.2%
Vehicles	Expenditure	4.2%	3.9%	4.4%	**3.5%**
Home Rental	Expenditure	3.5%	3.4%	3.6%	3.3%
Food Costs	Expenditure	5.9%	**7.3%**	6.1%	5.9%
Energy Prices	Expenditure	2.7%	2.5%	3.0%	2.8%
Buying a Home	Expenditure	2.8%	3.1%	2.8%	**4.2%**
Period Poverty	Expenditure	2.7%	2.5%	2.5%	2.7%
Value Added Tax	Expenditure	3.2%	3.3%	3.2%	3.3%
Mileage Allowance	Income	2.7%	2.4%	2.6%	2.5%
Taxation	Income	2.3%	2.2%	2.3%	2.4%
Public Sector Pay	Income	3.7%	3.2%	3.9%	3.6%
Benefits	Income	3.8%	4.0%	3.9%	3.4%
Pensions	Income	4.5%	4.0%	4.7%	4.0%
Wages and Pay	Income	2.6%	2.8%	2.6%	2.8%
Minimum Wage	Income	4.9%	4.8%	4.6%	4.6%
Small Businesses	Both	2.4%	2.4%	2.5%	2.5%
Students	Both	3.6%	3.9%	3.5%	3.3%
School Children	Care	2.6%	2.5%	2.6%	2.5%
Childcare	Care	4.1%	4.0%	3.7%	3.8%
Nurses	Care	2.9%	2.7%	3.0%	2.8%
Green Energy	Care	3.1%	3.3%	3.2%	3.1%
Social Care	Care	4.4%	**4.9%**	4.4%	4.1%
NHS Staff	Care	**4.3%**	3.8%	3.7%	3.8%
Misc 1	Miscellaneous	2.6%	2.4%	2.5%	2.6%
Misc 2	Miscellaneous	2.4%	2.3%	2.4%	2.7%
Misc 3	Miscellaneous	3.0%	3.2%	3.1%	2.8%
Misc 4	Miscellaneous	3.8%	4.1%	3.8%	4.3%
Misc 5	Miscellaneous	2.6%	2.4%	2.5%	2.5%
Misc 6	Miscellaneous	3.0%	3.0%	2.8%	3.2%
Misc 7	Miscellaneous	2.4%	2.4%	2.8%	**3.7%**
min		2.3%	2.2%	2.3%	2.4%
max		5.9%	7.3%	6.1%	5.9%
range		3.7%	5.1%	3.9%	3.5%
n		292	175	124	59

Source: Authors' own.

for any specific topic; however, it has a geographic concentration in Scotland and Northern Ireland as illustrated in Figure 7.6. Lastly, Group 4 exhibits strong support for assistance with buying a home but shows limited support for vehicle costs.

The location of these groups can be visualised by mapping them according to their constituencies. Figure 7.6 displays this distribution as a geographic map on the left-hand side and as a cartogram on the right-hand side, where each constituency is represented by the same hexagon shape. By combining these geographic locations with the signature support results, we can begin to assign names to each group. Group 3, referred to as the 'Celtic Fringe' Group, is predominantly represented in rural constituencies in Scotland and Northern Ireland. On the other hand, Group 4, named 'Housing', is primarily concentrated in the outer areas of Greater London. Group 1, known as the 'NHS' Group, and Group 2, labelled 'Social Costs and Care', derive their names from the strong support they exhibit for specific topics.

The top section of Tables 7.3a, 7.3b displays the electoral party for each constituency's MP in the current Parliament, while the middle section presents the projected changes in party affiliation based on current predictions (source: Electoral Calculus, 2023). In the bottom section, the level of deprivation for each constituency in the group is indicated by the Index

118 *Handbook on governance and data science*

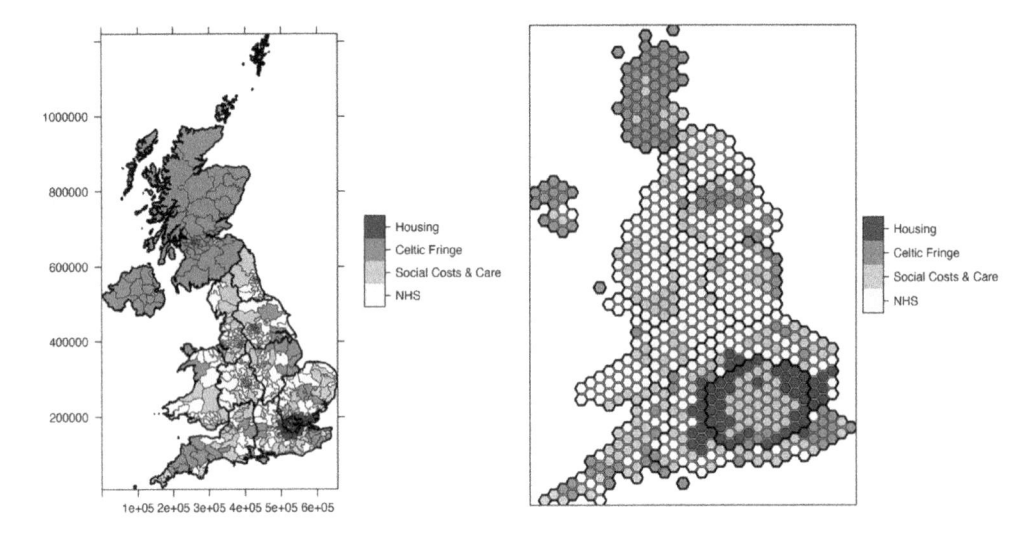

Source: Authors' own.

Figure 7.6   Map of the location of groups using a geographic map (LHS) and a cartogram (RHS)

of Multiple Deprivation (IMD), where a lower score signifies higher levels of deprivation (Francis-Devine, 2019). Nearly half of the constituencies in the NHS Group are currently represented by Conservative MPs, and these constituencies have, on average, higher levels of deprivation. However, according to predictions, the Conservative Party is expected to lose most of its seats in the NHS Group. The Housing Group comprises the least deprived constituencies.

DISCUSSION

In this chapter, we have explored the significance of public petitioning to the UK Parliament and the role of the e-platform in facilitating this process. By utilising the data accessible through the platform, we have examined the public sentiment regarding the pressing issue of the cost of living crisis, as expressed in nearly 500 e-petitions.

Through our analysis, we have distilled these concerns into 23 meaningful topics, which can be broadly categorised into three main areas. First, there are topics centred around the rising costs of essential items, particularly food and energy. Notably, one specific issue that emerges is the cost and accessibility of sanitary products for women, which is a vital and sensitive topic often overshadowed by the broader cost of living crisis (Astrup, 2017).

The second category encompasses topics related to income and household finances. Among these, a notable topic of interest is the tax allowance on mileage expenses, specifically in relation to work-related travel (Gascoyne-Richards, 2018). This particular topic garners significant attention, with numerous e-petitions calling for specific increases in the allowance.

The third substantial category involves topics related to societal care and the potential impact of the cost of living crisis on such provisions. One prominent aspect is the cost of

Examining the cost of living crisi

childcare and how the government can provide financial support and additional resources to address this issue (Farquharson & Olorenshaw, 2022). This topic directly affects household incomes, as families struggle to afford childcare, and indirectly impacts parents' ability to participate in paid work.

By measuring the level of concern for each topic in each constituency, we have identified common patterns that have led to the formation of four distinct groups of constituencies. These groups also exhibit spatial clustering, with two noticeable geographic clusters. The first group encompasses constituencies in Scotland and Northern Ireland, referred to as the 'Celtic Fringe' Group. While this group does not display outstanding differences in concerns compared to other groups, it is worth noting that separate legislatures exist in Scotland, Wales, and Northern Ireland, which may address some of the specific concerns within their jurisdictions (Booth, 2015; Trench, 2007).

The second spatially clustered group comprises constituencies situated on the outskirts of Greater London, with a particular focus on housing-related issues. This area is characterised by a distinct housing market (Simmie, 2020), occupying a lower tier within the housing market hierarchy (Webb et al., 2021). Interestingly, this group represents the least deprived constituencies on average.

The NHS Group, which predominantly consists of constituencies represented by Conservative members in the current Parliament (at the time of writing in November 2023), faces electoral consequences due to the cost of living crisis, as indicated in Tables 7.3a, 7.3b. Based on current predictions, they are projected to lose over one hundred seats, highlighting their vulnerability to the cost of living concerns in the NHS Group. Given the high regard for the NHS among the British public (Cream et al., 2018), the Conservative Party may need to address these concerns strategically to mitigate potential losses. On the other hand, the Labour Party is expected to maintain its seats and even gain additional seats in all groups, albeit to a lesser extent in the affluent Housing Group. This underscores the importance of understanding the nuanced concerns of constituents for MPs in a political context.

Thankfully, the UK Parliament's e-petition platform provides timely and geographically detailed data, which proves valuable for researchers and policy analysts. However, it is unfortunate that there is no archive of signatures, with hourly timestamps, as such data would allow for a retrospective view of the evolution of support for e-petitions and their associated topics.

Table 7.3a   Party representation for each group

Group	NHS	Social Cost and Care	Celtic Fringe	Housing
Conservative	189	83	56	37
Labour	97	77	8	20
Nationalists[†]	2	7	43	0
Northern Ireland	2	2	14	0
Liberal Democrats, Greens & House Speaker	2	6	3	2

Note: [†] Scottish National Party and Plaid Cymru (Party of Wales).
Source: Authors' own.

Table 7.3b   Projected party representation for each group (May, 2023) and the average ranked index of multiple deprivation

Group	NHS	Social Cost and Care	Celtic Fringe	Housing
Conservative Hold	61	45	36	27
Labour Hold	97	77	8	20
Labour gain from Conservative	127	39	31	9
Other	7	14	49	3
IMD[§]	229.1	297.5	283.9	336.5

Note: [§] Average of deprivation rank, 1 = most deprived, 650 = least deprived.
Source: Authors' own.

While this chapter has focused on the cost of living crisis in the UK, similar methodological approaches can be applied to understand the concerns of any sub-group of the electorate in relation to a particular set of events and timeframe. For example, in previous work we utilised similar methods to understand the concerns of the UK's expatriate population (Clark & Lomax, 2022), focusing on resident and citizen signatories with an address outside the UK in the period 2017–19. This was a period of intense negotiation between the UK and the European Union about what a Brexit deal might look like, so topics of interest were focused on the domestic and international implications of this deal. In that paper, we suggested that e-petitions offer an opportunity to monitor ongoing concerns of the electorate. In a subsequent paper (Clark & Lomax, 2023), we did just that, focusing on public concerns during the COVID-19 pandemic. We revealed distinct topic groupings by parliamentary consistency: topics pertinent to equity of support (e.g., economic support for business) were typically important in constituencies with a Conservative MP, while education and funding concerns were typically important in areas of Labour support. The focus on the cost of living crisis in this chapter extends the monitoring proposed in Clark and Lomax (2022) and with an eye on the future, the next UK General Election will be called sometime between the time of writing (November 2023) and 17 December 2024. This key political event will offer another window during which similar analysis could be undertaken to understand the priorities and sentiment of the electorate. Moreover, our methods could be applied in international contexts, where similar data are available. For example in Clark and Lomax (2020) we undertake a comparison of the linguistic and semantic factors that represent a successful e-petition in the United States of America (USA) versus the UK, adopting methods set out in Hagen et al. (2016).

ACKNOWLEDGEMENTS

This work was funded by the Economic and Social Research Council of the United Kingdom under grant ES/L011891/1.

REFERENCES

Almbjär, M. (2019). The problem with early-modern petitions: Safety valve or powder keg? *European Review of History: Revue européenne d'histoire*, *26*(6), 1013–39.

Anthony, E., & Haworth, J. (2020). *A spatial analysis of UK e-petition signing behaviour*. GIS Research UK, London.

Asher, M., Leston-Bandeira, C., & Spaiser, V. (2019). Do parliamentary debates of e-petitions enhance public engagement with Parliament? An analysis of Twitter conversations. *Policy & Internet*, *11*(2), 149–71.

Astrup, J. (2017). Period poverty: Tackling the taboo. *Community Practitioner*, *90*(12), 40–2.

Blei, D.M., Ng, A.Y., & Jordan, M.I. (2003). Latent dirichlet allocation. *Journal of Machine Learning Research*, *3*(January), 993–1022.

Blumenau, J. (2020). Online activism and dyadic representation: Evidence from the UK e-petition system. *Legislative Studies Quarterly*, *46*(4), 889–920.

Bochel, C. (2016). Process matters: Petitions systems in Britain's legislatures. *The Journal of Legislative Studies*, *22*(3), 368–84.

Bolton, P., & Stewart, I. (2023). *Domestic energy prices*. House of Commons Library. https://commonslibrary.parliament.uk/research-briefings/cbp-9491/ [Accessed 8th November, 2024]

Booth, P. (2015). *Federal Britain: The case for decentralisation*. London Publishing Partnership.

Briassoulis, H. (2010). Online petitions: New tools of secondary analysis? *Qualitative Research*, *10*(6), 715–27. https://doi.org/10.1177/1468794110380530

Broadbent, P., Thomson, R., Kopasker, D., McCartney, G., Meier, P., Richiardi, M., ... Katikireddi, S.V. (2023). The public health implications of the cost-of-living crisis: Outlining mechanisms and modelling consequences. *Lancet Regional Health Europe*, *27*, 100585. https://doi.org/10.1016/j.lanepe.2023.100585

Cao, J., Xia, T., Li, J., Zhang, Y., & Tang, S. (2009). A density-based method for adaptive LDA model selection. *Neurocomputing*, *72*(7–9), 1775–81.

Centre for Social Justice. (2022). *On target. Protecting vulnerable households from the inflation crisis* https://www.centreforsocialjustice.org.uk/wp-content/uploads/2022/09/CSJ-Cost_of_Living.pdf [Accessed 8th November, 2024]

Chaney, P., Jones, I.R., & Fevre, R. (2021). Exploring the substantive representation of non-humans in UK parliamentary business: A legislative functions perspective of animal welfare petitions, 2010–19. *Parliamentary Affairs*, *75*(4).

Christensen, H.S. (2011). Political activities on the Internet: Slacktivism or political participation by other means? *First Monday*. https://firstmonday.org/ojs/index.php/fm/article/view/3336 [Accessed 8th November, 2024]

Clark, S.D., & Lomax, N. (2020). Linguistic and semantic factors in government e-petitions: A comparison between the United Kingdom and the United States of America. *Government Information Quarterly*, *37*(4), 101523. https://doi.org/10.1016/j.giq.2020.101523

Clark, S.D., & Lomax, N. (2022). A worlds-eye view of the United Kingdom through parliamentary e-petitions. *The British Journal of Politics and International Relations*, 13691481221109737.

Clark, S.D., & Lomax, N. (2023). Using e-petition data to quantify public concerns during the COVID19 pandemic: A case study of England. *Policy Studies*, 1–24.

Clark, S., Lomax, N., & Morris, M.A. (2017). Classification of Westminster parliamentary constituencies using e-petition data. *EPJ Data Science*, *6*(1), 16. https://doi.org/10.1140/epjds/s13688-017-0113-9

Clark, S.D., Morris, M.A., & Lomax, N. (2018). Estimating the outcome of UK's referendum on EU membership using e-petition data and machine learning algorithms. *Journal of Information Technology & Politics*, *15*(4), 344–57. https://doi.org/10.1080/19331681.2018.1491926

Cominetti, N., Costa, R., Datta, N., & Odamtten, F. (2022). *Low Pay Britain 2022: Low pay and insecurity in the UK labour market*. https://blogs.lse.ac.uk/businessreview/2022/06/22/low-pay-and-insecurity-in-the-uk-labour-market/ [Accessed 8th November, 2024]

Cream, J., Maguire, D., & Robertson, R. (2018). How have public attitudes to the NHS changed over the past three decades. https://www.kingsfund.org.uk/insight-and-analysis/long-reads/how-have-public-attitudes-to-nhs-changed [Accessed 8th November, 2024]

Dodd, G. (2007). *Justice and grace: Private petitioning and the English Parliament in the late Middle Ages.* Oxford: Oxford Univerity Press.

Electoral Calculus. (2023). *UK predictions.* https://www.electoralcalculus.co.uk/prediction_home.html [Accessed 8th November, 2024]

Everitt, B., Landau, S., & Leese, M. (2001). Cluster analysis. 4th edn. London: Arnold Press.

Farquharson, C., & Olorenshaw, H. (2022). *The changing cost of childcare.* IFS Report. https://ifs.org.uk/publications/changing-cost-childcare [Accessed 8th November, 2024]

Francis-Devine, B. (2019). *Deprivation in English constituencies, 2019.* House of Commons Library. https://commonslibrary.parliament.uk/research-briefings/cbp-7327/ [Accessed 8th November, 2024]

Francis-Devine, B., Zayed, Y., Gorb, A., Malik, X., & Danechi, S. (2022). *Food poverty: Households, food banks and free school meals.* House of Commons Library. https://commonslibrary.parliament.uk/research-briefings/cbp-9209/ [Accessed 8th November, 2024]

Gascoyne-Richards, R. (2018). Practical advice on motor expenses. *Practice Management, 28*(8), 32–3.

Griffiths, T.L., & Steyvers, M. (2004). Finding scientific topics. *Proceedings of the Nationall Academy of Sciences USA, 101* (Suppl 1), 5228–35. https://doi.org/10.1073/pnas.0307752101

Hagen, L., Harrison, T.M., Uzuner, Ö., May, W., Fake, T., & Katragadda, S. (2016). E-petition popularity: Do linguistic and semantic factors matter? *Government Information Quarterly, 33*(4), 783–95.

Hale, S.A., John, P., Margetts, H., & Yasseri, T. (2018). How digital design shapes political participation: A natural experiment with social information. *PLoS One, 13*(4), e0196068. https://doi.org/10.1371/journal.pone.0196068

Harari, D., Francis-Devine, B., Bolton, P., & Keep, M. (2022). *Rising cost of living in the UK.* House of Commons Library. https://commonslibrary.parliament.uk/research-briefings/cbp-9428/ [Accessed 8th November, 2024]

Heley, J., Yarker, S., & Jones, L. (2022). Volunteering in the bath? The rise of microvolunteering and implications for policy. *Policy Studies, 43*(1), 76–89.

Iacobucci, G. (2023). How the cost of living crisis is damaging children's health. *BMJ, 380,* o3064. https://doi.org/10.1136/bmj.o3064

Institute for Government. (2022). *Cost of living crisis.* https://www.instituteforgovernment.org.uk/explainer/cost-living-crisis [Accessed 8th November, 2024]

Irvine, S., Gorb, A., & Francis-Devine, B. (2022). *Food banks in the UK.* House of Commons Library. https://commonslibrary.parliament.uk/research-briefings/cbp-8585/ [Accessed 8th November, 2024]

Johnson, P. (2020). *Huge ethical choices face those tasked with bringing the UK out of lockdown.* Institute for Fiscal Studies, 13 April. https://www.ifs.org.uk/publications/14806. [Accessed 8th November, 2024]

Khan, N. (2022). The cost of living crisis: How can we tackle fuel poverty and food insecurity in practice? *British Journal of General Practice, 72*(720), 330–1. https://doi.org/10.3399/bjgp22X719921

Kolosok, S., Vasylieva, T., & Lyeonov, S. (2021). Machine analysis of the UK electrical energy initiatives based on the e-petitions to the UK government and Parliament. *Development, 12,* 13.

Leston-Bandeira, C. (2017). What is the point of petitions in British politics? http://blogs.lse.ac.uk/politicsandpolicy/what-is-the-point-of-petitions/ [Accessed 8th November, 2024]

Leston-Bandeira, C. (2019). Parliamentary petitions and public engagement: An empirical analysis of the role of e-petitions. *Policy & Politics, 47*(3), 415–36.

Matthews, F. (2021). The value of 'between-election' political participation: Do parliamentary e-petitions matter to political elites? *The British Journal of Politics and International Relations, 23*(3), 410–29.

Matthews, F. (2023). Between everyday politics and political elites: Transmission and coupling within Westminster's parliamentary e-petitions system. *British Politics, 18,* 279–99.

Milne, A.K.L. (2020) A critical COVID-19 economic policy tool: Retrospective insurance (21 March). Available at: *SSRN*: https://papers.ssrn.com/sol3/papers.cfm?abstract_id=3558667 [Accessed 8th November, 2024]

Murtagh, F., & Legendre, P. (2014). Ward's hierarchical agglomerative clustering method: Which algorithms implement Ward's criterion? *Journal of Classification, 31*(3), 274–95.

National Energy Action. (2022). *The hardest hit: Impact of the energy crisis - UK Fuel Poverty Monitor 2021–2022.* https://www.nea.org.uk/wp-content/uploads/2023/01/3830_NEA_Fuel-Poverty-Monitor-Report-2022_V2-1.pdf [Accessed 8th November, 2024]

Office for National Statistics. (2023). *Cost of living latest insights*. https://www.ons.gov.uk/economy/inflationandpriceindices/articles/costofliving/latestinsights [Accessed 8th November, 2024]

Robinson, E. (2023). Obesity and the cost of living crisis. *International Journal of Obes (Lond)*, *47*(2), 93–4. https://doi.org/10.1038/s41366–022–01242–9

Robinson, C., & Mattioli, G. (2020). Double energy vulnerability: Spatial intersections of domestic and transport energy poverty in England. *Energy Research & Social Science*, *70*. https://doi.org/10.1016/j.erss.2020.101699

Rodrigues, G., & Quinio, V. (2022). *Out of pocket: The places at the sharp end of the cost of living crisis*. https://www.centreforcities.org/publication/out-of-pocket-the-cost-of-living-crisis/ [Accessed 8th November, 2024]

Sasse, T., & Thomas, A. (2022). Better policy making. Institute for Government. https://www.instituteforgovernment.org.uk/sites/default/files/publications/better-policy-making.pdf [Accessed 8th November, 2024]

Simmie, J. (2020). *Planning London*. Routledge.

Skoric, M.M. (2012). What is slack about slacktivism? *Methodological and Conceptual Issues in Cyber Activism Research*, *77*(7), 7–92.

Sovacool, B.K., Upham, P., Martiskainen, M., Jenkins, K.E.H., Torres Contreras, G.A., & Simcock, N. (2023). Policy prescriptions to address energy and transport poverty in the United Kingdom. *Nature Energy*, *8*(3), 273–83. https://doi.org/10.1038/s41560–023–01196-w

Trench, A. (2007). *Devolution and power in the United Kingdom*. Manchester: Manchester University Press.

UK Government and Parliament. (2022). *Find out more about e-petitions*. https://www.parliament.uk/get-involved/sign-a-petition/e-petitions/ [Accessed 8th November, 2024]

Vidgen, B., & Yasseri, T. (2020). What, when and where of petitions submitted to the UK government during a time of chaos. *Policy Sciences*, *53*(3), 535–57.

Ward, J.H. (1963). Hierarchical grouping to optimize an objective function. *Journal of the American statistical Association*, *58*(301), 236–44.

Webb, R., Watson, D., & Cook, S. (2021). Price adjustment in the London housing market. *Urban Studies*, *58*(1), 113–30.

Willan, J., King, A.J., Jeffery, K., & Bienz, N. (2020). Challenges for NHS hospitals during covid-19 epidemic. *British Medical Journal Publishing Group*, *368*.

Wilson, W., & Barton, C. (2022). *Housing and the cost-of-living*. House of Commons Library. https://commonslibrary.parliament.uk/research-briefings/cbp-9622/ [Accessed 8th November, 2024]

Wright, S. (2015). 'Success' and online political participation: The case of Downing Street e-petitions. *Information, Communication & Society*, *19*(6), 843–57. https://doi.org/10.1080/1369118x.2015.1080285

Yasseri, T., Hale, S.A., & Margetts, H.Z. (2013). *Modeling the rise in Internet-based petitions*. Oxford Internet Institute. https://arxiv.org/pdf/1308.0239 [Accessed 8th November, 2024]

Yasseri, T., Hale, S.A., & Margetts, H.Z. (2017). Rapid rise and decay in petition signing. *EPJ Data Science*, *6*(1), 13. https://doi.org/10.1140/epjds/s13688–017–0116–6

8. Platform-based coordination for cross-agency collaboration in public service production

Yiwei Gong and Marijn Janssen

INTRODUCTION

Digital platforms refer to a sociotechnical assemblage encompassing digital technologies, associated business processes, and standards (Bharadwaj et al., 2013; de Reuver, Sørensen, & Basole, 2018). Digital government platforms can improve the efficiency of public services by providing government agencies with higher accessibility to data and data analytics tools (Brown et al., 2017). To facilitate collaborative service production, governments are converging existing IT and organizational silos with new digital technologies to generate digital platforms (Cordella & Paletti, 2019; Senyo, Effah, & Osabutey, 2021). At the same time, adopting digital platforms also changes coordination among many interacting, networked, and collaborative actors in a participatory ecosystem that enables the coproduction of public services (Janssen & Estevez, 2013; O'Reilly, 2011). Digital platforms increase data intelligence, accessibility, and reconfigurability to fundamentally reshape how public services are designed, produced, and delivered (Bharadwaj et al., 2013). Public services are becoming intelligent, integrative, and citizen-centric. On the one hand, governments on a digital platform journey need a comprehensive understanding of the associated platform coordination changes. On the other hand, introducing digital platforms implies the transformation of governments from closed and hierarchical relationships into open, flat, and ecosystem-like relationships (Cordella & Paletti, 2019). Digital platforms accompany a new way of collaboration implemented with cross-agency data and knowledge sharing, given the need for coordination for efficiency and flexibility (Gong, Yang, & Shi, 2020). Addressing these challenges requires proper coordination configuration for collaboration among government agencies.

In general, coordination refers to integrating or linking different parts of organizations together to accomplish a collective set of tasks (Van de Ven, Delbecq, & Koenig, 1976). Conventional coordination mechanisms for cross-agency collaboration are usually based on "traditional hierarchical government control through authoritative allocation of values to society" (Lange et al., 2013, p. 408). Digital platforms often trigger changes in how organizational activities are aligned and render conventional coordination mechanisms obsolete (Gkeredakis & Constantinides, 2019). However, studies in the public sector predominantly focus on the benefits or strategies of adopting digital platforms (e.g., Brown et al., 2017; Cordella & Paletti, 2019; Janssen & Estevez, 2013). Little is known about how the rise of different digital government platforms reconfigures coordination mechanisms. To address this knowledge gap, we developed a theoretical framework for scoping the features of digital platform coordination and conducted a demonstrative case study to test the creation of coordination mechanisms for collaborative platforms.

The chapter is structured as follows. The next section briefly discusses the background of digital platforms, digital coordination, and research streams on digital government platforms. The third section conceptualizes the theories for digital government platform coordination. The fourth section describes the research method. The fifth section presents the findings of the case study. In the sixth section, we discuss the implications of our study. The final section concludes the chapter.

CONCEPTS OF DIGITAL PLATFORMS

Our discussion begins with a brief introduction to relevant digital platform concepts to provide the basis for further discussion on digital coordination and digital government platforms. Although consensus has not been reached on the definition of platforms, many scholars—both in the information systems and digital government domains—adopt the definitions of Gawer and Cusumano (2014), in which platforms are classified into three predominant types: internal platforms, supply chain platforms, and industry platforms (Brown et al., 2017; Cordella & Paletti, 2019; Kapoor et al., 2021). In this classification, internal platforms refer to a set of assets organized in a common structure from which an enterprise can efficiently develop and produce a stream of derivative products, while industry platforms are products, services, or technologies that act as a foundation upon which external innovators are organized as an innovative business ecosystem (Gawer & Cusumano, 2014). Supply chain platforms coordinate external suppliers around an assembler to replicate the benefits of internal platforms across interfaces among different organizations (Gawer, 2014). Similar to many manufacturing supply chains, a supply chain platform coordinates a set of firms that follow specific guidelines to supply intermediate products or components to the platform owner for assembling final products. Typical industry platforms are Windows and iOS. In comparison with supply chain platforms, the firms developing complementary innovations for an industry platform, such as applications for Windows or the Apple App Store, do not necessarily buy from or sell to each other (Gawer & Cusumano, 2014). Compared with other platform conceptualizations that consider a wide spectrum of platform research streams (e.g., Thomas, Autio, & Gann, 2014), this conceptualization regards the platform as the organizational structure that carries organizational resources and capabilities to enable the rapid recombination of these to create flexibility. It takes a transformational perspective of "platform organization" (Ciborra, 1996) in restructuring new *organizational forms* to respond to emerging opportunities and challenges.

This classification also implies boundary-based scoping of digital platforms. The boundary of a digital platform concerns the context within which the platform exists and evolves; in particular, the organizational and technical interfaces that the platform relies upon in innovation (Jin & Robey, 2008). The dynamics of boundaries reflect the degree of openness, which affects the participation of external actors and the incentive to innovate (Boudreau, 2010). In general, *openness* refers to the easing of restrictions on the use and development of technology. For digital platforms, openness is not only related to technologies but also to organizational arrangements such as entrance and exit rules (de Reuver et al., 2018). When a platform's rules make it easier for more participants to join, it is more likely to make desirable innovations. At the same time, the larger the number and heterogeneity of participants joining a digital platform, the more challenging coordination and completion of specific tasks become (Kretschmer et al., 2022).

The concept of digital platforms can be viewed from both a technical and sociotechnical perspective (de Reuver et al., 2018; Kapoor et al., 2021). The technical concept of digital platforms emphasizes that the technical design of platforms matters for their ability to evolve and produce innovation (Rolland, Mathiassen, & Rai, 2018). This concept has been elaborated into a layered *modular architecture* that involves varying arrangements of devices, networks, services, and content created by digital technologies (Yoo, Henfridsson, & Lyytinen, 2010). With a modular architecture, a platform constitutes an enduring core that permits complementary modules to be easily added, combined, or modified (Baldwin & Woodard, 2009). In contrast, a sociotechnical perspective builds on the idea that work systems can be understood only when the social aspects (e.g., the organization, working processes, and roles) and technical aspects (e.g., the physical infrastructure, tools, and technologies) are considered in conjunction and treated as interdependent elements of a complex system (Hughes et al., 2017).

The creation of digital platforms involves the need to capture generativity. The concept of *generativity* refers to the capability of digital platforms to allow for the recombination of elements for assembly, extension, and redistribution of functionality (Nambisan, 2017; Warner & Wäger, 2019; Yoo et al., 2010). This generativity view assumes that digital resources and their combinations with social resources will result in new innovation possibilities and value creation (Jarvenpaa & Standaert, 2018). At the same time, such innovations and value creation can also be reflected by extending and repurposing existing digital infrastructure to produce new digital products, services, processes, and business models (Brown et al., 2017). The degree of generativity operates and affects participants' contributions, indicating the distinct nature of coordination and organizing logic in digital platforms compared with other organizational forms, such as hierarchical bureaucracy (Cennamo & Santaló, 2019).

Table 8.1 summarizes the general features of digital platforms. Our basic assumption in this study is that the different configurations of these features—in line with contextual requirements—(re)shape the coordination mechanism of a digital platform. Mechanisms in digital

Table 8.1   *General features of digital platforms*

Features	Description	Representative references
Openness	Technical and organizational arrangements reflect the easing of restrictions on the use and development of platform resources.	Boudreau (2010) and Ghazawneh and Henfridsson (2013)
Modularity	An architectural and technological property that allows complementary and independent modules of the platform to be easily added, combined, or modified.	Baldwin and Woodard (2009) and Tiwana, Konsynski, and Bush (2010)
Generativity	The capability of platforms to allow for the recombination of technical and social resources and the creation, extension, and redistribution of digital functionality, products, services, processes, and business models.	Yoo et al. (2010), Jarvenpaa and Standaert (2018), and Nambisan (2017)

Source: Authors' own.

platforms are characterized by contingent causality, as the implementation of a mechanism may lead to one outcome in a particular context, but another in a different context (Henfridsson & Bygstad, 2013). Such a configurational perspective is the basis for the analysis of the causal paths that explain how, in certain contexts, a coordination mechanism may lead to the successful evolution of digital platforms.

DIGITAL GOVERNMENT PLATFORM COORDINATION

Theoretical Foundation

Initiatives for digital government platforms are struggling with the application of platform theory from research on commercial digital platforms because of the differences in scope and focus (Bonina & Eaton, 2020; Brown et al., 2017). In comparison, government platforms and commercial platforms are different in value orientations toward openness and restrictions in effect (Boudreau, 2010; Gong & Li, 2023). Commercial platforms have an economic interest and often leverage openness through financial instruments, such as pricing. In contrast, government platforms emphasize accountability, authority, transparency, citizen satisfaction, and public value (Janssen & Estevez, 2013). These differences indicate the need to operationalize platform theory in the context of digital government. Existing insights on commercial digital platforms may not be directly applicable to digital government platforms (Schreieck, Wiesche, & Krcmar, 2017). In conducting digital government platform research, Brown et al. (2017) suggest informing "the consideration and evaluation of platform thinking in relation to the specific complexity of government, and to avoid the wholesale import of private sector ideas" (p. 171). In this section, we create a typology of government platforms based on the current platform theory derived from commercial platforms.

Gawer (2014) suggests that underlying the different types of platforms, the form of digital platforms may be supported by an important conceptual underpinning that offers intuition from an organizational lens to develop a framework for platforms. By bridging information systems and economic literature in her framework, distinguishing among internal, supply chain, and industry platforms, she notes that such a framework should present platforms with different organizational forms and highlight their essential features, including openness, architecture, and generativity. An underlying assumption in the platform theory of Gawer (2014) is that the types of platforms are not a discrete set of rigidly delineated configurations, but an organizational continuum with possible evolutionary pathways between these configurations. This implies opportunities to gain insights from the transformation and evolution of digital platforms from one type to another.

Theoretical frameworks that deeply ground commercial platform literature may be limited to analyzing government platforms. Scholars in digital government research also highlight the importance of understanding the roles of platform coordination in governments and of empirically examining the effects (Brown et al., 2017; Mukhopadhyay, Bouwman, & Jaiswal, 2019). This calls for a theoretical framework that distinguishes between platform types and associated organizing forms and features in the context of digital government platforms. Table 8.2 presents such a framework for understanding coordination mechanisms in digital government platforms, based on the platform typology of Gawer (2014) and the analysis of the various literature on platforms in the domains of information systems and digital government.

Table 8.2   A theoretical framework for digital government platform coordination

General platform types in Gawer (2014)	Internal platforms	Supply-chain platforms	Industry platforms
Organizational forms of digital government platforms in correspondence	Internal platforms: routine information systems with modular architecture and process-oriented design	Collaborative platforms: enable collaboration among government agencies with the joined-up mode of service creation	Open government platforms: such as OGD platforms, citizen-engagement platforms, and public transportation service platforms
Accountability and suitable types of public services	Services with high accountability over the final outcome, such as policing services	Services can be facilitated by shared accountability among public agencies, such as one-stop shop administrative services	Services with low accountability and limited administrative resources, such as public transportation services
Openness and transparency	Closed: platform development merely relies on the platform owner's resources and capabilities Low transparency: functioning and data are not visible to other agencies	Semi-open: platform development relies on resources and capabilities from the platform owner and the aligned agencies Medium transparency: providing insight into functioning and data to agencies in collaboration	Open: everyone who obeys the platform's basic rules can contribute to the platform's development High transparency: open data are highly visible to all participants
Modular architecture	The architecture enables the platform owner to have full decision rights on modules and how they interact	The architecture supports decision rights partitioning between the platform owner and external agencies	The architecture supports decision rights partitioning between the platform owner and external agencies
Generativity and control	High level of control and role-based	Medium level of control and data-driven	Low level of control and data-driven

Source: Authors' own.

Organizational Forms and Service Accountability

The first aspect in addressing digital platform coordination is the organizational form, which can be considered a manifestation of coordination configuration. The close relationship between organizational forms and coordination may be illustrated in a fundamental definition of organization given by Barnard (1938); that is, an organization is a "system of coordinating activities of two or more persons" (p. 73). Classical organization theory emphasizes the influence of organizational forms and structures on the design and implementation of coordination mechanisms (Malone & Crowston, 1994). Gawer (2014) regards organizational form as an endogenous variable for analyzing digital platforms. When a structure does not support technology operations and use, or the structure does not take advantage of the capabilities of the technology, these misalignments will trigger the need for transformation and reform of platform organization. From a sociotechnical perspective, such organizational changes are recognized as platform evolution through the processes of development, adoption, adaptation, and use of technologies in social settings. The analogy with "ecosystems" is used to signify complex and heterogeneous systems of institutions, groups of actors, infrastructure, and data, which interact, adapt, and grow in the context of digital government platforms (Bonina & Eaton, 2020). The ecosystem metaphor, with its emphasis on evolution and self-organization among actors and processes, would be a useful heuristic for approaching the design of effective digital government platform coordination (Dawes, Vidiasova, & Parkhimovich, 2016).

To bridge the platform theory from the commercial context to the digital government context, Cordella and Paletti (2019) align the above classification with government platforms, corresponding through the three types of platforms. The authors provide an electronic medical healthcare system at a hospital as an example of an internal platform in the public sector that provides a common infrastructure to exchange medical data within departments in the same hospital. Internal platforms configure the service creation processes by recombining the subunits, resources, and competencies that are internal to the organization. In this sense, many governments' routine information systems with modular architecture and process-oriented design can be considered internal platforms. Platform coordination here is based on its process design, organizational hierarchy, and functionality with high-level and centralized control (Thomas et al., 2014). Considering the need for very high accountability and specificity, some public services, such as policing services, are also suitable for internal platforms.

Collaborative platforms replicate the shared infrastructure and benefits of internal platforms across different government agencies that need to share data and collaborate in public service delivery (Cordella & Paletti, 2019). Similar to internal platforms, the benefit of collaborative platforms is also to improve efficiency and reduce costs by systematically reusing modular components. Furthermore, the platform owner can recombine capabilities internally within the organization, thus aligning the organization's routines, and through the wider network of collaborative organizations (Thomas et al., 2014). Specific guidelines coordinate these selected organizations with a coherent and integrative strategic orientation to supply intermediate components to the platform owner. Although internal platforms also enable coordination, to avoid confusion, we distinguish internal and collaborative platforms by whether the coordination activities and business processes cross organizational boundaries. In this sense, collaborative platforms facilitate collaboration among government agencies and support the joined-up mode of service production (Gong & Li, 2023). Many one-stop-shop administrative services and integrative services created by collaboration among multiple agencies are suitable for this type of platform. This also results in government agencies, in collaboration with service production and provision, sharing accountability toward citizens (Wang, Medaglia, & Zheng, 2018).

Open government platforms are a set of organizational structures and infrastructures that enable third parties (i.e., companies or citizens) to coproduce public services, such as public transport services. A key distinction between collaborative and open government platforms is that the participants of open government platforms are not intentionally selected or contracted by the platform owner but are attracted and incentivized by the opportunities created by the platform's core offerings, and they use the platform for their purposes. Coordination here is usually implemented by the platform owner's rules for controlling the quality of complementors and the services they have developed. Examples of these rules include those contained within licensing agreement contracts (Ghazawneh & Henfridsson, 2013). Open government platforms are suitable for providing public services that do not require strict administrative and procedural accountability, such as the provision of information about the schedule and status of a public bus (Cordella & Paletti, 2019). The concept of open government platforms often refers to the emerging research on the government as a platform (GaaP) (O'Reilly, 2011). The GaaP coordinates platform participants' activities in service production and provision by providing a set of open tools, rules, and service standards (Cordella & Paletti, 2019).

Openness and Transparency

The second aspect of addressing platform coordination is the level of openness. A platform ecosystem can be closed or open, depending on the platform owner's agency in charge of a specific domain and the production of specific public services (Cordella & Paletti, 2019). A platform becomes closed when restrictions are placed on participation in its development (Eisenmann, Parker, & Van Alstyne, 2009). The internal platform is closed because platform development is based only on internal capabilities and the sources of innovation of the platform owner's organization. Many digital government platforms providing routine public services to citizens or supporting cross-agency data exchanges are still categorized as internal and closed platforms because those citizens or actors from other agencies are merely users of the platform and will not directly contribute to the development of the platform. A platform becomes semi-open when its restrictions are relaxed on the supply side of the platform (Eisenmann et al., 2009). Supply chain platforms are semi-open and allow for development and innovation between the platform owner and its pool of suppliers (Gawer, 2014). Accordingly, collaborative platforms with semi-openness allow the platform owner to assemble capabilities and resources from other government agencies in alignment with the development of platform components. This situation often occurs with national and local government agencies that share their knowledge and collaborate in service production (Chen et al., 2019; Cordella & Paletti, 2019). Collaboration does not casually happen, but the agencies in collaboration have resources and capabilities that complement each other and share accountability and public service provision. Industry platforms are open with no restrictions on participation in development and use on either side of the platform (Eisenmann et al., 2009). Similarly, open government platforms, such as OGD platforms, allow everyone (including public and private actors) who obey the platform's basic rules to create services according to their interests.

Platform owners can adopt different levels of openness between completely closed and open to configure their coordination mechanisms. A higher level of openness could make a government platform more transparent by providing insight into its functioning and government data, and at the same time, the government exerts less intervention (Janssen & Estevez, 2013). If a platform is too closed, it keeps potentially desirable participants out; if it is too open, then there can be other value-destroying effects, such as poor quality contributions or misbehavior by some participants (Van Alstyne, Parker, & Choudary, 2016).

Modular Architecture

Platform architecture leverages the development of shared assets, designs, and standards that can be recombined to facilitate coordination within and between agencies sharing a given platform (Thomas et al., 2014). With a large degree of consensus, modular architecture is an essential feature of digital platforms of any type (Constantinides, Henfridsson, & Parker, 2018; Gawer & Cusumano, 2014). Platform architecture and modularity make a distinction between the platform core, consisting of tightly coupled components, and loosely coupled peripheral components (Constantinides et al., 2018). At the same time, design rules coordinate the interoperation among modules or between modules and the platform infrastructure (Cordella & Paletti, 2019). Kapoor et al. (2021) summarize these understandings, suggesting that platforms possess a small but stable, set of core components for establishing foundational standards, and a larger set of peripheral components that are essential to enable flexibility. Across different types of platforms, there is a fundamental trade-off couched in terms of stability and flexibility. If more modules interact with the complements, then there exists a higher interdependence among such modules, resulting in higher stability but lower flexibility (Cennamo & Santaló, 2019). As the platform core is managed by the platform owner, while the periphery is mainly contributed by complementors, it also shares the responsibility for service delivery and managing the complexity of the services involved among the various partners (Mukhopadhyay et al., 2019).

Generativity and Control

Literature on commercial digital platforms largely accounts for platforms' success based on the platforms' generative capabilities grounded in modular architectures and flexibility (e.g., Eaton et al., 2015; Ghazawneh & Henfridsson, 2013). At the same time, scholars also indicate the need to balance the paradoxical tension between generativity and control in the platform (e.g., Constantinides et al., 2018; Yoo et al., 2010). There is a need for digital platforms to remain stable to maintain a solid foundation for further enrollment, and at the same time, to be sufficiently flexible to support growth and evolution (Tilson, Lyytinen, & Sørensen, 2010). Implementing the controls necessary to achieve these dual goals of being simultaneously stable and evolving is very much aligned with the layered modular architecture of digital platforms (Constantinides et al., 2018).

Little is known about how the tension between generativity and control unfolds and affects the evolution of the digital government platform (Gong & Li, 2023). The levels of control associated with public services differ by hierarchical levels and accountability (e.g., national or local) and the importance of services (e.g., issuing a passport or providing a public bus schedule) (Cordella & Paletti, 2019). This reflects that the configuration of control in digital government platforms is highly contextualized. From a technical perspective, internal platforms for serious public services often employ a centralized and role-based control paradigm. Currently, role-based control is still the most widely used control paradigm in which functions of modules may be accessed by users fulfilling a specific role within the business process of the organization (Mundbrod & Reichert, 2019). Collaborative and open government platforms that facilitate the creation of public services with external parties embed a medium or low level of control to allow an increase in generativity (Cordella & Paletti, 2019). The control mechanisms in these platforms are often data-centric. This is especially the case with OGD platforms, in which the platform concerns the provision of modules as datasets rather than as software functionality to external parties (Bonina & Eaton, 2020). Data-centric control emphasizes monitoring, optimization, and organizational responsiveness to facilitate value cocreation (Cennamo & Santaló, 2019). Tilson et al. (2010) suggest observing and understanding changes in control paradigms by the change in control points. Janssen et al. (2020) show that government can consider the setting of control points at an organizational or system level and a data level. Furthermore, a hybrid control strategy can be created by applying differentiated solutions at different levels. For example, combining high control in platform organization involvement with low control in the usage of technology may result in better collaboration with trusted and serious agencies, avoid overcrowding of partners, and reduce integration efforts (Mukhopadhyay et al., 2019).

RESEARCH METHOD

Research Context

This research presents a demonstrative case study that was conducted in the State Taxation Administration (STA) of the People's Republic of China. The STA is responsible for planning and developing the national platform of tax administration, which provides various tax services. This national platform is developed and maintained in a long-term project format. It is currently in the third stage, called the Golden Tax Project III (GTP III). Since October 2016, the GTP III platform has been online to serve nationwide tax administration. The GTP III platform is a huge and complex system that supports the daily work of more than 700,000 taxation staff throughout the country, serving tens of millions of enterprise taxpayers and hundreds of millions of natural person taxpayers. Through its cloud infrastructure, the GTP III platform has centralized the storage and management of data from all local tax administrative divisions since the beginning of 2019. The next step in the STA's digital transformation agenda is to enable standardized, integrative, and taxpayer-centric tax services through innovative use of the data. Given the large scale and high complexity of the platform, coordinating various local agencies under different hierarchical levels of administrative divisions and tax categories for integrative service production and delivery is a great challenge. The STA would like to explore the value of the data while using data from various local tax services under control.

Data Collection

This chapter presents the findings of our case study from November 2018 to December 2020. During this case study, we observed the development of a collaborative platform for service innovation. To understand the service production approach in the GTP III platform, 16 documents, including the system requirements, data architecture, and service form design documents, were collected. Thereafter, five interviews and two workshops with tax experts from the GTP III department and software experts from their contracted vendor company were conducted.

FINDINGS

Challenges

The original platform was designed with "infrastructure thinking" to support the individual local agency with technical infrastructure to develop its own datasets, business processes, and digital forms for tax service delivery. The platform organization and its coordination followed the taxation administrative divisions in a hierarchical structure. The system was a shared infrastructure supporting many internal platforms in which local agencies developed tax services with their own data sources and expertise. Although the GTP III platform centralized data storage at the beginning of 2019, the platform owner and many local agencies still suffer from the data silos that the separate local agencies created under different hierarchical levels of administrative divisions and tax categories. The coordination for internal platforms cannot support cross-agency collaboration, in which high-quality data are expected to be shared among agencies to enable taxpayer-centric service design and production. The GTP III platform needs new coordination mechanisms to enable flexibility in creating integrative services and ensuring accountability in collaboration at the same time.

The GTP III platform manages a large volume of tax data from different sources. The data provided by local agencies vary in definitions and statistical scopes, leading to data silo problems. Data silos cannot be solved simply by process reengineering with authorization for cross-agency data access and sharing, because some data objects with the same nomenclature can have different semantic meanings, while others have the same semantic meaning with different nomenclatures. Furthermore, a few data objects are consistent in both nomenclatures and semantic meanings, but they are generated by applying different statistical methods. Solving this problem demands data quality and interoperability beyond the unified processes, forms, and rules for nomenclature. Finally, coordination is needed to ensure that tax data are produced consistently.

The data silos do not just exist in different levels of administrative divisions but can also appear in different tax categories. A large amount of data was accumulated by separate departments that were established to implement tax services under different tax categories. The GTP III department expects to reuse data to avoid repeating input from taxpayers. This requirement is also challenging as much of the data were provided with coarse granularity and are difficult to reuse. To enable data reusability, data objects should be divided into data items with fine granularity and a proper coordination mechanism to identify and connect them.

Centralization in data storage increases the amount of accessible data but also makes it difficult to find the required data and understand the semantic connections among data. During workshops and interviews, both tax staff and analysts admitted to the problem of data awareness: "sometimes we are not aware whether the GTP III platform has the data that we need to create a new tax service. This results in redundant input, difficulty in maintaining data relationships, and the aggravation of data silos in the long run." At the same time, the GTP III department had difficulty tracking the usage of data in each tax service because there are too many tax forms, and checking each form via current user interfaces manually would be very time-consuming. To ensure data awareness and the maintainability of data relationships, users need an easy-to-use data index that can manage and indicate the relationships among data and between data and forms.

Developing a Collaborative Platform

To address the above challenges, a pilot platform was developed to provide new coordination tools and interfaces. The first one is an architectural solution that helps restructure the modular platform architecture. This architectural design aims to enable data modularity and to develop a stable core of data modules. Corresponding to this architectural design, tax experts from the GTP III department were involved in developing a data architecture. The most important part of this data architecture design is a formal enterprise data model that contains comprehensive data and metadata definitions, logical structures of data items (data mapping), and the data use relationships with tax categories and business units. This enterprise data model worked as a data standard for building various data models in the later stages. It defines the basic data relationships shared by the data modules and the basic rules to define how they interoperate. As the unified data standard is provided to all the agencies, it creates the foundation of platform openness.

The second one focused on data modeling and management functions. These functions address the data awareness problem by providing data modeling tools with data visualization to present data relationships. In this development, the toughest work was to clean the tax data and model the data relationships among data items by following the provided enterprise data model and improving it iteratively. A tax expert reflected on the necessity for this work, stating, "only by reviewing all data items that constitute the data objects, the data objects with the same semantics but from different sources could be checked and compared." In this way, the data standard can be compiled, and data objects from different sources with the same semantics can coalesce. Local agencies that want to use these data objects to build tax services must follow the relevant data relationships and constraints. At the same time, data items contained in these data objects can be visualized to offer data awareness. These data models also enable data access control. The use of extra data items that are not compliant with the data relationship would be constrained. Although it was time-consuming to build many data models, common data items can be linked and used in different data objects. This increased data reusability, consequently reducing redundancy and the efforts for data maintenance. Since the data models are visible to all agencies, the platform transparency is increased.

The third component is the interface for service design that provides service developers (local agencies) with a design studio to create interactable forms for taxpayers. Once the user selects a certain data object, the relevant data items are listed for further selection. If any necessary data item is missing, or a data item is no longer needed in a data object, the developer may play the role of the contributor and suggest adding, changing, or removing the data item. In addition to service production, the system also provides a visualization of the data items used in a tax form for data auditing. In this way, the platform's generativity is provided to enable the development and improvement of data models and further support the development of various tax services.

These new digital coordination tools and interfaces have facilitated flexibility and service production efficiency in the STA. In the past, each taxation department focused on its own services and tax forms for a specific tax category. Little consideration was given to reusing data across different tax categories, and forms were provided for single tax reporting. By using the new coordination tools and interfaces, the data objects and items used in the tax forms created by other departments are visible to all service designers. This improves their awareness of whether the same data are used by other tax forms, resulting in cooperation in designing comprehensive forms for multiple tax categories. This also enables the sharing of knowledge among people and enhances the accessibility of business knowledge in tax form (re)design. A tax expert working in the GTP III department for business operations commented on this exercise that "it increased very much the efficiency in screening, comparing, and correlating between data items and forms, and consequently enhanced the efficiency in business analysis and collaboration in service production." The new coordination configuration reduces redundant functions and duplicate work, as well as facilitates collaboration among government agencies.

Transforming to a Collaborative Platform

A collaborative platform needs more openness than an internal platform. While the development of new platform components presents how technical tools and interfaces support openness, the new configuration of coordination also requires the STA to reshape the corresponding organizational form to access external resources and capabilities for the development of the GTP III platform. The large volume of data accumulated in the GTP III platform and different tax categories requires specific expertise for developing and maintaining data models. Rather than relying only on the GTP III department's own resources to develop all data models, the STA opened data modeling functionality and interfaces to tax experts from various local agencies to facilitate the data modeling. A tax expert from the GTP III department explained this new organizational form in which "it was not possible for the team to manage the modeling of such a large number of data models. Experts from local agencies joining as contributors speeded up the modeling and increased the quality of models and the tax staff's acceptance of using those data models, as they participated in the modeling." The new organizational form was not a top-down planned design by the STA, but a bottom-up emergence during the iterations of the platform and data model development. When an increasing number of local agencies participated in the development of data models, the organizational form of the GTP III platform evolved into a collaborative platform ecosystem. The role of local agencies can be either contributors or developers depending on whether they are building or improving data modules or using the data modules to develop tax services. Since the models and data logic are visible to both national and local agencies, the transparency of the platform increases along with openness.

A collaborative platform needs a modular architecture to balance the core and periphery. Given the data silo problems faced by the STA, modularity was considered not only with the software architecture but also with the data architecture of the GTP III platform. While the software architecture has been relatively stable since 2016, adding the data architecture results in the need for new software functions in the interface that allow data visualization and inference based on data relationships. The role of these semantic and data visualization technologies in this study is to implement new interface artifacts to coordinate between the core and the periphery. By implementing these instruments, the GTP III department could focus on supporting, authorizing, and monitoring the use of datasets and data models, leaving the creation of integrative services to the relevant collaborating local agencies. Flexible and integrative tax services could emerge from self-organizing among local agencies in the collaborative platform ecosystem.

Coordination based on data relationships and accessibility is needed to balance generativity and control. Control mechanisms could be addressed on a technical level, for example, inside or between tax services, and on an organizational level, for example, the authority for an agency or cross-agency collaborations. At the technical level, the relationships among data items are managed by the given data models for certain data objects. At the organizational level, the STA can facilitate or constrain cross-agency collaboration by assigning or changing the accessibility of data objects to local agencies. In this way, the working scope of a local agency is defined by the data accessibility assigned to it. Data sharing among agencies can be achieved without many normal bilateral negotiations or the configuration of extra user roles and accounts to access data owned by the other side.

IMPLICATIONS

This case study provides three implications for government platform practitioners. Like application programming interfaces (APIs) that allow software developers to have their applications interact with the platform, unified data standards allow local agencies to understand the accessible data and connect their services and data models with the shared datasets. In this sense, data standards regulate data interoperation and enable openness. A collaborative platform requires transparent protocols, rules for the exchange of data, and conflict resolution. The first implication is, therefore, to provide data standards to address the need for platform openness and transparency. The standards regulate how data items within a data object are described, defined, and represented on the platform for sharing across agencies. These standards contribute to ensuring data quality and interoperability.

Modular architecture is an essential design feature of digital platforms that allows the platform to recombine modules for creating new products or services. The discussion of modularity in platform literature often focuses on the combinatorial nature of software modules, that is, autonomous software modules and sophisticated module interfaces (Nambisan et al., 2017). However, software modularity does not necessarily support or reflect the need for and effect of coordination in digital service provision (Gkeredakis & Constantinides, 2019). Considering that a digital government platform might deliver many services to citizens via unified digital channels, the creation and delivery of different services might rely on similar software functionality but vary in the content of services for different citizens. In comparison with many commercial platforms, a distinction of such government platforms is the provision of modules as datasets, rather than software functionality (Bonina & Eaton, 2020). The second implication, therefore, relates to structuring the core and the periphery concerning the sharing and reuse of datasets in digital government platforms. Based on the designed data modularity and the provision of an interface to interact with data modules, the platform allows agencies to both contribute to the development of data models and use the models in service production.

The paradoxical tension between generativity and control has been widely discussed in platform research (Constantinides et al., 2018; Yoo et al., 2010). While the control mechanism is often discussed in the context of very open platform ecosystems (open government platforms), little is known about the coordination configurations in semi-open platforms (collaborative platforms). Tilson et al. (2010) suggest taking the view of control points to understand the change of control both in its levels and paradigm. Our study found that applying digital technologies to implement new platform coordination mechanisms may result in setting new control points. Proving data relationships may also facilitate data awareness by providing accessibility to the existing data models and, consequently, enabling generativity. In contrast, data accessibility constrains the use of data in service production. Digital technologies play a specific role in designing and implementing possible control points. The involvement of new digital technologies may result in changes in the control points and further influence the digital coordination configurations.

CONCLUSION

Implementing a proper coordination mechanism to improve cross-agency collaboration in public service production is a significant challenge for governments on a digital platform journey. To guide platform development, governments need to understand how the rise of different types of digital government platforms affects the scope of coordination. This practice often lacks theoretical support because platform theory, rooted in commercial platforms, has not considered the different scopes and focuses of digital government platforms. By reinterpreting platform theory in the context of digital government, we propose a theoretical framework spanning organizational forms and platform features for considering coordination configurations. This framework was tested by a case study in which the GTP III platform transformed from an internal platform to a collaborative platform. The case study demonstrates how the coordination mechanism for the collaborative platform was implemented to address the problems concerning data silos and lack of data awareness.

The findings indicate that the framework could be used to explain digital government platform transformations. This study also provides several lessons on digital coordination in government platforms. From a sociotechnical perspective, organizational forms, openness, modularity, and generativity are the general features to be addressed in coordination configurations. In the development of platform coordination mechanisms, three paradoxical tensions—openness and closeness, the core and the periphery (stability and flexibility), and generativity and control—should be considered when making design decisions. Digital government platform owners should define unified data standards, design data modularity and interfaces, and use data relationships and accessibility as control points to balance these paradoxical tensions. Finally, government platform owners should switch from "infrastructure thinking" to "platform thinking" to cultivate collaborative platform ecosystems that allow flexible and integrative public services to emerge from bottom-up collaboration among agencies.

Our study has some limitations that should be addressed in future research. We did not fully address the fuzziness and possibility of transformation among the types of platforms. In commercial platform theories, Gawer (2014) suggests possible evolutionary pathways among the three types of digital platforms. This study presents only one pathway in which the GTP III platform evolved from an internal platform to a collaborative platform. While we confirm the evolutionary view and fluidity among the types of digital government platforms, it also reflects, to some extent, the dynamics and fuzziness among the types. In the research on GaaP, Cordella and Paletti (2019) claim that a digital government platform may be a platform of platforms, where internal, supply chain, and industry platforms coexist and interact. This fuzziness reflects the need for further development of theory and design knowledge to address the dynamics and multiplicity of modes of digital government platforms in the future.

REFERENCES

Baldwin, C.Y., & Woodard, C.J. (2009). The architecture of platforms: A unified view. In A. Gawer (Ed.), *Platforms, Markets and Innovation* (pp. 19–44). Cheltenham, UK and Northampton, MA, US: Edward Elgar Publishing.

Barnard, C.I. (1938). *The Functions of the Executive*. Cambridge, MA: Harvard University Press.

Bharadwaj, A., El Sawy, O.A., Pavlou, P.A., & Venkatraman, N. (2013). Digital business strategy: Toward a next generation of insights. *MIS Quarterly*, 37(2), 471–82.

Bonina, C., & Eaton, B. (2020). Cultivating open government data platform ecosystems through governance: Lessons from Buenos Aires, Mexico City and Montevideo. *Government Information Quarterly*, 37(3), 101479.

Boudreau, K. (2010). Open platform strategies and innovation: Granting access vs. devolving. *Management Science*, 56(10), 1849–72.

Brown, A., Fishenden, J., Thompson, M., & Venters, W. (2017). Appraising the impact and role of platform models and Government as a Platform (GaaP) in UK Government public service reform: Towards a Platform Assessment Framework (PAF). *Government Information Quarterly*, 34(2), 167–82.

Cennamo, C., & Santaló, J. (2019). Generativity tension and value creation in platform ecosystems. *Organization Science*, 30(3), 617–41.

Chen, Y.-C., Hu, L.-T., Tseng, K.-C., Juang, W.-J., & Chang, C.-K. (2019). Cross-boundary e-government systems: Determinants of performance. *Government Information Quarterly*, 36(3), 449–59.

Ciborra, C.U. (1996). The platform organization: Recombining strategies, structures, and surprises. *Organization Science*, 7(2), 103–18.

Constantinides, P., Henfridsson, O., & Parker, G.G. (2018). Introduction—platforms and infrastructures in the digital age. *Information Systems Research*, 29(2), 381–400.

Cordella, A., & Paletti, A. (2019). Government as a platform, orchestration, and public value creation: The Italian case. *Government Information Quarterly*, 36(4), 101409.

Dawes, S.S., Vidiasova, L., & Parkhimovich, O. (2016). Planning and designing open government data programs: An ecosystem approach. *Government Information Quarterly*, 33(1), 15–27.

de Reuver, M., Sørensen, C., & Basole, R.C. (2018). The digital platform: A research agenda. *Journal of Information Technology*, 33(2), 124–35.

Eaton, B., Elaluf-Calderwood, S., Sørensen, C., & Yoo, Y. (2015). Distributed tuning of boundary resources: The case of Apple's iOS Service System. *MIS Quarterly*, 39(1), 217–44.

Eisenmann, T.R., Parker, G., & Van Alstyne, M. (2009). Opening platforms: When, how and why? In A. Gawer (Ed.), *Platforms, Markets and Innovation* (pp. 131–62). Cheltenham, UK and Northampton, MA, USA: Edward Elgar Publishing.

Gawer, A. (2014). Bridging differing perspectives on technological platforms: Toward an integrative framework. *Research Policy*, 43(7), 1239–49.

Gawer, A., & Cusumano, M.A. (2014). Industry platforms and ecosystem innovation. *Journal of Product Innovation Management*, 31(3), 417–33.

Ghazawneh, A., & Henfridsson, O. (2013). Balancing platform control and external contribution in third-party development: The boundary resources model. *Information Systems Journal*, 23(2), 173–92.

Gkeredakis, M., & Constantinides, P. (2019). Phenomenon-based problematization: Coordinating in the digital era. *Information and Organization*, 29(3), 100254.

Gong, Y., & Li, X. (2023). Designing boundary resources in digital government platforms for collaborative service innovation. *Government Information Quarterly*, 40(1), 101777.

Gong, Y., Yang, J., & Shi, X. (2020). Towards a comprehensive understanding of digital transformation in government: Analysis of flexibility and enterprise architecture. *Government Information Quarterly*, 37(3), 101487.

Henfridsson, O., & Bygstad, B. (2013). The generative mechanisms of digital infrastructure evolution. *MIS Quarterly*, 37(3), 907–31.

Hughes, H.P.N., Clegg, C.W., Bolton, L.E., & Machon, L.C. (2017). Systems scenarios: A tool for facilitating the socio-technical design of work systems. *Ergonomics*, 60(10), 1319–35.

Janssen, M., & Estevez, E. (2013). Lean government and platform-based governance–doing more with less. *Government Information Quarterly*, 30(1), S1–S8.

Janssen, M., Brous, P., Estevez, E., Barbosa, L.S., & Janowski, T. (2020). Data governance: Organizing data for trustworthy Artificial Intelligence. *Government Information Quarterly*, 37(3), 101493.

Jarvenpaa, S.L., & Standaert, W. (2018). Digital probes as opening possibilities of generativity. *Journal of the Association for Information Systems*, 19(10), 982–1000.

Jin, L., & Robey, D. (2008). Bridging social and technical interfaces in organizations: An interpretive analysis of time-space distanciation. *Information and Organization*, 18(3), 177–204.

Kapoor, K., Bigdeli, A.Z., Dwivedi, Y.K., Schroeder, A., Beltagui, A., & Baines, T. (2021). A socio-technical view of platform ecosystems: Systematic review and research agenda. *Journal of Business Research*, 128, 94–108.

Kretschmer, T., Leiponen, A., Schilling, M., & Vasudeva, G. (2022). Platform ecosystems as meta-organizations: Implications for platform strategies. *Strategic Management Journal*, 43(3), 405–24.

Lange, P., Driessen, P.P.J., Sauer, A., Bornemann, B., & Burger, P. (2013). Governing towards sustainability—conceptualizing modes of governance. *Journal of Environmental Policy & Planning*, 15(3), 403–25.

Malone, T.W., & Crowston, K. (1994). The interdisciplinary study of coordination. *ACM Computing Surveys*, 26(1), 87–119.

Mukhopadhyay, S., Bouwman, H., & Jaiswal, M.P. (2019). An open platform centric approach for scalable government service delivery to the poor: The Aadhaar case. *Government Information Quarterly*, 36(3), 437–48.

Mundbrod, N., & Reichert, M. (2019). Object-specific role-based access control. *International Journal of Cooperative Information Systems*, 28(1), 1950003.

Nambisan, S. (2017). Digital entrepreneurship: Toward a digital technology perspective of entrepreneurship. *Entrepreneurship Theory and Practice*, 41(6), 1029–55.

Nambisan, S., Lyytinen, K., Majchrzak, A., & Song, M. (2017). Digital innovation management: Reinventing innovation management research in a digital world. MIS Quarterly, 41(1), 223–38.

O'Reilly, T. (2011). Government as a platform. *Innovations*, 6(1), 13–40.

Rolland, K.H., Mathiassen, L., & Rai, A. (2018). Managing digital platforms in user organizations: The interactions between digital options and digital debt. *Information Systems Research*, 29(2), 419–43.

Schreieck, M., Wiesche, M., & Krcmar, H. (2017). Governing nonprofit platform ecosystems – an information platform for refugees. *Information Technology for Development*, 23(3), 618–43.

Senyo, P.K., Effah, J., & Osabutey, E.L.C. (2021). Digital platformisation as public sector transformation strategy: A case of Ghana's paperless port. *Technological Forecasting and Social Change*, 162, 120387.

Thomas, L.D.W., Autio, E., & Gann, D.M. (2014). Architectural leverage: Putting platforms in context. *Academy of Management Perspectives*, 28(2), 198–219.

Tilson, D., Lyytinen, K., & Sørensen, C. (2010). Research commentary—digital infrastructures: The missing IS research agenda. *Information Systems Research*, 21(4), 748–59.

Tiwana, A., Konsynski, B., & Bush, A.A. (2010). Research commentary—platform evolution: Coevolution of platform architecture, governance, and environmental dynamics. *Information Systems Research*, 21(4), 675–87.

Van Alstyne, M.W., Parker, G.G., & Choudary, S.P. (2016). Pipelines, platforms, and the new rules of strategy. *Harvard Business Review*, 94(4), 54–60, 62.

Van de Ven, A.H., Delbecq, A.L., & Koenig, R., Jr. (1976). Determinants of coordination modes within organizations. *American Sociological Review*, 41(2), 322–38.

Wang, C., Medaglia, R., & Zheng, L. (2018). Towards a typology of adaptive governance in the digital government context: The role of decision-making and accountability. *Government Information Quarterly*, 35(2), 306–22.

Warner, K.S.R., & Wäger, M. (2019). Building dynamic capabilities for digital transformation: An ongoing process of strategic renewal. *Long Range Planning*, 52(3), 326–49.

Yoo, Y., Henfridsson, O., & Lyytinen, K. (2010). The new organizing logic of digital innovation: An agenda for information systems research. *Information Systems Research*, 21(4), 724–35.

9. Implementing social media monitoring in the public sector: a four-model approach
Julián Villodre

INTRODUCTION

Public organizations have been implementing social media as part of their communication strategies for more than a decade. Social media has been helping public organizations to push institutional information, engage with citizens and encourage participation, provide limited transactions for service delivery, and boost collaboration (Criado & Villodre, 2021; DePaula et al., 2018; Mergel, 2013), both in routine and critical situations (Kavanaugh et al., 2012). Although there are potential limitations usually linked to social and political biases (Feeney & Porumbescu, 2021), public administrations have tried to use social media to have a presence wherever the citizen requires it.

But social media is not just about communication and interaction. Social media can also be an important source of data for public organizations. Social media data might help public organizations to detect trends and problems, and to improve policies and services (Bekkers et al., 2013; Driss et al., 2019; Loukis et al., 2017; Panagiotopoulos et al., 2017). This is done through social media monitoring, which can be defined as a body of methods and techniques that allow gathering and analyzing evidence from self- or user-generated content complying with a particular purpose (or set of purposes). The advantages and disadvantages it has in comparison to traditional monitoring techniques (such as citizen surveys) make it interesting for both researchers and practitioners (Agostino & Arnaboldi, 2017; Loukis et al., 2017; Mergel, 2017; Reddick et al., 2017; Severo et al., 2016). There have been efforts to assess social media monitoring from several perspectives, ranging from its purpose and expected outcomes, its relation with the policy process, the type of evidence it provides, or the risks and challenges that it entails, among others. This opens up an opportunity to systematize and integrate knowledge on social media monitoring in a way that might help approach good practices and avoid compromising ones.

This chapter draws on this opportunity and tries to answer the following question: How can social media monitoring be implemented in the public sector? I propose four different models of social media monitoring to approach this question: a performance model, an opinion model, a collaborative model, and a behavioral model. The performance model of social media monitoring focuses on the evaluation of the social media strategy by self-assessing the results (e.g., in terms of how well a public administration is doing in disseminating information). The opinion model uses social media monitoring as a way of gathering citizen opinions to detect and understand new problems and trends. The collaborative model depicts social media monitoring as a way of enabling crowdsourcing, gathering valuable citizen feedback to improve services and fight against complex problems. Finally, the behavioral model sees social media monitoring as a way of collecting and analyzing data that can be useful to predict or even modify citizen behavior. These models should not be considered as mutually exclusive. All four can coexist within an organization, and in no case should they be evaluated as better or worse. Instead, we should think about the extent to which they serve the purposes of each organization.

This chapter is structured as follows. First, I look at the concept of social media monitoring, its application to public sector needs, and its advantages/disadvantages in comparison to traditional monitoring techniques. Then, I review how the literature approaches the implementation of social media monitoring in the public sector. I do that by looking at the purpose and expected outcomes for social media monitoring, the tools and evidence used, the role the citizen has in this process, and the challenges this type of monitoring may entail. Thus, I use all these elements to propose four models of social media monitoring in the public sector.

CONCEPTUALIZING SOCIAL MEDIA MONITORING IN THE PUBLIC SECTOR

Social media are digital artifacts characterized by their high degree of interactivity and strong orientation towards the generation of content. Carr and Hayes (2015: 50) define social media as "internet-based channels that allow users to opportunistically interact and selectively self-present, either in real-time or asynchronously, with both broad and narrow audiences who derive value from user-generated content and the perception of interaction with others." This definition emphasizes several elements, such as the capacity to facilitate the generation of content by its users, the persistence and bidirectionality of communications, and the connectivity between actors. All of them relate to the very essence of these digital platforms: the activity of their users generates content and information, produced consciously (e.g., the posts and images uploaded by a user themself), but also unconsciously (e.g., metadata, such as the user's location or smartphone model) (Meijer & Potjer, 2018; Panagiotopoulos et al., 2017).

All this activity produces what we usually refer to as user-generated data. This data is regarded as highly valuable for private corporations as a way of discovering trends and knowing their customers' opinions and desires. But it is also valuable for public administrations. Particularly, public organizations might seek to obtain a specific type of user-generated data, labeled as citizen-generated data (Meijer & Potjer, 2018), which references debates and trends that can be encapsulated in the polity and policy world and be useful – or, at least, to some extent – for the realization of public goals (Panagiotopoulos et al., 2017). In order to gather and analyze this data, public administrations resort to social media monitoring (Bekkers et al., 2013; Loukis et al., 2017).

Social media monitoring in the public sector can be defined as a body of methods and techniques that allow a public organization to gather and analyze evidence from self- or citizen-generated social media content, complying with a particular public purpose (or set of purposes). As a method, it relies on a series of tools that may range from simply gathering descriptive metrics provided by a platform itself (such as the number of followers or the number of shares) to several forms of content analysis and natural language processing (like sentiment analysis) (Chung & Zeng, 2016; López-Chau et al., 2020; Nguyen et al., 2014). As a process, social media monitoring is usually undertaken in a continuous and systematic form (Fensel et al., 2012). Moreover, the analysis revolves around content pushed or promoted by the public organization (usually as a way to assess results or performance) (Mergel, 2013; Ruggiero & Vos, 2014), or plain citizen-generated content (posted by citizens having a natural conversation around a policy or service, or as a part of a crowdsourcing process) (Driss et al., 2019; Loukis et al., 2017; Panagiotopoulos et al., 2017). Finally, social media monitoring has an intended purpose, which might vary depending on the organization's capacity, as well as on the orientation of management itself (e.g., routine versus emergency situations) (Kavanaugh et al., 2012; Tarasconi et al., 2017), among others.

Social media monitoring is a new form of monitoring citizens' opinions and attitudes towards services and policies. Traditionally, public administrations have developed methods and techniques such as citizen surveys, public consultations, focus groups, and even relied on mass media, to accomplish such purposes (Androutsopoulou et al., 2015; Loukis et al., 2017; Severo et al., 2016). However, the data and evidence generated by these methods have not always been satisfactory. Decision-makers have reported ineffectiveness generated by delays, insufficient topics of interest, ineffective questions, and sometimes, an excessive top-down approach that may harm the overall quality and interest of the data. For example, Koshkin et al. (2017) refer to sociological surveys as a way of monitoring students' opinions and attitudes towards the administration of universities, reflecting that these surveys have problems with the questions and ways of evaluating, not giving a concrete image, for instance, of the emotional attitudes of students. Social media data can complement these surveys by drawing on spontaneous reactions and contextual cues (Agostino & Arnaboldi, 2017; Koshkin et al., 2017).

As such, social media monitoring has its own advantages. In comparison with traditional forms of monitoring, it is quicker, less expensive, and provides real-time insights (Androutsopoulou et al., 2015; Loukis et al., 2017; Panagiotopoulos et al., 2017; Ruggiero & Vos, 2014; Tarasconi et al., 2017). Social media data may reveal perceptions of citizens and services out of scope from a survey question, as this data relies on spontaneity (Loukis et al., 2017; Pencheva et al., 2020; Reddick et al., 2017). It can capture specific contexts (e.g., with hashtag searches) and provide detailed information on the impacts and agreement/disagreement, becoming what some have tagged as a "24/7 focus group" (Ruggiero & Vos, 2014). Moreover, it can also reveal new trends and make comparative analysis relatively easier between time points and demographically different audiences (Loukis et al., 2017). It also provides measures of performance, not only for the communication strategy (Mergel, 2013), but also on the citizens' posts, for example, by assessing the diffusion and relevance of messages.

However, in comparison to traditional ways of monitoring in the public sector, social media has several disadvantages. One of the most common, especially when compared with traditional surveys, is the lack of representativeness of populations in social media samples (Loukis et al., 2017; Mergel, 2017; Severo et al., 2016), which makes it difficult to make inferences that may be generalizable to the majority of the population. Another problem is related to the nature of social media audiences, which refers to the impossibility of public administrations to know "who I am listening to" and detect the appropriate targets, which may be relevant in collaborative processes and emergency situations (Marwick & Boyd, 2011; Panagiotopoulos et al., 2017; Villodre & Criado, 2020). Moreover, the information that citizens may provide to public administrations could have problems of reliability and bias (Feeney & Porumbescu, 2021; Harrison & Johnson, 2019), especially considering the nature of social media interactions and how prone they are to the creation of echo chambers and misinformation. Finally, social media monitoring may require additional capabilities, human resources, and technical requirements that might not be present in public organizations, such as particular analytical skills (Agostino & Arnaboldi, 2017; Mergel, 2017).

When surpassing some of these difficulties and disadvantages, the outcomes of social media monitoring can be quite beneficial. The integration of crowd capabilities gathered from social media platforms may help to rapidly detect problems and points of improvement in service delivery based on citizen opinions and reports, sending feedback to the appropriate departments (Criado & Villodre, 2021; Panagiotopoulos et al., 2017). Citizen-generated data may also be beneficial for fine-tuning policies or even facing certain wicked problems (Androutsopoulou et al., 2015), to which traditional expert-based committees have not reached a satisfactory solution. Social media monitoring could also be linked to evidence-based policymaking (Mergel, 2017; Panagiotopoulos et al., 2017; Grubmüller et al., 2013), a movement that prioritizes data-based inputs as an effort to restructure and reform policy processes (Giest, 2017). Overall, social media monitoring might drive several innovations (mostly crowdsourcing-based), depending on the levels of implication of citizens and public administrations (Loukis et al., 2017).

All in all, a big part of this literature has been dealing with the implementation of social media monitoring and its use in public organizations. With all of this information, there is an opportunity to try to systematize and integrate knowledge in a way that might help both scholars and practitioners approach social media monitoring. In this chapter, I draw on these efforts, aiming to look at social media monitoring implementation in the public sector around four different models. In the following section, I revise some of the most important elements from previous contributions to help me propose these models.

THE IMPLEMENTATION OF SOCIAL MEDIA MONITORING IN PUBLIC ADMINISTRATIONS

The implementation of social media monitoring navigates from positive to pessimistic perspectives. An optimistic view on social media monitoring usually entails the recognition of the complementary nature and utility of social media "soft-evidence" to provide new insights about trends, problems, and services (Panagiotopoulos et al., 2017). Pessimistic perspectives have many faces, usually materializing from concerns about privacy to hard surveillance situations (Scott, 2016). In this section, I draw insights from the literature on social media monitoring. I address the orientations and outcomes of social media monitoring, the tools and types of evidence generated, as well as its impact on the policy cycle, the consideration of citizens during the monitoring process, and the main challenges that surround the social media monitoring process in public organizations. These elements are then used to approach different models of social media monitoring in the public sector.

Orientations and Outcomes

A first important question regarding social media monitoring is related to the purpose and orientation it has. Based on the Habermas theory on communicative action, Bekkers et al. (2013) hypothesize three different orientations, characterizing organizational practices. First, a rational-instrumental approach, in which social media monitoring is interesting for finding out what is happening in the world, identifying trends and opinions of citizens, to later intervene with communication and even fine-tune policies and services. Second, and related to the first perspective, is the political-strategic approach, for which social media is used to explore the environment as a way of understanding actors' roles and power resources, calculate their alternatives, and calibrate one's own alternatives, affecting mitigation of policy resistances, avoiding damage to the reputation of the organization, and even influencing citizens' opinions and behaviors. Finally, a communicative approach looks at social media monitoring as a way of reaching consensus, trying to get feedback from citizens and to get them involved in the solution of complex problems.

These perspectives are a good starting point to understand how social media monitoring occurs and what the expected outcomes are in public administration practices. Literature has been generally positive about the potential of social media monitoring for gathering opinions and citizen ideas that might be useful for public administrations (Driss et al., 2019; Loukis et al., 2017; Panagiotopoulos et al., 2017). Projects such as "Unite Europe" (Grubmüller et al., 2013), have been in place to feed non-governmental organizations (NGOs) and public administrations with citizens' opinions. In that particular case, the project helped with the integration of immigrants, allowing public administrations to quickly detect trends and act accordingly (the authors exemplify this with the presence of many postings pointing out migrant discrimination in a particular entertainment facility, and integration specialists using these social media data to avoid further escalation by mediation service). Another example can be found in the study of higher education and university services (Agostino & Arnaboldi, 2017; Koshkin et al., 2017), in which social media data can be used to understand the satisfaction of students with the institution and also with administrative practices.

But dealing with these inputs is difficult. Maybe the missing link in most of these works is related to how these social media inputs are translated into specific outcomes (Hadi & Fleshler, 2016; Koshkin et al., 2017). The results of social media monitoring range from identifying potential problems, fine-tuning services, and co-producing (Agostino & Arnaboldi, 2017; Driss et al., 2019; Loukis et al., 2017; Panagiotopoulos et al., 2017; Tarasconi et al., 2017), to even the reinforcement of some nodality tools (Hood & Margetts, 2007), particularly informational and behavioral ones (Mergel, 2017). But how this is produced, how public administrations implementing social media monitoring deal with the potential problems of social media data, and how they eventually convert these inputs into potential solutions is largely uncovered.

Finally, when talking about social media monitoring, we tend to forget that social media is a tool used as part of a digital communicative strategy. Public administrations use social media mainly for communicative purposes (Criado & Villodre, 2021; DePaula et al., 2018; Mergel, 2013), pushing information to citizens. Thus, they are usually willing to know how effective these communicative strategies are and how the implementation of social media profiles is happening (Mergel, 2013). Social media monitoring can be used here as a self-assessment tool, to understand the reach and interest of the messages public administrations post on social media, and as a way of evaluating (usually in a very quantitative way) the reach and impact of messages.

Tools and Evidence

The data derived from the application of these tools has been considered from big data to open data. But a very interesting view on social media evidence is its consideration as soft data. Social media as soft data has the following features (Severo et al., 2016): (a) it is freely available on social media platforms, on "small" or "big" terms (depending on the user-generated activity), by daily conscious and unconscious activities; (b) it is easy to use and easily accessible through application programming interfaces (APIs) (Congosto, 2018) or by scraping; and (c) it is a bottom-up source, and it can be treated as a trace of public opinion. The way data can be analyzed may vary, from tools that help with basic descriptive metrics (often embedded in social media platforms), positional and relational statistics with social network analysis (Mergel, 2017), to the new automated natural language processing tools that can help with large amounts of data, classifying it in accordance with categories, sentiment, etc. (Chung & Zeng, 2016; López-Chau et al., 2020; Nguyen et al., 2014).

Social media might produce different evidence depending on the type of interaction we set. This might range from citizens' opinions and feedback to the use of certain network properties that reflect specific citizen behavior (Mergel, 2017). Panagiotopoulos et al. (2017), signaled some characteristics for evidence-based policymaking and social media, including the potential to discover conversations outside spaces of visibility through the power of keyword searches and network-based approaches, the nature of the samples (driven by participants' own engagement), the impact of platform characteristics in the construction of audiences, the immediate nature of input, its scalability, and the construction of more dynamic relations, among others.

The impacts of social media data can potentially be seen across all stages of the policy cycle depending on the nature of the data and purpose of monitoring (Driss et al., 2019; Panagiotopoulos et al., 2017; Pencheva et al., 2020). For example, big data can influence the policy cycle in many ways (Pencheva et al., 2020): (a) for agenda-setting and policy formulation, it can allow identifying problems and potential solutions in a more efficient, legitimate, and accountable way; (b) for policy implementation, it can help deliver services and enforce policies through collaborative strategic decisions, as well as support decision-making by enabling additional supervisory mechanisms to detect problems and irregularities; and (c) for evaluation, it can help obtain additional information about processes, through, for example, allowing the simultaneous observation of individual and aggregate variables. Moreover, as platforms with algorithmic properties, or to which artificial intelligence (AI) agents such as AI-guided chatbots can be integrated (Androutsopoulou et al., 2019), social media could follow the trends of AI and the potential transformations of the policy cycle. Authors such as Valle-Cruz et al. (2020), have discussed how the impacts of AI might transform the traditional way of conceiving the policy cycle into a more dynamic one, in which data feedback is constantly given through all phases of the cycle (e.g., there could be policy evaluation potentially across all phases), representing incremental spiral-based iterations rather than repetitive linear ones.

Citizen Consideration

Social media monitoring takes place between the interactions of citizens and public administrations. Thus, one of the most important aspects is to actually know how public administrations consider the citizens who use these platforms. The theory of public roles has systematized how public administrations may see citizens during these interactions (Thomas, 2013): (a) as customers, who consume services; (b) as partners, who might help co-produce services and co-design policies; or (c) citizens, who may deliberate about the status of services and policies, and critically assess the direction of the government. In its study of US cities' response to Hurricane Florence, Wukich (2021) applied this categorization, finding that most cities mainly considered citizens as customers and, to some extent, as partners. As customers, the focus of authorities during that emergency situation was informing citizens and ensuring the information was reaching the appropriate targets. As partners, authorities tried to gather some feedback from citizens. For example, Wukich (2021: 17) exemplifies this with the following post from Chapel Hill: "Be our eyes & ears! You can report #HurricaneFlorence issues, like blocked storm drains and downed trees, to the Town of Chapel Hill from your smartphone, tablet, or computer. Get the app today!" Although infrequently, these types of posts were promoted by the majority of the cities. However, only three of the 62 analyzed cities sought to gather citizens' opinions to discuss storm-related policymaking opportunities (Wukich, 2021). Thus, relegating the "citizen" role to the background.

A large part of the literature on social media monitoring has focused on reporting some of these crowd-based capabilities for service delivery and policymaking. For example, Panagiotopoulos et al. (2017) examined the perception of value of crowdsourcing in the use of social media around the UK Department of Environment, Food and Rural Affairs, through the impact of acquisition (the activity of sourcing content from citizens) and assimilation (the incorporation of crowdsourcing input to the policy process). The results showed that policymakers were satisfied with the immediacy and diversity of input, although they were concerned about the representation of the data sourced and the "noise" and useless nature of some of the collected content. Loukis et al. (2017) provide another good example on the study of three pilots on the promotion of open innovation through social media monitoring. There was a general agreement among policymakers and stakeholders that social media data was a good complement to knowing the opinions and perspectives about several issues, but they were skeptical about whether the results reflect the general opinion of a population and on its reliability.

However, the reality is that the participation of citizens on social media channels is, in the majority of cases, quite passive. Research on citizen roles on social media identifies that during routine or critical events, the vast majority of citizens are not oriented towards active content generation (González-Bailón et al., 2013). Some articles show that a large number of users do not use social media to produce content and that they will very sporadically favorite or share content from others (Congosto, 2018; Villodre & Criado, 2020). This activity may leave some unconscious data (e.g., number of visualizations of a public administration post) that could qualify for performance analysis, but not as a way of gathering relevant information from citizens with impacts on service delivery or policymaking.

Challenges

Setting up social media monitoring in the public sector is not problem-free. Because of the peculiar nature of the public sector in comparison with the private enterprise world, social media monitoring should be approached with caution, taking into consideration some challenges that may arise when gathering and using social media data. A first big challenge refers to the reliability of the data itself (Harrison & Johnson, 2019; Koshkin et al., 2017; Loukis et al., 2017; Severo et al., 2016). In their study of crowdsourcing around Canadian emergency management agencies, Harrison and Johnson (2019) stated that the majority of interviewed public managers found it difficult to work with citizen-generated data due to the lack of verification and potential concerns of being inaccurate, misleading, or directly false. And not without reason. For example, during the COVID-19 pandemic, Spanish fact-checker Maldita.es verified 1,299 misleading contents and fake information circulating on social media that were, in some cases, getting immense diffusion. The rise of fake news is particularly worrisome, even threatening the nature of democratic mechanisms (Lee, 2019; Olaniran & Williams, 2020). The persistence of echo chambers, and the increasingly toxic nature of relations inside social media platforms, does not help. Moreover, with the advances in Generative AI (Jo, 2023), the likelihood of AI-generated data fluctuating around social media adds more noise to the map, making it even harder to know what content we can consider real. All this makes social media data in the public sector difficult to use without prior intensive checks.

Even if social media data has the quality, the lack of representativeness might harm its usability. This challenge is strongly linked to reliability and refers to the fact that the people who use social media platforms and actively engage in its activities are quite special (Mergel, 2017). For example, the Pew Research Center (2021) has shown differences in how US adults use social media, such as by looking at age (most Instagram, Snapchat, and TikTok users are under 30). Pushing this data into policy processes can be problematic due to the fact that it may not represent the real opinions and feelings of the entire population (Mergel, 2017). It could also have effects on the impact of the digital divide (Harrison & Johnson, 2019). Thus, when integrating social media data in service delivery and public policies, we must admit, "that it will be very difficult not only to monitor the composition of observed samples but also to have a complete and comparable geographic coverage" (Severo et al., 2016: 359). The inclusion of social media data may reveal problems in the legitimacy of crowdsourcing initiatives and add complexity layers to data integration with other sources (Ruggiero & Vos, 2014).

Non-neutrality is another important challenge for social media monitoring. As Feeney and Porumbescu (2021: 780) have stated, technologies such as social media "are not simply neutral objects enacted by individual users in organizational contexts, but artifacts that embody political and social values, structures, inequalities, and systems." Social media is developed by third parties, and its development and administration are not under the control of public organizations (Mergel, 2013). Public administrations are, like citizens, just users of these platforms. This non-controlled environment opens the window to a wild west in which there are two potential perspectives. On the one hand, the content that public administrations will find on their users is not objective, but rather biased and conditioned. Citizens' actions may just be guided by their preconceptions and even by the way in which the affordances of these platforms, such as anonymity, are perceived (Stamati et al., 2015). On the other hand, this non-neutrality is not exclusive to citizens. Public organizations are, for the most part, entities that coexist with a dual political and administrative condition. Social media strategies are usually coordinated from departments very close to political power (Criado & Villodre, 2021). It is not uncommon to find cases in which institutional profiles are used in a political way. When this happens, social media monitoring can serve purposes that go beyond the improvement of public services, incurring under certain circumstances invasive techniques and potential risks for the privacy and freedom of citizens (Bekkers et al., 2013).

Connected with the previous point, another potential malpractice in social media monitoring may be in the hands of surveillance. Surveillance on social media may occur when public administrations follow this path (Bekkers et al., 2013): on the one hand, statements of users are systematically observed and analyzed; and, on the other hand, this observation and analysis is focused on influencing and modifying citizen behavior. An extreme case can be seen in the well-known scandal of Cambridge Analytica and the purchase of personal information of more than 80 million Facebook users with the intention of manipulating citizens during the 2016

US elections (Persily, 2017), with potentially perverse effects on the consideration of democracy (Olaniran & Williams, 2020). Another potential damage of surveillance is its impact on citizens' privacy, especially regarding the inclusion of certain information that might make citizens easily identifiable, particularly when integrating this data with other administrative sources (Mergel, 2017). Intensive surveillance, especially if intrusive, can threaten freedom of speech and silence those who have unpopular views, as shown with the monitoring of the Twitter hashtag #BlackLivesMatter by the Department of Homeland Security to assess reports that affected the image of the US government (Scott, 2016).

While privacy might be an underpinning principle for social media monitoring, transparency and accountability are more process-based. In particular, transparency challenges deal with how to appropriately scrutinize specific decisions and practices, while also providing spaces for citizens to be informed and discuss the development and orientation of monitoring practices (Bekkers et al., 2013). However, leaving spaces for effective monitoring might be difficult when public agencies have no clear strategy on citizen-generated data, or when they go deliberately opaque. Transparency might also be difficult to achieve due to data ownership problems (Morozov & Bria, 2018). Questions such as why private enterprises or public agencies could be using social media data without citizens' knowledge, or who is responsible for the misuse of data and the pernicious effects it may produce on populations, are some inquiries that citizens might legitimately ask. The concept of "democratic data ownership regimes" (Morozov & Bria, 2018), revolves around the idea of removing the power technological companies and governments have over data, dissolving it among multiple social and governmental actors with the objective of driving innovation and improving public services. However, there is still a need for data governance frameworks that integrate citizen collaboration deeply into the system (Ingrams, 2019).

Finally, there are more transversal challenges related to the capacities of public administrations in relation to social media monitoring, particularly, human capacities. Social media monitoring is an activity that requires a great amount of human resources, and to some extent, some technological resources too (Hadi & Fleshler, 2016). Scholars such as Driss et al. (2019), Panagiotopoulos et al. (2017), Mergel (2017), and Agostino and Arnaboldi (2017) signal a lack of human and automated analytical skills in the public sector that may affect less to more sophisticated perspectives on monitoring. Technological resources, such as the presence of appropriate tools to gather and analyze the data, are also a requirement (Chung & Zeng, 2016).

DISCUSSING POTENTIAL MODELS OF SOCIAL MEDIA MONITORING IN THE PUBLIC SECTOR

In this section, I attempt to systematize and integrate the knowledge from the different dimensions we looked at during the previous section, in a way that might help in approaching social media monitoring. The result of this is the conceptualization of four potential models for the implementation of social media monitoring in the public sector: the performance model, the opinion model, the collaborative model, and the behavioral model. They have differential characteristics from each other. However, this does not make them mutually exclusive. Several models, even all four, can coexist within an organization. In addition, these are ideal models, which in no case should be evaluated as better or worse. They must always serve the purposes of the organization. Table 9.1 presents a summary of the proposed models, which I explain in more detail below.

Performance Model

The first model of social media monitoring is what I call the performance model. The main idea behind this model is that public administrations use social media monitoring to evaluate their own communication strategy (Mergel, 2013). Monitoring is used to verify that the results set for the communication strategy are being met, using measurements such as the number of mentions, visualizations, impressions, follower count, or the number of favorites and shares,

Table 9.1   Four models for social media monitoring in the public sector

	Performance model	Opinion model	Collaborative model	Behavioral model
Purpose	Evaluate the results of the social media strategy	Gather opinions from citizens about the activities and services	Get citizens involved in the design of policies and delivery of public services	Predict or modify citizens' behavior to comply with public goals
Expected outcome	Improve communicative practices	Identify problems/trends	Improve policies and services, fight problems with the wisdom of the crowds	Reduce policy resistances, avoid reputation damage, reinforce nodality tools
Main tools	Platform properties and statistics	Content analysis, natural language processing	Quantitative data analysis, content analysis, natural language processing, AI systems	Quantitative data analysis, content analysis, natural language processing, network analysis, AI systems
Main evidence	Platform indicators (number of followers, shares, visualizations, etc.)	Citizen feedback	Citizen feedback	Citizen behavior (role, position in the network, sentiment, etc.)
Impact on the policy cycle mostly on	Policy evaluation	Agenda-setting, policy formulation, policy evaluation	Policy formulation, decision-making, policy implementation	Broad, across all stages
Citizen role	Customer	Citizen	Partner	Customer
Challenges	The tyranny of indicators	Lack of representativeness, non-neutrality	Reliability of information, non-neutrality	Surveillance, unethical behavioral modification

Source: Author's own elaboration.

to understand the reach and popularity of posted messages. Communication is considered as a service, and as such, public administrations want to know how interested or satisfied the public is with what they provide, and check if they are performing well in communicative terms. The role that the citizen is supposed to play is that of a mere consumer (Wukich, 2021). The citizen is a passive receiver of information, or interacts according to the organization's designs. The fact that the citizen shares or responds more to a publication is seen in a purely quantitative way, as an indicator of success.

Therefore, social media monitoring focuses on validating whether the communicative service provided through social media is adequate. The expected outcome of monitoring is to improve communication and offer information through social media that is interesting and valuable to the citizen. The strategy is purely evaluative, with the policy evaluation stage being the one that better reflects the integration of these instruments. It is just about evaluating a digital communication strategy. The best thing to do is to take advantage of the indications of impact that the platforms give to assess whether this objective is being met or not. In this model, public administrations do not conduct any excessively sophisticated analysis, and focus on the aggregated data provided by the platform's integrated functionalities. They usually use simple descriptive statistics to meet that goal.

The main challenge that public administrations could face with this model derives from the importance and focus given to the platform's quantitative indicators. This issue is directly linked to the famous adage attributed to the British economist Charles Goodhart: "when a measure becomes a target, it ceases to be a good measure." The tyranny of indicators in social media occurs when public organizations focus on turning the increase in followers or the number of favorites into an end in itself. In doing so, they completely forget about providing citizens with an enriching experience and focus only on obtaining an acceptable number of likes and shares. This approach potentially fails to disseminate information that, under certain circumstances, could also be useful. Having civil servants appropriately trained to understand how to approach social media indicators might be a good start to avoid this problem (Driss et al., 2019; Mergel, 2017).

Opinion Model

A potential second model for social media monitoring in the public sector is what I have called the opinion model. This model focuses on the use that many citizens make of social media to express their opinions on a wide variety of issues, from problems they have to issues related to the policies and public services (Agostino & Arnaboldi, 2017; Grubmüller et al., 2013; Koshkin et al., 2017). Public administrations can collect this information and try to use it to detect problems in services more quickly than with traditional monitoring mechanisms. In addition, they can use trend tracking to get ahead of citizen problems and explore potential solutions before it is too late. Public administrations collect opinions by monitoring, for example, direct mentions, or by searching for specific hashtags. Subsequently, and depending on the amount of information, they can use traditional content analysis techniques or automated natural language processing to analyze opinions and derive useful insights from them (López-Chau et al., 2020; Nguyen et al., 2014). It is, therefore, a perspective with a more qualitative focus.

The opinion model places great value on the opinions of citizens. They are considered as feedback, which public organizations must process and incorporate as part of their service improvement and policy fine-tuning (Bekkers et al., 2013). This model considers that the fundamental role of the citizen is to position themselves around constructive criticism towards the manner of proceeding and acting by public administrations, seeking accountability and improvement of services and public policies. Thus, opinions have fundamental impacts on agenda-setting processes, allowing public decision-makers to turn social media into a kind of "citizen thermometer" with which to identify problems, analyze their relevance, and potentially incorporate them from the informal into the institutional agenda. Citizen opinions can also serve as part of the public policy formulation stage, as a way of guiding possible solutions to problems. Finally, citizen opinions can also serve towards policy evaluation, as a way of detecting if a policy or service is working as intended.

There are two fundamental challenges in this model that public administrations must take into consideration. First, the critical spirit of citizens on social media is very often confused with noise and an expression of anger towards organizations, becoming, in the worst case, even disrespectful. Unfortunately, this content is hardly usable by a public administration and might even discourage active listening practices (Harrison & Johnson, 2019). Moreover, unlike traditional opinion surveys, which are based on representative samples of the population, social media samples are non-representative and biased by default, sometimes making it very difficult to establish generalizations that can be extrapolated to the general population (Androutsopoulou et al., 2015; Severo et al., 2016).

Collaborative Model

A third model for implementing social media monitoring in the public sector is what I have labeled as collaborative. This model is closely linked to the practices of crowdsourcing, open innovation, and co-production of services and policies (Loukis et al., 2017; Panagiotopoulos et al., 2017). In this model, the opinion of citizens is not as important as the knowledge they may have (or generate) about certain problems. In concrete circumstances, either because the problem the public organization faces is very complex, or because the organization's capacities are exceeded (e.g., during an emergency situation) (Kavanaugh et al., 2012), public administrations try to capture the so-called wisdom of the crowds. The general objective of social media monitoring is to gather citizen-generated data to improve public services and, in many cases, to collaborate with citizens in the co-design of policies and in the co-production of services. Therefore, the role of the citizen is that of a partner, co-producer of services, and close collaborator with the public administration (Wukich, 2021).

The nature of the crowdsourcing phenomenon means that the potential results are quite heterogeneous. It is enough to look at the list of citizen-generated data initiatives cataloged by Meijer and Potjer (2018) to have an idea of the vast amount of possibilities. This means that the types of tools used may vary a lot. Initiatives such as Weather Amateurs (https://wow.knmi.nl/) or the SINOBAS (https://www.aemet.es/es/eltiempo/observacion/sinobas) network in Spain show, for example, how all those citizens interested in meteorology can collaborate openly with public administrations and send information on weather events from their home-based weather stations. In this way, public administrations can cover meteorological information in areas where it is not easy to have professional equipment. The data collected in these initiatives is mostly quantitative. Other crowdsourcing initiatives are based on citizen conversation (think of platforms like Challenge.gov, where challenges are posted by public administrations and citizen participation is encouraged) (Mergel & Desouza, 2013). This type of information may require content analysis. The implementation of AI tools such as AI-guided chatbots could also drive collaborative monitoring practices. These intelligent systems might be capable of freeing public administrations from pressure regarding certain citizen questions in complex environments (Androutsopoulou et al., 2019), or even acting as moderating agents, while collecting information on citizen consultations that can be integrated as part of crowdsourcing challenges. All these citizen-generated data have a clear impact on the public policy process, fundamentally on finding solutions to public problems (policy formulation), during the decision-making process (as citizens can also be involved to a certain extent in some of the decisions), and for the implementation of policies and services.

There are two fundamental challenges that public administrations could face with this monitoring model. First, the reliability of citizen knowledge is not always going to be good or sufficient to be integrated into the routines and processes of the public organization (Harrison & Johnson, 2019). This may be because the information generated is not detailed enough, contains inaccuracies, or sometimes because it may be outright false. Public administrations must be very careful when working with data generated by citizens and verify that the information is reliable, a revision process that is costly in terms of resources and time. On the other hand, the non-neutrality of digital spaces means that biases can potentially creep into these processes (Feeney & Porumbescu, 2021), so public administrations must be very careful to refine and analyze the information.

Behavioral Model

Finally, the fourth model of social media monitoring is what I describe as the behavioral model. For the behavioral model, the fundamental objective of social media monitoring is to predict citizen behavior and, under certain circumstances, use the data and information collected to modify it. Unlike the opinion and collaborative models, the role of the citizen in the behavioral model is more passive, acting as a mere consumer. There is no collaboration with the public administration, or at least not consciously (as public administrations still need citizens to be performing actions). Often, monitoring will occur silently, without the citizen's knowledge.

In general terms, the results of the behavioral model can be quite broad. If the objective is to predict citizen behavior, public administrations will apply holistic perspectives of data analysis (Mergel, 2017), combining social network analysis with automated natural language processing, identifying the behavior of users (e.g., based on roles and how they use the mechanisms and functionalities of the platforms) (Congosto, 2018). This can help public administrations to fully understand which users can act in a given circumstance as potential allies in the dissemination of information, and which ones can be an obstacle (Villodre & Criado, 2020). The objective of all this is to reduce resistance to the implementation of policies or specific lines of action. On many occasions, it can also serve as a preventive strategy for the organization to avoid reputation damage (Bekkers et al., 2013).

When directed at behavior modification, the situation becomes more complex. In general, the intention is to profile the audience and try to personalize information for public campaigns so that they not only reach the appropriate targets but also the message permeates. Broadly speaking, the behavioral model can help reinforce the nodality of policy tools, particularly public campaigns and suasion, and, in certain circumstances, it can also help in the implementation of public nudging. The final objective is the modification of citizen behavior (e.g., monitoring conversations on social media, detecting fake new, and quickly pushing information that counteracts it, thus changing citizens' perceptions about the issue). Public administrations might also use AI systems such as bots and AI-guided chatbots to automate data gathering through APIs or as a way to push information and influence the drift of citizen conversations. All in all, if directed towards behavioral modifications, the impacts on the policy cycle can be incredibly broad, from modifying the perceptions of problems during agenda-setting to dealing with implementation failures.

The main risks of this strategy are surveillance and unethical behavioral modification. Poorly executed, or with insidious intentions, the behavioral model can affect aspects of people's lives that are part of their digital private sphere and, in extreme cases, affect people's freedoms and condition the way they express themselves (Persily, 2017; Scott, 2016). To avoid this, it is extremely important that public administrations develop clear transparency policies regarding the type of information that is collected and its reasoning (Bekkers et al., 2013). Moreover, it is naive to think that behavioral modification will always serve the general interest. For instance, populist political discourses, from left to right, have used social media to sway citizens' opinions and behaviors, as a way of serving the desires of political leaders, with great examples of this being Brexit or the January 2021 US Capitol raid. This could undermine confidence in institutional trust and, ultimately, suffocate the idea of democracy (Olaniran & Williams, 2020), as an increasingly less legitimate system to absorb and represent citizen demands.

CONCLUSIONS

This chapter has delved into social media monitoring in the public sector. Through a review of previous literature around the purpose and expected outcomes for social media monitoring, the tools and evidence used, the role the citizen has in this process, and the challenges social media monitoring entails, I have proposed four models of social media monitoring in the public sector. The first model, which I call the performance model, focuses on the evaluation of the social media strategy of a public organization, relying on platform indicators and metrics to assess the results of communicative practices. The main challenge of this model is the fact that platform indicators may become an end in themselves. The opinion model gives importance to gathering opinions from citizens about the activities and services a public organization provides, expecting to identify potential problems and new trends. The main challenge of this model lies in the lack of representativeness of social media data, and the non-neutral nature of these platforms and the contents inside them. The collaborative model seeks to get citizens involved in the design of policies and delivery of services by resorting to citizen feedback from processes such as crowdsourcing. The citizen is seen here as a partner, helping to improve public services and provide innovative solutions to complex problems. The main challenge, however, lies in the reliability of citizen-generated data and the non-neutrality of the platforms. Finally, the behavioral model uses social media data to predict and even try to modify citizen behavior, reinforcing nodality tools, reducing policy resistance, and avoiding reputation damage. Its main challenges are surveillance and unethical behavioral modification.

The proposed models might guide future empirical work. It will be important to test these models through the study of different cases and under different administrative contexts. The four models reflect that there is no one way of monitoring social media data, nor a "best" way to do that. These models can be a good starting point to provide scholars with guidance in elaborating both qualitative and quantitative designs to address the implementation of social media monitoring. They might also serve practitioners to understand potential routes for social media monitoring, as well as to evaluate current strategies of monitoring and approaching the advantages and risks.

REFERENCES

Agostino, D., & Arnaboldi, M. (2017). Social media data used in the measurement of public services effectiveness: Empirical evidence from Twitter in higher education institutions. *Public Policy and Administration*, 32(4), 296–322.

Androutsopoulou, A., Charalabidis, Y., & Loukis, E.N. (2015). Using social media monitoring for public policy making – an evaluation. *Proceedings of the MCIS Conference*.

Androutsopoulou, A., Karacapilidis, N., Loukis, E., & Charalabidis, Y. (2019). Transforming the communication between citizens and government through AI-guided chatbots. *Government Information Quarterly*, 36(2), 358–67.

Bekkers, V., Edwards, A., & de Kool, D. (2013). Social media monitoring: Responsive governance in the shadow of surveillance? *Government Information Quarterly*, 30, 335–42.

Carr, C.T., & Hayes, R.A. (2015). Social media: Defining, developing, and divining. *Atlantic Journal of Communication*, 23(1), 46–65.

Chung, W., & Zeng, D. (2016). Social-media-based public policy informatics: Sentiment and network analyses of US Immigration and border security. *Journal of the Association for Information Science and Technology*, 67(7), 1588–606.

Congosto, M. (2018). Digital sources: A case study of the analysis of the recovery of historical memory in Spain on the social network Twitter. *Culture & History Digital Journal*, 7, 2.

Criado, J.I., & Villodre, J. (2021). Delivering public services through social media in European local governments. An interpretative framework using semantic algorithms. *Local Government Studies*, 47(2), 253–75.

DePaula, N., Dincelli, E., & Harrison, T. (2018). Toward a typology of government social media communication: Democratic goals, symbolic acts and self-presentation. *Government Information Quarterly*, 35, 98–108.

Driss, O.B., Mellouli, S., & Trabelsi, Z. (2019). From citizens to government policy-makers: Social media data analysis. *Government Information Quarterly*, 36(3), 560–70.

Feeney, M.K., & Porumbescu, G. (2021). The limits of social media for public administration research and practice. *Public Administration Review*, 81(4), 787–92.

Fensel, D., Leiter, B., & Stavrakantonakis, I. (2012). Social media monitoring. Innsbruck: Semantic Technology Institute.

Giest, S. (2017). Big data for policymaking: Fad or fasttrack? *Policy Sciences*, 50(3), 367–82.

González-Bailón, S., Borge-Holthoefer, J., & Moreno, Y. (2013). Broadcasters and hidden influentials in online protest diffusion. *American Behavioral Scientist*, 57(7).

Grubmüller, V., Götsch, K., & Krieger, B. (2013). Social media analytics for future oriented policy making. *European Journal of Futures Research*, 1(1), 1–9.

Hadi, T.A., & Fleshler, K. (2016). Integrating social media monitoring into public health emergency response operations. *Disaster Medicine and Public Health Preparedness*, 10(5), 775–80.

Harrison, S., & Johnson, P. (2019). Challenges in the adoption of crisis crowdsourcing and social media in Canadian emergency management. *Government Information Quarterly*, 36(3), 501–9.

Hood, C., & Margetts, H. (2007). *The Tools of Government in the Digital Age*. New York: Palgrave Macmillan.

Ingrams, A. (2019). Big Data and Dahl's challenge of democratic governance. *Review of Policy Research*, 36(3), 357–77.

Jo, A. (2023). The promise and peril of generative AI. *Nature*, 614(1), 214–16.

Kavanaugh, A.L., Fox, E.A., Sheetz, S.D., Yang, S., Li, L.T., Shoemaker, D.J., & Xie, L. (2012). Social media use by government: From the routine to the critical. *Government Information Quarterly*, 29, 480–91.

Koshkin, A.P., Rassolov, I.M., & Novikov, A.V. (2017). Monitoring social media: Students satisfaction with university administration activities. *Education and Information Technologies*, 22, 2499–522.

Lee, T. (2019). The global rise of "fake news" and the threat to democratic elections in the USA. *Public Administration and Policy: An Asia-Pacific Journal*, 22(1), 15–24.

López-Chau, A., Valle-Cruz, D., & Sandoval-Almazán, R. (2020). Sentiment analysis of Twitter data through machine learning techniques. In Ramachandran, M., & Mahmood, Z. (eds.), *Software Engineering in the Era of Cloud Computing*. Cham: Springer, pp. 185–209.

Loukis, E., Charalabidis, Y., & Androutsopoulou, A. (2017). Promoting open innovation in the public sector through social media monitoring. *Government Information Quarterly*, 34, 99–109.

Marwick, A.E., & Boyd, D. (2011). I tweet honestly, I tweet passionately: Twitter users, context collapse, and the imagined audience. *New Media & Society*, 13, 114–33.

Meijer, A.J., & Potjer, S. (2018). Citizen-generated open data: An explorative analysis of 25 cases. *Government Information Quarterly*, 35(4), 613–21.

Mergel, I. (2013). A framework for interpreting social media interactions in the public sector. *Government Information Quarterly*, 30, 327–34.

Mergel, I. (2017). Building holistic evidence for social media impact. *Public Administration Review*, 77(4), 489–95.

Mergel, I., & Desouza, K. (2013). Implementing open iInnovation in the public sector: The case of Challenge.gov. *Public Administration Review*, 76(3), 882–90.

Morozov, E., & Bria, F. (2018). *Rethinking the Smart City. Democratizing Urban Technology*. New York: Rosa Luxemburg Foundation.

Nguyen, T.T., Quan, T.T., & Phan, T.T. (2014). Sentiment search: An emerging trend on social media monitoring systems. *Aslib Journal of Information Management*, 66(5), 553–80.

Olaniran, B., & Williams, I. (2020). Social media effects: Hijacking democracy and civility in civic engagement. In Jones, J., & Trice, M. (eds.), *Platforms, Protests, and the Challenge of Networked Democracy. Rhetoric, Politics and Society*. Cham: Palgrave Macmillan, pp. 77–94.

Panagiotopoulos, P., Bowen, F., & Brooker, P. (2017). The value of social media data: Integrating crowd capabilities in evidence-based policy. *Government Information Quarterly*, 34(4), 601–12.

Pencheva, I., Esteve, M., & Mikhaylov, S.J. (2020). Big Data and AI – a transformational shift for government: So, what next for research? *Public Policy and Administration*, 35(1), 24–44.

Persily, N. (2017). The 2016 U.S. election: Can democracy survive the internet? *Journal of Democracy*, 28(2), 63–76.

Pew Research Center (2021). Social media use in 2021.

Reddick, C.G., Chatfield, A.T., & Ojo, A. (2017). A social media text analytics framework for double-loop learning for citizen-centric public services: A case study of a local government Facebook use. *Government Information Quarterly*, 34(1), 110–25.

Ruggiero, A., & Vos, M. (2014). Social media monitoring for crisis communication: Process, methods and trends in the scientific literature. *Online Journal of Communication and Media Technologies*, 4(1).

Scott, J.D. (2016). Social media and government surveillance: The case for better privacy protections for our newest public space. *Journal of Business & Techology Law*, 12, 151.

Severo, M., Feredj, A., & Romele, A. (2016). Soft data and public policy: Can social media offer alternatives to official statistics in urban policymaking? *Policy & Internet*, 8(3), 354–72.

Stamati, T., Papadopoulos, T., & Anagnostopoulos, D. (2015). Social media for openness and accountability in the public sector: Cases in the Greek context. *Government Information Quarterly*, 32(1), 12–29.

Tarasconi, F., Farina, M., Mazzei, A., & Bosca, A. (2017). The role of unstructured data in real-time disaster-related social media monitoring. In 2017 IEEE International Conference on Big Data, pp. 3769–78.

Thomas, J.C. (2013). Citizen, customer, partner: Rethinking the place of the public in public management. *Public Administration Review*, 73(6), 786–96.

Valle-Cruz, D., Criado, J.I., Sandoval-Almazán, R., & Ruvalcaba-Gómez, E.A. (2020). Assessing the public policy-cycle framework in the age of artificial intelligence: From agenda-setting to policy evaluation. *Government Information Quarterly*, 37(4).

Villodre, J., & Criado, J.I. (2020). User roles for emergency management in social media: Understanding actors' behavior during the 2018 Majorca Island flash floods. *Government Information Quarterly*, 37(4).

Wukich, C. (2021). Government social media engagement strategies and public roles. Public Performance & Management Review, 44(1), 187–215.

10. Towards a framework for data science governance in the post-pandemic context: an analysis of three initiatives

Rodrigo Sandoval-Almazan and David Valle-Cruz

INTRODUCTION

Digital transformation is an ongoing social process, driven by rapid technological innovation and continually adapting to new disruptions, trends, and practices. This transformation will have far-reaching implications for many aspects of society, including the public sector, leading to added value, improved relationships, digital public services, and greater efficiency in public administration (Gong et al., 2020). The emergence of digital government applications and web portals has facilitated organizational transformation, and information and communication technology (ICT) has played a key role in driving the development of e-government (Luna-Reyes & Gil-García, 2014; Nograšek & Vintar, 2014).

The power of digital transformation has the potential to change the dynamics of communication, facilitating greater connectivity and global interaction through social media, messaging applications, and online collaboration tools (Criado, Sandoval-Almazan & Gil-García, 2013). This connectivity has profound implications for social relationships, information transmission, and collective behavior. Moreover, digital transformation has removed barriers and created equal opportunities in access to information, education, and lifelong learning (Gebayew et al., 2018). It has also disrupted traditional industries, led to the emergence of new business models, and the transformation of existing business models, driving innovation, economic growth, and job creation (Grab, Olaru & Gavril, 2019). But this disruption can also result in job losses, socio-economic inequalities, and misinformation, highlighting the need to understand the mechanisms involved and ensure a smooth transition for affected stakeholders.

Moreover, digital technologies have enabled more efficient and transparent public services and revolutionized governance. E-government initiatives, digital platforms for citizen participation, and data-driven decision-making have improved public service delivery and increased citizen participation, thereby improving policy outcomes (Gil-García et al., 2014; Valle-Cruz, 2019). Nonetheless, challenges around data protection, data security, and the digital divide must be addressed to ensure equal access to digital services and protect individual rights.

The post-pandemic era has brought about changes in information systems. But what exactly does "post-COVID" or "post-pandemic era" mean? Different concepts help us understand this new phase. For instance, Vlados et al. (2022) align more with our approach. Their study focuses on progressive change and global transformation: "This evolutionary phase concerns the period emerging after the COVID-19 crisis, which leads the global socioeconomic system and the various actors at all levels (macro-meso-micro), respectively, to irreversible transformations, laying the ground for the appearance of an entirely new form of globalization."

The concepts of post-COVID and post-pandemic are not from the "pandemic narrative" or the time lost during the emergence of COVID-19 (Darici, 2023), but represent a stage that follows the crisis and that undergoes irreversible transformations, leading to the emergence of a new form of globalization. Leach et al. (2021) identify three critical changes. First, there's a shift towards using scientific advice to shape policies, which changes power dynamics. Second, COVID-19 exposes the traditional model of economic growth as inadequate. Lastly, pandemics create new types of politics and change the relationships between citizens and government.

Susskind (2020) thoroughly examines these changes, exploring the accelerated pace of different work processes and their effects on health systems, supply chains, and political power dynamics. These shifts have significant implications for organizations and institutions, necessitating their adaptation to the evolving context. The post-pandemic era represents a period of gradual change and worldwide transformation, establishing the groundwork for a distinct future. Consequently, it is at this juncture that our analysis commences.

As data volumes continue to grow exponentially in the post-pandemic era, effective data management becomes essential. Data governance ensures responsible and efficient data management, including data quality, accuracy, and security, and supports trusted decision-making (Gegenhuber et al., 2023; Janssen et al., 2022). It also facilitates the integration, standardization, and sharing of data across various government departments, thereby fostering systematic consistency and trust among stakeholders (OECD, 2019b). Furthermore, data governance promotes transparency and fosters trust between governments and the public by establishing clear processes for accessing and using public sector data (Cerrillo-Martinez & Casadesus-de-Mingo, 2021; Ingrams & Klievink, 2022). In addition, it facilitates better decision-making, reduces risk, and ensures effective procedures based on reliable and accurate data (Valle-Cruz & García-Contreras, 2023).

Data science has a crucial role in dealing with data management challenges in the public sector. With the large amount of data generated and collected, data science provides the necessary tools and techniques to effectively manage, analyze, and interpret this information. Governments can use data science techniques to uncover valuable insights and patterns that can inform decision-making and enhance public services (Matheus, Janssen & Maheshwari, 2020). From a privacy and security standpoint, data science offers advanced cryptographic algorithms and data anonymization techniques to safeguard sensitive information while enabling meaningful analysis. By utilizing data masking and secure data exchange protocols, data scientists can ensure the privacy and security of citizen data and address concerns regarding unauthorized access or breaches. To combat data and algorithmic biases, advanced data analysis techniques and algorithm testing are essential (Jain, Gyanchandani & Khare, 2016).

Data science can identify and mitigate bias in datasets, ensuring that decision-making processes are fair and impartial. Additionally, data scientists can develop algorithmic fairness models to reduce the impact of bias on policy outcomes and promote inclusiveness and fairness. Interpretability and explainability are inherent strengths of data science methods. Machine learning interpretability techniques such as LIME (Local Interpretable Model-agnostic Explanations) and SHAP (SHapley Additive exPlanations) enable data scientists to provide transparent and clear explanations for complex data-driven decisions (Balayn, Lofi & Houben, 2021). This transparency helps the public understand the rationale behind government actions and policies, increasing public trust. Ethical considerations in artificial intelligence (AI) and data science projects are paramount, and data science provides a method for developing and deploying ethical models. Through ethical AI frameworks and policies, data scientists can ensure AI models are used responsibly and human rights and social values are respected. By promoting the ethical use of data-driven technology, governments can put the welfare and interests of their citizens first (Brous, Janssen & Krans, 2020).

Collaboration among various government agencies and stakeholders benefits from data science tools that enable seamless data integration and data sharing. Data scientists can develop data interoperability solutions, break down silos, and facilitate cross-agency collaboration (Wieringa et al., 2021). This collaborative approach leads to a holistic understanding of complex issues, enabling more informed decision-making based on data-driven insights. Compliance with evolving privacy regulations is facilitated by a data science approach to data management (McKinsey & Company, 2022). Data scientists can implement data governance frameworks that comply with the latest data protection laws and ensure government practices remain compliant. Keeping data protection regulations up to date is critical in maintaining public trust and avoiding legal consequences. Data science enables the public sector to effectively address data governance challenges (ICLG–Data Protection Laws and Regulations, 2022).

By leveraging data science techniques, governments can ensure privacy and security, combat bias, improve interpretability, uphold ethics, foster collaboration, and comply with regulations (Wieringa et al., 2021). By adopting data science principles and practices, governments can make data-driven decisions that serve the public good while protecting individual rights and promoting transparency and responsible governance. The public sector faces challenges and limitations (OECD, 2019a). The COVID-19 pandemic exacerbated data-related concerns, revealing inefficiencies in processing raw data for trend generation and decision-making (Khomsani, 2022; Li, 2022). Some governments need help publishing data in a format that the public can read, demonstrating weaknesses in reporting (Gurstein, 2011).

These challenges, while daunting, present an intriguing opportunity. They underscore the importance of delving deeper into data sharing, governance, open governance, and transparency. By doing so, we can identify areas ripe for improvement and explore innovative solutions to these pressing issues.

This chapter examines data governance in the post-pandemic context based on three initiatives: (1) Data-driven government, (2) Strategies or initiatives for government data, and (3) Data government ecosystem, and answers the following question: How can data science governance be effectively resumed worldwide in the post-pandemic era? We analyze the challenges of data science governance in the context of these three governance initiatives. The chapter consists of six sections, including the present Introduction. The next section provides an overview of the three data governance initiatives that have emerged in response to the global pandemic's transformative impact. The third section proposes a novel framework for data science governance in terms of the three governance initiatives. The fourth section presents a selection of representative international cases that exemplify successful data governance initiatives. The fifth section discusses the findings. The last section presents the final comments of the chapter.

DATA GOVERNANCE INITIATIVES IN THE POST-PANDEMIC CONTEXT

The public sector increasingly recognizes the importance of data science in its digital transformation. This is due to technological advancements and the growing significance of data-driven decision-making. Before the pandemic, various strategies were developed to manage public sector data effectively. Examining these efforts to understand how governments utilize data science for better policymaking and service delivery is crucial. This section analyzes the benefits, challenges, and limitations of three key strategies that have emerged as significant players in data management: data-driven government, strategies or initiatives for government data, and data governance ecosystems.

Data-Driven Government

Benefits

For the data-driven government, data is the primary driver to shape government policies and services, enabling evidence-based decision-making to effectively address complex societal challenges (Robertson, Reisin Miller & Dolz, 2021). By collecting, analyzing, and interpreting data, governments can identify trends, patterns, and insights that inform and improve decision-making processes, ultimately improving public services and policymaking (van Veenstra & Kotterink, 2017).

Data-driven government offers several advantages that greatly benefit society (OECD, 2019a). First, data-driven analytics can help governments pinpoint problems, evaluate policies effectively, align decision-making with the needs of society, and achieve greater efficiency and effectiveness, leading to improved decision-making (Shah, Peristeras & Magnisalis, 2021).

Moreover, this approach fosters innovation and the development of public services (Carbonara & Pellegrino, 2018). Opening government data to developers, researchers, and entrepreneurs creates an ecosystem that fosters the development of new applications, services, and solutions, ultimately improving the quality of life for citizens and making public services more efficient, accessible, and user-centric (Abdulla, Janiszewska-Kiewra & Podlesny, 2021).

Additionally, data-driven government promotes transparency and accountability by providing citizens with open data that enables them to access and understand information relevant to government administration (van Ooijen, Ubaldi & Welby, 2019). This transparency allows citizens to scrutinize government actions and decisions, promotes participation in the democratic process, and holds governments accountable (Meijer, 't Hart & Worthy, 2018).

In addition, data analysis and visualization will enable governments to identify societal problems and needs, enabling more targeted allocation of resources and policies in areas requiring greater attention, such as health, education, infrastructure, and security more effectively (Wirtz et al., 2022). This data-driven approach will enable governments to formulate precise, results-driven strategies to effectively address societal challenges (van Ooijen, Ubaldi & Welby, 2019). The availability of open data facilitates ongoing monitoring and evaluation of government policies. By tracking key indicators and measuring policy impact in real time, governments can make timely adjustments and improvements, ensuring public policy effectiveness and alignment with established goals (Arundel, Bloch & Ferguson, 2019).

Adopting a data-driven approach to government offers many benefits, from improving decision-making and fostering innovation to promoting transparency and identifying societal needs (Robertson, Reisin Miller & Dolz, 2021). By harnessing the full potential of data, governments can build more efficient, responsible, and citizen-centric governance, ultimately leading to better public services and better outcomes for society (Sigwejo & Pather, 2016).

Challenges and limitations
In the context of government data strategies or initiatives, addressing the challenges of data collaboration and sharing is critical to promoting government transparency and efficiency (Montes, Bastos & de Oliveira, 2019). Establishing agreements on data access and intellectual property protection facilitates collaboration among various government agencies and organizations (Wernick, 2020). This enables them to exchange critical data to tackle complex problems and make evidence-based decisions. Ensuring appropriate confidentiality ensures the security of shared information and protects the privacy of citizens (Abouelmehdi, Beni-Hessane & Khaloufi, 2018).

Additionally, compliance with data protection regulations and laws is paramount to any data governance strategy (Pike, 2019). Governments ensure that data is used responsibly and ethically by keeping up with evolving regulations. This increases public trust and avoids potential sanctions and legal issues related to data management. Data management is the basis for ensuring that data is properly used for the benefit of society (Porsdam Mann, Savulescu & Sahakian, 2016).

The use of data-driven decision-making in government decision-making began with e-government a few years ago. However, during the pandemic, data has become even more crucial. As a result, this strategy has evolved and become essential for many governments in the post-pandemic era. It has enabled governments to transform their organizations and adapt to the new challenges and problems caused by the COVID-19 lockdown.

Strategies or Initiatives for Government Data

Benefits
Categories of government policies and frameworks that promote open data practices, transparency, and cooperation among government agencies play a key role in fostering data sharing, collaboration, and responsible data use while complying with privacy regulations (Federal Data Strategy, 2020).

The implementation of government policies and initiatives on open data and public access can have far-reaching implications for society and governance (Zuiderwijk, Chen & Salem, 2021). One of the main benefits is ensuring that the public has access to public information. An open government data policy promotes transparency and enables people to better understand government actions and decisions, thereby increasing trust in government and promoting public participation in the democratic process (Criado & Gil-Garcia, 2019; OECD, n.d.).

In addition, a strong open government data policy empowers citizens to actively participate in the decision-making process and shape public policy (Wukich, 2021). This inclusivity promotes diverse perspectives and enables civil society to participate actively in governance (Sénit, 2020).

The benefits of such policies also extend to innovation and economic growth (Valle-Cruz, Fernandez-Cortez & Gil-Garcia, 2022). Open government data drives innovation, inspiring entrepreneurs, researchers, and developers to create new applications, tools, and products that bring both economic and societal benefits (Ruijer & Meijer, 2020). This facilitates job creation, boosts economic growth, and ultimately improves the general quality of life of its citizens (De Guimarães et al., 2020).

Additionally, open government data policies contribute to greater accountability and governance. By increasing the transparency of public resource management, citizens and organizations can more effectively monitor government activity, reduce the risk of corruption, detect fraud, and improve administrative efficiency and effectiveness (Ruijer et al., 2020).

Moreover, the guidelines promote cooperation and synergies across industries. By facilitating the exchange of information and knowledge between government, academia, civil society, and the private sector, broader solutions can be developed to address complex social, economic, and environmental challenges. This evidence-based decision-making promotes more efficient resource allocation and benefits society (Loureiro, Romero & Bilro, 2020).

The introduction of an open government data policy is a strategic initiative that has the potential to bring about significant positive changes in society and governance (Piotrowski, Berliner & Ingrams, 2022). From increasing public access to information, encouraging public participation in policymaking, and fostering innovation, to enhancing accountability, transparency, and cross-sectoral cooperation, these efforts are essential to building more inclusive, transparent, and effective governments that meet the needs and aspirations of the people they represent (Gil-Garcia, Gasco-Hernandez & Pardo, 2020).

Challenges and limitations

Implementing open government and transparency strategies also promotes public participation. Access to government information and open data will enable citizens to understand government actions and participate in decision-making. This will strengthen government accountability and foster trust and cooperation between citizens and government agencies (Matheus & Janssen, 2020).

Efficient decision-making also improves when collaboration and data sharing between different government agencies are facilitated. Sharing data leads to a more complete understanding of problems and challenges, resulting in more informed and effective solutions. This optimizes the use of resources and improves the delivery of government services to the public (Janssen et al., 2020).

In addition, fostering collaboration and data sharing fosters innovation and the development of new solutions and services. Entrepreneurs, researchers, and developers can use open data to create applications and tools that benefit society. This fosters economic and social growth as well as a culture of innovation in the public sector (Kitsios & Kamariotou, 2023).

Integrating and sharing data as part of a government data strategy or initiative offers many benefits (Janssen et al., 2020). This could increase government transparency, accountability, and efficiency, resulting in better decision-making processes. By complying with data protection regulations, encouraging public participation, and fostering innovation, data-driven governments can harness the potential of data to deliver significant benefits to society (van Ooijen, Ubaldi & Welby, 2019).

Data governance faces numerous challenges and barriers within the post-pandemic circumstance that require careful attention to utilize government information capably and successfully, and data science plays a key part in addressing these challenges (PublicTechnology.net, 2021).

Data governance provides effective tools and strategies for securing data privacy and information security. Anonymization, encryption, and strong foundational security measures ensure delicate data is protected, guaranteeing that citizens' privacy is ensured in a progressively advanced environment (TechTarget, 2022).

The presence of bias and segregation within the information and calculations utilized in data science is another critical viewpoint that ought to be considered in information administration (Wieringa et al., 2021). Data science strategies can help distinguish and mitigate these tendencies, guarantee that government arrangements are reasonable and inclusive for all individuals of society, and promote reasonable and fair-minded decision-making (Matheus, Janssen & Maheshwari, 2020). The interpretability and explainability of data science models are crucial in critical areas such as healthcare and government decision-making. Data science provides a way to construct models that are more interpretable and transparent, subsequently increasing public trust in data-driven decision-making (Angelov et al., 2021).

Within the zone of data collaboration and sharing, data science is vital in overseeing access control, ensuring intellectual property, and guaranteeing confidentiality. By utilizing data science methods, governments can secure sensitive data and facilitate evidence-based decision-making while working successfully with different organizations (Mikalef, van de Wetering & Krogstie, 2021).

Moral improvement of counterfeit insights (AI) is another major challenge in information administration, and information science can help address this issue by consolidating moral considerations into the advancement of AI models. By designing, implementing, and using ethical guidelines and principles, data science can guarantee the dependable and advantageous utilization of AI innovation to improve society (van Berkel et al., 2022).

In addition, data science makes a difference in guaranteeing compliance with security directions and laws by providing tools to screen and audit data usage. Staying abreast of advancing regulations and complying with pertinent laws is fundamental to maintaining accountability and straightforwardness in taking care of government information (Janssen et al., 2020).

With the control of data science used to address these challenges and imperatives, information administration can advance dependable, ethical, and viable utilization of government information (Daniel, 2019). Reinforcing public belief in government organizations and harnessing the complete potential of data science will advance more transparent, participatory, and effective governance frameworks that serve as the leading interface of the open data ecosystem. Effectively integrating data science into data governance scenarios paves the way for data-driven decision-making that empowers governments to address societal challenges and achieve positive societal results (Matheus, Janssen & Maheshwari, 2020).

Data Government Ecosystem

Benefits
The data government ecosystem represents a strategic approach that can transform how government data is managed and used, resulting in greater benefits to society and improved collaboration among various stakeholders (Bonina & Eaton, 2020). This extensive network of data-sharing platforms and systems promotes transparency, accountability, and efficient use of data for the greater good. Styrin et al. (2017) define ecosystems as "systems of people, practices, values, and technologies in a particular place," emphasizing the socio-technical nature of these systems and the interconnectedness of human activities and their components supported by technology.

One of the key benefits of the data governance ecosystem is its ability to promote transparency and combat corruption (Ingrams, 2020; Matheus & Janssen, 2020). Through mechanisms that expose public information and enable public oversight, these systems facilitate access to relevant and timely data, thereby preventing corruption and building trust in public institutions. In doing so, it contributes to more transparency and responsible governance (Piotrowski, Berliner & Ingrams, 2022).

Additionally, the data governance ecosystem plays a key role in improving the efficiency and effectiveness of government (Bonina & Eaton, 2020; Cordella & Paletti, 2019). By providing quality data and analytical tools, these ecosystems enable informed, evidence-based decision-making, optimized resource allocation, and improved public services. As a result, governments can operate more efficiently and effectively, resulting in greater public satisfaction with government services. In addition, these ecosystems facilitate informed planning and decision-making by providing critical information to government strategies (Nisar et al., 2021). Accessing data such as the National Accounts System provides valuable insight into a country's socio-economic situation and enables the development of long-term strategies to address social challenges. This facilitates effective, data-driven planning and ensures that public policy is aligned with established goals.

Another important benefit of the data governance ecosystem is its role in the monitoring and evaluation of public policy (Valle-Cruz et al., 2020). By granting access to timely and reliable data, governments can assess the impact of policies in real time and make necessary adjustments. This ongoing evaluation ensures that actions are effective and aligned with goals, ultimately improving service quality and benefiting the public.

In addition, these ecosystems facilitate cooperation among relevant institutions and stakeholders. Working together on the collection, analysis, and use of data creates synergies and enables a more holistic approach to solving complex challenges. This collaborative governance facilitates the introduction of effective and sustainable solutions that benefit society (Saura, Ribeiro-Soriano & Palacios-Marqués, 2022).

The data government ecosystem is a fundamental tool for promoting transparent, efficient, and evidence-based government operations. The ability to improve transparency, efficiency, informed planning, policy oversight, and cooperation among stakeholders has enormous benefits for society. By leveraging these ecosystems, governments can optimize data use, achieve better policy outcomes, and ultimately strengthen governance for the benefit of their citizens (Ahmad et al., 2022).

Challenges and limitations

In the context of data government ecosystems, addressing the challenges of data collaboration and sharing is critical to promoting government transparency and accountability. Collaborating with various agencies and stakeholders will provide a comprehensive overview of data and information to ensure informed and data-driven decision-making. Sharing data on transparency systems, national accounts, and anti-corruption systems increases public trust in the governments and promotes greater accountability (Reggi, Dawes, 2022).

In addition, privacy and data security protections are essential in transparency and national accounting systems. Minimizing the risk of compromise or unauthorized access to sensitive information by implementing policies and measures such as anonymity, encryption, and infrastructure security creates a trusted environment in which citizens and stakeholders can share and access government data with peace of mind (Lnenicka et al., 2022).

Facilitating interpretation and explainability is another important aspect of the data governance ecosystem. Ensuring that the information presented is interpretable and understandable by the public and stakeholders promotes understanding and trust in government actions. This promotes citizen participation and empowers them to participate in decision-making (Xu & Peng, 2022).

A data government ecosystem increases the efficiency of government decision-making by addressing challenges related to collaboration, privacy, and explainability. Transparent and shared data leads to a comprehensive understanding of problems and challenges, resulting in more informed and effective solutions. This resource optimization improves the delivery of public services to residents (Styrin, Mossberger & Zhulin, 2022).

Moreover, a data government ecosystem promotes anti-corruption systems that share data transparently and securely to combat corruption within governments. Open and accessible data improves oversight and control of government behavior, reduces the risk of corruption, and increases public servant accountability (Parenti, Noori & Janssen, 2022).

A robust data governance ecosystem is essential to foster transparency, accountability, and efficient decision-making in government. By fostering collaboration, ensuring privacy and accountability, and combating corruption through transparent systems, a data-driven government can build trust with citizens and stakeholders, ultimately benefiting society.

TOWARDS A FRAMEWORK FOR DATA SCIENCE GOVERNANCE

Data-Driven Government

In the context of a data-driven government, leveraging government data for data science projects comes with major challenges. Data science plays an important role in turning raw data into actionable insights, but governments need to overcome a variety of barriers to ensure the efficient and responsible use of data.

Ensuring government data privacy and security is paramount in data science projects. Robust policies and procedures, such as data encryption, access control, and infrastructure protection, must be implemented to prevent security breaches and unauthorized access to sensitive information (The National Academies Press, 2020). Data science can contribute to this aspect by developing advanced encryption methods and security algorithms to effectively protect government data. Bias and discrimination in data pose significant challenges to government data-driven initiatives (The Pew Charitable Trusts, 2018). Governments must combat bias to ensure that the data used for decision-making is representative, balanced, and free of discriminatory elements. Data science techniques, such as bias reduction algorithms and equity perception modeling, can be used to improve the fairness and inclusiveness of data-driven government policies, promoting equitable outcomes for all citizens.

Explainability and interpretation of data science models used in government decision-making is another important challenge. Governments need to ensure that these models are transparent and interpretable, providing clear explanations of how they arrive at certain conclusions and predictions. Data science can contribute to the interpretability of models by developing techniques that provide insights into the decision-making process, allowing decision-makers to understand and trust the results (Barredo, Díaz-Rodríguez & Del Ser, 2019).

Additionally, the integration of AI into data-driven government projects raises concerns about ethical governance. Responsible use of AI requires regulations and ethical practices that carefully consider the social, cultural, and human impacts of AI technologies (Valle-Cruz, Fernandez-Cortez & Gil-Garcia, 2022). Data science can contribute to ethical AI governance by developing ethical AI frameworks that ensure AI-driven efforts prioritize human rights, equity, and accountability.

Addressing these challenges with data science methods and solutions is essential for a data-driven government to unleash the full potential of government data and promote ethical, efficient, and informed decision-making processes. By leveraging the ability of data science to overcome these barriers, governments can foster a data-driven culture that enables public administrations to deliver better services, address societal challenges, and promote the overall well-being of their citizens.

Strategies or Initiatives for Government Data

In the field of open government and transparency initiatives, addressing data sharing and collaboration challenges is critical to promoting effective and efficient data-driven governance (OECD, 2019b). Data science plays an important role in analyzing and gathering insights from data exchanged between different government agencies and organizations.

Strategies and policies in this area must be designed to address the complexities of data collaboration and exchange while ensuring data privacy and security. It is important to establish strong agreements to access data, protect intellectual property, and maintain appropriate confidentiality while sharing data between different organizations. Data science can contribute to this aspect by developing secure data-sharing frameworks to implement encryption and access control, reducing the risk of data breaches and unauthorized access. In addition, the data governance landscape requires constant adaptation to changing data protection laws and regulations. Data governance strategies must be aligned with an ever-changing regulatory framework to ensure compliance with applicable regulations (Seagate, n.d.). Data science can support compliance efforts by developing data management tools and systems that are flexible and adaptable to changes in the regulatory environment, ensuring that transparent and open government initiatives align with regulatory requirements.

Government transparency and openness initiatives must also prioritize compliance with these regulations to ensure accountable and transparent data management (OECD, 2022). Data science methods, such as data monitoring and auditing systems, can improve transparency and accountability by providing audit trails of data sharing and usage, and foster trust between citizens and stakeholders. By integrating data science principles and solutions into data collaboration and open government initiatives, governments can promote responsible data management, build public trust, and make informed decisions that drive social progress. Data-driven governance, backed by data science practices, is poised to revolutionize public service delivery and improve government efficiency in meeting citizens' needs.

Data Government Ecosystems

Addressing challenges related to data cooperation and sharing in the context of transparent systems, national accounts, and anti-corruption mechanisms is paramount to promoting transparency and accountability in a data-driven government. Data science plays an important role in managing and analyzing the data exchanged in these ecosystems to derive meaningful insights and informed decision-making (Brookings Institution, 2020).

In addition to the challenges of collaboration, ensuring the privacy and security of data collected and shared is equally important. Transparency systems and national accounts must implement robust policies and measures such as anonymization, encryption, and infrastructure security to prevent breaches and maintain public trust.

The interpretability and explainability of the data presented in the data governance ecosystem is also an important consideration. It is important that the information provided is easy to understand and explainable so that the public and stakeholders can understand the basis for data-backed conclusions and decisions (O'Sullivan et al., 2022).

This framework (Figure 10.1) provides an overview of how the challenges of privacy, security, bias, interpretability, ethics, collaboration, and compliance are interconnected within various data governance approaches in the public sector. Addressing these challenges is critical to achieving effective data governance and maximizing the value of data science in government.

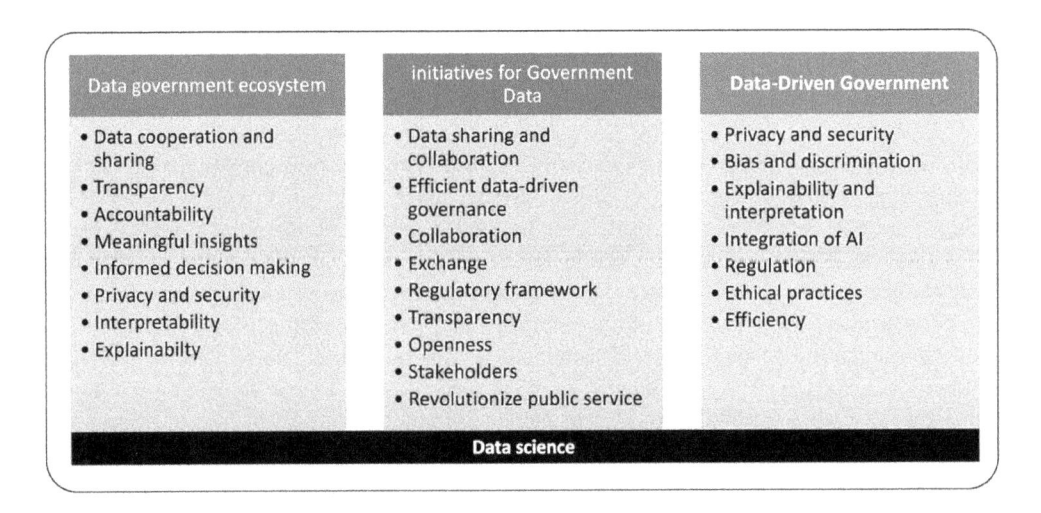

Data government ecosystem	initiatives for Government Data	Data-Driven Government
• Data cooperation and sharing • Transparency • Accountability • Meaningful insights • Informed decision making • Privacy and security • Interpretability • Explainabilty	• Data sharing and collaboration • Efficient data-driven governance • Collaboration • Exchange • Regulatory framework • Transparency • Openness • Stakeholders • Revolutionize public service	• Privacy and security • Bias and discrimination • Explainability and interpretation • Integration of AI • Regulation • Ethical practices • Efficiency

Data science

Source: Authors' own.

Figure 10.1   Framework for data science governance

SOME REPRESENTATIVE INTERNATIONAL CASES OF EACH GOVERNANCE INITIATIVE

Data-Driven Government

Some international cases exemplify the challenges of data-driven government and their approaches to privacy and data security, equity and inclusion in government decisions, transparency and accountability in decision-making, and ethics in the use of AI (Vashisht, 2023):

(a) Estonia is known for its advanced approach to using technology and data to improve government services. It has implemented robust policies to protect the privacy and security of citizen data through the X-Road platform, which uses encryption and access controls to ensure the protection of sensitive data. Additionally, it has adopted ethical practices in the use of AI in government administration, considering the social and human impact of data-driven decisions. Transparency in the government is an important pillar in Estonia, where citizens have access to their personal data and can audit who has accessed it.

(b) Singapore has demonstrated a strong commitment to equity and inclusion in its government decisions. It has used data analytics to address social and economic challenges, such as reducing income inequality and ensuring equitable access to public services. The government has been transparent in its data-driven decision-making, providing clear explanations of how certain conclusions were reached. Additionally, it has implemented policies to protect the privacy of citizen data and ensure information security.

(c) Canada has adopted an ethical approach to the use of AI in government. It has established ethical principles and guidelines to ensure that data-driven decisions respect citizens' fundamental rights and values. Additionally, it has worked to address bias and discrimination in the data and algorithms used in government projects, aiming to promote more inclusive and equitable policies.

(d) New Zealand has been a leader in government transparency and accountability. It has implemented open data initiatives and created platforms that allow citizens to access and use government data for informed decision-making. It has been transparent in the interpretation and explainability of data science models used in government decision-making, which has promoted public trust in the decision-making process.

These international cases showcase different approaches that countries have adopted to address the challenges of data-driven government. Each of them has implemented specific policies and practices to ensure the protection of privacy and data security, to promote equity and inclusion in government decisions, to be transparent and accountable in decision-making, and to adopt ethical practices in the use of AI in public administration.

Strategies or Initiatives for Government Data

Some international cases that exemplify the challenges of strategies or initiatives for government data and their approaches to promoting data collaboration and sharing, compliance and accountability, transparency and citizen participation, efficiency in decision-making, and the promotion of innovation and development are the following (OECD, 2019b):

(a) Mexico has implemented open government initiatives to promote data collaboration and sharing among different government entities and civil society. It has established data access agreements and intellectual property protection to foster collaboration in solving complex problems. Additionally, it has been transparent in publishing open data to empower citizens and encourage their participation in government decision-making. An example is Mexico's open government actions, reported in the Open Government Partnership (Visit: https://www.opengovpartnership.org/members/mexico/).

(b) Singapore has enacted the Data Sharing and Governance Act to address challenges related to data collaboration and sharing among different government agencies. This law establishes frameworks for secure and efficient data exchange between government entities and promotes transparency and accountability in data use. Additionally, Singapore

has set up a compliance framework to ensure ethical and responsible data usage. (Visit: https://www.smartnation.gov.sg/about-smart-nation/secure-smart-nation/personal-data-protection-laws-and-policies/).
(c) The United States has implemented Data.gov, a platform that allows citizens to access open government data and participate in decision-making. This initiative promotes transparency and citizen participation by providing access to data and enabling citizens to use that data to address social and economic challenges. Additionally, Data.gov fosters innovation and development by enabling entrepreneurs and developers to use data to create new solutions and services.
(d) The European Commission has established the European Data Portal, providing access to open data from different European Union countries. This initiative fosters data collaboration and sharing among member countries, enabling them to address common issues and make evidence-based decisions. Additionally, the platform ensures compliance with data protection regulations and promotes transparency and citizen participation within the European Union.
(e) Canada has adopted an open data policy that encourages data collaboration and sharing among different government agencies. The policy promotes the use of open data to improve decision-making efficiency and deliver more effective government services. Additionally, the policy ensures compliance with data protection regulations and promotes transparency and accountability in the government (Visit: https://open.canada.ca/en/open-data-principles).

These international cases showcase different approaches that countries have adopted to address the challenges of strategies or initiatives for government data. Each of them has implemented specific policies and practices to foster data collaboration and sharing, to ensure compliance and accountability, to promote transparency and citizen participation, to enhance efficiency in decision-making, and to stimulate innovation and development in the public sector.

Data Government Ecosystems

Some international cases illustrating challenges in the data governance ecosystem and their approaches to promoting transparency and accountability, protecting data privacy and security, fostering understandability and explainability, and facilitating effective decision-making are presented below (Digital Watch Observatory, 2023):

(a) Mexico has established a National Transparency System (SNT) to promote transparency and accountability in government. This system brings together different organizations and stakeholders to ensure access to government information and open data publishing. By sharing data through the SNT, public trust in the government is enhanced and encourages greater accountability in government actions. (Visit: https://snt.org.mx/ in Spanish).
(b) Korea has implemented an e-government system to improve the efficiency of government decision-making. Thanks to the exchange of data between different government agencies, the use of resources is optimized, and the delivery of public services is improved. In addition, the system aims to ensure the confidentiality and security of the data collected and shared. (Visit: https://www.dgovkorea.go.kr/).

(c) Australia has a national account system that provides economic and financial information about the country. This system ensures the ability to interpret the data presented, allowing citizens and stakeholders to better understand the country's economic situation and participate in data-driven decision-making. (Visit: https://www.abs.gov.au/statistics/economy/national-accounts/australian-system-national-accounts/latest-release).

(d) Spain has developed a national open data platform to promote transparency and citizen participation in government. By providing access to open government data, citizens are empowered to understand government actions and participate in decision-making. In addition, the platform ensures the security and safety of the shared data. (Visit: https://datos.gob.es/es in Spanish).

These international cases show the different approaches that countries have taken to address the challenges of the data governance ecosystem. Each of them has specific policies and practices to promote transparency and accountability, to ensure the protection of privacy and data security, to promote the interpretation and integration of information, to improve the effectiveness of government decision-making, and to combat corruption in government.

DISCUSSION

The challenges posed by the pandemic have highlighted the essential balance in data science governance between leveraging data for the public good and safeguarding individual privacy. A specific challenge lies in the tension between insights and confidentiality, necessitating the development of robust frameworks for data access, usage, and anonymization. Achieving transparency and security simultaneously is a complex task, and governments must prioritize the creation of comprehensive guidelines that strike a balance between these two crucial aspects.

Moreover, real-time data demand surges, data-driven strategies gain momentum, and data privacy and security become paramount in the post-pandemic era. Data governance already had its processes, limitations, and challenges before the pandemic. However, its influence and effects were somewhat slower than expected. The management that emerged after the pandemic brought about new combinations of components, including data-driven strategies and data ecosystems. Likewise, the fragmented data ecosystems observed during the pandemic emphasize the importance of coordination and collaboration within and between government agencies. Standardized data protocols and platforms are critical to fostering a cohesive data ecosystem.

A key obstacle illuminated during the pandemic is the infrastructure limitations in data collection, storage, and analysis. To address this, governments must invest in upgrading their data infrastructure and ensure interoperability between diverse agencies. The wave in real-time data demand has exposed the vulnerabilities of existing systems, emphasizing the need for scalable storage, flexible analytics tools, and secure data channels. By strengthening these elements, governments can lay the groundwork for a resilient and responsive data infrastructure capable of meeting the evolving demands of the post-pandemic era.

Another critical aspect is the skills gap in data literacy and analytical capabilities within the government workforce. The effectiveness of data governance depends on having a skilled and knowledgeable workforce that can navigate the complexities of data management. Investment in training and skills enhancement programs for government officials and citizens is essential to close this gap. By empowering individuals with the necessary skills to critically assess data and make informed decisions, governments can improve the overall effectiveness of their data governance strategies.

One of the critical impacts of the pandemic on the data-driven government ecosystem has been the increased demand for real-time data. Governments have had to rely on timely and accurate data to track the spread of the virus, identify hotspots, and make decisions about lockdowns, social distancing measures, and other interventions. This has highlighted the need for robust data infrastructure, including data-sharing protocols, analytics tools, and secure data storage.

Consequently, the pandemic accelerated the adoption of data-driven strategies in government. Governments recognized the value of data analytics in identifying patterns and predicting future trends, enabling them to take proactive steps to prevent future crises. The public sector has increased investment in data science, machine learning, and other advanced analytics technologies.

Final Comments

The post-pandemic period has brought modern challenges to data governance and data science. Recapping the three initiatives specified, (1) Data-driven government, (2) Strategies or initiatives for government data, and (3) Data governance ecosystem, each one faces challenges that must be successfully addressed to guarantee conscious, ethical, and feasible utilization of data in society.

Within the setting of data-driven government, information protection and security are vital, particularly in an environment where digitization and information collection have been extended due to widespread data use. Strong approaches and strategies must be implemented to ensure critical data protection and anticipate security violations and unauthorized access. Furthermore, data-driven decision-making must be straightforward and free from bias, guaranteeing more even-handed and comprehensive policies that react to the changing needs of society within the post-pandemic context.

Regarding the procedures or activities for data governance, it is significant to set up data-sharing agreements and ensure intellectual property when sharing information among different government agencies. In the post-pandemic time, there's a requirement for reflection on the advancement and challenges inside the information scenarios. Remaining continually updated with information assurance regulations is key to ensuring responsibility and administrative compliance in data governance, as digitization and worldwide interconnection have increased the requirement for solid and efficient administration.

Data government ecosystems are also affected by the changes and challenges within the post-pandemic era. Collaboration and information sharing are vital for transparency and responsibility within the government, but it is essential to consider how these ecosystems need to adjust to the modern reality. Executing approaches and measures for security, anonymity, and explainability is fundamental to secure the protection and security of shared information while ensuring that the displayed data is interpretable and straightforward to citizens and partners.

The post-pandemic time has underscored the significance of data governance and data science in society. It is fundamental to address the challenges posed to guarantee capable and ethical utilization of information in government decision-making and benefit conveyance to the populace. Fortifying worldwide data governance, proposing recommendations, and reflecting on changes and impediments within the data landscape will enable us to successfully handle the challenges of the present and post-pandemic future. Only when stakeholders collectively work towards these goals will we truly guarantee a more transparent, participatory, and effective society, promoting well-being and advancement for all.

REFERENCES

Abdulla, A., Janiszewska-Kiewra, E., & Podlesny, J. (2021). Data ecosystems made simple. McKinsey Digital. https://www.mckinsey.com/capabilities/mckinsey-digital/our-insights/tech-forward/data-ecosystems-made-simple [Last accessed 6 November 2024].

Abouelmehdi, K., Beni-Hessane, A., & Khaloufi, H. (2018). Big healthcare data: Preserving security and privacy. *Journal of Big Data*, 5(1), 1–18.

Ahmad, K., Maabreh, M., Ghaly, M., Khan, K., Qadir, J., & Al-Fuqaha, A. (2022). Developing future human-centered smart cities: Critical analysis of smart city security, data management, and ethical challenges. *Computer Science Review*, 43, 100452.

Angelov, P.P., Soares, E.A., Jiang, R., Arnold, N.I., & Atkinson, P.M. (2021). Explainable artificial intelligence: An analytical review. *Wiley Interdisciplinary Reviews: Data Mining and Knowledge Discovery*, 11(5), e1424.

Arundel, A., Bloch, C., & Ferguson, B. (2019). Advancing innovation in the public sector: Aligning innovation measurement with policy goals. *Research Policy*, 48(3), 789–98.

Balayn, A., Lofi, C., & Houben, G.J. (2021). Managing bias and unfairness in data for decision support: A survey of machine learning and data engineering approaches to identify and mitigate bias and unfairness within data management and analytics systems. *The VLDB Journal*, 30(5), 739–68.

Barredo Arrieta, A., Díaz-Rodríguez, N., & Del Ser, J. (2019). Explainable Artificial Intelligence (XAI): Concepts, taxonomies, opportunities and challenges toward responsible AI. *Soft Computing*, 24(14), 10,315–20. doi: 10.1007/s00500-019-04577-2

Bonina, C., & Eaton, B. (2020). Cultivating open government data platform ecosystems through governance: Lessons from Buenos Aires, Mexico City and Montevideo. *Government Information Quarterly*, 37(3), 101479.

Brookings Institution. (2020, April 20). What all policy analysts need to know about data science. https://www.brookings.edu/articles/what-all-policy-analysts-need-to-know-about-data-science/

Brous, P., Janssen, M., & Krans, R. (2020, April). Data governance as success factor for data science. In *Conference on e-Business, e-Services and e-Society* (pp. 431–42). Cham: Springer International Publishing.

Carbonara, N., & Pellegrino, R. (2018). Fostering innovation in public procurement through public private partnerships. *Journal of Public Procurement*, 18(3), 257–80.

Cerrillo-Martinez, A., & Casadesus-de-Mingo, A. (2021). Data governance for public transparency. *Profesional De La Información*, 30(4), 1–14. https://doi.org/10.3145/epi.2021.jul.02

Cordella, A., & Paletti, A. (2019). Government as a platform, orchestration, and public value creation: The Italian case. *Government Information Quarterly*, 36(4), 101409.

Criado, J.I., & Gil-Garcia, J.R. (2019). Creating public value through smart technologies and strategies: From digital services to artificial intelligence and beyond. *International Journal of Public Sector Management*, 32(5), 438–50.

Criado, J.I., Sandoval-Almazan, R., & Gil-Garcia, J.R. (2013). Government innovation through social media. *Government Information Quarterly*, 30(4), 319–26.

Daniel, B.K. (2019). Big Data and data science: A critical review of issues for educational research. *British Journal of Educational Technology*, 50(1), 101–13.

Darici, K. (2023). El tiempo que nos robaron (2021) de Rosa Huertas: Writing as a lifeboat during COVID-19 pandemic confinement. In *Managing Pandemic Isolation with Literature as Therapy* (pp. 43–62). IGI Global: Hersey, CA.

De Guimarães, J.C.F., Severo, E.A., Júnior, L.A.F., Da Costa, W.P.L.B., & Salmoria, F.T. (2020). Governance and quality of life in smart cities: Towards Sustainable Development Goals. *Journal of Cleaner Production*, 253, 119926.

Digital Watch Observatory. (2023, June 28). Data governance | Trends in 2023. https://dig.watch/topics/data-governance

Federal Data Strategy. (2020). Federal Data Strategy Data Ethics Framework. https://resources.data.gov/assets/documents/fds-data-ethics-framework.pdf

Gebayew, C., Hardini, I.R., Panjaitan, G.H.A., & Kurniawan, N.B. (2018, October). A systematic literature review on digital transformation. In *2018 International Conference on Information Technology Systems and Innovation (ICITSI)* (pp. 260–5). IEEE.

Gegenhuber, T., Mair, J., Luehrsen, R., & Thaeter, L. (2023). Orchestrating distributed data governance in open social innovation. *Information and Organization*, 33(1), 100453 (1–11). https://doi.org/10.1016/j.infoandorg.2023.100453

Gil-Garcia, J.R., Helbig, N., & Ojo, A. (2014). Being smart: Emerging technologies and innovation in the public sector. *Government Information Quarterly*, 31, 11–18.

Gil-García, J.R., Rentería, C., & Luna-Reyes, L.F. (2014). Enacting collaborative electronic government: Empirical evidence and lessons for developing countries. In *Proceedings of the 47th Hawaii International Conference on System Sciences (HICSS-47)*, 10.

Gil-Garcia, J.R., Gasco-Hernandez, M., & Pardo, T.A. (2020). Beyond transparency, participation, and collaboration? A reflection on the dimensions of open government. *Public Performance & Management Review*, 43(3), 483–502.

Gong, Y., Yang, J., & Shi, X. (2020). Towards a comprehensive understanding of digital transformation in government: Analysis of flexibility and enterprise architecture. *Government Information Quarterly*, 37(3), 101487 (1–13). https://doi.org/10.1016/j.giq.2020.101487

Grab, B., Olaru, M., & Gavril, R.M. (2019). The impact of digital transformation on strategic business management. *Ecoforum Journal*, 8(1).

Gurstein, M.B. (2011). Open data: Empowering the empowered or effective data use for everyone?. *First Monday*, 16(2). https://doi.org/10.5210/fm.v16i2.3316

ICLG – Data Protection Laws and Regulations. (2022). Data Protection Laws and Regulations USA 2022–2023. Retrieved August 7, 2022, from https://iclg.com/practice-areas/data-protection-laws-and-regulations/usa

Ingrams, A. (2020). Administrative reform and the quest for openness: A Popperian review of open government. *Administration & Society*, 52(2), 319–40.

Ingrams, A., & Klievink, B. (2022, February 14). Transparency's role in AI governance. In Justin B. Bullock and others (eds.), *The Oxford Handbook of AI Governance* (online edn). Oxford Academic. https://doi.org/10.1093/oxfordhb/9780197579329.013.32

Jain, P., Gyanchandani, M., & Khare, N. (2016). Big data privacy: A technological perspective and review. *Journal of Big Data*, 3, 1–25.

Janssen, M., Brous, P., Estevez, E., Barbosa, L.S., & Janowski, T. (2020). Data governance: Organizing data for trustworthy Artificial Intelligence. *Government Information Quarterly*, 37(3), 101493.

Janssen, M., Hartog, M., Matheus, R., Yi Ding, A., & Kuk, G. (2022). Will algorithms blind people? The effect of explainable AI and decision-makers' experience on AI-supported decision-making in government. *Social Science Computer Review*, 40(2), 478–93. https://doi.org/10.1177/0894439320980118

Kassen, M. (2022). *Open Data Governance and Its Actors: Theory and Practice*. Springer International Publishing: Cham.

Leach, M., MacGregor, H., Scoones, I., & Wilkinson, A. (2021). Post-pandemic transformations: How and why COVID-19 requires us to rethink development. *World Development*, 138, 105233.

Khomsani, M.A. (2022, September 20). The impacts of open government initiatives to deal with COVID-19: A learning from local government. In *Proceedings of the 6th International Conference on Social and Political Enquiries, ICISPE 2021, 14–15 September 2021, Semarang, Indonesia*. https://eudl.eu/doi/10.4108/eai.14-9-2021.2321426

Kitsios, F., & Kamariotou, M. (2023). Digital innovation and entrepreneurship transformation through open data hackathons: Design strategies for successful start-up settings. *International Journal of Information Management*, 69, 102472.

Li, F. (2022). Disconnected in a pandemic: COVID-19 outcomes and the digital divide in the United States. *Health & Place, 77*, 102867 (1–8). https://doi.org/10.1016/j.healthplace.2022.102867

Liva, G., Codagnone, C., Misuraca, G., Gineikyte, V., & Barcevicius, E. (2020). Exploring digital government transformation: A literature review. In Y. Charalabidis, M.A. Cunha, & D. Sarantis (eds.), *13th International Conference on Theory and Practice of Electronic Governance (ICEGOV 2020)* (pp. 502–9). Association for Computing Machinery. https://doi.org/10.1145/3428502.3428578

Lnenicka, M., Nikiforova, A., Luterek, M., Azeroual, O., Ukpabi, D., Valtenbergs, V., & Machova, R. (2022). Transparency of open data ecosystems in smart cities: Definition and assessment of the maturity of transparency in 22 smart cities. *Sustainable Cities and Society, 82*, 103906.

Loureiro, S.M.C., Romero, J., & Bilro, R.G. (2020). Stakeholder engagement in co-creation processes for innovation: A systematic literature review and case study. *Journal of Business Research, 119*, 388–409.

Luna-Reyes, L.F., & Gil-García, J.R. (2014). Digital government transformation and internet portals: The co-evolution of technology, organizations, and institutions. *Government Information Quarterly, 31*(4), 545–55. https://doi.org/10.1016/j.giq.2014.08.001

Matheus, R., & Janssen, M. (2020). A systematic literature study to unravel transparency enabled by open government data: The window theory. *Public Performance & Management Review, 43*(3), 503–34.

Matheus, R., Janssen, M., & Maheshwari, D. (2020). Data science empowering the public: Data-driven dashboards for transparent and accountable decision-making in smart cities. *Government Information Quarterly, 37*(3), 101284.

McKinsey & Company. (2022, January 28). The data-driven enterprise of 2025. https://www.mckinsey.com/business-functions/mckinsey-analytics/our-insights/the-data-driven-enterprise-of-2025

Meijer, A., 't Hart, P., & Worthy, B. (2018). Assessing government transparency: An interpretive framework. *Administration & Society, 50*(4), 501–26.

Mikalef, P., van de Wetering, R., & Krogstie, J. (2021). Building dynamic capabilities by leveraging big data analytics: The role of organizational inertia. *Information & Management, 58*(6), 103412.

Montes, G.C., Bastos, J.C.A., & de Oliveira, A.J. (2019). Fiscal transparency, government effectiveness and government spending efficiency: Some international evidence based on panel data approach. *Economic Modelling, 79*, 211–25.

Nardi, B.A. (1998). Information ecologies. *User Services Quarterly, 38*(1), 49–50.

Nisar, Q.A., Nasir, N., Jamshed, S., Naz, S., Ali, M., & Ali, S. (2021). Big data management and environmental performance: Role of big data decision-making capabilities and decision-making quality. *Journal of Enterprise Information Management, 34*(4), 1061–96.

Nograšek, J., & Vintar, M. (2014). E-government and organisational transformation of government: Black box revisited? *Government Information Quarterly, 31*(1), 108–18). https://doi.org/10.1016/j.giq.2013.07.006

O'Sullivan, S., Janssen, M., Holzinger, A., Nevejans, N., Eminaga, O., Meyer, C.P., & Miernik, A. (2022). Explainable artificial intelligence (XAI): Closing the gap between image analysis and navigation in complex invasive diagnostic procedures. *World Journal of Urology, 40*(5), 1125–34.

OECD. (2019a). Data governance in the public sector. In OECD, *The Path to Becoming a Data-Driven Public Sector* (pp. 23–57). Paris: OECD. https://doi.org/10.1787/9cada708-en

OECD. (2019b). Enhancing access to and sharing of data: Reconciling risks and benefits for data re-use across societies. Retrieved August 10, 2022, from https://www.oecd.org/sti/enhancing-access-to-and-sharing-of-data-276aaca8-en.htm

OECD. (2022). Responding to societal challenges with data: Access, sharing, stewardship and control. https://www.oecd.org/digital/responding-to-societal-challenges-with-data-2182ce9f-en.htm

OECD. (n.d.). Open government data. https://www.oecd.org/gov/digital-government/open-government-data.htm

Parenti, C., Noori, N., & Janssen, M. (2022). A smart governance diffusion model for blockchain as an anti-corruption tool in Smart Cities. *Journal of Smart Cities and Society, 1*(1), 71–92.

Pike, E.R. (2019). Defending data: Toward ethical protections and comprehensive data governance. *Emory Law Journal, 69*, 687.

Piotrowski, S.J., Berliner, D., & Ingrams, A. (2022). *The Power of Partnership in Open Government: Reconsidering Multistakeholder Governance Reform*. Cambridge, MA: MIT Press.

Porsdam Mann, S., Savulescu, J., & Sahakian, B.J. (2016). Facilitating the ethical use of health data for the benefit of society: Electronic health records, consent and the duty of easy rescue. *Philosophical Transactions of the Royal Society A: Mathematical, Physical and Engineering Sciences*, *374*(2083), 20160130.

PublicTechnology.net. (2021, April 9). Data governance is fundamental to our post-pandemic world. https://www.publictechnology.net/2021/04/09/business-and-industry/data-governance-fundamental-our-post-pandemic-world/

Reggi, L., & Dawes, S.S. (2022). Creating open government data ecosystems: Network relations among governments, user communities, NGOs and the media. *Government Information Quarterly*, *39*(2), 101675.

Robertson, A.S., Reisin Miller, A., & Dolz, F. (2021). Supporting a data-driven approach to regulatory intelligence. *Nature Reviews Drug Discovery*, *20*(3), 161–2.

Ruijer, E., & Meijer, A. (2020). Open government data as an innovation process: Lessons from a living lab experiment. *Public Performance & Management Review*, *43*(3), 613–35.

Ruijer, E., Détienne, F., Baker, M., Groff, J., & Meijer, A.J. (2020). The politics of open government data: Understanding organizational responses to pressure for more transparency. *The American Review of Public Administration*, *50*(3), 260–74.

Saura, J.R., Ribeiro-Soriano, D., & Palacios-Marqués, D. (2022). Assessing behavioral data science privacy issues in government artificial intelligence deployment. *Government Information Quarterly*, *39*(4), 101679.

Seagate. (n.d.). Better data governance and ediscovery in the post-pandemic world. https://www.seagate.com/blog/better-data-governance-and-ediscovery-in-the-post-pandemic-world/

Sénit, C.A. (2020). Leaving no one behind? The influence of civil society participation on the Sustainable Development Goals. *Environment and Planning C: Politics and Space*, *38*(4), 693–712.

Shah, S.I.H., Peristeras, V., & Magnisalis, I. (2021). DaLiF: A data lifecycle framework for data-driven governments. *Journal of Big Data*, *8*(1), 1–44.

Sigwejo, A., & Pather, S. (2016). A citizen-centric framework for assessing e-government effectiveness. *The Electronic Journal of Information Systems in Developing Countries*, *74*(1), 1–27.

Styrin, E., Luna-Reyes, L.F., & Harrison, T.M. (2017). Open data ecosystems: An international comparison. *Transforming Government: People, Process and Policy*, *11*(1), 132–56. https://doi.org/10.1108/TG-01-2017-0006

Styrin, E., Mossberger, K., & Zhulin, A. (2022). Government as a platform: Intergovernmental participation for public services in the Russian Federation. *Government Information Quarterly*, *39*(1), 101627.

Susskind, D (2020) Six prominent thinkers reflect on how the pandemic has changed the world. IMF Blog. Retrieved December 13, 2023, from https://www.imf.org/en/Publications/fandd/issues/2020/06/how-will-the-world-be-different-after-COVID-19

TechTarget. (2022). What is data governance and why does it matter? https://www.techtarget.com/searchdatamanagement/definition/data-governance

The National Academies Press. (2020, October 21). Private lives and public policies: confidentiality and accessibility of government statistics. https://www.nap.edu/read/2122/chapter/12

The Pew Charitable Trusts. (2018, August 14). Using data to improve policy decisions. https://www.pewtrusts.org/en/about/news-room/opinion/2018/08/13/using-data-to-improve-policy-decisions

Valle-Cruz, D. (2019). Public value of e-government services through emerging technologies. *International Journal of Public Sector Management*, *32*(5), 473–88. https://doi.org/10.1108/IJPSM-03-2018-0072

Valle-Cruz, D., & García-Contreras, R. (2023). Towards AI-driven transformation and smart data management: Emerging technological change in the public sector value chain. *Public Policy and Administration*, 09520767231188401.

Valle-Cruz, D., Criado, J.I., Sandoval-Almazán, R., & Ruvalcaba-Gomez, E.A. (2020). Assessing the public policy-cycle framework in the age of artificial intelligence: From agenda-setting to policy evaluation. *Government Information Quarterly*, *37*(4), 101509.

Valle-Cruz, D., Fernandez-Cortez, V., & Gil-Garcia, J.R. (2022). From e-budgeting to smart budgeting: Exploring the potential of artificial intelligence in government decision-making for resource allocation. *Government Information Quarterly*, *39*(2), 101644.

van Berkel, N., Tag, B., Goncalves, J., & Hosio, S. (2022). Human-centred artificial intelligence: A contextual morality perspective. *Behaviour & Information Technology, 41*(3), 502–18.
van Ooijen, C., Ubaldi, B., & Welby, B. (2019). A data-driven public sector: Enabling the strategic use of data for productive, inclusive and trustworthy governance. OECD Library. https://www.oecd-ilibrary.org/governance/a-data-driven-public-sector_09ab162c-en
van Veenstra, A.F., & Kotterink, B. (2017). Data-driven policy making: The policy lab approach. In *Electronic Participation: 9th IFIP WG 8.5 International Conference, ePart 2017, St. Petersburg, Russia, September 4–7, 2017, Proceedings 9* (pp. 100–11). Springer International Publishing: Heidelberg.
Vashisht, A. (2023, June 1). Data-driven decision-making in government: enhancing policy formulation and public services through advanced analytics. LinkedIn. https://www.linkedin.com/pulse/data-driven-decision-making-government-enhancing-policy-vashisht
Vlados, C., Koutroukis, T., & Chatzinikolaou, D. (2022). Change management, organizational adaptation, and labor market restructuration: Notes for the post-COVID-19 era. In *COVID-19 Pandemic Impact on New Economy Development and Societal Change* (pp. 1–21). IGI Global: Hersey, CA.
Wernick, A. (2020). Defining data intermediaries: A clearer view through the lens of intellectual property governance. *Technology and Regulation, 2020*, 65–77.
Wieringa, J., Kannan, P.K., Ma, X., Reutterer, T., Risselada, H., & Skiera, B. (2021). Data analytics in a privacy-concerned world. *Journal of Business Research, 122*, 915–25.
Wirtz, B.W., Weyerer, J.C., Becker, M., & Müller, W.M. (2022). Open government data: A systematic literature review of empirical research. *Electronic Markets, 32*(4), 2381–404.
Wukich, C. (2021). Government social media engagement strategies and public roles. *Public Performance & Management Review, 44*(1), 187–215.
Xu, Z., & Peng, J. (2022). Ecosystem services-based decision-making: A bridge from science to practice. *Environmental Science & Policy, 135*, 6–15.
Zuiderwijk, A., Chen, Y.C., & Salem, F. (2021). Implications of the use of artificial intelligence in public governance: A systematic literature review and a research agenda. *Government Information Quarterly, 38*(3), 101577.

PART II

AI GOVERNANCE AND INNOVATION

11. Key challenges for the participatory governance of AI in public administration

Janis Wong, Deborah Morgan, Vincent J. Straub, Youmna Hashem and Jonathan Bright

INTRODUCTION

The last decade has seen exceptional progress in artificial intelligence (AI) research and innovation. As AI has moved from a purely technical field to an interdisciplinary domain with applications in a wide range of areas, its promise to transform government has also been recognized (Margetts and Dorobantu, 2019). However, as public agencies adopt AI at a national and subnational level in the hopes of improving public service delivery and informing policymaking, the challenges that this poses and the substantive harms which can result from the misguided or premature adoption of AI systems have become more apparent (Rudin, 2019). There is by now broad agreement in academic and policy circles that the use of AI in government demands that systems are reliable, safe, transparent, and trustworthy, as well as free from bias (Veale et al., 2018b). This is especially the case in public administration, where decision-making can involve exceptionally high stakes and carries the risk of serious harms to individuals and communities.

Yet, while technical research has proceeded to investigate how to engineer such systems, there are several remaining challenges related to the governance and oversight of AI systems that still need to be addressed to ensure that deployed systems function as expected (Margetts, 2022). In particular, as we shall argue below, one of the core drivers of many AI failures thus far has been a lack of involvement of affected stakeholders and communities, and a wider lack of democratic oversight and participation in their design. Thus, many are now calling for AI services in government and public administration to involve more explicit citizen participation.

While citizen participation is undoubtedly a goal to strive for in theory, its implementation in practice is mired with difficulties, which the field of AI and public administration is only starting to come to grips with. In this chapter, we seek to bridge this gap through conceptual analysis and a narrative review of literature within the fields of participatory governance, public administration, and the developing space of AI and data within government to outline a framework for understanding participatory governance, while also highlighting how the participatory governance of AI raises considerable challenges. In doing so, we hope to contribute to efforts aimed at developing participatory governance of AI models that work, taking inspiration both from participatory governance literature and from work on the participatory governance of data, a closely related subfield that has already started to think about AI governance and participation.

Our chapter is structured as follows. In the next section, we define AI in government, survey existing literature, and provide an overview of the application of AI to government and public administration. We highlight and consider many empirical use cases that are emerging, some of the harms that result, and make the case that applying enhanced citizen participation methods may help mitigate some of these problems. In the third section, we develop this work to sketch a simple framework for understanding participatory governance, drawing upon literature from key scholars in the field. Finally, in the fourth section, we apply this framework to the developing field of the governance of AI in public administration, highlighting the key challenges facing the implementation of a truly participatory form of AI.

AI IN GOVERNMENT AND PUBLIC ADMINISTRATION

AI is a broad term used to describe both machines and computers that appear to act intelligently, and the field of study concerned with understanding and developing such systems (Simon, 1995). While there is no widely accepted definition, many basic descriptions relate AI to systems that can perform tasks which, if performed by people, would be regarded as requiring intelligence (Russell, 2010). A prominent example is provided by the European Union (EU) High-Level Expert Group, which defines AI as 'systems that display intelligent behaviour by analysing their environment and taking actions—with some degree of autonomy—to achieve specific goals' (European Commission,, 2018). Similarly, the working definition of the UK government, as set out in the National AI Strategy, is: 'Machines that perform tasks normally performed by human intelligence, especially when the machines learn from data how to do those tasks' (Kazim et al., 2021). An important attribute of AI systems captured by these definitions, as highlighted by Köbis et al. (2022), is that AI fundamentally differs from static information and communication technologies (ICTs). The implications therein for its use in public administration are potentially transformative; while classic ICTs (such as email) allow for the digitalization of procedures and ensure public services are accessible online, they do not actually conduct tasks autonomously—AI systems do (Bullock, 2019; Methnani et al., 2021).

The Uses of AI in Government and Public Administration

AI technologies are currently being used in various public agencies with the aim of making government operations and services more efficient, fair, and responsive. One comprehensive study found that, in the context of the United States, nearly half (45 percent) of all federal agencies had experimented with AI by 2020 (Engstrom et al., 2020). Globally, AI systems are now being employed to process general requests, standardize paperwork flows, administer health insurance, provide student aid services, and even detect possible fraud for drug authorities (Bullock et al., 2022). However, previous research on the use of AI in government has tended to consider the uses of AI very broadly and fragmentarily (Wirtz et al., 2019).

While various attempts to classify government applications of AI exist, there is no universally accepted framework to determine or analyze the scope of government-related tasks AI systems can complete (Bullock et al., 2022). For the purposes of this chapter, we follow Margetts (2022) and argue that the current uses of AI can broadly be split into three areas for which AI systems have already proved helpful in a public sector context: detection, prediction, and simulation.

Detection is one of the 'essential capabilities that any system of control must possess at the point where it comes into contact with the world outside' (Hood and Margetts, 2007). In the case of AI, machine learning (ML) tools can be deployed, for instance, in the detection of online harms such as hate speech, financial scams like fraud, and identity identification. A notable example of the latter is the use of facial recognition technology in policing (Zilka et al., 2022). A second, related use of AI is for prediction. Governments can employ the predictive capabilities of ML to spot patterns and relationships that may be of concern or which might otherwise have gone unnoticed. Recent examples here include recidivism prediction in the criminal justice system (Kleinberg et al., 2018), and forecasting future needs in emergency services (Bright et al., 2019). A particularly striking example is tools that aim to prevent infant maltreatment by leveraging existing data systems to rapidly predict future risk (Lanier et al., 2020). Finally, AI can be used for simulation, allowing governments to test and experiment with interventions before they are enacted. More specifically, with the use of ML along with other computational methods and large-scale transactional data, public agencies can simulate policies like different resource allocation strategies to explore any unintended consequences. In the UK context, for example, the National Digital Twin program is considering how the UK can increase system resilience for built environments in the face of future extreme weather events caused by climate change (Smith, 2022).

Challenges for AI in Government

As the use of AI in government has grown, several governance challenges have emerged that stem in large part from the civic and public demand for stronger ethical foundations to curtail the irresponsible use of data science and AI. As a result, there is now broad agreement in both academic and policy circles that the use of AI in government demands systems that are more human-centered (Veale et al., 2018b). Although there is no consensus for defining what human-centered AI means, it broadly refers to AI systems that address a common set of concerns spanning ethics, law, culture, and governance, which may be grouped under the heading of epistemic and normative issues (Straub et al., 2023). Each concern can be said to relate to the increasing complexity of AI systems and their potential to cause real-world harms. They include, among others, the need for systems to be more transparent, reliable, accountable, and interpretable, as well as fair, safe, and trustworthy (Estevez et al., 2022). Many of these concerns are a direct response to the substantive harms caused by using AI applications within high-stakes decisions. In the case of AI used for facial recognition, for instance, it has been shown that algorithms trained with biased data have resulted in algorithmic discrimination (Buolamwini and Gebru, 2018). Similar studies exist for natural language processing applications which learn word associations from written texts (Caliskan et al., 2017). Some scholars have in turn called for a moratorium on government use of facial recognition (Crawford, 2019), while several local administrative regions have banned its use altogether (Conger et al., 2019). Although AI systems are being developed to be more accurate, the body of evidence revealing their perils and pitfalls has continued to grow.

While a range of harms has resulted from careless uses of AI in government, one common thread linking them all, we argue, relates to a lack of civic participation and democratic engagement in the process of the design, deployment, and assessment of the technologies. As such, our argument builds on the work of previous scholars who have argued that people and society are the 'missing dimension' (Grosz, 2019) in the current AI revolution. While a lack of participatory design methods has also been identified as a feature of AI in education, research, and engineering (Grosz et al., 2019), we contend that the issue of a participation deficit is perhaps most significant when it comes to oversight and governance of AI systems in the context of government. As such, this is the focus of this chapter. This can be seen where current AI developments and applications are, to a large extent, regulated through non-binding ethics guidelines penned by transnational entities (Erman and Furendal, 2022). As Widder and Nafus (2022) claim, the field arguably needs to get better at understanding relations between institutions and advancing creative ways to modularize participation from impacted groups, as opposed to *metadata maximalism*, defined by Gansky and Mcdonald (2022) as 'practices and infrastructures for achieving normative goals by adding contextualizing information to datasets and machine-learning models and services.' Notably, although the involvement of civil society is regularly identified as key in ensuring ethical and equitable approaches towards the governance of AI by state and non-state actors (Sanchez, 2021), the reality of AI governance presents a stark contrast. As summarized by Beining et al. (2020), 'civil society organisations that study and address the social, political and ethical challenges of AI are not sufficiently consulted and struggle to have an impact on the policy debate.' The results, perhaps unsurprisingly, are AI systems that are not open and accessible to all members of the public, exhibit biases towards affected groups that were not consulted, and, at worst, result in unfair treatment of minorities (Alon-Barkat and Busuioc, 2022; Brantingham et al., 2018; Dressel and Farid, 2018; Miron et al., 2021). As AI becomes more and more embedded within government operations and decision-making, retaining democratic control over these technologies will only become more crucial as a means of mitigating such problems.

THE DIMENSIONS OF PARTICIPATORY GOVERNANCE

In this chapter, we consider the challenge of applying methods of participatory governance to the oversight of AI systems in public administration. This section explores the literature in the field to highlight several dimensions that constitute and define participatory governance, alongside illustrative examples of how such dimensions have been explored in relation to data and ML.

Participatory governance is defined by Fischer (2012) as a 'variant or subset of governance theory that puts emphasis on democratic engagement, in particular through deliberative practices.' Citizen-led engagement and deliberation are a core element of normative conceptions of participatory governance through the opening up of existing legal and institutional arrangements and the redistribution of power between those institutions and their citizens. Participatory approaches may take a number of forms, including public inquiries, citizen juries, public dialogue processes and conferences, local associations and councils, and citizens' assemblies (Dryzek, 2002; Papadopoulos and Warin, 2007). In practice, the varied form and design of participatory approaches across domains, while necessarily flexible, present definitional challenges in identifying common features, structural arrangements, and uniform methods. Further, in defining participatory governance structures, the democratic nature and quality of participatory governance arrangements is often used as a benchmark (Heinelt, 2018). Several methods have been used to operationalize these arrangements. Papadopoulos and Warin (2007) focus on the core questions to consider when assessing the potential of participatory governance tools to contribute to democratic decision-making. Institutional analysis, and particularly the Institutional Analysis Framework (IAD) developed by Elinor Ostrom (1990, 2005), has been used by Klok and Denters (2018) to analyze and isolate features of the 'rules in use' of participatory governance arenas 'where participants propose, debate and eventually perhaps decide on what to do.' As such, the applications of the IAD and the questions posed by Papadopoulos and Warin (2007) are combined below to outline and explore a number of dimensions of democratic participatory governance.

Institutional Rules and Frameworks

The first critical element of participatory governance is the institutional rules and frameworks of the participation mechanism itself. In a participatory situation, the rules and structure of the 'action situation,' wherein actions produce outcomes, can be highly determinative of participant perceptions and the impact of the process (Ostrom, 2005). The participatory 'institution' that is created may be themed around a particular issue or problem, specific community need, or defined project, and may differ significantly in its design from the more historical formal decision-making bodies that it may intersect with. Applying Ostrom's IAD framework to analyze participatory governance, Klok and Denters (2018) highlight several aspects that need to be considered in such participatory systems. For example, this includes the adoption of a design consideration of the institutionalization of the participatory process, where this dimension relates to the significance of early rule formulation and establishing the internal operation of the process itself. Balancing the need for process flexibility and clarity is a challenging design task, and Klok and Denters (2018) outline a general design principle as potentially being where 'the more power is transferred the more clarity and formalization of other rules is needed.'

Openness and Access

Second, allied to the need to define the varied 'rules-in-use' of the participatory governance arena, Papadopoulos and Warin (2007) highlight the need to consider questions of openness and access. This dimension is focused on the extent to which a particular participatory approach is inclusive and accessible to enable engagement with a broad range of citizen knowledge (Krick, 2021). Salient questions within this dimension encompass how decisions or inputs will be collated, agreed upon, and shared. Systematically mapping and iteratively assessing information flows through the participatory governance process may highlight how participant knowledge can be collected and incorporated. Concerns around entry and exit from the governance structure are also particularly important. Fung (2006) details a number of important selection questions regarding the 'character of the franchise' of governance participation. These include:

- Are important interests or perspectives excluded?
- Are they appropriately representative of the relevant population of the general public?
- Do they possess the information and competence to make good judgements and decisions?

It is important to note that many of the answers to such questions are subjective, value-based questions that may change and adapt as a process develops. In addition, questions around equality are key considerations. Examples include which participant inputs are considered 'equal' within the process and, more broadly, whether equality amongst participants is itself a desirable aim or whether individuals who are more significantly impacted have or require a higher degree of input. In order for participatory governance to be open and accessible, these questions should be considered iteratively and include the direct involvement of participants.

Alongside establishing entry criteria questions, the method of invitation or selection of participants is a further 'boundary rule' (Ostrom, 2005) which surfaces wider considerations of representation, the role of power (Haus, 2018), and inclusiveness of the wider affected community (Damayanti and Syarifuddin, 2020). Accessibility is an essential criterion alongside representation and, again, necessitates reflective consultation and planning, at the early stage of developing a participatory process. Irvin and Stansbury (2004) define a useful number of ideal and non-ideal conditions for citizen participation in agency-based decision-making, including 'Key stakeholders are not too geographically dispersed; participants can easily reach meetings. Citizens have enough income to attend meetings without harming their ability to provide for their families.' As Wilkinson et al. (2019) also explore, in the context of participatory budgeting, addressing the questions of who benefits from the process, why they should benefit, and how they benefit is 'critical to ensuring the process is fair, just and worthy of giving their time to and granting their trust in.'

Actors

The third critical element of participatory governance is defining, identifying, and locating the participants within a participatory governance process (Klok and Denters, 2018). This can be a challenging task given that the nature and interests of affected partics may vary considerably. Local norms and values of a particular setting or context may significantly influence the willingness and ability of participants to engage. Assessing how representative a process is requires significant reflection and consultation by those involved in designing the process. Participants may also change and develop throughout the lifecycle of the governance process as an understanding of the context and implications of a particular decision or project are surfaced and problematized. As Klok and Denters (2018, p. 137) outline, 'formulating the right to formulate new options is a major way of ensuring that participants can influence outcomes in line with their preferences.' As such, an expectation of various forms of change during the participatory process and across all aspects of the governance lifecycle are important considerations. The increasing complexity of 'knowledge societies' may also require the involvement of specific experts within a participatory process. Krick (2022) explores the tensions in balancing increasing 'expertization' with the aim of expanding the use of participatory processes. This work highlights the role of advocacy groups in blending a multiplicity of affected viewpoints and expert representation to move beyond individual viewpoints.

Aggregation and Preference Elicitation

In adopting and applying participatory governance approaches, aggregation and preference elicitation are also important for clarifying next steps as part of the collaborative process. Aggregation refers to how the decisions or outcomes of a particular process will be collated at the conclusion or at defined points within the participatory process. Defining aggregation rules is a significant yet challenging design consideration. Avoiding stalemate, acknowledging participant involvement, and minimizing the loss of vital participant knowledge are key considerations in capturing key learning and deliberations from the participatory process. If voting or consensus is used as an aggregation mechanism, the structures and rules of any voting system will require explicit agreement prior to any summative process (Klok and Denters, 2018). Beyond voting, participants' views and knowledge may be represented in both quantitative and qualitative data. Examples of this may comprise plans, reports, decision summaries, transcripts, or budget proposals. In the production of such aggregations of knowledge, this then raises the question of accountability. Klok and Denters (2018) ask, 'who writes the report?' In other words, who is responsible for the final representation of the process, wherein the rich learning from the diverse participatory process are communicated.

Intersection with Formal Structures/Governance

In our assessment of the participatory governance literature and landscape, the final critical element of participatory governance involves combining the outcomes derived from participatory governance approaches with formal institutional and governance structures for continued implementation. Visser and Kreemers (2020), within their work reflecting upon institutional space for participatory governance in education, highlight the challenges of bridging 'distances' between educational stakeholders and particular processes, noting that 'it is hard to combine the local and diverse context of the schools with the overarching policy themes and processes in the national policymaking process.' The analogy of a bridge is particularly useful in considering how the many forms of participatory processes may then be incorporated into the structures of decision-making or policy of a particular domain. The outputs of a particular participatory process will necessarily be specific, contextual, and, hopefully, align with the agreed aims of the process. However, the iterative nature and co-design of a participatory process may itself present challenges in reaching agreement regarding the appropriate mechanism to then implement or action the outcomes of the process (Goodyear-Smith et al., 2015). The contextual challenges of forming links with more formalized or historical local or national processes is an element within the broader absence of 'consensus understanding of the proper role or consequences of direct public engagement' (Fung, 2015).

PARTICIPATORY GOVERNANCE FOR AI

In this section, we apply the critical elements of participatory governance which we identified above for thinking about participatory governance and the governance of AI technologies in public bureaucracies. While participatory governance in the context of novel technologies can be seen to empower people to increase their agency over their data and positively contribute to the governance of AI, participatory processes can also introduce new challenges. We seek to expand on these challenges in relation to the uses of AI in government, building upon the framework for understanding participation we outlined in the previous section.

Our work in this section is inspired by scholarship that has examined participatory governance as applied to data, a closely related subfield that has considered many of the questions we wish to tackle. It is useful to begin, therefore, with a brief overview of the data governance landscape. Data governance comes in many forms, and although there is no universally applicable definition, it largely refers to frameworks, processes, and practices that support responsible data management to ensure that data is secure, accurate, complete, and protected

186 *Handbook on governance and data science*

with high levels of integrity (HESA, 2022; Microsoft, 2020; Stobierski, 2021). More holistically, data governance considers the data lifecycle and contextualizes the who, how, and what when it comes to the data collection, processing, and sharing lifecycle.

Data governance came to prominence with the recognition that in our data-driven society (Pentland, 2013), the ownership and ways in which data is being collected, processed, and analyzed have become more complicated. This makes it more difficult for individuals to understand how their personal data is being used (Veale et al., 2018a) and how to make choices that are more in line with their privacy preferences (Gerber et al., 2018). As new technologies enable the capture of information, the creation of an information commons recognizes that information is no longer a free and open public good, but now needs to be managed, monitored, and protected for archival sustainability and accessibility (Hess and Ostrom, 2001). In addition to the legal and technological measures (much of which were developed following the implementation of the EU General Data Protection Regulation (GDPR) 2016) for ensuring that principles such as data minimization, data protection-by-design, and mandating data protection rights are employed, wider stakeholder inclusion has been considered beyond the protection of personal data alone (Malcolm, 2015).

Data governance is seen as both supplementary and evolutionary to existing regulations and technological solutions that aim to increase the socioeconomic value of individual and collective forms of data (Coyle et al., 2020). As part of data governance, participatory methods are increasingly seen as crucial for ensuring that data is properly collected, processed, managed, and protected. For example, in consideration of participatory data governance or participatory methods as part of data management, numerous organizations have incorporated stakeholder engagement practices (Wong et al., 2022), such as the Ada Lovelace Institute's 'Participatory data stewardship' report (2021b) that establishes a framework for involving people in the use of data to operationalize practices that empower people to help inform, shape, and govern their own data. Meanwhile, Waag, in their Urbanite project (2021), has also assessed people's experiences with disruptive technology through a participatory lens. The project examined the effectiveness of participatory processes as part of democratic citizen engagement that involves taking part in ideating, debating, and implementing initiatives in the public sphere.

More recently, European regulatory developments such as the EU Data Governance Act (DGA) 2020 have considered new mechanisms for facilitating the reuse of public sector data and encouraging data sharing. This includes AI technologies, such as regulating data intermediation services, creating common European data spaces, and promoting data altruism through data cooperatives (Bietti et al., 2021).

For the remainder of this section, we draw on insights from studies involving participatory data governance to highlight the key challenges facing the application of participatory governance to AI in the context of public administration, making use of the framework developed in Section the fourth section. Figure 11.1 provides a schematic showing the five key elements we identify that are needed to achieve participatory governance of AI, on each of which we expand below.

Institutional Rules and Frameworks

The first area to consider is the institutional rules and frameworks through which participation in the public administration sphere takes place. In general, there is no one fixed format

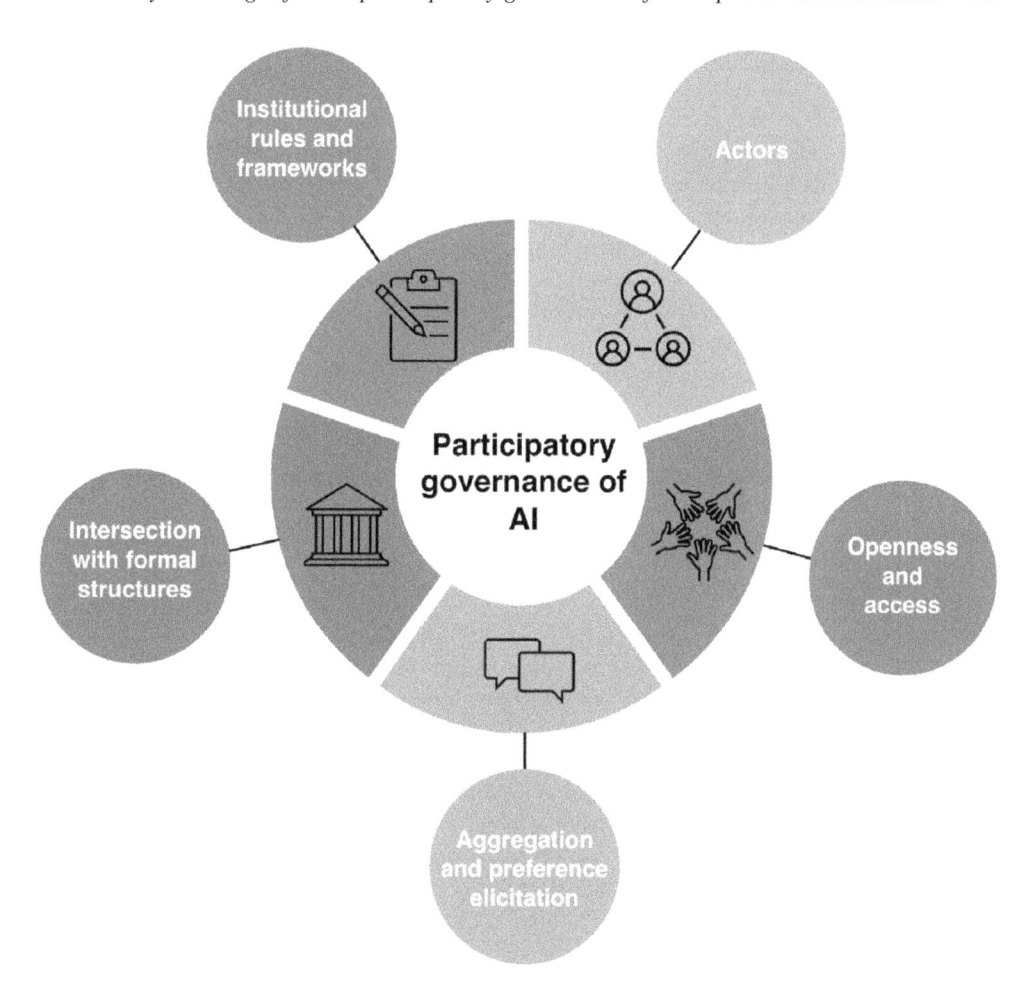

Figure 11.1 Schematic illustrating the five elements that need to be considered to achieve participatory governance of AI based on applying Ostrom's Institutional Analysis and Development (IAD) framework

for participatory processes, and many are convened ad hoc in response to the emergence of particular projects. However, institutionalizing new forms of participation takes time. Hence, creating new structures for every new AI project in a public administration context may not be appropriate. In the context of data governance, it is worth highlighting the development of generic platforms for enabling participation that may also prove effective in the AI context. For example, in the case of smart cities and citizen participation in an urban environment, decidim is an online digital platform for citizen participation that aims to help citizens, organizations, and public institutions self-organize democratically (decidim, 2019). Yet, it is equally important to remember the issue of digital divides in this context, and not to over-rely on technology to solve governance issues (Londonwide LMCs, 2019).

Openness and Access

The area of openness and access has also raised considerable challenges when considering the adoption of AI in government and public administration. Engaging the public in the governance of technology is not an easy task in practice. Existing studies of participatory data governance have highlighted uncertainties over long-term efforts and effectiveness inherent in participation as one core reason why people are often skeptical about joining in (Waag, 2021). More generally, it may be difficult to ensure that participation is diverse or representative of the population (Karanasiou, 2019; Waag, 2021), with technology enthusiasts perhaps more likely to be represented than others.

Citizen's ability to access participatory governance processes can also be limited by the high entry barriers in terms of specialist knowledge that may be required to understand a particular AI application. While research and development in the field of 'explainable AI' continues to grow (Adadi and Berrada, 2018; de Bruijn et al., 2022; UK Central Digital and Data Office, 2022), the technology nevertheless remains largely a 'black box' to the public at large (European Commission, 2021; Lipton, 2016). Indeed, while explaining AI to skilled practitioners is certainly feasible, it remains to be seen whether the general public will reach the level of comprehension of the technology to necessitate meaningful agency and participation or whether such high levels of technical knowledge and digital literacy are feasible in democratic systems (Bulfin and McGraw, 2015). Notably, prominent initiatives aiming to fill this public knowledge gap do exist. One such example is Elements of AI, a first-of-its-kind online course, accessible to all, that teaches some of the core technical aspects and social implications of AI, developed by the publicly funded University of Helsinki and technology company Reaktor, which has reached over 130,000 people (Elements of AI, 2020). Another such example is the Methods for Inclusion project led by the non-profit Partnership on AI, which aims to champion a participatory approach to the design of AI and ML systems by amplifying the voices of the public, and specifically impacted communities, in the development of these systems (Yang and Park, 2020).

Nevertheless, those advocating for further citizen participation in the process of AI technologies must recognize that participation in AI may never come with a sophisticated understanding of the technology. Furthermore, while some individuals may grasp how AI technologies are deployed within public administration, many may not; hence, participatory democracy in data-related projects may exacerbate digital divides (Londonwide LMCs, 2019) and increase inequalities of participation.

Additionally, it is important to distinguish participatory governance and methods from increased transparency and communication of processes. For example, while increased support for open research, data, and AI can help increase individuals' understanding of data and governance to allow for greater accountability (Brandusescu et al., 2019), this does not equate to encouraging participation, consultation, or agency within participatory governance (Fung, 2015).

Actors

Alongside the questions of openness and access, there is also the question of who is allowed to participate in the process. Often, this is a question related to geographic scope and scale. In the case of policing, community involvement in policing, such as Neighbourhood Watch in the

UK and Safeland in Sweden, is often structured at the local level (Mulgan et al., 2018); however, community involvement in AI-driven policing may have a different required geographic scope as technologies developed in one context can often be unthinkingly ported into another (Fung and Wright, 2003).

Considering participation requirements also relates to the question of experts' involvement. As highlighted in our chapter, participatory processes have an uneasy relationship with experts. On the one hand, they can facilitate public engagement by providing a link between citizens and a complex subject. On the other hand, they may erect another implicit barrier to participation and make governance technocratic rather than truly democratic. One interesting example in this context is data stewards. Within data governance, data stewardship frameworks operationalize this redistribution of power to maximize the potential value of data (University of Washington, 2022). Similar to data governance, there is no universal definition for data stewardship (Informatica UK, 2022; O'hara, 2019). Data stewardship generally refers to processes by which data governance policies can be implemented for the benefit of stakeholders within the data management process (FAIRsFAIR, 2022; Plotkin, 2021). Data stewards refer to a specific individual or role that enacts data stewardship (Loshin, 2009), often with fiduciary duties or responsibilities (Rosenbaum, 2010; Winowatan, 2019). Similar stewardship roles may also be valuable in the context of AI in public administration but must be carefully defined to ensure that such stewards enable and not replace citizens' involvement as part of the participatory governance process.

Aggregation and Preference Elicitation

In the specific context of AI in government and public administration, participatory governance approaches have also been considered (Balaram et al., 2018; Stephens, 2021). One example is a Citizens' Jury, a method developed by The Jefferson Center that involves a group of citizens representative of the local area who come together to deliberate and find common ground on a given issue (Involve, 2018). The National Institute for Health Research Greater Manchester Patient Safety Translational Research Centre and the Information Commissioner's Office (ICO) in the UK explored what people expect to know about how an AI system reaches a decision as part of the Citizens' Juries on Explainable AI project (Health e-Research Centre, 2019). The findings and outcomes of the projects were aggregated to produce guidance that gives organizations practical advice to help explain the processes, services, and decisions delivered or assisted by AI to the individuals affected by them (ICO and The Alan Turing Institute, 2020).

Regulators might also seek to turn to digital technologies, including AI applications themselves, in order to make the process of aggregation and preference elicitation more effective, inclusive, and democratic. Research in the field of digital democracy (Clark et al., 2019) and collective intelligence, an interdisciplinary field concerned with the enhanced capacity that is created when people work together, has shown how new digital tools can facilitate conversation and consensus-building between diverse opinion groups (Saunders and Mulgan, 2017). One tool using AI that has received widespread coverage is Pol.is, an open-source online platform that invites participants to enrich a debate (Small et al., 2021). Having been recently trialed in a UK policy context (Buch, 2022), the application uses ML to group participants according to how they vote on all statements in the debate. Another prominent example at the national level is vTaiwan, a platform originally launched in 2014 and designed to engage experts and relevant members of the public in large-scale deliberation on specific topics (Hsiao et al., 2018). Further case studies are discussed by Ryan et al., (2020). While many such tools have yet to be systematically adopted at a large scale, they show the potential of using AI to improve participation. A recent review of the growing collective intelligence field has shown this area of research is increasingly influenced by AI-focused research (Berditchevskaia et al., 2022), suggesting that many more AI tools may help to further promote participation in the near future.

Intersection with Formal Structures of Governance

A final consideration in the context of AI for public administration is how the results of participatory and deliberative processes can be integrated into formal structures once they have emerged. Data governance provides examples of data stewardship frameworks. These include:

- Data trusts (a legal structure that facilitates the storage and sharing of data through a repeatable framework of terms and mechanisms, providing independent, fiduciary stewardship of data) (Hardinges, 2020);
- Data cooperatives (a group that perceives itself as having collective interests where an autonomous association of persons unites voluntarily to meet their common economic, social, and cultural needs and aspirations through a jointly owned and democratically controlled enterprise in the context of data) (Ada Lovelace Institute, 2021a; International Cooperative Alliance, 2018); and
- Data commons (a collective set of resources that may be: owned by no one; jointly owned but indivisible; or owned by an individual with others nevertheless having rights to usage) (Ada Lovelace Institute, 2021a; Fisher and Fortmann, 2010).

These frameworks all include participatory methodologies to varying degrees and as different parts of the data governance process. However, given the absence of agreement regarding the roles and routes for participatory governance, it is unsurprising that tensions may emerge from local participation processes and ongoing attempts at regulation and governance. One example is the intersection between participation and standards-setting bodies where, on the one hand, it is increasingly recognized that international standards will be a critical part of developing a mature AI ecosystem, but, on the other hand, such standards may override locally developed norms and community practices.

CONCLUSION

Despite the promises of responsible and ethical AI research, the challenges that the use of AI in government and public administration poses are only growing, especially as the complexity and applicability of AI systems continue to increase. At the same time, it has been recognized that many of the challenges posed by AI systems stem from a lack of democratic involvement and engagement of affected communities, citizens, civil society, and society at large. However, while in theory, citizen participation is undoubtedly a goal to strive for, its implementation in practice is mired in difficulties with which the field of AI and public administration is only starting to get to grips. In this chapter, we have sought to advance this goal by outlining a framework for understanding participatory governance through identifying key considerations, while also taking into account how participatory governance of AI raises particular challenges as applied to government and public administration.

Going forward, in the realm of AI governance, we are still at the beginning of establishing and embedding formal channels of participatory governance within existing state institutions as well as incorporating such approaches meaningfully into the ecosystem of data use and AI development practices. Empirical research that explores the unique benefits and challenges of such approaches, therefore, has the potential to greatly shape future policy. Further inquiry will thus benefit from considering how citizen participation can be directly embedded into the oversight of the design, development, and deployment of AI systems. Beyond this, the lack of effective education on AI and the potential knock-on effects this has on the current development of information societies globally calls for more immediate macro-level action. In reconsidering the frameworks underpinning the governance of AI, growing calls to focus on citizen participation and to treat government AI systems as a public good managed in the public interest are warmly welcomed as one further avenue of research that can help pave a path forward towards a more democratic, participatory future.

FUNDING

This work was supported by Towards Turing 2.0 under the EPSRC Grant EP/W037211/1 and The Alan Turing Institute.

REFERENCES

Ada Lovelace Institute. (2021a, March 4). *Exploring legal mechanisms for data stewardship.*
Ada Lovelace Institute. (2021b). *Participatory data stewardship.*
Adadi, A., and Berrada, M. (2018). Peeking inside the black-box: A survey on Explainable Artificial Intelligence (XAI). IEEE Access, 6, 52138–60. https://doi.org/10.1109/ACCESS.2018.2870052 (Last accessed October 13, 2022).
Ala-Pietilä, P., and Smuha, N. (2021) A framework for global cooperation on artificial intelligence and its governance. In B. Braunschweig and M. Ghallab (eds.), *Reflections on Artificial Intelligence for Humanity.* Springer, 2021. https://ssrn.com/abstract=3696519 (Last accessed October 13, 2022).
Alon-Barkat, S., and Busuioc, M. (2022). Human–AI interactions in public sector decision making: 'Automation bias' and 'selective adherence' to algorithmic advice. *Journal of Public Administration Research and Theory,* muac007. https://doi.org/10.1093/jopart/muac007 (Last accessed October 13, 2022).
Balaram, B., Greenham, T., and Leonard, J. (2018). Artificial Intelligence; Real public engagement. *The Royal Society for Arts, Manufactures and Commerce.* https://www.thersa.org/reports/artificial-intelligence-real-public-engagement (Last accessed October 13, 2022).
Beining, L., Bihr, P., and Heumann, S. (2020). Towards a European AI & society ecosystem. *Stiftung Neue Verantwortung.*
Belli, L. (2015). A heterostakeholder cooperation for sustainable internet policymaking. *Internet Policy Review.* https://policyreview.info/articles/analysis/heterostakeholder-cooperation-sustainable-internet-policymaking (Last accessed October 13, 2022).
Bengio, Y., Lecun, Y., and Hinton, G. (2021). Deep learning for AI. *Communications of the ACM, 64*(7), 58–65. https://doi.org/10.1145/3448250 (Last accessed October 13, 2022).

Berditchevskaia, A., Maliaraki, E., and Stathoulopoulos, K. (2022). A descriptive analysis of collective intelligence publications since 2000, and the emerging influence of artificial intelligence. *Collective Intelligence*, *1*(1), 26339137221107924.

Bietti, E., Etxeberria, A., Mannan, M., and Wong, J. (2021). Data cooperatives in Europe: A legal and empirical investigation. *White Paper Created as Part of The New School's Platform Cooperativism Consortium and Harvard University's Berkman Klein Center for Internet & Society Research Sprint*.

Brandusescu, A., Iglesias, C., Lämmerhirt, D., and Verhulst, S. (2019, February 20). *Open data governance and open governance: Interplay or disconnect?* World Wide Web Foundation. https://webfoundation.org/2019/02/open-data-governance-and-open-governance-interplay-or-disconnect/ (Last accessed October 13, 2022).

Brantingham, P.J., Valasik, M., and Mohler, G.O. (2018). Does predictive policing lead to biased arrests? Rresults from a randomized controlled trial. *Statistics and Public Policy*, *5*(1), 1–6. https://doi.org/10.1080/2330443X.2018.1438940 (Last accessed October 13, 2022).

Bright, J., Ganesh, B., Seidelin, C., Vogl, T.M. (2019). Data Science for Local Government. https://dx.doi.org/10.2139/ssrn.3370217 (Last accessed November 20, 2024).

Buch, P. (2022). *Cutting through complexity using collective intelligence—Policy Lab*. [online] Openpolicy.blog.gov.uk. Available at: https://openpolicy.blog.gov.uk/2022/10/11/cutting-through-complexity-using-collective-intelligence/ (Last accessed October 13, 2022).

Bulfin, S., and McGraw, K. (2015). Digital literacy in theory, policy and practice: Old concerns, new opportunities. *Teaching and Digital Technologies: Big Issues and Critical Questions*, 266–81.

Bullock, J. (2019). Artificial intelligence, discretion, and bureaucracy. *The American Review of Public Administration*, *49*(7), 751–61.

Bullock, J., Huang, H., and Kim, K.-C. (Casey). (2022). Machine intelligence, bureaucracy, and human control. *Perspectives on Public Management and Governance*, *5*(2), 187–96. https://doi.org/10.1093/ppmgov/gvac006 (Last accessed October 13, 2022).

Buolamwini, J., and Gebru, T. (2018). Gender shades: Intersectional accuracy disparities in commercial gender classification. In *Proceedings of the 1st Conference on Fairness, Accountability and Transparency*, 77–91. https://proceedings.mlr.press/v81/buolamwini18a.html (Last accessed October 13, 2022).

Caliskan, A., Bryson, J.J., and Narayanan, A. (2017). Semantics derived automatically from language corpora contain human-like biases. *Science*, *356*(6334), 183–6.

Clark, B.Y., Zingale, N., Logan, J., and Brudney, J. (2019). A framework for using crowdsourcing in government. In *Social Entrepreneurship: Concepts, Methodologies, Tools, and Applications* (pp. 405–25). IGI Global.

Conger, K., Fausset, R., and Kovaleski, S.F. (2019). San Francisco bans facial recognition technology. *The New York Times*, *14*, 1.

Council Regulation (EU) 2016/679 of the European Parliament and of the Council of 27 April 2016 on the protection of natural persons with regard to the processing of personal data and on the free movement of such data, and repealing Directive 95/46/EC (General Data Protection Regulation) [2016] OJ L 119.

Council Regulation (EU) 2022/868 of the European Parliament and of the Council of 30 May 2022 on European data governance and amending Regulation (EU) 2018/1724 (Data Governance Act) [2022] OJ L 152.

Coyle, D., Diepeveen, S., Wdowin, J., Kay, L., and Tennison, J. (2020). *The Value of Data: Policy Implications*. Bennett Institute for Public Policy, Open Data Institute and Nuffield Foundation.

Crawford, K. (2019). Halt the use of facial-recognition technology until it is regulated. *Nature*, *572*(7771), 565. https://doi.org/10.1038/d41586-019-02514-7 (Last accessed October 13, 2022).

Damayanti, R., and Syarifuddin, S. (2020). The inclusiveness of community participation in village development planning in Indonesia. *Development in Practice*, *30*(5), 624–34. https://doi.org/10.1080/09614524.2020.1752151 (Last accessed October 13, 2022).

de Bruijn, H., Warnier, M., and Janssen, M. (2022). The perils and pitfalls of explainable AI: Strategies for explaining algorithmic decision-making. *Government Information Quarterly*, *39*(2), 101666. https://doi.org/10.1016/j.giq.2021.101666. (Last accessed October 13, 2022).

decidim. (2019, February 16). *Decidim*. https://decidim.org/ (Last accessed October 13, 2022).

Domingos, P. (2012). A few useful things to know about machine learning. *Communications of the ACM*, 55(10), 78–87. https://doi.org/10.1145/2347736.2347755 (Last accessed October 13, 2022).

Dressel, J., and Farid, H. (2018). The accuracy, fairness, and limits of predicting recidivism. *Science Advances*, 4(1), eaao5580.

Dryzek, J.S. (2002). *Deliberative Democracy and Beyond: Liberals, Critics, Contestations* (1st edn). Oxford University Press. https://doi.org/10.1093/019925043X.001.0001 (Last accessed October 13, 2022).

Elements of AI. (2020). Elements of AI online course. https://www.elementsofai.com/ (Last accessed October 13, 2022).

Engstrom, D.F., Ho, D.E., Sharkey, C.M., and Cuéllar, M.-F. (2020). Government by algorithm: Artificial intelligence in federal administrative agencies. SSRN Scholarly Paper ID 3551505. Social Science Research Network. https://doi.org/10.2139/ssrn.3551505 (Last accessed October 13, 2022).

Erman, E., and Furendal, M. (2022). The global governance of artificial intelligence: Some normative concerns. *Moral Philosophy and Politics*. https://doi.org/10.1515/mopp-2020-0046 (Last accessed October 13, 2022).

Estevez, A.M., Fernandez, L.D., Gomez, G.E., and Martinez, P.F. (2022). Glossary of human-centric artificial intelligence. *EUR 31113 EN*. Publications Office of the European Union.

European Commission. (2018). *Communication from the Commission to the European Parliament, the European Council, the Council, the European Economic and Social Committee and the Committee of the Regions on Artifical Intelligence for Europe*. Brussels. COM(2018) 237 final. https://eur-lex.europa.eu/legal-content/EN/TXT/?uri=COM:2018:237:FIN (Last accessed November 20, 2024).

European Commission. (2021). *Eurobarometer: Digital Rights and Principles*. https://europa.eu/eurobarometer/surveys/detail/2270 (Last accessed October 13, 2022).

FAIRsFAIR. (2022, February 24). *The role of data stewards*. FAIRsFAIR. https://fairsfair.eu/competence-centre/training-library/role-data-stewards (Last accessed October 13, 2022).

Fischer, F. (2012). *Participatory Governance: From Theory to Practice*. Oxford University Press. https://doi.org/10.1093/oxfordhb/9780199560530.013.0032 (Last accessed October 13, 2022).

Fisher, J.B., and Fortmann, L. (2010). Governing the data commons: Policy, practice, and the advancement of science. *Information & Management*, 47(4), 237–45. https://doi.org/10.1016/j.im.2010.04.001 (Last accessed October 13, 2022).

Fung, A. (2006). Varieties of participation in complex governance. *Public Administration Review*, 66, 66–75.

Fung, A. (2015). Putting the public back into governance: The challenges of citizen participation and its future. *Public Administration Review*, 75(4), 513–22. https://doi.org/10.1111/puar.12361 (Last accessed October 13, 2022).

Fung, A., and Wright, E. (2003). *Deepening Democracy: Institutional Innovations in Empowered Participatory Governance*. Verso Press.

Gansky, B., and Mcdonald, S. (2022). CounterFAccTual: How FAccT undermines its organizing principles. In *2022 ACM Conference on Fairness, Accountability, and Transparency (FAccT '22)*, June 21–24, 2022, Seoul, Republic of Korea. https://doi.org/10.1145/3531146.3533241 (Last accessed October 13, 2022).

Gerber, N., Gerber, P., and Volkamer, M. (2018). Explaining the privacy paradox: A systematic review of literature investigating privacy attitude and behavior. *Computers & Security*, 77, 226–61. https://doi.org/10.1016/j.cose.2018.04.002 (Last accessed October 13, 2022)

Goodyear-Smith, F., Jackson, C., and Greenhalgh, T. (2015). Co-design and implementation research: Challenges and solutions for ethics committees. *BMC Medical Ethics*, 16, 78. https://doi.org/10.1186/s12910-015-0072-2 (Last accessed October 13, 2022).

Grosz, B.J. (2019). The AI revolution needs expertise in people, publics, and societies. *Harvard Data Science Review*, 1(1). https://doi.org/10.1162/99608f92.97b95546 (Last accessed October 13, 2022).

Grosz, B.J., Grant, D.G., Vredenburgh, K., Behrends, J., Hu, L., Simmons, A., and Waldo, J. (2019). Embedded EthiCS: Integrating ethics across CS education. *Communications of the ACM*, 62(8), 54–61.

Hardinges, J. (2020, March 17). Data trusts in 2020. https://theodi.org/article/data-trusts-in-2020/ (Last accessed October 13, 2022).

Haus, M. (2018). Governance and power. In H. Heinelt (ed.), *Handbook on Participatory Governance* (pp. 53–76). Edward Elgar Publishing. https://doi.org/10.4337/9781785364358.00009 (Last accessed October 13, 2022).

Health e-Research Centre. (2019). Citizens juries on explainable AI. https://www.herc.ac.uk/case_studies/citizens-juries-explainable-ai/ (Last accessed October 13, 2022).

Heinelt, H. (2018). *Handbook on Participatory Governance*. Edward Elgar Publishing.

HESA. (2022). *Data governance | HESA.* https://www.hesa.ac.uk/support/tools/data-capability/signposting/governance (Last accessed October 13, 2022).

Hess, C., and Ostrom, E. (2001). *Artifacts, Facilities, and Content: Information as a Common-pool Resource, 36.* In *Conference on the Public Domain, Duke Law School, Durham, North Carolina, November 9-11, 2001.* https://web.law.duke.edu/pd/papers/ostromhes.pdf (Last accessed November 20, 2024)

Hood, C., and Margetts, H. (2007). *The Tools of Government in the Digital Age.* Bloomsbury Publishing.

Hsiao, Y.T., Lin, S.Y., Tang, A., Narayanan, D., and Sarahe, C. (2018). vTaiwan: An empirical study of open consultation process in Taiwan. https://osf.io/preprints/socarxiv/xyhft/ (Last accessed October 13, 2022).

Informatica UK. (2022). *What is data stewardship | Informatica UK.* https://www.informatica.com/gb/resources/articles/what-is-data-stewardship.html (Last accessed October 13, 2022)

Information Commissioner's Office and The Alan Turing Institute. (2020). *Explaining decisions made with AI.* https://ico.org.uk/for-organisations/guide-to-data-protection/key-dp-themes/explaining-decisions-made-with-ai/ (Last accessed October 13, 2022).

International Cooperative Alliance. (2018). *Cooperative identity, values & principles.* ICA. https://www.ica.coop/en/cooperatives/cooperative-identity (Last accessed October 13, 2022).

Involve. (2018). Citizens' jury. https://involve.org.uk/resources/methods/citizens-jury (Last accessed October 13, 2022).

Irvin, R.A., and Stansbury, J. (2004). Citizen participation in decision making: Is it worth the effort? *Public Administration Review*, *64*(1), 55–65. https://doi.org/10.1111/j.1540–6210.2004.00346.x (Last accessed October 13, 2022).

Karanasiou, A. (2019, September 4). The rise and fall of participatory democracy: AI as a governance tool. Commission on Democracy and Technology. https://demtech.chathamhouse.org/submission/the-rise-and-fall-of-participatory-democracy-ai-as-a-governance-tool/ (Last accessed October 13, 2022).

Kazim, E., Almeida, D., Kingsman, N., Kerrigan, C., Koshiyama, A., Lomas, E., and Hilliard, A. (2021). Innovation and opportunity: Review of the UK's national AI strategy. *Discover Artificial Intelligence*, *1*(1), 1–10.

Kleinberg, J., Lakkaraju, H., Leskovec, J., Ludwig, J., and Mullainathan, S. (2018). Human decisions and machine predictions. *The Quarterly Journal of Economics*, *133*(1), 237–93.

Klok, P.-J., and Denters, B. (2018). Structuring participatory governance through particular 'rules in use': Lessons from the empirical application of Elinor Ostrom's IAD Framework. In H. Heinelt (ed.), *Handbook on Participatory Governance*, (pp. 120–42).Edward Elgar Publishing. https://doi.org/10.4337/9781785364358

Köbis, N., Starke, C., and Rahwan, I. (2022). The promise and perils of using artificial intelligence to fight corruption. *Nature Machine Intelligence.* http://arxiv.org/abs/2102.11567 (Last accessed October 13, 2022).

Krick, E. (2021). Citizen experts in participatory governance: Democratic and epistemic assets of service user involvement, local knowledge and citizen science. *Current Sociology*, 001139212110592. https://doi.org/10.1177/00113921211059225 (Last accessed October 13, 2022).

Krick, E. (2022). Participatory governance practices at the democracy-knowledge-nexus. *Minerva.* https://doi.org/10.1007/s11024–022–09470-z (Last accessed October 13, 2022).

Lanier, P., Rodriguez, M., Verbiest, S., Bryant, K., Guan, T., and Zolotor, A. (2020). Preventing infant maltreatment with predictive analytics: Applying ethical principles to evidence-based child welfare policy. *Journal of Family Violence*, *35*(1), 1–13. https://doi.org/10.1007/s10896–019–00074-y (Last accessed October 13, 2022).

LeCun, Y., Bengio, Y., and Hinton, G. (2015). Deep learning. *Nature*, *521*(7553), 436–44. https://doi.org/10.1038/nature14539 (Last accessed October 13, 2022).

Lipton, Z. (2016). The mythos of model interpretability. *2016 ICML Workshop on Human Interpretability in Machine Learning (WHI 2016)*. https://arxiv.org/pdf/1606.03490.pdf (Last accessed October 13, 2022).

Londonwide LMCs. (2019, June 19). Babylon GP at hand. Londonwide LMCs. https://www.lmc.org.uk/news/babylon-gp-at-hand-update-june-2019/ (Last accessed October 13, 2022).

Loshin, D. (2009). Chapter 4—Data governance for master data management. In D. Loshin (ed.), *Master Data Management* (pp. 67–86). Morgan Kaufmann. https://doi.org/10.1016/B978-0-12-374225-4.00004-7 (Last accessed October 13, 2022).

Malcolm, J. (2015). Criteria of meaningful stakeholder inclusion in internet governance. *Internet Policy Review*. https://policyreview.info/articles/analysis/criteria-meaningful-stakeholder-inclusion-internet-governance (Last accessed October 13, 2022).

Margetts, H. (2022). Rethinking AI for good governance. *Daedalus*, *151*(2), 360–71.

Margetts, H., and Dorobantu, C. (2019). Rethink government with AI. *Nature*, *568*(7751), 163–5. https://doi.org/10.1038/d41586-019-01099-5 (Last accessed October 13, 2022).

Mcelheran, K., and Brynjolfsson, E. (2017). The rise of data-driven decision-making is real but uneven. *IEEE Engineering Management Review*, *45*(4), 103–5. https://doi.org/10.1109/EMR.2017.8233302 (Last accessed October 13, 2022).

Methnani, L., Aler Tubella, A., Dignum, V., and Theodorou, A. (2021). Let me take over: Variable autonomy for meaningful human control. *Frontiers in Artificial Intelligence*, *4*. https://www.frontiersin.org/article/10.3389/frai.2021.737072 (Last accessed October 13, 2022).

Microsoft. (2020). Creating a modern data governance strategy to accelerate digital transformation. IT Showcase. https://www.microsoft.com/en-us/insidetrack/driving-effective-data-governance-for-improved-quality-and-analytics (Last accessed October 13, 2022).

Miron, M., Tolan, S., Gómez, E., and Castillo, C. (2021). Evaluating causes of algorithmic bias in juvenile criminal recidivism. *Artificial Intelligence and Law*, *29*(2), 111–47. https://doi.org/10.1007/s10506-020-09268-y (Last accessed October 13, 2022).

Mulgan, G., Eaton, M., and Straub, V. (2018) Collective intelligence design and effective, ethical policing. Nesta. https://www.nesta.org.uk/blog/collective-intelligence-design-and-effective-ethical-policing/ (Last accessed October 13, 2022).

O'hara, K. (2019, February 13). *Data Trusts: Ethics, Architecture and Governance for Trustworthy Data Stewardship* (Monograph). University of Southampton. https://doi.org/10.5258/SOTON/WSI-WP001 (Last accessed October 13, 2022).

Ostrom, E. (1990). *Governing the Commons: The Evolution of Institutions for Collective Action*. Cambridge University Press.

Ostrom, E. (2005). *Understanding Institutional Diversity*. Princeton University Press.

Papadopoulos, Y., and Warin, P. (2007). Are innovative, participatory and deliberative procedures in policy making democratic and effective? *European Journal of Political Research*, *46*(4), 445–72. https://doi.org/10.1111/j.1475-6765.2007.00696.x (Last accessed October 13, 2022).

Pentland, A. (2013, October 1). How big data can transform society for the better. *Scientific American*. https://doi.org/10.1038/scientificamerican1013-78 (Last accessed October 13, 2022).

Plotkin, D. (2021). *Data Stewardship: An Actionable Guide to Effective Data Management and Data Governance* (2nd edn). Academic Press.

Proposal for a REGULATION OF THE EUROPEAN PARLIAMENT AND OF THE COUNCIL on European data governance (Data Governance Act), (2020). https://eur-lex.europa.eu/legal-content/EN/TXT/?uri=CELEX%3A52020PC0767 (Last accessed October 13, 2022).

Regulation (EU) 2016/679 of the European Parliament and of the Council of 27 April 2016 on the protection of natural persons with regard to the processing of personal data and on the free movement of such data, and repealing Directive 95/46/EC (General Data Protection Regulation) (Text with EEA relevance), 119 OJ L (2016). http://data.europa.eu/eli/reg/2016/679/oj/eng (Last accessed October 13, 2022).

Rosenbaum, S. (2010). Data governance and stewardship: Designing data stewardship entities and advancing data access. *Health Services Research*, *45*(5 Pt 2), 1442–55. https://doi.org/10.1111/j.1475-6773.2010.01140.x (Last accessed October 13, 2022).

Rudin, C. (2019). Stop explaining black box machine learning models for high stakes decisions and use interpretable models instead. *Nature Machine Intelligence*, *1*(5), 206–15. https://doi.org/10.1038/s42256-019-0048-x (Last accessed October 13, 2022).

Russell, S.J. (2010). *Artificial Intelligence a Modern Approach*. Pearson Education.

Ryan, M., Gambrell, D., and Noveck, B.S. (2020). Using collective intelligence to solve public problems. Nesta.

Sanchez, C. (2021). Civil society can help ensure AI benefits us all. Here's how. World Economic Forum. https://www.weforum.org/agenda/2021/07/civil-society-help-ai-benefits/ (Last accessed October 13, 2022).

Saunders, T., and Mulgan, G. (2017). Governing with collective intelligence. Nesta.

Simon, H.A. (1995). Artificial intelligence: An empirical science. *Artificial Intelligence*, *77*(1), 95–127. https://doi.org/10.1016/0004-3702(95)00039-H (Last accessed October 13, 2022).

Small, C., Bjorkegren, M., Erkkilä, T., Shaw, L., and Megill, C. (2021). Polis: Scaling deliberation by mapping high dimensional opinion spaces. *Recerca: Revista de Pensament i Anàlisi*, *26*(2).

Smith, J. (2022). *CReDo Methodology Papers: Elicitation of asset vulnerability to flooding events linked to climate change*.

Speer, J. (2012). Participatory governance reform: A good strategy for increasing government responsiveness and improving public services? *World Development*, *40*(12), 2379–98. https://doi.org/10.1016/j.worlddev.2012.05.034 (Last accessed October 13, 2022).

Stephens, G. (2021). The need for a citizen jury model: Partnering with the public for governance of artificial intelligent solutions for integrated healthcare. *International Journal of Integrated Care*, *21*(S1), 103. doi: http://doi.org/10.5334/ijic.ICIC20285 (Last accessed October 13, 2022).

Stobierski, T. (2021, February 16). *Data governance: A primer for managers | HBS Online*. Business Insights Blog. https://online.hbs.edu/blog/post/data-governance (Last accessed October 13, 2022).

Straub, V.J., Morgan, D., Bright, J., Margetts, H. (2023). Artifical intelligence in government: *Conceptis, standards, and a unified framework*. Government Information Quarterly 40(4). https://doi.org/10.1016/j.giq.2023.101881(Last accessed November 20, 2024).

UK Central Digital and Data Office. (2022). Algorithmic Transparency Standard. https://www.gov.uk/government/collections/algorithmic-transparency-standard (Last accessed October 13, 2022).

University of Washington. (2022). Data Stewardship. *Data Governance*. https://datagov.uw.edu/data-stewardship/ (Last accessed October 13, 2022).

Veale, M., Binns, R., and Ausloos, J. (2018a). When data protection by design and data subject rights clash. *International Data Privacy Law*, *8*(2), 105–23. https://doi.org/10.1093/idpl/ipy002 (Last accessed October 13, 2022).

Veale, M., Van Kleek, M., and Binns, R. (2018b). Fairness and accountability design needs for algorithmic support in high-stakes public sector decision-making. In *Proceedings of the 2018 CHI Conference on Human Factors in Computing Systems*, 1–14. https://doi.org/10.1145/3173574.3174014 (Last accessed October 13, 2022).

Visser, S.S., and Kreemers, D. (2020). Breaking through boundaries with PAR—or not? A research project on the facilitation of participatory governance through participatory action research (PAR). *Educational Action Research*, *28*(3), 345–61. https://doi.org/10.1080/09650792.2019.1624380 (Last accessed October 13, 2022).

Waag. (2021, April 8). *Urbanite: Case Studies for Participatory Mobility*. https://waag.org/en/article/case-studies-participatory-mobility/ (Last accessed October 13, 2022).

Widder, D.G., and Nafus, D. (2022). Dislocated accountabilities in the AI supply chain: Modularity and developers' notions of responsibility. arXiv. http://arxiv.org/abs/2209.09780 (Last accessed October 13, 2022).

Wilkinson, C., Briggs, J., Salt, K., Vines, J., and Flynn, E. (2019). In participatory budgeting we trust? Fairness, tactics and (in)accessibility in participatory governance. *Local Government Studies*, *45*(6), 1001–20. https://doi.org/10.1080/03003930.2019.1606798 (Last accessed October 13, 2022).

Winowatan, M. (2019, February 20). Data fiduciary. *The Living Library*. https://thelivinglib.org/data-fiduciary/ (Last accessed October 13, 2022).

Wirtz, B.W., Weyerer, J.C., and Geyer, C. (2019). Artificial intelligence and the public sector—applications and challenges. *International Journal of Public Administration*, *42*(7), 596–615. https://doi.org/10.1080/01900692.2018.1498103 (Last accessed October 13, 2022).

Wong, J., Henderson, T., and Ball, K. (2022). Data protection for the common good: Developing a framework for a data protection-focused data commons. *Data & Policy, 4*. https://doi.org/10.1017/dap.2021.40 (Last accessed October 13, 2022).

Yang, Y., and Park, T. (2020). Methods for inclusion: Expanding the limits of participatory design in AI. https://partnershiponai.org/methodsforinclusion/ (Last accessed October 13, 2022).

Zilka, M., Sargeant, H., and Weller, A. (2022). Transparency, governance and regulation of algorithmic tools deployed in the criminal justice system: A UK case study. https://doi.org/10.1145/3514094.3534200 (Last accessed October 13, 2022).

12. Artificial intelligence and governance challenges in Latin America – the game between decolonization and dependence

Fernando Filgueiras

INTRODUCTION

This chapter examines how Latin American governments create strategic perspectives for artificial intelligence governance. We examine in this chapter how artificial intelligence governance is marked by asymmetries and institutional heterogeneity and how there is no single global answer to the changes that technology provides. Latin American countries tend to reproduce dependent perspectives, in which institutional choices for technological development reproduce the institutional and economic heterogeneity characteristic of the region. Artificial intelligence is a general-purpose technology that can help governments tackle governance challenges. However, specificities in Latin America make technology policy dependent and difficult from a regulatory perspective for developing countries.

Considering this desideratum, artificial intelligence is a technology whose development is strategic for Latin America, providing gains in competitiveness and productivity for countries in the region. However, government responses tend to be silent concerning regulatory perspectives controlling technological innovations. The adoption of artificial intelligence among Latin American countries tends to reinforce the heterogeneous economic structure of the region, where there are islands of technological excellence associated with significant poverty. Thus, adopting artificial intelligence can be key to solving a series of governance challenges. However, adopting technology and the related innovation processes tends to produce heterogeneous disruptions, impacting society profoundly and unevenly.

Innovations reflect the pathway in which policy choices are motivated by ethical perspectives for artificial intelligence and not by market governance designs that can provide equitable and solid technological development for the challenges of Latin America. In the next section of this chapter, we build a background related to how artificial intelligence and associated big data produce epistemic changes and the process of deinstitutionalization and reinstitutionalization of governance. In the third section, we deal with artificial intelligence and the emerging governance challenges in Latin America. In the fourth, we address policy strategies that emerge in Latin American countries, pointing out the constraints that heterogeneity and dependence produce in the countries' capacity to solve their governance dilemmas. In the fifth section, we explore the future of governance and democracy in Latin America. We conclude this chapter by addressing the global challenges and differences that emerge from a political economy of artificial intelligence.

BACKGROUND: ARTIFICIAL INTELLIGENCE, EPISTEMIC CHANGES, AND INSTITUTIONAL RECONSTRUCTION

Artificial intelligence is a general-purpose technology applied to a variety of problems and tasks. In summary, artificial intelligence is a set of algorithms that perceives a flow of inputs and converts them into a flow of knowledge outputs (Russell, 2019). This comprehensive definition of artificial intelligence needs to deconstruct two essential elements for its understanding. First, the artificial character of technology assumes that it is an artifact dedicated to accomplishing something (Simon, 1996). As an artifact, artificial intelligence is created by humans to accomplish a purpose (Simon, 1995). The second aspect concerns the concept of intelligence. Intelligence is a multifaceted concept that can mean many different things. Intelligence can be, for example, rationality (Russell & Norvig, 2010; Simon, 1995), structured thinking (Markram, 2006), and cognition (Minsky, 1985

There is no certainty as to which intelligence we are talking about with artificial intelligence. However, artificial intelligence is a sociotechnical system that transforms the epistemic bases of society, governments, markets, and international relations. Artificial intelligence is not a sociotechnical system that only modifies the social structure but changes all knowledge bases from algorithmic systems that organize and rationalize how society thinks, reflects, does things, and performs processes. Thus, artificial intelligence, as a sociotechnical system, has impacts on the social structure and also on the way humans construct their individual and collective choices (Mendonça, Filgueiras & Almeida, 2023).

Artificial intelligence changes the epistemic foundations of society as its development progresses in different societies. Artificial intelligence transforms the epistemic bases of society because it works with broad information and produces prediction, simulation, and definition of horizons for human action in their interactions with algorithmic systems. That is, algorithmic systems change the bases of information and the construction of knowledge with the broad treatment of data (Knuth, 1968; Winston, 1992). Interactions between humans are gradually shaped by algorithmic systems, which act between a sender and a receiver of information through noise sources that shape these social interactions and communication structures (Shannon & Weaver, 1964). That is, algorithmic systems act as mediators of communication and social interactions. As the digitalization of society advances, epistemic changes deepen.

The essential point, therefore, is how artificial intelligence transforms human-machine and human-human interactions. These interactions create the power of digital technologies and the figurative reimagining of the world through instruments incorporated into social action. Algorithms create power contexts and transform societal preferences in different domains of society. The power of algorithms emerges from the fact that they create interactions between humans and humans, and between humans and machines (Weizenbaum, 1976). Social interactions are rule-governed games and imply a language that defines what is allowed, prohibited, and made possible. Computers incorporate the rules to interpret a given phenomenon in the form of data and produce knowledge outputs. How we incorporate technologies has social and political implications since algorithmic systems, often considered a simple instrument, constitute a language of social action and new meanings and forms of power relations. Tools such as computational systems provide new possibilities for the imaginative reconstruction of the world. The imaginative reconstruction of the world implies that algorithms reinstitutionalize society, economy, and politics. The way computational systems designers recreate the world is supported by the prominence of instrumental reason (Mendonça, Filgueiras & Almeida, 2023).

Artificial intelligence algorithms increasingly shape interactions between humans and humans, and between humans and machines. For example, the structure of political communication in contemporary societies is powerfully shaped by artificial intelligence embedded in social media platforms. Artificial intelligence has political consequences as a mediator of social interactions, disseminating hate speech and shaping political polarization, which profoundly affects democracy (O'Neil, 2016). Algorithms introduce noise sources to political discourse. Artificial intelligence embedded in social media platforms transforms the epistemic bases of society (Coeckelbergh, 2022) and may reflect preferences for growing political authoritarianism (Feldstein, 2019).

From governments, artificial intelligence transforms the epistemic bases of public policy. Artificial intelligence can be applied throughout the public policy cycle by transforming how policymakers think about government action in the process of social change. Using machine learning algorithms can enhance analytical capacities and thus be incorporated into all phases of the policy cycle (Porciello et al., 2020; Valle-Cruz et al., 2020). For example, in identifying the problems and the agenda, machine learning algorithms allow governments to analyze data from social media and build perspectives on citizen attention (Giest, 2017). Moreover, machine learning algorithms can incorporate the entire policy design, perform different tasks, and support decision-making. In policy implementation, machine learning algorithms can perform different tasks related to the welfare state (Coles-Kemp et al., 2020), implement predictive policing actions, and various security policy tasks (Meijer & Wessels, 2019).

In the dynamics of the economy, artificial intelligence produces disruptions in how work is done through automation to increase the competitiveness of the industry. Applying artificial intelligence in the workplace can boost productivity and create new jobs, but the benefits will likely be distributed unevenly (Acemoglu & Restrepo, 2020). Furthermore, artificial intelligence changes the basis of the functioning of the financial market, with algorithmic systems making decisions regarding the flow of capital, investments, and gains between economic actors.

In society, artificial intelligence reinforces or creates diverse inequalities. For example, artificial intelligence punishes the poorest by creating social poorhouses and new patterns of hierarchies that deepen inequalities (Eubanks, 2018). Likewise, artificial intelligence reinforces algorithmic biases in a way that harms Black women and people (Benjamin, 2019; Noble, 2018). Alternatively, artificial intelligence is applied to algorithmic governance (Yeung, 2018). Algorithmic governance creates new agency conditions from a new context of data-based knowledge (Issar & Aneesh, 2021). Artificial intelligence supported by big data structures transforms the actions of regulators and regulated people and corporations because it transforms behaviors and modifies the structures of compliance with regulations (Yeung, 2018). That is, artificial intelligence applied in regulation changes behaviors and institutionalizes normative structures that shape collective choices (König, 2019).

These are just a few challenging examples of the epistemic changes driven by artificial intelligence. The reason why these epistemic changes occur is that algorithmic systems become new institutions of society and politics, shaping behaviors by defining rules and strategies to achieve individual and collective goals and deinstitutionalizing and reinstitutionalizing practices in different areas (Mendonça, Filgueiras & Almeida, 2023). Algorithms represent a "book of rules" that define how algorithmic systems calculate courses of social action (Turing,

1950). More broadly, algorithms shape political orders by calculating courses of action and shaping collective choices (Amoore, 2022), creating a new order of change and disruption within modern society.

It is important to emphasize that these epistemic changes and institutional transformations that emerge with artificial intelligence occur in asymmetrical contexts related to the economy, politics, and society (Crawford, 2021). The threats and ambiguities that arise for society due to the development of artificial intelligence have required mechanisms for technology governance, which highlights the need for regulatory mechanisms (Floridi et al., 2021). However, the debate on the governance and regulation of artificial intelligence occurs in contexts of institutional heterogeneity that may vary from society to society regarding the solutions established. Institutional heterogeneity refers to differences that might impact the success of reaching a collective goal and can pose difficulties in successful collective action to manage resources (Ostrom, 2005). If we look at the global picture of artificial intelligence, mastery of this technology has proven critical in creating new economic asymmetries with different political consequences. Specifically for artificial intelligence governance, collective action dilemmas create barriers to advancing a regulatory design. Heterogeneity varies from society to society and between different policy domains. In the case of Latin America, this heterogeneity is abysmal as we are dealing with societies strongly marked by substantial inequalities, a colonial legacy, and difficulties with infrastructure and shared resources.

The emergence of artificial intelligence governance stems from the risks and harms to society and the political and social consequences of corporate control of information (Acemoglu, 2021). Thus, the definition of governance mechanisms for artificial intelligence starts from different layers connected to produce an institutional framework for developing and applying technology in society. The first layer concerns a technical layer capable of addressing data and algorithms. In this layer are data governance processes, the definition of standards for choices of algorithm architectures, and the definition of purposes of accountability processes. In the second layer of artificial intelligence governance, we have ethical issues. This ethical layer concerns the definition of criteria and professional principles for developers to deploy technologies (Reich, Sahami & Weinstein, 2021). Finally, the third layer concerns the social and legal layer. In this third layer, we have broader laws, norms, rights, and regulatory processes (Gasser & Almeida, 2017).

The governance of artificial intelligence emerges as a profound process of international diffusion centered on data governance, the definition of an ethical perspective, and the construction of regulatory frameworks (Issar & Aneesh, 2021). Disruptive technologies challenge governance in ways that create uncertainty about the process. While these technologies offer opportunities for improvements in economic efficiency and quality of life, they also generate many unintended consequences and pose new forms of risk and harm (Li, Taeihagh & De Jong, 2018; Tan & Taeihagh, 2021).

The regulation of disruptive technologies emerges in contexts of information asymmetries, political uncertainties, structural power dynamics, and errors in policy design and government responses (Taeihagh, Ramesh & Howlett, 2021). Furthermore, we must consider that, unlike other fields of regulatory policy, regulating emerging technologies is not identical to regulating industrial products. When we deal with emerging technologies such as artificial intelligence, we are not regulating a thing per se but a scientific method or approach to solving a problem (Calo, 2017). Thus, the definition of principles and the use of policy instruments aimed at producing compliance become essential for regulating disruptive technologies.

Concerning the regulation of artificial intelligence, what is being regulated is a new epistemic framework based on data and a new status of agency in politics, economics, and society.

Considering that the regulation of technologies occurs in contexts of asymmetries, uncertainties, structural power dynamics, and design errors, when we observe the experiences of peripheral countries, these dilemmas become exponential. Looking at how Latin America is developing artificial intelligence to solve various social, political, and economic challenges, as well as how countries in this region are producing emerging regulations, can give us clues as to how artificial intelligence transforms societies and creates a new asymmetric and dependent international reality that influences the modes of governance of technology.

ARTIFICIAL INTELLIGENCE AND GOVERNANCE CHALLENGES IN LATIN AMERICA

There are many governance challenges in Latin America. The challenges can be divided into economic, social, and political. Regarding economic challenges, a shared perspective for all countries in the region is to create an industrial structure and economic growth accompanied by redistribution to combat poverty and social vulnerability. Economic challenges mean expanding the competitiveness and productivity of Latin American industry to make possible greater availability of resources and the construction of redistributive policies (Bertola & Ocampo, 2012, Furtado, 2010, Suarez & Yoguel, 2020).

Societal challenges include combating the structural inequalities of Latin American societies and addressing health, education, and social protection problems. Latin America faces the challenge of inequalities and redistribution because of its position within a global economy, internal colonialism with the maintenance of racial injustice, and the underdevelopment of state capacities (Hoffman & Centeno, 2003). Breaking the colonial logic that still governs Latin American countries is one of the main social challenges (Quijano, 2008).

Finally, the political challenges include the consolidation of democracy after decades of authoritarian and populist governments that lasted until the 1980s and 1990s. Latin America comprises countries in the process of development. Developing countries is a poorly defined concept in political science, being a broad category of a set of countries in transition to democracy and capitalism (Diamond et al., 1995). Latin American democracies present problems regarding the formation of the public sphere, the institutionalization of decision-making, and deliberation procedures and strong institutional instability (Avritzer, 2002).

Considering these three issues, artificial intelligence has the potential to be an instrument of economic and social development. However, as an instrument, the development of the artificial intelligence industry depends on the structural conditions of the economy. The context of institutional heterogeneity characteristic of Latin America (Hirschman, 1958) creates a situation in which decisions on artificial intelligence governance are difficult, presenting dilemmas characteristic of collective action due to two factors that reinforce each other: the technological dependence that emerges from a precarious infrastructure associated with international political asymmetries that constrain collective choices regarding institutional development. We now analyze these two factors.

Artificial Intelligence, Infrastructure, and Development

Artificial intelligence, as a general-purpose technology, can contribute to development in Latin America. Artificial intelligence can be a technology aligned with development and sustainability purposes, especially in the environmental, educational, and health domains (Salas-Pilco & Yang, 2022; Salas, Patterson & Vida, 2022). The artificial intelligence industry has the potential to produce organizational rationalization and optimization, gains in productivity, create spaces for the expansion of economic growth, expand the added value of products, and improve the institutional performance of markets and governments in terms of public policy effectiveness. However, artificial intelligence policy has trade-offs in the context of inequalities and democratization.

Artificial intelligence can contribute to the design of development policies by mobilizing diverse data and creating more effective and efficient policies to achieve development goals (Salas et al., 2022). Development requires policy capacities that transform administrative, political, and analytical processes to achieve public policy effectiveness (Wu, Ramesh & Howlett, 2015). In this sense, analytical capacities are essential for policymakers to observe a flow of information and create an agency flow in the form of data-based government actions. Analytical capacities strengthen broader state capacities, enabling governments to build more robust responses to public problems (Howlett, 2009; Koga et al., 2023).

Expanding the flow of information and understanding the problems is essential for producing development policies. Deploying artificial intelligence systems can play an essential role in policy design in Latin American countries. However, the deployment of technologies takes place in context and has political and economic implications. The dilemmas revolve around controlling the physical and data infrastructure that supports artificial intelligence systems (Crawford, 2021). Countries in Latin America have poor infrastructure to advance the development of artificial intelligence and accomplish the potential benefits for development. This point reflects the entire development pathway of Latin American countries throughout the twentieth century based on the dependence of peripheral countries on developed countries (Cardoso & Faletto, 1969).

The dependence stems from asymmetries in the global political economy. Developing countries are subordinated to producing raw materials with low added value (Cardoso & Faletto, 1969). Dependence manifests itself in asymmetrical power relations, low value-added production, and networks of international influence that impede the economic independence of dependent countries. Dependence also manifests in reliance on technology and critical infrastructure for technological development (Prebisch, 2012). The insertion of Latin America in a world shaped by artificial intelligence is dependent. It is subject to two pressure vectors reinforcing each other: the technological gap plagues many countries and the consequent primary-export productive specialization that historically has defined the peripheral and dependent insertion in the global economy.

The technological dependence of Latin American countries is reflected in the availability of critical data infrastructure for governments and industry to formulate innovation processes. Data infrastructures comprise data storage and sharing processes necessary for society to operate services and facilities necessary for the economy to work through digital means. As infrastructures are shared means to many ends (Frischmann, 2012), data infrastructures are essential as an institutional mechanism that can facilitate or create barriers to development. Data infrastructures can take on a public, private, or hybrid character and are essential requirements for the development of artificial intelligence.

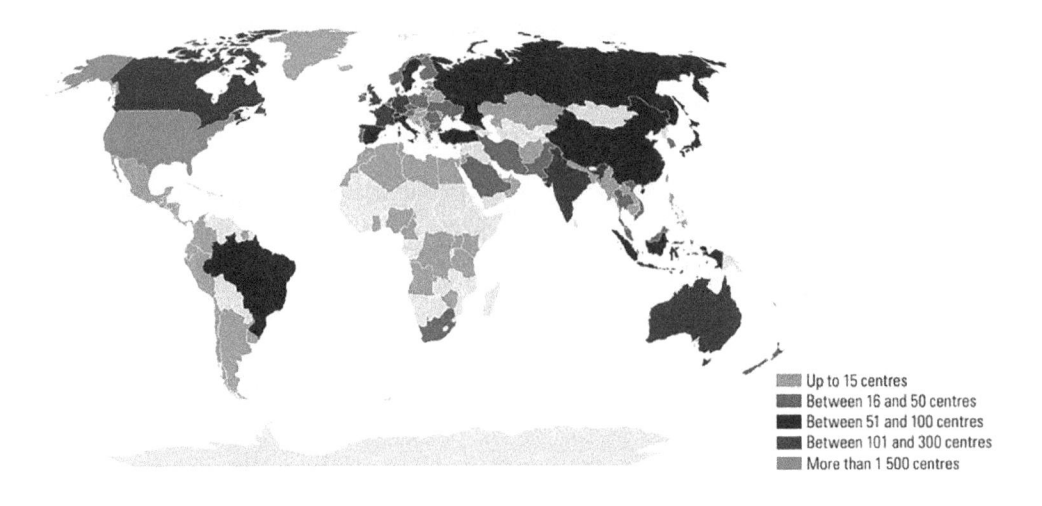

Source: Author's own.

Figure 12.1   Data centers by country

From a global perspective, data infrastructure comprises asymmetrically distributed data centers and cloud providers. In Figure 12.1, we see the distribution of data centers globally. The position of peripheral countries is dependent because the global information flow is mainly stored in the United States, Germany, United Kingdom, France, India, and Australia. India is an outlier in this process due to extensive investments in digital infrastructure. This map comprises public, private, or hybrid data centers. Latin America's position in the global data infrastructure concert is not significant, requiring extensive public investments to build critical infrastructure. In Latin America, Brazil has a greater availability of data centers, followed by Argentina and Chile. In other countries, the availability of data centers is restricted, normally linked to public digital infrastructures. In this scenario, several countries in Latin America are dependent on physical and data infrastructures located outside the national territory, weakening digital sovereignty and placing these countries as data providers, which can be thought of as raw materials for global digital transformation.

Associated with the distribution of data centers, control of cloud providers is fundamental for data infrastructures. In Figure 12.2, we have the position of the regions in the distribution of private cloud providers, which is an enabler of digital transformation. Cloud providers play an important role in digital transformation through greater availability and data sharing via the Internet. Cloud services also provide access to different shared systems. Access to cloud providers in Latin America is, in general, restricted and not very widespread, with Brazil, Argentina, and Chile leading the way in this process. While European countries comprise 308 cloud providers, all of Latin America comprises 41 providers.

These data infrastructures do not just include data storage. They also include the possibility of sharing data – thought of as resources – in an interoperable manner, associated with citizens' digital identities and digital public services. The process of digital transformation in Latin America has progressed satisfactorily with the emergence of public service platforms, extension of Internet access, digitalization of citizens' identities, payment systems, and smart

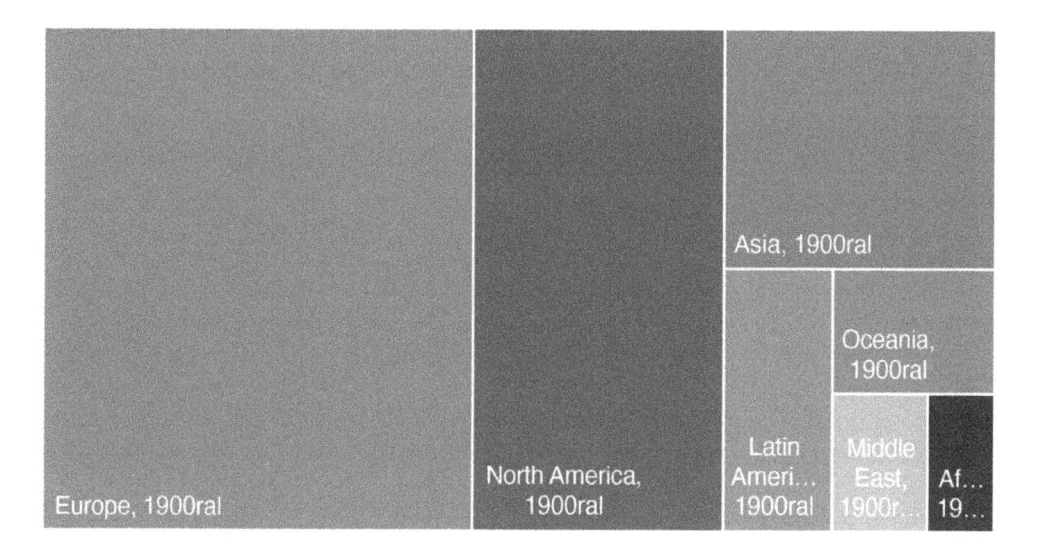

[Treemap figure: Europe, 1900ral; North America, 1900ral; Asia, 1900ral; Oceania, 1900ral; Latin America, 1900ral; Middle East, 1900ral; Africa, 19...]

Source: Author's own.

Figure 12.2   Public, private, and hybrid cloud infrastructure by region

contracts. This enables the expansion of data collection and increasing interoperability and sharing, in turn enabling the development of infrastructure. Countries such as Brazil, Peru, Mexico, Argentina, Honduras, Colombia, and Chile have developed public service platforms, but still face interoperability problems and challenges in data sharing. Likewise, these countries have developed their own payment methods, such as Pix in Brazil, SPI in Colombia, Transfer365 in El Salvador, and SPEI-Codi in Mexico. These countries are also advancing in public digital infrastructures with the use of smart contracts, such as Drex in Brazil.

Although there are advances in digital transformation, infrastructure problems persist, making it difficult for developers to access data securely and reliably. In many situations, the institutional design of data governance in countries such as Brazil, Argentina, or Colombia produces ambiguous responses regarding data collection, storage, and sharing processes. Associated with this, the advancement of this infrastructure faces the barrier of economic investment capacity, both from governments and private agents. The solution that has been found by some Latin American countries, including countries in the Caribbean region, is the association and partnership with technology companies from the global north, amplifying the international flow of data. The Central America and Caribbean region lacks digital infrastructures that reinforce new patterns of inequalities and exclusion from public services and policies. The response has been to encourage government partnerships with technology companies in order to accelerate digital transformation (Eclac, 2021). On the other hand, countries such as Brazil and Chile have sought solutions for the creation of public digital infrastructures, with investments that attempt to ensure digital sovereignty and digital inclusion. Institutional responses from Latin American countries have been ambiguous, subject, in many cases, to the power of big techs and their situation as data suppliers.

Infrastructure development in Latin America is heterogeneous and is inserted into the global arena peripherally and with low investment capacity. This gives artificial intelligence development a dependent position; in the global concert of data flow, we are suppliers of resources and raw materials (raw data), creating difficulties for digital development.

Institutional Designs for Artificial Intelligence in Latin America

When we look at emerging policies and governance for artificial intelligence in Latin America, context matters in defining the institutional choices made by governments (Filgueiras, 2023). The conditions dependent on critical infrastructures to support artificial intelligence create political and institutional constraints to technological development. Strategic choices are constrained by modes of governance and political regimes, creating a policy regime with particularities in Latin America (Filgueiras, 2023). The advancement of artificial intelligence occurs at a more or less accelerated pace among countries in the region, with different strategic developments and institutional choices constrained by the political context. Developing countries are constrained by design policies and use regulatory instruments in an asymmetric global political economy.

As technology policy follows a path of dependence (Arthur, 1989; Filgueiras, 2023; Zysman, 1994), the condition of economic dependence and constraints of critical data and physical infrastructure limit the way Latin American countries define governance structures and policies for artificial intelligence. These policy choices occur in the trade-off between governing artificial intelligence and producing barriers to regional or local development, or not governing artificial intelligence and bearing the unintended consequences of using the technology.

Associated with these infrastructure problems, when data infrastructure is not controlled, societies are more subject to processes of data colonialism. "Data colonialism means that new social relations (data relations, which generate raw inputs to information processing) become a key means whereby new forms of economic value are created" (Couldry & Mejias, 2018, p. 344). With the advancement of artificial intelligence, Latin America has become dependent on technologies within the global economy and new forms of colonialism that make people as data points subject to various behavioral interventions incorporated into algorithms. Data colonialism is a sore point in Latin America, with diverse economic, social, political, and cultural implications and emerging modes of resistance (Banos, 2023).

Data colonialism produces structural power dynamics that make it difficult to design policies based on strategic visions for artificial intelligence development. In this way, artificial intelligence governance prospects for addressing general governance challenges in Latin America emerge from the institutional constraints of economic dependence, on the one hand, and data colonialism, on the other. Thus, artificial intelligence applied in governance is situated, and the policy is constrained by contexts that shape the policymakers' and public managers' actions.

Latin American countries are adopting national strategies for artificial intelligence widely, and they reproduce heterogeneous and dependent perspectives. Several countries are designing these strategic perspectives to encourage technological development and start the discussion on the regulatory perspectives to be adopted. Although the design dynamics of these national strategies are very different when we analyze cases (Filgueiras, 2023), there are common points in these strategies that arise due to technological dependence. These common points of strategies give rise to initiatives for developing the technical, ethical, and regulatory layers of artificial intelligence with different focuses.

Argentina, Brazil, Chile, Colombia, Mexico, Peru, the Dominican Republic, and Uruguay have published national artificial intelligence strategies differently. These strategies point to common challenges regarding the development of the technical layer, with the provision of public digital infrastructures that drive and support the development of artificial intelligence. Except for Brazil, the others explain infrastructure development in partnerships with private organizations. Regarding the ethical layer, the common point in all strategies is the definition of principles, generally associated with disseminating ethical values by the OECD and UNESCO. Finally, regarding the regulatory layer, national strategies in Latin America tend to be silent or reproduce common topics in governance practices disseminated by international agencies. The exception is Chile, which clearly states that the creation of systems to protect consumption, privacy, and citizen data is more clearly related to the advancement of artificial intelligence. Argentina, Brazil, and Colombia have legislation to protect data and consumption, but they do not specify situations related to artificial intelligence systems and their consequences.

Another critical point is that national artificial intelligence strategies in Latin America, except for Colombia and the Dominican Republic, do not outline any form of regional cooperation between the countries. The statements in the Dominican Republic's strategy consider cooperation with other countries in the region, especially those in the Caribbean, as a data infrastructure, with a view to financing mechanisms in partnership with the Latin American Development Bank. Colombia sets out international cooperation in a generic way to assume leadership in the Andes region. Table 12.1 summarizes the elements contained in national strategies in Latin America.

These differences in infrastructure provide different ways of developing AI. For example, Argentina designed a national strategy for artificial intelligence based on bricolage. Political uncertainties in Argentina created an action situation in which policymakers produced incoherent and inconsistent instruments after successive revisions. Political instability in Argentina makes it difficult to build consensus. It makes policies biased towards the idea of controlling artificial intelligence development or towards the more active role of big techs in implementing policies. For example, the government of Argentina created, in partnership with Meta, artificial intelligence for policies aimed at the health and protection of pregnant women. Around 30 percent of pregnant women in Argentina do not attend prenatal care appointments. This artificial intelligence built on Facebook Messenger accompanies women during their pregnancy and the baby's first year with personalized information according to the week of gestation and the baby's age. It also reminds them of attendance to pre- and postnatal check-ups. There are no reports on the impact of this artificial intelligence or analyses of related risks. The partnership with Meta does not specify the processes for collecting data from pregnant women, nor does it include clear elements to protect this data and their privacy. The government uses this tool added to Facebook with the justification that it does not have information and nodality with society so that it could act and create a digital infrastructure in the face of this policy problem. The bricolage that supports Argentine artificial intelligence policy does not have the means to create or control digital infrastructures, in many situations reproducing a colonial perspective of raw materials (data), without any possibility of controlling risks.

Brazil created a situation of non-design (Filgueiras, 2023). The Brazilian strategy, delivered in 2021, did not involve stakeholders and was built as a strategy without measurable outcomes consistent with the objectives. The Brazilian strategy lists principles and objectives without clarity as to which mechanisms to provide to achieve these principles and change practices

Table 12.1   Summary of national strategy for artificial intelligence, Latin America

Country	Synthesis	Priority policy domains	Technical layer	Ethical layer	Regulatory layer	Regional cooperation instruments?
Argentina	Creation of partnerships between the public and private sectors for the development of AI, with the sharing of public data infrastructures. Developing ethical values, sharing good practices between the public and private sectors, and expanding the AI industry through technical training and data sharing.	It does not specify policy domains but proposes the creation of a national innovation laboratory.	Absent	It proposes developing and disseminating ethical values and good professional practices for developers.	Absent	No
Brazil	The strategy assumes the role of guiding the actions of the Brazilian State in favor of the development of actions, in its various aspects, that stimulate research, innovation, and development of solutions in AI, as well as its conscious, ethical use in favor of a better future.	Public sector, health, education, public security.	Data sharing from public infrastructures and financial instruments for the development of research and innovation. Labor training.	Definition of principles and values for developing AI and training around good practices.	Design of regulatory instruments for the AI industry based on principles and techniques defined in OECD models.	No

Artificial intelligence and governance challenges in Latin America

Country	Synthesis	Priority policy domains	Technical layer	Ethical layer	Regulatory layer	Regional cooperation instruments?
Chile	Defines national AI policy with enabling factors, instruments to strengthen research development and increasing adoption models, governance mechanisms, and ethical values for AI.	It does not specify policy domains but proposes the creation of a national innovation laboratory.	Defines mechanisms for financing basic and applied research involving partnerships between government, civil society, academia, and the private sector. It suggests the creation of physical and data infrastructure with a public and shared nature.	Addresses issues of gender inequalities and labor and economic impacts associated with the definition of ethical principles for the development of AI.	Addresses consumer, privacy and data protection, intellectual property systems, and cybersecurity. It points to the use of algorithmic risk assessments, assessment of impacts on markets, and the explainability and transparency of systems.	No

Country	Synthesis	Priority policy domains	Technical layer	Ethical layer	Regulatory layer	Regional cooperation instruments?
Colombia	Its main objective is to forge a high impact on generating public policies and digital transformation projects within the country's public entities where AI systems are used. Therefore, it seeks to promote access and dissemination of knowledge that can impact the implementation and deployment of AI in the country and region.	It does not specify policy domains.	Defines mechanisms for financing basic and applied research involving partnerships between government, civil society, academia, and the private sector.	Supports the implementation of the Colombian AI Ethical Framework and ethical standards for using AI.	It does not specify clear AI governance and regulation mechanisms.	Yes

Country	Synthesis	Priority policy domains	Technical layer	Ethical layer	Regulatory layer	Regional cooperation instruments?
México	Map the uses and needs in industry and identify best practices in government; boost Mexico's international leadership in this matter, with particular emphasis on the OECD and D7.	It does not specify policy domains.	Absent	Defines principles for AI development in line with OECD principles.	Creates the Artificial Intelligence Subcommission within the Intersecretarial Commission for Electronic Government Development. Creates public consultation mechanisms on impact reports but does not define specific regulatory mechanisms for AI.	No

Country	Synthesis	Priority policy domains	Technical layer	Ethical layer	Regulatory layer	Regional cooperation instruments?
Peru	Initiative aimed at promoting research, development, and adoption of Artificial Intelligence in Peru.	It does not specify policy domains.	Facilitates creating and strengthening digital and telecommunications infrastructure as support for AI development in partnership between the public and private sectors. Facilitates the development of a data infrastructure to make high-quality public data available in an open, reusable, and accessible format as support for AI development.	Absent	Absent	No
Dominican Republic	Develop industry 4.0 with a mission-based approach. Strengthen digital sovereignty and position the Dominican Republic as a technological hub in Latin America through public-private partnerships, the creation of centers of excellence, and human development.	Industry	It houses a technological infrastructure to convert the Dominican Republic into a data storage and processing service provider in the Caribbean region.	Definition of ethical principles focusing on the protection of human rights.	Absent	Yes

Artificial intelligence and governance challenges in Latin America 213

Country	Synthesis	Priority policy domains	Technical layer	Ethical layer	Regulatory layer	Regional cooperation instruments?
Uruguay	Defines the AI strategy to promote and strengthen its responsible use in public administration through digital government.	Public sector	Compliance with technical and regulatory frameworks that guarantee the solvency and solidity of AI systems.	Defines ethical principles aligned with OECD principles and mechanisms for human oversight and transparency in AI systems.	Train public servants in different related capacities and define transparency and accountability mechanisms for AI solutions applied in government.	No

Note: Bolivia, Costa Rica, Cuba, Ecuador, El Salvador, Guatemala, Haiti, Honduras, Nicaragua, Panama, Paraguay, and Venezuela, at the time of the research, did not have an official document that articulated a national AI strategy.
Source: Author's own elaboration.

that imply modes for the design and development of artificial intelligence (Filgueiras & Junquilho, 2023). Although the Brazilian Congress is discussing a proposed Law for Artificial Intelligence and a Law on Disinformation on social networks, which create regulatory perspectives, many veto points are placed by the artificial intelligence industry, particularly big tech. The proposed Law on Disinformation was a point of deep political controversy in 2023, with Google defining on its portals that the Brazilian State was proposing to restrict freedom of expression, defending self-regulation processes. Evidence shows that social media platforms, with onboard artificial intelligence, contributed to and influenced coup speeches and the deepening of political polarization in Brazil (Evangelista & Bruno, 2019). Currently, there is a political conflict between the government and big tech related to the emergence of regulatory instruments for artificial intelligence. Despite this, Brazil has a considerable public digital infrastructure, which has allowed advances in digital public services and the development of artificial intelligence for the government. An example is how compliance and justice systems are investing heavily in the development of artificial intelligence, such as the Alice and Mônica systems of the Federal Audit Court, systems for detecting deviations by public servants, of the Union General-Comptroller, or the Victor system of the Federal Supreme Court. These systems were based on public data, on their initiative, and without any partnership with private organizations in their development.

Strategies for artificial intelligence in Latin America define modes of governance that expect ethical behavior from developers and broad development goals without enunciating the mechanisms by which development will take place. They center on an artificial intelligence ethic without being accompanied by adequate policy instrumentation to achieve development goals. Although the design dynamics differ among Latin American countries, retaining political and governance specificities, all strategies converge towards common objectives and similar instruments. As outlined earlier, artificial intelligence governance is done in layers, thinking about technical elements, a layer of ethical approaches, and a regulatory layer (Gasser & Almeida, 2017). Addressing these layers, we can examine how policy strategies for artificial intelligence in Latin America create a country-dependent approach with trade-offs of complex policy choices.

Policy choices are path-dependent. Dependence in Latin America implies that the innovation dynamic is asymmetric and concentrated due to the institutional heterogeneity that characterizes the countries in the region (Hirschman, 1958). The path dependence of technological development in Latin America is influenced by countries at the center of capitalism, creating constraints on political and policy choices. The interaction between center and periphery reproduces the technological and income asymmetries over time, with peculiarities to each historical period. Various cumulative mechanisms come together in the learning and capacity-building process.

Thus, policies for technological development are asymmetrical and produce ambiguous innovation processes, which reinforce situations of dependence. Strategies for artificial intelligence among Latin American countries tend to reinforce a technical and ethical layer despite a regulatory layer that could create incentives for more symmetrical technological development consistent with the values of democracy. Among Latin American countries, strategies for artificial intelligence reinforce a perspective of development policy based on the connection of physical and data infrastructures with technology companies, associated with advocacy of ethical perspectives without the appropriate instruments to achieve it. Among the layers of artificial intelligence governance, strategies reflect a technical and ethical concern and tend to be silent in relation to the regulatory layer.

This approach happens because Latin American countries do not have control over the data generated and the physical infrastructure necessary for data storage and processing. Once big techs control data, they control the global information structure, and Latin American governments find themselves hostage to the development and deployment of artificial intelligence technologies. Regulating artificial intelligence could mean losing the opportunity for economic and social development that technology promotes. Innovation with artificial intelligence produces disruptive epistemic changes in Latin American society, politics, and the economy. However, there are difficulties concerning the design of regulatory perspectives. The tendency is for countries in the region to confuse the development of an ethical and professional perspective for artificial intelligence designers with a regulatory perspective that can overcome the condition of dependence and the heterogeneous institutional structure that characterizes the region.

National strategies for artificial intelligence in Latin America frame policies on the delimitation of ethical values and the creation of professional codes for designers. Regarding the technical layer, the strategic definitions of policies for artificial intelligence tend to reproduce comprehensive parameters of data governance, use, and reuse of data, without defining, in turn, criteria for choosing algorithm architectures, the definition of cybersecurity approaches, and detailed forms of transparency and accountability. Regarding the regulatory layer, all Latin American national strategies tend to reinforce a perspective of self-regulation on the part of companies, with risk analyses that are poorly informed or characterized.

The tendency to defend a perspective of self-regulation arises from an ambiguous situation of enabling technological development dependent on big techs, with the exception of countries that have public digital infrastructures, such as Brazil and Chile. That is, the regulatory layer is built in ambiguous ways. These paths are delimited by the gains in productivity, competitiveness, and economic rationalization that artificial intelligence provides, on the one hand, and existential and disruptive risks in the dimension of society, on the other hand. The existential risks lie in the fact that epistemic changes in Latin America call into question social and cultural elements that can amplify the institutional heterogeneity characteristic of countries in the region and processes of data colonialism that threaten Latin American culture. The answer to these dilemmas is to involve the regulatory perspective in an ethical perspective. Recently, 20 Latin American countries, except Nicaragua, Bolivia, and Panama, signed the Declaration of Santiago, within the scope of the Summit Ministerial and High Authorities of Latin America and the Caribbean., between October 23 and 24, 2023, in Santiago, Chile. The objective expressed in the declaration is "to promote ethical artificial intelligence in Latin America and the Caribbean," based on references disseminated by UNESCO. Furthermore, the Declaration of Santiago created the Working Group aimed at establishing an intergovernmental Artificial Intelligence Council for Latin America and the Caribbean.

Latin American governments defend technical and ethical development without clarity regarding the regulatory layer in this context of ambiguous choices. Structural power dynamics in Latin America are heterogeneous and the product of diverse and distinct power conditions (Hirschman, 1958). The dependence condition causes Latin American countries to build ambiguous technological policies that reproduce design errors and incoherent government responses to emerging problems. Policy choices are made in contexts of vast uncertainties and information asymmetry, making regulatory responses inconsistent with the problems pointed out, particularly epistemic changes. Artificial intelligence policies in Latin America focus on ethical construction without detailing codes of conduct or any regulatory perspective for emerging markets. The tendency is for countries in the region to reproduce regulatory perspectives without governments having the capacity to regulate.

FUTURE OF LATIN AMERICAN GOVERNANCE AND DEMOCRACY

The future of Latin America with artificial intelligence is ambiguous. Governance challenges related to technological development remain, so adopting artificial intelligence challenges governments to implement it. First, from the point of view of the technical layer, the development of communication infrastructure demands robust investments. In order to encourage the development of artificial intelligence, Latin American countries need investments in critical data infrastructure and need to overcome the digital divide that persists. As a result of Latin America's structural inequalities, the digital divide persists even though inclusion processes have taken place via the market. Only 45.5 percent of Latin American households have broadband access, and the average gap in Internet usage between the top and bottom quintile of earners is about 40 percent (Eclac, 2022).

The second aspect concerns the development of capacities and human resources. Capacity development implies accelerated human training to face the challenges of advancing artificial intelligence. The training consists of more than just training system designers but also people capable of working with large volumes of data and data governance. The third aspect concerns the regulatory mechanisms. The dependence condition implies that regulation must create incentives to accelerate digital development and create barriers to the risks and harms that emerge with artificial intelligence.

This technology governance framework responds to the economic mechanisms embedded in digital development. However, political challenges persist in the context of widespread misinformation and hate speech disseminated with platforms' support. Threats to democracy revive dark periods in Latin American history due to authoritarian and populist aspirations. In a context of low democratic consolidation, Latin America promotes modes of governance based on data and artificial intelligence that reinforce epistocratic and technocratic mechanisms of government (Mendonça, Filgueiras & Almeida, 2023).

This is reflected in different examples of how governments uncritically adopt artificial intelligence technologies, which tend to reinforce dependency mechanisms. The adoption of artificial intelligence by the Argentine government in partnership with Meta, for example, means that large corporations can access public data on pregnant women, increasing international data flows to build diverse commercial or governmental solutions that are not explained to Argentine society. This case exemplifies how the institutional heterogeneity characteristic of the region results in the amplification of the risks and harms of artificial intelligence and situations of dependence.

The epistemic changes that emerge with artificial intelligence amplify the technology's harms in social and economic dimensions. In the social and economic dimensions, artificial intelligence makes an economic structure no longer competitive and dependent. Advancing policies and incentives for artificial intelligence implies choices that have stagnated labor demand, declining labor share in national income, rising inequality, and lowering productivity growth (Acemoglu & Restrepo, 2020). The epistemic changes introduced with big data and artificial intelligence imply an amplification of the threats to emerge in the future, demanding regulatory mechanisms that provide compensation to changing contexts. The deepening of inequalities in Latin America tends to be reinforced in a heterogeneous and complex social structure, with low capacity and high social and digital divide.

How governments uncritically embrace artificial intelligence is driving profound changes in public governance. Different countries in Latin America have adopted artificial intelligence to solve governance challenges. Driven by the idea of digital transformation, with governmental responses to economic crises in the background, government platformization provides the insertion of algorithmic systems within the institutional work of the state, defining through algorithms the government's operating rules and strategies of the bureaucracy, along with the definition of incentives and constraints in the regulatory framework. Adopting algorithmic systems encodes procedures for bureaucratic agents, rearranging various bureaucratic practices (Meijer et al., 2021). The algorithmization of bureaucratic organizations is embedded further in changes in work routines, streamlining many processes and altering the logic of organizational work.

The institutional redesign of governments by adopting algorithmic systems as solutions to different policy problems has been disseminated by many international organizations, and this diffusion process, in turn, has shaped coordinated organizational convergences in a growing transformation of governments into platforms (Mendonça, Filgueiras & Almeida, 2023). Technology companies – and their data infrastructures – also play a substantial role in government transformation in Latin America. As corporations play a crucial role in reconfiguring public administration in Latin America, states may be redesigned on the grounds of interests and perspectives that have not been submitted to public scrutiny. Market interests and technical choices that may benefit some actors to the detriment of others can reshape existing institutions through these emerging algorithmic institutions.

The dynamics through which digital governance has been built in Latin America imply new situations of dependence. That is, algorithmic systems based on artificial intelligence models are reinstitutionalizing governments in Latin America with undemocratic purposes due to dependence and colonialism. Governments in the region are becoming increasingly algorithmic to address governance challenges. However, they create and deepen institutional heterogeneity, in turn, creating insiders and outsiders of digital development. Infrastructure dependence makes digital governance in Latin America a more complex and challenging context in which to solve existing governance problems.

CONCLUSIONS

Looking across Latin American countries, artificial intelligence governance challenges are contextualized and different. Strategies for artificial intelligence and its adoption to solve governance challenges imply understanding asymmetrical international contexts, which promote different perspectives and challenges. Latin American countries have critical infrastructure deficits that make digital development dependent on countries at the center of capitalism. These asymmetries reinforce specific institutional dynamics that create different approaches to technological development.

Understanding how artificial intelligence is adopted in governance processes means thinking from strategic perspectives embedded in political and economic dynamics. Latin American governments adopt artificial intelligence to solve governance challenges but thereby reinforce perspectives of data colonialism and technological dependence. Data colonialism refers to how the adoption of artificial intelligence occurs with international data flows that are poorly regulated and associated with a dependent infrastructure. Data colonialism reinforces profound cultural and epistemic changes, in which governments adopt technologies uncritically and little adapted to complex and profoundly unequal institutional heterogeneity. For example, adopting artificial intelligence for public services must consider, on average, the access difficulties arising from the digital divide. In addition to public services, the policy formulation and implementation process with artificial intelligence takes place in complex designs made by trial and error, with low impact on social change.

The technological development of governance tools takes place in complex political and economic contexts, with social imbrications that are difficult to control when institutional heterogeneity is high. Although artificial intelligence and big data have the potential to solve governance challenges in Latin American countries, situations of dependence tend to deepen significant institutional heterogeneity due to political and economic imbrications that arise in an asymmetric political order.

Digital governance, therefore, is more than just a governance process done with digital tools. The instrumentation of technology takes place in context, depending on the political and economic environment in which it is designed and developed. Dependence on critical infrastructure makes the challenges of digital governance more profound and difficult to implement in democratic and economic development contexts. Without adequate regulatory mechanisms, which are challenging to build in dependent realities, technologies tend to deepen heterogeneities and rapidly threaten the future of governments and democracies in developing countries.

REFERENCES

Acemoglu, D. (2021). Harms of AI. In: J.B. Bullock; Chen, Y.C.; Himmelreich, J.; Hudson, V.; Korinek, A.; Young, M.M.; Zhang, B. (eds.), *The Oxford handbook of AI governance*. p. 660–706. Oxford: Oxford University Press.

Acemoglu, D.; Restrepo, P. (2020). The wrong kind of AI? Artificial intelligence and the future of labour demand. *Cambridge Journal of Regions, Economy and Society,* 13(1), 25–35. doi:https://doi.org/10.1093/cjres/rsz022

Amoore, L. (2022). Machine learning political orders. *Review of International Studies*, 49(1), 20–36. doi: https://doi.org/10.1017/S0260210522000031

Arthur, W.B. (1989). Competing technologies, increasing returns, and lock-in by historical events. *Economic Journal*, 99(394), 116–31. https://doi.org/10.2307/2234208

Avritzer, L. (2002). *Democracy and public space in Latin America*. Princeton, NJ: Princeton University Press.

Banos, A.M. (2023). Data colonialism is not a metaphor: Remembering colonialism and why it matters in the digital ecosystem. In: The Tierra Comum Network (ed.), *Resisting data colonialism: A practical intervention*. Amsterdam: Institute of Network Cultures.

Benjamin, R. (2019). *Race after technology*. New York: Polity Press.

Bertola, L.; Ocampo, J.A. (2012). *The economic development of Latin America since independence*. Oxford: Oxford University Press.

Calo, R. (2017). Artificial intelligence policy: A primer and roadmap. *UCD Law Review*, 51–2, 399–435. https://heinonline.org/HOL/LandingPage?handle=hein.journals/davlr51&div=18&id=&page=

Cardoso, F.H.; Faletto, E. (1969). *Dependency and development in Latin America*. Mexico City: Siglo XXI.

Coeckelbergh, M. (2023). Democracy, epistemic agency, and AI: Political epistemology in times of artificial intelligence. *AI & Ethics*, 3, 1341–1350. doi: https://doi.org/10.1007/s43681-022-00239-4

Coles-Kemp, L.; Ashenden, D.; Morris, A.; Yuille, J. (2022). Digital welfare: Designing for more nuanced forms of access. *Policy Design and Practice*, 3(2), 177–88. doi:https://doi.org/10.1080/25741292.2020.1760414

Couldry, N.; Mejias, U. (2018). Data colonialism: Rethinking big data's relations to the contemporary subjects. *Television & New Media*, 20(4), 336–49. doi:https://doi.org/10.1177/1527476418796632

Crawford, K. (2021). *Atlas of AI: Power, politics, and the planetary costs of artificial intelligence*. New Haven, CT: Yale University Press.

Diamond, L.; Linz, J.; Lipset, S.M. (1995). Introduction: What makes for democracy? In L. Diamond; J. Linz; S.M. Lipset (eds.), *Politics in developing countries*. Boulder, CO: Lynne Rienner, pp. 1–35.

Eclac (2022). A digital path for sustainable development in Latin America and the Caribbean. Santiago: Eclac. https://repositorio.cepal.org/bitstream/handle/11362/48461/4/S2200897_en.pdf

Eclac (2021). Digital public goods: Driving the development of digital public infrastructure in the Caribbean. Santiago: Eclac – Focus. https://www.cepal.org/en/publications/48141-digital-public-goods-driving-development-digital-public-infrastructure-caribbean

Eubanks, V. (2018). *Automating inequality:* How high-tech tools profile, police, and punish the poor. New York: St Martin's Press.

Evangelista, R.; Bruno, F. (2019). Whatsapp and political instability in Brazil: Targeted messages and political radicalization. *Internet Policy Review*, 8(4), 1–23. doi:https://doi.org/10.14763/2019.4.1434

Feldstein, S. (2019). The road to digital unfreedom. How artificial intelligence is reshaping repression. *Journal of Democracy*, 30(1), 40–52. doi: https://www.doi.org/10.1353/jod.2019.0003

Filgueiras, F. (2023). Designing artificial intelligence policy: Comparing design spaces in Latin America. *Latin American Policy*, 14(1), 5–21. doi: https://doi.org/10.1111/lamp.12282

Filgueiras, F.; Junquilho, T.A. (2023). The Brazilian (non)perspective on national strategy on artificial intelligence. *Discover Artificial Intelligence*, 3(7), 1–15. doi: https://doi.org/10.1007/s44163-023-00052-w

Floridi, L.; Cowls, J.; King, T.C.; Taddeo, M. (2021). How to design AI for social good: Seven essential factors. In: L. Floridi (ed.), *Ethics, governance, and policies in artificial intelligence*. Cham: Springer. doi: https://doi.org/10.1007/978-3-030-81907-1_9

Frischmann, B. (2012). *Infrastructure: The social value of shared resources*. Oxford: Oxford University Press.

Furtado, C. (2010). *Economic development of Latin America*. Cambridge: Cambridge University Press.

Gasser, U.; Almeida, V.A. (2017). A layered model of AI governance. *IEEE Internet Computing*, 21(6), 58–62. doi:https://doi.org/10.1109/MIC.2017.4180835

Giest, S. (2017). Big data for policymaking: Fad or fast track? *Policy Sciences*, 50(3), 367–82. doi:https://doi.org/10.1007/s11077-017-9293-1

Hirschman, A. (1958). *The strategy of economic development*. New Haven, CT: Yale University Press.

Hoffman, K.; Centeno, M.A. (2003). The lopsided continent: Inequality in Latin America. *Annual Review of Sociology*, 29, 363–90. doi: https://doi.org/10.1146/annurev.soc.29.010202.100141

Howlett, M.P. (2009). Policy capacity analytical and evidence-based policy-making: Lessons from Canada. *Canadian Public Administration*, 52(2), 153–75. doi: https://doi.org/10.1111/j.1754-7121.2009.00070_1.x

Issar, S.; Aneesh, A. (2021). What is algorithmic governance? Sociology Compass, 16(1), e12955. https://doi.org/10.1111/soc4.12955

Knuth, D.E. (1968). *The art of computer programming, volume 1: Fundamental algorithms*. Berkeley, CA: Addison-Wesley.

Koga, N.; Palotti, P.L.M.; Bridges, P.A.M.M.; Couto, B.G.; Soares, M.L.V. (2023). Analytical capacity is a critical condition for responding to Covid-19 in Brazil. *Policy & Society*, 42(1), 117–30. doi: https://doi.org/10.1093/polsoc/puac028

König, P.D. (2019). Dissecting the algorithmic Leviathan: On the socio-political anatomy of algorithmic governance. *Philosophy & Technology*, 33(4), 467–85. https://doi.org/10.1007/s13347-019-00363-w

Li, Y.; Taeihagh, A.; De Jong, M. (2018). The governance of risks in ride-sharing: A revelatory case from Singapore. *Energies*, 11(5), 1277. doi: https://doi.org/10.3390/en11051277

Markram, H. (2006). The Blue Brain project. *Nature Reviews Neuroscience*, 7(2), 153–60.

Meijer, A.; Wessels, M. (2019). Predictive policing: Review of benefits and drawbacks. *International Journal of Public Administration*, 42(12), 1031–9. https://doi.org/10.1080/01900692.2019.1575664

Meijer, A.; Lorenz, L.; Wessels, M. (2021). Algorithmization of bureaucratic organizations: Using a practical lens to study how context shapes predictive policing systems. *Public Administration*, 81(5), 1–10. doi: https://doi.org/10.1111/puar.13391

Mendonça, R.F.; Filgueiras, F.; Almeida, V.A. (2023). *Algorithmic institutionalism: The changing rules of social + political life*. Oxford: Oxford University Press.

Minsky, M. (1985). *The society of mind*. New York: Simon and Schuster.

Noble, S.U. (2018). Algorithms of oppression. New York: New York University Press.

O'Neil, C. (2016). *Weapons of math destruction: How big data increases inequality and threatens democracy*. New York: Crown.

Ostrom, E. (2005). *Understanding institutional diversity*. Princeton: Princeton University Press.

Porciello, J.; Ivanina, M.; Islam, M.; Einarson, E.; Hirsch, H. (2020). Accelerating evidence-informed decision-making for the Sustainable Development Goals using machine learning. *Nature Machine Intelligence*, 2, 559–65. doi:https://doi.org/10.1038/s42256-020-00235-5

Prebisch, R. (2012). *El desarrollo económico de América Latina y algunos de sus principais problemas*. Santiago: CEPAL. https://www.cepal.org/es/publicaciones/40010-desarrollo-economico-la-america-latina-algunos-sus-principales-problemas

Quijano, A. (2008). Coloniality of power, eurocentrism, and social classification. In: M. Moraña; E. Dussel; C.A. Jáuregui (eds.), *Coloniality at large: Latin America and the postcolonial debate*. Durham, NC: Duke University Press.

Reich, R.; Sahami, M.; Weinstein, J.M. (2021). *System error: Where big tech went wrong and how we can reboot*. New York: Harper.

Russell, S. (2019). *Human compatible: Artificial intelligence and the problem of control*. New York: Viking.

Russell, S.; Norvig, P. (2010). *Artificial intelligence: A modern approach*. Englewood Cliffs, NJ: Prentice-Hall.

Salas, J.; Patterson, G.; Vidal, F.B. (2022). A systematic mapping of artificial intelligence solutions for sustainable challenges in Latin America and Caribbean. *IEEE Latin America Transactions*, 20(11), 2312–29.

Salas-Pilco, S.Z.; Yang, Y. (2022). Artificial intelligence applications in Latin American higher education: A systematic review. *International Journal of Education Technology in Higher Education*, 19(21), 1–20. doi: https://doi.org/10.1186/s41239-022-00326-w

Samuel, A.L. (1959). Some studies in machine learning use the game of checkers. *IBM Journal of Research and Development*, 44 (1–2), 206–26.

Samuel, A.L. (1962). Artificial intelligence: A frontier of automation. *The Annals of the American Academy of Political and Social Science*, 340(1), 10–20. doi:https://doi.org/10.1177/000271626234000103

Shannon, E.C; Weaver, W. (1964). *The mathematical theory of communication*. Urbana, IL: The University of Illinois Press.

Simon, H.A. (1995). Artificial intelligence: An empirical science. *Artificial Intelligence*, 77(1), 95–127. doi:https://doi.org/10.1016/0004-3702(95)00039-H

Simon, H.A. (1996). *The science of artificial*. Cambridge, MA: MIT Press.

Suarez, D.; Yoguel, G. (2020). Latin American development and the role of technology: An introduction. *Economics of Innovation and New Technology*, 29(7), 661–9. doi: https://doi.org/10.1080/10438599.2020.1715058

Taeihagh, A.; Ramesh, M.; Howlett, M.P. (2021). Assessing the regulatory challenges of emerging disruptive technologies. *Regulation & Governance*, 15, 1009–19. doi:https://doi.org/10.1111/rego.12392

Tan, S.Y.; Taeihagh, A. (2021). Governing the adoption of robotics and autonomous systems in long-term care in Singapore. *Policy and Society*, 40(2), 211–31. doi:https://doi.org/10.1080/14494035.2020.1782627

Turing, A. (1950). Computing machinery and intelligence. *Mind – A Quarterly Review of Psychology and Philosophy,* 59(236), 433–60.
Valle-Cruz, D.; Created, J.I.; Sandoval- Almazán, R.; Ruvalcaba -Gomez, E.A. (2020). Assessing the public policy-cycle framework in the age of artificial intelligence: From agenda-setting to policy evaluation. *Government Information Quarterly*, 37, 101509. doi: https://doi.org/10.1016/j.giq.2020.101509
Weizenbaum, J. (1976). *Computer power and human reason: From judgment to calculation.* San Francisco, CA: W.H. Freeman.
Winston, P.H. (1992). *Artificial intelligence.* New York: Addison-Wesley.
Wu, X.; Ramesh, M.; Howlett, M. (2015). Policy capacity: A conceptual framework for understanding policy competences and capabilities. *Policy and Society,* 34(3–4), 165–71. doi:https://doi.org/10.1016/j.polsoc.2015.09.001
Yeung, K. (2018). Algorithmic regulation: A critical interrogation. *Regulation & Governance*, 12, 505–23. https://doi.org/10.111/rego.12158
Zysman, J. (1994). How institutions create historically rooted trajectories of growth. *Industrial and Corporate Change,* 3(1), 243–83. https://doi.org/10.1093/icc/3.1.243

13. Proactive algorithmic transparency in government: the case of the Colombian repositories of public algorithms

Juan David Gutiérrez and Sarah Muñoz-Cadena

INTRODUCTION[1]

The adoption of artificial intelligence (AI) and other algorithmic technologies in the public sector is expanding around the globe (Ada Lovelace Institute et al., 2021; Zuiderwijk et al., 2021), and transparency is one of the most common principles included in AI guidelines (Valderrama et al., 2023). However, only a few national and subnational governments worldwide proactively inform citizens about the use of automated decision-making (ADM) systems. Proactive transparency refers to the routine disclosure of information by the government that is "made available to external actors without them first having to explicitly request it" (Porumbescu et al., 2022, p. 11).

Few national and subnational governments have made public the algorithms they use through online repositories (Gutiérrez, 2023; OGP, 2023; Valderrama et al., 2023; GPAI, 2024). Other governments only disclose the use of specific algorithms that support their decision-making processes on a case-by-case basis but limit the availability of information about how the algorithms operate (Valderrama et al., 2023).

The literature has justified the importance of proactive algorithmic transparency (OGP, 2023; Valderrama et al., 2023), proposed standards for recording information about public algorithms (CDDO & CDEI, 2023), and critically assessed its usefulness (Diakopoulos, 2020). However, the literature concerning the assessment of mechanisms implemented by governments to comply with proactive algorithmic transparency has been less prolific. How can the repositories of public algorithms contribute to proactive algorithmic transparency? How can we assess – in practice – the levels of transparency achieved through such repositories?

This chapter aims to bridge this gap in the literature by studying the case of the Colombian government's repositories, a unique example since it is the only national government in Latin America that has published online repositories of its ADM systems.[2] The chapter assesses the levels of transparency that repositories provide regarding the acquisition, development, piloting, adoption, and use of AI systems and robotic process automation (RPA).

Most of the literature on the implementation of ADM systems by governments focuses on Global North countries (Camacho Gutiérrez & Praxedes Saavedra Rionda, 2021; Chenou & Rodríguez Valenzuela, 2021; Sanabria-Pulido et al., 2014) and the literature published in English on algorithmic transparency predominantly addresses Global North cases (Valderrama et al., 2023). Moreover, civil society organizations and academics, such as Cetina et al. (2021), Escobar et al. (2021), Flórez and Vargas (2020), Gutiérrez (2020), and López and Castañeda (2020) have published case studies on specific AI projects in the Colombian public sector. However, to the best of the authors' knowledge, no publications systematically study the existence and use of AI systems or other algorithmic tools by Colombian public entities nor examine algorithmic transparency in Colombia.[3]

The chapter also presents the results of a novel database with information for 113 ADM systems adopted by the Colombian public sector (Gutiérrez et al., 2023).[4] The essential features of most of the systems included in our novel database were documented using information made public by government organizations through different means. However, we report that there is very little information on critical aspects such as the type of data used by the systems, the performance of the algorithms, their cost, whether the software is proprietary or open-source, and the procurement processes required to acquire the respective license and service. We conclude that while the government publishes significant amounts of data about its ADM systems, the publicly available information is insufficient to make the algorithmic processes truly accountable in Colombia.

This research follows a case study approach in which quantitative and qualitative data about algorithmic transparency in Colombia were collected and processed. The primary data were drawn from pre-existing government databases and repositories that are publicly available, the annual management reports of public bodies, institutional web pages, and press reports. Secondary sources included gray literature published by multilateral entities, civil society organizations, and academic literature.

The chapter is divided into five sections, including this Introduction. The second section reviews the literature on algorithmic transparency and ADM systems adoption in Colombia. The third section describes the methodological approach of this research. The fourth section presents and discusses the findings of the case study. The final section summarizes the main conclusions, outlines policy implications, and suggests future avenues of research.

ALGORITHMIC TRANSPARENCY IN THE PUBLIC SECTOR

Before delving into the literature on algorithmic transparency in the public sector, it is pertinent to delineate four critical terms used in this text: ADM systems, AI systems, RPA, and algorithmic transparency. This study focuses on computational systems that automate or semi-automatize decision-making processes in the public sector that may affect people's lives. Hence, in this chapter, we follow Richardson (2022, p. 795), who defines automated decision systems as "any systems, software, or processes that use computation to aid or replace government decisions, judgments, and policy implementation that impact opportunities, access, liberties, rights, and safety. Automated Decision Systems can involve predicting, classifying, optimizing, identifying, and/or recommending."

ADM systems include AI systems and rules-based algorithmic systems, such as RPA. Here we understand AI systems as "a machine-based system that can, for a given set of human-defined objectives, make predictions, recommendations or decisions influencing real or virtual environments [which] are designed to operate with varying levels of autonomy" (OECD, 2019, pp. 23–4). Moreover, in this chapter RPA is understood as "the application of specific technology and methodologies which is based on software and algorithms aiming to automate repetitive human tasks …, mostly driven by simple rules and business logic" (Ivančić et al., 2019, p. 2).

Finally, there are diverse ways of defining algorithmic transparency, which allude to different obligations for organizations that use ADM systems (Lapostol et al., 2023). On a basic level, "algorithmic transparency" is associated with the disclosure of information about public algorithms and may be understood "as the quality of algorithmic systems that allows us to see and/or understand their operation" (Garrido et al., 2021, p. 42). A more stringent standard, such as the "meaningful algorithmic transparency" described by Brauneis and Goodman (2018, 2018), requires additional efforts from the government to provide citizens with access to enough information to assess the "algorithm's performance," making the "algorithmic process accountable" (2018, p. 132). From an institutional perspective, Valderrama et al. (2023, p. 8) argue that algorithmic transparency is "a relational achievement between different actors that can be internal and external to the algorithm development."[5]

In this chapter, algorithmic transparency is understood as a principle that involves access to crucial information about the algorithms used by organizations (*accessibility*) and the availability of explanations on when, how, and why an algorithmic decision is taken (*explainability*) (Criado et al., 2020, p. 453; Grimmelikhuijsen, 2023, pp. 243–4; Hermosilla & Lapostol, 2022a, p. 290).[6]

In this sense, Grimmelikhuijsen argues that algorithmic transparency may be "achieved when external actors can access the underlying data and code of an algorithm and the outcomes produced by it are explainable in a way a human being can understand" (2023, p. 244). Therefore, "transparency of algorithms (or algorithmic transparency) is a key factor for the understanding of their results and potential problems derived from the decisions made using autonomous systems" (Criado et al., 2020, p. 453).

New Transparency Challenges Associated with ADM Systems

The use of ADM systems in the public sector has expanded under the premise that these tools allow for improving the provision of state services through more efficient processes, better allocation of resources, fairness in algorithmic governance, or greater accuracy in forecasts and predictions (Brauneis & Goodman, 2018; Chenou & Rodríguez Valenzuela, 2021; Zuiderwijk et al., 2021).

The growth of people's demand for greater transparency in democratic government processes and decisions (Gavelin, 2009) can be compatible with adopting ADM systems. In this sense, Haataja et al. argued that governments should inform about using public authority through human actions and how they "automate those actions with the help of algorithms. Every citizen should have access to understandable and up-to-date information about how algorithms affect their lives and the grounds on which algorithmic decisions are made" (2020, p. 3).

The use of ADM systems creates new transparency challenges for governments that acquire, develop, pilot, adopt, and use these technologies. For example, when governments use ADM systems powered by machine learning algorithms, it may be more difficult for citizens to understand the basis of the decisions made by public officials who adopt the recommendations produced by the algorithms. Perhaps even the public official will not be able to fully explain the basis of his or her decision when the algorithm operates as a "black box." Moreover, when the ADM system operates through proprietary software, governments may not be allowed to disclose how it operates entirely. In this sense, Brauneis and Goodman have argued that "the opacity of algorithmic decision making is particularly problematic, both because governmental decisions may be especially weighty and because democratically elected governments have special duties of accountability" (2018, p. 103).

In summary, as mentioned in a recent report by Open Government (2022, p. 82), systems should be transparent, among other reasons, because they might "affect the lives of millions of people on sensitive issues ...; to ensure that they operate with fairness and equality ...; to ensure governments use them for their intended purpose; to give the public a chance to challenge their results."

Models of Algorithmic Transparency

Algorithmic transparency is one of the main principles that have been included in diverse ethical frameworks for responsible AI, as well as in diverse mandatory regulations (Hermosilla & Lapostol, 2022a; Lapostol et al., 2023; Larsson & Heintz, 2020; OGP, 2023; Valderrama et al., 2023). There are two main models for complying with algorithmic transparency.[7] First, "passive transparency," whereby the state discloses information about its algorithms on a case-by-case basis, often upon the explicit request of an interested party. The format and type of information disclosed depend on the corresponding request, but it may correspond to structured layouts such as model cards.

Second, "proactive" or "active transparency" consists of systematic and constant disclosure of information about public algorithms, for example, by publishing online AI repositories (Garrido et al., 2021; Lapostol et al., 2023). These public registries might present different forms, from an electronic file (e.g., a spreadsheet) that can be downloaded from a governmental web page to online platforms that aim to facilitate user navigation (Valderrama, 2023, p. 16).

The public repositories of algorithms are "windows" and "channels" where individuals can find information "to understand how the system works, how its decisions were done ('explainability') and to contest its behaviours ('accountability')" (Haataja et al., 2020, p. 5), and even to understand where the data come from and what will happen to the results the data produces ('traceability').

However, as stated at the beginning of the chapter, only a few national and subnational governments worldwide actively inform citizens about adopting ADM systems through online repositories. This is the case for the governments of cities such as New York, Amsterdam, Helsinki, and Nantes; provincial governments such as Ontario in Canada; national governments of the United Kingdom, France, New Zealand, and Colombia; and supranational governments such as the European Union (Gutiérrez & Muñoz-Cadena, 2023c).[8]

Finally, universities and civil society organizations have also contributed to algorithmic transparency through the creation of online registries of public algorithms. Two examples are worth highlighting. On the one hand, the "Repositorio Algoritmos Públicos" created by the GobLab of the Universidad Adolfo Ibáñez de Chile[9], and the Register of the "Observatory of Algorithms with Social Impact, or OASI" launched by *Eticas Foundation* that includes public algorithms from all over the world.[10]

METHODOLOGY AND DATA

This research follows a case study design that implements an extreme case selection criterion. The extreme case design allows us to "highlight the most unusual variation in the phenomena under investigation" (Jahnukainen, 2010, p. 379) or maximize the "variation in the variable of interest" to make the studied relationships "more transparent" (Gerring, 2017, p. 68). The Colombian government is one of the few national governments around the globe that has made repositories of public algorithms available. Hence, the case may be considered "extreme" regarding one of the main variables of interest: the availability of such repositories.

This research is based on quantitative and qualitative data on ADM systems in the Colombian public sector that were collected and processed between late 2021 and 2023. Data on the transparency of the acquisition, development, adoption, piloting, and use of ADM systems come from two major sources. On the one hand, primary data were drawn from three pre-existing public databases and repositories, the public entities' annual management reports, institutional web pages, social networks, and press reports. On the other hand, secondary sources included information published by tech companies, news reports, gray literature – published by multilateral entities and civil society organizations – and academic literature.

Using this information, we built a new database on ADM systems adopted by the Colombian State, with 113 ADM systems characterized through 40 variables and from more than 300 primary and secondary information sources: 68% of which are institutional sources, 15% are news articles, 8% are academic publications, 4% are documents from multilateral organizations, 3% are company documents, and 2% are civil society publications.

The database characterizes each system regarding 40 variables that allow the tracing the accessibility and explainability of the information disclosed about the public algorithms. The variables may be grouped into five categories: (i) basic information about the system, including its name, information about the public entity that implements it, its main objectives, and the functions of each ADM system – using the OECD's (2022a) framework for the classification of AI systems – and status of the system, among others; (ii) type of data that the system requires; (iii) information on the financier or financiers of the project, in addition to the amounts and where the resources come from; (iv) the reports on the results and impact of the system, and the Sustainable Development Goals (SDGs) that may be positively impacted; and (v) the sources of publicly available information.

There is no consensus on an algorithmic transparency standard for repositories (Open Government, 2022). The information collected for our novel dataset includes most of the variables that appear in public repositories, such as the "Selected AI cases in the public sector" database of the European Union (European Commission, Joint Research Centre, 2021) and the repository of public algorithms made available by GobLab in Chile (Garrido et al., 2021; GobLab UAI, 2022, 2023). The same can be said about the type of information requested by the UK's algorithmic transparency standard (CDDO & CDEI, 2023). Moreover, the information we collected covers the five main components of transparency identified by Porumbescu et al. (2022): (1) availability, (2) information, (3) organization or actor, (4) external actors, and (5) internal functioning.

Our research has limitations that must be acknowledged. The information we collected to build our novel database is based on systems for which there is public information. Likely, some Colombian public sector entities have yet to disclose the existence of ADM systems adopted to carry out and support diverse decision-making processes. This is the case of public bodies shielded by exceptions in the access to information laws or that tend to conceal how they operate, such as security government bodies. Hence, our database does not include ADM systems that the Colombian State has not publicly disclosed.

The research presented in this chapter is part of a broader project that studies the life cycle of ADM projects in the Colombian public sector and the implications of these systems for public management, democracy, and society.

MAIN FINDINGS ON THE TRANSPARENCY OF PUBLIC ALGORITHMS IN COLOMBIA

This section assesses the transparency of public algorithms in Colombia through two main pathways: (i) surveying the information disclosed through the Colombian national government's repositories of public algorithms and, in general, the disclosure of data on the use of AI and RPA systems; and (ii) comparing the latter with our novel database.

The Colombian National Government's Repositories of Public Algorithms

The Colombian national government created three publicly accessible repositories with information on AI tools used by the public sector (Table 13.1). The repositories, accessible online, are managed by the Administrative Department of the Presidency of the Republic (DAPRE, its acronym in Spanish) and by the Ministry of Information and Communication Technologies (MinTIC, its acronym in Spanish). Each repository contains different data types about systems that the government bodies voluntarily disclose.

No rule obliges the Colombian State to publish information about its ADM systems through online repositories. However, the Colombian *Law on Transparency and Right to National Public Information* establishes the "principle of transparency" that public bodies must follow, in terms of "the duty to provide and facilitate access to [public information] in the broadest terms possible and through the means and procedures."[11] Moreover, the principle of "proactive disclosure of information" establishes that public bodies have "the obligation to publish and disclose documents and archives that reflect state and public interest activity, routinely and proactively, updated, accessible and understandable ...".[12]

The first online repository listed in Table 13.1 aimed to facilitate monitoring governmental bodies' compliance with the "Ethical Framework for Artificial Intelligence in Colombia" published by the Colombian government. According to governmental reports, the platform was

Table 13.1   *Repositories of public algorithms in Colombia (2023)*

Name of the repository	Responsible public body	Registered systems	Variables per system
Artificial Intelligence Ethical Framework Tracking Dashboard[a]	DAPRE	6	27
Open Data (Big Data Project)[b]	MinTIC	16	13
Innovation exercises based on artificial intelligence[c]	MinTIC	6	7

[a] The "Dashboard" platform was available at: https://inteligenciaartificial.gov.co/dashboard-IA/. However, in 2023, the availability of the data in the portal has been intermittent.
[b] The "Open Data" platform is available at: https://herramientas.datos.gov.co/taxonomy/term/501?page=0
[c] The "Innovation exercises" web page is available at: https://gobiernodigital.mintic.gov.co/portal/Centro-de-Innovacion-Publica-Digital/Proyectos/#data=%7B%22filter%22:%22412572%22,%22page%22:1%7D
Source: Authors' own elaboration.

inspired by the repositories of cities such as Amsterdam and Helsinki (Muñoz et al., 2021). The second online repository in Table 13.1 was created as part of the national government's Open Data initiative, and the third one aims to publicize MinTIC's projects.

To what extent do these public repositories contribute to proactive algorithmic transparency? Figure 13.1 depicts the different dimensions of algorithmic transparency that will be considered to answer this question:

First, the public repositories of the Colombian national government contribute to the "accessibility" of basic information about the ADM systems used by the Colombian government. The repositories demonstrate that the Colombian national government has the capacity and willingness to reveal basic information about some of its algorithms permanently, without requiring said disclosure to be the product of requests for access to information.

Second, the repositories partially explain when, how, and why specific algorithms are used to support or make a decision. The datasets include information about how the systems operate, the organization in charge of the system, and the target population. However, the repositories need more crucial information to understand the scope and implications of each ADM system. For example, the repositories do not offer information about whether the systems use personal data, how they obtain the data used, who developed the algorithm, and who holds the intellectual property rights associated with the algorithms, among others. We will come back to the issue of the type of data available in these repositories when we assess whether such information allows us to draw key inferences about the algorithms.

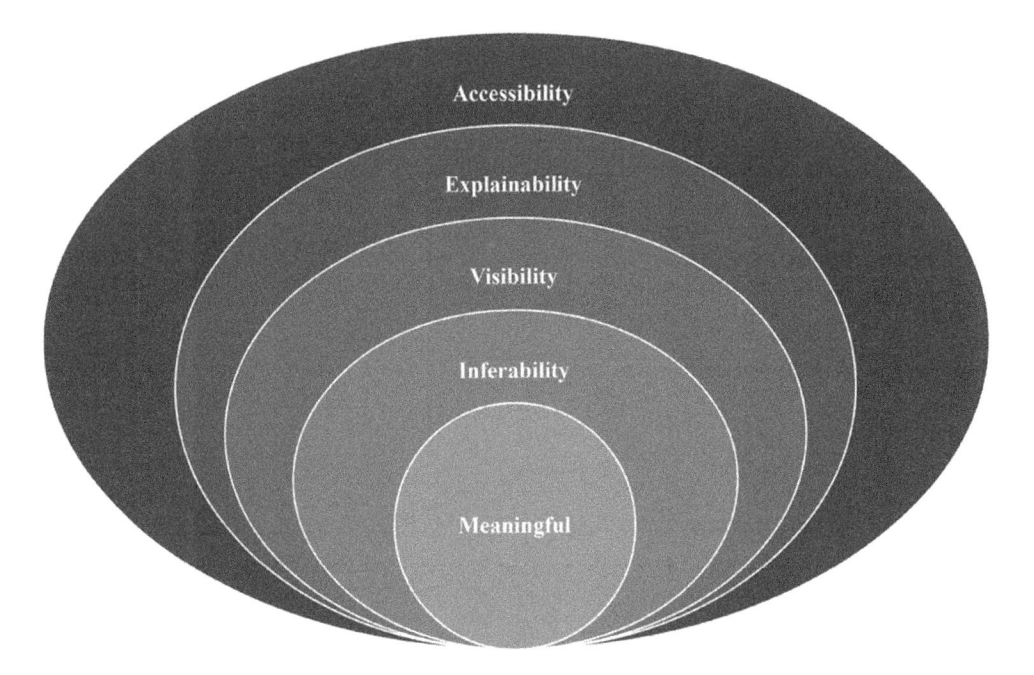

Source: Authors' own elaboration.

Figure 13.1   Dimensions of transparency of repositories of public algorithms

Third, the "visibility" dimension entails that information is "a) reasonably complete and b) found with relative ease" (Michener & Bersch, 2013, p. 238). While it may be argued that the examined repositories can be easily found on the Internet, they do not offer "a complete picture" of the ADM systems adopted by the Colombian State. First, as explained in the previous paragraph, the public repositories do not systematically provide basic information about the registered algorithms.

Another reason the repositories fail the "visibility" dimension is that the number of systems used by the Colombian State is much greater than the publicly registered ones. On the one hand, the public repositories do not include information on the use of these systems to support activities associated with health and security. Furthermore, the repositories do not include information about ADM systems used by subnational governments or organizations in the judicial branch.

Regarding ease of access, the platform of the first repository listed in Table 13.1, the *Dashboard*, has been intermittent since its publication. In fact, since May 2023, the platform is no longer available because the government did not renew the software license required to display the information (Gutiérrez & Castellanos-Sánchez, 2023). Moreover, accessing the information in the Open Data platform (the second repository listed in Table 13.1) requires a certain degree of digital literacy.

Additionally, the total number of systems registered in these repositories could be higher than the number of effectively used systems. A recent survey conducted by the national government to collect information about the public management performance of public entities also suggests that there needs to be more reporting of public algorithms. According to the public entities that filled out the "2021 Management Progress Report Form" (*Formulario Único de Reporte de Avances de Gestión* – FURAG), 233 out of 2,939 reported that they used AI or RPA: 172 (74%) declared that they use the first, 116 (50%) the second, and 55 (24%) use both.[13]

However, since the FURAG survey comprises self-reported data that need more verification, it is possible that some of the public entities that answered affirmatively about their use of AI or RPA systems do not use this type of system. The latter is reinforced by the fact that these terms are porous, that the public officials who filled in the form may not be acquainted with what AI or RPA mean, and that the DAFP, which administers the FURAG, did not include the terms "artificial intelligence" or "robotic process automation" in the survey's glossary.[14] In sum, the FURAG survey does not allow us to conclude that over 200 public bodies use AI or RPA systems in Colombia's public sector. However, it suggests that the number of adopted systems is significantly larger than those registered in the government's publicly available repositories.

Fourth, the "inferability" of data is understood as "the extent to which the information at hand can be used to draw accurate inferences – both about visible information and information we do not know" (Michener & Bersch, 2013, p. 239). In this respect, the information from the repositories is accurate but not updated frequently; hence, the data quality tends to diminish over time. Moreover, the repositories lack vital data for making inferences about information that may not be visible. For example, the source code, how the systems were developed, the effects of the systems, how potential risks are mitigated, or the performance of the systems.

Finally, the information in the repositories is insufficient to carry out algorithmic audits and evaluations, for example, to determine the fairness of the system's decisions and their impact. In this sense, the national government's repositories do not comply with a standard of "meaningful transparency," understood as "knowledge sufficient to approve or disapprove the algorithm's performance" (Brauneis & Goodman, 2018, p. 132).

In sum, while the Colombian repositories of public algorithms contribute to different dimensions of algorithmic transparency, they fall short regarding the most demanding ones: explainability, inferability, and meaningfulness.

New Database of ADM Systems in the Colombian Public Sector

Our novel database registers a total of 113 ADM systems in Colombia's public sector, which includes 98 systems that are in operation (86.7%), 13 being piloted (11.5%), one suspended, and one discontinued. The statistics presented in the following sections of the chapter characterize the 111 systems in operation or being piloted; in other words, the statistics do not include cases in which the project was suspended or discontinued.

Most of the systems (74%) included in the database were adopted by national government units, and most of the systems (93%) pertain to public bodies that are part of the executive branch (at the national or subnational level). Based on the OECD's Classification of the Functions of Government (COFOG), we found that the public bodies that disclosed the use of ADM systems are related to the sectors of economic affairs (32%), general public services (23%), education (19%), public order and security (12%), social protection (5%), recreation, culture, sports, and other social services (3%), environmental protection (3%), health (3%), and defense (1%). Figure 13.2 presents the information in greater detail.

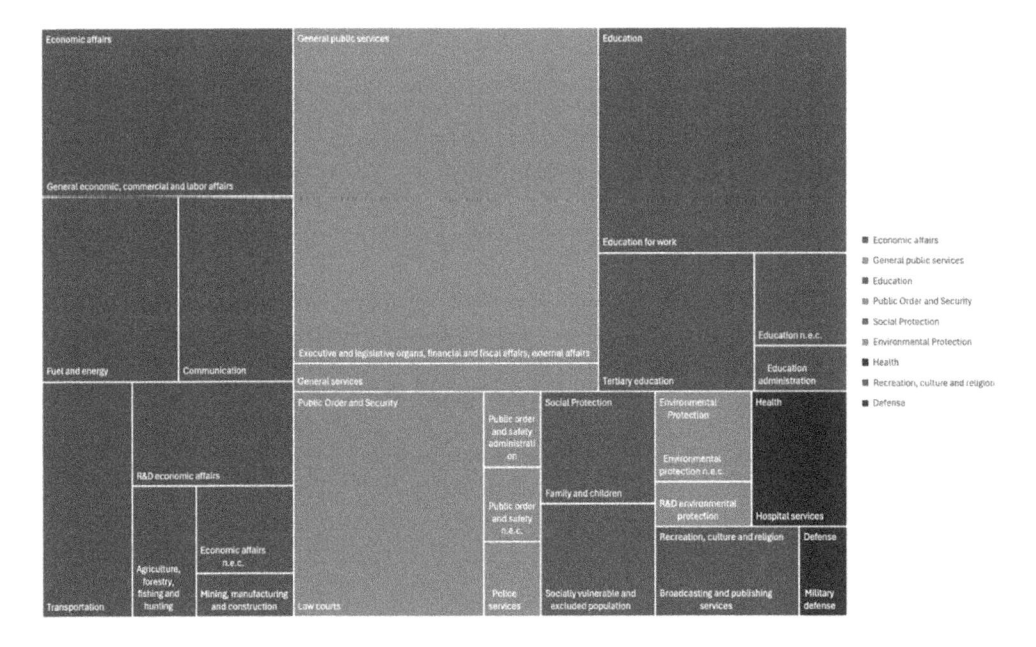

Source: Authors' own elaboration.

Figure 13.2   Classification of the functions of the public bodies that adopted ADM systems

Source of the information types of missing data

One of the critical questions is how public bodies make public information about their ADM systems. Information about 89% of the systems was published on the respective public bodies' websites. In contrast with our findings, the 2023 report of "Algoritmos Públicos de Chile," the public algorithm repository managed by GobLab, informed that in their database, only 19% of the 75 registered systems have information published on the web pages of the respective public entity that adopted the ADM systems (GobLab UAI, 2023).

Concerning 5% of the systems, the information was published on another government platform. Regarding the remaining 6%, no information was made public directly or indirectly by the government. This means that in these cases, we found information about the ADM systems on web pages of private undertakings, news reports, or civil society organizations.

We attempted to characterize all the systems with information on each of the pre-defined 40 variables, but it was not always possible to find all the required data; as a result, 90% of the fields in our database contain information about the systems, while the remaining 10% were left as "not available" when we could not find publicly available information concerning specific variables. As we explain in more detail below, one of the variables for which it was impossible to find information is the one that refers to the cost of the ADM systems and who is or are the project funder(s).

Another category for which no information was available is the responsible unit within the public entity that implements the system: we could not find data for 50 of the systems (45%). Finally, in 69 of the systems (62%), the public body did not make clear who the beneficiaries were.

Data about the results or performance of the ADM system

Given that the implementation of most of the ADM systems in the Colombian public sector started in the last five years, it is not surprising that most of the systems (63%) lack information about their results. However, the public bodies self-reported the results for 25% of the ADM systems. Finally, in 12% of the cases, a third party (e.g., a tech company that developed the ADM systems) participated in publishing information about the system results (Figure 13.3).

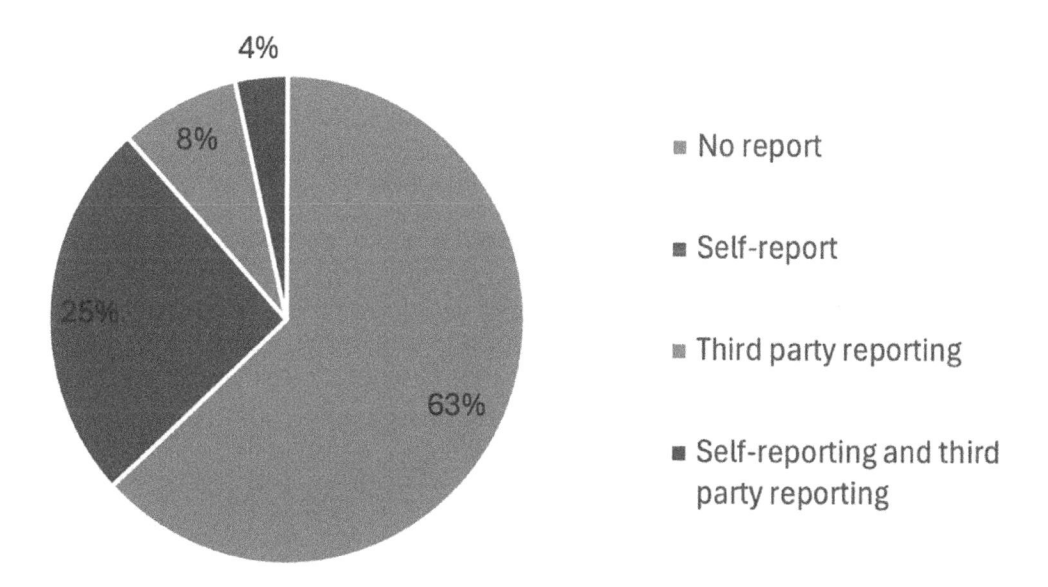

Source: Authors' own elaboration.

Figure 13.3   *Who reports the results of the ADM systems?*

Information on costs and licensing

We found information about costs for 30% of the ADM systems in our database. This information includes the results of our search in the Colombian government's "Electronic Public Procurement System" (SECOP), where official information about the public procurement processes (including the costs) should be published. Although the law mandates that procurement processes and public contracts must be registered in SECOP, in previous research projects (Gutiérrez & Muñoz-Cadena, 2023b) we have found that contracts are not always registered, or the information may be incomplete.

Some of the keywords that we used in our inquiry in SECOP's database were the name of each ADM system, "machine learning," "automation," "artificial intelligence," "robotization," and "algorithm," among others. For example, for "Watson – Machine Learning," a system adopted by the Attorney General's Office, we used the key term "Watson" to search SECOP. The only information that we were able to retrieve was related to a contract signed with IBM de Colombia SAS for the "upgrade, expansion and specialized technical support of the Watson tool and the expansion of the cloud pack for application licensing, with technical support from IBM for the Attorney General's Office" (Fiscalía General de la Nación, 2020).

We only found information about procurement processes associated with seven systems (6%).[15] A critical side-effect of the low level of information about the procurement processes associated with the acquisition, development, and operation of ADM systems is that there is scant information about the private companies that developed the systems and whether the public bodies were licensed proprietary software or if the systems rely on open-source software.

The low levels of transparency concerning how ADM systems were financed may not be a particular feature of the Colombian case. For example, in the latest report of "Algoritmos Públicos de Chile," GobLab stated that "[i]nformation on the source of funding is only available for just over half of the public algorithms [52%], and of these the amount is known for 54%. This implies that the source and funding are available for only 28% of the systems" (GobLab UAI, 2023, p. 54).

Finally, information regarding which entity or entities financed adopting the ADM system is available for only 22 (19.8%) of the 111 systems. Some of these projects could have been funded by multilateral banks or in partnership with private entities. Still, such information is not easily accessed; hence, data availability regarding this dimension is limited.

About the used data

The disclosure of information by public bodies about the type of data used to operate their ADM systems is very uneven. In the case of AI, only a handful of public bodies disclosed the kind of data used to train their systems. Moreover, few public bodies listed and described the data used to operate their ADM systems. However, most of the ADM systems included in our database contain general information about the data used by the systems, or at least it is possible to infer the types of data due to the descriptions of the functions and outputs of the ADM systems.

Finally, we found that in 58% of cases, personal data is used to operate the systems. This finding illustrates that the operation of the ADM systems may imply data protection and privacy risks that must be addressed by the government units using them.

CONCLUSIONS

The main objective of this chapter was to contribute to the literature on the transparency of public algorithms and the use of ADM systems in Colombia's public sector. Although Colombia's national government has three online AI repositories (one of which is no longer accessible), essential gaps were identified in the information provided. Moreover, in these public repositories, there is a significant under-registration of systems used by public bodies. Furthermore, the national government does not actively inform citizens when it uses ADM systems, and in some cases, it actively conceals how the algorithm operates.

The chapter first assessed the extent to which three repositories of public algorithms of the national government contribute to the principle of proactive algorithmic transparency through five dimensions: accessibility, visibility, explainability, inferability, and meaningfulness. The findings are nuanced: the repositories partially contributed to the first three dimensions, but their information was insufficient to comply with the last two.

Then, the chapter presented the main findings derived from constructing a new database containing information on 113 ADM systems in the Colombian public sector. The database characterizes the systems through 40 different variables and was created with more than 300 sources of primary and secondary information. The database illustrates how these systems are widespread in diverse sectors of the national government and some subnational governments.

We found that the basic features of most of the systems included in our novel database can be documented through information made public by government organizations through other means. We report that there is very little information on critical aspects such as the type of data used by the systems, the performance of the algorithms, their cost, whether the software is proprietary or open-source, and the procurement processes required to acquire the respective license and service. The publicly available information about the systems must be more comprehensive and up-to-date to make Colombia's algorithmic processes accountable. Moreover, even if the systems are developed by private parties for public entities to use within the framework of their functions, this does not exclude the public sector from its responsibility to provide timely, relevant information in a language that citizens can understand about the systems it uses (Hermosilla & Lapostol, 2022b).

Rather than a "meaningful transparency" standard, the Colombian State appears to favor a "performative transparency" practice where information about ADM systems is used to portray an image of efficiency and innovation. However, such data is not sufficient to inform citizens when an ADM system is used to take or support a decision, nor does it allow key stakeholders to assess the performance of such systems. The case of Colombia suggests that issuing rules, principles, or ethical frameworks, or signing commitments is insufficient to guarantee high levels of algorithmic transparency.

However, the contribution of transparency to algorithmic governance should not be overrated: algorithmic transparency is not an end, and much more is needed to guarantee public management's improvement and greater accountability. As Hermosilla and Lapostol argue, "it is not enough to merely provide information ... it is necessary to consider to whom the information is given, where the data is obtained, and by whom the system's information must be requested, among other issues" (2022b, p. 290). For example, case studies in Colombia have found that when institutional contexts are weak, implementing procurement transparency initiatives and e-procurement tools may be insufficient to foster competitive public tendering processes (Gutiérrez, 2020). However, transparency is a crucial enabler for any stakeholder who wishes to hold governments accountable, which is also true concerning the accountability of algorithmic processes.

Future research could continue to advance the study of algorithmic transparency in other jurisdictions and the means for increasing and preserving it. Regarding the latter issue, it would also be worth assessing the capabilities Colombian public entities require to improve ADM systems governance. This also includes capacity-building for civil society organizations and other stakeholders that could conduct external algorithmic audits.

This study offers policy implications that are pertinent from a global standpoint. First, the reliability and quality of algorithmic transparency require new forms of governance in which transparency operates by design, not through reactive measures. This may entail co-designing systems with users, beneficiaries, and other stakeholders, and deploying public repositories of interoperable algorithms with the government's information systems that tend to be updated in real-time.

A low level of algorithmic transparency is incompatible with a democratic regime and the rule of law. For example, failing to inform a citizen that a governmental decision was based on an ADM system makes it unfeasible for the citizen to understand how the decision was made and how they could find the grounds to appeal the decision. In this sense, the objectives of algorithmic transparency are threefold: (i) to inform citizens about the use of ADM systems that may affect their lives and rights; (ii) to help allocate the responsibility of any liability associated with the use of the systems; and (iii) to make possible the social control of the use of algorithms and make governments accountable for their use.

NOTES

1. The authors thank Michelle Castellanos-Sánchez for her diligent research assistance. This research is financed with resources from the Universidad del Rosario. The authors also thank the attendees of the XI International Conference on Government, Administration and Public Policy (GIGAPP), the XVII Annual Conference of the Inter-American Network for Public Administration Education (INPAE), the Section on International and Comparative Administration (SICA), 10th Annual Fred Riggs Symposium (2023), IE Lawtomation Days conference (2023), and an anonymous referee for their helpful queries and feedback.
2. A private university developed the Chilean repository of public algorithms, but an autonomous public body collaborated on its development (Lapostol et al., 2023).
3. However, a report published by Gutiérrez and Muñoz-Cadena (2023a) summarizes the findings of the novel dataset of ADM systems used by the Colombian government, and a paper published by Gutiérrez and Castellanos-Sánchez (2023) reflects on the links between Open Government and algorithmic transparency in Colombia.
4. The complete database is available at the following URL: https://doi.org/10.34848/YN1CRT
5. This definition by Valderrama et al. (2023) partly resembles that of Larsson and Heintz (2020, p. 10), who understand transparency in AI as "a balancing of interests and a governance challenge demanding multidisciplinary development to be adequately addressed."
6. Key information refers to information that allows one to "monitor, test, critique, or evaluate the logic, procedures, and performance of an algorithmic system in order to foster trust and increase the accountability of the developers or controllers of the system" (Valderrama et al., 2023, p. 8). Additionally, algorithmic transparency should not be

assumed to be static, but dynamic, in that such information must be updated as systems are also updated (Valderrama et al., 2023).
7. Valderrama et al. (2023) propose another classification, in terms of the objective of the algorithmic transparency mechanism, that includes three categories: disclosure, explanation, and evaluation. The first mechanism is direct disclosure, where information about algorithmic systems is shared. However, there are variations in who discloses, how it is enforced, the required documentation, and the intended audience. The second mechanism aims to increase the explainability of systems. The third mechanism involves algorithm evaluations to examine the impacts of algorithms "on potentially affected individuals and groups" (Valderrama et al., 2023).
8. A detailed list of these repositories, curated by Gutiérrez (2023), can be found at the following URL: https://forogpp.com/inteligencia-artificial/repositorios-y-registros-de-algoritmos/
9. The Chilean repository is available at the following URL: http://algoritmospublicos.cl/
10. The OASI's registry is available at the following URL: https://eticasfoundation.org/oasi/
11. Article 3 of Law 1712 of 2014.
12. Article 3 of Law 1712 of 2014.
13. Information on the type of questions included in the FURAG and the collection methodology is available in Spanish at the following DAFP platform: https://www.funcionpublica.gov.co/web/mipg/medicion_desempenoThe data of the responses to FURAG can be consulted at the following platform: https://www.datos.gov.co/Funci-n-p-blica/FURAG/daed-z4fw/data
14. The glossary, in Spanish, of June 2020 (version 5) of the FURAG can be consulted at the following link: https://www.funcionpublica.gov.co/documents/28587410/36200637/Glosario_mipg.pdf/9ff42c08-61a9-e0fa-76b1-1f662c0b2202?t=1593207412671
15. The fact that a contract is registered at SECOP does not necessarily mean that information about the project's total costs is available. It may be the case that only some of the contracts related to a project are registered at SECOP, but that the total value of the development and implementation of an algorithm is higher if other contracts were not registered and if the public body internally developed part of the project.

REFERENCES

Ada Lovelace Institute, AI Now Institute, & Open Government Partnership. (2021). *Algorithmic accountability for the public sector. Learning from the first wave of policy implementation.* https://www.opengovpartnership.org/wp-content/uploads/2021/08/algorithmic-accountability-public-sector.pdf

BID, & UNESCO. (n.d.). *Observatorio | fAIrLAC*. Retrieved December 27, 2022, from https://fairlac.iadb.org/observatorio

Brauneis, R., & Goodman, E.P. (2018). Algorithmic transparency for the Smart City. *Yale Journal of Law and Technology, 20*, 103–76.

Camacho Gutiérrez, O.L., & Praxedes Saavedra Rionda, V. (2021). El acercamiento del sector público a la IA: la divergencia entre la expectativa y la realidad. In G.A. Dobratinich (Ed.), *Derecho y nuevas tecnologías* (1st edn) (167–192). La Ley.

CDDO, & CDEI. (2023). *Algorithmic Transparency Recording Standard – Guidance for Public Sector Bodies.* Central Digital and Data Office (CDDO) and Centre for Data Ethics and Innovation (CDEI). https://www.gov.uk/government/publications/guidance-for-organisations-using-the-algorithmic-transparency-recording-standard/algorithmic-transparency-recording-standard-guidance-for-public-sector-bodies

Cetina, C., Garay Salamanca, L.J., Salcedo-Albarán, E., & Vanegas, S. (2021). *La analítica de redes como herramienta de integridad: El caso de la Procuraduría General de la Nación en Colombia* (Policy Brief no. 22) CAF Working Paper. https://cafscioteca.azurewebsites.net/handle/123456789/1675

Chenou, J.-M., & Rodríguez Valenzuela, L.E. (2021). Habeas data, Habemus algorithms: Algorithmic intervention in public interest decision-making in Colombia. *Law, State and Telecommunications Review*, 13(2), 56–77. https://doi.org/10.26512/lstr.v13i2.34113

Criado, J.I., Valero, J., & Villodre, J. (2020). Algorithmic transparency and bureaucratic discretion: The case of SALER early warning system. *Information Polity*, 25(4), 449–70. https://doi.org/10.3233/IP-200260

Departamento Administrativo de la Función Pública (Director). (2020, August 21). *ADA – Asistente de Adopciones ICBF*. https://www.youtube.com/watch?v=LkTMRP8yRWU

Diakopoulos, N. (2020). Transparency. In M.D. Dubber, F. Pasquale, & S. Das (Eds.), *The Oxford Handbook of Ethics of AI* (pp. 197–213). Oxford University Press. https://doi.org/10.1093/oxfordhb/9780190067397.013.11

Escobar Gutiérrez, E., Ramírez Roa, D.P., Quevedo Hernández, M., Insuasti Ceballos, H.D., Jiménez Ospina, A., Montenegro Helfer, P., Numpaque Cano, J.S., Rocha Ruiz, C.A., Ruiz Saenz, J. A., Berniell, M.L., & Zapata, E. (2021). *Aprovechamiento de datos para la toma de decisiones en el sector público*. CAF y DNP. https://cafscioteca.azurewebsites.net/handle/123456789/1776

European Commission, Joint Research Centre. (2021). *Selected AI cases in the public sector (JRC129301)* [dataset]. http://data.europa.eu/89h/7342ea15-fd4f-4184-9603-98bd87d8239a

Fiscalía General de la Nación. (2020). *Contrato: CO1.PCCNTR.2064648. CONTRATO-FGN-NC-0231-2020*. https://community.secop.gov.co/Public/Tendering/ContractNoticeManagement/Index?currentLanguage=es-CO&Page=login&Country=CO&SkinName=CCE

Flórez Rojas, M.L., & Vargas Leal, J. (2020). El impacto de herramientas de inteligencia artificial: Un análisis en el sector público en Colombia. In C. Aguerre (Ed.), *Inteligencia Artificial en América Latina y el Caribe. Ética, Gobernanza y Políticas*. CETyS Universidad de San Andrés. https://guia.ai/wp-content/uploads/2020/05/GECTI-El-impacto-de-herramientas-de-inteligencia-artificial.pdf

Garrido, R., Lapostol, J.P., & Hermosilla, M.P. (2021). *Transparencia algorítmica en el sector público*. GOB LAB UAI. Consejo para la Transparencia. https://goblab.uai.cl/wp-content/uploads/2021/10/ESTUDIO-TRANSPARENCIA-ALGORITMICA-EN-EL-SECTOR-PUBLICO-GOBLAB-CPLT-final....pdf

Gavelin, K. (2009). Open Government: Beyond static measures. Involve. https://www.oecd.org/gov/46560184.pdf

Gerring, J. (2017). *Case study research: Principles and practices* (2nd edn). Cambridge: Cambridge University Press.

GobLab UAI. (2022). *Repositorio de algoritmos públicos de Chile. Primer informe de estado de uso de algoritmos en el sector público*. Universidad Adolfo Ibáñez (UAI). https://goblab.uai.cl/wp-content/uploads/2022/02/Primer-Informe-Repositorio-Algoritmos-Publicos-en-Chile.pdf

GobLab UAI. (2023). *Repositorio Algoritmos Públicos. Informe Anual 2023*. Universidad Adolfo Ibáñez (UAI).

GOV.CO. (n.d.). *Dashboard de seguimiento al Marco Ético de Inteligencia Artificia*. https://inteligenciaartificial.gov.co/dashboard-IA/?TSPD_101_R0=0883a32c4dab2000dd6f602217a18ab4968020ee791a81bbff34764c7512577f7619311eb951b1eb08501259d0143000f1f034e8ec1ace3cbd81e20bd75a71d522a32bfc7fe1876ed13187dcaa48908e7f1806e2021160ec618895366787df95

GPAI (2024). Algorithmic transparency in the public sector: A state-of-the-art report of algorithmic transparency instruments. *Global Partnership on Artificial Intelligence (GPAI)*, May 2024. https://gpai.ai/projects/responsible-ai/algorithmic-transparency-in-the-public-sector/algorithmic-transparency-in-the-public-sector.pdf

Grimmelikhuijsen, S. (2023). Explaining why the computer says no: Algorithmic transparency affects the perceived trustworthiness of automated decision-making. *Public Administration Review*, 83(2), 241–62. https://doi.org/10.1111/puar.13483

Gutiérrez, J.D. (2020). Oil revenues, public procurement and armed conflict: A case study of a subnational government in Colombia. *The Extractive Industries and Society*, 7(2), 686–703. https://doi.org/10.1016/j.exis.2020.03.018

Gutiérrez, J.D. (2023, July 6). Repositorios y registros públicos de algoritmos. *Foro Administración, Gestión y Política Pública*. https://forogpp.com/inteligencia-artificial/repositorios-y-registros-de-algoritmos/

Gutiérrez, J.D., & Castellanos-Sánchez, M. (2023). Transparencia algorítmica y Estado Abierto en Colombia. *Revista Reflexión Política*, 25(52). https://revistas.unab.edu.co/index.php/reflexion/issue/archive

Gutiérrez, J.D., & Muñoz-Cadena, S. (2023a). Adopción de sistemas de decisión automatizada en el sector público: Cartografía de 113 sistemas en Colombia. *GIGAPP Estudios Working Papers*, 10(270), 365–95.

Gutiérrez, J.D., & Muñoz-Cadena, S. (2023b). Assessing government design practices from a human-centered perspective: Case study of an improved cookstoves program in Colombia. *Desafíos*, 35(1), 1–38. https://doi.org/10.12804/revistas.urosario.edu.co/desafios/a.12332

Gutiérrez, J.D., & Muñoz-Cadena, S. (2023c). Building a repository of public algorithms: Case study of the dataset on automated decision-making systems in the Colombian public sector. In L. Belli & W.B. Gaspar (Eds.), *The Quest for AI Sovereignty, Transparency and Accountability: Official Outcome of the UN IGF Data and Artificial Intelligence Governance Coalition* (pp. 325–40). Getulio Vargas Foundation/FGV Direito Rio. https://www.intgovforum.org/en/filedepot_download/288/26421

Haataja, M., van de Fliert, L., & Rautio, P. (2020). *Public AI Registers. Realising AI transparency and civic participation in government use of AI* (White paper). https://algoritmeregister.amsterdam.nl/wp-content/uploads/White-Paper.pdf

Hermosilla, M.P., & Lapostol, P. (2022a). The limits of algorithmic transparency. In Núcleo de Informação e Coordenação do Ponto BR (Ed.), *Survey on the Use of Information and Communication Technologies in the Brazilian Public Sector: ICT Electronic Government 2021* (pp. 289–95). Comitê Gestor da Internet no Brasil.

Hermosilla, M.P., & Lapostol, P. (2022b). The limits of algorithmic transparency. In *ICT Electronic government Survey on the Use of Information and Communication Technologies in the Brazilian Public Sector* (pp. 131–7). https://cetic.br/media/docs/publicacoes/2/20220725170710/tic_governo_eletronico_2021_livro_eletronico.pdf

ICBF. (2021). *Modelos de Probabilidad de Vulneración para la Prevención de Violencia contra Niñas, Niños y Adolescentes en Colombia*. https://www.icbf.gov.co/system/files/boletin_violencias_nna_dic21_0.pdf

ICBF. (2023, September 11). *Plataforma Betto deja de ser herramienta de selección de operadores del ICBF*. Portal ICBF – Instituto Colombiano de Bienestar Familiar ICBF. https://www.icbf.gov.co/buscador

Ivančić, L., Suša Vugec, D., & Bosilj Vukšić, V. (2019). Robotic process automation: Systematic literature review. In C. Di Ciccio, R. Gabryelczyk, L. García-Bañuelos, T. Hernaus, R. Hull, M. Indihar Štemberger, A. Kő, & M. Staples (Eds.), *Business Process Management: Blockchain and Central and Eastern Europe Forum* (Vol. 361, pp. 280–95). Springer International Publishing. https://doi.org/10.1007/978-3-030-30429-4_19

Jahnukainen, M. (2010). *Extreme Cases* (pp. 379–80). https://doi.org/10.4135/9781412957397.n142

Lapostol, J.P., Garrido, R., & Hermosilla, M.P. (2023). *Algorithmic Transparency from the South: Examining the State of Algorithmic Transparency in Chile's Public Administration Algorithms*. 2023 ACM Conference on Fairness, Accountability, and Transparency (FAccT '23), Chicago, IL. https://doi.org/10.1145/3593013.3593991

Larsson, S., & Heintz, F. (2020). Transparency in artificial intelligence. *Internet Policy Review*, 9(2), 1–16. https://doi.org/10.14763/2020.2.1469

López, J. (2020). *Experimentando con la pobreza: El SISBÉN y los proyectos de analítica de datos en Colombia*. Fundación KARISMA. https://web.karisma.org.co/wp-content/uploads/download-manager-files/Experimentando%20con%20la%20pobreza.pdf

López, J., & Castañeda, J.D. (2020). Automatización, tecnologías digitales y justicia social: La experimentación con la pobreza en Colombia. In *Inteligencia Artificial en América Latina y el Caribe. Ética, gobernanza y políticas*. CETyS Universidad de San Andres. https://proyectoguia.lat/wp-content/uploads/2020/05/Lopez-Casta%C3%B1eda-Automatizacion-tecnologias-digitales-y-justicia-social-la-experimentacion-con-la-pobreza-en-Colombia.pdf

Michener, G., & Bersch, K. (2013). Identifying transparency. *Information Polity*, *18*(3), 233–42. https://doi.org/10.3233/IP-130299

Muñoz, V., Tamayo, E., & Guio, A. (2021). The Colombian case: Adopting collaborative governance as a path for implementing ethical artificial intelligence. http://repositorio.udesa.edu.ar/jspui/handle/10908/18743

OECD. (2019). *Artificial Intelligence in Society*. OECD Publishing. https://www.oecd.org/publications/artificial-intelligence-in-society-eedfee77-en.htm

OECD. (2022a). *OECD Framework for the Classification of AI Systems*. OECD. https://doi.org/10.1787/cb6d9eca-en

OECD. (2022b). *Uso estratégico y responsable de la inteligencia artificial en el sector público de América Latina y el Caribe*. OECD. https://www.oecd-ilibrary.org/governance/uso-estrategico-y-responsable-de-la-inteligencia-artificial-en-el-sector-publico-de-america-latina-y-el-caribe_5b189cb4-es

OGP. (2023). *The Skeptic's Guide to Open Government – 2022 Edition*. Open Government Partnership - OGP. https://www.opengovpartnership.org/skeptics-guide-to-open-government-2022-edition/

Open Government. (2022). Chapter 8: Algorithmic transparency. In *The Skeptic's Guide to Open Government*.

Porumbescu, G., Meijer, A., & Grimmelikhuijsen, S. (2022). *Government Transparency: State of the Art and New Perspectives*. Cambridge University Press. https://doi.org/10.1017/9781108678568.

Richardson, R. (2022). Defining and demystifying automated decision systems. *Maryland Law Review (1936)*, *81*(785).

Sanabria-Pulido, P., Pliscoff, C., & Gomes, R. (2014). E-government practices in South American countries: Echoing a global trend or really improving governance? The experiences of Colombia, Chile, and Brazil. In M. Gascó-Hernández (Ed.), *Public Administration and Information Technology* (pp. 17–36). https://doi.org/10.1007/978-1-4614-9563-5_2

Valderrama, M., Hermosilla, M.P., & Garrido, R. (2023). *State of the Evidence: Algorithmic Transparency*. Open Government Partnership and GobLab (Universidad Adolfo Ibáñez). https://www.opengovpartnership.org/documents/state-of-the-evidence-algorithmic-transparency/

Zuiderwijk, A., Chen, Y.-C., & Salem, F. (2021). Implications of the use of artificial intelligence in public governance: A systematic literature review and a research agenda. *Government Information Quarterly*, *38*(3), 101577. https://doi.org/10.1016/j.giq.2021.101577

14. Decoding the privacy puzzle: a study on AI deployment in public governance

Jose Ramon Saura, Belem Barbosa and Sudhir Rana

INTRODUCTION

The development of artificial intelligence (AI) in the last decade has spurred debate about its use by public institutions (Agarwal, 2018) and large corporations (Hickok and Maslej, 2023). In an increasingly connected ecosystem where the use of technology has become a habit for citizens (Cai et al., 2021), the development and execution of AI actions by governments to optimize their services to citizens pose great challenges for public administration in terms of effectiveness, privacy, and optimization (Charles et al., 2022).

The debate about privacy concerns regarding the use of AI in public governance (Kuziemski and Misuraca, 2020) has led authors like Winter and Davidson (2019) to warn of the risks to citizens' personal data privacy. Privacy in AI deployment by public institutions is understood as a multifaceted and dynamic concept. It refers to the ability of governments to control, access, and determine the disclosure and use of citizens' personal information. In the era of AI, this kind of privacy is challenged by the use of data science processes such as data collection, advanced processing, and data analysis (Zuboff, 2015) that could predict citizens' habits and behaviors. Data science has evolved to encompass the use of statistical, computational, and analytical techniques to extract insights and knowledge from structured and unstructured data (Saura et al., 2022). This field plays a pivotal role in the evolution of AI as we know it today, as it provides the foundational methods and data-driven insights necessary for the development of intelligent systems that are used in smart governance. In the context of government use, data science has become instrumental, enabling public entities to leverage AI for efficient service delivery, policymaking, and public administration (Matheus et al., 2020).

The convergence of data science and AI thus represents a significant evolution in how governments interact with and serve their constituents, paving the way for more informed, efficient, and responsive governance (Ejarque et al., 2022). Therefore, it is particularly concerning in the context of public institutions, where large-scale data collection and analysis can be used for a variety of government services, from social security to urban management (Saura, 2024). Likewise, the governance of public institutions in the use of AI refers to the frameworks, policies, and practices these institutions implement to ensure that the adoption and application of AI are deployed ethically, responsibly, and aligned with citizens' rights (de Almeida et al., 2021). This includes the creation of privacy policies, the implementation of ethical principles in AI development, and the oversight and regulation of AI technologies to prevent abuses and ensure transparency and accountability (Saura et al., 2022). In this sense, effective governance of AI in the public sector must balance innovation and efficiency with the protection of privacy and the fundamental rights of individuals (EU Ethics Guidelines for Trustworthy AI, 2019).

In this digital sphere, the intersection of privacy and AI governance in public institutions poses unique challenges. On the one hand, public institutions are mandated to use data science and AI to improve the efficiency and effectiveness of government services (Pencheva et al., 2020). On the other hand, they must do so while respecting the privacy and civil rights of citizens, requiring a careful balance and ongoing consideration of how emerging technologies might impact these rights (Zuboff, 2019a). The changing dynamics between technological innovation and legal regulation, as well as social expectations around privacy, make this an evolving field for contemporary research in AI governance. Some examples are the management and optimization of citizens' data using data science techniques, characterized, for example, by the growth of so-called smart cities (Allam and Dhunny, 2019), the connected devices (Choi, 2014), the increased investment in cybersecurity for information storage (Maschmeyer et al., 2021), predictive analysis programs (Cantero Gamito and Ebers, 2021), or automate dashboards (Gorwa et al., 2020) that aid in decision-making by policymakers (Kuziemski and Misuraca, 2020).

According to authors such as van Noordt and Misuraca (2022), there is no doubt that AI, through all its formats, can enable public institutions and governments to optimize their activities and exponentially improve the services they provide. However, the speed at which AI develops its full potential is contrary to the speed at which laws can develop regulations and set boundaries to AI application. Nevertheless, governments are focusing on using AI in the automation of small tasks (Pencheva et al., 2020) but AI can also be used as a strategic tool to identify different scenarios in the event of a war (Russell, 2023), an extreme climate crisis (Gupta et al., 2022; Saura et al., 2023), intelligent security and protection (Green, 2022), healthcare (Zhu et al., 2022), or transportation (Iyer, 2021).

Also, authors like Willems et al. (2022) justify the need for additional research based on privacy perception in many areas of society when governments use AI in their services. The concept of collective surveillance (Karpa et al., 2022) and surveillance capitalism (Zuboff, 2015) have been linked to citizens' privacy perception when governments use AI (Zuboff, 2019a). Given this new paradigm, this study aims to identify privacy concerns when governments use AI for the development and execution of services and establishment of automated strategies. Thus, this research question is proposed (RQ1): What are the main privacy concerns when governments use AI according to the literature published to date? In addition the following objectives linked to the research question are presented for contemplation:

- To create knowledge about the main privacy concerns when AI is used by governments
- To evaluate the role of governments in the development of AI and its execution on society.

To address the problems analyzed, this study develops a bibliometric analysis using VOSViewer software on the Web of Sciences (WoS) database developing the well-known approaches of co-citation analysis of references and authors (Gmür, 2003), as well as bibliographic coupling (Oyewola and Dada, 2022) and occurrence of keywords (Tripathi et al., 2018).

The research is structured as follows. The introduction and research objectives are first outlined. The theoretical framework is then presented in which the main challenges and issues analyzed are discussed. The methodology and the development of the sample are given followed by analysis and discussion of results. Finally, conclusions are presented along with the limitations of the study.

THEORETICAL FRAMEWORK

AI Governance: Ethical Challenges and Dilemmas

The integration of AI in governance has introduced ethical challenges and dilemmas, necessitating an understanding and proactive approach. Key among these challenges is the issue of transparency and the cultivation of trust in government-provided AI services. As Ingrams et al. (2022) articulate, the imperative for governments is to assure stakeholders of the transparency in AI-driven decisions. This is complicated by the fact, as Lepri et al. (2018) note, that various AI systems operate with a degree of autonomy, often without a transparent explanation of their decision-making processes. Such opacity in government decision-making engenders skepticism regarding transparency. In this context, Nagtegaal (2021) emphasizes the need for transparent AI processes and decisions, suggesting that even automated decisions should be explicable by governments.

The ethical implications of AI in governance extend beyond transparency. Mittelstadt et al. (2016) indicated that public administrations should not prioritize automated decisions in smart governance due to potential ethical lapses, such as AI-driven injustice or inequality, especially in the absence of human oversight. Engstrom and Haim (2023) highlight the intersection between governance and the application of existing regulations in public administration regarding AI. They advocate for the establishment of robust legal frameworks to guide the safe and ethical use of AI tools, echoing the sentiments of Susanto et al. (2021). Furthermore, the ethical management of AI in governance necessitates addressing the privacy and rights of citizens, particularly concerning the use of their data. Hickok (2021) introduces the concept of digital ethics, linking it to data automation and algorithmic decision-making. This underscores the need for changes in the structure and training of public servants, as pointed out by Nagtegaal (2021). The public sector must invest in training and recruitment to ensure the effectiveness and security of predictive algorithms and other AI applications, as suggested by Manana et al. (2022).

Also, Djeffal et al. (2022) raise a critical issue regarding the accountability of automated decisions in AI governance. When AI systems make decisions, it becomes unclear who bears responsibility for their outcomes (Susanto et al., 2021). This necessitates legal scrutiny and regulation to assign accountability for decisions made by AI, especially given the potential for biased or outdated data, as noted by Saveliev and Zhurenkov (2021).

Addressing these challenges also involves ensuring a secure data infrastructure, a concern accentuated by the realities of cybercrime and cybersecurity in the digital age (Gardner et al., 2022). Governments, capable of accessing vast data sources, must secure, store, and process this data while maintaining control over AI algorithms, as argued by Ribeiro-Navarrete et al. (2022). The public's trust in AI systems, according to Kerr and Scharp (2022), hinges on the government's ability to demonstrate an understanding of the potential risks of AI in public administration.

The ethical use of AI in governance encompasses privacy concerns related to internet-connected devices. Sætra and Danaher (2022) suggest that these devices should adhere to default privacy standards to secure user data, an aspect further explored by Saura et al. (2021). The rise of smart cities, using connected Internet of Things (IoT) devices, directly ties to AI governance and presents additional privacy challenges (Deng et al., 2021). These devices, capable of collecting extensive personal and sensitive data, highlight the urgent need for ethical governance in the age of AI. Finally, the governance of AI presents a complex array of ethical challenges and dilemmas. Addressing these requires a multifaceted approach that encompasses transparent decision-making, robust legal frameworks, privacy safeguards, and a commitment to ethical standards, ensuring that AI serves the public interest while respecting individual rights and societal values (Yang et al., 2019).

AI and Society: Main Privacy Concerns

As highlighted above, the adoption of AI in governments has emerged as a challenge for ethical and legal decision-making. Authors such as Manheim and Kaplan (2019) suggest that data privacy and security have become one of the most complex challenges. Governments, in their activities and services to the citizenry, obtain and collect massive amounts of data, including personal information on citizens and sensitive information about their activities (Yang et al., 2019).

For the development of AI and its use in governmental service activities, governments must be able to ensure robust privacy standards. However, as Chen and Wen (2021) point out, if AI and its uses are still being developed, precisely due to its artificial and automated reasoning capacity, there will be numerous challenges that could jeopardize citizens' privacy (Mazurek and Małagocka, 2019).

Thus, authors like Green and Chen (2021) have studied the privacy risks that AI algorithms pose to society, particularly regarding biases and fairness. These algorithms may reflect existing societal biases that are unjust (Green, 2022). That is, if databases contain biased or historical data, machines that use machine learning (a type of AI that learns on its own) will use them to make future predictions, which does not ensure equitable legal actions from a government (Zarsky, 2016). In this regard, governments can use any type of data to understand citizens' locations, identify behavior patterns or consumption preferences, or even predict an individual's health (Wirtz et al., 2020). Although there is no doubt that these technological advances offer significant benefits to society, privacy remains a complex challenge.

Even though these kinds of actions are utilized today to improve and optimize traffic (Sukhadia et al., 2020), energy efficiency (Pahwa et al., 2022), surveillance tasks (Fontes et al., 2022), security (Gordon et al., 2022), or service personalization (Henman, 2020), connected devices sometimes do not respect the privacy terms that citizens agreed to, or whether they are truly aware that internal data collection processing exist. Therefore, the increasing reliance on AI for public decision-making raises concerns about the opacity of these systems. As noted by Lee and Lee (2021), the lack of transparency of AI algorithms can obscure whether individual privacy is being adequately protected. For instance, an AI system used for welfare distribution might inadvertently expose sensitive personal information, such as financial or health data, without the individuals' knowledge or consent. The challenge lies in balancing the efficiency and effectiveness of AI systems in public administration with the imperative of safeguarding citizens' privacy.

In addition, the use of AI in government surveillance has amplified privacy concerns. As observed by Lee and Lee (2021), governments are increasingly deploying AI-driven surveillance tools for law enforcement and security purposes. While these tools can enhance public safety, they also risk creating a pervasive surveillance state where citizens' movements and actions are constantly monitored. This scenario poses a significant threat to individual freedoms and privacy rights. The aggregation and analysis of vast amounts of personal data by AI systems without proper oversight or accountability mechanisms could lead to abuses of power and violations of privacy.

Finally, the cross-border nature of data flows poses another challenge for privacy protection in the context of government deployment of AI. As highlighted by Patel and Singh (2021), data collected by AI systems often traverses national boundaries, complicating the enforcement of local privacy laws and regulations. This situation is exacerbated by the differing privacy standards and laws across countries. Therefore, international collaboration and harmonization of privacy standards are essential to ensure that citizens' privacy is protected, regardless of where the data is processed or stored.

METHODOLOGY

As previously stated, this study conducts a bibliometric analysis aiming to understand the main connections between privacy concerns and AI activities executed by governments. The WoS database and the prestigious Journal of Citation Report (JCR) index were used for this purpose, following studies like Liao et al. (2019) and Lafont et al. (2023).

In this sense, it must be indicated, following authors such as Donthu et al. (2021a), that bibliometric analyses are studies focused on quantitatively understanding bibliographic sources and their relationships in academic databases. Authors like Wang et al. (2020) indicate that these types of studies can facilitate the understanding of emerging themes on the studies published to date in relation to one or several concepts. Also, due to the characterization of the study presented, it allows identifying through graphic maps what the structure and dynamic characteristics are in terms of relationships of a research field (Rey-Martí et al., 2016). Thus, with the execution of a bibliometric analysis, it is possible to identify citation networks among authors, keywords or journals, and understand the relationship existing among them (Donthu et al., 2021b). In this way, the identification of clusters explaining a concept can promote the ideation of new concepts and in-depth study of the theme being analyzed.

In this research, three approaches centered on bibliometric analysis using the VOSViewer software were chosen. Firstly, following authors such as Nandiyanto and Husaeni (2021), a co-citation analysis of the references of the publications indexed in the WoS database was computed. This type of analysis allows identifying the relationships linked to an intellectual structure of references and their citations. This approach is most frequently used in bibliometric studies. Secondly, a bibliographic coupling (Shah et al., 2020) of sources is also computed. This type of analysis is used to create and understand the structure of documents that are cited between them, after being published in different academic journals relevant in the research field. In this way, connections between various journals can be understood, and relationships and patterns in connection with the study theme established.

Thirdly, a keyword occurrence analysis is conducted, identifying the most frequent keywords in a database. The execution of this approach allows visually understanding how these keywords are linked with each other when authors publish their contributions. This may allow for establishing relationships and ties between different concepts that would initially have no relation. In addition, this type of analysis also identifies clusters that allow grouping different concepts with the same theme (Oladinrin et al., 2023).

244 *Handbook on governance and data science*

Data Sampling

As previously indicated, the sample is collected from the WoS database. This database gathers the prestigious ranking of JCR academic journals. Authors like Principale et al. (2023) highlight the importance of using databases with quality features for the development of bibliometric analyses. In this way, the study of Abdolhamid et al. (2023) was consulted for the extraction of data and justification of the emerging theme related to the perceptions of privacy when governments use AI. For data extraction, Boolean operators including AND and OR are used. Additionally, the Topic filter in WoS is used, which allows the database to extract academic contributions that develop the concepts that are included in the search. In this way, all contributions that fit within the following search were considered:

"government (Topic) AND privacy (Topic) AND artificial intelligence (Topic) OR public administration (Topic) AND privacy (Topic) AND artificial intelligence (Topic) OR public policy (Topic) AND privacy (Topic) AND artificial intelligence (Topic) OR public organization (Topic) AND privacy (Topic) AND artificial intelligence (Topic) OR governance (Topic) AND privacy (Topic) AND artificial intelligence (Topic)."

On the date of data collection, the database of scientific contributions yielded a total of 335 academic entries from the WoS Core Collection. Using this sample size, the analysis was computed using the VOSViewer software.

Sample Description

Regarding the descriptive results of the sample obtained from WoS, Figure 14.1 displays the top 20 WoS categories featuring academic contributions linked to government AI implementation and privacy concerns. Leading the list, with 66 results and comprising 18% of the total, is the category Computer Science Information Systems, followed by Computer Science

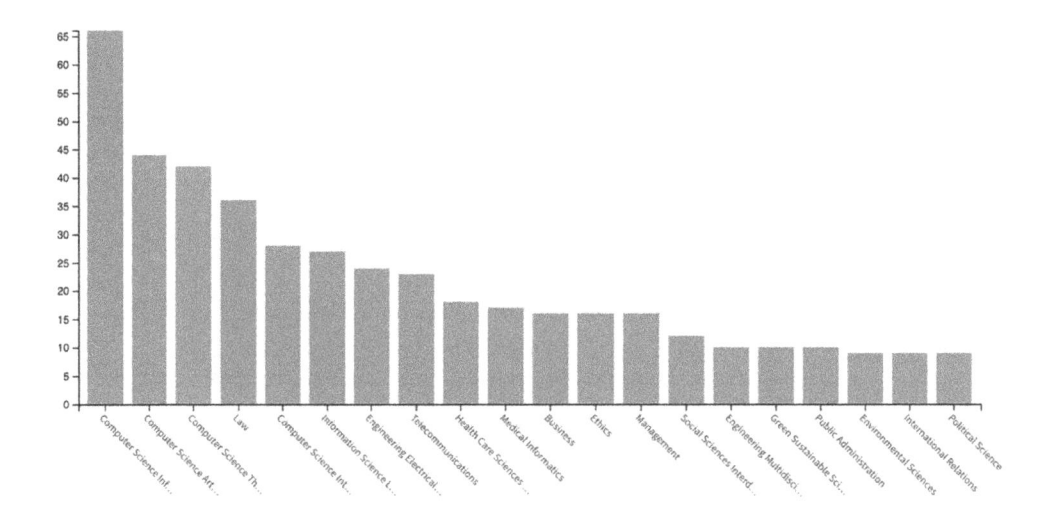

Source: WoS, retrieved on May 19, 2023.

Figure 14.1 Number of published articles in WoS related to Governance, AI and Privacy

Artificial Intelligence with 44 results (12%) and Computer Science Theory Methods with 42 results (11%). This indicates that AI is under ongoing development and there are many issues that need to be regulated.

This notion is confirmed by the fourth identified category, Law, with 36 contributions (10%). In fifth place, the category Computer Science Interdisciplinary Applications can be found with 28 contributions (7%), followed by Information Science Library Science with 27 contributions (7%), Engineering Electrical Electronic with 24 contributions (6%), Telecommunications with 23 contributions (6%), Health Care Sciences Services with 18 contributions (5%) and in tenth place, Medical Informatics with 18 contributions (5%).

The multidisciplinary nature of the subject under study is evident, and specific industries linked to categories that may be of potential use for AI by governments and large corporations are noticeable. Moreover, these categories reflect major privacy concerns, such as those in the health or e-health industry. Next, the categories of Business (16, 4%), Ethics (16, 4%), and Management (16, 4%) highlight the importance of ethics in applying AI for management and business. Sustainability appears in places 16 and 18 through the categories of Green Sustainable Sciences Technology (10, 2%) and Environmental Sciences (9, 2%), providing a view of how government-applied AI can drive sustainable actions. Finally, it is worth noting the role of the categories Public Administration (10, 2%) and Political Science (9, 2%), which underscore efforts to regulate AI by government and the development of policies aimed at preserving privacy.

Likewise, Figure 14.2 illustrates the evolution of the theme analyzed in the WoS database. In total, 6,337 citations are obtained from 2005 to 2023. The first contribution analyzing the subject of study appears in 2005. In 2017, the first breakpoint marking the theme's evolution to the present day appears. From 2005, there are annually 1 or 2 contributions about AI, governments, and privacy, and from 2017, 4 studies are published and in 2022, 106 publications are identified. The graphical representation shows not only the evolution and implementation of new government AI actions but also the growing concern about citizens' data privacy, its

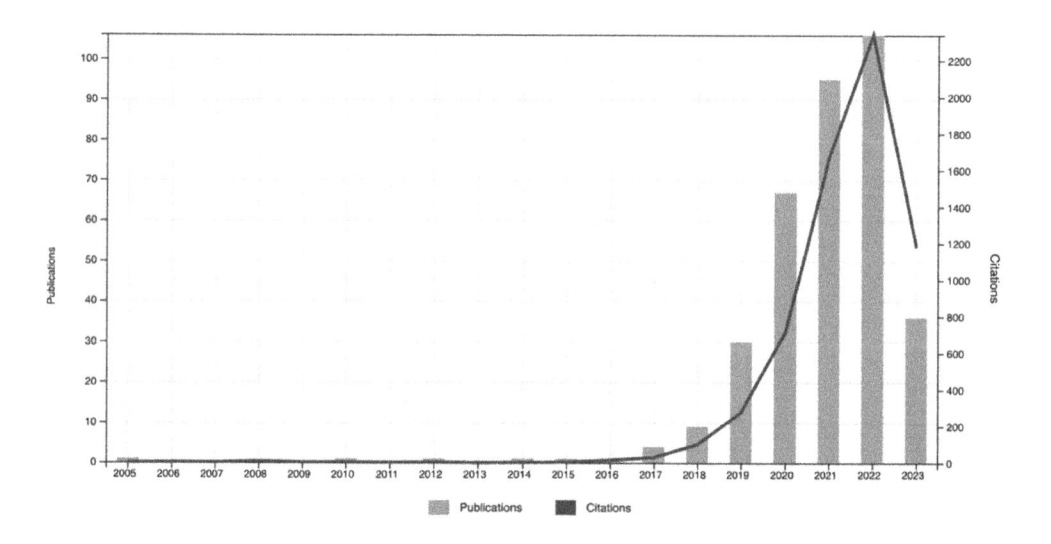

Source: WoS, retrieved on May 19, 2023.

Figure 14.2   *Number of citations and articles per year in WoS (2005–23)*

management, and control. This justifies the relevance of the proposed study topic and its relevancy in academic terms, as it has significantly sparked researchers' interest in recent years.

ANALYSIS OF RESULTS

The reports of co-citation analysis, bibliographic coupling, and keyword co-occurrence are computed using VOSViewer on the database collected from WoS. Table 14.1 provides a summary of the main contributions in terms of categories with more contributions and key scientific contributions in terms of the number of citations directly linked to the objectives of this research.

Table 14.1   *WoS categories and percentage of records and most article citations*

WoS categories	Number of records	% of total
Computer Science Information Systems	66	18.697%
Computer Science Artificial Intelligence	44	12.465%
Computer Science Theory Methods	42	11.898%
Law	36	10.198%

Article	Author	Citations
The global landscape of AI ethics guidelines	Jobin and Vayena (2019)	691
Artificial Intelligence (AI): Multidisciplinary perspectives on emerging challenges, opportunities, and agenda for research, practice and policy	Dwivedi et al. (2021)	558
Privacy in the age of medical big data	Price and Cohen (2019)	328
From what to how: An initial review of publicly available AI ethics tools, methods and research to translate principles into practices	Morley et al. (2020)	145
A governance model for the application of AI in health care	Reddy et al. (2020)	122
Robotics and the lessons of cyberlaw	Calo (2015)	114
The ethics of AI in health care: A mapping review	Morley et al. (2020)	96
The Chinese approach to artificial intelligence: An analysis of policy, ethics, and regulation	Roberts et al. (2021)	87
Privacy aware learning	Duchi et al. (2014)	77
The ethics of algorithms: Key problems and solutions	Tsamados et al. (2021)	71

Source: Adapted from the WoS collected data.

Co-citation Analysis of References and Authors

For the co-citation analysis, Table 14.2 presents the top ten academic contributions identified by the highest number of citations in the analyzed database and their average weight. In terms of the studies presented in Table 14.2, the first one, by Angwin et al. (2016) (29 link strength), develops the foundations and concepts to understand the challenges of what is known as bias in AI algorithms. This concept explains that intelligent models sometimes have not taken into account all the available information in a dataset, and therefore, it is too poor to make accurate, fair, and consistent predictions.

Next, the study by Arrieta et al. (2020) (40 link strength) introduces the concept of Explainable Artificial Intelligence (XAI) with the aim of presenting the opportunities and challenges that society has towards responsible AI. Likewise, Barocas and Selbst (2016) in third place (51 link strength) present in their study a measurable quantification of the impact that the development of big data could have in multiple areas. Subsequently, Burrell (2016) in fourth place (46 link strength) presents a research paper where they develop and explain how AI algorithms work. The author focuses on the opacity of decisions and the potential consequences for privacy and security risks.

Afterwards, Citron and Pasquale (2014) with a link strength of 37 analyze automated decisions for the progress of a society based on data-driven decisions and analytical indicators. In sixth place, Dwivedi et al. (2021) highlight in their study the power of AI from a multitude of perspectives and research categories. They analyze the main challenges, opportunities, and future agendas among which regulatory policies and the practice in applying AI strategies stand out.

Also, Eubanks (2018) with a link strength of 27 highlights the concept of automating inequality. The study focuses on the repercussions of tools that work with AI when used by the police and the consequences this can have on poor groups and collectives. In eighth place, Abrassart et al. (2018) with 15 link strength analyze the Montreal declaration for responsible use and development of AI. Zuboff (2019a) in her study on the era of surveillance capitalism tries to explain how in using AI, large corporations and governments can boost economic stimuli that favor them at the expense of citizens' data and violating their privacy. Lastly, with a link strength of 52 Hagendorff (2020) develops in his study the concept of AI ethics proposing good practices and guidelines for evaluating its use, development, and application.

To graphically represent the results indicated in Table 14.2, the analysis is computed in VOSViewer. For the visual representation, the minimum number of citations has been set at 10. Out of a total of 22,322 cited references, 23 meet the threshold. These results identified a total of 4 clusters, 1,666 links, and a total link strength of 382. In the representation of Figure 14.3, 4 clusters are observed, ordered by relevance according to link strength. First, the purple cluster, composed of 7 items: Angwin, 2016, Barocas, 2016, Burrell, 2016, Citron, 2014, Kroll, 2017, Scherer, 2016, and Wachter, 2017. The second largest and heaviest cluster is the blue one, made up of 6 items: Arrieta, 2020, Jobin, 2019, Yang, 2019, Mcmahan, 2017, and Buolamwini, 2018. The third cluster (in pink) is the one formed by 5 items: Dwivedi, 2021, Floridi, 2018, Giles, 2019, Mittelstadt, 2016, and Taddeo, 2018. Finally, cluster number 4 is formed by 5 items in black and composed of: Eubank, 2018, Obermeyer, 2019, Oneil Cathy, 2016, Price, 2019, and Topol, 2019.

Table 14.2a   Reference co-citation results

Title	Author(s)	Citations	Link strength
Machine bias	Angwin et al. (2016)	10	29
Explainable Artificial Intelligence (XAI): Concepts, taxonomies, opportunities and challenges toward responsible AI	Arrieta et al. (2020)	13	40
Big data's disparate impact	Barocas and Selbst (2016)	16	51
How the machine "thinks": Understanding opacity in machine learning algorithms	Burrell (2016)	14	46
The scored society: Due process for automated predictions	Citron and Pasquale (2014)	10	37
Artificial Intelligence (AI): Multidisciplinary perspectives on emerging challenges, opportunities, and agenda for research, practice and policy	Dwivedi et al. (2021)	10	7
Automating inequality: How high-tech tools profile, police, and punish the poor	Eubanks (2018)	10	27
Montréal Declaration for a responsible development of artificial intelligence	Abrassart et al. (2018)	15	43
The age of surveillance capitalism: The fight for a human future at the new frontier of power	Zuboff (2019a)	10	15
The ethics of AI ethics: An evaluation of guidelines	Hagendorff (2020)	17	52

Source: Author's own.

Table 14.2b   Author co-citation results

Author(s)	Citations	Link strength
Floridi, L.	95	584
European Commission	126	549
European Union	21	273
Morley, J.	38	251
Wachter, S.	36	248
OECD	31	223
Jobin, A.	33	201
Crawford, K.	30	192
Mittelstadt, B.	25	188
Barocas, S.	24	175

Source: Author's own.

Decoding the privacy puzzle 249

Source: Author's own.

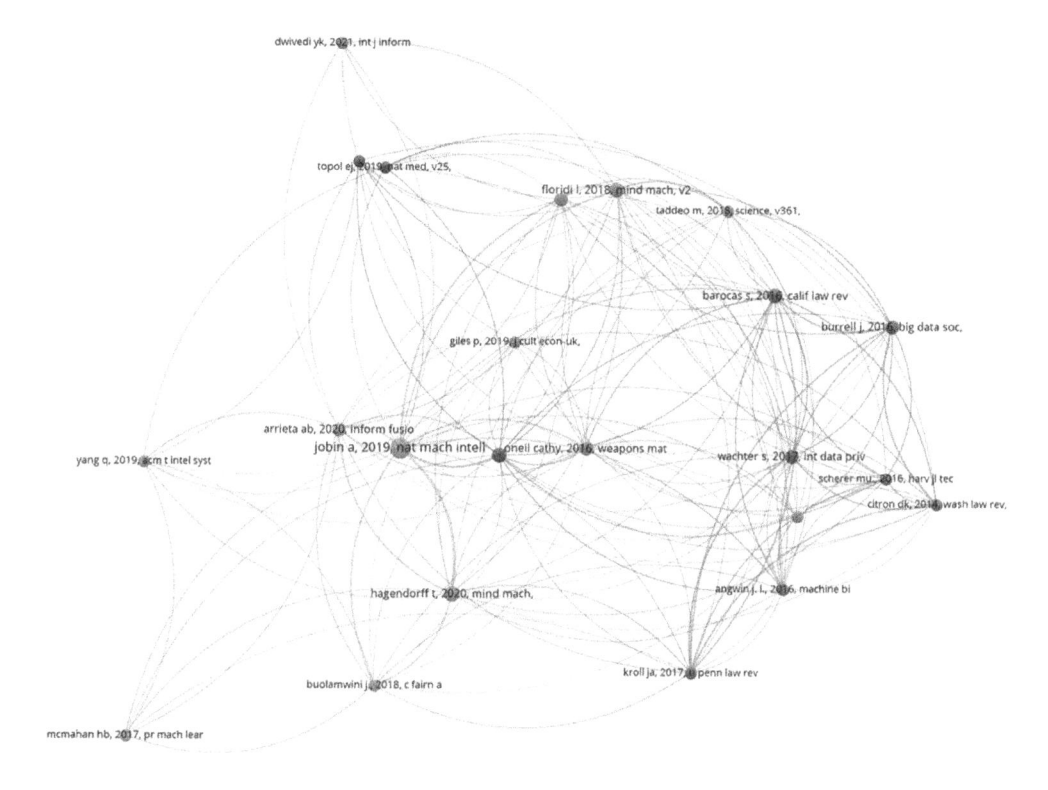

Figure 14.3   Reference co-citation analysis

Once the references and the citations between the clusters have been identified based on study topics linked to AI, privacy, and governments, the co-citation analysis of authors has been computed to understand the most relevant authors linked to the theme of the present study. Out of a total of 16,628 authors, 24 met the threshold with a minimum of 20 citations per author. The density map of the author co-citation analysis is represented in Figure 14.4.

Of the total clusters that are represented in Figure 14.4, there are 3 that stand out for their weight and size in the number of citations and link strength. The first is the one formed by Floridi, Cath, Morley, Shin, Hagendorff, and Jobin. The second one is formed by Chatterjee, Mittelstadt, Crawford, Wachter, and Pasquale. Lastly, the third cluster with greater representation of the European Commission as the main author is the one composed of the institution itself and the European Union as the main reference. In terms of citations and link strength, the most cited authors and with the greatest weight in the analyzed database in relation to privacy and the execution of AI activities and governments are Floridi with 95 citations and link strength of 584, European Commission with 126 citations and link strength of 549, European Union with 21 citations and link strength of 273, Morley with 38 citations and link strength of 251, and in fifth place Wachter with 36 citations and link strength of 248. In sixth place appears another institution, the Organisation for Economic Co-operation and Development (OECD), with a total of 31 citations and link strength of 223.

The graph represents a total of 24 items, 220 links, and a total link strength of 2,155. In this way, three major clusters are observed in which there are three authors that highlight

Source: Author's own.

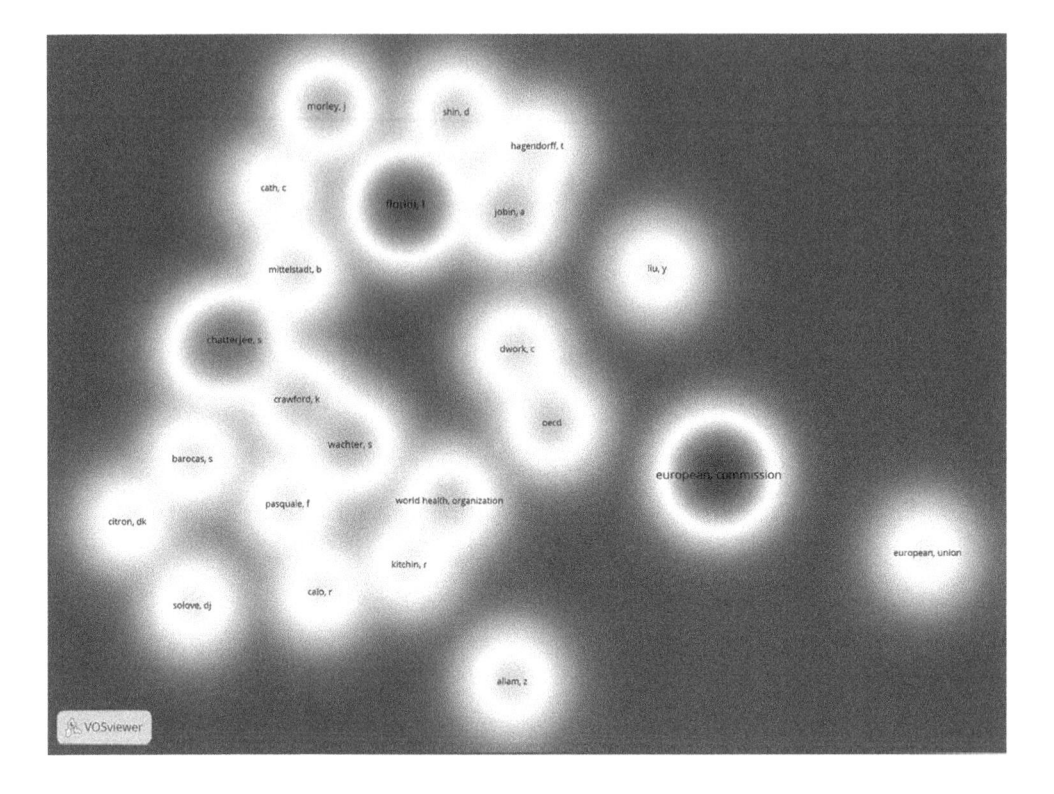

Figure 14.4   Density map of the author co-citation analysis

their relevance in terms of citations and link strength above the rest of the contributions and they are Floridi, Chatterjee, and the European Commission. Undoubtedly, these authors are recognized as significant references regarding the development and deployment of AI and government actions, as well as privacy related to these actions.

Bibliographic Coupling of Sources

Moreover, an analysis known as bibliographic coupling of sources was conducted. This analysis highlights the interest that academic journals (sources) receive when publishing and getting cited on studies published under the theme analyzed in this research. VOSviewer software was used to perform this analysis, with a requirement of three articles published in the journal per reference. Of the total 266 journals identified, 10 met the threshold. These results are represented in Table 14.3 in terms of documents per journal, the total number of citations in the database, and link strength.

The journal leading in the number of citations, documents, and link strength is *AI & Society*, with a total of 9 documents, 167 citations, and link strength of 128. The theme of this journal directly correlates with the objectives of this research, explaining its impact. In second place is *Sustainability*, with 7 documents, 49 citations, and a total link strength of 67. The sustainability of AI and its government-led development is also indirectly linked to actions that could condition privacy.

Table 14.3   Bibliographic coupling of sources

Source	Documents	Citations	Link strength
AI & Society	9	167	128
Sustainability	7	49	67
Government Information Quarterly	5	138	65
Computer Law & Security Review	4	30	50
Frontiers in Artificial Intelligence	3	19	37
Technology in Society	3	40	33
IEEE Access	8	62	27
Journal of Medical Internet Research	4	45	19
Data & Policy	3	3	14
Healthcare	4	22	14

Source: Author based on the VOSviewer results.

Thirdly, *Government Information Quarterly*, with 5 papers, 138 citations, and link strength of 65. *Government Information Quarterly* is a reputed journal focused on the analysis of public administration execution of numerous norms, innovations, and challenges in various industries where governments perform their activities. Fourthly, *Computer Law & Security Review*, with 4 papers, 30 citations, and link strength of 50. This source highlights the necessity for legislation and security related to AI risks and its development in governments. Fifthly, *Frontiers in Artificial Intelligence*, with 3 papers, 19 citations, and link strength of 37. This journal focuses on the development of AI and the multitude of potential applications. In sixth place, *Technology in Society*, with 3 papers, 40 citations, and link strength of 33. This journal focuses on the analysis of technology application in society, highlighting the importance of a correct application in any societal domain. In seventh place, *IEEE Access*, with 8 papers, 62 citations, and link strength of 27. In its publications, it promotes new AI models centered on the category of computer sciences.

In eighth place, the *Journal of Medical Internet Research* is found with 4 documents, 45 citations, and link strength of 19. This journal focuses on the application of medicine on the internet, a scientific field in which data, AI, government regulation, and privacy have sparked research interest in recent years. In ninth place, *Data & Policy* with 3 documents, 3 citations, and link strength of 14 positions itself as a journal directly related to the theme studied as it attempts to link data to the development of public policies. Finally is the *Healthcare* journal, related to the medical field, with 4 documents, 22 citations, and link strength of 14. These journals are identified in Table 14.3.

Regarding their interconnections, Figure 14.5 identifies 3 clusters with 10 items (the journals are highlighted in Table 14.3), 40 links between them, and a total link strength of 227. The first cluster consists of AI & Society and *Healthcare* journal (in yellow), the second cluster comprises the journals: *Computer Law & Security Review, Technology in Society, Sustainability,* and *Government Information Quarterly*. The third cluster consists of the *Journal of Medical Internet Research, Frontiers in Artificial Intelligence,* and *IEEE Access.*

Source: Author's own.

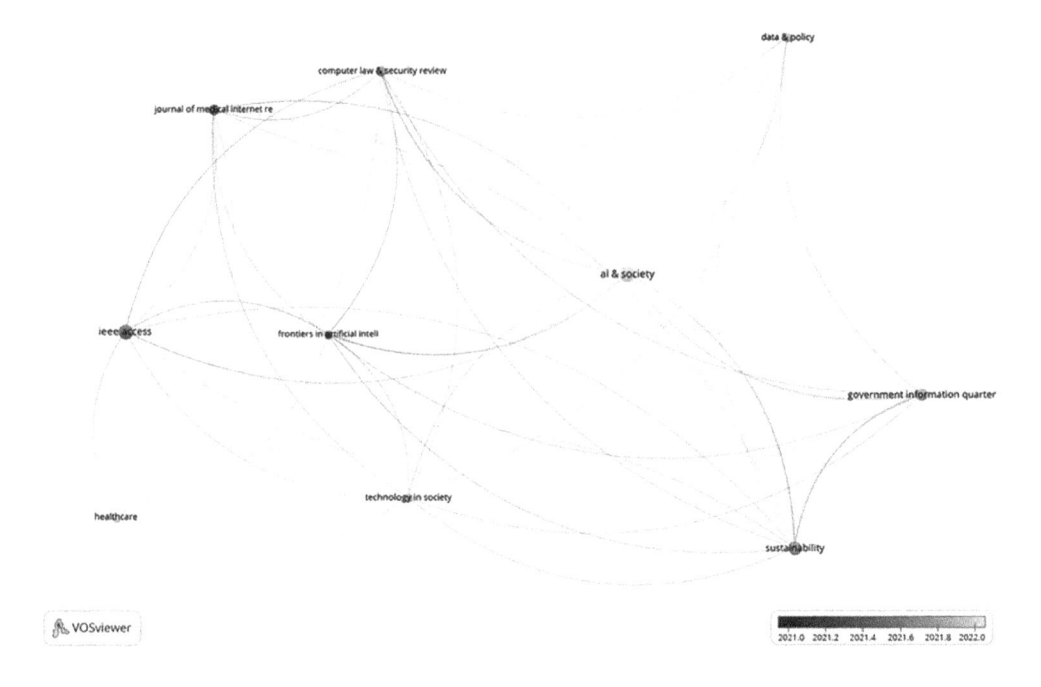

Figure 14.5   Bibliographic coupling of sources by average year of publication

Table 14.4   Author keyword co-occurrence

Keywords	Occurrences	Total link strength
artificial intelligence	149	441
privacy	116	427
Big data	50	235
challenges	34	187
ethics	47	170
internet	29	156
security	31	144
machine learning	38	139
governance	34	132
framework	21	102
trust	17	88

Source: Author's own.

Source: Author's own.

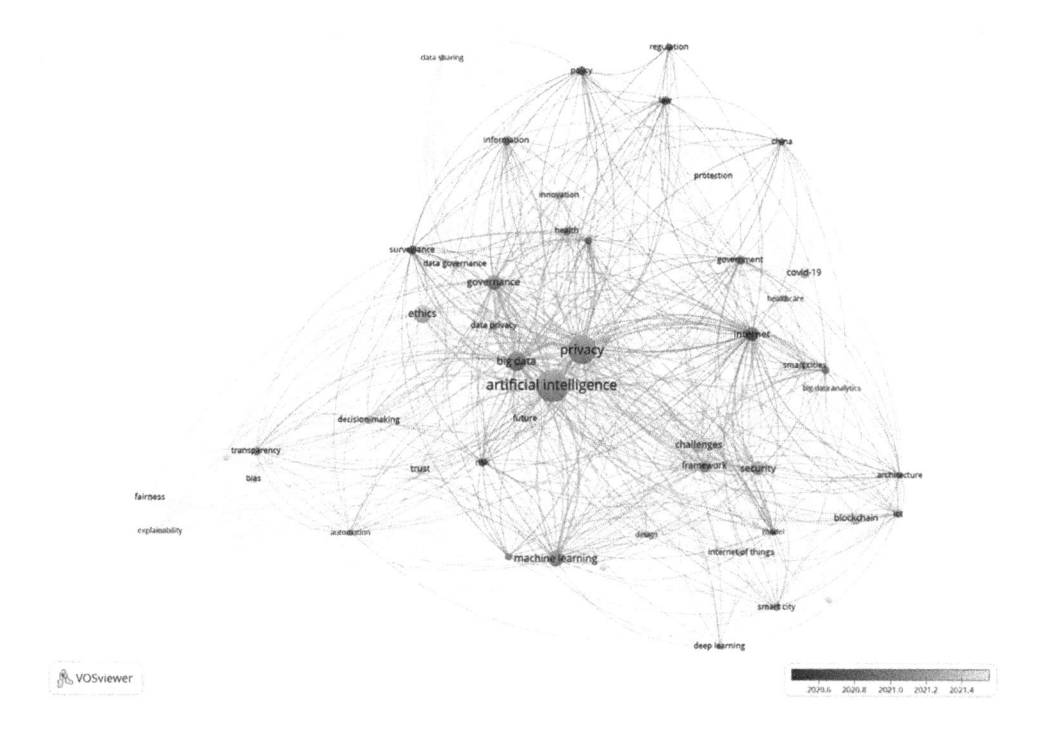

Figure 14.6   Author keyword co-occurrence by average year of publication

Author Keyword Co-occurrence

For the development of the keyword co-occurrence analysis, a minimum of 7 occurrences of keywords was established. Of the 1,492 keywords identified in the database, 57 were selected to appear in the mapping, and the most relevant keywords related to the research theme by relevance position are represented in Table 14.4. Thus, the most relevant ones according to the research objectives were highlighted. Of the total, 51 items identified in 9 clusters in Figure 14.6, 652 links were identified among the keywords with a total link strength of 1,796.

In Figure 14.6, four clusters are identified from which the main concepts and relationships are highlighted. The first cluster by link strength is composed of the three words that surround the research objectives: artificial intelligence, privacy, and governance (in the center of the figure). Linked to these concepts are the keywords of framework, security, IoT, machine learning, data privacy, big data, deep learning, and smart cities. All these concepts are directly interlinked, highlighting the automation of information, the need for a framework and security over personal data, and citizens' privacy.

Likewise, the second cluster by weight is composed of bias, trust, fairness, explainability, challenges, big data analytics, protection, and data sharing. These concepts elaborate on some of the main issues with the application of AI to date, such as making correct decisions based on data and the algorithms' explainability when making complex decisions where bias exists. Two smaller clusters are also identified, the first one composed of data governance, ethics, innovation, decision-making, Internet of Things, and blockchain. This cluster defines ethics in the application of these technologies when innovation drives new ways of making decisions and governing from public administration.

Finally, the cluster formed by surveillance, China, policy, regulation, law, internet, model, and government. This cluster highlights some case studies on China and its social model that uses AI as a surveillance system, the concept of surveillance capitalism, the need for laws and regulations on AI models, and the use of the internet.

DISCUSSION

The results of this research focus on understanding the main privacy concerns to date when governments use AI. Thus, it has been possible to verify through the analysis of scientific literature and the growing interest of researchers in this field of research that there are various issues that urgently need to be discussed (Dwivedi et al., 2021; Saura et al., 2022).

Firstly, citizens should have control over their data as a right when AI is used by governments. Citizens must be aware and be capable of understanding how a predictive algorithm or any kind of AI will analyze and use their data to predict future actions and behaviors (Willems et al., 2022). In fact, the responsibility of governments is to ensure security and decrease the risk that the collection and processing of these data is entirely legal and understood by citizens. Authors like Hickok and Maslej (2023) highlight that both public administrations and citizens should invest time in understanding the functioning of AI as it is a global paradigm shift (Eubanks, 2018). To be correctly developed, both policymakers and the passive subjects (users or citizens) who provide their data to improve the use of services – such as when using free or freemium AI-based apps and tools – must be fully aware of how AI works (Gordon et al., 2022).

In the scientific literature, there is a debate about the bias (Angwin et al., 2016) of algorithms and how these algorithms are not able to explain the procedures transparently (XAI), by which they make automated decisions (Kuziemski and Misuraca, 2020). This is precisely one of the factors that affect trust (Chen et al., 2021) in the use of AI in governments, the values (Gordon et al., 2022) of digital ethics (Hagendorff, 2020), transparency (Lepri et al., 2018) and the risks (Manheim and Kaplan, 2019) that have already existed in several previous case studies (Saveliev and Zhurenkov, 2021). In these, algorithms make decisions that foster inequality (Zarsky, 2016) and, therefore, make unjust decisions (Eubanks, 2018). Data-driven decision-making by governments must ensure digital ethics so that the future is fair and can preserve XAI. Authors like Wirtz et al. (2020) have already pointed out that a global framework must be generated to ensure the fair and reliable use of AI models by governments.

We agree with authors like Zhu et al. (2022) who highlight that the COVID-19 pandemic was an example where tools that worked with AI were used to track citizens. These policies have in many cases been evaluated as illicit (Ribeiro-Navarrete et al., 2021), and have shown that smart cities, through IoT devices (Yang et al., 2019), can create an infrastructure that is not ethical from the citizens' privacy point of view (Zuboff, 2019a). This is a risk for the future of society in general, as governments increasingly use AI to optimize their processes and services to the public (Henman, 2020). We agree with Oladinrin et al. (2023) that innovation is one of the most important factors for advancement, both in public administration and in technological development. However, in managing privacy, all the possibilities that technologies such as big data or machine learning offer can pose risks to citizens' security, their data, and their behaviors (Mazurek and Małagocka, 2019).

There are examples such as the treatment of personal data related to health (Winter and Davidson, 2019) or finance (Pallathadka et al., 2023), which have become an entire industry due to the massive buying and selling of this data (Zuboff, 2019a). This is seen both from the perspective of large corporations and from public administration that aims to understand how a society is organized (Suran et al., 2022). Similarly, the design of AI models from their inception must incorporate protective and security frameworks that can be regulated and verified both at the time of data sharing and during data collection.

Authors such as Citron and Pasquale (2014) highlight that the future of AI in governments is centered on automated decision-making, which, although supervised by human beings, could offer biased opportunities and options affecting citizens' privacy (Manheim and Kaplan, 2019). Laws and protection from public administrations must be decisively promoted (Roberts et al., 2021).

On the one hand, one of the most evident problems is that AI grows and evolves at an exponential rate, while more and more connected devices exist, thus more data is generated (Charles et al., 2022). On the other hand, regulation is slow, it must be agreed upon, and its execution and implementation are also slow. The timeframes developed in public administration will be slower than the development of new AI models that can be applied to society (Djeffal et al., 2022). We agree with authors such as Schiff et al. (2022), when one of the problems is adoption, not execution.

That is, governments must be cautious with the adoption of AI models and understand their development. It should be a priority that if the information can be biased or promote unjust or unequal activities, there should be mechanisms to alert the humans (policymakers) who will make the decisions (Miao et al., 2021). Furthermore, actions related to the concept of surveillance capitalism should be avoided (Zuboff, 2019b). AI tools and data automation increasingly raise privacy risks. Its application is a simple strategy for governments, as is the collection of massive citizen data thanks to connected cities (Ismagilova et al., 2020) or through large governments' service providers such as mobile phones (Ingrams, 2015) and GPS (Morabito and Morabito, 2015), automobiles, or medicine (Price and Cohen, 2019) industries.

Finally, we accept the proposals of Noain-Sánchez (2016) and Saura et al. (2021), which urge all corporations that develop intelligent and connected devices to follow the "Privacy by default" manifesto. This mechanism ensures that all devices, once purchased, must be perfectly configured to maintain user privacy, thus preventing the incentive for the massive buying and selling of data. Governments, moreover, must legislate taking into account the urgent need for the approval of numerous laws that safeguard the privacy security of citizens' data, both when governments use AI for decision-making and for the management and transfer of this data with interested third parties.

Future Research Questions

Based on the comprehensive analysis undertaken in the present study, six pivotal areas have been discerned as particularly salient in the realm of government utilization of AI and their link to AI's broader implications. These identified areas are meticulously delineated in Table 14.5, which also presents 18 future research questions. These questions are thoughtfully crafted to probe deeper into each identified area, offering a roadmap for scholarly inquiry and practical exploration in the ever-evolving landscape of AI in public governance and its influence on privacy concerns.

(i) *Lack of transparency in data-driven decisions*: This concern highlights the opaque nature of AI processes in government, where the reasoning behind critical decisions often remains

Table 14.5   Future research questions

Research area	Future research questions
Lack of transparency in data-driven decisions	• How can governments enhance transparency in AI decision-making processes? • What frameworks can be established to ensure transparency in data sourcing and processing in AI systems? • How does the lack of transparency in AI systems affect public perception and acceptance in terms of privacy?
Possible bias in predictive algorithms	• What measures can effectively mitigate biases in AI predictive algorithms used by governments? • How can governments detect and correct unintentional biases embedded in AI systems that affect citizens' privacy? • In what ways can AI algorithms be audited for bias by independent entities?
Inability to obtain reasoned explanations about data-driven decisions	• How can explainable AI be effectively implemented in government AI systems? • What are the challenges in providing understandable AI decision-making explanations to non-expert users? • How does the inability to obtain reasoned explanations from AI systems impact their judicial and administrative use?
Lack of complete trust in current AI systems	• What factors most significantly contribute to the lack of trust in current AI systems within government settings? • How can governments build public trust in AI systems used and work on the possible privacy concerns generated in society? • What role does public awareness and education play in building trust in government AI systems?
Possible absence of ethics in AI execution	• What ethical frameworks can be developed for AI systems deployed by governments to protect citizen's privacy? • How can governments ensure that AI systems are aligned with ethical standards and societal values? • What are the implications of potential ethical breaches in AI systems for public governance?
Lack of complete trust in AI deployment in governments	• What are the main drivers of distrust in AI deployment by governments? • How can governments ensure that AI deployment is perceived as beneficial and secure by citizens? • What regulatory policies can be established to increase accountability and trust in government AI deployment?

Source: Author's own.

hidden, leading to skepticism and questioning of the integrity of these decisions; (ii) *Possible bias in predictive algorithms:* This issue underscores the potential for AI algorithms to perpetuate existing biases, whether intentional or inadvertent, thus affecting the fairness and impartiality of governmental decisions and actions; (iii) *Inability to obtain reasoned explanations about data-driven decisions*: This problem points to the difficulty in deciphering the logic used by AI systems, thereby hindering the understanding and accountability of AI-driven government decisions; (iv) *Lack of complete trust in current AI systems*: This reflects a general skepticism and apprehension towards the reliability and objectivity of AI systems deployed in government, fueled by concerns over their transparency and potential biases; (v) *Possible absence of ethics in AI execution*: This area of concern addresses the ethical considerations and potential risks involved in AI execution, especially when decisions made by AI have significant societal implications; and (vi) *Lack of complete trust in AI deployment in governments*: This points to the broader issue of public confidence in the way governments deploy AI, including concerns over privacy, security, and the ethical use of citizens' data.

CONCLUSION

This research has developed a bibliometric analysis of the main contributions to date related to the development of AI-centered strategies by governments and their connection to privacy. It has been observed how the interest in research in this area has grown since 2005. Specifically, since 2017, interest in this research topic has increased among researchers, with 2022 being the year that received the most contributions. The categories and themes related to privacy and AI in governments are directly related to the development of computer science, information sciences, computing theories and methods, law, ethics, and telecommunications. Likewise, it is important to highlight the role played by the medicine industry in all its forms, as it is one of the categories that has aroused the most interest among researchers when studying privacy and the execution of AI by governments.

The main information sources highlighted in this research are focused on understanding how to prevent AI algorithms from promoting inequality or obtaining results that are not fair based on past databases. The main research categories identified are articles that focus on understanding the different perspectives and emerging challenges for the practice and development of public administration policies on the use of AI. In addition, ethics and potential massive surveillance by governments are themes that the literature has published to date in this area. Also, the journals and authors that have contributed the most to the development of this theme are focused on the development of computer science, society, sustainability in the execution and development of AI, medicine in all its forms, and the development of technology within society.

Likewise, in terms of privacy concerns directly related to government execution of their AI strategies, the following actions responding to RQ1 have been identified. Firstly, (i) the lack of transparency in data-driven decisions, (ii) the potential bias of predictive algorithms, (iii) the inability to obtain reasoned explanations about erroneous data-driven decisions, (iv) lack of trust in current AI systems, (v) the possible absence of ethics in the execution of AI and (vi) lack of confidence in the execution of AI in governments. These factors define the main concerns about privacy when governments use AI. Also, as a result of the present study 18 future research questions relative to AI deployment in public governance are defined (see Table 14.5).

The role played by risks linked to automations through algorithms that can drive mass surveillance is emphasized in the literature. This surveillance can, on the one hand, stimulate collective intelligence or understanding of social behavior (de Geus et al., 2020), thus improving services to citizens, but, on the other hand, it can increase vulnerabilities against societal privacy and access to citizens' personal data. Furthermore, there is concern in the scientific literature about the lack of solid regulation and laws that can protect the execution of AI from a political standpoint. The case of China (Saveliev and Zhurenkov, 2021; Zhu et al., 2022) and its social surveillance system and also the COVID-19 pandemic (Ibrahim, 2020) are analyzed as examples of massive surveillance executions using AI by governments. In many cases, these systems have violated societal privacy in multiple terms (Liu and Zhao, 2021). In addition, one of the main challenges identified and linked to government actions is the fair development of smart cities and IoT devices that, along with medical and financial databases, set the boundaries of privacy concerns when it comes to AI deployment by governments. Moreover, the consequent exponential growth of connected infrastructures, as well as the massive appearance and use of new technologies, such as blockchain, arouses even more concern about privacy. These concerns focus on data sharing, data acquisition and collection, and automated decision-making that may violate the security and privacy of personal data.

Likewise, in most of the analyzed articles, it is indicated urgently that governments make joint and global decisions for AI regulation. AI's power of optimization, analysis, prediction, and automated decision-making can promote inequality, unfair decisions, and lack of ethics in data handling of society. It is therefore urgent that public institutions develop well-defined policies and laws that truly understand how AI works and design tools for its control and optimization by human beings, not by machines learning algorithms themselves.

Limitations

The limitations of this research are directly linked to the database used. There are numerous optimal academic databases for the development of bibliometric studies. It is a limitation that this research only uses one database for its development. In addition, only articles published in English were considered, which can also be identified as a limitation. Furthermore, the queries made in the database, as well as the theme analyzed, can be referred to in numerous terms. Although this research focuses on the main terms that determine the subject of study, there may be terminologies that are not covered by this research and that are also valid for studying AI by governments and implications for privacy. Moreover, the analysis of the research, although with quantitative indicators, is exploratory and qualitative and does not identify a statistical significance or empirical value in the results. This study offers a reasoned argument and discusses the main contributions to date, linking the results to previous literature to justify the arguments for future research in this area.

REFERENCES

Abdolhamid, M., Abdolhoseinzadeh, M., Esmaeili Givi, M., Saberi, M.K., Mirezati, S.Z., & Amiri, M.R. (2023). Bibliometric analysis of global scientific research on Public Administration: 1923–2020. *International Journal of Information Science and Management (IJISM)*, 21(1), 75–96.

Abrassart, C., Bengio, Y., Chicoisne, G., de Marcellis-Warin, N., Dilhac, M.A., Gambs, S., ... & Voarino, N. (2018). Montréal Declaration for a responsible development of artificial intelligence. Announced at the conclusion of the Forum on the Socially Responsible Development of AI. https://www. montrealdeclaration responsibleai. com/the-declaration. Last accessed 15 May 2023.

Agarwal, P.K. (2018). Public administration challenges in the world of AI and bots. *Public Administration Review*, 78(6), 917–21.

Allam, Z., & Dhunny, Z.A. (2019). On big data, artificial intelligence and smart cities. *Cities*, 89, 80–91.

Angwin, J., Larson, J., Mattu, S., & Kirchner, L. (2016). Machine bias: There's software used across the country to predict future criminals. And it's biased against blacks. *ProPublica*, 23, 77–91.

Arrieta, A.B., Díaz-Rodríguez, N., Del Ser, J., Bennetot, A., Tabik, S., Barbado, A., ... & Herrera, F. (2020). Explainable Artificial Intelligence (XAI): Concepts, taxonomies, opportunities and challenges toward responsible AI. *Information Fusion*, 58, 82–115.

Ashok, M., Madan, R., Joha, A., & Sivarajah, U. (2022). Ethical framework for Artificial Intelligence and digital technologies. *International Journal of Information Management*, 62, 102433.

Barocas, S., & Selbst, A.D. (2016). Big data's disparate impact. *California Law Review*, 671–732.

Burrell, J. (2016). How the machine 'thinks': Understanding opacity in machine learning algorithms. *Big data & society*, 3(1), 2053951715622512.

Cai, L., Yuen, K.F., Xie, D., Fang, M., & Wang, X. (2021). Consumer's usage of logistics technologies: Integration of habit into the unified theory of acceptance and use of technology. *Technology in Society*, 67, 101789.

Calo, R. (2015). Robotics and the lessons of cyberlaw. *California Law Review*, 513–63.

Cantero Gamito, M., & Ebers, M. (2021). Algorithmic governance and governance of algorithms: An introduction. *Algorithmic Governance and Governance of Algorithms: Legal and Ethical Challenges*, 1–22.

Charles, V., Rana, N.P., & Carter, L. (2022). Artificial Intelligence for data-driven decision-making and governance in public affairs. *Government Information Quarterly*, 101742.

Chen, Y.N.K., & Wen, C.H.R. (2021). Impacts of attitudes toward government and corporations on public trust in artificial intelligence. *Communication Studies*, 72(1), 115–31.

Choi, A.J. (2014, November). Internet of Things: Evolution towards a hyper-connected society. In *2014 IEEE Asian Solid-State Circuits Conference (A-SSCC)* (pp. 5–8). IEEE.

Citron, D.K., & Pasquale, F. (2014). The scored society: Due process for automated predictions. *Washington Law Review*, 89, 1.

de Almeida, P.G.R., dos Santos, C.D., & Farias, J.S. (2021). Artificial intelligence regulation: A framework for governance. *Ethics and Information Technology*, 23(3), 505–25. https://doi.org/10.1007/s10676-021-09593-z

de Geus, C.J., Ingrams, A., Tummers, L., & Pandey, S.K. (2020). Organizational citizenship behavior in the public sector: A systematic literature review and future research agenda. *Public Administration Review*, 80(2), 259–70.

Deng, T., Zhang, K., & Shen, Z.J.M. (2021). A systematic review of a digital twin city: A new pattern of urban governance toward smart cities. *Journal of Management Science and Engineering*, 6(2), 125–34.

Djeffal, C., Siewert, M.B., & Wurster, S. (2022). Role of the state and responsibility in governing artificial intelligence: A comparative analysis of AI strategies. *Journal of European Public Policy*, 29(11), 1799–821.

Donthu, N., Kumar, S., Mukherjee, D., Pandey, N., & Lim, W.M. (2021a). How to conduct a bibliometric analysis: An overview and guidelines. *Journal of Business Research*, 133, 285–96.

Donthu, N., Kumar, S., Pandey, N., & Gupta, P. (2021b). Forty years of the *International Journal of Information Management*: A bibliometric analysis. *International Journal of Information Management*, 57, 102307.

Duchi, J.C., Jordan, M.I., & Wainwright, M.J. (2014). Privacy aware learning. *Journal of the ACM (JACM)*, 61(6), 1–57.

Dwivedi, Y.K., Hughes, L., Ismagilova, E., Aarts, G., Coombs, C., Crick, T., ... & Williams, M.D. (2021). Artificial Intelligence (AI): Multidisciplinary perspectives on emerging challenges, opportunities, and agenda for research, practice and policy. *International Journal of Information Management*, 57, 101994.

Ejarque, J., Badia, R.M., Albertin, L., Aloisio, G., Baglione, E., Becerra, Y., ... & Volpe, M. (2022). Enabling dynamic and intelligent workflows for HPC, data analytics, and AI convergence. *Future Generation Computer Systems*, 134, 414–29. https://doi.org/10.1016/j.future.2022.04.014

Engstrom, D.F., & Haim, A. (2023). Regulating government AI and the challenge of sociotechnical design. *Annual Review of Law and Social Science*, 19.

Eubanks, V. (2018). *Automating inequality: How high-tech tools profile, police, and punish the poor.* St. Martin's Press.

Fontes, C., Hohma, E., Corrigan, C.C., & Lütge, C. (2022). AI-powered public surveillance systems: Why we (might) need them and how we want them. *Technology in Society*, 71, 102137.

Gardner, A., Smith, A.L., Steventon, A., Coughlan, E., & Oldfield, M. (2022). Ethical funding for trustworthy AI: Proposals to address the responsibilities of funders to ensure that projects adhere to trustworthy AI practice. *AI and Ethics*, 1–15.

Gmür, M. (2003). Co-citation analysis and the search for invisible colleges: A methodological evaluation. *Scientometrics*, 57(1), 27–57.

Gordon, G., Rieder, B., & Sileno, G. (2022). On mapping values in AI governance. *Computer Law & Security Review*, 46, 105712.

Gorwa, R., Binns, R., & Katzenbach, C. (2020). Algorithmic content moderation: Technical and political challenges in the automation of platform governance. *Big Data & Society*, 7(1), 2053951719897945.

Green, B. (2022). The flaws of policies requiring human oversight of government algorithms. *Computer Law & Security Review*, 45, 105681.

Green, B., & Chen, Y. (2021). Algorithmic risk assessments can alter human decision-making processes in high-stakes government contexts. *Proceedings of the ACM on Human-Computer Interaction*, 5(CSCW2), 1–33.

Gupta, S., Modgil, S., Kumar, A., Sivarajah, U., & Irani, Z. (2022). Artificial intelligence and cloud-based collaborative platforms for managing disaster, extreme weather and emergency operations. *International Journal of Production Economics*, 254, 108642.

Hagendorff, T. (2020). The ethics of AI ethics: An evaluation of guidelines. *Minds & Machines*, 30, 99–120. https://doi.org/10.1007/s11023-020-09517-8

Henman, P. (2020). Improving public services using artificial intelligence: Possibilities, pitfalls, governance. *Asia Pacific Journal of Public Administration*, 42(4), 209–21.

Herteux, A. (2019, August). Behavioural capitalism and surveillance capitalism – a comparison of two interpretations of a development of capitalism. *Erich von Werner Society*.

Hickok, M. (2021). Lessons learned from AI ethics principles for future actions. *AI and Ethics*, 1(1), 41–47.

Hickok, M., & Maslej, N. (2023). A policy primer and roadmap on AI worker surveillance and productivity scoring tools. *AI and Ethics*, 1–15.

HLEG, A. (2019). Ethics guidelines for trustworthy AI. *European Commission*. Retrieved on November 10, 2023 from: https://digital-strategy.ec.europa.eu/en/library/ethics-guidelines-trustworthy-ai.

Ibrahim, N.K. (2020). Epidemiologic surveillance for controlling Covid-19 pandemic: Types, challenges and implications. *Journal of Infection and Public Health*, 13(11), 1630–8.

Ingrams, A. (2015). Mobile phones, smartphones, and the transformation of civic behavior through mobile information and connectivity. *Government Information Quarterly*, 32(4), 506–15.

Ingrams, A., Kaufmann, W., & Jacobs, D. (2022). In AI we trust? Citizen perceptions of AI in government decision making. *Policy & Internet*, 14(2), 390–409.

Ismagilova, E., Hughes, L., Rana, N.P., & Dwivedi, Y.K. (2020). Security, privacy and risks within smart cities: Literature review and development of a smart city interaction framework. *Information Systems Frontiers*, 1–22.

Iyer, L.S. (2021). AI enabled applications towards intelligent transportation. *Transportation Engineering*, 5, 100083.

Jobin, A., Ienca, M., & Vayena, E. (2019). The global landscape of AI ethics guidelines. *Nature Machine Intelligence*, 1(9), 389–99.

Karpa, D., Klarl, T., & Rochlitz, M. (2022). Artificial intelligence, surveillance, and big data. In *Diginomics research perspectives: The role of digitalization in business and society* (pp. 145–72). Springer International Publishing.

Kerr, A.D., & Scharp, K. (2022). The end of vagueness: Technological epistemicism, surveillance capitalism, and explainable artificial intelligence. *Minds and Machines*, 32(3), 585–611.

Kuziemski, M., & Misuraca, G. (2020). AI governance in the public sector: Three tales from the frontiers of automated decision-making in democratic settings. *Telecommunications Policy*, 44(6), 101976.

Lafont, J., Saura, J.R., & Ribeiro-Soriano, D. (2023). The role of cooperatives in Sustainable Development Goals: A discussion about the current resource curse. *Resources Policy*, 83, 103670.

Lee, M. & Lee, H.H. (2021). Social media photo activity, internalization, appearance comparison, and body satisfaction: The moderating role of photo-editing behavior. *Computers in Human Behavior*, 114, 106579. https://doi.org/10.1016/j.chb.2020.106579

Lepri, B., Oliver, N., Letouzé, E., Pentland, A., & Vinck, P. (2018). Fair, transparent, and accountable algorithmic decision-making processes: The premise, the proposed solutions, and the open challenges. *Philosophy & Technology, 31*, 611–27.

Liao, P., Wan, Y., Tang, P., Wu, C., Hu, Y., & Zhang, S. (2019). Applying crowdsourcing techniques in urban planning: A bibliometric analysis of research and practice prospects. *Cities, 94*, 33–43.

Liu, J., & Zhao, H. (2021). Privacy lost: Appropriating surveillance technology in China's fight against COVID-19. *Business Horizons, 64*(6), 743–56.

Manana, T., & Mawela, T. (2022, November). Digital skills of public sector employees for digital transformation. In *2022 International Conference on Innovation and Intelligence for Informatics, Computing, and Technologies (3ICT)* (pp. 144–50). IEEE.

Manheim, K., & Kaplan, L. (2019). Artificial intelligence: Risks to privacy and democracy. *Yale Journal of Law & Technology, 21*, 106.

Maschmeyer, L., Deibert, R.J., & Lindsay, J.R. (2021). A tale of two cybers-how threat reporting by cybersecurity firms systematically underrepresents threats to civil society. *Journal of Information Technology & Politics, 18*(1), 1–20.

Matheus, R., Janssen, M., & Maheshwari, D. (2020). Data science empowering the public: Data-driven dashboards for transparent and accountable decision-making in smart cities. *Government Information Quarterly, 37*(3), 101284. https://doi.org/10.1016/j.giq.2018.01.006

Mazurek, G., & Małagocka, K. (2019). Perception of privacy and data protection in the context of the development of artificial intelligence. *Journal of Management Analytics, 6*(4), 344–64.

Miao, F., Holmes, W., Huang, R., & Zhang, H. (2021). *AI and education: A guidance for policymakers.* UNESCO Publishing.

Mittelstadt, B.D., Allo, P., Taddeo, M., Wachter, S., & Floridi, L. (2016). The ethics of algorithms: Mapping the debate. *Big Data & Society, 3*(2), 2053951716679679.

Morabito, V., & Morabito, V. (2015). Big data governance. *Big Data and Analytics: Strategic and Organizational Impacts*, 83–104.

Morley, J., Floridi, L., Kinsey, L., & Elhalal, A. (2020a). From what to how: An initial review of publicly available AI ethics tools, methods and research to translate principles into practices. *Science and Engineering Ethics, 26*(4), 2141–68.

Morley, J., Machado, C.C., Burr, C., Cowls, J., Joshi, I., Taddeo, M., & Floridi, L. (2020b). The ethics of AI in health care: A mapping review. *Social Science & Medicine, 260*, 113172.

Nagtegaal, R. (2021). The impact of using algorithms for managerial decisions on public employees' procedural justice. *Government Information Quarterly, 38*(1), 101536.

Nandiyanto, A.B.D., & Al Husaeni, D.F. (2021). A bibliometric analysis of materials research in Indonesian journal using VOSviewer. *Journal of Engineering Research.*

Noain-Sánchez, A. (2016). "Privacy by default" and active "informed consent" by layers: Essential measures to protect ICT users' privacy. *Journal of Information, Communication and Ethics in Society, 14*(2), 124–38.

Oladinrin, O.T., Arif, M., Rana, M.Q., & Gyoh, L. (2023). Interrelations between construction ethics and innovation: A bibliometric analysis using VOSviewer. *Construction Innovation, 23*(3), 505–23.

Oyewola, D.O., & Dada, E.G. (2022). Exploring machine learning: A scientometrics approach using bibliometrix and VOSviewer. *SN Applied Sciences, 4*(5), 143.

Pahwa, M.S., Dadhich, M., Saini, J.S., & Saini, D.K. (2022). Use of artificial intelligence (AI) in the optimization of production of biodiesel energy. *Artificial Intelligence for Renewable Energy Systems*, 229–38.

Pallathadka, H., Ramirez-Asis, E.H., Loli-Poma, T.P., Kaliyaperumal, K., Ventayen, R.J.M., & Naved, M. (2023). Applications of artificial intelligence in business management, e-commerce and finance. *Materials Today: Proceedings, 80*, 2610–13.

Patel, V. L., Shortliffe, E. H., Stefanelli, M., Szolovits, P., Berthold, M. R., Bellazzi, R., & Abu-Hanna, A. (2009). The coming of age of artificial intelligence in medicine. *Artificial Intelligence in Medicine, 46*(1), 5–17. https://doi.org/10.1016/j.artmed.2008.07.017

Pencheva, I., Esteve, M., & Mikhaylov, S.J. (2020). Big Data and AI–A transformational shift for government: So, what next for research? *Public Policy and Administration, 35*(1), 24–44.

Price, W.N., & Cohen, I.G. (2019). Privacy in the age of medical big data. *Nature Medicine, 25*(1), 37–43.

Principale, S., Cosentino, A., Lombardi, R., & Rocchi, A. (2023). Public administration in smart city: A bibliometric analysis. *Journal of Public Affairs*, e2863.

Reddy, S., Allan, S., Coghlan, S., & Cooper, P. (2020). A governance model for the application of AI in health care. *Journal of the American Medical Informatics Association*, 27(3), 491–7.

Rey-Martí, A., Ribeiro-Soriano, D., & Palacios-Marqués, D. (2016). A bibliometric analysis of social entrepreneurship. *Journal of Business Research*, 69(5), 1651–5.

Ribeiro-Navarrete, S., Saura, J.R., & Palacios-Marqués, D. (2021). Towards a new era of mass data collection: Assessing pandemic surveillance technologies to preserve user privacy. *Technological Forecasting and Social Change*, 167, 120681. https://doi.org/10.1016/j.techfore.2021.120681

Roberts, H., Cowls, J., Morley, J., Taddeo, M., Wang, V., & Floridi, L. (2021). The Chinese approach to artificial intelligence: An analysis of policy, ethics, and regulation. *AI & Society*, 36, 59–77.

Russell, S. (2023). AI weapons: Russia's war in Ukraine shows why the world must enact a ban. *Nature*, 614(7949), 620–3.

Saura, J.R., Ribeiro-Soriano, D., & Palacios-Marqués, D. (2021). Setting privacy "by default" in social IoT: Theorizing the challenges and directions in Big Data research. *Big Data Research*, 25, 100245. https://doi.org/10.1016/j.bdr.2021.100245

Saura, J.R., Ribeiro-Soriano, D., & Palacios-Marqués, D. (2022). Assessing behavioral data science privacy issues in government artificial intelligence deployment. *Government Information Quarterly*, 39(4), 101679. https://doi.org/10.1016/j.giq.2022.101679

Saura, J.R., Ribeiro-Navarrete, S., Palacios-Marqués, D., & Mardani, A. (2023). Impact of extreme weather in production economics: Extracting evidence from user-generated content. *International Journal of Production Economics*, 260, 108861. https://doi.org/10.1016/j.ijpe.2023.108861

Saura, J.R. (2024). Algorithms in digital marketing: does smart personalization promote a privacy paradox? *FIIB Business Review*, 13(5), 499–502. https://doi.org/10.1177/23197145241276898

Sætra, H.S., & Danaher, J. (2022). To each technology its own ethics: The problem of ethical proliferation. *Philosophy & Technology*, 35(4), 93.

Saveliev, A., & Zhurenkov, D. (2021). Artificial intelligence and social responsibility: The case of the artificial intelligence strategies in the United States, Russia, and China. *Kybernetes*, 50(3), 656–75.

Schiff, D.S., Schiff, K.J., & Pierson, P. (2022). Assessing public value failure in government adoption of artificial intelligence. *Public Administration*, 100(3), 653–73.

Shah, S.H.H., Lei, S., Ali, M., Doronin, D., & Hussain, S.T. (2020). Prosumption: Bibliometric analysis using HistCite and VOSviewer. *Kybernetes*, 49(3), 1020–45.

Sukhadia, A., Upadhyay, K., Gundeti, M., Shah, S., & Shah, M. (2020). Optimization of smart traffic governance system using artificial intelligence. *Augmented Human Research*, 5, 1–14.

Suran, S., Pattanaik, V., Kurvers, R., Hallin, C.A., De Liddo, A., Krimmer, R., & Draheim, D. (2022). Building global societies on collective intelligence: Challenges and opportunities. *Digital Government: Research and Practice*, 3(4), 1–6.

Susanto, H., Yie, L.F., Rosiyadi, D., Basuki, A.I., & Setiana, D. (2021). Data security for connected governments and organisations: Managing automation and artificial intelligence. In *Web 2.0 and cloud technologies for implementing connected government* (pp. 229–51). IGI Global.

Tripathi, M., Kumar, S., Sonker, S.K., & Babbar, P. (2018). Occurrence of author keywords and keywords plus in social sciences and humanities research: A preliminary study. *COLLNET Journal of Scientometrics and Information Management*, 12(2), 215–32.

Tsamados, A., Aggarwal, N., Cowls, J., Morley, J., Roberts, H., Taddeo, M., & Floridi, L. (2021). The ethics of algorithms: Key problems and solutions. *Ethics, Governance, and Policies in Artificial Intelligence*, 37, 97–123.

van Noordt, C., & Misuraca, G. (2022). Artificial intelligence for the public sector: Results of landscaping the use of AI in government across the European Union. *Government Information Quarterly*, 39(3), 101714.

Wang, X., Xu, Z., & Škare, M. (2020). A bibliometric analysis of Economic Research-Ekonomska Istra zivanja (2007–2019). *Economic research-Ekonomska istraživanja*, 33(1), 865–86.

Willems, J., Schmid, M.J., Vanderelst, D., Vogel, D., & Ebinger, F. (2022). AI-driven public services and the privacy paradox: Do citizens really care about their privacy?. *Public Management Review*, 1–19.

Winter, J.S., & Davidson, E. (2019). Governance of artificial intelligence and personal health information. *Digital Policy, Regulation and Governance*, 21(3), 280–90.

Wirtz, B.W., Weyerer, J.C., & Sturm, B.J. (2020). The dark sides of artificial intelligence: An integrated AI governance framework for public administration. *International Journal of Public Administration*, *43*(9), 818–29.

Yang, L., Elisa, N., & Eliot, N. (2019). Privacy and security aspects of e-government in smart cities. In *Smart cities cybersecurity and privacy* (pp. 89–102). Elsevier.

Zarsky, T. (2016). The trouble with algorithmic decisions: An analytic road map to examine efficiency and fairness in automated and opaque decision making. *Science, Technology, & Human Values*, *41*(1), 118–32.

Zhu, L., Chen, P., Dong, D., & Wang, Z. (2022). Can artificial intelligence enable the government to respond more effectively to major public health emergencies? Taking the prevention and control of Covid-19 in China as an example. *Socio-Economic Planning Sciences*, *80*, 101029.

Zuboff, S. (2015). Big other: Surveillance capitalism and the prospects of an information civilization. *Journal of Information Technology*, *30*(1), 75–89.

Zuboff, S. (2019a, January). Surveillance capitalism and the challenge of collective action. In *New labor forum* (Vol. 28, No. 1, pp. 10–29). Sage CA: Los Angel.

Zuboff, S. (2019b). *The age of surveillance capitalism: The fight for a human future at the new frontier of power: Barack Obama's books of 2019*. Profile Books.

PART III

RESPONSIBLE AND PARTICIPATORY DATA USE BY GOVERNMENT

15. Intersecting digital governance and data science: preparing for communication to strengthen citizen-government partnerships

Jae-Seong Lee

INTRODUCTION

The advancement of artificial intelligence (AI) and data-driven digital technologies has catalyzed a paradigm shift in digital transformation, introducing significant changes to our society (Majchrzak et al., 2016). The societal alterations precipitated by these technological innovations have further manifested in shifts in individual behavioral patterns (Kumar et al., 2019). For example, consumers who demand products or services have started to participate in the innovation process by suggesting new ideas to companies (Lucas Jr. et al., 2013; Sia et al., 2016; Vial, 2019). At the same time, companies are using their improved data utilization capabilities to investigate and satisfy the evolving consumer expectations regarding current products or services (Sia et al., 2016; Vial, 2019).

The fundamental components of the digital transformation paradigm that have spurred these changes comprise personalization and automation (Kumar et al., 2019; Suoniemi et al., 2020). Personalization denotes the ability to customize information to suit a user's character and preferences, fostering the bond between the customer and marketing executives (Kumar et al., 2019). The element of personalization creates an emotional bond with customers and affects their engagement behavior (Pansari and Kumar, 2017; Van Doorn et al., 2010). Meanwhile, automation involves a series of processes that manage and handle these operations automatically throughout their entire cycle (Kumar et al., 2019). Therefore, the process of automation enables efficient and cost-effective real-time management, ensures consistency by following predetermined routines, and alleviates managerial burdens (Kumar et al., 2019).

However, significant concerns persist regarding the digital transformation paradigm. During the implementation of personalization and automation in digital transformation, companies must unavoidably gather personal information from their customers (Taeihagh and Lim, 2019). Outsourcing databases may result in the undesirable sharing of customers' collected personal information with third parties (Tan et al., 2021). Additionally, personalization algorithms that prioritize high accuracy may deliberately omit minority groups, causing severe discriminatory harm (Joyce et al., 2021; Mikalef et al., 2022). If personal data is leaked or discriminatory information delivery via algorithms is revealed and claims are made for customer damage compensation, determining liability can become very complex (Cooper et al., 2022). For example, numerous companies often buy software from others instead of creating their own algorithms. Even if companies develop their own algorithms, much of the code is reliant on open source, which heightens the probability that many and unspecified stakeholders may be involved.

Governments have begun to take interest and assume responsibility for these issues at the national level. Multiple administrations have participated in policy discussions aimed at establishing digital technology policies related to digital transformation, also referred to as AI and data innovation, and its defining features: personalization and automation. As the discussions progressed, the term "digital governance" surfaced, covering all the policy debates related to governance concerns in the digital era (Hanisch et al., 2023). Governance is usually characterized as the "system comprising authoritative norms, regulations, institutions, and practices that aid every group, from local to global levels, in jointly managing affairs" (Ruggie, 2014). In this context, digital governance refers to the implementation of governance that fulfills the requirements of the digital age. These requirements correspond to the needs of managers to coordinate and facilitate multiple interactions that take place simultaneously in vast networks, driven by environmental changes that have led to a significant expansion of opportunities for the exchange of data and knowledge (Hanelt et al., 2021; Hanisch et al., 2023; Verhoef et al., 2021; Vial, 2019). This chapter simplifies and defines the concept of digital governance more succinctly and intuitively as "better AI and data policies." The concept of "better" can be elucidated to address the social concerns arising in the digital transformation paradigm, which accelerates the use of data and AI, as previously mentioned.

Among the various policy outcomes related to digital governance, a prominent example showing significant progress is the "AI Regulation" adopted by the European Union (EU), the world's first of its kind (EU Parliament, 2023). Central to discussions on AI regulation is the commitment to assess the risks associated with AI use and to mandate appropriate responsive measures based on those results. However, imposing the burden of managing AI risks and responsibilities on suppliers can only be a temporary solution. In other words, such regulation merely represents the bare minimum required to reduce harm. The more fundamental question of how to create inherently safe and trustworthy AI remains insufficiently addressed. Critiques pointing out the deficiency of the design principles for achieving desirable digital governance underscore the urgency for discussion (Bharosa, 2022).

Deliberations on practical design principles for safe and trustworthy AI are particularly pressing in the government service sector. As previously mentioned, the private sector has rapidly embraced the paradigm of digital transformation, investing considerable efforts in exploring new customer expectations. Citizens who have experienced the convenience of digital transformation in the private sector now demand personalized and valuable information from government services (Mergel et al., 2019). This demand has necessitated digital transformation in the public sector (Hong et al., 2022), leading to the evolution from e-government to digital government. Discussions surrounding the new governmental concept have begun, but they encounter challenges such as semantic discrepancies, unpredictability, and adaptations caused by a lack of shared understanding (Ansell and Trondal, 2018). This chapter acknowledges these challenges and delves into a deep discussion focused on digital government, aiming to facilitate a common discourse on enhanced digital governance.

LITERATURE REVIEW

The Imperative of Citizen-Government Partnerships for the Realization of Digital Governance

The cross-national recommendation of the OECD (Organisation for Economic Co-operation and Development) for a phased strategy to realize digital government comprises three main pillars: (1) openness and engagement, (2) governance and coordination, and (3) capacities to support implementation, which further break down into 12 specific recommendations (OECD, 2014). The OECD's proposed recommendation underscores the importance of leveraging digital technology in government while preventing the emergence of a new form of digital divide, thereby fostering a more open, innovative, and participatory government.

The first pillar includes specific recommendations for (1) openness, transparency, and inclusiveness; (2) engagement and participation in a multi-actor context in policymaking and service delivery; (3) creation of a data-driven culture; and (4) protection of privacy and ensuring security. The second pillar delineates recommendations to (5) demonstrate leadership and political commitment; (6) ensure coherent use of digital technology across policy areas; (7) establish effective organizational and governance frameworks for coordination; and (8) strengthen international cooperation with other governments. The third pillar encapsulates (9) development of clear business cases; (10) reinforcement of institutional capacities; (11) procurement of digital technologies; and (12) a robust legal and regulatory framework.

The core discussion of this chapter on digital governance for realizing digital government aligns with the second pillar of the OECD's recommendations. The detailed recommendations of the second pillar can be summarized as a "social consensus among all stakeholders aimed at the adoption and utilization of digital technology across various policy areas." Essentially, the OECD emphasizes the role of the government as a coordinator in constructing digital governance. In summary, it can be inferred that the definition of digital governance, framed as "policies for AI and data to mitigate societal concerns," necessitates a social consensus among various stakeholders, with the government playing a pivotal role as a mediator.

On another note, the OECD guidelines delineated six fundamental elements that the digital government should embody (OECD, 2020): (1) user-driven administration; (2) proactive policymaking and service delivery; (3) a data-driven public sector; (4) digital-by-design; (5) government as a platform; and (6) open-by-default. A prime policy instrument to fulfill these foundational elements is the citizen-government partnership, the types of which are further categorized, based on the stage of public value creation, into co-creation and co-production (Brandsen et al., 2018). Co-creation, rooted in citizen participation, is predominantly employed during the planning phase of the digital government (Brandsen et al., 2018), fostering openness and engagement. Co-production, on the other hand, can be utilized during the design, implementation, and realization phases of the digital government (Brandsen et al., 2018).

A Detailed Examination of the Types of Citizen-Government Partnership

This chapter delves into two pivotal citizen-government partnership mechanisms: co-creation and co-production, which facilitate the effective development of digital government. Though conceptually similar, co-creation focuses on citizen involvement during the early planning stages of government services, while co-production emphasizes collaboration during service implementation (Brandsen and Honingh, 2018).

Co-creation
Through co-creation, citizens collaboratively ensure that the digital government provides inclusive and beneficial services. Central to this is open data, which facilitates engagement by permitting the utilization of government information by various stakeholders (Toots et al., 2017; Yu and Robinson, 2012). Examples include:

- Information Provision: Leveraging open data, the government offers detailed insights into its activities, narrowing the gap between citizen expectations and government performance (Yetano, 2010).
- Encouraging Participation: Open data boosts citizen involvement in governmental decisions (Yoshida and Thammetar, 2021).
- Improvement of Digital Services: Using open data as a resource, governments can refine digital service delivery based on citizens' preferences (Mergel et al., 2018).

Co-production
Co-production fosters a user-centric digital government by integrating citizen insights, ensuring inclusivity, and reducing algorithmic biases. This active citizen involvement enriches service delivery, fortifying trust in the government and promoting the adoption of new digital platforms (Eom and Lee, 2022; Panagiotopoulos et al., 2019).

Governmental efforts to champion co-production include hosting open discussion forums and conducting technology assessments to address AI-related concerns, driving the development of a transparent, accountable, and equitable digital government (Manoharan et al., 2021; Owen and Pansera, 2019).

The Underutilization of Citizen-Government Partnerships in the Actual Stages of Digital Governance Implementation

The primary issue identified in this chapter while examining discourses related to digital government development is that discussions tend to revolve around public-private partnerships rather than focusing on citizen-government partnerships. Citizen-government partnerships have been mainly employed during the planning phase of digital governance to capture the public's service delivery needs (Bannister and Connolly, 2014; Cordella and Bonina, 2012), while public-private partnerships have often been utilized during the design and development phases (Pittaway and Montazemi, 2020).

Public-private partnerships signify collaborative measures concerning the newly evolving governance of data and AI, allowing government leaders and administrators to design and implement user-friendly public services (Eom and Lee, 2022). While both public-private and citizen-government partnerships fall under the methods of public value creation (Pang et al., 2014), they differ in their goals. Public-private partnerships aim for a symbiotic structure centered on the government and private companies rather than on citizens, ensuring the profitability of private enterprises through effective budget utilization by the government while contributing to the improvement of the efficiency and quality of public service delivery (Linder and Rosenau, 2000).

In the development and implementation phases, the government's primary collaborators tend to shift from citizens to private companies, often overlooking the importance of citizen participation. Evidence for this is found in the citizens' dissatisfaction related to democratic procedures due to the lack of participation in the smart city development process (Van Twist et al., 2023). Smart cities aim to utilize digital technologies like AI to address urban issues, enhance citizens' lives, and contribute to a more efficient government (Meijer and Bolívar, 2016; Nam and Pardo, 2011). They incorporate digital governance as a vital component, alongside areas such as public safety and transportation (Zheng et al., 2019). According to Van Twist et al. (2023), in policymaking grounded on citizen participation, citizens are often relegated to passive and dependent roles. Consequently, they are growing increasingly discontented with their diminished influence, demanding more substantial inclusion and, in some cases, outright rejecting participation in smart city development processes.

The Government's Role in Promoting a Citizen-Government Partnership

Linders (2012) understood citizen-government partnerships as a key means of co-production for public value creation. Similar to this chapter, Linders (2012) differentiated such partnerships from public-private ones and summarized the roles and responsibilities that the government should undertake within citizen-government partnerships as follows:

- Framer: In traditional co-production efforts, the government plays a leading role, "setting the atmosphere" and defining how actions should unfold. This is achieved not only by "fostering ideas" but also by actively "promoting and sustaining" such activities (Lam, 1996). Tasks can include setting rules to ensure fair participation, promoting reciprocity, monitoring performance, and enforcing regulations (Linders, 2012).
- Sponsor: Government sponsorship, whether financial or otherwise, often makes the difference between success and failure in citizen-government co-production. For instance, government resources can play a crucial role, whether in the form of physical infrastructure or the rule of law (Evans, 1996). Even if in name only, government support is essential in ensuring public legitimacy (Ackerman, 2004).
- Mobilizer: When co-production is not mandated, there is a need to motivate. For example, in arguments suggesting that the democratic potential of the internet cannot be realized without government guidance (Rethemeyer, 2007), the government can play a vital role in ensuring unorganized individuals align their actions (Linders, 2012).
- Monitor: The government is almost certain to retain ultimate accountability for the public's well-being. In citizen-led co-production, the government can also hold civil society accountable for adverse outcomes. Hence, the government can act as a watcher, overseeing and supervising the co-production activities of civil society (Ackerman, 2004).
- Provider of Last Resort: The government should also continue its role as the actor/provider of last resort, intervening when third-party alternatives do not prove satisfactory (Robinson et al., 2009).

An Empirical Understanding of the Government's Role through a Korean Case

The roles and responsibilities of the government for citizen-government partnerships can be better understood through the digital government policy cases of South Korea. During the planning phase of the digital government, South Korea made several policy efforts through its first national AI policy, "I-Korea 4.0," launched in 2018. The government planned to (1) generate high-quality large-scale data; (2) secure access to high computing resources; and (3) continuously invest in R&D for algorithm refinement. Through "I-Korea 4.0," South Korea aimed to design the digital government as a major public project, identifying the necessity for the government-led development and promotion of safe and trustworthy AI, thereby playing the role of a "Framer."

Subsequently, in 2020, South Korea introduced the "South Korean AI Ethics Guidelines" based on "I-Korea 4.0." These guidelines prioritized preserving human dignity and covered various sub-goals related to human rights, privacy, diversity, data management, responsibility, safety, and transparency. As a follow-up to these guidelines, South Korea announced a "Trustworthy AI Strategy" in 2021, divided into three goals: (1) fostering a trustworthy AI environment; (2) constructing a safe AI infrastructure; and (3) enhancing awareness about ethical AI. To achieve the first goal, South Korea committed to investing in explainable AI, fairness AI, and robust AI, planning to support the private sector by connecting private data with open government data and providing access to public computing resources. The second goal tackled technological evaluations and institutional considerations, while the third aimed at stakeholder education and hosting public debates on AI ethics. Therefore, South Korea performed the role of a "Sponsor" through the first and second goals and embodied the "Mobilizer" role through the third goal.

In 2023, South Korea further refined its policy outcomes by announcing the "Digital Government Transition Strategy." The government aimed for (1) providing personalized public services; (2) automating public administrative tasks and building predictive systems; (3) fully disclosing government data and promoting the use of the MiData program; and (4) enhancing citizen protection. Thus, the 2023 policy can be interpreted as a result of policy decisions primarily associated with public-private partnerships, emphasizing leveraging private capabilities to design and implement user-friendly public services. As highlighted in this chapter, the Korean case shows that, rather than utilizing citizen-government partnerships, the development and implementation phases of digital government have primarily been advanced through public-private partnerships.

Considerations for Enhancing Citizen-Government Partnerships Activation

Despite the potential of co-production through citizen-government partnerships to be utilized across the designing and eventual implementation stages of digital government (Brandsen et al., 2018), public-private partnerships seem to be supplanting citizen-government partnerships in these phases. Undoubtedly, the government would have made extensive efforts to achieve outstanding outcomes through the citizen-government partnerships. Yet, the reason co-production isn't being fully exploited appears to be due to insufficient communication between citizens and the government—a factor known to considerably impact co-production (Li, 2020).

Governments can successfully mitigate concerns regarding digital technologies by engaging in dialogue with various stakeholders (Eom and Lee, 2022; Leurent et al., 2019). However, information asymmetry obstructs effective communication between the government and its citizens, subsequently negatively influencing co-production (Li, 2020). This asymmetry might hinder citizens from recognizing the necessity of co-production and the methods for successful collaboration (Li, 2020). Conversely, the government might be unable to effectively motivate and engage with citizens for jointly producing desired policy outcomes (Li, 2020).

A fundamental reason for this information imbalance between citizens and the government is their differing levels of understanding concerning science and technology. While the government possesses vast information about advanced technologies like AI, citizens are relatively under-informed. Research fields focusing on the public's understanding of science and technology pay significant attention to enhancing citizens' technological knowledge and information, aiming to improve communication with the government (Durant et al., 1989). Through these efforts, the goal is to to ensure that both parties share a similar level of information and achieve a standardized conceptual framework.

To level the information disparity related to understanding digital technology, this chapter aims to connects primary digital governance issues with corresponding technological advancements. This chapter posits that through such efforts can one easily discern the technological measures being discussed concerning key digital governance issues and identify the remaining challenges. Essentially, this chapter argues that narrowing the focus of discussion can foster a shared understanding of issues recognized by both citizens and the government. Refining the discussion aids in enhancing the public's understanding of science and technology, facilitating the incorporation of more valuable opinions from citizens. Concurrently, the government can devise comprehensive discussion topics encompassing both digital governance and data science. Consequently, this chapter seeks to contribute to successful co-production outcomes between citizens and the government, ultimately supporting the revitalization of the vital citizen-government partnerships in designing and actualizing the digital government.

EXPLORING THE INTERSECTION BETWEEN DIGITAL GOVERNANCE AND DATA SCIENCE

This chapter bridges the primary discussions in digital governance with recent technological advancements to facilitate meaningful discourse between citizens and the government. The pivotal category examined here is Fairness, Accountability, and Transparency (FAT) in data and AI, concepts rooted in AI ethics guidelines (Jobin et al., 2019). Notably, this category correlates with "FAT-ML (Machine Learning)" in data science, denoting endeavors to establish safe and trustworthy AI.

Digital Governance Research Views

Fairness
The notion of fairness is a critical component in AI ethics guidelines and highlights the necessity of monitoring and intervening to prevent undesired discrimination or bias (Jobin et al., 2019). With AI's gradually expanding role in decision-making across diverse domains, policymakers are prioritizing the assurance of AI fairness to counteract potential algorithmic bias (Ferrer et al., 2021). The discussions regarding fairness in AI encompass a broad range of topics, ranging from the potential for AI to produce discriminatory outcomes against particular groups during service delivery to exacerbating existing disparities by limiting access to information and services for marginalized individuals (Joyce et al., 2021; Mikalef et al., 2022).

The fairness concerns surrounding AI are presenting challenges in the private sector, specifically in the realm of self-driving cars and medical services. Selection bias has led to the development of systems that favor certain demographics or geographic regions, leading to autonomous navigation that may not perform uniformly well for all users (Etienne, 2022). In the AI-based medical service industry, meanwhile, unequal access to services for certain groups can harm patients and lead to welfare issues (Rajkomar et al., 2018).

Such fairness issues in AI have inherent risks that also apply to establishing digital governance in the government sector (Harrison and Luna-Reyes, 2022). For instance, during the initial phase of digitizing personal data, there is a risk of excluding certain groups, which may result in selection bias. Additionally, in the process of implementing digital government transformation, particular groups may not receive public services, leading to neglect of their welfare.

Safety, responsibility, privacy
The notion of safety within the context of AI ethics guidelines encompasses the overall need for protection. Safety concerns in AI typically arise from possible risks in unforeseen situations that the system has not been trained to handle, as noted by Taeihagh and Lim (2019). These risks result from a lack of generalization across different contexts that the system may unexpectedly encounter (Taeihagh and Lim, 2019). It is difficult to understand the reasoning behind AI decisions when mimicking human decision-making, making it challenging to take precautions in advance (Koopman and Wagner, 2016).

Concurrently, with the emergence of issues surrounding connected products, particularly within the realm of the Internet of Things (IoT), cybersecurity concerns are rapidly becoming an essential component of digital safety. This highlights the potential risks that cyber threats from the interconnected virtual world pose to the physical world.

The concept of privacy refers to measures taken to safeguard personal information against cyber threats. However, when applied to AI, it often implies the possibility of misusing such information (Janssen et al., 2020). AI systems store a significant amount of personal data and often share it with third parties to generate personal preference information (Taeihagh and Lim, 2019). For instance, personal biometric or medical data collected from medical devices based on IoT must be transferred externally for diagnosis and monitoring (Tan et al., 2021). Privacy concerns emerge when personal information is digitized and managed, including standards related to information collection consent, as well as data management obligations to curtail data breaches (Hutchinson et al., 2021).

Central to responsibility is discerning the accountable entity in legal matters and addressing any misconduct (Busuioc, 2021). AI's inherent complexity can lead to unforeseen outcomes (Tsamados et al., 2021). In instances of AI failures, various stakeholders, like data providers or coders, might be held accountable, echoing the "many hands" dilemma in complex computer systems (Cooper et al., 2022; Nissenbaum, 1996). Unaddressed, this can result in either a void of responsibility or an efficiently overwhelming attribution of blame (Busuioc, 2021).

Transparency
The notion of transparency, as discussed in the context of AI ethical principles, is important enough to intersect with all previously mentioned concepts. However, its definition is still unclear, and its boundaries with other concepts are not well defined (Loi and Spielkamp, 2021). Transparency of AI is a pressing concern under the guidance of the EU's GDPR (General Data

Protection Regulation). Despite serving as a law primarily for safeguarding personal information, this statute represents a major achievement as the first legislative effort to encompass legal clarifications for automated decision-making, including profiling.

The GDPR preamble explains the "fair and transparent processing principle," in which the concept of transparency is highlighted and frequently used synonymously with fairness. (Kaminski, 2021; Selbst and Powles, 2018). Nevertheless, transparency is recognized as a distinct concept because the GDPR's wording is typically interpreted as procedural fairness achieved through ensuring transparency in the information processing process, not the fairness of the AI decision-making outcome (Kaminski, 2021; Selbst and Powles, 2018).

On the contrary, some argue that the concept of transparency frequently encompasses measures that are identical, similar, or overlapping with accountability (Loi and Spielkamp, 2021). While responsibility focuses on identifying the culpability for potential harm caused by decisions made by AI systems (Cooper et al., 2022), accountability emphasizes the implementation of measures to control and manage potential harm (Hutchinson et al., 2021). Therefore, transparency, which clarifies the information processing procedure underlying automated decision-making, is debated as one of the crucial methodological concepts for achieving accountability.

Based on this methodology, transparency can be divided into two subcategories (Loi and Spielkamp, 2021): (1) control transparency, which concerns how information can be accessed and communicated for any purpose, and (2) transparency-as-a-right, which refers to the privilege of users or organizations outside the accountable organization to request access to specific information. Transparency-as-a-right emerges as a more essential concept in the public sector. This concept covers a range of circumstances, from individuals requesting information about their personal data usage by corporations to a broader scenario in which civil society, through government intervention, seeks extensive information from companies, including algorithm source codes, data usage, and parameters utilized in predictive and classification models.

Data Science Research Views

Fairness

In the field of data science, discussions about fairness aim to address data and algorithmic biases. The primary concern is statistical bias, which can result from the underrepresentation of minoritized groups in real-world bias patterns (Hutchinson et al., 2021). In numerous instances, statistical bias has arisen from historical patterns associated with social injustices. There is concern that the use of AI may lead to the expansion of statistical bias into automated bias (Hutchinson et al., 2021).

Data science methods to prevent statistical bias for fairness can be divided into three categories: pre-processing, in-processing, and post-processing.

- Pre-processing methodology: It intends to address the imbalance of both data samples and data classes. Stratified sampling is the representative technique for the former, and methods such as the synthetic minority oversampling technique (SMOTE), generative adversarial networks (GANs), and variational autoencoders (VAEs) are employed for the latter. However, like the latter methodologies, the method often finds it challenging to resolve the imbalance of data classes by simply increasing the amount of data for each individual class.

- In-processing methodology: It is utilized during the model training process and typically employs functions that perform regularization (Ntoutsi et al., 2020). These functions gradually eliminate underrepresented data classes labeled as outliers in the model training process, thus preventing both data class imbalance and model overfitting. However, there is concern that identifying minor groups as outliers may worsen discriminatory outcomes. Moreover, this method is not feasible for new users who aren't currently represented in the data (Cao et al., 2019; Soares et al., 2012).
- Post-processing methodology: It refers to a statistical method for treating bias in an already trained model. This method can be flexibly applied to new data and various domains by adjusting the decision boundary based on distance learning, which provides an advantage. However, it is also sensitive to outliers and difficult to control for performance improvement (Kaneda et al., 2015).

Accountability

In this chapter, AI accountability is viewed as a comprehensive concept that includes safety, responsibility, and privacy, further explained in the prior section. Accountability necessitates proper management not only for groups currently handling data but also for those influenced by AI-powered decisions (Hutchinson et al., 2021). Specifically, the use of AI involves concerns of privacy and safety. Misjudged AI-driven decisions can lead to issues of responsibility.

Data scientists focus on privacy protection methods such as de-identification, differential privacy techniques, and encryption. De-identification encompasses strategies like pseudonymization, aggregation, and data masking to avert privacy infringements (Lee and Jun, 2021). Differential privacy alters original data values to protect personal information, producing either fully or partially synthetic data. Recent studies employ partially synthetic data to link de-identified open government data without identifiers (Lee and Jun, 2021).

Encryption, aimed at information security, divides into homomorphic encryption, federated learning, and blockchain. Homomorphic encryption facilitates operations on encrypted data (Moore et al., 2014). Federated learning merges local model weights onto a central server (Li et al., 2020). Blockchain records in a decentralized distributed ledger, emphasizing persistency and anonymity (Zheng et al., 2017). However, challenges persist: homomorphic encryption's computational intensity, federated learning's increasing communication costs, and blockchain's inability to ensure user data erasure (Li et al., 2020; Moore et al., 2014; Politou et al., 2019).

Meanwhile, several AI research initiatives are underway to address the problem of AI-generated decisions being misjudged. These efforts typically involve working to create AI models that are robust, stable, and possess error resilience (Min et al., 2020). Some of these AI research efforts include (Min et al., 2020):

- Competency-Aware Machine Learning (CAML, '19~'23): AI that establishes models while being aware of its own problem-solving abilities.
- Guaranteeing AI Robustness and Deception (GARD, '19.2): AI that is resistant to external attacks and operates without malfunction.
- Lifelong Learning Machine (L2M, '18~'21): A learning method that enables adaptation to new changes and lifelong knowledge growth.
- Science of AI and Learning for Open-World Novelty (SAIL-ON, '19.3): AI that can learn and understand without limitations on problem domains, similar to human learning.

Transparency

AI transparency is often referred to as explainable AI (XAI) in the field of data science. XAI includes several sub-concepts, including understandability, interpretability, explainability, and transparency (Arrieta et al., 2020). Comprehensibility involves ensuring that AI's inference process and its conclusions are relevant to the contextual inferences humans can draw by observing the same objects. Objectivity requires that AI's operation is explained in a way that is understandable to humans (Michalski, 1983). Interpretability suggests that AI ought to convey meaning or explanation through language that humans can comprehend (Arrieta et al., 2020), while explainability entails that AI should serve as an interface for decision-makers and competently facilitate communication between decision-makers and users (Guidotti et al., 2018). Transparency refers to the understandability of the AI model itself (Lipton, 2018).

Based on the conceptual definition of XAI above, this chapter summarizes the trends of XAI research being conducted in the field of data science as follows (Speith, 2022):

- Ante-Hoc: This method pertains to the pre-approach of XAI technology. It specifically refers to algorithmically transparent models like kNN, decision trees, rule-based models, and Bayesian models. However, it is well known that the more complex the Ante-Hoc models are and the more rules they contain, the harder they are to comprehend (allegedly). Ante-hoc methods have the advantage of providing intuitive interpretability to anyone but are difficult to expect high performance from in many cases.
- Post-Hoc: This method pertains to the post-approach of XAI technology. It can be divided into model-agnostic and model-specific. The former is generally applicable to all models, while the latter is limited to specific models. Both approaches involve creating a surrogate model to explain the black-box model. However, the distinction lies in that model-agnostic post-hoc can evaluate the significance of prediction variables for changes in input values, offering regional interpretability, like LIME (Local Interpretable Model-agnostic Explanation). It can also assess the importance of prediction variables concerning changes in slope and provide global interpretability, similar to SHAP (Shapley Additive Explanation). On the other hand, model-specific post-hoc can generate visual explanations, like heat maps, in CNN (Convolutional Neural Network) models. It can also swap the convolution layer with a max-pooling layer, simplifying the model structure and reducing complexity to aid interpretation. Recent research has also attempted to provide auxiliary interpretability through different output formats, such as describing image outputs as text data. Post-hoc methods are considerably complex and require a significant amount of resources. However, they can yield greater interpretability.

CURRENT CHALLENGES DERIVED FROM AN INTEGRATED PERSPECTIVE

This chapter integrates perspectives from the field of digital governance and the realm of data science, yielding an invaluable comprehensive understanding. Through this amalgamation, the study identifies discernible gaps in the co-evolutionary process of both domains. These challenges pertain to fairness, accountability, and transparency and are outlined below.

Fairness

- Digital Governance Perspective: Emphasizes the mitigation of social prejudice and bias.
- Data Science Perspective: The primary focus is on controlling statistical bias. In other words, there is a noticeable limitation in examining the variables that might amplify societal biases. This chaoter points out that in data science, biased variables could potentially act as proxy variables that accurately categorize group characteristics. Consequently, determining the optimal balance between data utility and societal prejudice becomes a crucial topic for future research.

Accountability

- Digital Governance Perspective: Stresses the aspects of safety, security, identification of responsibility, and privacy.
- Data Science Perspective: Research predominantly focuses on robust models, multi-modal AI, and privacy-enhancing technologies. This chapter argues that technical measures for identifying responsibility are relatively scant in comparison to other theoretical facets. Given the contemporary shift towards software development leveraging open source libraries, discerning accountability in scenarios where AI's automated decision-making results in detrimental outcomes becomes increasingly paramount.

Transparency

- Digital Governance Perspective: Distinguish between control transparency and transparency as a right.
- Data Science Perspective: Research endeavors chiefly target augmenting the explanation functionalities for control, exemplified by frameworks like XAI. This trajectory appears to cater to the explicative obligations set forth by the GDPR. Consequently, this chapter underscores a conspicuous void: while significant research transpires in corporate compliance, there's a notable dearth in investigations targeting technological measures for the public's benefit.

CONCLUSION

The push for digital transformation in the public sector, highlighted by digital government, has intensified discussions on digital governance and emphasized the need for safe and trustworthy AI. The development process of the digital government was segmented into (1) planning; (2) design and implementation; and (3) implementation, where citizen-government collaboration tools were essential. Therefore, enhancing co-production for safe and trustworthy AI in digital government has become crucial.

This chapter identified a shortfall in co-production during the design phase, attributed to the information imbalance between citizens and the government. This asymmetry was understood to arise from their divergent comprehension of science and technology. The chapter's goal is to equalize this understanding.

The chapter linked data science to key digital governance issues, offering citizens clear insights into technical topics and encouraging policy participation. Through this cross-field literature review, potential shared discussion topics between citizens and the government were identified.

First, major discourses in the digital governance field are primarily regulatory. Therefore, there is a significant absence of discussion on incentivization policies. Recently, suspicions have emerged that many companies are engaging in "AI ethics washing," which has led to demands for stricter monitoring by regulatory authorities. However, it's challenging to determine how much stricter regulations can curb such activities. Based on the need to promote the development of safe and trustworthy AI, the following potential subjects are suggested for future discussions between citizens and the government:

- What incentives are appropriate to promote investment in safe and trustworthy AI development?
- How should AI ethics washing in companies be supervised, and what are the roles of the government and citizens in this?
- Concerning policy mix, how can incentive and regulatory policies complement each other?

Second, there's a need for collective insights into practical design principles for understanding ethical mechanisms technically in the data science field. Citizens can refer to the preceding section of this chapter to prioritize unresolved challenges in data science, contributing to efficient resource allocation for policy decisions. Moreover, citizens' diverse opinions on ethical mechanisms can be communicated to the research community through the government, possibly involving them in the R&D process. On the other hand, the government should explore numerous empirical cases through small-scale testbed projects regarding the relationship between digital governance and technological development (Maffei et al., 2020). Amassing various empirical outcomes, accumulating experience on potential arising challenges, and continually engaging in profound discussions seem essential.

ACKNOWLEDGEMENT

This work was supported by an Electronics and Telecommunications Research Institute (ETRI) grant funded by the Korean government: 23ZR1400, A Study on Technology Policy and Standardization for National Intelligence.

REFERENCES

Ackerman, J. (2004). Co-governance for accountability: beyond "exit" and "voice". *World Development*, 32(3), 447–63.
Ansell, C., & Trondal, J. (2018). Governing turbulence: An organizational-institutional agenda. *Perspectives on Public Management and Governance*, 1(1), 43–57.
Arrieta, A.B., Díaz-Rodríguez, N., Del Ser, J., Bennetot, A., Tabik, S., Barbado, A., ... & Herrera, F. (2020). Explainable Artificial Intelligence (XAI): Concepts, taxonomies, opportunities and challenges toward responsible AI. *Information Fusion*, 58, 82–115.

Bannister, F., & Connolly, R. (2014). ICT, public values and transformative government: A framework and programme for research. *Government Information Quarterly*, 31(1), 119–28.

Bharosa, N. (2022). The rise of GovTech: Trojan horse or blessing in disguise? A research agenda. *Government Information Quarterly*, 39(3), 101692.

Brandsen, T., & Honingh, M. (2018). Definitions of co-production and co-creation. In T. Brandsen & M. Honingh (Eds.), *Co-production and co-creation*. Routledge, 9–17.

Busuioc, M. (2021). Accountable artificial intelligence: Holding algorithms to account. *Public Administration Review*, 81(5), 825–36.

Cao, K., Wei, C., Gaidon, A., Arechiga, N., & Ma, T. (2019). Learning imbalanced datasets with label-distribution-aware margin loss. *Proceeding of the Advances in Neural Information Processing Systems (NeurIPS 2019)*, 32.

Cooper, A.F., Moss, E., Laufer, B., & Nissenbaum, H. (2022). Accountability in an algorithmic society: Relationality, responsibility, and robustness in machine learning. In *Proceedings of the 2022 ACM Conference on Fairness, Accountability, and Transparency* (pp. 864–76).

Cordella, A., & Bonina, C.M. (2012). A public value perspective for ICT enabled public sector reforms: A theoretical reflection. *Government Information Quarterly*, 29(4), 512–20.

Durant, J.R., Evans, G.A., & Thomas, G.P. (1989). The public understanding of science. *Nature*, 340(6228), 11–14.

Eom, S.J., & Lee, J. (2022). Digital government transformation in turbulent times: Responses, challenges, and future direction. *Government Information Quarterly*, 39(2), 101690.

Etienne, H. (2022). When AI ethics goes astray: A case study of autonomous vehicles. *Social Science Computer Review*, 40(1), 236–46.

EU Parliament (2023). EU AI Act: First regulation on artificial intelligence. Accessed September 30, 2023. Available at https://www.europarl.europa.eu/news/en/headlines/society/20230601STO93804/eu-ai-act-first-regulation-on-artificial-intelligence.

Evans, P. (1996). Government action, social capital and development: Reviewing the evidence on synergy. *World Development*, 24(6), 1119–32.

Ferrer, X., van Nuenen, T., Such, J.M., Coté, M., & Criado, N. (2021). Bias and discrimination in AI: A cross-disciplinary perspective. *IEEE Technology and Society Magazine*, 40(2), 72–80.

Guidotti, R., Monreale, A., Ruggieri, S., Turini, F., Giannotti, F., & Pedreschi, D. (2018). A survey of methods for explaining black box models. *ACM Computing Surveys (CSUR)*, 51(5), 1–42.

Hanelt, A., Bohnsack, R., Marz, D., & Antunes Marante, C. (2021). A systematic review of the literature on digital transformation: Insights and implications for strategy and organizational change. *Journal of Management Studies*, 58(5), 1159–97.

Hanisch, M., Goldsby, C.M., Fabian, N.E., & Oehmichen, J. (2023). Digital governance: A conceptual framework and research agenda. *Journal of Business Research*, 162, 113777.

Harrison, T.M., & Luna-Reyes, L.F. (2022). Cultivating trustworthy artificial intelligence in digital government. *Social Science Computer Review*, 40(2), 494–511.

Hong, S., Kim, S.H., & Kwon, M. (2022). Determinants of digital innovation in the public sector. *Government Information Quarterly*, 39(4), 101723.

Hutchinson, B., Smart, A., Hanna, A., Denton, E., Greer, C., Kjartansson, O., ... & Mitchell, M. (2021). Towards accountability for machine learning datasets: Practices from software engineering and infrastructure. In *Proceedings of the 2021 ACM Conference on Fairness, Accountability, and Transparency* (pp. 560–75).

Janssen, M., Brous, P., Estevez, E., Barbosa, L.S., & Janowski, T. (2020). Data governance: Organizing data for trustworthy Artificial Intelligence. *Government Information Quarterly*, 37(3), 101493.

Jobin, A., Ienca, M., & Vayena, E. (2019). The global landscape of AI ethics guidelines. *Nature Machine Intelligence*, 1(9), 389–99.

Joyce, K., Smith-Doerr, L., Alegria, S., Bell, S., Cruz, T., Hoffman, S.G., ... & Shestakofsky, B. (2021). Toward a sociology of artificial intelligence: A call for research on inequalities and structural change. *Socius*, 7, 1–11.

Kaminski, M. E. (2021). The right to explanation, explained. In *Research Handbook on Information Law and Governance*. 278–299. Edward Elgar Publishing.

Kaneda, Y., Pei, Y., Zhao, Q., & Liu, Y. (2015). Improving the performance of the decision boundary making algorithm via outlier detection. *Journal of Information Processing*, 23(4), 497–504.

Koopman, P., & Wagner, M. (2016). Challenges in autonomous vehicle testing and validation. *SAE International Journal of Transportation Safety*, 4(1), 15–24.

Kumar, V., Rajan, B., Venkatesan, R., & Lecinski, J. (2019). Understanding the role of artificial intelligence in personalized engagement marketing. *California Management Review*, 61(4), 135–55.

Lam, W.F. (1996). Institutional design of public agencies and coproduction: A study of irrigation associations in Taiwan. *World Development*, 24(6), 1039–54.

Lee, J.S., & Jun, S.P. (2021). Privacy-preserving data mining for open government data from heterogeneous sources. *Government Information Quarterly*, 38(1), 101544.

Leurent, H., Betti, F., Shook, E., Fuchs, R., & Damrath, F. (2019). Leading through the fourth industrial revolution: putting people at the centre. In *World Economic Forum White paper*. 1–25.

Li, H. (2020). Communication for coproduction: Increasing information credibility to fight the coronavirus. *The American Review of Public Administration*, 50(6–7), 692–7.

Li, T., Sahu, A.K., Talwalkar, A., & Smith, V. (2020). Federated learning: Challenges, methods, and future directions. *IEEE Signal Processing Magazine*, 37(3), 50–60.

Linder, S.H., & Rosenau, P.V. (2000). Mapping the terrain of the public-private policy partnership. In P.V. Rosenau (Ed.), *Public-private policy partnerships*. MIT Press, 1–17.

Linders, D. (2012). From e-government to we-government: Defining a typology for citizen coproduction in the age of social media. *Government Information Quarterly*, 29(4), 446–54.

Lipton, Z.C. (2018). The mythos of model interpretability: In machine learning, the concept of interpretability is both important and slippery. *Queue*, 16(3), 31–57.

Loi, M., & Spielkamp, M. (2021). Towards accountability in the use of artificial intelligence for public administrations. In *Proceedings of the 2021 AAAI/ACM Conference on AI, Ethics, and Society* (pp. 757–66).

Lucas Jr., H., Agarwal, R., Clemons, E.K., El Sawy, O.A., & Weber, B. (2013). Impactful research on transformational information technology: An opportunity to inform new audiences. *MIS Quarterly*, (37)2, 371–82.

Maffei, S., Leoni, F., & Villari, B. (2020). Data-driven anticipatory governance: Emerging scenarios in data for policy practices. *Policy Design and Practice*, 3(2), 123–34.

Majchrzak, A., Markus, M.L., & Wareham, J. (2016). Designing for digital transformation. *MIS Quarterly*, 40(2), 267–78.

Manoharan, A.P., Ingrams, A., Kang, D., & Zhao, H. (2021). Globalization and worldwide best practices in e-government. *International Journal of Public Administration*, 44(6), 465–76.

Meijer, A., & Bolívar, M.P.R. (2016). Governing the smart city: A review of the literature on smart urban governance. *International Review of Administrative Sciences*, 82(2), 392–408.

Mergel, I., Kleibrink, A., & Sörvik, J. (2018). Open data outcomes: US cities between product and process innovation. *Government Information Quarterly*, 35(4), 622–32.

Mergel, I., Edelmann, N., & Haug, N. (2019). Defining digital transformation: Results from expert interviews. *Government Information Quarterly*, 36(4), 101385.

Michalski, R.S. (1983). A theory and methodology of inductive learning. In R.S. Michalski, J.G. Carbonell, & T.M. Mitchell (Eds.), *Machine learning* (pp. 83–134). Morgan Kaufmann.

Mikalef, P., Conboy, K., Lundström, J.E., & Popovič, A. (2022). Thinking responsibly about responsible AI and "the dark side" of AI. *European Journal of Information Systems*, 31(3), 257–68.

Min, O.G., Kim, Y.K., Park, J.Y., Park, J.G., Kim, J.Y., & Lee, Y.K. (2020). ATL 1.0: An Artificial Intelligence technology level definition. *Electronics and Telecommunications Trends*, 35(3), 1–8.

Moore, C., O'Neill, M., O'Sullivan, E., Doröz, Y., & Sunar, B. (2014, June). Practical homomorphic encryption: A survey. In *2014 IEEE International Symposium on Circuits and Systems (ISCAS)* (pp. 2792–95). IEEE.

Nam, T., & Pardo, T.A. (2011). Smart city as urban innovation: Focusing on management, policy, and context. In *Proceedings of the 5th International Conference on Theory and Practice of Electronic Governance* (pp. 185–94).

Nissenbaum, H. (1996). Accountability in a computerized society. *Science and Engineering Ethics*, 2, 25–42.

Ntoutsi, E., Fafalios, P., Gadiraju, U., Iosifidis, V., Nejdl, W., Vidal, M.E., ... & Staab, S. (2020). Bias in data-driven artificial intelligence systems—an introductory survey. *Wiley Interdisciplinary Reviews: Data Mining and Knowledge Discovery*, 10(3), e1356.

OECD (2014). Recommendation of the Council on Digital Government Strategies. Adopted by the OECD Council on 15 July 2014.

OECD (2020-10-07). The OECD Digital Government Policy Framework: Six dimensions of a Digital Government. *OECD Public Governance Policy Paper.* No. 02. OECD Publishing. Paris.

Owen, R., & Pansera, M. (2019). Responsible innovation and responsible research and innovation. *Handbook on Science and Public Policy,* 26–48.

Panagiotopoulos, P., Klievink, B., & Cordella, A. (2019). Public value creation in digital government. *Government Information Quarterly, 36*(4), 101421.

Pang, M.S., Lee, G., & DeLone, W.H. (2014). IT resources, organizational capabilities, and value creation in public-sector organizations: A public-value management perspective. *Journal of Information Technology,* 29, 187–205.

Pansari, A., & Kumar, V. (2017). Customer engagement: the construct, antecedents, and consequences. *Journal of the Academy of Marketing Science,* 45, 294–311.

Pittaway, J.J., & Montazemi, A.R. (2020). Know-how to lead digital transformation: The case of local governments. *Government Information Quarterly,* 37(4), 101474.

Politou, E., Casino, F., Alepis, E., & Patsakis, C. (2019). Blockchain mutability: Challenges and proposed solutions. *IEEE Transactions on Emerging Topics in Computing,* 9(4), 1972–86.

Rajkomar, A., Hardt, M., Howell, M.D., Corrado, G., & Chin, M.H. (2018). Ensuring fairness in machine learning to advance health equity. *Annals of Internal Medicine,* 169(12), 866–72.

Rethemeyer, R.K. (2007). Policymaking in the age of internet: Is the internet tending to make policy networks more or less inclusive? *Journal of Public Administration Research and Theory,* 17(2), 259–84.

Robinson, D., Yu, H., Zeller, W.P., & Felten, E.W. (2008). Government data and the invisible hand. *Yale Journal of Law & Technology,* 11, 159.

Ruggie, J.G. (2014). Global governance and new governance theory: Lessons from business and human rights. *Global Governance,* 20, 5.

Selbst, A.D., & Powles, J. (2018). Meaningful information and the right to explanation. *International Data Privacy Law,* 7(4), 233–42.

Sia, S.K., Soh, C., & Weill, P. (2016). How DBS Bank pursued a digital business strategy. *MIS Quarterly Executive,* 15(2), 105–21.

Soares, R.G., Chen, H., & Yao, X. (2012). Semisupervised classification with cluster regularization. *IEEE Transactions on Neural Networks and Learning Systems,* 23(11), 1779–92.

Speith, T. (2022). A review of taxonomies of explainable artificial intelligence (XAI) methods. In *2022 ACM Conference on Fairness, Accountability, and Transparency* (pp. 2239–50).

Suoniemi, S., Meyer-Waarden, L., Munzel, A., Zablah, A.R., & Straub, D. (2020). Big data and firm performance: The roles of market-directed capabilities and business strategy. *Information & Management,* 57(7), 103365.

Taeihagh, A., & Lim, H.S.M. (2019). Governing autonomous vehicles: Emerging responses for safety, liability, privacy, cybersecurity, and industry risks. *Transport Reviews,* 39(1), 103–28.

Tan, S.Y., Taeihagh, A., & Tripathi, A. (2021). Tensions and antagonistic interactions of risks and ethics of using robotics and autonomous systems in long-term care. *Technological Forecasting and Social Change,* 167, 120686.

Toots, M., Mcbride, K., Kalvet, T., & Krimmer, R. (2017). Open data as enabler of public service co-creation: Exploring the drivers and barriers. In *2017 Conference for E-Democracy and Open Government (CeDEM)* (pp. 102–12). IEEE.

Tsamados, A., Aggarwal, N., Cowls, J., Morley, J., Roberts, H., Taddeo, M., & Floridi, L. (2021). The ethics of algorithms: Key problems and solutions. In L. Floridi (Eds.), *Ethics, Governance, and Policies in Artificial Intelligence* (97–123). Springer Cham.

Van Doorn, J., Lemon, K.N., Mittal, V., Nass, S., Pick, D., Pirner, P., & Verhoef, P.C. (2010). Customer engagement behavior: Theoretical foundations and research directions. *Journal of Service Research,* 13(3), 253–66.

Van Twist, A., Ruijer, E., & Meijer, A. (2023). Smart cities & citizen discontent: A systematic review of the literature. *Government Information Quarterly,* 101799.

Verhoef, P.C., Broekhuizen, T., Bart, Y., Bhattacharya, A., Dong, J.Q., Fabian, N., & Haenlein, M. (2021). Digital transformation: A multidisciplinary reflection and research agenda. *Journal of Business Research*, 122, 889–901.

Vial, G. (2019). Understanding digital transformation: A review and a research agenda. *The Journal of Strategic Information Systems*, 28(2), 118–44.

Yetano, A., Royo, S., & Acerete, B. (2010). What is driving the increasing presence of citizen participation initiatives? *Environment and Planning C: Government and Policy*, 28(5), 783–802.

Yoshida, M., & Thammetar, T. (2021). Education between GovTech and Civic Tech. *International Journal of Emerging Technologies in Learning (iJET)*, 16(4), 52–68.

Yu, H., & Robinson, D.G. (2012). The new ambiguity of "Open Government." *UCLA Law Review*, 59(178), 178–208.

Zheng, L., Kwok, W.M., Aquaro, V., & Qi, X. (2019, April). Digital government, smart cities and sustainable development. In *Proceedings of the 12th International Conference on Theory and Practice of Electronic Governance* (pp. 291–301).

Zheng, Z., Xie, S., Dai, H., Chen, X., & Wang, H. (2017). An overview of blockchain technology: Architecture, consensus, and future trends. In *2017 IEEE International Congress on Big Data (BigData Congress)* (pp. 557–64). IEEE.

16. Delivering on transparency's good governance promise? The state of government data against political corruption

Kristen Rose and Joseph Foti

INTRODUCTION

Part of the promise of big data has been opening up data held by governments. This has meant publishing previously secret datasets, and, increasingly, publishing that data in open data formats. Improvements in the field of data science have allowed governments to more easily make important datasets freely available, well structured, bulk downloadable, and perhaps most importantly, continuously updated. Even more, this has meant supporting users—including internal government users, as well as external users such as civil society organizations, journalists, and interested citizens—to reuse government data as a public good.

The intended consequences of opening up this data, however, are varied. For some, opening up government data is useful for stimulating markets (Publications Office of the European Union, 2020), while others believe it is an essential step in improving the provision of public goods (Jelenic, 2019). A final aim in opening this data, and the subject of this chapter, is to increase government accountability and reduce corruption (Yu & Robinson, 2012).

In that sense, this chapter may vary from other chapters in that it looks less at how governments process data and more to the issue of data about how governments operate, that is, *governance data* rather than *government data*.

Of course, governments use governance data as well for purposes of their own internal accountability and checks and balances. Peixoto (2012) points out that the release of data itself is usually insufficient to change behavior and achieve government accountability, especially when it comes to improving government. He posits that it requires a free press, processes for public input, and actual sanctions or rewards for governments to act on newly revealed information. This is where the government's ability to use data—in concert with the public—is essential. Auditors must be able to access and use fiscal data, contracting data, and data on conflicts of interest. Electoral management boards must be able to evaluate conflicts of interest, political finance data, and asset disclosures.

Before evaluating the capacity of states and citizens to compel change based on this data, however, it is worthwhile to evaluate the existence of that data. Opening data against political corruption consists of publishing certain core datasets that anti-corruption experts have come to see as necessary in order to understand trade in influence and money in politics. This chapter examines the state of high-value datasets that are believed to be part of supporting less corrupt governance.

DEFINING OPEN GOVERNANCE DATA

The word "open" has become a commonly used prefix to advocate for transparency and accessibility across many sectors, including open source, open access, and, most relevant to this chapter, open data (Yu & Robinson, 2012). Open data is especially critical for data science as it helps remove barriers to entry and improve cost-effectiveness. Data that is freely available for anyone to reuse prevents the need for data scientists to collect data themselves. Over time, this benefit both saves money and spurs more innovation.

Governments around the world have adopted open data policies and strategies in the name of democracy, transparency, and accountability. Government data includes both data held by the government (e.g., census data) and data about the operations of the government itself, most especially around how decisions are made by decision-makers, also known as "governance data." Yu and Robinson (2012) argue that this duality diverted much of the initial energy toward government openness away from limiting secrecy about major decisions and toward information on government services. To that end, this chapter attempts to bridge this duality by reviewing the availability of data around government decisions and decision-makers. While not an exhaustive list, those elements which are readily measured by an open government approach are as follows:

Data about decision-makers and interests:

- Asset disclosure
- Political finance
- Company beneficial ownership
- Land ownership and tenure.

Data about decisions:

- Legislative decision-making (Lobbying)
- Administrative decision-making (Rulemaking)
- Agency-level decision-making (Right to Information Performance)
- Awarding of contracts (Public Procurement).

While availability of data is only a proxy for whether actual decisions were subject to undue influence or fraud, it is nonetheless a core part of understanding the availability of open data. Data must be open for data scientists to analyze the information and uncover instances of corruption. The types of information covered in these datasets is discussed in more depth as part of the section titled "Defining Useful Governance Data: High-Value Data Elements."

This chapter will focus on the current state of open governance data around the globe by highlighting existing data gaps and discussing examples of how data scientists can use this data to detect and flag cases of corruption. Specifically, the chapter will highlight open governance data in eight key areas: asset disclosure, political finance, company beneficial ownership, land ownership and tenure, public procurement, lobbying, right to information performance, and rulemaking.

OPEN DATA ELEMENTS

Publishing governance data openly is essential to ensure that key datasets are interoperable, meaning they can be linked to each other. Interoperability increases the ability of government oversight institutions, civil society, journalists, and interested citizens to monitor and flag potential cases of corruption or fraud.

Most stakeholders of the open data movement adhere to the Open Knowledge Foundation's Open Definition for a full, technical definition of open data. A one-sentence version of the Open Definition is that "open data and content can be freely used, modified, and shared by anyone for any purpose" (Open Knowledge Foundation, n.d.). For the purposes of this chapter, open data tangibly consists of five key elements:

1. *Data is freely accessible.* Freely available data allows anyone to contribute to monitoring and oversight of government activity.
2. *Data is openly licensed.* Open licenses prevent restrictions on the reuse or redistribution of data, allowing anyone to use the data for monitoring or analysis purposes.
3. *Data is timely and updated.* Data that is updated regularly can ensure that the public is kept well informed and has the opportunity to flag cases of corruption, potentially before they occur.
4. *Data is machine-readable.* Data is most usable when it is structured and can be read by a computer.
5. *Data is bulk downloadable.* Datasets that are available in bulk, meaning as a whole, can be downloaded easily and efficiently.

DEFINING USEFUL GOVERNANCE DATA: HIGH-VALUE DATA ELEMENTS

While it is critical to publish data in an open format, it is arguably more important to ensure that the actual content of the data captures the most high-value information. In many cases, countries may credit themselves for having a number of datasets available to the public, but a closer look at the data will reveal that the most important information for combating corruption is not included in the published dataset. Examples of high-value information for each policy area are as follows:

- *Asset Disclosure:* Data on public officials' income, in-kind interests, and their family members' assets.
- *Political Finance:* Data on political party/candidates' income and spending, as well as data on donors and their donation amounts.
- *Company Beneficial Ownership:* Data on companies' beneficial owners, including detailed information on their held interests.
- *Land Ownership and Tenure:* Data on natural and legal owners of land, land transactions, and land rights and concessions.
- *Public Procurement:* Data on each phase of the procurement process—from planning to implementation—as well as the cost of contracts, descriptions, and award documentation.

- *Lobbying:* Data on meetings between lobbyists and public officials—including times, topics, expenses, and participants.
- *Right to Information Performance:* Data on information requests received and processed by agencies, including the number of requests, length of response times, and information on information redactions and appeals.
- *Rulemaking:* Data on proposed regulations, public comments, reasoned responses from the government, and challenges to regulations.

For example, although many countries publish data on tenders and awards for public contracts, few publish information on contract implementation. Similarly, many countries publish basic political finance data, but few clearly identify donors to political parties and candidates. And while many countries publish geospatial information as part of their land registers, few countries publish data on who owns the land, which is critical for identifying cases of hidden assets.

GLOBAL SURVEY OF KEY GOVERNANCE DATA[1]

Using data from the Global Data Barometer, a global survey of open data in 109 countries, the *Broken Links* report provides an overview of the state of anti-corruption data in 67 member countries of the Open Government Partnership (OGP). Given that membership in OGP is dependent on meeting certain criteria of government openness, it can be presumed that the state of open data is even worse in non-OGP member countries.

Method

This chapter is the result of primary research carried out by the Global Data Barometer (GDB). The GDB is a global research collaboration that examines government websites for the existence of key datasets and reviews the quality of that data. To the authors' knowledge, the GDB provides the first-ever assessment of the global state of data for some policy areas, such as lobbying and right to information performance, and a detailed and comprehensive overview of available data for other areas, like company beneficial ownership and public procurement. This includes an assessment of data availability for all policy areas featured in the *Broken Links* report, along with a review of legal frameworks governing data collection and publication for all areas except land ownership and tenure and public procurement.

To collect the data used in this chapter, the GDB team partnered with a network of regional hubs to collect the data. With the GDB team's support, the regional hubs recruited and trained experts, mostly in-country researchers, who collected the primary data in 109 countries. During this process, the researchers for each country completed an in-depth survey using the GDB Handbook (Global Data Barometer, 2021). To complement the responses collected in this primary survey, the GDB team also conducted a short government survey in parallel. Governments were invited to provide evidence that a researcher might not be able to find through desk research or interviews.

For many survey responses, researchers provided a written justification and supporting evidence. This includes information such as the URLs to specific laws, policies, or datasets; the latest update date of a dataset; or the file format in which data is available. All supporting evidence (together with the full set of response values) is publicly available online. It is important to note that the researchers assessed only information between May 1, 2019 and May 1, 2021. Any developments that took place after May 1, 2021 are not reflected in this data.

While *Broken Links* focuses specifically on key open governance datasets, the first edition of the GDB also covers datasets across a range of other topics, including climate, health, and public finance. The *Broken Links* sample size is also narrower than that of the GDB, given that the report focuses solely on the 67 OGP member countries included in the Barometer's research, rather than all 109 countries assessed by the GDB. Ten OGP member countries were not included in the first edition of the GDB due to difficulties finding country researchers.

FINDINGS

The following findings summarize the state of anti-corruption data—including key gaps and an overview by policy area—in OGP member countries, based on the first edition of the Global Data Barometer. The section closes with a discussion on the importance of making governance datasets interoperable in order to employ data science approaches for the detection and/or prevention of corruption.

Five Key Gaps of Policy Implementation

While the open data movement's recent rise in popularity has led governments to publish a broad range of information in an open format, few countries are actually publishing the most important data needed to counter political corruption. Globally, countries still face a range of significant challenges in opening anti-corruption data, ranging from a lack of data collection to data that exists, but lacks useful information. These global challenges can be summarized in the form of five key data gaps. These are gaps in collection, publication, high-value elements, usability, and use.

Collection gaps

Many countries do not have laws or regulations in place mandating the collection of anti-corruption data. This is most notable in the area of lobbying, where fewer than a third of OGP countries require the collection of lobbying information (Table 16.1). Between one-quarter and one-third of OGP countries lack legal mandates for the collection of data on beneficial owners, rulemaking, and the performance of right to information systems.

This collection gap exists even in policy areas where most countries have relevant legislation. For example, all OGP countries legally require public officials to submit asset declarations. Yet, in a majority of these countries, government collection of data on assets of other politically exposed persons, like spouses and family members, is not required.

The same issue applies to other areas, like political finance, where nearly all OGP countries legally require political parties and campaigns to submit financial information. Only about half legally require the collection of donation timings and amounts, which are critical to understanding the influence of different actors in the political process.

This all points to the urgent need for greater collection of anti-corruption data. In many cases, these are legal issues, specifically the absence of binding laws and policies that require

Table 16.1 Varying levels of open data maturity by policy area (n = 67)

	Data collection required	Data published	High-value data published*	Open data published**
Asset Disclosure	100%	61%	37%	22%
Political Finance	94%	70%	39%	39%
Company Beneficial Ownership	73%	36%	19%	21%
Land Ownership and Tenure	Not reviewed	57%	19%	16%
Public Procurement	Not reviewed	96%	69%	67%
Lobbying	22%	27%	7%	10%
Right to Information Performance	63%	46%	27%	25%
Rulemaking	72%	63%	22%	16%

Note: * Over half of the defined high-value data elements for the policy area are available online. High-value data elements refer to the useful information content for detecting instances of corruption.
** Published data meets at least three of the following standards: free, timely, machine-readable, openly licensed, bulk downloadable.
Source: Authors' own.

data to be collected or the existence of weak legislation that does not require the collection of more granular, high-value data that can enable effective monitoring.

Publication gaps
Many countries do not publish essential data, even those that legally require its collection. On one end of the spectrum, nearly all OGP countries publish public procurement data online in some form (see Table 16.1). On the other hand, only about one in four OGP countries publish lobbying data, and one in three publish beneficial ownership data. Rates of data availability for the other policy areas fall somewhere in between. For most of these other areas, like asset

disclosure and political finance, about one-third of OGP countries do not publish any data online.

This is evidence of a significant gap between the number of countries requiring data collection and those actually publishing data. Nowhere is this gap wider than in asset declarations, where all OGP countries have a legal requirement that officials submit such information, but less than two-thirds actually publish any information online. Beneficial ownership data is another example; three-quarters of OGP countries require data collection, but only one-third publish any data online.

There are three possible drivers of these publication gaps:

1. *No legal framework:* In some cases, OGP countries lack any sort of legal framework that requires collection—much less publication—of the specific data. Lobbying is a notable example, as mentioned in the previous section.
2. *Weak or unclear legal framework:* In many cases, a legal framework requiring data collection exists, but it does not mandate publication. Beneficial ownership frameworks commonly fall into this category. Nearly three-quarters of OGP countries legally require the collection of beneficial ownership data, but only about one-third require the data to be published.
3. *Non-compliance with the legal framework:* In other cases, legal mandates to publish data exist, but the data is still unavailable. Sometimes, this means that data is closed, like asset declarations submitted to the government that remain unpublished. At other times, this means that data is nonexistent, such as when some political parties or candidates never submitted their financial declarations to begin with, despite legal requirements.

High-value data gaps
Releasing data by itself is not inherently useful. In the case of data to counter political corruption, the content of the data must be useful for determining whether ethics, the rule of law, and democracy are being protected.

Table 16.1 displays the percentage of OGP countries that publish information on at least half of the high-value data elements for each policy area. Looking at public procurement data, for example, over three-quarters publish tenders and awards as data, but fewer than a quarter publish information on implementation—whether a contract was executed and whether taxpayers got good value for their money. By comparison, the other policy areas have far worse gaps. As a result, even in this relatively strong area of procurement, one can see that OGP countries often have significant room for improvement.

Usability gaps
When data is not published according to open data standards, it is more difficult—and often impossible—to process data for accountability and oversight. The specific problems are as follows:

- *Freely accessible:* In some countries, there are high fees for the use of data, it is managed by third parties that charge high fees, or it is available on request only. In the typical OGP country, where data is available online, it is also available for free. While cost may be a barrier in some countries, this is not a typical barrier.

- *Timely and updated:* Anti-corruption data needs to be available as soon as possible for accountability purposes. In the typical OGP country, data is consistently and typically too old to be useful for assessing compliance with laws in the short term.
- *Openly licensed:* Data needs to be freely reusable, whether for accountability purposes or for other uses, including commercial uses. Licenses are unclear or not explicitly open for most datasets in the typical OGP country.
- *Machine-readability:* For accountability and oversight to occur, data needs to be available in structured formats that allow for data reuse, not simply in scanned documents. In most cases, data, while publicly available, is published using non-machine-readable formats, making it difficult to analyze.
- *Bulk downloadable:* In order to be analyzed, data needs to be available as a whole, rather than in multiple spreadsheets or PDF documents. In the typical OGP country, data must be gathered from multiple pages and sources, raising the cost of use.

Table 16.1 shows that—across policy areas—countries do not typically publish data according to open data standards. Public procurement data is the major outlier across policy areas, where two-thirds of OGP countries meet a majority of open data standards. Across most areas of governance data covered in this study, less than a quarter of OGP countries meet open data standards for data publication.

Use gaps

A final gap is that capacity to use the data, in many cases, is lacking. Investigators in only five of the 68 surveyed OGP countries documented notable uses of anti-corruption data by watchdogs. This is likely an underreporting of use cases, since it is entirely reasonable that researchers did not catch all examples of use in a country. Nonetheless, the low number of documented examples suggests that this does not yet show overwhelming use of the data by the public. It will be fruitful for future studies to identify whether user capacity, the relative newness of the data in many countries, the technical nature of some datasets, or lack of available and useful data is the binding constraint for each policy area.

Data by Policy Area

While unique skills are necessary to identify and prevent corruption across each of the following areas, certain applications of data science are consistently useful across all areas. Before governance data can be properly published or analyzed, it needs to be collected. Data scientists are key to designing collection systems that can output clean and structured data. In addition, collection systems can be designed to automatically validate data, identify outliers, and flag potential cases of falsification. Governments that invest in building structured, accessible datasets with minimal errors prior to data publication will likely see much more user traffic than governments who publish complex, unstructured, or error-riddled datasets.

Current global data gaps exist to varying extents depending on the policy area. For example, most OGP countries (96 percent) publish at least some public procurement data online, and most of these datasets include high-value elements in open data formats (see Table 16.1). On the other end of the spectrum, only a quarter of OGP countries publish any lobbying data, with even fewer legally requiring its collection. Levels of maturity, therefore, vary significantly by policy area.

One exception is the publication of high-value data, as it is largely absent across all policy areas. These high-value elements are different for each policy area and critical for accountability. For example, most OGP countries publish which goods and services are being procured, but very few publish information on spending against contracts, which is essential for monitoring results.

Asset disclosure
Asset disclosure data includes information on the assets, liabilities, and finances of elected and senior-appointed government officials, along with their family members and closest associates. Making asset disclosure data publicly available helps to prevent, detect, and sanction illicit enrichment of public officials, along with conflicts of interest and cases of favoritism (Jenkins, 2015). Other benefits of effective asset disclosure systems include detecting and recovering stolen assets (Burdescu et al., 2009), along with increasing public confidence in government officials (World Bank; United Nations Office on Drugs and Crime, 2012).

Due to OGP eligibility requirements, all OGP countries have legal frameworks that require the collection of asset disclosure data. Three-fifths of these countries currently make the data publicly available online. However, less than 20 percent of the datasets that are currently available online are machine-readable. Without machine-readability, data scientists, along with the broader public, are unable to efficiently use the data for monitoring and accountability purposes.

Where asset disclosure datasets are publicly available, data scientists—both inside and outside of the government—can use the data to scrutinize suspicious activity or unexplained changes in wealth and verify reported declarations against other public registers, including land, company, and beneficial ownership registers. Other data science approaches to asset disclosure data could include tying public officials' interests to pending or ongoing legislation and regulations in order to check for potential conflicts.

Political finance
Political finance data features information on financial flows to and from political parties, candidates, and third parties, including income, expenses, and donations. Publicly available political finance data allows for increased scrutiny of fundraising (International IDEA and Open Government Partnership, 2019), identification of foreign interference (Ellena & Shein, n.d.), and reduced corruption in government decision-making.

Nearly three-quarters of OGP governments publish at least some political finance data online. This stands in stark contrast to non-OGP countries, where only about one in six publish any data online. However, existing political finance datasets in OGP countries are typically missing many pieces of high-value information. For example, only half of these datasets in OGP countries include names of donors, and far fewer include donors' employment information, which is needed to spot cases of legal entities subdividing donations and channeling them through employees.

While nearly all political finance datasets in OGP countries are available at no cost, only about one-third are machine-readable and licensed for reuse. One in five OGP countries makes the data available for bulk download. In many cases, political party financial statements are only available as scanned forms in PDF format, which requires users to manually review them to track income and expenses.

Delivering on transparency's good governance promise? 291

While journalists are some of the most common monitors of political finance datasets, data scientists have a unique perspective and more modern skills to contribute to the field. For example, data science approaches include automatically detecting unusual campaign donations, applying natural language processing techniques to donor occupation fields, and even linking donor names with their biographic information and professional networks using Wikipedia (Investigative Reporters and Editors, n.d.).

Company beneficial ownership

Disclosing beneficial owners—those who ultimately control or profit from a business—has emerged as an important tool to fight corruption, particularly the misuse of shell companies. Shell companies have been found to be the major means by which the proceeds of criminal activities move across boundaries (Pacini, Lin & Patterson, 2021). Company beneficial ownership data features information on people who own, control, or benefit from companies, including the nature and size of the interest they hold. Beneficial ownership transparency helps governments limit tax evasion (Obermaier & Obermayer, 2018) and identify money laundering activities (Kupfer & Flydal, 2022).

Just over one-third of OGP governments currently publish beneficial ownership data online in some form. However, this number is expected to increase in the coming years, as beneficial ownership transparency has seen increased support around the globe. Three-quarters of OGP countries now have an operational legal framework that requires the collection of beneficial ownership information, compared to less than half of countries in 2019.

While most beneficial ownership datasets include some identifying information for beneficial owners, few countries are publishing information on interests held by beneficial owners or disaggregating data by sex or gender. In addition to missing content, the format of the data remains an area of growth for many countries. Less than half of beneficial ownership datasets are machine-readable, and even fewer are bulk downloadable. For these reasons, data analysis can be costly and time-intensive for users.

Only one in six OGP countries publish beneficial ownership data that follows an international standard, such as the Beneficial Ownership Data Standard (BODS). The BODS provides technical requirements for the design, collection, and publication of structured beneficial ownership data (Open Ownership, 2021). When this standard is followed, users can apply data science approaches, including machine learning techniques, to flag suspicious ownership patterns, cross-reference owners with other datasets, and create innovative technologies for due diligence.

Land ownership and tenure

As a major source of wealth, land transactions are both targets of corruption and destinations for ill-gotten gains. Governments can combat this by opening up land ownership and tenure data, including information on who owns land and the type of tenure, including state, communal, and open access lands. Numerous benefits stem from open land data, such as the detection of corruption (Davies & May, 2019), fairer transactions, and the protection of legal rights to land (Notess et al., 2018).

Just over half of OGP countries currently publish data about land ownership and tenure online, yet few countries publish the data in a machine-readable format, make it available for bulk download, or update it regularly. Additionally, information on the entities that hold land tenure is scarce. Of the 38 OGP countries that were found to publish data on land, less than half included information on legal owners and around one-quarter included information on the individual beneficiaries. When this information is not available to the public, corrupt actors can more easily hide wealth, evade taxes, and engage in money laundering.

Land data has a wealth of potential data science applications. For example, the geospatial attributes of land datasets provide opportunities for rich visualizations. Regarding land ownership and tenure data, specifically, data science techniques are critical in linking this data with other important governance data, including company beneficial ownership, asset disclosure, and public procurement data. For the purposes of anti-corruption, land ownership data is much more valuable when combined with other high-value datasets. Data science approaches can be used to flag suspicious cases, where it is possible that corrupt actors are hiding their wealth and assets in land.

Public procurement
Governments spend anywhere from tens of billions to trillions of dollars on public contracts each year, but complete information is published openly on less than 3 percent of these contract dollars (Open Contracting Partnership, 2020). Complete public procurement datasets include information on the government purchase of goods, services, and public works, including names of suppliers, dates, costs, and details on each stage of the contract cycle. Opening data on public procurement—a process also known as open contracting—has been shown to increase competition (Adam et al., 2021), improve the quality of public services (Majeed, 2013), and ensure governments receive better value for their money (Brown, 2016).

Procurement data is widely available across the globe; 96 percent of OGP countries publish procurement data online, and nearly two-thirds of procurement datasets are machine-readable. Most datasets tend to focus on the tender and award stages of procurement. While some datasets lack information on contract specifics and implementation, public procurement data is, by far, the most advanced area of open anti-corruption data.

Forty percent of procurement datasets in OGP countries are published according to a relevant data standard, most typically the Open Contracting Data Standard (OCDS). The OCDS provides technical guidance for the collection and publication of structured procurement data in order to fit a range of user needs. Users can more easily conduct analysis and apply data science approaches to procurement data that follows the OCDS. Potential data science use cases include analyzing fairness and efficiency of government contracts, creating red-flagging methods for potential cases of corruption, and linking procurement data to other datasets, including government spending data and beneficial ownership data, for monitoring and accountability purposes (Parra, n.d.).

Lobbying
Creating a transparent lobbying register is one of the major measures to ensure that access to public officials is open, accessible, and ethical. Lobbying data features information on who influences policies and decisions, including details of interactions with public officials such as dates and times, topics, and money spent. Lobbying transparency allows for input from more diverse interests (Sahd & Valenzuela, 2016), enables flagging of conflicts of interest and potential cases of corruption (OECD, n.d.), and supports responsible corporate lobbying (Principles for Responsible Investment, 2018).

Very few OGP countries publish lobbying data. Eighteen of the 67 surveyed OGP countries make some lobbying information available online, meaning nearly three-quarters of OGP countries do not publish any form of lobbying data. While most countries that publish lobbying data do so because of legal requirements, four OGP countries publish lobbying data despite an absence of legislation. Of the 18 countries that do publish lobbying data, however, only a handful include information on the meeting topics, duration of meetings, or money spent on lobbying activities.

While information on lobbying is limited in most countries, it is a topic that receives a fair amount of public interest. Where lobbying data exists, data science is necessary to translate complex data into accessible information for the general public. For example, the Massachusetts Institute of Technology's LobbyView database, built using data parsing and customized algorithms, provides firm-level lobbying data for the United States. In addition to searchable data and custom visualizations, LobbyView employs common identifiers for lobbyists that allow users to use the data in conjunction with other datasets (Massachusetts Institute of Technology, n.d.).

Right to information performance

Data on performance of public authorities can help measure progress or regress, aid learning and accountability, and help prioritize reforms. Specifically, opening right to information performance data includes publishing information on the implementation of right to information laws, including the number of requests, delays, denials, and appeals.

Most OGP countries require reporting on each agency's implementation of the country's respective right to information law. However, less than half of countries currently publish the performance data. Most of these datasets include information on the number of requests submitted, but less than half include details about how long it took to fulfill a request, materials withheld and reasons for holding it, appeals to right to information determinations and their results, and the relevant agency or department. The limited coverage of publicly available data limits the ability of stakeholders to analyze and track whether data is being adequately shared and whether agencies are complying with the law.

Data science approaches can be applied to right to information performance data in order to analyze compliance rates with right to information laws and understand why information is being withheld from the public. Performance data can be visualized to show which agencies or departments are least compliant with the law—in terms of number of materials withheld or average wait time for response to request. Natural language processing techniques can also be used to parse through agencies' reasons for withholding information, appeals to determinations, and the subsequent results of those appeals to extract key patterns and themes.

Rulemaking

Transparency of public consultations—or rulemaking—provides the public with a greater understanding of who is trying to influence policy and how well the government is doing at soliciting and implementing public comments. Rulemaking data features information on the process of drafting regulations, including proposed regulations, public comments, reasoned responses, final regulations and justifications, and challenges. Increased transparency of rulemaking has many documented benefits, including increased fairness in the implementation of laws (Coglianese et al., 2009), greater compliance with laws (Radaelli, 2003), and higher levels of economic growth (Shim & Eom, 2008).

Nearly two-thirds of OGP countries publish some rulemaking data online. Most datasets include the text of proposed regulations, while fewer include final regulations, links to public comments, and supporting documentation. A small number of countries link rulemaking data to legal challenges. Most rulemaking datasets are free but not machine-readable, and this lack of structured data makes it more difficult for the public to reuse and analyze the data.

Data science approaches have a key role in analyzing rulemaking datasets. Proposed regulations, especially those related to major or controversial legislation, could have thousands of public comments available online. Natural language processing is one approach that can be used to parse through these comments and extract key themes to better understand public input. The United Kingdom's Office for National Statistics, for example, used word collocation and term frequency–inverse document frequency techniques to understand the context of key phrases used by supporters and opponents of a Wales government bill (Joshi, 2019).

Interoperability

Corruption often doesn't involve only a single act, type of act, or actor, but rather entails networks and flows. Data can be a critical tool in tracking illicit financial flows and otherwise fighting corruption, but when the relevant datasets are not interoperable, it may offer only a fragmentary picture. However, making such data interoperable—for example, using the same unique identifiers across different types of datasets—makes it increasingly useful.

Interoperability is essential for data to be useful for different sectors of society, including government regulators, the press, watchdog groups, the private sector, and interested citizens. Ensuring that data is standardized allows these organizations to recombine it with other datasets and information at a speed and rate that is otherwise impossible without some standardization for interoperability.

Most OGP countries do not employ common identifiers for the simple reason that they do not publish all of the relevant datasets. As countries move to develop data collection, validation, and publication systems, they can do so knowing that it will save time and make data more useful to collect certain data in relational and reusable databases.

Where data is available in OGP countries, there is evidence that at least some of the datasets employ useful common indicators. Company beneficial ownership data is harmonized between datasets most frequently. Perhaps because it is one of the newest areas, company identifying data is frequently used across multiple datasets and policy areas.

On the other hand, lobbying data tends to have low amounts of interoperability. Publishing lobbying data, in general, is rarely required. It thus follows that lobbying data is rarely published in a way that allows for linking up data. As lobbying transparency becomes more popular around the globe, there is opportunity to build datasets with common identifiers that will allow for interoperability with other government data.

BEYOND OPEN DATA

While it is critical to collect and publish high-quality datasets—in terms of content, format, and interoperability—it is not, by any means, the final step for governments looking to combat corruption. Rather, governments must also establish systems that hold actors accountable once users have identified cases of corruption via open governance datasets. The final section of this chapter will focus on how governments can integrate online datasets with oversight mechanisms to create a more direct link between transparency and accountability.

Turning Transparency into Accountability

Transparency and accountability are foundational characteristics of good governance. The intuitive belief is that transparency will, by default, lead to increased accountability, specifically, detection and prosecution of corruption. This relationship is only true under certain conditions, however (Fox, 2007).

In most cases, governments do not publish the most important information, opting instead to publish datasets filled with critical gaps in order to qualify as "transparent." And often, making sense of what is considered "transparent government information" requires heavy investment from civil society organizations or individuals who are willing to sort complex or messy data into clear and accessible information for the public (Peixoto, 2012).

In addition to the broad spectrums of transparency and accountability, accountability only occurs in situations where independent watchdog organizations can act on that data. This requires some amount of democracy. If press freedoms are not protected, politically important data and its consequential findings may not reach the public eye. And when elections are not free and fair, political actors do not have to worry about answering to the public for their blatant acts of corruption (Peixoto, 2012).

Given the need for these enabling, it may not be surprising that some less democratic regimes also happen to be some of the most transparent. For example, the Global Data Barometer (2021) found that Russia is among the countries with the most publicly available procurement data. This transparency allows Russian citizens to bear witness to acts of favoritism or nepotism in the procurement of government contracts, but they have little to no power to actually hold officials to account for criminal activities.

Providing Channels for Action

While publishing high-quality, interoperable data and ensuring that it is used by a range of stakeholders is important, it is not enough on its own. Governments must also create and maintain a strong enabling environment that allows stakeholders—both internal government users and external public users—to monitor and flag potential cases of corruption.

Evidence from numerous open data initiatives has shown that, when paired with accountability mechanisms, open data is more effective. The 2020 World Development report highlights the importance of sanctions for non-compliance with asset disclosure regimes and the usefulness of interoperability (World Bank, 2020). In the case of fiscal abuse and fraud, ensuring that whistleblowers can report on cases of abuse is overwhelmingly the primary means of detection of illegal acts (ACFE, 2022). In cases where the public can flag complaints such as the EU public procurement tenders process, there are estimated cost savings of 2–3 percent (Bauhr et al., 2017). Of course, evidence of the wide-scale efficacy of other open data initiatives remains scant, especially where policies are rarely adopted or where follow-up is rare, such as with lobbying disclosure.

In conclusion, while open data, by itself, will not lead to preventing corruption, there is growing evidence that it is an effective part of the solution. Before corruption can be reduced fully, however, governments will need to more widely adopt policies and practices of disclosure to address core risks.

NOTE

1. This section is an abridged version of the Open Government Partnership's (OGP) 2022 report, *Broken Links: Open Data to Advance Accountability and Combat Corruption*.

REFERENCES

Adam, I., Hernandez Sanchez, A., & Fazekas, M. (2021, July 20). Global public procurement open competition index. Government Transparency Institute. Retrieved from https://www.govtransparency.eu/global-public-procurement-open-competition-index/

Association of Certified Fraud Examiners (ACFE). (2022). *Occupational Fraud 2022: A Report to the Nations*. Retrieved from https://acfepublic.s3.us-west-2.amazonaws.com/2022+Report+to+the+Nations.pdf

Bauhr, M., Czibik, A., Fazekas, M., & de Fine Licht, J. 2017. Lights on the shadows of public procurement: Transparency in government contracting as an antidote to corruption? Digiwhist. Retrieved from http://digiwhist.eu/wp-content/uploads/2017/09/D3.2-Light-on-the-Shadows-of-Public-Procurement_corr.pdf

Brown, S. (2016, November 28). "Everyone sees everything": Overhauling Ukraine's corrupt contracting sector. Medium. Retrieved from https://medium.com/open-contracting-stories/everyone-sees-everything-fa6df0d00335

Burdescu, R., Reid, G.J., Gilman, S., & Trapnell, S. (2009). Income and asset declarations: Tools and trade-offs. World Bank. Retrieved from https://documents.worldbank.org/en/publication/documents-reports/documentdetail/126741468151478453/income-and-asset-declarations-tools-and-trade-offs

Coglianese, C., Kilmartin, H., & Mendelson, E. (2009, June). Transparency and public participation in the rulemaking process: Recommendations for the new administration. Penn Carey Law: Legal Scholarship Repository. Retrieved from https://scholarship.law.upenn.edu/faculty_scholarship/238/

Davies, T., & May, L. (2019, October). *Open Land Data in the Fight against Corruption—Discussion Report*. Land Portal. Retrieved from https://landportal.org/node/85879

Ellena, K., & Shein, E. (n.d.). The dark side of democracy. Foreign Policy. Retrieved from https://foreignpolicy.com/sponsored/the-dark-side-of-democracy/

Fox, J. (2007). The uncertain relationship between transparency and accountability. *Development in Practice*, 17(4–5), 663–71. https://doi.org/10.1080/09614520701469955

Global Data Barometer. (2021). *Global Data Barometer Handbook*. Retrieved January 6, 2023, from https://handbook.globaldatabarometer.org/2021/

International IDEA and Open Government Partnership. (2019). Political finance transparency. Retrieved from https://www.idea.int/publications/catalogue/political-finance-transparency

Investigative Reporters and Editors. (n.d.). Data science, meet campaign finance. Retrieved from https://www.ire.org/data-science-meet-campaign-finance/

Jelenic, M.C. (2019). From theory to practice: Open government data, accountability, and service delivery. Washington, DC: World Bank. Retrieved from https://openknowledge.worldbank.org/handle/10986/31800

Jenkins, M. (2015). Topic guide: Interest and asset disclosure. Transparency International Knowledge Hub. Retrieved from https://knowledgehub.transparency.org/guide/topic-guide-on-interest-and-asset-disclosure/5361

Joshi, C. (2019, September 12). Automating consultation analysis. Data Science for Public Good. Retrieved from https://datasciencecampus.ons.gov.uk/projects/automating-consultation-analysis/

Kupfer, M., & Flydal, E.F. (2022, May 3). Dubai uncovered: Data leak exposes how criminals, officials, and sanctioned politicians poured money into Dubai real estate. Organized Crime and Corruption Reporting Project. Retrieved from https://www.occrp.org/en/investigations/dubai-uncovered-data-leak-exposes-how-criminals-officials-and-sanctioned-politicians-poured-money-into-dubai-real-estate

Majeed, R. (2013). Promoting accountability, monitoring services: Textbook procurement and delivery, the Philippines, 2002–2005. Innovations for Successful Societies. Retrieved from https://successfulsocieties.princeton.edu/publications/promoting-accountability-monitoring-services-textbook-procurement-and-delivery

Massachusetts Institute of Technology. (n.d.). LobbyView. Retrieved from https://polisci.mit.edu/research/projects/lobbyview

Notess, L., Veit, P., Monterroso, I., Andiko, Sulle, E., Larson, A.M., Gindroz, A.-S., Quaedvlieg, J., & Williams, A. (2018). The scramble for land rights: Reducing inequity between communities and companies. World Resources Institute. Retrieved from https://www.wri.org/research/scramble-land-rights

Obermaier, F., & Obermayer, B. (2018, April 3). Oligarchs hide billions in shell companies. Here's how we stop them. *Guardian*. Retrieved from https://www.theguardian.com/world/commentisfree/2018/apr/03/public-registries-shell-panama-papers

OECD. (n.d.). Lobbying in the 21st century transparency, integrity and access. Retrieved from https://www.oecd.org/corruption-integrity/reports/lobbying-in-the-21st-century-c6d8eff8-en.html

Open Contracting Partnership. (2020). How governments spend: Opening up the value of global public procurement. Retrieved from https://www.open-contracting.org/what-is-open-contracting/global-procurement-spend/

Open Government Partnership. (2022). *Broken Links: Open Data to Advance Accountability and Combat Corruption*. Retrieved from https://www.opengovpartnership.org/broken-links/

Open Knowledge Foundation. (n.d.). Open definition. Retrieved from https://opendefinition.org/

Open Ownership. (2021, July). Principles for effective beneficial ownership disclosure. Retrieved from https://www.openownership.org/en/principles/

Pacini, C., Lin, J.W., & Patterson, G. (2021). Using shell entities for money laundering: methods, consequences, and policy implications. *Journal of Forensic and Investigative Accounting, 13*(1), January–June, 73.

Parra, R. (n.d.). *Analyzing Open Contracting data: A Manual Using the R Programming Language*. Open Contracting Partnership. Retrieved from https://open-contracting.github.io/ocds-r-manual/

Peixoto, T. (2012). The uncertain relationship between open data and accountability: Response to Yu and Robinson's the New Ambiguity of Open Government. *UCLA Law Review Discourse, 60*, 200–13.

Principles for Responsible Investment. (2018, May 30). Converging on climate lobbying: Aligning corporate practice with investor expectations. Retrieved from https://www.unpri.org/climate-change/converging-on-climate-lobbying-aligning-corporate-practice-with-investor-expectations-/3174.article

Publications Office of the European Union, Berends, J., Carrara, W., Radu, C. (2020). The economic benefits of open data. Publications Office. Retrieved from https://data.europa.eu/doi/10.2830/081754

Radaelli, C.M. (2003, March 1). The open method of coordination: A new governance architecture for the European Union? Retrieved from https://ore.exeter.ac.uk/repository/handle/10036/22489

Sahd, J., & Valenzuela, C. (2016, December). Lobby law in Chile: Democratizing access to public authorities. Open Government Partnership. Retrieved from https://www.opengovpartnership.org/wp-content/uploads/2001/01/report_Lobby-law-in-Chile.pdf

Shim, D.C., & Eom, T.H. (2008). E-government and anti-corruption: Empirical analysis of international data. *International Journal of Public Administration, 31*(3), 298–316. https://doi.org/10.1080/01900690701590553

World Bank. (2020). *Asset and Interest Disclosure. Global Report: Enhancing Government Effectiveness and Transparency: The Fight against Corruption*. Washington, DC: World Bank.

World Bank; United Nations Office on Drugs and Crime. (2012). Income and asset disclosure: An introduction. In *Public Office, Private Interests: Accountability through Income and Asset Disclosure* (pp. 7–21). World Bank.

Yu, H., & Robinson, D.G. (2012). The new ambiguity of "Open Government". *SSRN Electronic Journal*. https://doi.org/10.2139/ssrn.2012489

17. System update: emerging transparency and oversight functions for responsible data use
Joseph Foti, Tara Davis and Divij Joshi

THE RISE OF BIG DATA AND DATA-DRIVEN POLICYMAKING

The use of data has been essential to the development of the state and the activities of government as long as there has been a claim to a monopoly of violence (Weber, 1978). Rationalization, reduction, and legibility are essential processes to the administration and taming of wild and complicated phenomena such as creating identification numbers for individuals and houses to counting tax in its many forms (Scott, 1998).

What has changed in recent years are the intensity of data use and the changing context. The sheer quantity of data ("big data") and the pervasiveness of data created in everyday transactions (Tisné, 2018) mark increasing risks and rewards of data processing. The context continues to evolve as non-state actors increasingly reuse government data and governments continue to evolve new uses of such data – from data mining to detect fraud to predicting group behavior in elections.

High-profile cases of data misuse have led governments to begin regulating certain uses of data and encouraging the reuse of other types of data. Such undertakings must balance the protection and promotion of fundamental rights, especially privacy and protection from discrimination, with the need for innovation (Hoffmann-Rhiem, 2020; Marsch, 2020). Given that need to balance, numerous approaches have emerged, often in combination. These range from allowing government agencies or industry to "self-regulate" or to set voluntary guidance or standards, to strict command-and-control approaches including banning certain technologies. Across this range of approaches, they may create mechanisms that intentionally introduce elements of public oversight, allowing the public to oversee data use and sound "alarms" when a violation of rights has occurred. These approaches largely fall into the categories of "public accountability" and "transparency."

After outlining some of the potential and real harms of government use of big data, this chapter shifts to an overview of a subset of regulatory tools that governments are increasingly using to begin to tackle some of these issues, with a focus on approaches using public accountability and transparency. This chapter pays special attention to these measures meant to empower non-government actors, as they may often be seen as a middle pathway between command-and-control regulation and a laissez-faire approach.

UNDERSTANDING POTENTIAL AND REALIZED HARMS

In order to evaluate the potential role of government regulation, one must first understand the list of potential harms. This gives a better sense of where regulatory approaches may be most appropriate, and more specifically, where public involvement in maintaining norms would be appropriate.

Individual Harms

Privacy
The principal focus of legislation and regulation thus far has been on privacy. The aim of such legislation has been to limit state intrusion into the private lives of individuals. In some cases, this has been extended to include requirements for the private sector and other non-state "data processors." The stated policy aims of these privacy protections include:

1. Conformity to international human rights standards and constitutions (ECHR, 2022).
2. Protection from the risk of surveillance, and with it, the threats of violence, intimidation, or manipulation by state and non-state actors (EDPS, 2010, US Supreme Court 2013).
3. Division between public and private spheres (see, for example, the My Health Records Act (2012) in Australia).
4. Consumer protection (see, for example, California's Consumer Privacy Act or CCPA, 2018).

Bias and discrimination
Beyond privacy, there is growing evidence that data systems and decision-making built on top of that data may perpetuate or exacerbate bias already extant in society. For example, a court in the Netherlands invalidated software aimed at detecting housing fraud, finding that it was resulting in discrimination and undue denial of public services (ten Seldam & Brenninkmeijer 2021). The causes of discrimination or bias may be multiple. The data sets upon which decisions and automated decision-making are based ("training data") may be biased in terms of their sample. The processes for decision-making on such data (both automated and human) may be built in such a way that they overemphasize variables which are illegal or which otherwise result in discrimination.

Collective Harms

Beyond personal data protection arguments, there are issues of collective harm.

- Competition: Data may be collected by governments or companies, which can be reused to put particular market participants at a competitive disadvantage, allowing collusive or monopolistic behavior (Center for Global Development, 2014). Inadequate protection of commercial information can result in the theft of intellectual property or trade secrets. Waples (1974) and Kwoka (2016) have documented how companies use government records to conduct industrial espionage.
- Public goods: A further argument has been made that there are harms to public goods that may come from the use of government data. In particular, the use of private sector data combined with publicly available data can be used to manipulate public opinion. In turn, this can be used to erode public confidence, social solidarity, and democratic freedoms. In the public sector, this can most clearly be seen in declining democracies (including Hungary, Malaysia, and parts of the United States) where voter and demographic data

have been harnessed with algorithms that reduce electoral competition and favor more extreme candidates (Hong and Kim, 2016; Wylie, 2019).

Harm Reduction Opportunities

As Hoffmann-Rhiem (2020) points out, safeguards must be balanced against the opportunities that more advanced forms of data science and innovation may bring. In the case of governance, as much as systems may risk reproducing bias, they also may be able to identify patterns of bias or other forms of unfairness, abuse, or inefficiency in public sector processes. For example, Hamilton and Piper's 2022 review of bias in public broadcasting in Canada and publicly available open criminal records data allowed Hou and Truex (2022) to identify cases of ethnic bias in Chinese drug courts. Therefore, a best-fit regulatory environment will constantly seek to balance innovation with the protection of individuals and communities, and providing public goods. In cases where innovation can help address existing harms or biases, it can actually encourage, rather than curtail, data processing activities. This is to be kept in mind when weighing regulatory options.

Other chapters will likely deal with these particular risks and harms in greater detail. The majority of this chapter will, instead, focus on the relatively new set of regulatory tools introduced to establish guardrails in both public sector data and private sector data processing that touches on the personal and public spheres.

OPEN GOVERNMENT REGULATORY APPROACHES

Increasingly, governments are introducing regulatory tools to establish guardrails and incentives for the use of data processing in government operations. These approaches aim to minimize harms to individual and collective goods.

This chapter focuses specifically on regulatory approaches characterized by an open government approach. Such an approach is outlined in great detail and precision in Piotrowski, Ingrams, and Berliner (2022). In short, such an approach centers around the values of access to information, civic participation, and public accountability. While regulatory approaches will necessarily be broader than an open government approach – including direct law enforcement, self-regulation by industry, or voluntary codes of conduct, for example – an open government approach will necessarily be a component.

In the interest of brevity, this chapter cannot go into all of the motivations for such an approach. Decades of policy, activism, and research show that such an approach is often justified both in normative terms – human rights, democratic accountability, need for rationality and reason-giving – and in practical terms. Issues may be too complex and require trade-offs, thus requiring greater public participation. Monitoring or enforcement may be too costly for state actors or may be undesirable (McCubbins and Schwartz, 1984)

The following proceeds from foundational elements (laws and basic organizational elements) before proceeding to a growing set of information disclosure and public accountability and oversight practices. The chapter does not emphasize the role of the private sector except as contractors for the government, as that is beyond the scope of government data science.

BASIC FRAMEWORKS

Although the emphasis of this section is on public accountability and transparency measures, in order for those systems to operate, there need to be basic systems in place to ensure that frameworks are established.

Framework Data Policies

Framework data governance policies establish key legal terminology, assign mandates to various government institutions, and establish the rights and obligations of different parties. The most famous among these is the General Data Protection Regulation (European Union 2016) in Europe. Many such as the GDPR cover government data processing as well as private sector processing of data. Similar laws exist around the world, from Brazil (2018) to South Africa (2013) to Thailand (2019). Notably, some countries, such as the United States, do not have framework data laws, even within the federal government.

Policies differ in their primary orientation. An early wave of data protection laws, especially in African countries, finds its inspiration in the *African Union Convention on Cybersecurity and Personal Data Protection* (the "Malabo Convention", 2014) and the push for greater cybersecurity in the early twenty-first century. Whereas the European GDPR law has its roots in the human right to privacy, other laws have their roots in consumer protection, such as the California Consumer Protection Act in the United States.

The consequences of these differences give rise to differing emphases on what must be disclosed and what merits an official response. Most important is how these policies establish who suffers a "harm" as a result of improper data processing. Consumer-oriented laws may cover issues of data breaches from a personal data protection perspective and seek corrections for problems arising from neglectful behavior. This differs from human rights law, which seeks to balance the right to privacy with other rights (most especially the right to information), and from security-based measures, including the protection of children (Davis, 2021; US, 1998)

Most of these data protection framework laws include:

- Definitions of data processing (including collection, use, transfer, and disposal).
- Defining data processors (including whether government and private actors are counted as data processors).
- Data protection authorities and mandates. Official bodies may solely investigate issues of data processing, while others, such as Mexico, establish a dual role for information regulators in both the promotion of the right to information and data protection.
- Disclosure regimes. Transparency and disclosure are regular parts of data protection regimes. These may include the establishment of public processing registers, impact assessment requirements, consent-based explanations, and other forms of informing users about their rights. (See "Content-Nased Transparency" below.)
- Identifying harms and means of redress and remedy. Many framework laws establish what types of harm a member of the public can suffer at the hands of processors and what options they have for seeking redress and remedy.

Principles and Guidelines for Data Processing

In contrast with the hard data protection laws highlighted in the section above, many countries and agencies have adopted principles and guidelines for data processing by government. This may be a substitute for law when a government has not yet passed a law or existing law does not cover particular risks.

Principles and guidelines for data processing are non-binding, normative guidance on ethical principles and values for public agencies to follow. These documents generally identify high-level policy goals and how they might be implicated in the use of data processing operations by public agencies (Taylor, Leenes, and Schendel, 2017). Uruguay's AI Strategy for Digital Government, for example, outlines several guiding principles for the use of artificial intelligence (AI) in government, including "general interest," "respect for human rights," "transparency," and "privacy by design" (Digital Government Agency, 2020).

Policies that articulate high-level principles or guidelines are generally not intended to be binding and are issued as normative standards against which agencies can assess their own use of data processing systems. Often, as non-binding and standalone principles, these do not create any enforceable obligations (Metzinger, 2019; Hagendorff, 2020), but they can provide useful aids and guidance for public agencies confronted with questions about the appropriate use of data processing systems. They can also serve as declarations of intent about the broader goals of administrations in the development of public policy for data processing systems.

The UK Data Ethics Framework provides a useful example of such formal guidance. First published in 2018 and updated in 2020 (United Kingdom, 2020), ut provides guidance on "appropriate and responsible data use" within the government and public sector, which includes guidance on the algorithmic processing of data. The framework emphasizes three overarching principles – transparency, fairness, and accountability – and provides actionable guidance on how these principles can be translated into specific actions taken by agencies while using data in the course of a project. The framework emphasizes that agencies should understand and articulate the public benefit of using data-based systems, comply with legal requirements of privacy and equality, review data for bias and limitations, and ensure organizational diversity.

Data Protection Authorities

Numerous countries have laws which establish an oversight role or "Data Protection Authority" (DPA). In the context of government data science, these bodies have the role of ensuring that public agencies act within the law, and, when they do not, that adequate corrections are made. This body may have various responsibilities and mandates, ranging from purely informational to full powers of enforcement.

Typically, the authorities are independent, tasked with data protection. Alternatively, many countries have expanded the mandate of their commissions on the right to information, with the express logic that these agencies are best placed to balance the right to information with the right to privacy, which are in tension with one another. Still others have expanded the mandate of offices within the ministry of communications or information (such as Malawi).

Oversight functions of DPAs vary in the powers granted by law. They may include:

- Investigatory powers. These may be complaint-based, or the DPA may initiate these cases themselves based on patterns of practice or some other established set of priorities. In some cases, the DPA may have the power to subpoena evidence, data, and testimony, or request the provision of evidence or explanation.
- Referral: DPAs may be able to refer findings to parliamentary bodies, other regulatory authorities, law enforcement, or courts, including specialized courts, such as human rights bodies. Such referral capacity can be helpful where government data processing may violate some rights, such as privacy, while ostensibly protecting others, such as security. By referring to courts outside of the specific jurisdiction of privacy law or data protection, these values can be balanced.
- Accountability. Some DPAs have the ability to levy administrative penalties. In the context of government data processing, however, it is unlikely that such administrative fines per *se* would be motivating. They may be too small relative to the size of the offender. Rather, "stop processing" orders, injunctive relief, and continuing mandamus or structural injunctions may be more suitable tools (Butler 2022).
- Independence. A study of African DPAs (Davis, 2021) shows that numerous DPAs worry about interference, especially through budgetary processes. This is most likely when their work confronts vested political interests with access to politicians.

Beyond centralized data authorities, governments may choose to make safeguards a part of civil service job descriptions or other departments. Similar work has been done in creating professional tracks for protecting the right to information, such as the United States civil service category "Government Information Specialist" (US Office of Personnel Management, 2012). On the non-governmental side, organizations such as the International Association of Privacy Professionals (iapp.org/train/) support the professionalization and training of government and private sector actors across boundaries. Establishing clear lines of authority and responsibility, as well as standard operating procedures for the lawful and professional application of such laws, can help to improve consistency, adaptation, and learning for data processing operations.

ACCOUNTABILITY MEASURES

Numerous countries have begun to put in place accountability measures to ensure that data processing inside and outside of government ensures that individuals are answerable for any harms and that there are corrective measures in place.

Screening: Impact Assessment and Risk Assessment

Not all government data processing is equally risky. Part of the responsibility of officials is often to sort out which processes are high risk and which require relatively little oversight. This allows limited attention and resources to be dedicated to those processes that pose a high risk of creating harm, while allowing for innovation among those that do not.

Algorithmic impact assessment

Algorithmic impact assessments (AIAs) are a policy mechanism used by public agencies to gather information on the potential use of an algorithmic data processing system in context, seeking to better understand, categorize, and respond to the potential harms or risks posed by the use of these systems. (Under the GDPR, such processes are referred to as "Data Protection Impact Assessments.") Such assessments are often made public and can inform broader decision-making.

An example of such policies in practice, the Canadian Directive on Automated Decision-Making (ADM) is one of the first policies on algorithmic accountability to define and incorporate an AIA. Under the Directive, an AIA must be conducted by a federal public agency prior to the "production" of any ADM system, including at the design stage of a project and immediately prior to the production of a system. These AIAs are required to be updated when there is a change in the functionality or scope of the system and must be publicly available. The questions involve technical elements of a system, such as the data and the algorithm, as well as organizational elements like consultation and procedures, and to assess impacts along the lines of "economic interests," "health," "sustainability," and "rights" of individuals or communities (Ada Lovelace Institute et al., 2021; Cardoso and Curry, 2021; Treasury Board of Canada Secretariat, 2021).

In the United States, privacy impact statements (PIS) are required by the E-Government Act of 2002. The law requires an agency to incorporate privacy protection elements into the full life cycle of a government program when there is personally identifiable information being collected, used, shared, or maintained. In the United States, PIS standards specifically aim to engage the public, with public posting of the assessments and communications with the public (SEARCH, 2005).

Human rights impact assessments

The need for safeguards in data processing extends beyond personal data to collective harms and public goods. Examples from private sector platforms like Facebook in Myanmar and WhatsApp in India have demonstrated the problem (Stevenson, 2018). In established democracies, government data processing may also violate human rights or democratic practices. For example, the Trump Administration in the United States mandated the release of government data on crimes committed by illegal immigrants as part of what was arguably a disinformation campaign (Executive Order 13768, Section 9(b), since rescinded). (Immigrants, even illegal immigrants, commit crimes at a far lower rate than the general public in the United States, per Light, Jingying, and Robey 2020.) Similarly, the same administration made the decision to use only open data on climate change and other environmental calculations, meaning that private health data could not be used in calculating the costs of pollution (EPA, 2019). These decisions, arguably, expose groups of people to harm collectively.

Human rights impact assessments have been suggested as a way to address this need for safeguards, but challenges in design arise due to numerous potential issues affecting human rights, jurisdictional issues, and activities beyond data processing.

While governments have not widely adopted these assessments, leading civil society organizations such as Access Now have laid out guidelines by which these assessments can be undertaken in the public and private sectors. According to their analysis, there is a growing chorus understanding the centrality of human rights. In particular, they point out the growing enshrinement of human rights approaches in voluntary principles and government policy, ranging from professional standards (of the Institute of Electrical and Electronics Engineers) to the Asilomar Principles on Beneficial Artificial Intelligence, and from the European Commission's High Level Expert Group on AI. Microsoft and Intel are among the first global tech companies to conduct Human Rights Impact Assessments on new AI applications (Nonnecke and Dawson, 2022).

As this tool becomes more widely adopted by the public sector and is considered part of the solutions in the Digital Services Act (European Union 2022) in Europe, there is an increasing sense that these questions and practices will need to become standardized without introducing opportunities for manipulation seen in environmental impact assessment, such as limiting scope to minimize impacts (see Henckes, et al., 2021 for further discussion).

Human oversight requirements

The GDPR introduced the concept of "human intervention" to ensure that data processing does not violate other guidelines or rules and meets the intended aims of a project. It specifically requires human intervention as an essential component in the decision-making process (GDPR Art. 22.2). The GDPR obliges data controllers to implement suitable safeguards, including the right to obtain human intervention a posteriori when the decision has been made. Similarly, US states, such as Washington, have introduced human oversight requirements.

The proposed AI Proposal for Regulation (European Parliament, 2021) would explicitly require human intervention in high-risk AI systems such as those used by public authorities to evaluate the eligibility of natural persons for public benefits, to evaluate creditworthiness, and to use facial recognition software (Domingo, 2022).

There is considerable discussion about just what such requirements may be able to achieve. For one, there is little guidance on just how involved a human will need to be in automated decision-making processes. More importantly, systems that are designed to surveil or to discriminate – or at least those lacking adequate safeguards to prevent them from doing so – may not be the result of frontline operators failing at their work but may be built into the original model or legal requirements (Green and Kak, 2021).

Justice and Dispute Resolution Mechanisms

At some point in government data processing, it is likely that individuals or groups of individuals may suffer harm or a law may be violated. In these cases, numerous countries have established processes to seek remedy and redress. Establishing such systems requires defining harms and creating dispute resolution forums.

Defining harms

Harms to individuals and classes are addressed through data protection laws and related laws.

Within data protection laws, certain rights are frequently established. A review of data protection laws (Davis, 2021) shows that different laws allow an affected party to invoke rights of access, correction of personal data, and deletion of personal data. When a party establishes that these rights are transgressed, they have the commensurate right to remedy and redress, at least where established in law.

Not all data protection issues, however, are issues of data misuse specifically. As a consequence, legal code that critically shapes government data processing may be ensconced in other parts of the law. Other forms of harm may be defined in other laws which apply to the misuse of data processing. These include:

- Discrimination: Includes racial, ethnic, religious information, health, and sexual orientation.
- Infringements of freedom of thought and association: Political opinions and philosophy or creed, organizational membership (including union membership).
- Competition laws: Undue use of government technology to enable corporate espionage or establish illegal trade monopolies.
- Business secrets: Protection of proprietary information, especially where such information puts a party at a competitive disadvantage.
- Medical and personal information. This includes sharing such information as health, genetic, academic, and biometric data. Other special categories may include financial data, employment data, and location data.
- Administrative law: For government data processing, dispute resolution may also be invoked in cases where due process for a decision was not followed, where the government failed to enforce a law, or where access to information was inadequate. (See, for example, the US Administrative Procedures Act of 1946, "Judicial Procedures.")

Dispute resolution forums

Formal dispute resolution mechanisms have become increasingly common within the field of data protection. These may take place in a judicial or quasi-judicial setting. They may likewise fall under the mandate of a regulatory authority such as a DPA or its sector-specific equivalent (such as an ombudsman responsible for the protection of education or health records). It is likely that any effective system will have multiple forums and will use a combination of actions initiated by the regulatory authority and actions initiated by members of the public.

Pring and Pring (2009) lay out numerous design choices in establishing dispute resolution systems, including type of forum (judicial or otherwise); legal and geographic jurisdiction; de jure and de facto independence; powers of discovery and referral; standing; costs; and access to technical expertise. Of these design elements, issues of standing, cost, and available remedies are of particular interest from the perspective of encouraging public accountability.

- **Standing:** Standing describes the qualifications required of parties to bring an action or otherwise participate in a case. The law may establish public interest standing or citizen suits (the right of private individuals to bring suits on behalf of the government). Issues of ripeness are important; does actual harm need to have happened, or is violation of the law adequate to seek corrective action? In addition, forums may establish rules to allow classes or other forms of collective action, which can lower the cost of enforcement.
- **Costs**: Regulatory authorities need to establish the rules to determine the expenses for parties from the time of filing to a final decision and to establish which mechanisms (such as American vs. British systems of court and attorney fees) may reduce those costs.
- **Remedies:** The specific powers a dispute resolution forum may have can vary from the simple ability to make recommendations to requiring restitution for damages or even find criminal liability in some cases. These may include mandating disclosure of information, injunctive orders such as "stop processing" orders, administrative compliance orders, civil or criminal penalties, and referral to alternative dispute resolution.

Audits and Inspection

Regulators, private sector actors, or members of the public may undertake audits of data processing, even by the government. As mentioned earlier, these may be part of routine inspections, triggered by a complaint, or part of a larger investigation into patterns of practice. DPAs may investigate complaints or problems on their own, or may, as in the case of Nigeria, have a process by which they license and register authorized audits, conduct training, and engage data protection compliance consultants (Bryant and Hadebe, 2020). In many cases, data audits may be mandatory when processing affects more than a certain number of people per month.

Just exactly what must be audited sheds some light on what standards auditors may apply. Rieke, Bogen, and Robinson (2018) argue that more than just source code can be inspected and disclosed. The authors provide an essential list of components that can be disclosed when describing any sort of automated decision-making process.

Insights: Elements outside of the formal processing of data.

- Existence. Any analysis of an automated system must begin with the knowledge that it exists. This basic point is worth emphasizing because automated systems often operate invisibly, behind the scenes.
- Purpose. All automated systems are created to serve some purpose. Understanding a system's intended purpose creates the opportunity to debate that system's role in society, even without more specific details about how it operates.
- Constitution. A system's constitution – the nature of its technical elements, human participation, governing rules, and how they all interact – is critical to guide and inform more detailed inquiry.
- Impact. Any automated system of social concern will have some sort of observable consequence, whether for a single person or an entire population. These impacts can be experienced personally, studied anecdotally, or measured quantitatively.

Artifacts: Components of actual data processing operations.

- Policies. Even systems that rely heavily on computers can be constrained by policies that govern how both technical and human components of that system should behave. Policies (and how well those policies are enforced) will play an important role in how the systems affect people in the real world.
- Inputs and Outputs: All automated systems take some sort of input and produce some sort of output. Regulatory systems need to take into account inputs and outputs of a system in order to assess its impact.
- Training Data: Training data refers to a set of historical data used to discover potentially predictive relationships among that data, which end up being represented in a model (commonly referred to as an algorithm). Training data is at the heart of statistical analysis and modern machine learning.
- Source Code: Source code refers to technical descriptions of software or predictive models within an automated system. Source code can be complex and difficult even for experts to diagnose and understand. In some cases, governments may choose to require open-source software solutions for public functions, including data processing. In other

cases, this may not be appropriate, and code may need to remain secret or unpublished. Nonetheless, regulators may still need to examine source code on rare occasions.

Standards-based accountability: explainability, traceability, and auditability
In addition to requiring specific elements of data processing to be subject to oversight, government bodies may adopt certain standards of practice that enable oversight and encourage developers and innovators within government to develop new projects in such a way that the systems can be made clear to stakeholders inside and outside of government.

To this end, regulators may require that certain types of data processing be subject to standards of traceability, auditability, and explainability. As governments move from simpler descriptive statistics and regression models toward more complex machine learning, models become increasingly difficult to explain in human terms. This means that supervisors, regulatory agencies, and courts miss an opportunity to understand processes themselves sometimes or to make those processes comprehensible to their respective publics.

Three common standards, as integrated into regulatory processes, include:

- **Explainability.** Neural nets, machine learning, and even more basic forms of data processing can quickly become "black boxes." While government data processing operations, by themselves, do not need to be explainable in order for them to work, they do need to be explainable within the context of democratic oversight. The inner workings of code may not even be understood by developers or engineers in some cases. Nonetheless, journalists, regulators, and even the general public need to understand what a model *does*. It is also essential so that when governments contract out data processing operations, officers can understand whether their processing operation is meeting programmatic and legal requirements. In this sense, it operates as a "safety feature" on a data processing operation (Johnson, 2020).
- **Traceability.** Government data processing operations also require some amount of traceability. This means that regulators can identify where and when a process has been accessed, altered, and where decisions took place along the line. This is essential in data processing operations such as voting. In some cases, this may be done through blockchain or through other more traditional methods such as careful custody of data (Thylstrup, Archer, and Ravn, 2022).
- **Auditability.** Standards of auditability include requiring data processors to provide an overview of how they work with data and to demonstrate how well these data processes work in human terms (IBM, 2022).

Procurement Conditions

Improving procurement through transparency and public accountability is increasingly popular for numerous reasons, ranging from improving value for money, inclusion, and environmental performance (McDevitt, 2022). Data processing may be outsourced to private vendors, either as product purchases or as service and development agreements. Including requirements for responsible data processing through contract conditions is a relatively easy policy to adopt in comparison with other legal reforms.

Leveraging contracts for better transparency or accountability may happen before or during the contract. Establishing contractual preconditions limits the chance of acquiring undesirable technologies and services. Preconditions may also establish consequences; if a vendor fails to meet contractual conditions, they are subject to contractual liability (Mulligan and Bamberger, 2019). During implementation, procurement conditions also allow for interventions in the design of data processing systems and during their use, including ongoing monitoring or other disclosure requirements (World Economic Forum, 2020).

A recent review shows that this approach is increasingly popular as a means of regulation:

- The UK government has developed extensive guidance on leveraging government procurement mechanisms for AI, particularly when used by public agencies, including suggestions for ensuring transparency of algorithmic decisions and fairness in data processing (United Kingdom, 2020).
- The City of Amsterdam requires that the procurement of data processing systems by public agencies in the city incorporates certain standard clauses in its procurement conditions (Municipality Amsterdam, 2020). These include conditions for transparency, such as the right of government auditors or agencies to examine the underlying data and models; conditions for the vendor to assess data processing systems for bias, and risk management strategies to be complied with by the vendor.
- Similar considerations for procurement are also included in the Tamil Nadu Safe and Ethical AI Policy (Tamil Nadu, 2020).
- The AI source list of the Government of Canada is a list of authorized vendors from whom procurement is expedited. A condition for inclusion in the AI source list is "demonstrated competence in AI ethics" (Canada, 2015).

Whistleblower Protection and Privacy Exemptions

Whistleblower protection is an essential part of the detection of waste, fraud, and abuse. The most recent *Report to the Nations* by the Association of Certified Fraud Examiners found that whistleblowers and tipsters were by far the most frequent sources of fraud investigations (ACFE, 2022).

Ensuring adequate protection for whistleblowers within the government is one of several components of a strong accountability system around government data processing. In addition, because so much work may be outsourced, it is also essential to extend such protections to private contractors. In the United States, the Obama-era Presidential Policy Directive 19 extended such protections to contractors involved in national security operations. This created a formal channel for private actors to notify inspectors and legislators of critical issues. Such a channel did not exist at the time of the Snowden revelations in 2013 (Canterbury, 2013).

In addition, specific exemptions to privacy laws and government data processing policies must be made to ensure that whistleblowers or journalists do not face additional retaliation through the disproportionate application of data protection laws. Exclusion of liability for journalistic, literary, or artistic expression acknowledges the need to balance privacy with other rights, such as freedom of expression and access to information (Davis, 2021).

DISCLOSURE AND TRANSPARENCY REGIMES

Disclosure and public transparency measures are increasingly common alternatives to command-and-control regulation. At the national level, this form of disclosure has been most advanced by the French government. In addition to impact assessment disclosure (see above), policymakers have innovated with processing registers, consent-based transparency, and data breach notifications.

Data Processing Registers

Processing registers are one of the most spoken-about transparency measures in the scrutiny of government data use. In essence, these are public databases about various automated decision-making processes. Some registers may include only the most basic information, such as the responsible agency and the name of the automated decision-making process. Others may link to more in-depth information, such as impact assessments and privacy impact statements.

As relatively recent phenomena, "best practice" in the design and implementation of these registers has yet to emerge. Recent practical experience illuminates how the practice of register development may evolve. Of these, public agencies responsible for algorithm registers in Amsterdam, Helsinki, Nantes, Antibes, and Lyon are active and have also described their experiences of implementation.

- The white paper published by the governments of Amsterdam and Helsinki on their implementation of algorithm registers indicates that these registers can help structure accountability for the use of algorithmic systems in public agencies by systematically ensuring public transparency and participation in their development and use (Haataja, van de Fliert, and Rautio, 2020).
- The experience of Nantes and Lyon indicates the importance of involving public agencies in the process of designing these registers. Their implementation has also given rise to questions about the scope of systems and information to include, how to ensure legitimacy for their use, and on prioritizing resources to ensure the greatest impact (Pénicaud, 2021).

The experiences of these registers show that governments that develop algorithmic registers have better outcomes when they design for specific audiences, such as auditors or journalists, who can appropriately understand and respond to the information provided.

They also hold some lessons for the form in which information can be accessed. These registers have mostly arisen as directories for consolidating information about data processing systems used across a particular, local jurisdiction. Decentralizing and focusing on local governments may ensure that these directories are not too large, unwieldy, or difficult to construct or use. On the other hand, standardization allows for better filtering. This is a challenge that has arisen, for example, in the context of larger, national directories, such as those being attempted in Chile (Consejo para la Transparencia, 2021).

Consent-Based Transparency

Consent to data processing by a subject is one of the lawful justifications provided for the processing of personal data. In numerous laws, it is one of the mechanisms that enable participation by allowing a data subject to control the ways in which their personal data is used. There are numerous reasons an individual may wish to grant or withhold consent, ranging from privacy, to data autonomy, to concerns of security (Park, 2020).

In order for consent to be specific and informed, the data subject must be provided with sufficient information. Such information should include: the identity of the data controller, the purpose for the processing, and the right to withdraw consent (UK Information Commissioner's Office, 2022).

The GDPR requires opt-in consent, but other jurisdictions do not. In a 2020 survey of data protection laws in Africa, Kenya's data protection law was the only one that expressly required opt-in consent (Davis, 2021).

Consent-based models of transparency have well-documented limitations (McDonald, 2019, Medine and Murthy, 2020, UK-ICO, 2022). Notably, arguments include: (1) users do not want to regularly read long and complex policies; (2) policies do not adequately explain risk; (3) agreement with policies does not necessarily imply actual conscious consent (Privacy Patterns, 2022); and (4) users do not have adequate ability to interpret such policies and their implications (Davis, 2021).

Numerous alternatives have been proposed. Specifically, the GDPR requires an additional level of readability in its transparency requirements. These include a set of "Terms of Service Icons," which, like nutrition facts, aim to present a simplified version of the actual processing as a result of using an online service or piece of software. At the time of writing, there are numerous private, governmental, and non-profit organizations working on competing conceptions of these icons (Privacy Patterns, 2022).

More radically, some have challenged whether the concept of consent – especially informed consent – can be meaningfully given by a data processing subject. The European Joint Human Rights Commission found that the consent model unreasonably places the onus on individuals to educate themselves in order to understand the risks associated with sharing their personal data online. The complexity of privacy policies makes it almost impossible for individuals to understand what consent they are giving. Further, many businesses make use of their online services conditional on users agreeing to their non-negotiable terms. Therefore, consent is often not 'informed' or "freely given" under the GDPR (McDonald, 2019).

In addition, the report found that companies routinely traded in private information without the consent of individuals. As a consequence, certain advertisements are shown to certain people and not to others, resulting in discrimination and worse access to services for some people.

As an alternative, the report suggested other elements to bolster a consent-based model, including human rights impact assessments, stepped-up fines for trading in information by regulators, and the right to request information on how data was being processed, often called a "subject access report."

Data Breach Notification

Notification in the event of a data breach is another important mechanism that increases transparency and enables data subjects to seek redress.

A breach notification is a mechanism that requires a data controller to provide notice if the personal data in their control has been accessed or acquired by an unauthorized person. Data protection laws generally require that notice be provided to the regulatory authority as well as to affected data subjects. This includes information concerning an event that impacts the integrity, availability, or confidentiality of a data subject's personal data (Kak, 2020). Data breach notifications are increasingly required under law in most US states (Desai, 2022), a number of African countries (Davis, 2021), and Articles 33 and 34 of the GDPR.

The purpose of the notification is to allow affected data subjects to take necessary measures to mitigate any potential harm they may suffer as a result of the breach. Identity theft is a common example of the type of harm that may result. As noted by the Information Policy Institute (Turner, 2006), "Identity theft and identity fraud have emerged as serious crimes for consumers, citizens and business ... Given the peculiar nature of this type of theft – namely, that it can be perpetrated by accessing information stored in places uncontrolled by the victim and in places of which the victim is often unaware – legislators have passed or are considering passing laws which require that the consumer be notified in the event of a data breach."

Where such rules exist, the effectiveness of such an obligation is undermined in three ways: first, through the absence of a prescribed timeframe for notification; second, through the use of vague terms for the notification period; and third, through the inclusion of exceptions that allow for non-reporting. Legislative texts that include these concerns may be open to abuse and provide loopholes for non-compliance.

CONCLUSION

The list of emerging regulatory approaches is far from complete. As the field of government data processing continues to evolve, so too does the regulator's toolkit. What is clear, however, is that the adoption and effectiveness of tools require an approach that cannot be government-only. To that end, ensuring responsible and legally compliant data processing, including the use of AI and other new technologies, empowers oversight institutions along with the broader public. While transparency and accountability will not be the only tools, they will help ensure that government data use is broadly consistent with public values.

REFERENCES

Ada Lovelace Institute, AI Now Institute and Open Government Partnership. 2021. Algorithmic Accountability for the Public Sector. bit.ly/3W0b41z

African Union. 2014. *African Union Convention on Cybersecurity and Personal Data Protection* (the "Malabo Convention")

Association of Certified Fraud Examiners (ACFE). 2022. *Occupational Fraud 2022: A Report to the Nations.* bit.ly/3nTWooa

Australia. 2012. *My Health Records* Act. 2012.

Brazil. 2018. *General Personal Data Protection Act (LGPD).* 2018. Law No. 13,709.

Bryant, Justin and Tshepiso Hadebe. 2020. Data Protection Factsheet Nigeria. bit.ly/42tKFvz

Burkina Faso. 2014. *The Protection of Personal Data Act 010–2004/AN of 2014.*

Butler, Oliver. 2022. Official secrecy and the criminalisation of unauthorised disclosures. *Law Quarterly Review* 138 (April), 273–98.

Cabo Verde. 2001. *The Data Protection Act, Law 133 of 2001.*

Canada. 2015. *AI Source List, Public Services and Procurement Canada.* bit.ly/3M1AXWw

Canterbury, Angela. 2013. Testimony to United States Congress, House of Representatives Advisory Committee on Transparency. November 20. bit.ly/3O0J1w1

Cardoso, Tom and Bill Curry. 2021. National Defence skirted federal rules in using artificial intelligence, privacy commissioner says. *The Globe and Mail*. February 7. tgam.ca/3O4MD13

Center for Global Development. 2014. Publishing Government Contracts: Addressing Concerns and Easing Implementation. Accessed 6/1/23 at: bit.ly/3BkHVVt

Consejo para la Transparencia, Chile. 2021. CPLT y la UAI firman convenio para promover transparencia del uso de algoritmos y datos personales en organismos públicos. bit.ly/44X1Ebc

Côte d'Ivoire. 2013. *The Protection of Personal Information Act*. 2013–450.

Davis, Tara. 2021. *Data Protection in Africa: A Look at OGP Member Progress*. Rosebank, South Africa and Washington, DC: AltAdvisory and Open Government Partnership.

Desai, Anokhy. 2022. *US State Privacy Legislation Tracker*. The International Association of Privacy Professionals (IAPP). bit.ly/44WA12k

Digital Government Agency. 2020. *Artificial Intelligence Strategy for Digital Government Government of Uruguay*.

Domingo, Sara. 2022. Human Intervention and Human Oversight in the *GDPR* and *AI Act*. Trilateral Research: Ethical AI. bit.ly/3pyX8zH

ECHR. 2022. Guide to the Case-Law of the European Court of Human Rights. Council of Europe/European Court of Human Rights. Accessed 6/1/23 at: bit.ly/3VVBrWE

EDPS. 2010. *The EDPS Video-Surveillance Guidelines*. Brussels: EDPS. Accessed 6/1/23 at: bit.ly/3M1NWv6

Electronic Privacy Information Centre (EPIC). 2020. *State Facial Recognition Policy*. bit.ly/44T8b6Z

EPA. 2019. Strengthening Transparency in Regulatory Science: Notification of a Public Teleconference of the Chartered Science Advisory Board. bit.ly/3pDwJk4

European Parliament. 2021. *Proposal for a Regulation of the European Parliament and of the Council Laying Down Harmonised Rules on Artificial Intelligence (Artificial Intelligence Act) And Amending Certain Union Legislative Acts*. 2021/0106.

European Union. 2016. *General Data Protection Regulation (GDPR)*.

European Union. 2022. *Digital Services Act*.

Ghana. 2012. *Data Protection Act*, 2012, Act 843.

Green, Ben and Amba Kak. 2021. The False Comfort of Human Oversight as an Antidote to A.I. Harm. *Slate: Future Tense*. bit.ly/3Bm0I2U

Haataja, Meeri, Linda van de Fliert and Pasi Rautio. 2020. Public AI Registers: Realising AI Transparency and Civic Participation in Government Use of AI Saidot. bit.ly/3BlGt5a

Hagendorff, T. 2020. The ethics of AI ethics: An evaluation of guidelines. *Minds and Machines*, 30(1), 99–120. link.springer.com/article/10.1007/s11023-020-09517-8

Hamilton, Sil and Andrew Piper. 2022. The COVID that wasn't: counterfactual journalism using GPT. In *Proceedings of the 6th Joint SIGHUM Workshop on Computational Linguistics for Cultural Heritage, Social Sciences, Humanities and Literature*, pp 83–93. Gyeongju, Republic of Korea. International Conference on Computational Linguistics.

Henckes, Ruth-Marie, Lucia Posteraro, Tonusree Basu, Helen Turek and Maria Koomen. 2021. Five Ways to Embed Open Gov Values in Online Political Advertising Regulation. Open Government Partnership. bit.ly/3VVCvd6

Hoffmann-Rhiem, Wolfgang. 2020. Artificial intelligence as a challenge for law and regulation. In *Regulating Artificial Intelligence*, Thomas Wischmeyer and Timo Rademacher, eds. pp 1–29. Springer Nature Switzerland.

Hong, S. and S.H. Kim. 2016. Political polarization on Twitter: Implications for the use of social media in digital governments. *Government Information Quarterly*, 33(4), 777–82.

Hou, Yue and Rory Truex. 2022. Ethnic discrimination in criminal sentencing in China. *The Journal of Politics*, 84(4).

IBM. 2022. Explainable AI. https://www.ibm.com/topics/explainable-ai

India, Supreme Court. 1996. *Vineet Narain v. Union of India*, AIR 1996 SC 3386.

Johnson, Jonathan. 2020. Interpretability vs explainability: The black box of machine learning. *BMC Machine Learning & Big Data Blog*. bit.ly/3pAqg9K

Kak, Amba. 2020. *Regulating Biometrics: Global Approaches and Urgent Questions*. AI Now Institute. bit.ly/3I0PO6o

Kenya. 2019. *The Data Protection Act*.

Kwoka, Margaret B. 2016. FOIA, Inc. *Duke Law Journal,* 1361, 1376–81.
Light, Michael, Jingying He and Jason P. Robey (2020). Comparing crime rates between undocumented immigrants, legal immigrants, and native-born US citizens in Texas. *PNAS,* 117(51), 32340–7.
Malawi. 2016. *The Electronic Transactions and Cyber Security Act.*
Marsch, Nikolaus. 2020. Artificial intelligence and the fundamental right to data protection: Opening the door for technological innovation and innovative protection. In *Regulating Artificial Intelligence,* Thomas Wischmeyer and Timo Rademacher, eds. pp 33–52. Springer Nature Switzerland.
McCubbins, Matthew D. and Thomas Schwartz. 1984. Congressional oversight overlooked: Police patrols versus fire alarms. *American Journal of Political Science.* Vol. 28, No. 1, pp. 165–179.
McDevitt, Andrew. 2022. *State of the Evidence: Open Contracting.* Washington, DC: Open Government Partnership. bit.ly/3I782D0
McDonald, J. 2019. Data Protection and Privacy: Is the Consent Model Broken? Charles Russell Speechlyss. bit.ly/42yPBPW
Medine, David and Gayatri Murthy. 2020. Making Data Work for the Poor: New Approaches to Data Protection and Privacy. Washington, DC: CGAP.
Metzinger, T. 2019. Ethics washing made in Europe. *Der Tagesspiegel,* April 18. bit.ly/2Uc81ln
Morocco. 2009. Law No. 09–08 of 18 February.
Mulligan, Deidre and Kenneth Bamberger. 2019. Procurement as policy: Administrative process for machine learning. *Berkeley Technology Law Journal,* 34.
Municipality Amsterdam. 2020. *Standard Clauses for Municipalities for Fair Use of Algorithmic Systems.* bit.ly/3Ml1enN
Nigeria. 2020. *The Draft Data Protection Bill.*
Nonnecke, Brandie and Philip Dawson. 2022. Human Rights Impact Assessments for AI: Analysis and Recommendations. Access Now. bit.ly/3BlRT9e
Park, Claire. 2020. How "Notice and Consent" Fails to Protect Our Privacy. Washington, DC: New America. https://bit.ly/463HUCg
Pénicaud, Soizic. 2021. Building public algorithm registers: Lessons learned from the French approach. *Open Government Partnership Blog,* May 12. bit.ly/3MlATpN
Piotrowski, Suzanne, Daniel Berliner, and Alex Ingrams. 2022. *The Power of Partnership in Open Government: Reconsidering Multistakeholder Governance Reform*.Cambridge, Massachussets: MIT Press.
Pring, George William and Catherine Pring. 2009. *Greening Justice: Creating and Improving Environmental Courts and Tribunals.* Washington, DC: Access Initiative, World Resources Institute.
Privacy Patterns. 2022. *Privacy Policy Display.* bit.ly/41vz264
Rieke, Aaron, Miranda Bogen and David Robinson. 2018. *Public Scrutiny of Automated Decisions: Early Lessons and Emerging Methods.* Upturn and Omidyar Network Report.
Scott, James. 1998. *Seeing Like a State: How Certain Schemes to Improve the Human Condition Have Failed.* New Haven, CT: Yale University Press.
SEARCH. 2005. *Guide to Conducting Privacy Impact Assessments for State, Local, and Tribal Information Sharing Initiatives.* Washington, DC: The National Consortium for Justice Information and Statistics. bit.ly/3pyCzTV
Senegal. 2008. *Law No. 2008–12* of 25 January.
Seychelles. 2003. *Data Protection Act,* 9 of 2003.
South Africa. 2013. *Protection of Personal Information Act,* 4 of 2013.
State of California. 2018. *California Consumer Privacy Act.* California Legislative Service. Ch. 55 (A.B. 375)
Stevenson, Alexandra. 2018. Facebook admits it was used to incite violence in Myanmar. *New York Times,* November 6. nyti.ms/2SU2eS4
Tamil Nadu. 2020. *Safe and Ethical AI Policy.* bit.ly/3I77kFQ
Taylor, Linnet, Ronald Leenes and Sascha van Schendel. 2017. Public Sector Data Ethics: From Principles to Practice. Tilburg University. bit.ly/44SbZp4
ten Seldam, Björn & Alex Brenninkmeijer. The Dutch benefits scandal: a cautionary tale for algorithmic enforcement. EU Law Enforcement. *https://eulawenforcement.com/?p=7941*
Thailand. 2019. *Personal Data Protection Act* BE 2562 (PDPA).

Thylstrup, Nanna Bonde, Matthew Archer and Louis Ravn. 2022. Traceability. *Internet Policy Review*, 11(1).

Tisné, Martin, 2018. It's time for a Bill of Data Rights. *MIT Technology Review*, December 4. Accessed 6/1/23 at: bit.ly/3pGdMgA

Treasury Board of Canada Secretariat (TBS), Government of Canada. 2021. *Algorithmic Impact Assessment tool*. bit.ly/3O4KG4J

Tunisia. 2004. *Law No. 2004–63 of 27 July 2004*

Turner, Michael. 2006. *Towards a Rational Personal Data Breach Notification Regime*. Information Policy Institute. bit.ly/44YqE1R

United Kingdom. 2020. *Guidelines for AI Procurement*. bit.ly/42vYYQe

United Kingdom Information Commissioner's Office (UKICO). 2022. What Is Valid Consent? Guide to Data Protection. bit.ly/2J5JcaH

United States. 1946. *Administrative Procedures Act. Judicial Review*. 5 USC Ch. 7.

United States. 1998. *Children's Online Privacy Protection Act*. 15 U.S.C. 6501, et seq.

United States. 2017. *EO 13768: Enhancing Public Safety in the Interior of the United States*. January 25. (Revoked by EO 13993 25/1/21.)

United States Office of Personnel Management. 2012. *Position Classification Flysheet for Government Information Series, 0306*. Washington, DC. https://bit.ly/3Z4UNvC

United States Supreme Court. 2013. *In Re Electronic Privacy Information Center, 134 S.Ct. 638*.

Waples, Gregory. 1974. The *Freedom of Information Act*: A seven-year assessment. *Columbia Law Review*, 895–958.

Weber, Max. 1978. In Guenther Roth and Claus Wittich (eds.). *Economy and Society*. Berkeley, CA: University of California Press, p 54.

World Economic Forum. 2020. AI Government Procurement Guidelines. bit.ly/42R4cpO

Wylie, C. 2019. *Mindf*ck: Cambridge Analytica and the Plot to Break America*. New York: Random House Publishing Group.

18. Classificatory versus transformative data regimes: towards a positive right to data production and analysis

Willie Gin

In 2016, the world was introduced to a sophisticated, all-seeing data-gathering scheme that automatically ranked people according to the positive and negative effects they produced throughout their life. The ranking algorithm was depicted in the comedy show, *The Good Place*, and while fictional, the show highlights the potential issues of data gathering and analysis to make predictive judgments about humans. In the show, a single score determines a person's entry to an afterlife of delight (the "Good Place") or an afterlife of suffering and punishment (the "Bad Place"). The scoring is determined by omniscient data gathering that perfectly observes all behavior and motivation without error throughout each person's life. The data gathering and scoring in *The Good Place* could be critiqued on many grounds familiar to the growing literature on algorithmic ethics. Perhaps the people in the afterlife could object to the lack of transparency. When they are alive, they are unaware they are being scored. Perhaps the people could object to the scoring algorithm's legibility and understandability, another critique that has often been made about the "black box" algorithms being used in the real world. The administrators of the afterlife do not reveal how different actions weigh in coming up with the final score. Instead of focusing on these kinds of criticisms, the show highlights a different fundamental objection to the afterlife's scoring system, one that has not been as well developed in the growing literature on data regulation, ethics, and governance. The protagonists in the show argue that what the afterlife's model misses is the ability of humans to change their behavior in different circumstances and with proper support. The protagonists propose that the afterlife be run as an experiment to see whether, under different circumstances, people can incrementally become morally good. After it is shown that even seemingly "bad" human beings can become better, the afterlife is reorganized into a purgatory where souls undergo experimentation to see if people can become better under different environmental conditions and exposure to different people. Individuals are constantly rebooted under different conditions, relationships, and interventions until they can pass a goodness test, which would then allow them to ascend to the Good Place.

The Good Place brings into focus the central concern of this chapter, two different data regimes. As defined here, a data regime corresponds to a distinctive way in which data is produced, analyzed, and used in a social formation. Data regime 1—the data regime associated with how the afterlife is initially organized in the show—aims to primarily classify and sort subjects into groups. In the show, this is primarily to punish or reward, given existing resources and rules afforded to the afterlife's bureaucratic administrators. Data regime 2—corresponding to the system in place in the afterlife at the end of the show—aims to experiment and transform individual subjects. Rather than have subjects confined to their initial classifications, data regime 2 seeks to allow individuals to transcend those classifications. *The*

Good Place ultimately makes the case that data regime 2 is morally and ethically superior to data regime 1.

In the current era of big data analytics, the majority of data analytics corresponds to data regime 1. Driven by the availability of huge troves of data, existing analyses have mined this data to produce novel predictive correlations, such as vitamin pill purchases as a sign of pregnancy (Mayer and Cukier 2013, 57) or pop-tart sales increasing during emergency weather events (Stephens-Davidowitz 2018, 72). The use of data in this context is largely driven by efficiency concerns (Kitchin 2014, 119). With knowledge that vitamin pill purchases often predict pregnancy, Target can more effectively decide on whom it should spend its limited ad budget. With knowledge that pop-tart sales tend to increase during extreme weather, Walmart can more efficiently plan its supply and distribution strategies. Enthusiasm for big data in the public sector is often motivated by similar concerns. Some government and nonprofit organizations believe algorithms may direct limited public and nonprofit budgets more effectively (Kitchin 2014, 116, 118).

Big data and the analytics associated with it have been subject to numerous critiques. Critical data studies has sought to denaturalize and show the ideological assumptions behind the use of big data analytics (van Dijck 2014; Kitchin and Laurialt 2018; Sadowski 2019). Problems with algorithmic predictions based on correlations in big data include misprediction and inaccuracy in prediction (Buolamwini and Gebru 2018); bias in predictions (Sweeney 2013; Eubanks 2015; Angwin et al. 2016; Benjamin 2019; Noble 2018); and lack of transparency and illegibility (Pasquale 2015). To highlight the political and constructed nature of big data analysis, critical data studie labels current practices as "data assemblages" (Kitchin 2014, 24), which are informed by particular "data cultures" (Bates 2017, 191) and "data discourses" (Fussell 2022). Others have given explicit names to the dominant data regime, such as "panoptic sorting" (Gandy 2021) or "surveillance capitalism" (Zuboff 2020). This chapter expands on these critiques by identifying the current dominant data practice of "classifying and economizing" as data regime 1, and contrasting it with data regime 2, a different use of data that emphasizes "experimenting and transforming." The identification of data regime 2 here builds on intuitions that previous scholars have identified (e.g., see O'Neil 2016, 98–9). The contrasting of the two forms of data practice can highlight further deficiencies and limitations of current normative data practices. For example, some authors argue that the problems identified in the use of data in data regime 1 can be fixed, through better data and variables— the problem is between badly built and properly built algorithms (Obermeyer et al 2019, 453; Ludwig and Mullainathan 2021, 89–92). In contrast to that perspective, the chapter argues that even "properly built" algorithms based on data regime 1 suffer from epistemological assumptions and patterns of practice associated with that data regime.

The argument in this chapter proceeds as follows. The first substantive section will show the emergence of the two different data regimes in a real-world example, major league baseball. This example leads to an ideal-typical definition of the differences between data regimes 1 and 2. The second section examines the two different data regimes with regards to two examples in public policy, to highlight the lack of deployment of data regime 2 in these areas and show the potential harm to individuals. The chapter concludes by arguing that the current dominance of data regime 1 over data regime 2 leads to two problems. There is an epistemological inequality in that production and analysis of data associated with classifying and economizing is predominant over experimenting and transforming. Second, there is a distributive inequality in the kinds of actors and entities that can successfully access data regime 2, with others being stuck primarily in data regime 1. If data regime 2 is desirable, then the governance framework regarding data needs to move beyond a right to access data (transparency) or a negative right to block access to data (privacy), the kinds of regulations that are appropriate for data regime 1. What is missing from the historical data of data regime 1 is information about possibility, information that can only be produced under certain conditions that are captured in data regime 2. This suggests not just negative right protecting individuals from the harms in which data can be used against their interests, but a positive right to data production to enable individuals to transform and flourish.

THE EVOLUTION OF DATA IN BASEBALL: SORTING VERSUS DEVELOPMENT

That there are two distinct data regimes can be seen not just in a fictional show like *The Good Place*, but also in the real-life example of major league baseball. Data analytics in baseball is an important case, because it is one of the fields in which data analysis and practices associated with data regime 1 became entrenched in the popular consciousness. As is now well known, the Oakland A's under the management of Billy Beane resorted to analysis of the value of players to deal with the team's lower budget relative to larger-market teams like the New York Yankees or Los Angeles Dodgers. By gathering and analyzing data on large datasets of players, the team's management sought to classify better: which characteristics in players are more likely to lead to actual baseball success on the field? Such classification could allow the A's to get a predictive advantage in selecting "undervalued" players, who could then be acquired on the cheap, like undervalued stocks. Michael Lewis's *Moneyball* (2004) chronicled the story of how the team performed well above what one might expect from their payroll limits, and the practices described in the book became the norm among baseball teams. The term Moneyball has since been appropriated by some in business and government to try to wring the most efficiency out of resources through analysis of data.

Moneyball encapsulates the use and deployment of data according to data regime 1. Data is analyzed to find predictive tendencies within certain subgroups. For example, analysis predicts that hitters who had a high walk rate in college would, on average, have a relatively higher hitting rate in the major leagues. As another example, the "aging curve" showed that players tended to peak around their late 20s. On average, a player approaching their late 20s would improve this much, and on average, players in their 30s would decline this much every given year. Managers of teams use these average tendencies to classify players and make decisions about which players to acquire and how much to pay them. The side effect of this more sophisticated data analysis by managers is that many players are being paid below what the analysis says they are truly worth (Gin 2018).

Moneyball never claimed to be an exact science. Different metrics like WAR (wins above replacement) purported to predict the overall future value of a player based on their historical production, yet these summary quantifications were probabilistic guesses. They performed poorly in predicting any individual player's actual season but analysts believed them to be better in the "aggregate," across many guesses. To explain why the Oakland A's never won the World Series, Billy Beane, the general manager of the A's, famously stated how his method doesn't work in the playoffs. Predictive analytics could yield some benefit over a large enough sample of games, as in a 140-game season. But in a short seven-game series in the postseason, variance could win out even if a team was constructed with a slight data advantage.

Furthermore, the limitations of Moneyball in a competitive environment where every front office adopted the same analytic lens also became apparent. If other teams were evaluating and valuing players the same way, then no longer could one team exploit market efficiencies and buy talent below their actual predicted value, and no competitive advantage could be gained. The disappearance of these market inefficiencies spurred further innovation in player evaluation, with new forms of player tracking and data gathering. Today, expensive sensors in stadiums track things like pitch movement and exit velocities and angles when hitters make contact. This intensification of surveillance and data gathering is actually not that radical an innovation, at least in terms of thinking of a data regime. The goal is still to "classify and economize," but just with better data.

Lindbergh and Sawchik's book, *MVP Machine* (2019), recounts a more fundamental shift in data analysis in baseball—what some have called Moneyball 2.0. Statistical analysis in the early version of Moneyball is essentially data mining for correlations. The metaphor implied in "mining" is apt. The unchangeable ore is already there; all the analyst had to do was uncover it. Observe more of what was already right in front of you, and then you might have the data that could uncover a correlation across time—that is, that a pitcher with a higher spin rate might have more strikeouts than a pitcher with a lower spin rate. Moneyball did not challenge group classification; it aimed to classify groups better. The more radical innovation, at least according to *MVP Machine*, is to break classifications. Instead of assuming that one's baseball "essence" was fixed and revealed through the accumulated historical data of one's games played and comparisons with groups of other players with similar traits, this new paradigm allowed for the possibility that one could change through careful coaching and development (Lindbergh and Sawchik 2019, 61). In Moneyball 1.0, the metaphor was data mining in which the "ore" is already there and unchangeable; in Moneyball 2.0, the idea is crafting and developing the ore so that it becomes something more refined—instead of data mining, think of data-smithing.

Breaking classifications requires a different kind of data regime. Instead of getting data from actual games, the data was gathered from experimentation in a carefully controlled lab. From "classify and economize," the new mantra might be "experiment and develop." Lindbergh and Sawchick describe the new paradigm of "Betterball" through the pitcher Trevor Bauer. Bauer early on embraced experimentalism and technology like the Edgertronic machine to help him experiment better. The Edgertronic is significantly better at high-speed image capture, capable of showing in detail pitcher and ball movements, thus allowing experimentation in how factors like grip can affect spin (Lindbergh and Sawchick 2019, 107). By spending the off season in Driveline, a training lab with high-tech optic sensors that could record the nuances of both his body and arm positioning as well as the speed, spin rate, and movement of the pitch, Bauer and Driveline's coaches were able to make minor adjustments to his pitches and physical training and observe the real-time results. Through numerous iterations and adjustments he made in this controlled environment—what others have called "deliberate" or "intentional" practice (Ericsson and Pool 2017)—Bauer improved his existing pitches and developed new pitches, even when traditional analytics suggested that pitchers at his age tended to lose velocity (Lindbergh and Sawchik 2019,109, 345).

MVP Machine chronicles multiple other stories of players who were able to change the trajectories of their careers through similar kinds of experimentation and coaching that Bauer experienced. As the coach who helped oversee Rich Hill's pitching resurrection put it, "with a few changes or giving the guy the right mental approach, the right physical approach, the right pitch mix, the development of a new pitch, you can completely change his projection or his future ceiling" (Lindbergh and Sawchik 2019, 124). One indicator of the rise of this new mentality is the increase in player development staff on baseball teams. As Lindbergh and Sawchik (2019, 177) note, "between the springs of 2011 and 2018, the average size of the staffs assigned to player development by MLB teams increased by 51 percent, from an average of 51 in 2011 to an average of 77 in 2018 … . Those totals have kept climbing since."

The developments in baseball, from Moneyball to Betterball, show the evolution in data analysis in a highly cutthroat market-driven competitive environment. This evolution can be described as a change in data regimes. The term "data regime" borrows and extends the notion of "data assemblages" developed in critical data studies (Kitchin 2014, 24; Iliadis and Russo 2016, 3; Hepp et al 2022, 5), as well as the allied concepts of "data cultures" (Bates 2017, 191) and "data discourses" (Fussell 2022). All three concepts highlight that data is never "neutral" but situated in social and political contexts, and that different constructions of data and data analytics can have effects on society and who has power and opportunities. To help distinguish different data assemblages, Kitchin and Laurialt (2018, 8) provide a definition of a data assemblage as "the production, management, analysis, and translation of data and derived information products for commercial, governmental, administrative, bureaucratic, or other purposes." Bates (2017, 3) defines data cultures as the norms, values, and beliefs that sustain "data production, processing, distribution, and use." These definitions identify at least three dimensions in which data regimes can be distinguished: (1) how the data is collected and produced; (2) how the data is analyzed; and (3) how the analytic insights are deployed and used.

Table 18.1 summarizes how Moneyball and Betterball differ in these dimensions. The Moneyball era in sports analytics collects and produces data by looking primarily at historical game data. The environment and the players are not manipulated; data is produced by more intensive surveillance of the game as it is played. In this way, the production of the data can be described as primarily extractive. The information is already "out there" embedded in everyday life as it is; the data is produced by "extracting" from these everyday contexts. In the second step, the analysis of the data is largely correlational. Looking at the historical data, analysts search for group tendencies and averages that gives a predictive edge. The goal of the data analysis is the building of a predictive model that can be used to evaluate anybody. Individualization is hinted at in this analysis, but only in the sense that individuals are conceived as the aggregate of each of the subgroups to which they belong, as specified in the all-encompassing model. In the third and final step, the use of the data is primarily by elites to act upon others. In this case, management uses the data to classify players and economize the team's resources. Statistical tendencies in practice become ontological "essence," as player typologies are used to decide who gets opportunities and who does not. Players are the objects of analysis, rather than being subjects of analysis.

Betterball constitutes a second distinct data regime that evolves beyond the limits of the Moneyball data regime. Rather than emphasizing categorical "being," Betterball allows for experimentally driven "becoming." This requires an active experimental approach that differs from Moneyball in terms of data collection, analysis, and use. Experimentation needs sophisticated data gathering (i.e., high-speed cameras), which in itself is not different from Moneyball. What is different is that it also requires the establishment of an experimental environment (i.e., Driveline) and numerous iterations and intentional practice within this

Table 18.1   Ideal-typical description of data regimes 1 and 2

	Data Regime 1: Classification and Economization	Data Regime 2: Experimentation and Transformation
Production of Data	Extraction Exploration of historical space No environmental interventions	Creation Exploration of possibility space Based on experimental transformation in environment
Analysis of Data	Data-mining Finding predictive group correlations and classifications Building an all-encompassing model	Data-smithing Finding individualized interventions
Use of Data		
Who does the analyzing	Hierarchical Managers and data elites with access to large troves of data	Potentially democratized The individual themselves, perhaps in conjunction with data elites
Purpose of analysis	Objectification Sorting and ranking of objects of analysis by elites Economization of resources in short term	Subject's improvement; transformation and development of the object of analysis Breaking classification Greater individualization

Source: Author's own.

controlled and surveilled environment to develop new skills in individual players. In this sense, the collection of the data is not "extractive" in a narrow sense because the information was not already present in everyday life. Instead, the information to be analyzed is created by actively intervening in the environment and exploring alternatives to the historical status quo. At the analysis stage, Betterball does not look at group-based averages; rather, the analysis is highly individualized. There is no aspiration to build a model that then subsumes the possibilities for all players. What works for Bauer in Driveline may not work for another player; each individual must undergo their own experimentation and deliberate practice. Finally, Betterball is distinctive in the use of the data. Moneyball is a top-down use of data. Centralized managers use data to classify and, as the term Moneyball indicates, economize an organization's resources. By contrast, Betterball is not as top-down. In some cases, the collection, analysis, and use of data can come from the bottom of the organizational hierarchy. Bauer, for instance, initiated his development program on his own using his own resources. The data collection, analysis, and deployment can be collaborative, as coaches and players work together to craft an individualized strategy for improvement. The flow of the data is much more democratic, as the data is not concentrated in the hands of analytically privileged management. In this other sense, the data collection is not extractive because ownership of the data still belongs to Bauer, rather than being shifted to an elite. Bauer is both the subject and object of the data analysis; he is the one participating in the collection, analysis, and use of the data.[1]

THE TWO DATA REGIMES IN PUBLIC POLICY

Within the market-driven world of competitive sports, there has been a distinct movement away from the limitations of data regime 1 to data regime 2. What about outside of sports, in the realm of public policy? Unlike with baseball, comparable data analytics in public policy largely remain within the framework of data regime 1 rather than data regime 2. This section considers two examples, criminal justice and social welfare. These examples show that, despite the unique characteristics of these policy domains, both remain entrenched in a data regime of classification and economization. There have been sporadic attempts to implement a data regime that looks more like Betterball in criminal justice and social welfare. Exploring these alternatives shows some of the limits of a data regime organized around classification and economization in these areas of public policy.

Criminal Justice

Algorithms have proliferated within the criminal justice system. Many police forces rely on crime prediction programs like Predpol to determine how to allocate scarce police resources, sending more units to "hotspots" of criminal activity. After arrest, programs like Correctional Offender Management Profiling for Alternative Sanctions (COMPAS) claim to accurately predict how likely it is for someone to commit crime in the future (Slobogin 2021, vii). These predictions influence decisions of the court system as to how much bail to set for someone accused of a crime, sentencing after conviction, and parole and release after sentencing.

Current recidivism prediction algorithms include measures like the Violence Risk Appraisal Guide (VRAG), the Non-Violent Risk Assessment (NVRA), COMPAS, Public Safety Assessment (PSA), and the HCR-20. To make predictions, these algorithms are trained on data such as the nature of the crime, age, gender, previous convictions, prior imprisonment, prior conduct in school, and alcohol use to see how these factors correlate with the tendency to recommit crime (Forrest 2021, 88, 91, 92–4; Slobogin 2021, 39–42). None of the algorithms are trained on data that measure environmental or relational interventions that may affect recidivism. While some of the algorithms are used to determine whether imprisonment or some other kind of intervention is recommended for a criminal, the intervention itself is not a factor in computing the recidivism risk (Slobogin 2021, 41). COMPAS, for instance, includes a "needs scale" that is designed to help judges determine what kind of intervention would be appropriate for an individual. The scale is produced by looking at characteristics like having friends and family who are criminals; degree of violence of one's crime; personality characteristics such as being anti-social; financial instability; and high levels of boredom and lack of constructive activities that contribute to opportunity to commit crime. Rather than assessing interventions that affect the propensity to resort to crime, the measure assesses whether an individual should be eligible for alternatives to incarceration (Practitioner's Guide 2020, 36–50; Forrest 2021, 71–4). The logic is typical of data regime 1: classifying which groups of convicted individuals should be eligible for interventions by finding correlations predictive of recidivism in large datasets, then economizing by devoting scarce intervention resources to those deemed most likely to benefit.

O'Neil (2016) in her early critique of crime and sentencing algorithms argues that missing from the "training data" that builds recidivism prediction models are analyses of how prison treatment itself—solitary confinement, the experience of prison rape, the conditions of the prison and the presence of rehabilitative activities—affects recidivism (O'Neil 2016, 98–9). There is an extremely strong case that these interventions in the environment, relations, and treatment of prisoners matter in recidivism risk. For example, recidivism in the Scandinavian penal systems are much lower compared with the US penal system. Scholars have identified how the Scandinavian penal system emphasizes rehabilitation over retribution (Kirby 2019; Høidal and Hanssen 2022). In Norway, for instance, prison cells often look like college dorms; cells often remain unlocked; programming activities are abundant; guards often go unarmed; and prisoners may even be allowed to work in the real world during the day and return to the prison at night. By contrast, the environment of US prisons can be so harsh that prisoners resort to forming prison gangs based on race for self-protection. Some have argued that US prisons are crimogenic, as they become "schools for criminality" (Slobogin 2021, 23). The success in Scandinavian penal systems has inspired some communities in the US to experiment with rehabilitation methods (Hyatt and Anderson 2022). Even though different environments and interventions can affect recidivism, current risk algorithms largely do not account for these factors in computing the probability of someone committing a future crime.

A recent philosophical treatment of the justice of algorithms recognizes that interventions that affect future criminal behavior should be part of any algorithmic calculation of risk. Slobogin (2021, 38) argues that for criminal justice algorithms to be considered just, they should meet the following conditions: "a risk assessment should address: (1) the probability (P), (2) that a particular type of offense outcome (O), (3) will occur within a specified period of time (T), (4) in the absence of a specified intervention (I)." Of particular interest here is the last criterion: any risk calculation needs to be computed taking into account the possibilities of intervention. As an example, Slobogin states that a recidivism should take into account the individual's potential to respond to cognitive behavioral therapy (2021, 53); but the intervention criterion can be interpreted much more expansively to include other kinds of interventions, such as the drastic differences between Scandinavian and American prisons.

Much of the debate about the justice of algorithms in criminal justice has focused on the accuracy of the prediction without considering the intervention criterion. Critics have focused on bias in the training data that is used to produce risk scores (Pasquale 2015, 41–2; O'Neil 2016, 25; Ferguson 2017, 49; Brayne 2021, 107). Crime data could be biased because police are biased. Racial bias exists in the historical data because, for instance, stop and frisk and traffic stops by the police end up targeting racial minorities more. Crime data is also class biased because policing blue-collar crimes like robbery is easier than white-collar crimes like wage theft (Reiman 2020). Crime conviction data itself could be biased because of inequalities in the criminal justice system. The ability to afford high-quality legal counsel is likely to produce racial and class inequalities in who is convicted. Even if these biases in police and court administration were eliminated, there would still be racial difference in the historical crime data because of a long history of racial discrimination in the USs that has left racial minorities with inferior wealth accumulation and education opportunities. Thus, if either arrest or conviction data are used to train predictive models, the end result could be biased. These kinds of critiques are aptly summarized by the phrase, "garbage in, garbage out."

Lack of intervention data is also a way in which the training data may be producing "garbage output" because of missing information in the training data. To illustrate this, consider what might "Betterball" look like in the context of prisons. An example of this would be juvenile rehabilitation at Texas' Giddings State School, which houses a population of youth convicted of violent crimes. As is the case with Scandinavian prisons, the detainment facility does not look like a prison, but more like a high school preparatory academy and the population housed there are not referred to as inmates, but "students" and "peers" (Hubner 2005, 9, 15). Participants undergo a program called "resocialization" in which they learn communication skills and self-reflection; ultimately, through good behavior, students can become eligible for small group therapy in a program called Capital Offenders group (Hubner 2005, 18–19). Over a course of six to nine months of group therapy, each of the 18 participants recount two different stories, their life story and their crime story. As Hubner puts it (2005, 29), "Life stories are about what was done to these boys," while crime stories are "about what they did to others." They are also encouraged to become "archaeologists of the self" and to develop empathy and responsibility for their crimes (Hubner 2005, 25–7). Through group therapy and role play, "They experience the range and subtlety of emotions," as Linda Reyes, a former clinical director at Giddings and later deputy executive director of the Texas Youth Commission overseeing the Giddings program, put it. "They connect with others. Having done that, they can no longer live in an antisocial world where everything is black and white and there is no concept of the other." Failure of a student to meet the goals at any particular step on this path does not automatically mean being permanently stamped as irredeemable; students are allowed to restart the program for a limited number of times.

Recidivism rates in this program are lower compared to other juvenile detention programs (Hubner 2005, 18). The success of the program owes to its commitment to try things and see what works, rather than classifying and assuming that certain individuals are unreachable. As Hubner puts it (2005, 32),

> "Any therapist who specializes in working with troubled adolescents knows that there is no one best way to reach them, no silver bullet that will hit a youth between the eyes and turn his life around. The best programs are eclectic and pragmatic, trying out approaches borrowed from sociology, psychology, and biochemistry, using them all, betting hunches, hoping to get lucky, seeing what works. This is especially true of Capital Offenders."

Reyes tells Hubner (2005, 29), "We have to be cautious about ruling out kids in the beginning. They all come through the gate looking like psychopaths. They're kids, they can develop, they can change."

As recounted by Hubner, the success of rehabilitation may be relational. One reason is the relation between the therapists and the juvenile inmates. Perhaps the success of the program is related to the strong and skillful personalities of the specific people managing the program. The second set of relationships that may matter is the relationship between the inmates themselves in the small group therapy circle. Participants in each group are selected based on what the therapists consider likely candidates for compatibility, as the feedback students provide to each other is crucial in developing empathy and responsibility (Hubner 2005, 34). The role of specific relationships in transformation was also echoed in *MVP Machine*. Driveline's coaches believe that part of the success of their player development programs is the relationships between the athletes that participate, forming a local culture (Lindbergh and Sawchik 2019, 115). These kinds of relationships and interaction effects are hard to model in the statistics of data regime 1. Modeling relationships requires more data and variables, so they are often ignored in predictive models.

When data is confined to merely individual traits without taking into account environmental and relational interventions, debates over algorithms can seem locked into tradeoffs between incompatible values. For example, in response to criticisms that COMPAS's algorithms are racially biased, proponents argued that there is a fundamental tradeoff between fairness and accuracy in predicting recidivism (Equivant 2018; but see also Rodolfa, Lamba, and Ghani 2021). When one group is more likely to commit a crime, then any algorithm that attempts to predict crime is going to be biased towards predicting that that group will more likely commit a crime. Attempting to make the algorithm give a similar rate of prediction across groups will make the algorithm less accurate. This framing makes it seems as if the debate is frozen between two competing values, but really this is true only from the perspective of data regime 1. From this perspective, the problem of mass incarceration here is viewed as a classification problem: some groups are more likely to commit crime than others, and policy requires getting this classification right. Some prisoners are dangerous, some are not, and justice is advanced when the classification becomes more precise. Where the data is lacking is whether in fact those classified as "dangerous" have the potential to become nondangerous through interventions. Examples such as the Giddings State School show that experimentalism along the lines of data regime 2 can matter and that people can transcend their classification. Without data on intervention, can it be really said that sentencing algorithms are "accurate"? Is the recidivism risk of a youth who goes through the Giddings State School really the same as the recidivism risk of someone who does not? If other interventions matter, then the idea that there is a fundamental tradeoff between accuracy and fairness is wrong; rather, the notion of accuracy was limited from the start.

Others have suggested that the current problems of big data analytics should be compared with human decision-making without data, which can be just as biased or inaccurate as data-driven algorithmic judgments, or even worse (Ludwig and Mullainathan 2021, 74–81). These same authors and others have argued that the problems identified in the use of data to make judgments and predictions can be fixed, through better data and variables. With better algorithms, the error rates in classification of different groups can be balanced so that, for example, there is no racial bias. The problem, then, is between badly built and properly built algorithms (Obermeyer et al. 2019, 453; Ludwig and Mullainathan 2021, 89–92). In contrast to that perspective, there is not just a choice between the flaws of human judgment and the flaws of big data analysis emanating from the practices of data regime 1; nor is there just a choice between badly built and properly built algorithms. There is a third alternative to consider as well. From the perspective of data regime 2, one can also see that even "properly built" algorithms suffer from epistemological assumptions and patterns of practice associated with data regime 1.

Social Welfare

As with criminal justice, automated algorithmic sorting is increasingly being used to determine provision of welfare services (Eubanks 2015, 11–12; Alston 2019; Gilman 2020, 22; Constantaras et al. 2023). The uses include rooting out fraud in welfare provision; prioritizing who should receive resources like scarce housing support resources; and assessing predictive risk of things like child maltreatment to determine intervention by child protective services. As is evident from this brief list, the uses of data analytics in welfare are largely along the lines of data regime 1: to classify legitimate and/or high-need groups versus fraudulent and/or low-need groups. Such classification takes place in a context of limited funding and the need to economize scarce welfare resources.

The use of algorithms to sort the population in social welfare provision is plagued by many of the same difficulties found in the use of automated scoring in criminal justice. One of the problems in criminal justice algorithms is the insufficiency and bias in the historical training data, and the same applies in the use of social welfare algorithms. In the case of child maltreatment risk scores in Allegheny county, for instance, the scoring for the predictive model was trained on community referrals (someone in the community reported a family to the authorities because of suspicion of possible maltreatment) or court determinations that maltreatment had occurred in the training data. Community referrals can be highly inaccurate and biased, as a referral is simply a suspicion of maltreatment and may be motivated by something other than actual maltreatment, such as neighborly disputes or bias in the reporter. Similarly, court determinations may be subject to judges' and caseworkers' bias (Eubanks 2015, 143–4, 154–5). Class bias in the assessment of child maltreatment exists because there is no information on individuals who access private services rather than public services (Eubanks 2015, 157–8).

As with the criminal justice algorithms, what is also missing from these social welfare algorithms are data on the interventions that might move individuals from one classification state to another. "The digital poorhouse," as Eubanks terms it, freezes "its targets in time, portraying them as aggregates of their most difficult choices." It ignores "the ability to develop and evolve … . The digital poorhouse locks us into patterns of the past" (Eubanks 2015, 195). Is there an equivalent of Betterball in social welfare that allows individuals to break out of these classifications? One rare example is the work of Cottam (2018), who has helped develop a different model of social welfare provision that involves greater individual and local-level experimentation without this tendency to sort and classify. Cottam began her experiments in social welfare delivery after many years of seeing how traditional social welfare delivery directed by the government and social workers failed to change many clients' lives. Frustrated with this history of failure, Cottam embraced experimentalism at two levels: first, with the social policy designer engaging in experiments in policy implementation, and second, with the client of social welfare services engaging in their own experimentation. Cottam's vision of social welfare provision does not start off with the social worker as expert, nor with classification of social service recipients. Instead, in her model, the recipients define what they think they need, often in group settings with other recipients, and the social workers try to assist and provide resources as the recipients test their own proposed solutions. Cottam's work can be seen as in line with a broader movement for evidence-based policymaking and use of experiments in government (Baron 2018), with the added twist that it is not just Cottam, the social welfare expert, who is experimenting, but also the social welfare clients themselves.

In one of Cottam's first attempts to experiment with this new philosophy, her organization attempted to assist families where the parents were not working and the children not attending school; many of these families had not responded to previous social workers' interventions. Instead of dictating what the families should do, Cottam's group of professionals asked families to define what support they needed as they pursued their own proposed solutions to their problems and reflected on what worked and did not work (Cottam 2018, 53). In another, her organization tasked itself with trying to connect disaffected youth with employment experiences. Instead of mandating that youth learn a set of predetermined skills, Cottam's team solicited members of the local community to provide different "experiences" in different careers. The youth then get to choose, in a process of trial and error, which experiences they would like to undergo and reflect with others on the experience (Cottam 2018, 79–81). Based on the success of these programs, Cottam applied the philosophy in other social service realms. In an employment assistance program, those without jobs are allowed to define for themselves their strategy for acquiring a profession they are interested in (Cottam 2018, 89). In healthcare, Cottam experimented with creating a social network in which individuals decide within small local groups how they want to manage their health conditions (Cottam 2018, 114). The same is also applied to seniors and how they want to manage their conditions (Cottam 2018, 137).

Cottam's reforms in social welfare provision reimagine social assistance as a realm of personal experimentation, in which individuals get to provisionally define their goals, make mistakes, engage in self-correction, and assess their efforts with people in similar situations to themselves. Although not explicitly framed this way by Cottam, this is not a data regime in which data is gathered by an elite or an expert who then "manages" the program by classifying and economizing resources. Instead, this is a more individualized and localized data regime. It is also a data regime in which the "objects" of knowledge—each social service client—is not simply an object of knowledge but also a subject: each are tasked with evaluating the data and information from their own experiments, and reflecting and making adjustments based on that data. This process of becoming the subject of knowledge production not only motivates higher participation in the programs but also increases the confidence and skill of the subjects to have agency over their own lives (Cottam 2018, 161–5).

TOWARDS A RIGHT TO THE PRODUCTION OF DATA AND DATA ANALYSIS

As this brief review reveals, data regime 2 is underproduced relative to data regime 1 in public policy, even as other fields such as major league baseball have realized the benefits of data regime 2. This is concerning for two reasons. The first is that an epistemological inequality is created. Knowledge related to the formation of classification and sorting predominates over knowledge related to transformation of classifications. The second concern refers to differences in the possession of analytic power—that is, some entities are more likely to be able to possess the ability to engage in Betterball compared to other entities. Trevor Bauer can engage in experimentation because, as a wealthy baseball player, he has the resources to do so. At the same time, groups without resources are stuck within a Moneyball-like data regime. Given that classification is a form of power (Bowker and Star 1999, 45), some can transcend their classifications, while others cannot.

What this suggests is that the ethics of data extends to a positive right to data collection and analysis. Artificial intelligence and data ethics approaches in the current literature have emphasized values like transparency, explainability, privacy, lack of bias, and equality. These approaches are particularly well suited when it comes to elite actors (often corporations, governments, and academics) using data for classification and sorting that lead to decisions that affect opportunities given to individuals. However, these approaches should be supplemented by a positive right to data collection and analysis that addresses the overall epistemological inequality between data regime 1 and 2, and the distributive inequality between those who have access to data regime 2 and those who do not.

In the study of rights, there is a well-known distinction between negative and positive freedoms (Berlin 1969). Early formulations of rights extended to some basic political rights (i.e., the ability to vote), and basic civil rights (i.e., the ability to own property and the right to freedom of speech and association). Many of these earlier rights involved negative freedoms: such rights stop a centralized power—in this case, the government—from interfering with individual freedoms. By the twentieth century many theorists of rights began to question whether these earlier generation of rights were sufficient (Vasak 1977). A right to property did not actually guarantee that one had sufficient resources to afford necessities like food, shelter, and health. A right to vote did not actually ensure that one had the time to follow politics and exercise the right meaningfully. Rights activists began to theorize positive rights, which focus on the capacity of individuals to be able to do something. A positive right goes beyond just stopping the government from interfering with individuals; the government or others are obligated to provide something to individuals, as in the growth of public education and the social welfare state (Sen 1979, 1999).

Contemporary approaches to data ethics and regulation of data largely focus on negative rights preventing data elites in the public and private sectors from abusing their power. By contrast, a positive right to information and data analysis refers to the capacity to produce data and analysis for the benefit of individuals. A variety of scholars have discussed epistemic injustice (Fricker 2007; Kidd et al. 2017) and other scholars have proposed epistemic rights. Risse (2021), for example, has suggested dividing thinking about epistemic rights in terms of subjects as knowers and as knowns. As "knowns," subjects would have rights such as the protection of their data and limits on how it used by others; as "knowers," epistemic rights would include the ability of subjects to have knowledge and act upon it. Rights associated with increasing the space of data regime 2 would correspond to this category of improving epistemic rights of knowers.

Would this positive right to data production be too costly for governments increasingly constrained by budgetary concerns? Although more work needs to be done in this area, the examples from this chapter suggest that it might not. It is possible that analytic insights derived from data regime 2 could end up saving society more money in the long term. Hubner estimates that though the Giddings School in Texas is initially costly, it saves society money over time. He estimates the cost of the Giddings School at about $40,000 per pupil a year. A failure to prevent recidivism for a juvenile offender can lead to multi-decade sentences in state prison, which costed about $15,000 per inmate a year in the early 2000s (Hubner 2005, 177). Similarly Cottam has estimated that her experiments in social welfare provision, while initially costly, end up saving society more in resources that would have been spent on her clients (Cottam 2018, 67, 87, 112–13, 135). The current dominant regime of classification in data analysis is often justified in terms of efficiency and cost savings, but this is only efficiency in a narrow sense. This efficiency is incrementalism: as long as one can do better than the preexisting alternative, then the innovation might be said to be more efficient. Global efficiency, however, requires not just comparison to preexisting alternatives but comparison against not-yet-existing alternatives that actually may be better.

In summary, a right to the production of data helps realize the vision of making data regime 2 possible for more people. More work needs to be done in specifying to what extent data regime 2 should be implemented for more people. This chapter shows in broad strokes why this further work is necessary, and why it behooves data practitioners in social policy to think about the potential costs of only considering data analytics from the perspective of data regime 1.

NOTE

1. The definitions developed here are ideal-typical ones, defining the main tendencies within the practice of each data regime. There can be crossover at the margins. For instance, although the main tendency in data regime 1 has been described as "classifying and economizing" while data regime 2 has been described as "experimenting and developing," perhaps it could be argued that individual development could occur from data regime 1. For instance, a player could look at the results of a model developed in data regime 1 to try to modify their individual approach to the game (e.g., a player could try to draw more walks having learned the correlation between walks and runs). In this sense, data regime 1 can lead to "development and transformation" but it would still be lacking in giving that individual player knowledge on how to draw more walks. Similarly, data regime 2 can also be used for economization, but it is not as central or as short term as it is with data regime 1; see the last section of this chapter for how data regime 2 may actually promote long-term economization.

REFERENCES

Alston, Philip. (2019). *Report of the Special Rapporteur on Extreme Poverty and Human Rights* (advance unedited version). Report to United Nations General Assembly, 74th session. https://www.ohchr.org/sites/default/files/Documents/Issues/Poverty/A_74_48037_AdvanceUneditedVersion.docx, last accessed November 14, 2024.

Angwin, Julia, Larson, Jeff, Mattu, Surya, and Kirchner, Lauren. (2016, May 23). *Machine Bias.* Propublica. https://www.propublica.org/article/machine-bias-risk-assessments-in-criminal-sentencing

Baron, Jon. (2018). A Brief History of Evidence-Based Policy. *Annals of the American Academy of Political and Social Science* 678 no. 1: 40–50.

Bates, Jo. (2017). Data Cultures, Power and the City. In R. Kitchin, T. Laurialt, and G. McArdle (eds.), *Data and the City* (pp. 189–200). New York: Routledge.

Benjamin, Ruha (2019). *Race After Technology: Abolitionist Tools for the New Jim Code.* Cambridge: Polity.

Berlin, Isaiah. (1969). Two Concepts of Liberty. In *Four Essays on Liberty* (pp. 118–72). London: Oxford University Press.

Bowker, Geoffrey C., and Susan Leigh Star. (1999). *Sorting Things out: Classification and Its Consequences.* Cambridge, MA: MIT Press.

Brayne, Sarah (2021). *Predict and Surveil: Data, Discretion, and the Future of Policing.* New York: Oxford.

Buolamwini, Joy, and Timnit Gebru. (2018). Gender Shades: Intersectional Accuracy Disparities in Commercial Gender Classification. *Proceedings of Machine Learning Research* 81: 1–15.
Constantaras, Eva, Gabriel Geiger, Justin-Casimir Braun, Dhruv Mehrotra, and Htet Aung. (2023, March 6). Inside the Suspicion Machine. *Wired*. https://www.wired.com/story/welfare-state-algorithms
Cottam, Hillary. (2018). *Radical Help: How We Can Remake the Relationships between Us and Revolutionise the Welfare State*. London: Virago.
Equivant. (2018). Response to ProPublica: Demonstrating Accuracy Equity and Predictive Parity. https://www.equivant.com/response-to-propublica-demonstrating-accuracy-equity-and-predictive-parity/
Ericsson, Anders, and Robert Pool. (2017). *Peak: Secrets from the New Science of Expertise*. New York: HarperOne.
Eubanks, Virginia. (2015). *Automating Inequality: How High-Tech Tools Profile, Police, and Punish the Poor*. New York: St. Martin's Press.
Ferguson, Andrew Guthrie. (2017). *The Rise of Big Data Policing: Surveillance, Race, and the Future of Law Enforcement*. New York: New York University Press.
Forrest, Katherine B. (2021). *When Machines Can Be Judge, Jury, and Executioner: Justice in the Age of Artificial Intelligence*. Hackensack, NJ: World Scientific.
Fricker, Miranda. (2007). *Epistemic Injustice: Power and the Ethics of Knowing*. New York: Oxford University Press.
Fussell, Cathy. (2022). Four Data Discourses and Assemblage Forms: A Methodological Framework. SocArXiv. Preprint. https://osf.io/preprints/socarxiv/jvcqw/
Gandy, Oscar H. Jr. (2021). *The Panoptic Sort: A Political Economy of Personal Information*, 2nd edn. New York: Oxford University Press.
Gilman, Michele. (2020). *Poverty Lawgorithms: A Poverty Lawyer's Guide to Fighting Automated Decision-Making Harms on Low-Income Communities*. Report for Data and Society. https://datasociety.net/wp-content/uploads/2020/09/Poverty-Lawgorithms-20200915.pdf
Gin, Willie. (2018). Big Data and Labor: What Baseball Can Tell Us about Information and Inequality. *Journal of Information Technology & Politics*, 15 no. 1: 66–79.
Hepp, Andreas, Juliane Jarke, and Leif Kramp. (2022). New Perspectives in Critical Data Studies: The Ambivalences of Data Power—an Introduction, in A. Hepp, J. Jarke, and L. Kramp (eds.) *New Perspectives in Critical Data Studies: The Ambivalences of Data Power* (pp. 1–24), Cham: Palgrave Macmillan.
Høidal, Are, and Nina Hanssen. (2022). *The Norwegian Prison System*. New York: Routledge.
Hubner, John. (2005). *Last Chance in Texas: The Redemption of Criminal Youth*. New York: Random House.
Hyatt, Jordan, and Synøve Nygaard Andersen. (2022). A Pennsylvania Prison Gets a Scandinavian-Style Makeover – and Shows How the US Penal System Could Become More Humane. *The Conversation*. https://theconversation.com/a-pennsylvania-prison-gets-a-scandinavian-style-makeover-and-shows-how-the-us-penal-system-could-become-more-humane-187834
Iliadis, Andrews, and Federica Russo. (2016). Critical Data Studies: An Introduction. *Big Data & Society* 3 no. 2: 1–7.
Kidd, Ian James, Jose Medina, and Gaile Pohlhaus Jr. (eds.). (2017). *The Routledge Handbook of Epistemic Injustice*. New York: Routledge.
Kirby, Emma Jane. (2019). How Norway Turns Criminals into Good Neighbours. *BBC*. https://www.bbc.com/news/stories-48885846
Kitchin, Rob. (2014). *The Data Revolution: Big Data, Open Data, Data Infrastructures, and Their Consequences*. London: Sage.
Kitchin, Rob, and Tracey P. Lauriault, (2018). Toward Critical Data Studies: Charting and Unpacking Data Assemblages and Their Work, in J. Thatcher, J. Eckert, and A. Shears (eds.), *Thinking Big Data in Geography* (pp. 3–20), Lincoln: University of Nebraska.
Lewis, Michael. (2004). *Moneyball: The Art of Winning an Unfair Game*. New York: Norton.
Lindbergh, Ben, and Travis Sawchik. (2019). *The MVP Machine: How Baseball's New Nonconformists Are Using Data to Build Better Players*. New York: Basic Books.
Ludwig, Jens, and Sendhil Mullainathan, (2021). Fragile Algorithms and Fallible Decision Makers: Lessons form the Justice System. *Journal of Economic Perspectives* 35 no. 4: 71–96.

Mayer-Schönberger, Viktor, and Kenneth Cukier. (2013) *Big Data: A Revolution That Will Transform How We Live, Work and Think*. London: Houghton Mifflin Harcourt.

Noble, Safia Umoja. (2018). *Algorithms of Oppression: How Search Engines Reinforce Racism*. New York: New York University Press.

O'Neil, Cathy. (2016). *Weapons of Math Destruction*. New York: Crown.

Obermeyer, Ziad, Brian Powers, Christine Vogeli, and Sendhil Mullainathan. (2019). Dissecting Racial Bias in an Algorithm Used to Manage the Health of Populations. *Science* 366: 447–53.

Pasquale, Frank. (2015). *The Black Box Society: The Secret Algorithms that Control Money and Information*. Cambridge, MA: Harvard University Press.

Practitioner's Guide to COMPAS Core. (2020). https://www.equivant/resources

Reiman, Jeffrey. (2020). *The Rich Get Richer and the Poor Get Prison*. New York: Routledge.

Risse, Mathias (2021). *The Fourth Generation of Human Rights: Epistemic Rights in Digital Lifeworlds*. Carr Center for Human Rights Policy, Harvard Kennedy School. https://carrcenter.hks.harvard.edu/files/cchr/files/risse_fourth-generation.pdf

Rodolfa, Kit T., Hemank Lamba, and Rayid Ghani (2021). Empirical Observation of Negligible Fairness–Accuracy Trade-offs in Machine Learning for Public Policy. *Nature Machine Intelligence* 3: 896–904.

Sadowski, Jathan. (2019). When Data Is Capital: Datafication, Accumulation, and Extraction. *Big Data & Society* 6(1): 1–12.

Sen, Amartya. (1979). *Equality of What?* Stanford University: Tanner Lectures on Human Values.

Sen, Amartya. (1999). *Development as Freedom*. Oxford: Oxford University Press.

Slobogin, Christopher. (2021). *Just Algorithms: Using Science to Reduce Incarceration and Inform a Jurisprudence of Risk*. New York: Cambridge University Press.

Stephens-Davidowitz, Seth. (2018). *Everybody Lies: Big Data, New Data, and What the Internet Can Tell Us about Who We Really Are*, New York: Dey.

Sweeney, Latanya. (2013). Discrimination in Online Ad Delivery. *Communications of the Association of Computing Machinery* 56 no. 5: 44–54.

van Dijck, José. (2014). Datafication, Dataism and Dataveillance: Big Data between Scientific Paradigm and Ideology. *Surveillance & Society* 12 no. 2: 197–208.

Vasak, Karel (1977). A 30-Year Struggle: The Sustained Efforts to Give Force of Law to the Universal Declaration of Human Rights. *The UNESCO Courier* 11: 29–32.

Zuboff, Shoshana. (2020). *The Age of Surveillance Capitalism: The Fight for a Human Future at the Frontier of Power*. New York: Public Affairs.

19. The Janus face of personal data agency in public and private use applications
Dale Mineshima-Lowe, Roxana Bratu and Sarah Giest

INTRODUCTION

In a world where digital applications and platforms are used daily by people in their lives, there is consideration by an increasing number of people about the type and amount of information these digital technologies harvest and store. However, there has been little research and consideration about how much agency citizen-users have over how their information is used for public or private services. This chapter adds to the discourse about agency over personal data within the expanding use of digital applications and platforms in people's day-to-day lives. In doing so, the chapter is structured as three sections.

The first section provides background to what we mean by 'data agency' for this work, and how it relates to understandings of 'public' and 'private' spheres as well as privacy within the developing digital world. It uses the ideas of Horkheimer (1972) and Habermas (1991), who, in their discussions, attempt to reconstruct and reformulate what the 'public sphere' is and how this concept is shaped by the social-cultural-political system in which it rests. These foreground the exploration and identification of the underlying power structures that digital platforms and applications have (corporations, governments, processing institutions, for example) and the role these have on data use and reuse by those who claim to have 'ownership' of the data. Fundamentally, in identifying these power structures, we can begin to unravel and study the kinds and levels of information collected that directly impact individual agency-control over the data, with whom and for what purposes.

The second section builds upon previously explored concepts and ideas, applying them to four distinct digital applications and platforms. The selection of these four apps/platforms, each designed for diverse purposes and audiences, enables an examination of the power structures governing data access and control. This analysis spans data that is voluntarily provided to that which is mandated. The chapter conceptualizes a framework centered around data agency, utilizing key variables to map individuals' data agency across a spectrum of digital applications/platforms. The purpose and value of this data agency framework is discussed, detailing its application in the present context and proposing avenues for future expansion.

The final section concludes the chapter and highlights issues around responsibility for agency and privacy, as well as some of the trade-offs around, for example, heightened security features potentially limiting inclusive access.

BACKGROUND

Data Agency as a Concept

When we speak of 'agency,' we refer to ownership by an individual over their data, or of an individual having a choice about how the data is shared and used. The underlying ideas about 'agency' are of control and power – to determine the 'fate' (i.e., use, purposes, extent, and time-space issues) of one's personal data. This definition constitutes that (individual) 'data' is a commodity or asset, not dissimilar to one's labor, that can then be withdrawn or leveraged in some way. However, this generalization of agency in relation to digital technologies provokes some vital questions about how much control individuals really have over data they knowingly share as 'consumers' – users of digital technologies and as digital producers when using digital platforms and applications. While this connection between data as an asset like one's labor is not necessarily how the average person using various digital platforms or applications thinks about their data, it is a growing consideration by other stakeholders who are designing and creating such digital technologies that have become a part of everyday life.

When considering agency and data exchange, the focus is on individuals' proprietary control over data and the benefits they gain through data sharing, such as access to services or systems otherwise inaccessible. This relationship shapes the systems and structures that define the lived world, as discussed by Habermas (1989), contributing to a false dichotomy between public and private spheres. Private includes individual interests beyond the government, encompassing commodity exchange as part of the private sphere, challenging traditional distinctions.

Despite using digital applications managed by the public sector, individuals may perceive their actions within the private sphere. Instances like government-mandated digital technologies during the COVID-19 pandemic raise questions about agency and governance of personal data. Horkheimer (1975) and Habermas (1989) note how traditional approaches normalize unjust practices, creating a narrative unnoticed or unchallenged by citizens, perpetuating power structures. Horkheimer's (1975) concerns about the failure to question power and the status quo highlight the need for awareness and challenges to emancipate individuals from existing power structures.

Related to the previous discussion about data exchanges and power structures, the issue of data privacy has evolved further in recent years, and over time there has been an increasingly nuanced understanding of what privacy means for different parts of the population as well as for different scenarios in which information and data are shared. A widely used model is that by Smith et al. (2011), who suggest a comprehensive framework widely used for understanding information privacy research, called the Antecedents-Privacy Concerns-Outcomes (APCO model). The APCO model presents a macro-model of privacy-related concepts and is divided into the three main categories: the Antecedents (A), the Privacy Concerns (PC), and the Outcomes (O) (Smith et al., 2011). The theory thereby suggests that privacy concerns are a function of personal and situational cues, and thus these cues are antecedents and independent variables for predicting privacy concerns (Buck et al., 2022). Those cues include past privacy experiences of users, awareness of privacy, personality and demographic differences, as well as culture or climate. These elements affect privacy concerns, which are further shaped by the outcomes, which include behavioral reactions (including disclosures), regulation, as well as trust (Smith et al., 2011).

In recent years, the changing role that products and services play in satisfying users' needs has highlighted the user-centric dynamics in which users become co-creators through sharing personal data (Buck et al., 2022). This is captured in the idea of the 'privacy paradox' in that concerns over privacy are growing while information disclosure behavior is also growing. In short, 'studies that have tried to predict users' information disclosure behaviour have produced mixed results, often showing an individual's information disclosure behaviour does not reflect their stated privacy concerns. This mismatch between stated concerns and actual behaviour has been called the "privacy paradox"' (Wisniewski and Page 2022, 19).

Throughout variations of the model, privacy concerns have remained at the center of the discussion. There are different ways to capture privacy concerns specifically, such as the 'Concern for Information Privacy' (CFIP) model, which includes collection concerns, unauthorized secondary use concerns as well as improper access and errors – both accidental and deliberate (Stewart and Segars, 2002). The 'Users' Information Privacy Concerns' (IUIPC) model suggests a three-dimensional understanding of collection, control, and awareness (Malholtra et al., 2004). Given current technological realities, the 'Mobile Users' Privacy Concerns' (MUIPC) model (Xu et al., 2012) was developed and 'captures privacy concerns by secondary use of personal data, presided surveillance ... and perceived intrusion' (Buck et al., 2022, 48).

A relevant takeaway from these developments in the privacy field is that individual antecedents and individual behavior are a central component and that individual perceptions of privacy drive the discussion. This is especially relevant in settings where not only users themselves share information but in contexts where peer-to-peer (P2P) data is published: 'On P2P platforms, such as social media platforms or sharing economy platforms, personal data is no longer necessarily released or distributed by the user himself but also by other peers' (Buck et al., 2022, 52). These dynamics add, according to Choi et al. (2015), network commonality on perceived privacy invasion as well as perceived privacy bonding. This also links back to earlier discussions about Habermas's perspective on how the social order is created and bound by those who partake in it and in the system's creation and evolution.

Data Agency in Practice

While individuals often desire proprietary control over their data compared to entities like companies and governments, there are instances where relinquishing data agency, to some extent, can benefit users. The creation of the Sherpa platform[1] by California's community college system for collecting user feedback serves as an example (Bramucci and Gaston, 2012a; Reyman, 2013). However, even when systems aim to benefit users, questions arise about the secondary use of collected data, raising concerns about privacy and protection (Reyman 2013, 514–15).

A distinction exists between 'user content' and 'user data' in terms of data property and ownership, governed by copyright law (Reyman, 2013, 524). This distinction is crucial, as it affects ownership rights and protections outlined in terms-of-use agreements by digital application and platform providers. While it may seem like a semantic difference, many platforms emphasize this distinction to access user data while maintaining user trust in the security and protection of their information on these platforms.

Delving into terms-of-use agreements and privacy protections for widely used digital platforms, individuals may perceive their engagement as part of their private sphere, exercising freedom of choice in data sharing. Despite this scrutiny, only a few thoroughly read and understand the terms, limiting true agency over their data (Reyman, 2013).

Reyman (2013) points toward Facebook's approach, assigning copyright ownership to users while indicating that posting grants the platform a comprehensive license over the content. The distinction between user content and user data is emphasized by digital platforms, as seen with Facebook, where data appropriation occurs for the company's gain, raising concerns about loss of agency and economic exploitation (Reyman, 2013, 524).

The underlying assumption in terms-of-use agreements is that data, especially on social networks, are seen as technology-generated artifacts rather than integral to users' productive activities. Users are not recognized as agents, and the generated data is considered a technological product valuable to collectors for known and future purposes (Reyman, 2013, 525).

Based on this understanding of data agency, power structures, and the underlying assumptions made about power and control over one's data, we unravel the complex relationship between users, digital applications and platforms, data agency of individuals, and how digital technologies are structured around data collected and for whose use. It leads us to questions about 'What kind of processes exist within these specific digital applications and platforms that allow for agency by individuals over their data?'; 'Are there specific challenges and opportunities around data agency that both individual citizens and various stakeholders need to take into account more than they currently do?'; and 'How do citizens understand the power structures that exist in the digital apps/platforms they elect to use?'

In short, we explore the concept of 'agency' concerning individual control over data in digital platforms and applications and delve into the challenges users face in understanding and exercising true agency over their data linked to power and privacy. We argue that 'agency' in the context of personal data involves individual ownership and control over data, treating it as a commodity or asset comparable to labor, and highlight that there is a false dichotomy between public and private spheres, indicating challenges to traditional distinctions and raising concerns about power structures perpetuated by digital technologies.

CASE STUDIES

In this section, four apps/platforms have been selected as they have been created for different purposes and audiences. The differences between the four digital applications/platforms will allow us to consider the power structures (as discussed earlier) that exist within each. This relates to access and control of data, with the four digital apps/platforms illustrating a spectrum for individual data sharing, from voluntarily provided to those mandated. This will be used to identify key variables to create an agency framework across a range of digital applications/platforms. Each case study below will include a brief description of what they do/ are used for, before considering their design and usability in relation to the level of information (data) they collect from users, and the examination of power structures they create or are informed by.

Transparency Watch Platform and Apps (ISO and Android) for Combating Corruption and Creating Awareness of Corruption in North Macedonia

The Transparency Watch platform was created by Transparency International – Macedonia and the Center for International Relations in 2011 as a means for citizens to report allegations of corruption observed or experienced. It is a corruption reporting and monitoring platform that has been running for the past decade and uses the Ushahidi[2] open-source software, which allows for crowdsourcing data from citizens and includes mapping capabilities to visualize the crowdsourced data collected (Mineshima-Lowe, 2024).

The platform has been designed not only to collect reported allegations of corruption but also to check and verify reports, map crowdsourced data to a 5 kilometer radius of the reported incident, and provide a contact point for legal advice for citizens on their reported incidents (Neos, 2013). Through the web-based platform and the ISO and Android mobile applications that link to the platform, citizens can report incidents anonymously. The platform provides users with the opportunity to select what information they include in an incident report and to select a category for the type of corruption being reported.

With regard to the personal data collected, this is secured through multiple layers of protection due to the sensitivity of the issue and the possibility of reprisal for reports being made. On this platform and its associated mobile applications, users have agency over their data – in particular because of how the web-based platform's 'report form' has been created and laid out. Any personal data submitted by users and collected by the Transparency International-Macedonia team is done for incident verification processes and, more particularly, is utilized for the specific purpose of assisting users should they desire to take their investigated claims forward with legal action through the country's legal system (Mineshima-Lowe, 2024).

Data can also be collected from users who are utilizing one of the other methods for reporting an incident by sending a message via ONE to 145111, or calling the office at +389 2 3217000; by sending an email to prijavikorupcija@transparency.mk; by sending a tweet with the hashtag #korupcijaMK; or by filling out the platform's online form. Additional data may be automatically captured (e.g., the email address being sent from the phone number showing on the system; or the IP address of the system – mobile or computer – used). Data collated this way, due to security reasons, will be coded, anonymized, and/or separated from the incident reports by the TI-Mac team as part of the privacy and security processes to protect users.

Overall, when we consider agency over data and the power structures that this platform creates, individuals have a higher level of agency from start to end in their interactions with the platform. Individuals initiate contact and elect to share any amount of personal data details as they feel comfortable and desire to do. The underlying structure appears to have been created to maximize agency for users and layers of protection to ensure that users feel and know that they have agency within the use of the platform.

Fitbit Watch and App

In the case of the Fitbit app and Watches, this has been included as a case study as an example of the current trend of individuals using wearable fitness and health monitoring technologies and their associated mobile apps.[3] This wearable device interacts with its partner mobile app that was founded in early 2007 as Health Metrics Research Inc. before changing its name to Fitbit, Inc. in October of the same year (2007).

In terms of design and usability, Fitbit has been evolving since its launch in 2007 to become more user-friendly and has focused on fine-tuning the 'user experience' by providing multiple hardware options for wearable devices. This evolution has also seen the inclusion of increased health and fitness metrics that users are able to 'track' as they wish with the syncing of data collected by the wearable to the mobile Fitbit application (Level Design SF, 2023; Pier, 2023; Shaw, 2023). With its focus on user experience and usability, it had reached an 'active'[4] user base of 31 million in 2020, and 111 million registered users as of 2021 (Curry, 2023; Fitbit, 2023).

With the Fitbit wearable and app, there are different levels of data being collected – specific information users provide which are required to create a user account, additional 'voluntary' information with use and sync between wearable and app that the company collects to improve user experience, and then additional forms of data that the app will collect and store on the company's server. Within the Fitbit Privacy Policy most recently updated on June 6, 2023 (Fitbit, 2023), there is a note that differentiates privacy policy details for users of Fitbit devices and services using the Fitbit app account, as compared to those users who use their Fitbit device and services with a Google account. In this case study, we focus on the details about data collection, usage, and sharing for users interacting with the Fitbit app via a Fitbit account. The *Fitbit Legal: Privacy Policy* (2023) outlines what type of personal information users *must* provide to set up an account and interact with the wearable device and mobile app – this includes: name, email address, password creation, date of birth, gender, height, weight, and in some instances, a mobile telephone number. Other account information is optional, and users can decide which to include or not – such as a profile photo, biography, country information, and a community name. While these are considered basic information by Fitbit, it is also information that should a user decide to leave the service, would be deleted – usually within 30 days, but this can be up to 90 days according to Fitbit's policies. This longer duration accounts for the deletion of a user's data from its servers and backup servers that store all users' data. Any additional information, according to its Privacy Policy (2023) is by user choice but enables the use of certain features and improves user experience. Therefore, without this additional user information given, users may not be able to make full use of all the features available to them. Access to the breadth of features in the app is also reliant on the type of account a user has on the mobile app (e.g., a 'fit premium' account which requires payment in exchange for access to a larger range of health and fitness metrics and support via third-party apps linked into the Fitbit mobile app).

While the level and types of information to make full use of the Fitbit app are at a user's discretion – weight plan – gain/loss desired, number of steps per day, food and water intake, other data is collected by virtue of using a Fitbit wearable device 24/7. The wearable device, if worn throughout the day, will collect data on sleep time/wake time, duration and types of sleep, heart rate, and exercise, calories burned. However, it requires users to allow their wearable device to sync with the mobile phone app for these data to be shared with the Fitbit service. Again, the privacy policy states that 'this type of data' is collected 'if you grant us access to your location' via your mobile device or computer (Fitbit Legal: Privacy Policy, 2023). While users can voluntarily choose what types and amounts of data are collected, should they elect to share their data to maximize their experience with the technologies, their device will also provide Fitbit with their approximate location via the IP address from that device, along with the browser type being used, language settings, and operating system.

Fitbit states that the above information and data collected from a user's use of the Fitbit device and services is used by the company to 'improve and personalize the Services and to develop new ones. For example, we use the information to troubleshoot and protect against errors; perform data analysis and testing; conduct research and surveys; and develop new features and Services' (Fitbit Legal: Privacy Policy, 2023). Within the privacy policy, Fitbit states very clearly that 'We never sell the personal information of our users. We do not share your personal information except in the limited circumstances described below' (within the 'How Information Is Shared' section of the Privacy Policy (2023)). These 'limited circumstances' are conducted, it says, by the direction of users (e.g., in the app's community features, leaderboards, social tools, or with the use of third-party application access for employee wellness programs via a user's employer). However, again, to access and maximize the benefits of the app tools, it requires in many cases that users make their data accessible.

Overall, from the wording of the privacy policy, users do have agency in terms of what data they elect to provide and decisions about account settings that impact how and what data is collected and stored with Fitbit. Users also appear to have agency in terms of their personal information, as this can be edited and deleted, as mentioned. Most information the policy cites will, on request, be deleted within 30 days; however, it can take up to 90 days to delete all of a user's information as data is stored across backup systems. While it looks like users have significant agency over the types and levels of information they share and decisions about the use of that data, two things that stood out in the Privacy Policy (2023) that perhaps challenge users' data agency within these particular digital technologies are: (1) Fitbit 'keeps information about you and your use of the Services for *as long as necessary for our legitimate business interests*, for legal reasons, and to prevent harm'; and (2) third-party partners that Fitbit works with to provide analytics and advertising services, for example, are provided with information on users from Fitbit to process information according to Fitbit's instructions and in compliance with its policies on confidentiality and security. Such additional conditions added as clauses to the privacy policy can leave users with less agency over their data than expected, as users can't know the types, level of detail, or amounts of their data that are transferred to Fitbit's partners and affiliates. While data agency can be maintained by users, it requires a user to not only consider the account settings within their Fitbit account via their mobile phones but more fundamentally, for users to understand the nature and power structures related to Fitbit's work with third-party apps.

The Flo.health App

The Flo app is a menstrual and period tracker, allowing users to track their period/menstrual cycle, along with providing the option of using its ovulation calculator and pregnancy calendar. The app is designed for users to personalize their use in terms of their main purpose for interest in using the app and receiving personalized health insights through logging their health goals and any symptoms they are experiencing. The Flo app is used as a case study because it is a high-profile app that has been widely used for personal individual reasons by many users, only to have them choose to withdraw from its use with changes to state-level legislation within the USA following the US Supreme Court's change of stance on *Roe v. Wade* and the right to choose on the issue of abortion.

In registering for the app, there are personal questions required to assist the app in developing a personalized profile for individual users – year of birth, the user's general health (e.g., weight, sleep issues, height, stress levels, coffee consumption), and menstrual health-specific questions (PMS symptoms, pre-menstrual discharge, mood pre-/during cycle). Before a finalized personal profile is shared with a user, the user is required to review and agree to the terms and conditions of use of the app and agree to the app's privacy policy. Other privacy policy clauses, which are *optional* in terms of agreement, and a user can initially agree and then withdraw their consent later by contacting Flo at its support email, are: (1) the clause that users agree to Flo's use of their personal data to send them products and/or services deemed compatible with their data; and (2) the agreement that 'AppsFlyers, its integrated partners, as well as certain marketing partners indicated in Cookie Policy may receive my personal data' (Flo - Privacy Policy, 2023). Under this agreement of sharing user data with integrated and marketing partners, the data specified is 'strictly limited to technical identifiers (unique identifiers that generally only identify a device or an app – IP address, IDFA, Flo-issued Installation ID, User ID, certain location data), age groups, subscription status, fact of application launch (including web-application)" (Flo – Privacy Policy 'health', 2023).

By using the Flo app, users look to have agency over the data they share, as the policy allows users to request access to their personal data held, as well as to modify, correct, erase, or update any data held by Flo that has been shared by them (the user) in the course of interacting with the app. Like the previous case study (Fitbit), Flo states that modification or erasure of some personal data provided by users could have an impact on certain features of the app for the users, as it is reliant on historic data to build up the profile and monitoring for/by the user.

The Flo app provides users with the option to have their data included with others to contribute to the continued development of the app and community, which seems to provide greater agency to users regarding how their voluntary sharing of personal information will be further used by Flo beyond creating their individual profiles that they have access to and control over. This is also seen in how Flo manages requests to erase personal data – requests to erase data and deactivate a Flo user account result in Flo 'generally deleting all your Personal Data and it will not be recoverable should you later create another account' (Flo – Privacy Policy, 2023). However, as seen with the Fitbit app, there are limitations to users' requests for the erasure of their data – where Flo states it will make efforts to 'anonymize or otherwise de-identify your data where possible,' but 'may retain certain Personal Data and other information after your account has been terminated or deleted as necessary to comply with legal obligations, resolve disputes and enforce our agreements' (Flo – Privacy Policy, 2023). Perhaps this is why many users in the USA, within the post-US Supreme Court ruling on *Roe v. Wade* environment (late June 2022), have requested erasure of their data and deactivation of their user accounts, and yet still fear future repercussions (Garamvolgyi, 2022). For some users who have found themselves in this category, there is a worry that the specific clause mentioned about Flo's ability to retain certain Personal Data even after an account is terminated for 'legal obligations' is a potential threat to their futures but demonstrates a lack of real agency over data in light of the fact that numerous state legislatures have begun to pass legislation criminalizing abortion fully or in part (Torchinsky, 2022). The data held by Flo could, in some instances, create legal obligations on the Flo app developers to make available any data they hold on specific individuals, should legal action be taken against said individuals in state legal proceedings. An interesting development in quick follow-up to the US Supreme Court's ruling in June 2022 saw Flo, along with other women's health apps, pledge to enhance their privacy and security protocols' (Pifer, 2022). For Flo, this included launching an anonymous mode within the application, but also reviewing and changing its structures for handling user data for accounts using the anonymous mode. Such changes to the security system included enhanced encryption of all data and passcode protections. Perhaps more importantly, it revised its processes used for managing user data. Here we saw it utilizing a system to separate data and ensure 'no single party that processes user data for anonymous mode accounts has complete information on who the user is or what they're trying to access' (Pifer, 2022).

This change, while subtle and responsive to the user exodus that Flo and other women's health apps were seeing, is significant. It challenges the power structures in which the application sits and provides a means for users to exert more agency over their personal data. This shift also connects to the distinction between public and private as put forth by Habermas and Horkheimer in earlier discussions within this chapter.

DigiD Digital Identity System

DigiD is a shared online registration service for those living in the Netherlands to gain access to digital services by the Dutch government, both at national and local levels. In 2003, the Dutch government introduced an identity registration service for digital government services. This was an effort by four government agencies, including the Social Insurance Institute (SVB, Sociale Verzekeringsbank), the Centre for Work and Income (CWI, Centrum voor Werk en Inkomen), the Employees' Insurance and Benefits Office (UWV, Uitvoeringsinstituut Werknemersverzekeringen), and the Tax Authorities (Belastingdienst). The management of the service was taken over by a Department of the Ministry of Internal Affairs in 2006. Since its establishment around 400 local Dutch authorities use DigiD as their identity system (Seltsikas and van der Heijden, 2010). When a digital identity is requested, the following information is used:

- Social security number (in Dutch: Burgerservicenummer (BSN))
- Name
- Address
- Postal Code
- Place of residence
- Date of Birth
- Data to determine the residency or non-residency of the applicant
- Phone number (optional)
- Email address (mandatory)

This information is shared with government institutions that are linked to the DigiD system. While Logius (Department of the Ministry of Internal Affairs) is in charge of the system, it uses a private provider for some of the first-line support as well as for customer satisfaction surveys. These parties process the personal data of those users who contact the DigiD Helpdesk (BZK, 2022). There are further exceptions in the context of legal obligations to share information if there is an investigation. In addition, Logius shares any information related to, for example, insecure DigiD used to (or attempted to) view or change personal data.

The system follows a centralized identity management approach in that 'there is only one identity service, which is used by many different government agencies' (Seltsikas and van der Heijden, 2010, 6). The use by government departments is voluntary, and municipalities can opt in if needed. Despite the data-sharing idea underlying this centralized system, the DigiD is widely accepted by those that are able to use and access it. Numbers from 2021 suggest that there were 545 million log-ins, half of which were done via the mobile app, and that there are 16.5 million DigiD accounts (Logius, 2022). For the log-ins, there are four levels of identification:

- Via the DigiD app
- Through an SMS verification code
- With username and password
- Using an identity card, which is required for particularly privacy-sensitive data.

In addition, the DigiD allows giving permission for others to manage, for example, tax matters; however, it is at the moment not possible for legal representatives to log in on behalf of another person. The user retains rights over the data by having the right to find out whether and which personal data was processed as well as the right to update, supplement, or limit the processing of personal data (Rijksoverheid, 2023). In addition, some government services may require specific permissions. These permissions can be managed by the user in the online account.

Users of DigiD also retain rights over their data: users have the right to access their personal data held by the DigiD service and are allowed to know what information is being processed about them. This includes details about the purposes of processing, the categories of data involved, and any third parties with whom the data is shared. Users also have the right to request corrections to inaccurate or incomplete personal data held by DigiD. If the processing of personal data is based on user consent, individuals usually have the right to withdraw that consent. This, however, may affect their ability to use certain services linked to DigiD.

There is no legal obligation to have a DigiD; however, many services are not available online without the identifier and require extra effort to gain access by, for example, making an appointment with the government in person. In addition, having an email address for getting a DigiD can be a hurdle for those who have limited digital access or lack two-factor authentication methods (Giest and Samuels, 2022). A recent report highlights that offline/physical options need to remain available to those who lack digital skills or have a complex matter that is not covered by digital forms (Algemene Rekenkamer, 2023). Additionally, the report by the Dutch Court of Audit recommends that the Ministry investigates whether digital service points (IDOs) personnel are able to request a DigiD for those seeking support.

ANALYSIS OF THE DIGITAL APPS AND PLATFORMS

Upon reviewing various apps and platforms, two notable factors in the practices of digital application and platform providers stand out. Firstly, there's a focus on the extent to which apps can reuse collected data (even if non-identifying) for their legitimate business interests. Secondly, the ability of these providers to retain user data beyond contract termination and data withdrawal is a significant concern. Some examples explicitly state in their terms that they can store data for unspecified durations based on business interests, legal requirements, or to prevent harm, such as Fitbit stating that the company stores and keeps data for an undisclosed amount of time 'as long as necessary for our legitimate business interests, for legal reasons, and to prevent harm' (Fitbit, 2023). Similarly, Flo says that they 'may retain certain Personal Data and other information after your account has been terminated or deleted as necessary to comply with legal obligations, resolve disputes and enforce our agreements' (Flo – Privacy Policy, 2023). This discretion affects users' data agency, contradicting assurances that users can delete their data anytime.

Furthermore, the analysis of other apps/platforms reveals additional challenges related to user data agency. Increasingly, individual agency is intertwined with the use of digital technologies. Non-engagement with these technologies can limit opportunities to demonstrate agency in modern governance, where digital participation often becomes integral for accessing services and benefits. While participation may not be mandatory, refraining from it can lead to restrictions in accessing essential resources and assistance.

Based on this, we establish a framework for comprehending citizens' data agency concerning voluntarily shared data and its subsequent use, reuse, or sale (Figure 19.1). Our conceptualization of data agency emphasizes four key dimensions crucial to individual empowerment in the digital landscape. These dimensions include information and awareness regarding data

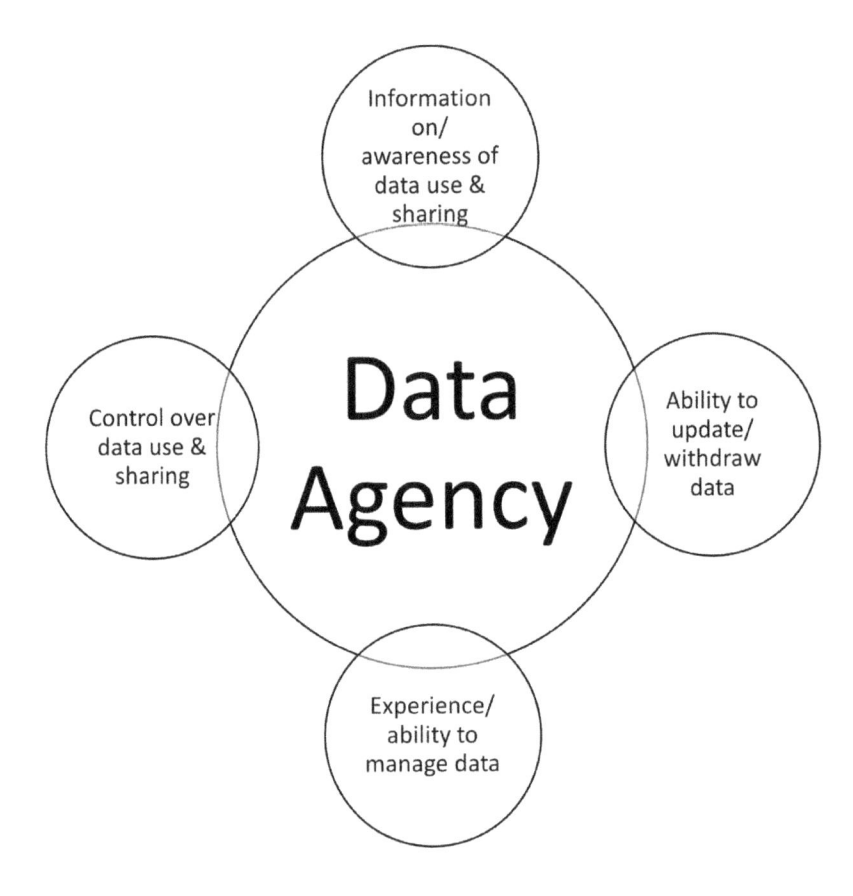

Source: Authors' own.

Figure 19.1   Data agency framework visualization

use and sharing, the level of control individuals have over their data, the ability to update or withdraw data as needed, and the overall experience and proficiency in managing personal data effectively.

Including all these elements becomes crucial as government agencies globally increasingly integrate digital applications and platforms, especially in areas like digital health innovations, aiming to address healthcare capacity shortages. The study delves into various applications, including DigiD (Netherlands' public service), Transparency Watch (North Macedonia, corruption monitoring), Fitbit (health and fitness), and the Flo.health app (ovulation and period tracker). The analysis focuses on the design, usability, data collection, and citizens' control over their data in these applications.

Notably, the comparison reveals that enhanced security features, while protecting data better, may limit inclusivity for individuals with limited digital skills or access. The complexity of data collection, processing, and sharing, involving public, private, and non-profit organizations, raises challenges in identifying stakeholders and understanding shared data. This prompts questions about responsibility for ensuring users' digital agency and privacy – is it the role of national governments, international organizations, digital app providers, or the users themselves?

For future research, an expanded scope involving additional digital applications and platforms, along with an examination of existing policies and legislation, would help identify gaps between current practices and future developments. This understanding could lead to improved protections, clearer messaging to users regarding data control and privacy, and more effective policymaking in this digital landscape.

NOTES

1. *Sherpa* is a search engine that makes use of human and machine learning, created to increase student success by providing students with guidance and information for making decisions about courses and services (Bramucci & Gaston 2012a, 2012b). An outline of the proposed system can be found at: https://doi.org/10.1145/2330601.2330625.
2. More information about the Ushahidi open-source software application: Ushahidi – Crowdsourcing Solutions to Empower Communities: http://www.ushahidi.com
3. One of the three authors of this work uses this technology for personal reasons, and this is how this specific wearable was selected from the plethora available.
4. 'Active' users – defined by Fitbit as users who use their devices at least once a week.

REFERENCES

Algemene Rekenkamer. (2023). Digitale identiteit vraagt veel van DigiD en eHerkenning. Report. Available at: https://www.rekenkamer.nl/publicaties/rapporten/2023/03/29/digitale-identiteit-vraagt-veel-van-digid-en-eherkenning (accessed: 13/6/2023).

Bevir, M. and Rhodes, R.A.W. (2012). Interpretivism and the Analysis of Traditions and Practices. *Critical Policy Studies* 6(2): 201–8.

Bramucci, R. and Gaston, J. (2012a). Sherpa: Increasing Student Success with a Recommendation Engine. In *LAK '12: Proceedings of the 2nd International Conference on Learning Analytics and Knowledge*. April 19, 2012. https://doi.org/10.1145/2330601.2330625

Bramucci, R. and Gaston, J. (2012b). Sherpa: Increasing Student Success with a Recommendation Engine. In *EDUCAUSE 2012 Annual Conference*. Anaheim and online. November 8, 2012. Conference Presentation. MP3. Available at: http://educause.mediasite.com/mediasite/Play/48bc1946312a4827ad81afc4bae1147f1d (accessed: 12/11/2024)

Buck, Christoph, Dinev, Tamara, and Reza Anaraky. (2022). Revisiting APCO. In Knijnenburg, B., Page, X., Wisniewski, P., Lipford, H., Proferes, N., and Romano, J. (Eds.), *Modern Socio-Technical Perspectives on Privacy*. Cham, Switzerland: Springer, pp. 43–60.

BZK (Ministerie van Binnenlandse Zaken en Koninkrijksrelaties). (2022). Over DigiD, Privacy. Available at: https://www.digid.nl/over-digid/privacy/ (accessed: 13/6/2023).

Choi, B.C.F., Jiang, Z., Xiao, B., and Kim, S.S. (2015). Embarrassing Exposures in Online Social Networks: An Integrated Perspective of Privacy Invasion and Relationship Bonding. *Information Systems Research* 26: 675–94. https://doi.org/10.1287/isre.2015.0602

Curry, D. (2023). *Fitbit Revenue and Usage Statistics*. Available at: https://www.businessofapps.com/data/fitbit-statistics/ (accessed: 03/06/2023).

Fitbit. (2023) *Fitbit Legal: Privacy Policy*. Fitbit - Google.com. Available at: https://www.fitbit.com/global/us/legal/privacy-policy (accessed: 12/11/2024)

Flo.health. (2023). *Privacy Policy*. Available at: https://flo.health/privacy-policy (accessed: 12/11/2024)

Flo.health. (2023). *Privacy Policy 'health'*. Available at: https://flo.health/privacy-policy (accessed: 12/11/2024)

Garamvolgyi, F. (2022). Why US Women Are Deleting Their Period Tracking Apps. *Guardian. Opinion*. June 28. Available at: https://www.theguardian.com/world/2022/jun/28/why-us-woman-are-deleting-their-period-tracking-apps (accessed: 06/02/2024).

Giest, S. and Ng, R. (2018). Big Data Applications in Governance and Policy. *Politics and Governance* 6(4): 1–4. doi:10.17645/pag.v6i4.1810

Giest, S. and Samuels, A. (2020) 'For Good Measure': Data Gaps in a Big Data World. *Policy Sciences* 53: 559–69. https://doi.org/10.1007/s11077–020–09384–1

Giest, S. and Samuels, A. (2022). Administrative Burden in Digital Public Service Delivery: The Social Infrastructure of Library Programs for E-inclusion. *Review of Policy Research*. https://doi.org/10.1111/ropr.12516

Habermas, J. (1991). *The Structural Transformation of the Public Sphere: An Inquiry into a Category of Bourgeois Society*. Trans. T. Burger and F. Lawrence. Cambridge: Polity Press.

Horkheimer, M. (1972). Traditional and Critical Theory. In *Critical Theory. Selected Essays*. Trans. M.J. O'Connell and others. New York: Continuum.

Hughes, S., Giest, S. and Tozer, L. (2020). Accountability and Data-Driven Urban Climate Governance. *Nature Climate Change* 10: 1085–90. https://doi.org/10.1038/s41558–020–00953-z

Level Design SF (2023) *Fitbit Graphic Design*. https://leveldesignsf.com/fitbit (accessed 12/11/2024).

Logius. (2022). Gebruik DigiD in de lift. Available at: https://logius.nl/actueel/gebruik-digid-de-lift#:~:text=Het%20gebruik%20van%20DigiD%20en,gedaan%20met%20de%20DigiD%20app (accessed: 13/6/2023).

Krijger, J. (2022). Enter the Metrics: Critical Theory and Organizational Operationalization of AI Ethics. *AI & Society* 37: 1427–37. https://doi.org/10.1007/s00146–021–01256–3

Malhotra, N., Kim, S. S., and Agarwai, J. (2004). Internet Users' Information Privacy Concerns (IUIPC): The Construct, the Scale, and a Causal Model. *Information Systems Research*. 15(4): 366-355. https://doi.org/10.1287/isre.1040.0032

Mineshima-Lowe, D. (2024). Involving Citizens through Multi-platform Strategies: Transparency Watch in North Macedonia. In A. Mattoni (Ed.), *Digital Media and Anti-Corruption from the Grassroots: Contexts, Platforms and Practices of Anti-Corruption Technologies Worldwide*. Cheltenham, UK and Northampton, MA, USA: Edward Elgar Publishing.

Morris, M. (2011). Mining Student Data Could Save Lives. *Chronicle of Higher Education*, October 2. *Chronicle.com*. Web. May 17, 2023.

Neos, D. (2013). Crowdsourcing to Fight Corruption in Macedonia: Interview with Metodi Zajkov (Transparency International – Macedonia). *International Affairs Forum* 4(1): 107–12. https://doi.org/10.1080/23258020.2013.830911

Pier, E. (2023) *Fitbit Design System*. https://www.ericpier.com/fitbit (accessed: 12/11/2024).

Pifer, R. (2022). Period Tracker Flo Launches Anonymous Mode amid Post-Roe Privacy Concerns. *Health Care Dive,* September 15. Available at: https://www.healthcaredive.com/news/flo-anonymous-mode-period-tracker-app-abortion-roe/631926/#:~:text=Period%20tracking%20ap (accessed: 04/02/2024).

Reyman, J. (2013). User Data on Social Web: Authorship, Agency, and Appropriation. *College English* 75(5): 513–33. Available at: https://library.ncte.org/journals/ce/issues/v75-5

Rijksoverheid. (2023). Wat kan ik regelen met mijn DigiD? Available at: https://www.rijksoverheid.nl/onderwerpen/digitale-overheid/vraag-en-antwoord/wat-is-digid#:~:text=DigiD%20niet%20verplicht,dingen%20niet%20via%20internet%20regelen (accessed 13/6/2023),

Seltsikas, P., and H. van der Heijden (2010). A Taxonomy of Government Approaches towards Online Identity Management. In *Proceedings of the 43rd Hawaii International Conference on System Sciences – 2010.* Available at: https://ieeexplore.ieee.org/stamp/stamp.jsp?tp=&arnumber=5428293 (accessed: 13/6/2023).

Shaw, A. (2023) *Fitbit Design Language.* https://www.annashaw.design/productwork/fitbit (accessed 12/11/2024).

Smith, H.J., T. Dinev, and H. Xu. (2011). Information Privacy Research: An Interdisciplinary Review. *MIS Quarterly* 35(4): 989–1016.

Stewart, K.A., and A.H. Segars. (2002). An Empirical Examination of the Concern for Information Privacy Instruments. *Information Systems Research* (13): 36–49. https://doi.org/10.1287/isre.13.1.36.97

Torchinsky, R. (2022). How Period Tracking Apps and Data Privacy Fit into a Post-Roe v. Wade Climate. *National Public Radio (NPR),* June 24 (updated). Available at: https://www.npr.org/2022/05/10/1097482967/roe-v-wade-supreme-court-abortion-period-apps (accessed: 06/02/2024).

Wisniewski, Panela and Xinru Page. (2022). Privacy Theories and Frameworks. In Knijnenburg, B., Page, X., Wisniewski, P., Lipford, H., Proferes, N., and Romano, J. (Eds.), *Modern Socio-Technical Perspectives on Privacy.* Cham, Switzerland: Springer, pp. 15–41.

Xu, H., Gupta, S., Rosson, M. B., and Carroll, J. M. (2012). Measuring mobile users' concerns for information privacy. In *Proceedings of International Conference on Information Systems, ICIS 2012.*

DIGITAL APPS/PLATFORMS

Transparency Watch platform homepage – https://transparency-watch.org/main?l=en_US
Transparency Watch – FAQs – https://transparency-watch.org/page/index/2
Fitbit – privacy policy – https://www.fitbit.com/global/us/legal/privacy-policy
Fitbit design development – https://www.annashaw.design/productwork/fitbit
Fitbit design development – https://www.ericpier.com/fitbit
Fitbit smartwear hardware design – https://leveldesignsf.com/fitbit
Fitbit FitOS and hardware development & design for user experience – https://leveldesignsf.com/fitbit
Flo – terms of use – https://flo.health/terms-of-service
Flo – privacy policy – https://flo.health/privacy-policy
Flo – terms & conditions – https://www.flo.com/terms-conditions/

20. A social capital perspective to building sustainable data centers for science

Federica Fusi and Eric W. Welch

INTRODUCTION

The dematerialization of scientific research has increased the need to integrate, manage, and distribute data within and across diverse research communities (Barone et al., 2017; Halewood et al., 2018). Scientists and research organizations rarely control all resources required for data-intensive research because of the high infrastructure cost and the narrow specialization of scientific activities. National governments, international agencies, and foundations extensively fund data centers for science – online platforms that ease the sharing of free common resources (e.g., data, computational capacity, storage space, and analysis and annotation tools) among scientists worldwide. Examples include Cyverse, funded by the US National Science Foundation, the European Union's Open Science Cloud (EOSC), and GISAID currently supported by Brazil, Germany, the US and Singapore governments as well as philanthropic foundations.

These data centers fill an infrastructural void while protecting scientists' intellectual property rights and encouraging innovation. Their long-term sustainability is, however, a challenge. Data centers depend on a geographically dispersed community of researchers, who voluntarily contribute new data and information, develop common metadata and ontologies, update content and infrastructures, and teach and recruit new members. Those that are unable to create a self-sustained community will likely fail in the long run, thus wasting a significant amount of public resources invested in their creation. A critical question for data-driven science is, how can data centers build and maintain an active membership that simultaneously uses and contributes common resources over time? Conversely, why are some data centers never able to create and sustain such a community?

This chapter draws from scholarships on open communities and social capital, both anchored in organization studies, to propose a novel theoretical framework to answer these questions. Data centers are akin to open communities, which are "goal-oriented yet loosely coordinated individuals" (Levine & Prietula, 2013, p. 1416) who create and maintain a shared pool of resources freely available to active contributors and non-contributors alike. Examples of open communities include Wikipedia, Stuck Overflow, and GitHub. Open communities – like data centers – are substantially different from traditional organizations because they primarily rely on the voluntary and informal support and engagement of a dispersed community of members. Sustainability, therefore, can only be achieved through a "recursive relationship between those who contribute content and those who consume it" (Kane & Ransbotham, 2016, p. 1258). In other words, sustainable open communities receive continuous inputs from their membership to develop and enhance common resources, which in turn attract new users who eventually become contributors (Butler, 2001; Peddibhotla & Subramani, 2007). But, since membership is mostly voluntary, common resources are greatly uncertain and fluctuating over time depending on individual willingness to dedicate time and efforts to the community.

Social capital offers an interesting lens to understand the mechanisms that support (or hinder) this recursive relationship. Social capital is "the aggregate of resources embedded within, available through, and derived from the network of relationships possessed by an individual or organization" (Inkpen & Tsang, 2005, p. 151). Prior research shows that social capital facilitates the active and repeated sharing and use of common resources over time (Chiu et al., 2006; Tsai & Ghoshal, 1998), such that individuals are more active members in open communities with greater social capital (Hsu, Ju, Yen, & Chang, 2007). Therefore, social capital appears to be key to activate and maintain the reciprocal relationship between users and contributors upon which depends the sustainability of open communities. Yet we know little about how open communities create and sustain social capital over time, especially at the community-level, and how social capital is linked to contributions and use of resources in ways that enhance long-term sustainability of open communities and data centers. This gap significantly limits our understanding of how we can intervene to design more effective governance structure.

In this chapter, we first define and characterize sustainability resources and social capital dimensions in open communities. We then use observations from six data centers in genomics as explorative cases and theoretically develop a set of propositions on how social capital dimensions develop and interact in data centers, and ultimately enable the contribution and use of resources key to long-term sustainability. Our proposed framework provides insights on the governance of data centers to inform decision-making processes and policies of funding agencies, large-scale data-intensive research projects, and the broader research community. Our propositions can also open venues for future research on how these communities emerge and sustain their membership over time.

SUSTAINABLE OPEN COMMUNITIES

The sustainability of open communities, such as data centers, is largely determined by the voluntary contributions of resources by members, such as data, information, skills, time, passion, ideas, and recruitment efforts (Faraj, Jarvenpaa, & Majchrzak, 2011). These resources create internally recognized and externally visible value, which in turn attracts users and potentially new contributors (Kane & Ransbotham, 2016; Peddibhotla & Subramani, 2007). Based on prior work, we identify three types of sustaining resources that members can contribute and are necessary for the sustainability of open communities in the long term: *promotion, participation*, and *shaping* resources (Butler, 2001; Preece et al., 2004; Ren et al., 2007). Each type of resource requires a different level of commitment, time, and effort from members, such that numerous members contribute promotion resources and only a few contribute shaping resources (Preece et al., 2004).

Most members contribute *promotion resources* by joining and continuing their association with the community, advertising their membership, and promoting the community to new members. Promotion resources help to maintain membership and attract new members. In fact, larger communities generally rely on greater provision of promotion resources (Butler, 2001; Kane & Ransbotham, 2016; Peddibhotla & Subramani, 2007). Contribution of *participation resources* entails the actual use of resources pooled by the community as well as donation of like resources to other members. For example, members use data and information shared by others but they also enhance the common pool by contributing new data, conducting analysis, and sharing knowledge produced from using the common resource. Ren and colleagues (2007) note that a major challenge for open communities is to transform "lurkers" – that is, members contributing only promotion resources – into active contributors of participation resources. Finally, open communities require *shaping resources* which include investment of time and effort to manage, maintain, control, and lead the community (Blanchard & Markus, 2004; O'Mahony & Ferraro, 2007). Participants contribute shaping resources when they serve on committees, undertake management activities, or voluntarily provide services, such as moderating comments or revising content. Shaping resources are generally contributed by a small group of members who have gained status or reputation within the community (Blanchard & Markus, 2004; Ren et al., 2007; Shah, 2006).

Up to now, the literature has mostly focused on individual antecedents explaining why and when individuals are likely to contribute these resources for community development, particularly promotion and participation resources (Hsu et al., 2007; Nambisan & Baron, 2007; Wasko & Faraj, 2005). Comparatively, there are fewer efforts to explain how "individual level behaviors aggregate to form sustainable online communities" by enhancing the recursive relationships between use and contribution of resources (Faraj & Johnson, 2011, p. 1466). We suggest that a social capital perspective can help address this gap.

A SOCIAL CAPITAL PERSPECTIVE TO OPEN COMMUNITY SUSTAINABILITY

The development of social capital is critical to encourage the sharing of tangible (e.g., capitals and goods), intangible (e.g., information and support), and even symbolic (e.g., prestige and reputation) resources among members of any collectivity (Burt, 2000; Lin, 1999; Putnam, 1995). In particular, community-level social capital manifests in the ability of members of a community to access resources from other members, regardless of whether they are directly connected or not (Lin, 1999; Putnam, 1995). Because of their belonging to the community, members are granted reciprocity, trust, and goodwill from others (Portes, 2000; Putnam, 1995). Communities that develop and maintain high levels of social capital are more likely to be sustainable over time as members are more willing to provide resources and contribute efforts to maintain the common pool of resources. Additionally, as community members trust each other, they have greater commitment and willingness to use common resources and contribute back with new ones to further individual and community outcomes. In open communities, social capital is therefore critical to activate and maintain the reciprocal relationship between users and contributors upon which depends their sustainability.

Researchers generally point to three dimensions of social capital (among others: Adler & Kwon, 2002; Huysman & Wulf, 2006; Inkpen & Tsang, 2005; Nahapiet & Ghoshal, 1998; Tsai, 2002; Tsai & Ghoshal, 1998; Wasko & Faraj, 2005). The *structural* dimension accounts for the configuration of relationships in which an actor is embedded. The *relational* dimension concerns the common rules and norms defining acceptable behaviors (Adler & Kwon, 2002; Nahapiet & Ghoshal, 1998). Finally, the *cognitive* dimension encompasses shared languages, goals, and narratives among actors (Nahapiet & Ghoshal, 1998). Variations of these dimensions lead to different levels and forms of social capital and, therefore, greater (or lower) access to resources, which determines the success of individual actors, networks, and communities (Boh et al., 2007; Chiu et al., 2006; Faraj & Johnson, 2011; Hsu et al., 2007; Inkpen & Tsang, 2005; Kirsch, Ko, Tsai, 2002; Tsai & Ghoshal, 1998; Wasko & Faraj, 2005).

Organizations are traditionally designed to facilitate the formation of social capital through physical and institutional elements. For instance, formal rules and contractual agreements between the organization and its employees maintain relational social capital by defining expectations and norms (Inkpen & Tsang, 2005). While all three dimensions of social capital coexist within each organization, structural social capital is commonly leveraged to create both relational and cognitive social capital (Burt, 2000; Tsai, 2002). Organizations count on the geographical proximity among organization members to facilitate repeated and frequent interactions, through which common norms and shared cognitive codes are developed (Inkpen & Tsang, 2005; Tsai, 2002; Tsai & Ghoshal, 1998). Frequent interactions also support the creation and consolidation of informal norms that regulate interpersonal relationships and the connected activities (e.g., coordination and resource sharing). Once developed, the relational and cognitive dimensions provide motivation and impetus to share resources (Adler & Kwon, 2002) and smooth information transfer and collaboration (Tsai, 2002; Tsai & Ghoshal, 1998), all of which are fundamental to the organization's sustainability in the long run.

Open communities lack the same physical and institutional settings that facilitate social capital formation in organizations (Faraj et al., 2011; Nahapiet & Ghoshal, 1998; Ren, Kraut, & Kiesler, 2007). In particular, they challenge the centrality of structural social capital (Tsai & Ghoshal, 1998). The high geographical dispersion of members, the online-only interactions, and the fluidity and heterogeneity of community membership affect interaction, and therefore might hinder the formation of structural social capital (Faraj et al., 2011; O'Leary & Mortensen, 2010). Additionally, given the voluntary nature of contributions, open communities cannot rely on formalized relationships and contracts to produce relational social capital. Finally, the production of a common pool of resources often requires heterogeneous communities with different goals and working norms to collaborate and share, reducing the initial level of cognitive social capital (Fusi et al., 2018). Because of these conditions, social capital is likely to manifest differently in open communities. As we aim to explore how it develops and maintains, we first need to define a taxonomy of the three social capital dimensions and how they can be identified and measured in open communities.

Structural Dimension

The virtual nature of open communities substantially constrains frequency and intensity of interactions (Blanchard & Markus, 2004; Butler, 200; Huysman & Wulf, 2006; Peddibhotla & Subramani, 2007). In digital settings "a tie [is only] created between two individuals when one person responds to another's posting" (Wasko et al., 2009, p. 44). Actors might join a virtual space but refrain from interacting with others, such that their presence remains invisible to the community (Rullani & Haefliger, 2013). As a result, community members often do not know each other nor who can provide the resources they need (Wasko et al., 2009). Because of these unique characteristics, we suggest that the structural social capital in open communities is determined by member interdependence and the degree of stability of the community. Communities with a more interdependent and stable membership will have greater structural social capital.

Member interdependence is the degree to which community members' work requires collaboration and interaction. Interdependence is greater when community tasks require members to interact in real time or a defined virtual space (Huysman & Wulf, 2006; Ma & Agarwal, 2007). As interdependence increases, so do incentives for more dense and frequent interactions, resulting in greater structural social capital. For instance, public document repositories are "devoid of social cues" (Peddibhotla & Subramani, 2007, p. 329). Members have no direct or indirect ties with other members and contribute to the community by posting documents on a shared repository (Ma & Agarwal, 2007). Interdependence is low as members are not required to interact to achieve community goals, thereby decreasing structural social capital. By contrast, in open source communities, members are connected through small groups or project teams and interact directly to achieve common goals and perform joint tasks, such as writing code and developing software programs. The success of the community requires coordinated inputs from multiple members, resulting in greater interdependence and higher structural social capital (Ren et al., 2007).

Community stability refers to the frequency that members join or leave the community, that is, membership turnover. In open communities, participation is voluntary and there are low costs associated with joining or leaving. Research shows that open communities experience greater turnover as size increases (Butler, 2001). Turnover reduces community stability because of the short duration of the relationships among community members, and between community members and the community itself. High turnover also increases the number of newcomers in the community, which may negatively affect the formation of long-term relationships. Overall, more stable communities enjoy a higher level of structural social capital as members establish long-term connections at the interpersonal and community level.

Relational Dimension

As members in open communities have few direct relationships, rules and norms are important to make behaviors predictable and define reciprocal expectations (Faraj & Johnson, 2011). Open communities are generally regulated by both formal rules that prescribe minimum behavioral standards and social norms learned and diffused through socialization (Nambisan & Baron, 2010; Wasko et al., 2009). Yet, too heavy reliance on formal rules may deter participation and contribution from new members who need to learn community rules and may worry about disrespecting them (Ma & Agarwal, 2007; Shah, 2006). Social norms may be more effective in guiding members' behavior without posing excessive constraints but compliance relies solely on informal controls placed on members (Preece et al., 2004). Open communities balance a mix of formal rules and social norms to enhance relational social capital that manifests as a sense of common responsibility and generalized trust (Ren et al., 2007).

Common responsibility exists when community members share a sense of responsibility and obligation toward other members and the common pool of resources (Blanchard & Markus, 2004; Nambisan & Baron, 2007). Research shows that a common sense of responsibility increases both direct and indirect reciprocity patterns within a community network (Faraj & Johnson, 2011) and increases the overall responsiveness of community members toward others (Blanchard & Markus, 2004), thereby reducing the likelihood of free-riding. Members of communities with a high sense of common responsibility are less likely to limit access to their resources and more likely to share them (Fusi et al., 2018). Open communities where common responsibility is widely shared, respected, and enforced will enjoy greater relational social capital.

Generalized trust occurs when there is expectation of benign behavior from others (Molm et al., 2000; Rousseau et al., 1998). In open communities, process-based interactions promote generalized trust at the community level (Inkpen & Tsang, 2005). As Kirsch, Ko, and Haney (2010, p. 475) explain, generalized trust "embodies expectations that each team member will perform his or her tasks competently." Formal rules related to processes and contributions support generalized trust (Blanchard & Markus, 2004; Inkpen & Tsang, 2005) by shaping members' expectations of behavior from other members. For instance, rules embedded in the infrastructure design – for example, data standards (Fusi et al., 2018) – guarantee the security and functionality of the common pool of resources, reinforcing positive expectations (Nambisan & Baron, 2007). Blanchard and Markus (2004) observe that community norms requiring members to use their real name in either their email address or signature increase trust among members. As generalized trust emerges from positive process-based interactions among members, relational social capital increases.

Cognitive Dimension

The formation of a community is based on the recognition of mutual goals and values that bring together individuals (Blanchard & Markus, 2004). When communities lack shared goals, members encounter severe difficulties in coordinating and managing joint tasks and resources (O'Leary & Mortensen, 2010). We highlight two mutually reinforcing aspects of cognitive social capital: common content and community identification. When members identify more strongly with the community, they are more likely to contribute common content (Ren et al., 2007). Similarly, the collective creation of common content can reinforce members' community identity (Benamar, Balagué, & Ghassany, 2017).

Common content includes artifacts – from metadata and ontologies to data and texts – collectively produced by community members (Peddibhotla & Subramani, 2007). The common content acts as a boundary object around which a community is defined (Kane & Ransbotham, 2016). It also reflects how members organize and enact their collective production and contribution (Brubaker & Cooper, 2000) through "visible routines ... needed for individuals to exert the continued effort to maintain a community cognition" (Kane, Johnson, & Majchrzak, 2014, p. 3044). Indeed, the process to collectively create and maintain the common content reduces cognitive discrepancies among members, supports the development of common languages and practices, and increases members' attachment to community goals and mission (Blanchard & Markus, 2004; Kane & Ransbotham, 2016; Rullani & Haefliger, 2013). For instance, newcomers can browse the common content to develop a cognitive understanding of the community and its boundaries before joining and actively contributing (Preece et al., 2004). Changes in the common content also foster changes in the community cognition (Kane et al., 2014). If such changes become the object of disagreement among community members, they can produce negative effects on social capital and community survival (Kane & Ransbotham, 2016).

Common identity is "the perception of oneness with or belongingness to some human aggregate" (Ashforth & Mael, 1989, p. 21). Over time, members transition from identifying with a narrow set of personal relationships (e.g., friendship ties) to cognitively associating their own identity with the mission, goals, and values of the community (Ren et al., 2007; Wasko et al., 2009). When members share a strong community identity, they are less likely to leave and more likely to contribute and provide support to the community (Nambisan & Baron, 2010; Ren et al., 2007). In contrast, misconceptions or conflicts around community identity negatively affect cognitive social capital because members attribute different meanings to or have different frames of reference about what the community is and should be doing.

Figure 20.1 provides a first overview of our theoretical approach. On the left side, it shows the three dimensions of social capital and how we define them in open communities (squared boxes). The right side shows the three types of resources that are needed for open community sustainability. Black arrows represent known relationships between social capital dimensions and their manifestation as well as the reciprocal relationships among sustainability resources. Dotted arrows represent unknown relationships, which will be explored in the next section of this chapter. Using genomic data centers as an illustrative example, we will examine the links among social capital dimensions and their effect on resources for open community sustainability.

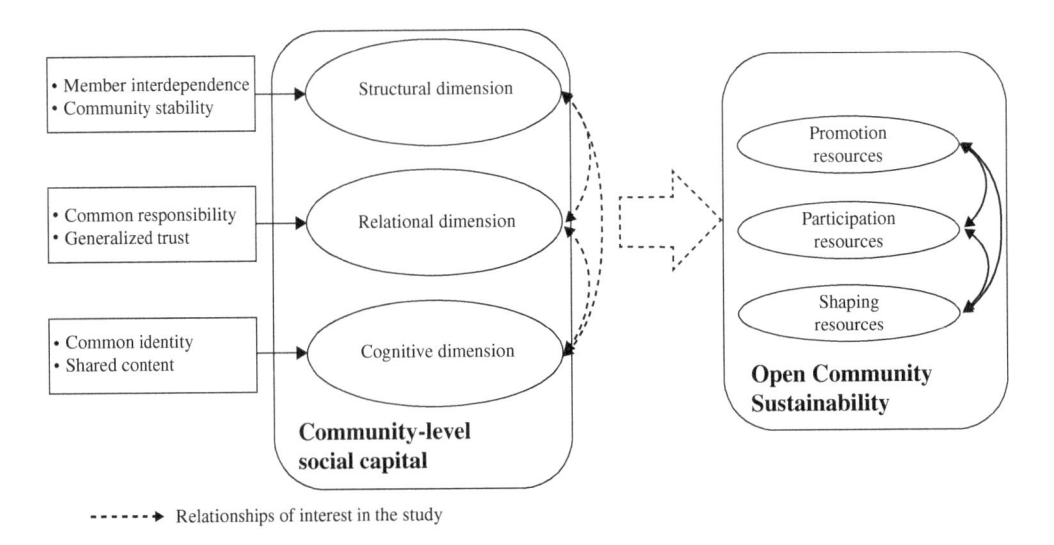

Source: Authors' own.

Figure 20.1   A theoretical approach to social capital in open communities

FORMING SOCIAL CAPITAL AND BUILDING SUSTAINABILITY: DATA CENTERS AS AN ILLUSTRATIVE EXAMPLE

In order to develop theory-driven propositions on the relationships among social dimensions and their impact on sustainability, we use six global genomics data centers in agricultural and health genomic research as explorative cases (Welch et al., 2016). We selected four mature data centers – Data_Center1, Data_Center2, Data_Center3, and Data_Center5 – and two relatively new ones – Data_Center4 and Data_Center6. All data centers were composed of a highly heterogeneous membership of researchers from multiple countries, sectors, and disciplines. Heterogeneity provides opportunities for synergy and dynamic exchange, but it can create challenges related to unequal access, conflicting goals, and weak ties among members because of great geographical distances. Table 20.1 briefly describes each case.

Table 20.1 Illustrative case studies

Global Genomics Center	Description
Data_Center1	• Facilitated access to distributed computational capacity across research institutions and communities; • Provided slack computational capacity thanks to resources pooled by a community of volunteers; • Tracked capacity availability and matched it with user requests for processing capacity; • Allowed members to contribute or not to the pool and to establish rules for access and use of their resources.
Data_Center2	• Aimed to facilitate joint, pre-competitive research activity among pharmaceutical companies through anonymous data sharing; • Focused on topics identified by members as critical for product development but too expensive to be individually undertaken; • Partnered with a university to conduct high-quality research; • Distributed outcomes in an open access format.
Data_Center3	• Supported data-intensive life science research through the development and deployment of a highly flexible and customizable platform for data management; • Provided informatics tools for managing, analyzing, sharing, visualizing, and storing large amounts of genetic data; • Promoted access to shared databases.
Data_Center4	• Provided a forum for discussion, design, and dissemination of common standards and principles for data sharing; • Aimed to develop harmonized approaches to data sharing and common solutions to data-sharing challenges, from technical barriers to security and privacy issues; • Developed small demonstration projects to showcase the value of a common approach to data sharing.
Data_Center5	• Provided a platform for scientists and breeders to manage, analyze, and visualize a large amount of breeding data; • Offered capacity-building programs to encourage the use of new technologies for traditional and molecular breeding; • Still under development and, at the current stage, provides minimal facilities for data sharing.
Data_Center6	• Aimed to provide a comprehensive repository for rice genetics data by integrating publicly available rice genetics datasets in an easily accessible format; • Collaborated with key actors in the sector and facilitated collaboration in the rice research community; • Offered data and tools for genotypic and phenotypic rice data analysis and management.

Source: Authors' own.

Between 2015 and 2016, the research team conducted semi-structured interviews with four to six individuals from each data center (see Fusi et al., 2018; Welch et al., 2016). The management teams typically consisted of five to ten members, so the small number of interviews was enough to reach saturation. Interviews included funders, top management personnel, and operational staff in charge of education, training, and outreach, or capacity building. The interview protocol asked about the organization's history, past decisions about membership and infrastructure design, and center functioning and activities. We conducted a total of 26 interviews. Each interview lasted about 60 minutes and all interviews were transcribed. Interview data were supplemented by the analysis of institutional documents collected on data center websites or provided by the interviewees, for example, organizational diagrams, meeting summaries, constitutive agreements, membership policies, and rules. Documents further informed the case studies and confirmed information collected through the interviews.

Within each interview, we identified mentions of social capital dimensions and sustainability resources. Tables 20.2a, 20.2b, 20.2c provide a few examples of how social capital dimensions were identified and operationalized based on our theoretical approach (Figure 20.1). From these observations, we then developed a set of propositions on how social capital dimensions are developed and how they are related to one another in open communities, as well as three propositions on how social capital dimensions are linked to specific types of sustaining resources. We discuss our findings in the next section.

Relationships among Social Capital Dimensions

Here, we discuss how social capital dimensions fit together, correlate, and behave within open communities in ways that are substantially different from traditional organizations.

Cognitive and relational social capital

We found that data centers rely heavily on cognitive social capital. Most interviewees suggested that the identification of a niche user community with common values and goals is fundamental for gathering enthusiasm and energy around the initiative and developing a community identity. Data centers consciously maintained an early focus on a relatively precise community in order to leverage cognitive social capital and expanded membership only in the long run (Fusi et al., 2018). For instance, Data_Center3 initially involved only genomic scientists and focused on the development of common ontologies. Only later on, it encouraged participation from scientists working in other disciplines. Data_Center5 slowly and selectively built region-based communities to decrease cognitive discrepancies and increase community identity by engaging with local institutions and groups.

Interviews from both Data_Center3 and Data_Center5 also showed that high cognitive social capital had a positive effect on the development of relational social capital. Community identity helps to increase a common sense of responsibility and solidarity because members felt a bond of togetherness (Nambisan & Baron, 2007; Ren et al., 2007). Furthermore, community identity promoted attachment and encouraged protective behaviors toward the whole community. By contrast, Data_Center6 had yet to develop a strong common identity both because of its newness and the lack of clear community boundaries. Data_Center6 managers were indeed more likely to report that members had low attachment and trust toward the community.

A social capital perspective to building sustainable data centers for science 355

Table 20.2a Social capital dimensions: structural social capital: community configuration as determined by interdependence among members and degree of stability of the community

Dimension	Definition	Measures	Examples (from genomics centers)
Network interdependence	Degree of collaboration and interaction among members of an open community.	• Dispersed networks • Hub-and-spoke networks • Team-based • Collaborative communities	In Data_Center1, members were not required to interact. The pool was maintained through individual contributions. Structural social capital was low. In Data_Center4, members collaborated on common projects. Structural social capital was high.
Community stability	Rate of membership growth and decline over time.	• Membership turnover • Number of registered users & number of new members • Costs to leave the community	In Data_Center6, few members registered as users, thus reducing community stability and structural social capital.

Source: Authors' own.

Table 20.2b *Social capital dimensions: cognitive social capital: symbolic boundaries, cognitive categories, and mutual understanding that bring together members of a community*

Dimension	Definition	Measures	Examples (from genomics centers)
Common content	Artifacts that are produced by members of the community.	• Shared project • Metadata • Shared databases • Ontologies • Stability of content	While Data_Center2 members shared resources with others, they did not co-produce content. In Data_Center3, members collaboratively designed the common infrastructure and ontologies.
Common identity	Sense of togetherness and cohesiveness with other members and toward community values, goals, and mission.	• Sense of community • Shared vision and mission • Common values • Group boundaries	Data_Center3 limited participation to life science researchers and excluded private sector partners. Data_Center4 created subcommunities based on members' interests. Those strategies strengthened their common identity and cognitive social capital.

Source: Authors' own.

Table 20.2c *Social capital dimensions: relational social capital: mix of social and formal norms that make behaviors more predictable and shape common expectations within the community*

Dimension	Definition	Measures	Examples (from genomics centers)
Common responsibility	Feeling a strong obligation to help others and safeguard and protect common resources.	• Indirect reciprocity patterns • Informal enforcement	In Data_Center6, members overused common resources as there were no formal requirements to access them.
Generalized trust	Members' expectations of positive behavior from other members.	• Process design • Formal rules • Infrastructure design	Data_Center1 increased trust toward use by creating an automated online platform that paired members with complementary needs and conditions for using and exchanging resources.

Source: Authors' own.

Relational social capital also increases when members engage in and contribute to the creation of common content. By contributing to the common content, members adopt similar behaviors and develop positive expectations toward others (Blanchard & Markus, 2004). In the case of Data_Center3, the development of metadata and platform functionalities to regulate data use and access promoted generalized trust toward collective processes and activities, thus increasing relational social capital. Moreover, the common content acted as a visible repository of community standards and norms (Rullani & Haefliger, 2013). Members could observe others' work and behavior and adopt widespread social norms (Faraj & Johnson, 2011).

Yet, we are cautious about the inverse relationship. As social control on compliance is generally low in open communities, communities that rely on relational social capital to build cognitive social capital are less likely to become sustainable over time. Some data centers started by designing reliable processes and rules to promote the development of relational social capital (e.g., generalized trust) and shape the initial community. Data_Center5 and Data_Center1 were such examples, where diverse actors were requested to follow rules about sharing resources – data and computational capacity, respectively – in a common pool. Under such circumstances, the development of cognitive social capital appeared a much slower process because it relied on members' willingness to comply with common rules and refrain from free-riding behaviors (Kane & Ransbotham, 2016). While still functioning, Data_Center1 reported no common content nor identity among its members. Data_Center5 failed to produce sufficient common content to survive, even after providing formal (e.g., economic) incentives to the community to contribute.

Proposition 1a: In open communities, cognitive social capital is an initial catalyst of community-level social capital development.

Proposition 1b: In open communities, cognitive social capital is likely to generate relational social capital.

Proposition 1c: In open communities, relational social capital is unlikely to generate cognitive social capital.

Cognitive and structural social capital
Cognitive social capital can also generate structural social capital. In all our cases, community members were researchers who initially joined a data center because it filled field-specific infrastructure and research needs. In other words, researchers joined because the community maintained a common content (e.g., a data repository or computational resources) of high perceived value. For instance, Data_Center6, which was relatively new, still needed to produce enough common content and was not able to attract a network of community members and contributors.

However, membership stability was a challenge for most centers because the establishment of collaborative and support relationships takes considerable time. Relationships between members were initially weak as members were not bound by the obligation to engage in joint or mutually interdependent activity. Over time, we observed that members who identified most strongly with the cultural norms and aims of the center were more likely to stay and become key contributors and community recruiters. These roles and tasks were undertaken voluntarily with the aim of furthering the content and mission of the community with which the individual identifies. As common content increased over time, structural social capital also increased. Key contributors' identities became more known, and they became more prominent and visible within the community network. Given their central position, they fostered collaborations across heterogeneous actors, thereby increasing task interdependence – a key component of structural social capital. Over time, as the tenure and visibility of these members increase, we also expect them to become stabilizing forces in the community (O'Mahony & Ferraro, 2004) because of their social connections and lower likelihood to leave (Ren et al., 2007).

While cognitive social capital has a positive effect on structural social capital, the reverse relationship is unlikely or it could be negative. We observed that some data centers developed local hubs or virtual groups that promoted task interdependence among members (Brubaker & Cooper, 2000; Ren et al., 2007). Data_Center4, for example, implemented three short-term demonstration projects to showcase the potential of data sharing and integration across datasets. Data_Center4 aimed to use these demonstration projects to motivate members from different sectors and disciplines to interact with each other. As members were more interdependent and involved in stable projects, they were expected to become more aware of their similarities, develop a common identity, and collaborate on common content, thus increasing cognitive social capital (Bagozzi & Dholakia, 2006).

This structural approach, however, has drawbacks at the community level. It promotes small, closed sub-communities of members who might be little integrated with the rest of the community, thereby generating little community-level social capital. The community risks becoming fragmented with several collaborative groups with high structural social capital, but low production of common content and no common identity. Moreover, open communities are often sustained by a large periphery of members who are connected only to core members or the management team, and seldom interact among themselves (Rullani & Haefliger, 2013). Developing common content within closed groups might hinder the participation of newcomers and peripheral members who need to learn common norms and be integrated into the community (Benamar et al., 2017).

Proposition 2a: In open communities, cognitive social capital likely leads to structural social capital.

Proposition 2b: In open communities, structural social capital likely leads to a decrease in cognitive social capital.

Structural and relational capital
We find structural and relational social capital to be related, wherein stable and repeated interactions among community members positively influenced a sense of common responsibility and trust. For example, Data_Center5 learned from the mistakes of its first failed attempt. Instead of structuring the initial development around relational social capital, it identified a set of regional-based communities that were already connected through collaborations and interactions at conferences and workshops. The stability of the initial community gave the project a footing upon which it could entice trust-based contributions of data from members and develop common rules for sharing and reusing such data. Moreover, member interdependence favored the identification of members who could play gatekeeper roles within the community and ensure the diffusion of standards and norms from the core to the periphery, that is, less connected members and newcomers (Benamar et al., 2017; Rullani & Haefliger, 2013). Data_Center2 adopted this approach by starting with only a few companies to figure out the rules and increase trust toward its sensitive sharing model. Structural social capital provided the support needed for the development of relational social capital.

Similarly, relational social capital could lead to structural social capital. Generalized trust and a common sense of responsibility drive the development of members' networks, such that relational social capital contributes to the stability of the community, decreases the number of newcomers, and pushes members to reply to, socialize, and connect with one another (Ren et al., 2007). In a similar fashion, Faraj and Johnson (2011) show that network development in open communities follows patterns of reciprocity and community norms, rather than structural factors, such as preferential attachment. In data centers, we noted that when community members shared high trust and sense of responsibility, they were more willing to interact with one another, collaborate on projects, and advance common content. Data_Center3 interviewees reported that community members asked the management team to identify potential collaborators on grant proposals and research projects. By contrast, where relational social capital is low, structural interactions were less likely to occur. Data_Center4 encountered several difficulties in implementing its small internal projects as community members were unwilling to collaborate with one another in the absence of common norms and trust.

These observations suggest that the relationship between structural and relational social capital is mutually reinforcing. However, we are cautious about the need to balance the creation of relational and structural social capital to enhance long-term sustainability. As suggested in the prior section, a structural approach that is too focused on individual interactions may create fragmented communities in the long term. On the other hand, creating and maintaining relational social capital is key to developing community-level structural social capital and reinforcing the social structure of open communities, which rely on several dispersed members who shared trust and responsibility.

Proposition 3: In open communities, structural and relational social capital are likely to be positively correlated.

From Social Capital to Sustainability Resources

While all dimensions of social capital influence the contribution of resources to the community, we argue that each dimension is more likely to support certain sustainability resources than others. First, the production of promotion resources is primarily facilitated by cognitive social capital. Promotion resources represent time and energy expended by members to articulate the character and promise of the community. Such effort is not simply passive; promotion requires interaction that serves to further formulate community identity and understand content potential. Cognitive social capital increases identification with the data center's culture, which increases members' willingness to devote time and passion to support center activities (Faraj et al., 2011). When individuals identify with the mission, goals, and content of the community, they act to legitimize and validate the community to others and are more willing to provide new contacts and introduce new members. In the case of Data_Center6, a high level of cognitive social capital provided the organization with some leeway to identify and encourage actors, pairs, or groups to contribute to the community.

Relational social capital yields participation resources more than other types of sustainability resources because it produces a sense of common responsibility for the community content. Members utilize and contribute common resources because they trust the rules and process for data use and access (Ren et al., 2007). As a result, relational social capital facilitates the generation of content from members to the community through active use, voluntary donation, and reciprocal contribution. For instance, in data centers with high relational social capital, members expected that the data they contributed to the pool were not going to be misused. They also believed that the data they accessed from the pool were of sufficient quality to be used for their research. When relational social capital is low, contributions are also lower and free-riding behaviors are more common. Data_Center6 managers – who noted lower relational social capital in their community – were more likely to report lurking behaviors, where members utilized common resources without feeling a social obligation to contribute back.

Shaping resources are created principally through structural social capital. As content is used and developed and community identity builds, core membership stabilizes and interactions among key community members become more frequent and visible. Though largely self-organized, these key community members attain recognized leadership, management, and support positions because of their centrality within the community network (O'Mahony & Ferraro, 2007). They gradually volunteer to provide shaping resources to the communities, which in turn increase the community reputation, competence, and content-derived influence to leverage new financial and other resources from members, funding agencies, and others. Shaping resources also help larger and more engaged communities to transition from the initial core team to a more established system of governance (Fusi et al., 2018) that supports the contribution of participation and promotion resources, thus further maintaining long-term sustainability.

Proposition 4: Open communities with higher cognitive social capital will likely produce more promotional resources.

Proposition 5: Open communities with higher relational social capital will likely produce more participation resources.

Proposition 6: Open communities with higher structural social capital will likely produce more shaping resources.

CONCLUSION

This chapter draws from open community and social capital scholarships to develop a more in-depth and theory-driven understanding of how social capital supports long-term sustainability of data centers. Drawing from previous studies and our observations of genomics data centers, we argue that three types of resources – participation, promotion, and shaping – are important for self-sustained open communities. We then illustrate how the three social capital dimensions – structural, relational, and cognitive – support the production of each resource.

Figure 20.2 summarizes our framework. It suggests that early investments in cognitive social capital are fundamental for a community to thrive and become sustainable. Cognitive social capital is critical because it leads to the creation of both relational and structural social capital and helps develop a critical mass of members through promotion resources. Both structural and relational social capital come at a later stage since they cannot be developed or are seriously undermined by the lack of cognitive social capital. Nevertheless, they are necessary to integrate and manage heterogeneity as well as promote trust. Relational and structural social capital are conducive of more effort-intensive and time-consuming resources, namely participation and shaping resources, upon which the community depends. We note, however, that structural social capital could have a potentially negative effect on the community, especially at an early stage. If an open community relies too much on task interdependence within

A social capital perspective to building sustainable data centers for science 361

Figure 20.2 Development of community-level social capital in open communities

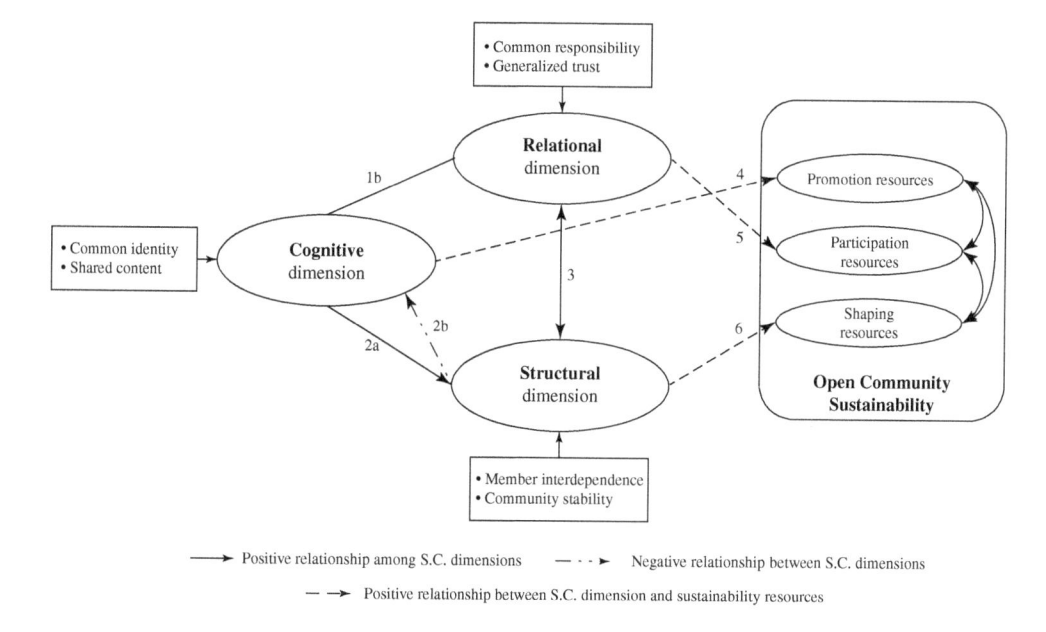

Source: Authors' own.

small groups, it might come at the expense of a common identity. Similarly, too much stability may have a negative effect on innovation and production of the common content. As fewer users and contributors are added to the community, members have fewer opportunities to develop, maintain, and enhance the common content potentially threatening cognitive social capital (Kane & Ransbotham, 2016; Ren et al., 2007).

We point out that the process illustrated in Figure 20.2 is dynamic, as communities evolve over time. Any increase or decrease in one social capital dimension comes with community changes that will likely affect the production of one or more types of sustaining resources. Therefore, the governance of data centers requires constant readjustments for open communities to maintain and promote all social capital dimensions and continue producing sustaining resources over time.

Our propositions should be empirically tested by future research. We suggest that case studies (see Chen & O'Mahony, 2006; O'Mahony & Ferraro, 2007) could provide rich data to assess social capital and sustainability outcomes. Quantitative data to assess sustainability outcomes, such as membership, contribution and use of shared resources, participation in workshops, and attendance at community meetings, could also be collected and used in network-based studies on how characteristics of dyadic relationships aggregate into community-level outcomes and social capital perceptions (Faraj & Johnson, 2011). Finally, we suggest that simulation techniques might offer a viable research methodology to model open community dynamics based on our proposed framework.

Future research should also address some limitations of our work. First, genomics data centers represent a specific type of open community where members seek data, information, or other knowledge resources. Future work should account for differences across open communities types and weigh the importance of social capital dimensions in different settings. Levine and Prietula (2013) suggest that open communities may vary according to cooperativeness, heterogeneity of members' needs, and rivalry of shared goods. We also assume that each repository operates in isolation, for example, has a clear stream of data and an identifiable community. In reality, most individuals rely on multiple data centers and data centers are increasingly connected to advance data-intensive science and innovation. Competition and cooptation among data centers might significantly affect social capital dimensions and act as shocks on the production of sustaining resources.

Second, our examples fall short by not sufficiently considering the possible conflicts and abuses of power that may occur in open communities. Some researchers highlight conflicts related to the common content and community identity (Kane et al., 2014; O'Mahony, 2007). Future research should expand our framework to integrate a better understanding of both successful and failing communities and the negative side effects of social capital. Finally, we argue that future research should expand on a dynamic approach to open communities in order to understand how the relationships across cognitive, structural, and relational dimensions deploy over time and influence community outcomes. Few studies have looked at open communities from a longitudinal perspective, although prior work hints to their shifting nature (Kane et al., 2014). As open communities consolidate and become more common in data-driven science, research needs to deepen our knowledge regarding the dynamics and cycles that characterized their life.

REFERENCES

Adler, P.S., & Kwon, S.-W. (2002). Social capital: Prospects for a new concept. *Academy of Management Review*, 27(1): 17–40.

Ashforth, B.E., & Mael, F. (1989). Social identity theory and the organization. *Academy of Management Review*, 14(1), 20–39. https://doi.org/10.5465/AMR.1989.4278999

Bagozzi, R.P., & Dholakia, U.M. (2006). Open source software user communities: A study of participation in Linux user groups. *Management Science*, 52(7): 1099–115. https://doi.org/10.1287/mnsc.1060.0545

Barone, L., Williams, J., & Micklos, D. (2017). Unmet needs for analyzing biological big data: A survey of 704 NSF principal investigators. *PLoS Computational Biology*, 13(10): e1005755. https://doi.org/10.1371/journal.pcbi.1005755

Benamar, L., Balagué, C., & Ghassany, M. (2017). The identification and influence of social roles in a social media product community. *Journal of Computer-Mediated Communication*, 22(6): 337–62. https://doi.org/10.1111/jcc4.12195

Blanchard, A.L., & Markus, M.L. (2004). The experienced "sense" of a virtual community: Characteristics and processes. *SIGMIS Database*, 35(1): 64–79. https://doi.org/10.1145/968464.968470

Boh, W.F., Ren, Y., Kiesler, S., & Bussjaeger, R. (2007). Expertise and collaboration in the geographically dispersed organization. *Organization Science*, 18(4): 595–612, 744–7.

Brubaker, R., & Cooper, F. (2000). Beyond "identity." *Theory and Society*, 29(1): 1–47.

Burt, R.S. (2000). The network structure of social capital. *Research in Organizational Behavior*, 22: 345–423. https://doi.org/10.1016/S0191-3085(00)22009-1

Butler, B.S. (2001). Membership size, communication activity, and sustainability: A resource-based model of online social structures. *Information Systems Research*, 12(4): 346–62. https://doi.org/10.1287/isre.12.4.346.9703

Chen, K. K., & O'mahony, S. (2006). The selective synthesis of competing logics. *Academy of Management Proceedings*, 2006(1), L1–L6. https://doi.org/10.5465/ambpp.2006.27176323

Chiu, C.-M., Hsu, M.-H., & Wang, E.T.G. (2006). Understanding knowledge sharing in virtual communities: An integration of social capital and social cognitive theories. *Decision Support Systems*, 42(3): 1872–1888. https://doi.org/10.1016/j.dss.2006.04.001

Faraj, S., & Johnson, S.L. (2011). Network exchange patterns in online communities. *Organization Science*, 22(6): 1464–80. https://doi.org/10.1287/orsc.1100.0600

Faraj, S., Jarvenpaa, S.L., & Majchrzak, A. (2011). Knowledge collaboration in online communities. *Organization Science*, 22(5): 1224–39.

Fusi, F., Manzella, D., Louafi, S., & Welch, E. (2018). Building global genomics initiatives and enabling data sharing: Insights from multiple case studies. *OMICS: A Journal of Integrative Biology*, 4: 237–47. https://doi.org/10.1089/omi.2017.0214

Halewood, M., Chiurugwi, T., Sackville Hamilton, R., Kurtz, B., Marden, E., Welch, E., Michiels, F. et al. (2018). Plant genetic resources for food and agriculture: Opportunities and challenges emerging from the science and information technology revolution. *New Phytologist*, 217(4): 1407–19.

Hsu, M.-H., Ju, T.L., Yen, C.-H., & Chang, C.-M. (2007). Knowledge sharing behavior in virtual communities: The relationship between trust, self-efficacy, and outcome expectations. *International Journal of Human-Computer Studies*, 65(2): 153–69. https://doi.org/10.1016/j.ijhcs.2006.09.003

Huysman, M., & Wulf, V. (2006). IT to support knowledge sharing in communities, towards a social capital analysis. *Journal of Information Technology*, 21(1): 40–51.

Inkpen, A.C., & Tsang, E.W.K. (2005). Social capital, networks, and knowledge transfer. *The Academy of Management Review*, 30(1): 146–65. https://doi.org/10.2307/20159100

Kane, G.C., Johnson, J., & Majchrzak, A. (2014). Emergent life cycle: The tension between knowledge change and knowledge retention in open online coproduction communities. *Management Science*, 60(12): 3026–48. https://doi.org/10.1287/mnsc.2013.1855

Kane, G.C., & Ransbotham, S. (2016). Content as community regulator: The recursive relationship between consumption and contribution in open collaboration communities. *Organization Science*, 27(5): 1258–74. https://doi.org/10.1287/orsc.2016.1075

Kirsch, L.J., Ko, D.-G., & Haney, M.H. (2010). Investigating the antecedents of team-based clan control: Adding social capital as a predictor. *Organization Science*, 21(2): 469–89. https://doi.org/10.1287/orsc.1090.0458

Levine, S.S., & Prietula, M.J. (2013). Open collaboration for innovation: Principles and performance. *Organization Science*, 25(5): 1414–33. https://doi.org/10.1287/orsc.2013.0872

Lin, N. (1999). Building a network theory of social capital. *Connections*, 22(1): 28–51.

Ma, M., & Agarwal, R. (2007). Through a glass darkly: Information technology design, identity verification, and knowledge contribution in online communities. *Information Systems Research*, 18(1): 42–67. https://doi.org/10.1287/isre.1070.0113

Molm, L.D., Takahashi, N., & Peterson, G. (2000). Risk and trust in social exchange: An experimental test of a classical proposition. *American Journal of Sociology*, 105(5): 1396–427. https://doi.org/10.1086/210434

Nahapiet, J., & Ghoshal, S. (1998). Social capital, intellectual capital, and the organizational advantage. *Academy of Management Review*, 23(2): 242–66.

Nambisan, S., & Baron, R.A. (2007). Interactions in virtual customer environments: Implications for product support and customer relationship management. *Journal of Interactive Marketing*, 21(2): 42–62. https://doi.org/10.1002/dir.20077

Nambisan, S., & Baron, R.A. (2010). Different roles, different strokes: Organizing virtual customer environments to promote two types of customer contributions. *Organization Science*, 21(2): 554–72. https://doi.org/10.1287/orsc.1090.0460

O'Leary, M.B., & Mortensen, M. (2010). Go (con)figure: Subgroups, imbalance, and isolates in geographically dispersed teams. *Organization Science*, 21(1): 115–31. https://doi.org/10.1287/orsc.1090.0434

O'Mahony, S. (2007). The governance of open source initiatives: What does it mean to be community managed? *Journal of Management & Governance*, 11(2): 139–50. http://dx.doi.org.ezproxy1.lib.asu.edu/10.1007/s10997-007-9024-7

O'Mahony, S.C., & Ferraro, F. (2004). Managing the boundary of an "open" project. Harvard NOM Working Paper No. 03–60. http://papers.ssrn.com/sol3/papers.cfm?abstract_id=474782

O'Mahony, S., & Ferraro, F. (2007). The emergence of governance in an open source community. *The Academy of Management Journal*, 50(5): 1079–106.

Peddibhotla, N.B., & Subramani, M.R. (2007). Contributing to public document centers: A critical mass theory perspective. *Organization Studies*, 28(3): 327–46.

Portes, A. (2000). Social capital: Its origins and applications in modern sociology. In Lesser, Eric L. (ed.), *Knowledge and Social Capital* (pp. 43–67). Boston, MA: Butterworth-Heinemann.

Preece, J., Nonnecke, B., & Andrews, D. (2004). The top five reasons for lurking: Improving community experiences for everyone. *Computers in Human Behavior*, 20: 201–23.

Putnam, R.D. (1995). Bowling alone: America's declining social capital. *Journal of Democracy*, 6(1): 65–78.

Ren, Y., Kraut, R., & Kiesler, S. (2007). Applying common identity and bond theory to design of online communities. *Organization Studies*, 28(3): 377–408. https://doi.org/10.1177/0170840607076007

Rousseau, D.M., Sitkin, S.B., Burt, R.S., & Camerer, C. (1998). Introduction to special topic forum: Not so different after all: A cross-discipline view of trust. *The Academy of Management Review*, 23(3): 393–404.

Rullani, F., & Haefliger, S. (2013). The periphery on stage: The intra-organizational dynamics in online communities of creation. *Research Policy*, 42(4): 941–53. https://doi.org/10.1016/j.respol.2012.10.008

Shah, S.K. (2006). Motivation, governance, and the viability of hybrid forms in open source software development. *Management Science*, 52(7): 1000–14. https://doi.org/10.1287/mnsc.1060.0553

Tsai, W. (2002). Social structure of "coopetition" within a multiunit organization: Coordination, competition, and intraorganizational knowledge sharing. *Organization Science*, 13(2): 179–90.

Tsai, W., & Ghoshal, S. (1998). Social capital and value creation: The role of intrafirm networks. *The Academy of Management Journal*, 41(4): 464–76. https://doi.org/10.2307/257085

Wasko, M.M., & Faraj, S. (2005). Why should I share? Examining social capital and knowledge contribution in electronic networks of practice. *MIS Quarterly*, 29(1): 35–57.

Wasko, M.M., Teigland, R., & Faraj, S. (2009). The provision of online public goods: Examining social structure in an electronic network of practice. *Decision Support Systems*, 47(3): 254–65. https://doi.org/10.1016/j.dss.2009.02.012

Welch, E., Louafi, S., & Fusi, F. (2016). Institutional and organizational factors for enabling data access, exchange and use in genomics organizations. Center for Science, Technology, and Environmental Policy Studies. Arizona State University. https://csteps.asu.edu/sites/default/files/%5Bterm%3Aname%5D/%5Bnode%3Acreate%3Acustom%3AYm%5D/genomicsorgfinal_design.pdf

21. Public sector innovation labs as an approach to data-driven innovation

Francesco Leoni

INTRODUCTION

Hundreds of *living labs, fab labs, innovation labs, policy labs*, and *public sector innovation labs* have been established during the last few decades by organizations eager to align with the most recent innovation paradigms. While each typology of lab began and developed differently than the others, today we may be able to see that they all contributed to the formation of a cohesive phenomenon and a multi-branched area of practice that, when taken as a whole, reflects the contemporary mentality toward innovation. These labs may be interpreted as socio-technical systems (Trist, 1978) whose main scope is to facilitate knowledge-sharing processes based on co-creation (McGann et al., 2021) and materialization (i.e., the representation of otherwise abstract concepts through artifacts). The reason behind the lab's practices is anchored in the approach toward innovation that labs strive for, which prioritizes the involvement of stakeholders and the general public in innovation processes (Criado et al., 2021). Possibly as a result of their significant participatory component, labs began to be regarded as venues in which to collectively investigate complex public issues and produce novel responses to societal problems that would otherwise go unaddressed by the market (Wascher et al., 2019). This particular aspect proved especially appealing to the public sector. Several governments throughout the world have established labs at various levels of public sector, ranging from local governments to in-line government departments and public agencies. The phenomenon grew to the point where it was recognized as an international movement and a public sector innovation trend (Bason & Schneider, 2014).

This chapter addresses the phenomenon of labs and relates it to data-driven innovation in the public sector. I start from the premise that public sector innovation labs are increasingly emerging as a specific way for governments to achieve the digital government ideal, that is, a set of governmental challenges related to digital transformation and data-driven innovation (Carstens, 2023; Santarsiero et al., 2022).

The phenomena of public sector innovation "labs" has been viewed through an organizational lens, and most research has concentrated on cataloguing laboratories as new "actors" in the public sector (Gofen & Golan, 2021). Instead, I propose viewing labs as an approach toward innovation (labs-as-an-approach) for framing data-driven public sector (van Ooijen et al., 2019) as a challenge that regards inter-organizational collaboration and public engagement in public service delivery and policy design (Carstens, 2023).

In the chapter, I explore what distinguishes "lab-as-an-approach" and how it has unfolded in relation to data-driven innovation in the public sector. Before delving into this specific issue, the first section of the chapter retraces the evolution of "lab" as a paradigm and practice. To do this, I conduct a literature review focused on labs' ideal types: *the scientific lab, the living lab, the innovation lab, and the public sector innovation lab*. This retracing of ideal types lays the groundwork for a discussion later in the chapter on "labs-as-an-approach" in public sector and data-driven innovation, substantiated by real-life examples.

LITERATURE REVIEW: LABS' IDEAL TYPES

Living Labs: Moving from "In Vitro" to "In Vivo"

> Scientific activity is not "about nature," it is a fierce fight to construct reality. The laboratory is the workplace and the set of productive forces, which makes construction possible. (Latour & Woolgar, 1986, p. 243)

The term lab, which stands for laboratory, has crucial significance in the semantic realm of science. When hearing this term, most would picture white-coated scientsists diligently working in aseptic rooms surrounded by test specimens, powerful computers, and expensive equipment. Our conception of the laboratory is that it is the optimal environment for the experimental method, a space deliberately isolated from outside influences to facilitate the activities of science experts: the scientists, and in particular those from the so-called "hard sciences." It may therefore appear paradoxical that, in the essay which has become a classic of science and technology studies, Bruno Latour and Steve Woolgar (1986) disrupted this ivory tower vision of science by conducting a real-world investigation of the safe environment that was intended to protect it. Among the contributions made by this work is the concept of the laboratory *as a stage of science reification*. To put it another way, the lab can be understood as a socio-technological context in which scientific assertions compete to become facts and "phenomena are thoroughly constituted by the material setting of the laboratory" (Latour & Woolgar, 1986, p. 64).

The insurgence of labs discussed in the Introduction may have slowly transformed the traditional notion of "lab," so far purely linked to the scientific research realm, not seen anymore only as the physical outposts where scientists observe natural phenomena. If the conventional scientific laboratory is defined by its isolation from the outside world, striving for inclusion and participation is a repeating theme in the new generation of labs (Criado et al., 2021; Tõnurist et al., 2017). *Living labs* represent an ideal type of lab where this trait is present, thus being exemplary of the contemporary lab approach to innovation.

The term "living lab" originates from the seventeenth century (Tukiainen et al., 2015). Leminen et al. (2012) highlight a more modern application in the early 1990s as a teaching method for students to learn about community public policy projects by being actively involved in a city neighborhood (Bajgier et al., 1991). The term was later used in studies on information and communication technologies (ICT) (Følstad, 2008). Here, its applications aligned with a perspective typically attributed to the late Dr. William Mitchell, Professor of Architecture and Planning at the Massachusetts Institute of Technology. Mitchell studied "smart homes" environments and proposed that buildings and cities could become "laboratories" for analysing users' patterns in real-world contexts, thereby relocating "innovation research from in vitro to in vivo settings" (Dutilleul et al., 2014, p. 7). Mitchell's conception of a living lab is essentially a research and development environment for testing and verifying ICT appliances by observing their use as part of real-life simulations (Følstad, 2008; Intille et al., 2005).

This type of living lab was exemplified by the *PlaceLab,* a Cambridge apartment outfitted with ubiquitous computing technology, for the "study of people and their interaction patterns with new technologies and home environments" (Eriksson et al., 2005, p. 13) as part of a research project conducted by MIT and other organizations in 2004 (Dutilleul et al., 2014; Eriksson et al., 2005).

Later, this early framing was attributed to a North American view of living lab (Hossain et al., 2019), in which the end-users played a relatively passive role, only included as subjects of observation (Ballon & Schuurman, 2015). In contrast, in the early 2000s, a European view emerged that tried to broaden the preceding living lab approach in terms of user involvement and intervention breadth (Hossain et al., 2019).

Living labs started to be regarded as strategies for large-scale experimentations for ICT product and service innovation. The new approach proposed that people actively participate in the design of these new solutions. In this new light, living labs could involve stakeholders who would be impacted by advancements in technology, thus tailoring their development to local needs (Eriksson et al., 2005). The European approach to living labs demonstrated consistency with a prior 1980s–1990s tradition of social participation in technological innovations, which included notable precursors such as the Scandinavian participatory design movement, ICT-centered social experiments, and digital cities initiatives (Hossain et al., 2019).

This revision of the living lab concept attempted to incorporate two significant modern innovation paradigms: *user innovation* (Von Hippel, 2006) and *open innovation* (Chesbrough, 2003). Regarding each of these two visions, living labs began to be viewed as platforms for activating innovation ecosystems that included not only private firms but also universities, institutions, and the general public (Dutilleul et al., 2014; Hossain et al., 2019; Leminen et al., 2012). The European Network of Living Labs (ENOLL), founded in 2006 by the European Commission to be an instrument for enhancing economic innovation and competitiveness among the member states (Dutilleul et al., 2014), is the result of these propositions. Since then, ENOLL has significantly expanded to include hundreds of living labs.

Innovation Labs: Addressing Complex Social Problems through a "Lab Approach"

The living lab experience consolidated a vision of the lab as an open physical or virtual setting designed to enable stakeholders to collaborate within innovation processes (Hossain et al., 2019). The early perception of labs as settings for developing specific innovations, aligned with a market perspective, gave way to the notion of labs as symbolic spaces where innovation with public and social dimensions could be "acted upon" and rearticulated through participatory, contextualized, and material practices. Under this framework, laboratories can be seen as procedural instruments for addressing policy issues (Howlett, 2019). More than established organizations, they represent a strategy for public participation and citizen engagement (Franz, 2015) as they embody the capabilities considered necessary to pursue contemporary innovation, that is, co-design and co-creation (Voorberg et al., 2017). In other words, the lab approach can aid in the development of collaborative and participatory governance, allowing for the collective resolution of complex social issues. This aspect of the living lab experience has predominantly been discussed in relation to urban-scale problems (Cognetti, 2022; Franz, 2015; Kareborn & Stahlbrost, 2009). Nonetheless, it has also been applied to *fab labs, makerspaces, and hackerspaces* experimenting with issues such as healthcare, food systems, plastic pollution, and agriculture (for practical examples, see Real & Schmittinger, 2022, and other chapters in the same volume).

Innovation labs (Gryszkiewicz et al., 2016; McGann et al., 2021; Tõnurist et al., 2017) emerged as an ideal type of lab that exemplified this transition by moving away from the living lab typology (Gryszkiewicz et al., 2016) and reaffirming the lab as a participatory approach to complex social problems. In accordance with this, innovation, labs were sometimes referred to as "social labs" or "change labs" to describe groups devoted to social change and innovation (Hassan, 2014; Kyriaki, 2017; Mulgan, 2006, p. 151). Several terms (Table 21.1) were used to define innovation labs associated with the public sector, which garnered a more consistent and specific level of interest. All of these terms referred to the establishment of units or teams dedicated to pursing public sector innovation objectives, which are now referred to as *public sector innovation labs* (PSI labs).

Public Sector Innovation Labs: The Labification of the Public Sector

PSI labs have become pervasive in the public sector over the past two decades, regardless of national context, political orientation, administrative culture, or governance level. PSI labs diffused to the extent of delineating a global movement (Bason & Schneider, 2014; McGann et al., 2018) and a trend in contemporary public administration known as *labification* (Lindquist & Buttazzoni, 2021; Williamson, 2015). This trend can be traced back to the austerity regimes that followed the financial crisis of 2007–08, when governments were compelled to make significant budget adjustments while maintaining previous levels of public service (Julier, 2017, pp. 146–52). Several design thinking, service design, and behavioral insights consultancies began assisting governments with optimizing, redesigning, and researching services using user-centered methods and approaches that are easily implemented via a standardized and replicable method (Julier, 2017, p. 147; McGann et al., 2018). These competencies were incorporated into line departments, public agencies, and local government by forming groups with the mandate to support the numerous activities associated with service innovation and optimization—as well as the other goals on the public sector innovation agenda (Tõnurist et al., 2017).

In recent years, these PSI labs have been extensively mapped, for instance, by Parsons Desis Lab (Selloni et al., 2013); NESTA and Bloomberg Philanthropies (Puttick et al., 2014), the University of Limerick (O'Rafferty & McMahon, 2016), and the EU Joint Research Centre (Fuller et al., 2016). These cataloguing projects and collections of labs continued to be released up to a few years ago (Bezzi et al., 2019; CPIPE, 2019; Gofen & Golan, 2021; Wellstead & Nguyen, 2020).

Parallel to these mapping efforts, which have been based primarily on observation of practices in the public sector, there have also been attempts to link the labification phenomenon to the "labs"-related public sector innovation literature. This literature is primarily devoted to providing an understanding of this emerging phenomenon by, on the one hand, attempting to contextualize it within broader public sector changes and innovations and, on the other hand, identifying the characteristics that differentiate PSI labs from other similar organizational formulas (e.g., think tanks). The authors situate PSI laboratories within broader trends in the public sector, such as.

Table 21.1   *Terms and definitions connected with the concept of innovation lab*

Term	Definition	Sources
Government Innovation Lab	"a range of organizations characterized by a direct connection with the public sector and developed to challenge complex public issues that more traditional governmental structures seek to resolve."	(Selloni et al., 2013, p. 1)
Innovation Teams	"units and funds established by governments and charged with making innovation happen. They work across the spectrum of innovation—from focusing on incremental improvements to aiming for radical transformations."	(Puttick et al., 2014, p. 5)
Policy Innovation Lab	"The lab is an organisational hybrid combining elements of the political think tank, media production, disciplinary expertise in social and political science, and digital R&D. It works by gathering, balancing, and assembling various institutionalised resources from across the academic, political, and commercial domains, and assembling those resources into unique packages."	(Williamson, 2015, p. 256)
	"individual units, both inside and outside of government, that apply the traditional principles of scientific laboratories—experimentation, testing, and measurement—to a host of emergent issues including the rise disruptive technologies, social problems, and environmental concerns."	(Wellstead & Nguyen, 2020, p. 2)
Innovation Lab	"An innovation lab is a semi-autonomous organisation that engages diverse participants—on a long-term basis—in open collaboration for the purpose of creating, elaborating, and prototyping radical solutions to open-ended systemic challenges"	(Gryszkiewicz et al., 2016, p. 84)
Policy Labs	"Policy Labs are dedicated teams, structures, or entities focused on designing public policy through innovative methods that involve all stakeholders in the design process. Practitioners describe these efforts as design or evidence-based approaches, which places the end users at the center of each stage of the policy-making process."	(Fuller et al., 2016, p. 1)
Public Sector Innovation Labs	"We use the acronym PSI lab to refer to labs that can be described as either 'public policy' or 'public sector innovation' labs. More often than not, these labs fall under the auspices of government departments or agencies, although what distinguishes a 'public policy' from a 'public sector innovation' team is not at all clear."	(McGann et al., 2018, p. 253)

Term	Definition	Sources
Public Sector Innovation Units	"innovation units have been considered important advocates of the use of design approaches and methods in the public sector to create and test alternative solutions to public problems, innovate in public services and policies, and propose alternative ways in which government might cope with public issues."	(Pamela et al., 2022, p. 90)

Source: Author's own.

- *The paradigm of New Public Management (NPM)*

    PSI Labs are a response and alignment of contemporary public administration to the values promoted by the NPM (Wellstead et al., 2021), which states that better performance of public sector services and functions under a general regime of austerity can be achieved by reproducing private sector dynamics in the public sector (e.g., greater internal competition). In this sense, PSI Labs can be seen as unique organisational and bureaucratic forms (adhocracies) that attempt a weak institutionalisation of public entrepreneurial forms via small "units" or "teams." (McGann et al., 2018).

- *Agentification tendency to address complex policy and service challenges*

PSI labs align with the historical trend of agentification (Wellstead & Howlett, 2022), which is the tendency for the public sector to delegate to external parties certain capacities deemed relevant to ensuring the quality of public services and policymaking (e.g., policy analysis and research activities, which are typically delegated to think tanks in the United States and Canada). The objective of PSI labs is to reframe complex policy issues and translate the ideal values of public sector innovation into concrete approaches and practices. This appears to be especially true for the topic of technological innovation (ICT and data analytics) (Kim et al., 2022; Tõnurist et al., 2017), for which the majority of the public sector lacks dedicated skills (Giest, 2018).

- *Willingness to experiment with experimental approaches*

PSI labs are designed to be "safe" environments with a mandate for public sector innovation. They are created as contexts divorced from the routine dynamics of public administration, allowing for the introduction of experimental approaches and methodologies in a public context (Tõnurist et al., 2017). The establishment of some PSI labs is primarily motivated by a desire to conduct practical experiments with a number of methods deemed successful. In PSI labs this appears particularly true for human-centered design and design thinking (McGann et al., 2018).

- *A desire to accomplish citizen engagement and public participation*

PSI labs vary greatly in nature and area of expertise (Fuller et al., 2016), but they almost always seek to increase citizen engagement and public participation in government and the public sector. This ambition also resonates with the importance given to co-creation as a new paradigm of value in the service economy and for reaching social innovation as a policy objective (Voorberg et al., 2017).

The authors have also indicated that PSI labs have several issues such as the propensity to remain a separate entity from the main organization with which they are affiliated, to focus excessively on experimentation and not on scaling innovation, to promote the spread of tools and standardized methods in public governance, and—because of their small size and high dependency on external political will—they are susceptible to sudden closure (Bezzi et al., 2019; Tõnurist et al., 2017),

MindLab, for many years one of Europe's most renowned PSI labs (Julier, 2017, p.147), is an example of the last point. MindLab has operated in Denmark since 2003 in support of various ministries, most notably the Ministry of Economy, and was shut down in 2018 despite its widespread national popularity and international fame. According to the accounts of former employees, the primary reason for the closure was the loss of political support, which resulted in the replacement of MindLab with the Disruptive Task Force for the Digital Agenda (70 percent of former MindLab employees are now employed by this new task force) (Guay, 2018).

LABS AND DATA-DRIVEN INNOVATION IN THE PUBLIC SECTOR

Labs have also been established to address the topic of digital transformation in the public sector (Carstens, 2023; Santarsiero et al., 2022; Whicher & Crick, 2019). Among them, a subset of PSI labs appears to be actively engaged in data-driven initiatives and the development of data-centric public sector projects and solutions (Kim et al., 2022). Various innovation groups/units around the world are working within public organizations or in collaboration with them to support the exploitation of non-traditional digital data, that is, data that is not traditionally collected and used by public institutions as the base of evidence (e.g., administrative and digital service data) (Leoni et al., 2023). These groups either expressly identify as labs or are labeled as such by outside observers, as they appear to be aligned with a lab approach. The goal here appears to be the development of data-centric public products and services as well as the generation of data-based policy knowledge across several policy domains (Kim et al., 2022).

Data science appears to be part of a mixed methodology used by these labs, rather than their primary focus (Whicher & Crick, 2019). For example, Williamson (2015) noticed several UK-based innovation labs that experimented in the education sector using a combination of data science techniques and user-centric and design methods (specifically, incorporated into a "design for policy" approach). Moreover, the Behavioural Insights Team (BIT), an internal unit originally established by the UK government, and that early on was mapped as a PSI lab (Puttick et al., 2014), became famous worldwide for promoting nudging approaches to public programs while also including data science in their toolset (Neuhaus & Curley, 2022; Williamson, 2015). In this sense, a lab approach to data-driven innovation should be considered as distinct from the work of units established in public organizations as data management intermediaries, or providers of data science services.

Discrepancy in empirical reviews of PSI labs reinforces this complementary role, or sideways approach, of labs toward data-driven innovation in the public sector. Tõnurist et al. (2017) found that five labs in Australia and New Zealand were primarily involved in ICT-centered projects rather than data-centric. Kim et al. (2022) instead identified 133 *data-based policy innovation labs* mostly across Europe and the United States, and offered a well-defined description of their work:

> Data-based PILs work to improve citizens' experiences of public services, using diverse data sources, advanced technology, and innovative solutions. ... Government agencies create or collaborate with data-based PILs to make effective use of a variety of data sources and digital technologies. (Kim et al., 2022, p. 345)

Different perspectives on PSI labs' engagement with data-driven innovation emphasize their role as adhocracies that alter their activities to changing public sector innovation priorities. This adaptability is required for labs to endure and thrive, as demonstrated by BIT (Neuhaus & Curley, 2022). However, the constant transformation of labs results in a landscape that defies systematization. Consequently, the uniqueness of a lab approach to data-driven innovation in the public sector remained an open question. This gap has begun to be filled by authors such as van Veenstra and Kotterink (2017), who propose a policy lab approach for integrating co-creation within an ideal data-driven policymaking process. They proposed that the use of data analytics in policymaking could be accomplished through experimental settings, the scope of which would depend on the various phases of policymaking, while allowing citizens and other interested parties to participate (van Veenstra & Kotterink, 2017, pp. 106–7).

While more research is necessary in this space, considering the characteristics of the contemporary idea of "labs-as-an-approach" described, three major areas of implication for practice where it might contribute to data-driven innovation in the public sector may be be discussed.

IMPLICATIONS FOR PRACTICE AND REAL-LIFE EXAMPLES

Labs for Trust in Data and Inclusive Data Governance

First, *a lab approach fosters trust in data science products and serves as the foundation for inclusive data governance activities.* As observed, involvement and active participation of stakeholders, normally outside of creative processes, or even the general public and citizens, are values important to the labs' approach. This approach seeks to engage actors in problem co-definition and co-design using a variety of strategies and techniques in order to incorporate the perspectives of those affected by public innovations and assess their contextual knowledge. Furthermore, labs facilitate co-production processes (McGann et al., 2021) in which multiple actors can participate actively in the execution of new concepts at various scales. What distinguishes the kinds of involvement realized by labs is that they are founded on materialization practices, which are typically brought into public contexts as part of a design background (Leoni et al., 2023). To concretize ideas and make them interactive as boundary objects, the lab approach typically employs prototyping, visualizations, and a variety of other techniques (e.g., role-playing). They are primarily intended to facilitate a group debate about a difficult issue by breaking down background, cultural, and literacy barriers through materiality. A lab method might thus serve as the foundation for developing public sector data-driven solutions as testbeds that are more than just technical but also serve as probes into the public acceptability of these solutions. This will support the idea of labs as trust builders in data-driven innovation (Wellstead, 2021). Several established practices demonstrate how working with visualization and prototypes may transform data-driven technology into data-centric group experiments. The Virtual Gothenburg Lab, a multi-stakeholder cooperation involving the City of Gothenburg in Sweden, Lindholmen Science Park, the innovation agency Vinnova, and several academic and business groups, provides a potential example of this at the city scale. The initiative developed a testbed based on data visualization in order to make the city's digital twin accessible and usable (visualarena.lindholmen.se). Another example is the participatory monitoring project Living Data Hubs, which was launched by the MIT Civic Data Design Lab with local organizations in Nairobi to monitor air quality (civicdatadesignlab.mit.edu/Living-Data-Hubs). Moving away from an abstract representation of data, these experimental efforts paint a picture of data-driven innovation in the public sector as situated. They could be essential foundations of inclusive data governance programs that promote data sovereignty and the idea that data management should be based on local culture and knowledge, also from ethnic minorities. That happened, for example, in the indigenous data governance project developed by the New Zealand Statistical Office in collaboration with Maori cultural representation organizations (https://data.govt.nz/toolkit/data-governance/maori) (Kukutai et al., 2023).

Labs for Integrating Human-Centered and Data-Centric Competences

A lab approach can also aid in the integration of human-centered and data-centric competences (including data science) in pursuit of innovative public sector goals. Incorporating data science competences and skills into the public sector is a two-pronged challenge. On the one hand, governments' overall tendency to outsource data skills may limit their ability to properly use these data for better policy outcomes and public value delivery (Giest, 2018). On the other hand, data science professionals are required to collaborate with legislators, domain experts, and other government practitioners (Arnaboldi & Azzone, 2020; Giest, 2018). This interdisciplinary collaboration appears to be necessary because data scientists bring distinct aesthetics and values than other actors to data-driven innovation (van der Voort et al., 2019). Furthermore, whereas contemporary data science curricula need the development of ethical and domain expertise (Oliver & McNeil, 2021), data science is practically absent from policy education (El-Taliawi et al., 2021).

As previously stated, the lab approach is associated with approaches that are highly context-specific, often derived from the culture and professional practice of design (McGann et al., 2018; Williamson, 2015). Because of the different focus and set of skills required, the integration of human-centered and data science competencies remains mostly a proposition rather than a reality (Williamson, 2015). However, some areas of prospective convergence may be indicated (Leoni et al., 2023) and are supported by field practices. For example, as part of a portfolio approach to public sector innovation, Pulse Lab Jakarta, the Indonesian chapter of a larger network of labs established by the United Nations, specifically blends data science with service design methodologies (Pulse Lab Jakarta, 2022).

Labs for Experimental Data Governance, Data Sharing, and Interoperability

Lastly, *the lab approach can facilitate public experiments that promote intragovernmental data governance, data sharing, and interoperability.* This is especially possible as part of innovative data-centric public service solutions (Leoni et al., 2023).

Integrating data science competencies in the public sector necessitates both micro-level and inter-organizational collaboration challenges. In this sense, the dispersed location of data sources across public agencies and departments presents both organizational and technological challenges. New data governance agreements must be promoted by figures accountable not only for data management (such as data officers) but also for the ethical and responsible use of data (such as data stewards). In addition, integrating data across public systems and domains remains a matter of technical and ontological interoperability (i.e., ensuring that digital systems interface with one another and data are represented in the same manner across different domains). Lastly, collaboration based on data sharing should include strategic alignment across parties, that is, how data can be utilized to serve the various purposes of public agencies. It is a scenario with a challenging level of institutional complexity and a high level of collaboration between public and private actors (Giest, 2017). As part of the experimental setting, labs enable public organizations to gradually join these partnerships. As such, laboratories represent a variation of a sandbox approach to data-centric innovation, which incorporates data ecosystems into project-oriented partnerships with the goal of creating value for citizens, adopting data-centric public services as the level at which these partnerships develop. The *"Crédito Peso a Peso"* pilot program in Bogotá, Colombia, is an example of this form of partnership. Bringing together the Bogotá Digital Innovation Team iBO, the data analytics agency Agatà, and the High Council of Information and Communications Technology, the pilot aims to encourage entrepreneurs in the city to apply for bank loans. The innovative solution is based on an alternative credit score system derived from the city's data, which will help develop banks' trust in these small businesses and facilitate the loan application process (Bloomberg Cities Network, 2023).

DISCUSSION AND CONCLUSIONS

In this chapter, we looked at the background of the lab's phenomenon and how it relates to government-led data-driven innovation. I placed the new generation labs in a broader perspective for the reader, tracing the development of the modern lab concept back across the many ideal types of lab that emerged during the last years—moving from the conventional scientific lab to the living lab and finally, to the innovation and the public sector innovation labs. In resonance with the work of Latour and Woolgar cited earlier in this chapter, this excursus highlighted that, while the traditional scientific lab was seen as the stage where the continuous construction of science manifested, this new lab generation similarly symbolizes the attempt to translate current innovation goals and paradigms into concreteness. PSI labs represent examples of adhocracies, adaptive organizational structures that demonstrate the political will of the public sector to take on innovation in all its forms (Lindquist & Buttazzoni, 2021), and must promote themselves through a project-based portfolio of innovative ideas and practices. I have argued that the contemporary generation of labs should be viewed as an approach to innovation (labs-as-an-approach). Although the relationship between data-driven innovation in the public sector and labs has yet to be thoroughly investigated, the "labs-as-an-approach" perspective proposed here highlights several implications for practice (discussed earlier). The real-life examples discussed in connection with these areas suggest the potential for codifying "labs-as-an-approach" into a methodology to build data-centric policymaking and public services. At the level of theoretical implications, the perspective on labs discussed here helps in framing data-driven innovation as a matter of collaborative and multi-level governance (Carstens, 2023).

If this perspective is to be further translated into practical experimentations, it presents a challenging outlook. Combining the materiality and situatedness inherent in the lab method with data science may be equally demanding and beneficial for future work in the data-driven public sector. The discussion surrounding data-driven innovation seems to be slowly moving away from an abstract idea of data and digital solutions (which was the hallmark of the big data movement); and we can expect less emphasis on technology development and more emphasis on the political and social dimensions of policymaking and governance.

The lab approach might play a crucial role in this shift.

REFERENCES

Arnaboldi, M., & Azzone, G. (2020). Data science in the design of public policies: Dispelling the obscurity in matching policy demand and data offer. *Heliyon*, 6(6), e04300. https://doi.org/10.1016/j.heliyon.2020.e04300

Bajgier, S.M., Maragah, H.D., Saccucci, M.S., Verzilli, A., & Prybutok, V.R. (1991). *Introducing Students to Community Operations Research by Using a City Neighborhood as a Living Laboratory*. INFORMS Stable. Accessed January 22, 2023. http://www.jstor.org/stable/171200. Linked references are available on JSTOR for this article: *You may*. 39(5), 701–9.

Ballon, P., & Schuurman, D. (2015). Living labs: concepts, tools and cases. *Info*, 17(4). https://doi.org/10.1108/info-04-2015-0024

Bason, C., & Schneider, A. (2014). Public design in global perspective: Empirical trends. In C. Bason (Ed.), *Design for Policy* (pp. 23–40). Gower Publishing.

Bezzi, M., Buongiovanni, C., & Deserti, A. (2019). *Deliverable 4.2: Transformations In STI Policy Making: Trends, Opportunities And Barriers*. SISCODE project consortium Accessed January 22, 2023. https://www.siscodeproject.eu/wp-content/uploads/2019/09/D4.2_Transformations-in-STI-policy-making.pdf

Bloomberg Cities Network. (2023, May). *Bogotá breaks new ground in city innovation (again). Here's how*. Accessed January 22, 2023. https://bloombergcities.jhu.edu/news/bogota-breaks-new-ground-city-innovation-again-heres-how

Carstens, N. (2023). Digitalisation labs: A new arena for policy design in German multilevel governance. *German Politics*, 32(2), 249–66.

Chesbrough, H.W. (2003). *Open Innovation: The New Imperative for Creating and Profiting from Technology*. Harvard Business Press.

Cognetti, F. (2022). Beyond a buzzword: Situated participation through socially oriented urban living labs. In N. Aernouts, F. Cognetti & E. Maranghi (Eds.), *Urban Living Lab for Local Regeneration: Beyond Participation in Large-Scale Social Housing Estates* (pp. 19–37). Springer International Publishing.

CPIPE. (2019). *The Emergence of Policy Innovation Labs in Canada: Cataloging Government Led Labs*. Accessed January 22, 2023. https://www.torontomu.ca/content/dam/cpipe/documents/The_Emergence_of_Policy_Innovation_Labs_GOV_LED_LABS_July_3_2019.pdf

Criado, J.I., Dias, T.F., Sano, H., Rojas-Martín, F., Silvan, A., & Filho, A.I. (2021). Public Innovation and Living Labs in Action: A Comparative Analysis in post-New Public Management Contexts.

International Journal of Public Administration, *44*(6), 451–64. https://doi.org/10.1080/01900692.2020.1729181

Dutilleul, B., Birrer, F.A.J., & Mensink, W. (2010). Unpacking European Living Labs : Analysing Innovation 's Social Dimensions. *Central European Journal of Public Policy*, *4*(1), 60–85.,

El-Taliawi, O.G., Goyal, N., & Howlett, M. (2021). Holding out the promise of Lasswell's dream: Big data analytics in public policy research and teaching. *Review of Policy Research*, *38*(6), 640–60. https://doi.org/10.1111/ropr.12448

Eriksson, M., Niitamo, V.-P., & Kulkki, S. (2005). State-of-the-art in utilizing Living Labs approach to user-centric ICT innovation—a European approach. Lulea, Sweden: Center for Distance-Spanning Technology. Lulea University of Technology Sweden.

Følstad, A. (2008). Towards a living lab for the development of online community services. *EJOV: The Electronic Journal for Virtual Organization & Networks*, *10*(August), 47–58. Accessed January 22, 2023. https://sintef.brage.unit.no/sintef-xmlui/bitstream/handle/11250/2440026/eJOV10_Folstad_ICTLiving%2bLabs%2breview.pdf

Franz, Y. (2015). Designing social living labs in urban research. *Info*, *17*(4), 53–66.

Fuller, M., & Lochard, A. (2016). *Public policy labs in European Union Member States*. Publications Office of the European Union. Accessed January 22, 2023.. https://doi.org/10.2788/799175

Giest, S. (2017). Big data analytics for mitigating carbon emissions in smart cities: Opportunities and challenges. *European Planning Studies*, *25*(6), 941–57. https://doi.org/10.1080/09654313.2017.1294149

Giest, S. (2018). Policy learning in times of big data analytics: The challenges of skill-based outsourcing. In *Knowledge, Policymaking and Learning for European Cities and Regions* (pp. 153–164). Edward Elgar Publishing.

Gofen, A., & Golan, E. (2021). *Laboratories of Design: A Catalog of Policy Innovation Labs in Europe*. https://doi.org/http://dx.doi.org/10.2139/ssrn.3822821

Gryszkiewicz, L., Lykourentzou, I., & Toivonen, T. (2016). Innovation labs: Leveraging openness for radical innovation? *Journal of Innovation Management*, *4*(4), 68–97. https://doi.org/10.24840/2183-0606_004.004_0006

Guay, J. (2018, June). *How Denmark Lost Its MindLab: The End of the World's First Innovation Lab*. Apolitical. Accessed January 22, 2023. https://apolitical.co/solution-articles/en/how-denmark-lost-its-mindlab-the-inside-story

Hassan, Z. (2014). What are social laboratories? In *The Social Labs Revolution* (pp. 1–16). Berrett-Koehler Publishers.

Hossain, M., Leminen, S., & Westerlund, M. (2019). A systematic review of living lab literature. *Journal of Cleaner Production*, *213*, 976–88. https://doi.org/10.1016/j.jclepro.2018.12.257

Howlett, M. (2019). *The Policy Design Primer*. Routledge. https://doi.org/10.4324/9780429401046

Intille, S.S., Larson, K., Beaudin, J.S., Nawyn, J., Tapia, E.M., & Kaushik, P. (2005). A living laboratory for the design and evaluation of ubiquitous computing technologies. *Conference on Human Factors in Computing Systems—Proceedings*, 1941–4. https://doi.org/10.1145/1056808.1057062

Julier, G. (2017). *Economies of Design*. Sage Publications.

Kareborn, B.B., & Stahlbrost, A. (2009). Living Lab: an open and citizen-centric approach for innovation. *International Journal of Innovation and Regional Development*, *1*(4), 356. https://doi.org/10.1504/ijird.2009.022727

Kim, S., Wellstead, A.M., & Heikkila, T. (2022). Policy capacity and rise of data-based policy innovation labs. *Review of Policy Research*, April, 1–22. https://doi.org/10.1111/ropr.12494

Kukutai, T., Campbell-Kamariera, K., Mead, A., Mikaere, K., Moses, C., Whitehead, J., & Cormack, D. (2023). *Māori data governance model*. Te Kāhui Raraunga. Accessed January 22, 2023. https://www.waikato.ac.nz/assets/Uploads/Research/Research-institutes-centres-and-groups/Institutes/Te-Ngira-Institute-for-Population-Research/Maori_Data_Governance_Model.pdf

Kyriaki, P. (2017). *Labs for social innovation*. ESADE Instituto de Innovación Social. Accessed January 22, 2023. https://itemsweb.esade.edu/research/Labs-Social-Innovation-ESADE.pdf

Latour, B., & Woolgar, S. (1986). *Laboratory Life: The Construction of Scientific Facts*. Princeton University Press.

Leminen, S., Westerlund, M., & Nyström, A. (2012). Living labs as open-innovation networks. *Technology Innovation Management Review*, September, 6.

Leoni, F., Carraro, M., McAuliffe, E., & Maffei, S. (2023). Data-centric public services as potential source of policy knowledge. Can "design for policy" help? *Transforming Government: People, Process and Policy*. https://doi.org/10.1108/TG-06-2022-0088

Lindquist, E.A., & Buttazzoni, M. (2021). The ecology of open innovation units: Adhocracy and competing values in public service systems. *Policy Design and Practice*, 4(2), 212–27. https://doi.org/10.1080/25741292.2021.1941569

McGann, M., Blomkamp, E., & Lewis, J.M. (2018). The rise of public sector innovation labs: Experiments in design thinking for policy. *Policy Sciences*, 51(3), 249–67. https://doi.org/10.1007/s11077-018-9315-7

McGann, M., Wells, T., & Blomkamp, E. (2021). Innovation labs and co-production in public problem solving. *Public Management Review*, 23(2), 297–316. https://doi.org/10.1080/14719037.2019.1699946

Mulgan, G. (2006). The process of social innovation. *Innovations: Technology, Governance, Globalization*, 1(2), 145–62. https://doi.org/10.1162/itgg.2006.1.2.145

Neuhaus, T., & Curley, L.J. (2022). The emergence of global behavioral public —policydevelopments of and within the nudge unit. *World Complexity Science Academy Journal*, 3(2). https://doi.org/10.5860/choice.51-2973

O'Rafferty, S., & McMahon, M. (2016). *Labs, iTeams, Designers.* Co-creating Ireland. Researching the Co-creation of Policy & Public Services in Ireland. Accessed January 22, 2023. https://cocreatingireland.wordpress.com/2016/03/29/policy-labs/

Oliver, J.C., & McNeil, T. (2021). Undergraduate data science degrees emphasize computer science and statistics but fall short in ethics training and domain-specific context. *PeerJ Computer Science*, 7, e441.

Pamela, D., Alvarez, V., Auricchio, V., & Mortati, M. (2022). Mapping design activities and methods of public sector innovation units through the policy cycle model. *Policy Sciences* (Issue 0123456789). Springer US. https://doi.org/10.1007/s11077-022-09448-4

Pulse Lab Jakarta. (2022). *Annual Report. Taking Steps towards an Inclusive Future: A Journey of Progress and Possibilities.* Accessed January 22, 2023. https://pulselabjakarta.org/download/file/annual-report-2022.pdf

Puttick, R., Baeck, P., & Colligan, P. (2014). i-Teams: The teams and funds making innovation happen in governments around the world. *Nesta; Bloomberg Philanthropies*, 61–70. Accessed January 22, 2023. https://www.nesta.org.uk/sites/default/files/i-teams_june_2014.pdf%0Ahttp://www.nesta.org.uk/sites/default/files/innovation_teams_and_labs_a_practice_guide.pdf

Real, M., & Schmittinger, F. (2022). A framework for experimenting co-creation in real-life contexts. In: Deserti, A., Real, M., Schmittinger, F. (Eds.), *Co-creation for Responsible Research and Innovation: Experimenting with Design Methods and Tools.* Springer Series in Design and Innovation, vol 15. Springer, Cham. https://doi.org/10.1007/978-3-030-78733-2_2

Santarsiero, F., Schiuma, G., & Carlucci, D. (2022). Driving organizational digital transformation through innovation labs. In H. Väyrynen, N. Helander & H. Jalonen (Eds.), *Public Innovation and Digital Transformation* (pp. 154–64). Routledge. https://doi.org/10.4324/9781003230854-9

Selloni, D., Staszowski, E., Bason, C., Schneider, A., & Findeiss, A. (2013). *Gov Innovation Labs. Constellation 1.0.* Accessed January 22, 2023. https://nyc.pubcollab.org/files/Gov_Innovation_Labs-Constellation_1.0.pdf

Tõnurist, P., Kattel, R., & Lember, V. (2017). Innovation labs in the public sector: What they are and what they do? *Public Management Review*, 19(10), 1455–79. https://doi.org/10.1080/14719037.2017.1287939

Trist, E.L. (1978). On socio-technical systems. *Sociotechnical Systems: A Sourcebook*, 43–57.

Tukiainen, T., Leminen, S., & Westerlund, M. (2015). Cities as collaborative innovation platforms. *Technology Innovation Management Review*, 5(10), 16–23. https://doi.org/10.22215/timreview933

van der Voort, H.G., Klievink, A.J., Arnaboldi, M., & Meijer, A.J. (2019). Rationality and politics of algorithms. Will the promise of big data survive the dynamics of public decision making? *Government Information Quarterly*, 36(1), 27–38. https://doi.org/10.1016/j.giq.2018.10.011

van Ooijen, C., Ubaldi, B., & Welby, B. (2019). A data-driven public sector. OECD Working Papers on Public Governance, 33. https://doi.org/https://doi.org/10.1787/09ab162c-en

van Veenstra, A.F., & Kotterink, B. (2017). Data-driven policy making: The policy lab approach. *Lecture Notes in Computer Science (Including Subseries Lecture Notes in Artificial Intelligence and Lecture Notes in Bioinformatics), 10429 LNCS*, 100–11. https://doi.org/10.1007/978-3-319-64322-9_9

Von Hippel, E. (2006). *Democratizing Innovation*. MIT Press.

Voorberg, W., Bekkers, V., Timeus, K., Tonurist, P., & Tummers, L. (2017). Changing public service delivery: Learning in co-creation. *Policy and Society*, *36*(2), 178–94. https://doi.org/10.1080/14494035.2017.1323711

Wascher, E., Kaletka, C., & Schultze, J. (2019). Social innovation labs—a seedbed for social innovation. *Atlas of Social Innovation: 2nd Volume—A World of New Practices*, 136–8. Accessed January 22, 2023. https://www.socialinnovationatlas.net/articles/

Wellstead, A. (2021). Trusting datification through labification. In H. Sullivan, H. Dickinson, & H. Henderson (Eds.), *The Palgrave Handbook of the Public Servant* (pp. 1055–73). Springer International Publishing. https://doi.org/10.1007/978-3-030-29980-4_77

Wellstead, A.M., & Howlett, M. (2022). (Re)yhinking think tanks in the age of policy labs: The rise of knowledge-based policy influence organisations. *Australian Journal of Public Administration*, *81*(1), 224–32. https://doi.org/10.1111/1467-8500.12528

Wellstead, A., & Nguyen, S. (2020). The rise of policy innovation labs: A catalog of policy innovation in the United States (1st edn). *SSRN Electronic Journal*, January. https://doi.org/10.2139/ssrn.3513548

Wellstead, A.M., Gofen, A., & Carter, A. (2021). Policy innovation lab scholarship: Past, present, and the future. Introduction to the special issue on policy innovation labs. *Policy Design and Practice*, *4*(2), 193–211. https://doi.org/10.1080/25741292.2021.1940700

Whicher, A., & Crick, T. (2019). Co-design, evaluation and the Northern Ireland Innovation Lab. *Public Money and Management*, *39*(4), 290–9. https://doi.org/10.1080/09540962.2019.1592920

Williamson, B. (2015). Governing methods: Policy innovation labs, design and data science in the digital governance of education. *Journal of Educational Administration and History*, *47*(3), 251–71. https://doi.org/10.1080/00220620.2015.1038693

22. Conclusion, research agenda, and policy recommendations for governance and data science

Bram Klievink and Sarah Giest

INTRODUCTION

This book highlights the opportunities and challenges that arise and exist at the intersection of data science and governance studies. Data science offers to play a key role in modern governance, where statistical, machine learning, and other model-based approaches allow leveraging large and complex datasets to support, inform, and enhance many acts of governing. The premise of the book is that a comprehensive account of this interaction must consider the insights of both data science studies and governance studies. One can support an in-depth understanding of how data science techniques turn datasets into useful patterns, trends, and insights; the other an in-depth understanding of their implications for government decisions, the accountability thereof, and the impact on policy and public organizations. The combination is vital to understanding the nuanced ways in which a reliance on data presents not only opportunities but also risks, for instance, in terms of understandability of outcomes, shifting balances between professionals and citizens as well as among professionals, and also in terms of unintended outcomes and even misuse. Ultimately, the collection of chapters provides an account of the capacity that the public sector has or needs to create to effectively integrate data into public services and policy processes. They show how data science capability and readiness is an integrative question of technological, analytical, operational, organizational, and political capabilities. It is ultimately a question of integrating data-driven technologies, including artificial intelligence (AI), into public sector governance. In this chapter, we offer concluding thoughts on the findings across the chapters and parts of the book, draft a future research agenda on the findings at the intersection of data science and government, and present policy recommendations.

CONCLUDING THOUGHTS

The chapters report on the transformative potential of big data and data science in governance, policymaking, and public administration, while acknowledging challenges, dilemmas, and limitations.

Part I documents where new insights at the intersection of governance and data science come from and what this means for institutions and different policy domains. Combined, the chapters present how data support novel insights, yet also highlight that these new practices have to be embedded in existing structures, processes, and policies.

The chapters reveal both the potential of big data to introduce new policy paradigms and the caution required in expecting it to resolve analytical challenges in policymaking. The chapters in this part demonstrate that new data science approaches may not necessarily fit unproblematically with long-standing analytical practices, be it nation-level statistics or specific policy questions. Chapters on data science applications in political economy and legislative favoritism, as well as the perspective of national statistics institutes on the integration of big data and machine learning in their practices, emphasize the expanding role of data science in governance, the challenges of integrating new data sources into official statistics, and the balance between traditional statistical methods and new data science approaches. Vydra's research on big data in labor market policymaking most explicitly documents a case in which there is great added value of big data in theory, but in practice these hopes for having big data solve the analytical problems turned out to be overly optimistic due to challenges related to the data, the fit with the policy problem, and the fit with the preexisting institutions. The discussion on the synergy between Big Data and Soft Operational Research (OR) in policymaking, along with the examination of digitalization in energy efficiency policy design and the analysis of public sentiments through e-petitions, illustrates the multifaceted applications of data and digital tools in policymaking and the complex dynamics of coordinating digital platforms for public service production, underscoring the transformative yet challenging nature of leveraging data science in governance contexts.

Part II looks at how challenges and opportunities of data-driven innovations occur in different countries and contexts. A key theme is the integration of digital tools and AI in public governance. The chapters demonstrate how much potential for innovation there is, yet also highlight that across countries and contexts there is increasing emphasis on the need for ethical considerations, transparency, and privacy safeguards to address challenges like socio-economic inequalities and misinformation.

The chapters emphasize that fostering data science co-creation and innovation within public services is key. This means something for the organization or sector that seeks to innovate. Employing innovation labs, such as living labs and fab labs, can be crucial as socio-technical systems that enable collaborative problem-solving. Also, at the national level and in the public sector as a whole, a comprehensive socio-technical approach is key to identifying long-term and fundamental implications and decisions that a choice for employing data science techniques comes with. Notably, the importance of addressing the dual framework of leveraging AI for governance improvements in Latin America while avoiding technological dependence is discussed, underscoring the need for strategic investments in human capital and national regulatory frameworks to ensure autonomy and break colonialist logics.

In *Part III*, chapters delve into the open, transparent, and accessible use of data by government and the role of citizens in these processes. An argument brought forward here is that the integration of AI and digital technologies in public governance necessitates participatory governance for democratic control, focusing on fairness, accountability, and transparency in public services. Chapters in the other parts have similarly highlighted the importance of securing public values like these, yet put this mostly as a requirement to be met within organizations that employ data science techniques. This part adds to this external focus. There are innovative participatory tools (e.g., beneficial ownership records and lobbying registers) that country governments are starting to adopt and incorporate into their routines and practices. Furthermore, open data can be considered a crucial tool in promoting transparent governance, yet one requiring a supportive ecosystem for effective utilization in enhancing government accountability and addressing corruption. Transnational collaboration and partnerships on transparency and open data may be required to address the collective action problems caused by the cross-border flows of data.

Beyond openness and participation, regulatory approaches need to balance the protection of fundamental rights with the need for innovation, addressing the challenges of data misuse in governance and the implications for social inequalities. At the time of publication of this book, this is an avenue that gets particular attention from policymakers, for instance, in the European AI Act, which seeks to regulate and set norms for the use of AI in society, including its use in and by government. The larger topic – and challenge – that this Act exemplifies is the need in the future to develop norms for these innovations and to institutionalize regimes that help to clarify or simplify procedures and reassure the public in very complicated and somewhat fuzzy legal and regulatory environments.

Across the parts, the chapters display the numerous decisions and value trade-offs that are made by data analysts and that could impact policy outcomes. Big data analysts unavoidably and perhaps unwittingly make many decisions and value trade-offs that may be consequential for the policies they mean to support. Importantly, this also extends to the role of scholars. Various chapters highlight the need for considering new forms of political or public space where data science innovations can be safely, ethically, and justly developed. As Fusi and Welch look at the case of data centers for scholarly collaboration, the role of scholars is more explicit. Other chapters also consider the need for empirically informed experimentation with new data governance regimes rather than keeping with the 'classificatory' status quo. Additionally, new forms of data agency may require a stronger culture of data-savviness on the part of citizens.

RESEARCH AGENDA

Together, the chapters address a key question: *What is data science fixing or solving in the public space?* The research in this field has clearly demonstrated that the technological capabilities are there, that data science can offer novel insights, capture information that could not be captured before, and have potential policy effects, and that actors aim to and do innovate based on what data science might offer. There are institutional, organizational, procedural, ethical, and technological hurdles that have been or still must be overcome, which many actors and researchers have identified and offered suggestions for. So, in short, about the interaction between data science and governance: we can. But should we? More specifically: what data and what data science is available and able to fix or offer viable improvements over what we have now, or offer scalable solutions for practice? Ultimately, at the interface between disciplines, we are looking at something that does not just work, but that benefits the public space and can aid in enhancing the very act of governing. It is this perspective on governance and data science that can also guide future research in this area.

Context Matters: But How?

Current thinking on data science and algorithms in governance has developed amid an influential wave of normative and ethical concerns surrounding data use. However, many accounts are still optimistic about the added value of big data and data science. The increased emphasis on responsible uses of data and algorithms leads to a search for and the development of solutions that fill the responsibility gaps in the design and transparency of data science systems. These are still techno-optimistic accounts at their core in the sense that these fundamental concerns can be addressed in and by the technology, or by designing the appropriate sociotechnical safeguards. In some chapters in this book (e.g., chapter 2), the authors demonstrate that one could and should critically interrogate this optimistic narrative about the potential added value. Data science and governance is not just about getting it right, it is about getting it right for the situations in which big data actually adds value, and perhaps even more so about finding out where it does not. If situations, contexts, use cases, or technical characteristics make it so that big data tools or systems do not significantly add value, not deploying these systems ensures that the associated ethical risks do not need to be taken. Important for future research is to critically interrogate the real added value and to identify how specific combinations of use, context, and tools relate to the potential added value of data science. Identifying patterns in what elements in the context of data science affect its added value, and in how it does so, through the interaction between contextual factors, (intended) use, and technological capability, is a key point for furthering our detailed and contextualized understanding of the phenomenon.

Making It Matter

By examining the patterns that make data science effective in governance, we can gain a better understanding of how data science can meet the varied needs of different users, as well as when it might fall short. Particularly, there might be actors that are not the intended recipients who may benefit, just as there are intended users who currently cannot benefit from data science. A more action-oriented part of future research could focus on identifying actors and seeking to understand how data science might provide value to them, and then also making these tools available to those actors. An example can be found in Chapter 3, which calls for providing 'actionable indicators' to political actors, journalists, and other groups. Thereby, data scientists can support policy action that promotes accountability and transparency and exposes corruption.

Does It Fit

Data science does not operate in greenfield environments, as many of the chapters in this book illustrate. Even if data science approaches provide better insights and these insights also land in a situation to make use of them, it rarely offers a role where there has not been one before. Oftentimes, analytical products exist that seek to provide similar insights or sit at the same point in a process, organization, or policy. Here, it makes sense to compare relative performance because legacy solutions are often already integrated into existing processes or institutions, giving them an advantage in terms of implementation and familiarity. How these processes, organizations, and institutions have worked with data and analysis in the past provides crucial contextualization for insights based on data science. What is more, over time many indicators have become institutionalized themselves: national or international bodies have agreed on how to define and measure them and thereby allow comparison across contexts or over time. This is what Vydra and Klievink (2019) call a 'data backdrop,' referring to 'decades of negotiated knowledge between experts, politicians, and institutions on how to measure and adapt these concepts to assure their continuous usefulness' (p. 3). This wider context and background may mean that even data science that is by all means 'better' may still lead to costs in terms of long-term comparability or general agreement among actors. These could also be unintended consequences of the use of novel data science approaches. A better understanding of the historical developments and of the official and unofficial standing of everything that precedes a data science approach in a specific setting can help to explore how the wider context is affected. This is especially true for institutions that are already heavily dependent on data analysis and where deploying data science tools might initially seem like an ideal scenario.

Making It Fit

Future research could investigate capacity and capability configurations that are effective in managing the interactions between governance and data science. A key question here is how capabilities can be organized to make data science for policy and governance work. This can be addressed from a skills perspective, focusing on what different types of professionals within an organization should know and be able to do. This, in turn, could concern technical skills but is as much a matter of securing the skills to meaningfully interrogate the products and insights supported by data science. Given that data science often involves the introduction of new professionals, further collaboration and communication skills across technical and non-technical disciplines is another area for future research.

Furthermore, there is research to be done on the inter-organizational dynamics. It is not necessarily so that every individual organization will, can, or should develop all necessary capabilities. Instead, they can organize or configure the needed set of capabilities through collaborations across sectors (public, private, academia, society). This, in turn, requires research into innovative sharing partnerships and procurement processes that fit the nature of data science, for instance, when private companies develop a model based on training data of the public sector partner.

The Big Questions

Many of the research topics described in this chapter so far have focused on adding more attention to how data science plays out in governance contexts, and on better understanding the varieties therein. Another class of research topics for the future is more fundamental, normative, or epistemological. Some of the chapters exhibit underlying and more traditional discussions on positivism or interpretivism, and could lead to questions about where the increased use of data comes in, particularly regarding the latter. Furthermore, normative and ethical reflections on data science could address questions like whether how we measure things impacts the governance of issues or whether the governance of data and issues impacts how we measure things.

POLICY RECOMMENDATIONS

We conclude this chapter by providing some policy recommendations. Many chapters have done so too, some more explicitly than others, and this section is not meant to summarize these. Rather, we aggregate and highlight three.

First, we recommend to better integrate data science into the toolboxes that are available to managers, policymakers, and decision-makers. This is to say, it should not be ignored that there are already many tools available. Actors should not blindly follow the 'new' because of the prospect of innovation and improvement, but should carefully evaluate and study how big data tools perform in relation to existing (analytical) tools, if and how they can complement each other, in what cases they can outperform other instruments, and in what situations certain characteristics of existing instruments make them a better fit for purpose. Even if big data instruments work and yield insights, the costs in terms of capacity, capability, comparability, auditability, understandability by non-experts, and other factors might still make an older tool the preferred choice. And vice versa, if such evaluation has taken place, a data science tool might fully replace or add to what was there before, and be fully integrated into procedures, practices, and processes.

Second, to be able to do this, actors involved in governance need to be able to experiment and learn about data science. That does mean some capacity and data are needed to explore what tools might provide added value, even if success is far from guaranteed. A process of experimenting not only leads to finding out what a tool may or may not do, but it will also help in finding out under what conditions stakeholders find it acceptable, and what safeguards need to be put in place. Or it might help in establishing that for a given situation, data science is not a solution.

Third and finally, all of this asks a lot of the people and organizations involved. Investment in skills and education in statistics, computer science, data engineering, and domain expertise is important. Especially the public sector sometimes faces challenges attracting the right kind and amount of expertise. Yet, it goes further than this. Data scientists need to not only be trained in the technical and methodological areas, but also develop a sufficient comprehension of the policy domain they are supporting. This knowledge equips them to identify questions they can address, explore new avenues for inquiry, and detect when their insights are being used in ways that do not align with their intended support. Domain experts need to be able to ask the right questions and develop a basic understanding of the potentially consequential choices a data scientist makes. Staff working in legal and procurement departments need to be able to understand what potential effects these choices have, for instance, in terms of the dependencies on vendors or providers of data. Ultimately, it is important to accept that individuals cannot master everything. Therefore, investing in boundary spanners that are skilled at linking all these different domains and expertise is key. And asks something of the support and structure of the organizations or contexts in which they have to operate.

REFERENCE

Vydra, S. and B. Klievink. 2019. Techno-optimism and policy-pessimism in the public sector big data debate. *Government Information Quarterly* 36(4), 101383. https://doi.org/10.1016/j.giq.2019.05.010.

Index

#BlackLivesMatter 149
4 Vs *see* volume, velocity, variety and veracity
1971 census 60, 61

Abdolhamid, M. 244
Abrassart, C. 247
accessibility 124, 224, 226, 233
   of basic information about ADM systems 228
   of business knowledge in tax form (re)design 135
   coordination based on 136
   data 137
   demand for 72
   of high-quality data 4
   open data 283
   in participatory governance 183–4, 188
   of political institutions 42–4
   of sanitary products for women 114, 118
Access Now 304
accountability 273, 274, 276, 295, 303
   AIAs 304
   audits and inspection 307–8
   dispute resolution forums 306
   harms 305–6
   human oversight requirements 305
   human rights impact assessments 304–5
   justice and dispute resolution mechanisms 305
   procurement conditions 308–9
   screening 303
   standards-based accountability 308
   whistleblower protection and privacy exemptions 309
Ackermann, F. 78
Ackoff, R. 76
ACM *see* Authority for Consumers and Markets
action situation 183, 207
active transparency 225
'active' users 343
actors 184, 188–9
Administrative Department of the Presidency of the Republic (DAPRE) 227
administrative law 306
ADM system *see* automated decision-making system
advanced data analytics deployment in governance 2–3
affordability
   of childcare 19, 23–4, 27
   of sanitary products for women 114

'agency' concept 335 *see also* data agency
agentification tendency 370
aggregation 184–5, 189–90
Agostino, D. 149
AI *see* artificial intelligence
AIAs *see* algorithmic impact assessments
algorithm(ic) 199–201
   artificial intelligence 200
   evaluations 235
   performance 224
   predictions 317
   systems 199
   transparency 234–5
      challenges associated with ADM systems 224–5
      models 225
   in public sector 223
   see also transparency
algorithmic impact assessments (AIAs) 304
algorithmization of bureaucratic organizations 217
Al Husaeni, D. F. 243
Alice and Mônica systems of Federal Audit Court 214
Amsterdam, City of 309
Angwin, J. 247
ante-hoc method 275
Antecedents-Privacy Concerns-Outcomes (APCO model) 333
APCO model *see* Antecedents-Privacy Concerns-Outcomes
APIs *see* application programming interfaces
Apple App Store 125
application programming interfaces (APIs) 136, 146
Arnaboldi, M. 149
Arrieta, A. B. 247
artificial intelligence (AI) 2, 59, 69, 95, 146, 179, 198–202, 222, 265, 302, 379
   AI-guided chatbots 153
   "AI Regulation" 266
   algorithms 200
   challenges 181–2
   elements of 188
   ethical/ethics 247
      considerations 159–60
      management 241
      washing 277

385

governance 198, 239
  challenges in Latin America 202–16
  deployment 2–3, 239
  emergence of 201
  ethical challenges and dilemmas 241–2
  in government and public administration 180–82
  infrastructure, and development 203–6
  integration in public sectors 3, 5
  participatory governance for 185–90, 187
  prediction in 180–81
  and society 242–3
  technologies in public governance 8
  transparency in 234
  use in public sector capabilities 9
asset disclosure 283, 284, 290, 292, 295
asynchronicity 86
auditability 308, 384
audits/auditing
  and inspection 307–8
  systems 167
Australia, data government ecosystems in 171
Authority for Consumers and Markets (ACM) 67
author keyword co-occurrence 252, 252–4, 253
automated algorithmic sorting 326
automated decision-making system (ADM system) 222–3, 304
  classification of functions of public bodies 230
  data about results or performance of 231
  new database in Colombian Public Sector 230
  new transparency challenges associated with 224–5
  system adoptions 9
automation 72, 265–6
  cyborg accounts 19
  data 241, 255
  of information 253
  RPA 222–3
  see also artificial intelligence (AI)
Avison, D. E. 78

Baldwin, C. Y. 126
Barnard, C. I. 129
Barocas, S. 247
baseball, data evolution in 318–22
'baseline' LDA models 26
Bauer, Trevor 319, 322, 327
Bayes algorithm 20
Beane, Billy 318
behavioral model 141, 153–4
Behavioural Insights Team (BIT) 371
Beining, L. 182
Bekkers, V. 144
Beneficial Ownership Data Standard (BODS) 291
Benoît, Cyril 6

Berliner, Daniel 300
"Betterball" paradigm 320–22, 324
bias 10, 299
  class 326
  cognitive 82
  confirmation 3–4
  ethnic 300
  reduction algorithms 166
  selection 272
bibliographic coupling of sources 250–52
bibliometric analysis 240, 243
Big Data 14, 59, 75, 282, 298, 317, 380
  4 Vs 79–80
  analytics 4
  capacity of 6
BIT *see* Behavioural Insights Team
black-box algorithms/model 275, 316
Blanchard, A. L. 351
Blei, D. M. 20
blockchain 253, 258, 274, 308
BODS *see* Beneficial Ownership Data Standard
Bogen, Miranda 307
Boolean operators 244
Both, A. 20
Boudreau, K. 126
boundary rule 184
Boyd, D. 14
Bratu, Roxana 11
Brauneis, R. 224
Brenner, Dominik 6
Bright, Jonathan 9
Broken Links report 285–6
Brown, A. 127
Building Energy Efficiency Program Dashboard in India 98
Buolamwini, Joy 247
Burger, K. 83, 84
Burrell, J. 247
Bush, A. A. 126
business secrets 306

California's Consumer Privacy Act (CCPA) 299
CAML *see* Competency-Aware Machine Learning
Canada
  data-driven government in 169
  strategies or initiatives for government data 170
capacity
  of big data 6
  development 216
  policy 4
  statistical 4
Capital Offenders group 324
Carpenter, Dan 46

Carr, C. T. 142
Castañeda, J. D. 222
Castellanos-Sánchez, Michelle 234
Cathy, Oneil 247, 249
CBS *see* Centraal Bureau voor de Statistiek
CCPA *see* California's Consumer Privacy Act
cell key method 62, 64
Celtic Fringe' Group 119
Centraal Bureau voor de Statistiek (CBS) 59, 65
centralization 133
Centre for Work and Income (CWI) 340
Cetina, C. 222
CFIP model *see* Concern for Information Privacy model
change labs 368
channelling 83
'character of franchise' of governance participation 183
Chatterjee, S. 249–50
Chen, Y. N. K. 242
childcare 19, 23–4, 27, 40
child maltreatment risk scores 326
Chilean repository of public algorithms 234
Ching, Leong 7
Choi, B. C. F. 334
citizen-government partnerships 10
  challenges derived from integrated perspective 275–6
  considerations for enhancing activation 270–71
  digital governance and data science 271–5
  examination of types 267–8
  government's role in promotion 269–70
  imperative for realization of digital governance 267–8
  underutilization in digital governance implementation 268–9
citizen(s) 146, 254
  citizen-generated data 144
  citizen-led engagement and deliberation 182
  engagement 370–71
  opinions 152
  participation 179
  on social media 146
  thermometer 152
Citizens' Jury method 189
Citron, D. K. 247, 255
civil society organisations 43, 182, 222, 282
Clark, S. D. 120
Clark, Stephen 7
class bias 326
classical organization theory 129
Classification of the Functions of Government (COFOG) 230
classificatory data regimes 10–11

classificatory *vs.* transformative data regimes
  evolution of data in baseball 318–22
  ideal-typical description of 321
  in public policy 322–7
  right to production of data and data analysis 327–9
cloud providers 204
cloud services 204
cluster mapping technique 86
CNN *see* Convolutional Neural Network
co-citation analysis of references and authors 243, 247
  author co-citation results 248, 250
  reference co-citation results 248, 249
co-creation 10, 268, 367
co-definition 372
co-design 367, 372
  of participatory process 185
  of policies 152
  visual interfaces 84
COFOG *see* Classification of the Functions of Government
cognitive biases in training datasets 82
cognitive mapping 78
cognitive social capital 351–2, 356
  relational social capital, relationship with 354, 357
  structural social capital, relationship with 357–8
collaboration model on social media monitoring 8, 141, 152–3
collaborative platforms 129–30
  development 134–5
  transformation 135–6
collection gaps 286–7
collective harms 10, 299–300
collective intelligence 189
collective surveillance 240
Colombia/Colombian government 226
  public sector 226
  repositories 222, 227–30
  transparency of public algorithms *see* public algorithms in Colombia
commercial platforms 127, 136, 137
common content 351, 356–9, 361–2
common identity 351–2, 354, 356, 359, 360
common responsibility 350–51, 356
communicative approach 145
community
  norms 351
  referrals 326
  stability 350
company beneficial ownership 284, 291
COMPAS *see* Correctional Offender Management Profiling for Alternative Sanctions

Competency-Aware Machine Learning (CAML) 274
competition 10, 299
competition laws 306
compliance 214
comprehensibility 275
computational systems 199–200
concept drift 70–71
Concern for Information Privacy model (CFIP model) 334
confirmation bias 3–4
consent-based transparency 310–11
consent model 311
consumer-oriented laws 301
Consumer Price Index (CPI) 67–8
control
   data-centric 132
   generativity and 128, 131–2
   mechanisms 52, 136
   role-based 131
   transparency 273
conventional coordination mechanisms 124
Convolutional Neural Network (CNN) 275
coordination 124, 130
co-production 10, 268, 270
Cordella, A. 129, 137
Correctional Offender Management Profiling for Alternative Sanctions (COMPAS) 322, 325
Correlated Topic Model (CTM) 20, 22, 23
corruption 295
cost of living crisis 109
   data 112–13
   methods 113
   party representation for each group 119
   petitions 110–12
   projected party representation for each group 120
   results 113–18
costs 306
Cottam, Hillary 326–8
COVID-19 pandemic 8, 53, 110, 160, 254
CPI *see* Consumer Price Index
Crawford, K. 14, 249
"Crédito Peso a Peso" pilot program 374
criminal/crime
   data 323–4
   justice 322–5
   stories 324
critical data studies 317
crowdsourcing phenomenon 152
CTM *see* Correlated Topic Model
Cusumano, M. A. 125
CWI *see* Centre for Work and Income
cybersecurity 272
Cyverse 346

Danaher, J. 241
DAPRE *see* Administrative Department of the Presidency of the Republic
"Dashboard" platform 227, 229
data
   analytics 317–18
   architecture design 134
   assemblages 317, 320
   audits 307
   availability 4, 59
   backdrop 382–3
   breach notification 311–12
   collection process 48
   colonialism 206, 218
   commons 190
   cooperatives 190
   coordination based on data relationships 136
   cultures 317
   data-based policy innovation labs 371–2
   data-centric competences, labs for integrating 373
   data-centric control 132
   energy efficiency data and data-policy implications 95–102
   inferability of 229, 233
   infrastructures 203–4
   intelligence 124
   labs for data sharing 374
   management 86, 162
   monitoring 167
   by policy area 289–90
   processing 308
      principles and guidelines for 302
      registers 310
   regimes in public policy 316–18, 320, 322, 329
      criminal justice 322–5
      social welfare 326–7
   revolution 44
   sampling 244
   stewardship frameworks 189
   trusts 190
databases and big data 96
data-driven
   decision-making 45, 162, 254
   digital technologies 265
   government 160
      framework for data science governance 166–7
      in post-pandemic context 161–2
      representative international cases of governance initiative 168–9
   innovations 371–2, 380
   policymaking 298
data agency 5, 11, 332
   analysis of digital apps and platforms 341–3

case studies 335–41
  as concept 333–4
  framework visualization 342
  new forms of 381
  in practice 334–5
data centers 204, 346, 352–4
Data Governance Act (DGA) 186
data governance/government 158, 185–6, 190
  data-driven government 160, 161–2
  ecosystem 160
    benefits 164–5
    challenges and limitations 165–6
  effectiveness of 171–2
  framework for data science governance 167–8
  initiatives in post-pandemic context 161
  representative international cases of governance initiative 170–71
  strategies or initiatives for government data 162–4
Data.gov platform 170
Data Protection Authority (DPA) 302–3
data science 1, 59, 158, 160, 166, 239, 282, 371, 379
  concept drift 70–71
  CPI 67–8
  emergence of techniques 1
  essential balance in governance 171
  explainable models 69
  extension of "internal validity" of model into "external validity" 69–70
  framework for governance 166–8
  and governance studies intersection 2–3
  historical events illustrating legal, technological, and social challenges 60
  history of registries 61
  insights and enhancing decision-making 11–12
  integrating data science and official statistics 68–9
  maintaining quality standards 64–5
  outcomes 62
  and political institutions 44–5
  practical considerations 71
  privacy concerns 61–2
  publishing 62–4
  rare occurrences 70
  research views 273
    accountability 274
    fairness 273–4
    transparency 275
  social licence to operation 65–7
  society demanding innovation 61
  techniques 47–8
  van der Aalst's definition of 1–2
Data Sharing and Governance Act 169
Davidson, E. 239

Davis, Tara 10
decision-making 11, 283
  agency-based 184
  AI 255
  automated 9, 258, 273, 276, 299, 305, 307, 310
  capacities 3
  citizen participation 179
  data-driven 45, 162, 254
  in domains 6
  evidence-based 163
  factors 76
  processes 2, 3, 299
Deda, P. 106
de-identification 274
"deliberate" practice 319
demand-side energy efficiency policy 97–8
democratic data ownership regimes 149
Denters, B. 183–5
detection in AI systems 180–81
DGA see Data Governance Act
differential privacy techniques 274
DigiD Digital Identity System 340–41
digital/digitalization 95
  applications and platforms 332, 341–3
  certification and compliance 96
  cities initiatives 367
  communication and networking 96
  coordination 125
  democracy 189
  divides 187
  of energy and electricity value chain 101
  of energy efficiency markets 98
  ethics 241
  infrastructures 205
  poorhouse 326
  tools/technologies 99, 105, 137, 270
    for energy efficiency policy design 96–7
    and technologies 7
  transformation 158, 204–5
    in public sector 8
    paradigm 265
  twin 96
  twin simulations 95
digital governance/government 217–18, 266
  applications 158
  and data science 271–5
  imperative of citizen-government partnerships for realization 267
  research views 271
    fairness 271–2
    safety, responsibility, privacy 272
    transparency 272–3
  underutilization of citizen-government partnerships in implementation 268–9
  see also participatory governance

Digital Government Transition Strategy 270
digital platform(s) 11, 124
   challenges 133–4
   collaborative platform
      development 134–5
      transformation 135–6
   coordination 124–5, 129
      cross-agency collaboration in public service production 137
      implications 136–7
      limitations 137–8
   data collection 132–3
   digital government platform coordination
      generativity and control 128, 131–2
      modular architecture 131
      openness and transparency 130–31
      organizational forms and service accountability 128–30
      theoretical foundation/framework 127–8
   research context 132
Digital Services Act 305
direct disclosure mechanism 235
disclosure and transparency regimes 310
   consent-based transparency 310–11
   data breach notification 311–12
   data processing registers 310
discrimination 10, 299, 306
dispute resolution forums 306
disruptive technologies 201
Djeffal, C. 241
Dominican Republic's strategy 207
Donthu, N. 243
DPA *see* Data Protection Authority
Drex in Brazil 205
Driss, O. B. 149
Driveline (training lab) 319
Dwivedi, Y. K. 247

E2PO *see* Energy Efficiency Programme Office
early childhood education and care (ECEC) 17, 33
EBP *see* evidence-based policymaking
ECEC *see* early childhood education and care
economic challenges 202
ecosystem(s) 129, 164
Edgertronic machine 319
EED *see* Energy Efficiency Directive
E-government initiatives 158
Electronic Public Procurement System (SECOP) 232
ELSA *see* ethical, legal, and social aspects
EMA *see* Energy Market Authority
emotions 82
employment
   hours per week worked 38
   LM keywords referring to types of 34
   openings topic 35
encryption 274
energy efficiency
   comprehensive policy frameworks for 93
   data and data-policy implications 95–102
   elements in policy design framework 94–5
   policy instruments 7
   in Singapore 102–6
Energy Efficiency Directive (EED) 102
Energy Efficiency Programme Office (E2PO) 103
Energy Market Authority (EMA) 103
energy service companies (ESCOs) 97
Energy Star program 99
Engstrom, D. F. 241
ENOLL *see* European Network of Living Labs
Environmental Protection Agency (EPA) 99
EOSC *see* European Union's Open Science Cloud
EPA *see* Environmental Protection Agency
e-petition 110–12
epistemic changes 199–202
epistemic injustice 328
equity perception modeling 166
Escobar Gutiérrez, E. 222
ESCOs *see* energy service companies
Estonia, data-driven government in 168–9
ethical/ethics in AI 247
   considerations 159–60
   management in governance 241
   washing 277
ethical, legal, and social aspects (ELSA) 66
ethnic bias in Chinese drug courts 300
Eubanks, Virginia 247, 326
European AI Act 381
European Commission, strategies or initiatives for government data 170
European Data Portal 170
European Harmonised Price Index (HICP) 65
European Network of Living Labs (ENOLL) 367
European Union (EU) 16, 65, 101, 266
   Data Governance Act 186
   High-Level Expert Group 180
European Union's Open Science Cloud (EOSC) 346
Eurostat 61
evidence-based decision-making 163
evidence-based policymaking (EBP) 3
ex ante 18, 47
experimental data governance, labs for 374
experimentalism 326
experimentation 320
expertization 184
explainability of systems 224, 226, 233, 235, 275, 308

Explainable Artificial Intelligence (XAI) 188, 247, 275 *see also* artificial intelligence (AI)
ex post career of laws 51
external validity of model 69–70

fab labs 365, 367–8
Facebook 17
   Facebook Messenger 207
   in Myanmar 304
facial recognition software 82
fairness 276
   data science research views 273–4
   digital governance research views 271–2
Fairness, Accountability, and Transparency-Machine Learning (FAT-ML) 271
Fairness, Accountability, and Transparency (FAT) 271
Faraj, S. 359
FAT-ML *see* Fairness, Accountability, and Transparency-Machine Learning
FAT *see* Fairness, Accountability, and Transparency
Fazekas, Mihály 6
federated learning 274
Feeney, M. K. 148
Filgueiras, Fernando 9
financial viability of energy efficiency programs 99
Fischer, F. 182
Fitbit 341
Fitbit Legal: Privacy Policy (2023) 337
Fitbit Watch and App 336–8
Flo.health App 338–40
Flórez Rojas, M. L. 222
Floridi, L. 247, 249–50
formal rules 349–51
Formulario Único de Reporte de Avances de Gestión (FURAG) 229
Foti, Joseph 10
framer 269
framework data policies 301
Friend, J. K. 78
Frog (advanced natural language processing suite) 20
Fundamental Principles of Official Statistics 60
Fung, A. 183
FURAG *see Formulario Único de Reporte de Avances de Gestión*
Fusi, Federica 11, 381

G20 Networked Devices Task Group 99
GaaP *see* government as a platform
Ganiz, M. C. 19
GANs *see* generative adversarial networks
Gansky, B. 182

gaps in global performance of critical data for public accountability 10
gaps of policy implementation 286
   collection gaps 286–7
   high-value data gaps 288
   publication gaps 287–8
   usability gaps 288–9
   use gaps 289
GARD *see* Guaranteeing AI Robustness and Deception
Gawer, A. 125, 128, 129, 137
GDB *see* Global Data Barometer
GDPR *see* General Data Protection Regulation
General Data Protection Regulation (GDPR) 65–6, 186, 273, 301, 305
generalized trust 350–51, 356–7, 359
generative adversarial networks (GANs) 273
Generative AI 148
generativity 126
   and control 128, 131–2
   development and improvement of data models 134
genomics data centers 361
geographic information system (GIS) 96
Geopolitical Risk Index 71
Ghamkhari, F. 78
Ghazawneh, A. 126
Giest, Sarah 11
Giles, P. 247
Gin, Willie 10–11
GIS *see* geographic information system
Global Initiative on Sharing All Influenza Data (GISAID) 346
Global Corruption Observatory project 48, 55
Global Data Barometer (GDB) 285
Golden Tax Project III (GTP III) 132–3
Golubchikov, Oleg 106
GoNetZero 98
Gong, Yiwei 7
Goodhart, Charles 151
Goodman, E. P. 224
government as a platform (GaaP) 130
government data, strategies or initiatives for framework for data science governance 167
   in post-pandemic context 162–4
   representative international cases of governance initiative 169–70
government/governance 266
   advanced data analytics deployment in 2–3
   AI in 2–3, 180–82, 239
   data 282–3
   effective governance of AI 239
   implications for 24–7
   intersection with 185, 190
   platforms 127

primary collaborators 269
of public institutions 239
studies 1, 2, 379
see also data governance; digital governance/government; participatory governance
Green, B. 242
greenhouse gas emissions 93, 102–3
Grimmelikhuijsen, S. 224
Grimmer, J. 45
GTP III see Golden Tax Project III
Guaranteeing AI Robustness and Deception (GARD) 274
Gutiérrez, Juan David 9, 222, 234, 235

Haataja, M. 224
Habermas, J. 332–3
Habermas theory 144
hackerspaces 367–8
Hagendorff, T. 247, 249
Hagen, L. 120
Haim, A. 241
Hamilton, Sil 300
Hanafizadeh, P. 78
Haney, M. H. 351
"Harder" OR techniques 75, 77
Hard Operational Research (Hard OR) 7
hard sciences 366
harm(s) 181, 305–6
　accountability 305–6
　collective 10, 299–300
　individual 10, 299
　potential 298–300
　realized 298–300
　reduction opportunities 300
　societal 10
Harrison, S. 147
Hashem, Youmna 8
Hayes, R. A. 142
HCR-20, 322
Head, B. 3
heat maps 275
Henfridsson, O. 126
Hermosilla, M. P. 233
Hickling, A. 78
Hickok, M. 241, 254
HICP see European Harmonised Price Index
hierarchical bureaucracy 126
high-value data
　elements 284–5
　gaps 288
Hill, Rich 320
Hinneburg, A. 20
Ho, Diandrea 7
Hoffmann-Rhiem, Wolfgang 300
homomorphic encryption 274

Horkheimer, M. 332–3
Household Budget Survey 64–5
household equivalence scales 64
Hou, Yue 300
Howlett, Michael 7
Hubner, John 324
human-centered competences, labs for integrating 373
human-human interactions 199
human-machine interactions 199
human oversight requirements 305
human resources 216
human rights
　impact assessments 304–5, 311
　law 301
Hungary, originators of legislation in 51
Hurst, B. 66
hybrid cloud providers 204, 205

IAD see institutional analysis and development; Institutional Analysis Framework
ICO see Information Commissioner's Office
ICT-centered social experiments 367
ICTs see information and communication technologies
identity
　common 351–2, 354, 356, 359, 360
　fraud 312
　theft 312
IEA see International Energy Agency
"I-Korea 4.0" 270
IMD see Index of Multiple Deprivation
impact assessments 10, 42, 303, 310
　algorithmic 304
　human rights 304–5, 311
Index of Multiple Deprivation (IMD) 118
individual harms 10, 299
industry platforms 125, 130
inferability of data 229, 233
information
　asymmetry 215, 270
　automation of 253
　on costs and licensing 232
　medical and personal 306
　novel 14–15
　right to information performance 285, 293
　source of information types of missing data 230–31
　transparency in government 295
information and communication technologies (ICTs) 158, 180, 366
Information Commissioner's Office (ICO) 189
information technology (IT) 97
infrastructure and AI 203–6

infringements of freedom of thought and association 306
Ingrams, Alex 241, 300
innovation labs 365, 367–8, 369–70
in-processing methodology 274
institutional
 analysis 182–3
 designs for AI in Latin America 206
  data colonialism 206
  national artificial intelligence strategies 207
  national strategy for artificial intelligence 208–13
  path dependence of technological development 214
  policy choices 215–16
 heterogeneity 201–2
 reconstruction 199–202
 rules and frameworks 183, 186–7
 transformations 201
institutional analysis and development (IAD) 9
Institutional Analysis Framework (IAD) 183
"intentional" practice 319
internal platforms 125, 129
internal validity of model 69–70
International Association of Privacy Professionals 303
International Energy Agency (IEA) 95, 105
Internet of Things (IoT) 96, 241, 272
interoperability 294
interoperability, labs for 374
interpretability 275
inverse document frequency techniques 294
IoT *see* Internet of Things
Irvin, R. A. 184
IT *see* information technology
IUIPC model *see* 'Users' Information Privacy Concerns' model

Janssen, Marijn 7
Jarvenpaa, S. L. 126
JCR index *see* Journal of Citation Report index
Jessop, W. N. 78
Jobin, A. 247, 249
Johnson, P. 147
Johnson, S. L. 359
Johnston, K. A. 66
Jordan, M. I. 20
Joshi, Divij 10
Journal of Citation Report index (JCR index) 243
justice and dispute resolution mechanisms 305
justice systems 214

Kantepe, M. 19
Kaplan, L. 242
Kapoor, K. 131

Keijdener, Darius 6
Kerr, A. D. 241
keyword occurrence analysis 243
Kiat, Tay Swee 7
Kim, I. S. 45
Kim, S. 371–2
Kirsch, L. J. 351
Kitchin, Rob 320
Klievink, Bram 11, 382
Klok, P. -J. 183–5
knowledge
 business 135
 object of 327
 societies 184
Köbis, N. 180
Ko, D. -G. 351
Konsynski, B. 126
Korea
 data government ecosystems in 170
 empirical understanding of government's role 269–70
Koshkin, A. P. 143
Kotterink, B. 372
Kreemers, D. 185
Krick, E. 184
Kroll, J. A. 247
Kwoka, Margaret B. 299

L2M *see* Lifelong Learning Machine
labification of public sector 368–71
labour market
 governance 6, 15
 as testing grounds 15
Labour Party 119
labs 371–2
 for experimental data governance, data sharing, and interoperability 374
 for integrating human-centered and data-centric competences 373
 lab-as-an-approach 365–6, 372, 375
 for trust in data and inclusive data governance 372–3
Lami, I. 78
land ownership and tenure 284, 291–2
land-scarce economy in Singapore 7
Lapostol, P. 233
large language models (LLMs) 28
latent Dirichlet allocation (LDA) 20–21, 116
Latin America
 AI and governance challenges in 202–16
 AI, epistemic changes, and institutional reconstruction 199–202
 future of Latin American governance and democracy 216–17
 specificities in 198

Latour, Bruno 366
Lauriault, Tracey P. 320
Law for Artificial Intelligence 214
Law on Disinformation on social networks 214
LDA *see* latent Dirichlet allocation
LDAvis 21
Lee, H. H. 242
Lee, Jae-Seong 10
Lee, M. 242
legibility 298, 316, 317
legislative favouritism 41–2
　application to 47
　case study on 46–7
　comprehensive mapping of legislative processes and outputs 47–8
　descriptive results for favouritism indicators across countries 51–5
　detecting and measuring 49
　indicators 49–51
Lemlijn, Pedro 6
lemmatisation 20
Leoni, Francesco 11
Lepri, B. 241
Levine, S. S. 361
Lewis, Michael 318
life course transitions 16, 17, 27, 28
Lifelong Learning Machine (L2M) 274
LIME *see* Local Interpretable Model-agnostic Explanations
Lim, H. S. M. 272
Lindbergh, Ben 319–20
Linders, D. 269
Lisbon Treaty 16
Living Data Hubs 373
"living lab" concept 11, 365–7
LLMs *see* large language models
LM keywords
　referring to employment types 34
　referring to general job search 34
　referring to policy 33
lobbying 285, 292–3
LobbyView 293
Local Interpretable Model-agnostic Explanations (LIME) 159, 275
Logius 340
Lomax, Nik 7, 120
López, J. 222
Loukis, E. 147
lurkers 348

machine learning (ML) 44, 59, 69, 181
　algorithms 200
　interpretability techniques 159
　models 82
macro-task crowdsourcing 86

makerspaces 367–8
Malabo Convention 301
Manana, T. 241
Manheim, K. 242
Mannhardt, F. 2
Margetts, H. 180
Markus, M. L. 351
Maslej, N. 241, 254
Mcdonald, S. 182
McMahan, B. 247
"meaningful algorithmic transparency" 224
meaningfulness 230, 233
Meijer, A. J. 152
member interdependence 349–50, 358
Mergel, I. 149
Messing, S. 45
Meta 207, 216
metadata maximalism 182
Methods for Inclusion project 188
Mexico
　data government ecosystems in 170
　strategies or initiatives for government data 169–70
MiData program 270
MindLab 371
Mineshima-Lowe, Dale 11
Ministry of Information and Communication Technologies (MinTIC) 227–8
Misuraca, G. 240
Mitchell, William 366
Mittelstadt, B. D. 241, 247, 249
ML *see* machine learning
'Mobile Users' Privacy Concerns' model (MUIPC model) 334
mobilizer 269, 270
model-agnostic post-hoc method 275
modular architecture 126, 131, 136
modularity 126
model-specific post-hoc method 275
Moneyball (Lewis) 318–19
Moneyball 1.0, 319
Moneyball 2.0, 319
monitoring in citizen-government partnerships 269
Montreal declaration 247
Morgan, Deborah 8
Morley, J. 249
Moss, David 46
MUIPC model *see* 'Mobile Users' Privacy Concerns' model
Mukherjee, Ishani 4, 7
Muñoz-Cadena, Sarah 9, 234
MVP Machine (Lindbergh and Sawchik) 319–20, 325
MyHEAT digital platform 98

NACE codes 70
Nafus, D. 182
Nagtegaal, R. 241
Nambisan, S. 126
Nandiyanto, A. B. D. 243
Nanyang Technological University (NTU) 103–4
National Accounts System 165
national artificial intelligence strategies 207
National Digital Twin program 181
National Environment Agency (NEA) 103
National Institute for Health Research Greater Manchester Patient Safety Translational Research Centre 189
national statistics institute (NSI) 61
National Transparency System (SNT) 170
natural language processing 96, 293–4
NEA *see* National Environment Agency
"needs scale" 322
Neighbourhood Watch in UK 188–9
Netherlands
    adopters of social investment policies 17–18
    Authority for Consumers and Markets 67
New Public Management (NPM) 370
New Zealand, data-driven government in 169
Ng, A. Y. 20
NGOs *see* non-governmental organisations
NHS Group 119
NMF *see* Non-negative Matrix Factorization
Noain-Sánchez, A. 261
non-governmental organisations (NGOs) 43, 145
non-intrusive load monitoring 96
Non-negative Matrix Factorization (NMF) 20, 23
non-neutrality 148
Non-Violent Risk Assessment (NVRA) 322
novel information 14–15
NPM *see* New Public Management
NSI *see* national statistics institute
NTU *see* Nanyang Technological University
NVRA *see* Non-Violent Risk Assessment

OASI *see* Observatory of Algorithms with Social Impact
Obama-era Presidential Policy Directive 19, 309
Obermeyer, Ziad 247
objectivity 275
Observatory of Algorithms with Social Impact (OASI) 225
OCDS *see* Open Contracting Data Standard
OECD *see* Organisation for Economic Co-operation and Development
OGP *see* Open Government Partnership
Oladinrin, O. T. 254
omnibus laws 53
O'Neil, Cathy 323
Oomens, Jolien 6

open communities 346–7, 349–50, 361–2
open contracting 292
Open Contracting Data Standard (OCDS) 292
open data 282, 294, 380–81
    asset disclosure 283, 284, 290, 292, 295
    channels for action 295
    company beneficial ownership 291
    data by policy area 289–90
    elements 284
    global survey of key governance data 285–6
    high-value data elements 284–5
    infrastructures 41
    interoperability 294
    key gaps of policy implementation 286–9
    land ownership and tenure 291–2
    lobbying 292–3
    maturity by policy area 287
    open governance data 283
    political finance 290–91
    public procurement 292
    right to information performance 293
    rulemaking 293–4
    transparency into accountability 295
    see also responsible data
"Open Data" platform 227, 229
open government
    data policy 163
    platforms 130
    regulatory approaches 300
Open Government Partnership (OGP) 285, 296
open innovation 367
openness 125, 126, 130–31, 183–4, 188
Operational Research (OR) 75–7, 380
opinion mining 86
opinion model 141, 151–2
opt-in consent 311
OR *see* Operational Research
Organisation for Economic Co-operation and Development (OECD) 16, 42, 43, 249, 267
organizational/organizations 349
    algorithmization of bureaucratic organizations 217
    organizational forms 125, 128–30
Ostrom, Elinor 183
outsourcing databases 265
"OV-chipkaart" 65

P2P data *see* peer-to-peer data
Paletti, A. 129, 137
Panagiotopoulos, P. 147, 149
panoptic sorting 317
Papadopoulos, Y. 182–3
'parenthood to employment' transition 17
participatory governance 9
    of AI 179, 185–90, 187

dimensions of 182–5
    see also digital governance/government
participatory/participation
    approaches 182
    budgeting 184
    institution 183
    methods 186
    participatory data stewardship' report 186
    resources 347–8
Pasquale, F. 247, 249, 255
passive transparency 225
Patel, V. 243
path dependence of technological development in Latin America 214
"Pay as You Save" schemes 99
peer-to-peer data (P2P data) 334
Peixoto, T. 282
performance model of social media monitoring 8, 141, 150–51
period poverty 114
personalization 265–6
    algorithms 265
    service 242
Piotrowski, Suzanne 300
Piper, Andrew 300
PIS *see* privacy impact statements
Pix in Brazil 205
PlaceLab 367
policy
    analysis 75–7
    capacity of government 4
    choices 215–16
    design comparison 105–6
    design orientation 93
    instruments 201
    labs 365
    policy-relevant insights 4, 6
    portfolios 94
    recommendations 384
    strategies for AI in Latin America 198, 214
policymaking 75
    behavioral aspects of 4
    Big Data in 79–80
    implications for 24–7
    operational research and policy analysis 75–7
    potential of Soft OR as aid to 77–9
Pol.is (open-source online platform) 189
political
    accountability 6
    challenges 202
    finance 284, 290–91
    instability in Argentina 207
    institutions
        data availability and accessibility of 42–4

data science and implications for study of 44–5
    large-scale micro-data to study 47–55
    political-strategic approach 144–5
    uncertainties in Argentina 207
Portugal, originators of legislation in 51
Porumbescu, G. 148
post-hoc method 275
post-pandemic context, data governance initiatives in 161–6
post-processing methodology 274
potential harms 298–300
Potjer, S. 152
pre-policy-making 84
pre-processing
    data 18–19
    method 19–22, 273
Predpol 322
preference elicitation 184–5, 189–90
Price, W. N. 247
Prietula, M. J. 361
Principale, S. 244
principle coordinates analysis 26–7
Pring, Catherine 306
Pring, George William 306
prison cells 323
privacy 10, 299
    in AI deployment 239
    in AI ethics 272
    exemptions 309
    paradox 334
    perception 240
    protection methods 274
privacy impact statements (PIS) 304
privacy puzzle decoding 239
    analysis of results 246–54
    data sampling 244
    future research questions 255–7, 256
    limitations 258
    methodology 243–6
    published articles in Wos 244
    sample description 244–6
    theoretical framework 241–3
private cloud providers 204, 205
'private' sphere 332
proactive algorithmic transparency 222
    methodology and data 225–7
    in public sector 223–5
    transparency of public algorithms in Colombia 227–32
    see also transparency
"proactive disclosure of information" principle 227–8
proactive transparency 222, 225
problem structuring methods (PSMs) 76, 78, 80

promotion resources 347–8, 359
property rights, structural imbalances in 9
prosumers 101
provider of last resort 269
PSA *see* Public Safety Assessment
PSI labs *see* public sector innovation labs
PSMs *see* problem structuring methods
public
   accountability 298
   agencies 179, 181
   cloud providers 204, 205
   document repositories 350
   goods 10, 282, 299–300
   institutions 239–40
   interest standing 306
   oversight 298
   participation 370–71
   procurement 284, 292
   public-private partnerships 268
   services 124
   sphere 332
   trust in AI systems 241
public administrations 2, 179, 241
   AI in government and 180–82
   challenges 147–9
   citizen consideration 146–7
   implementation of social media monitoring in 144
   orientations and outcomes 144–5
   tools and evidence 145–6
public algorithms in Colombia
   data about results or performance of ADM system 231
   database of ADM systems in Colombian public sector 230
   information on costs and licensing 232
   repositories of public algorithms 222, 225, 227–30
   source of information types of missing data 230–31
   used data 232
publication gaps 287–8
public policy
   cycle 200
   data regimes in 322–7
Public Safety Assessment (PSA) 322
public sector
   conceptualizing social media monitoring in 142–4
   potential models of social media monitoring in 149–54
   social media monitoring in 142–4
public sector innovation labs (PSI labs) 365, 368, 374

   implications for practice and real-life examples 372–4
   labification of public sector 368–71
   labs and data-driven innovation in 371–2
   literature review 366–71
Pulse Lab Jakarta 373
pyLDAvis 21

quantitative data anaysis 361

Radio Frequency Identification (RFID) 65
ranking algorithm 316
rational-instrumental approach 144
rationalization 298
ready availability of quality data 4
Reaktor 188
realized harms 298–300
recidivism 323–5
   failure to prevention 328
   prediction in criminal justice system 181, 322
   rates in juvenile detention programs 324–5
   risk calculation 323
   risk of youth 325
reconfigurability 124
reduction 298
   bias reduction algorithms 166
   carbon reductions 26
   dimensionality reduction 25, 26, 113
relational social capital 350–51, 356–7
   cognitive social capital, relationship with 354, 357
   structural social capital, relationship with 358–9
remedies 306
renewable energy 95
Ren, Y. 348
Report to the Nations 309
repositories of public algorithms 222, 225, 227–30
Repositorio Algoritmos Públicos *see* repositories of public algorithms
research agenda 381–3
resocialization 324
responsibility in AI ethics 272
responsible data
   accountability measures 303–9
   basic frameworks 301–3
   big data and data-driven policymaking 298
   disclosure and transparency regimes 310–12
   open government regulatory approaches 300
   potential and realized harms 298–300
Reyes, Linda 324
Reyman, J. 335
RFID *see* Radio Frequency Identification
Ribeiro-Navarrete, S. 241

Richardson, R. 223
Rieke, Aaron 307
right to information performance 285, 293
risk assessment 303
Rittel, Horst 76
Robinson, David 283, 307
robotic process automation (RPA) 222–3
Röder, M. 20
role-based control 131
Rory Truex 300
Rose, Kristen 10
RPA *see* robotic process automation
rulemaking 285, 293–4
'rules in use' of participatory governance arenas 183
Ryan, M. 190
Ryghaug, M. 102

Sætra, H. S. 241
safeguards 5, 300, 303–5, 380, 382, 384
Safeland in Sweden 189
safety in AI ethics 272
SAIL-ON *see* Science of AI and Learning for Open-World Novelty
sanctions for non-compliance 295
Sandoval-Almazan, Rodrigo 8
SARS-CoV-2, 8
Saura, Jose Ramon 9, 241, 255
Saveliev, A. 241
Sawchik, Travis 319–20
Scandinavian participatory design movement 367
Scandinavian penal system 323
Scharp, K. 241
Schiff, D. S. 255
Science of AI and Learning for Open-World Novelty (SAIL-ON) 274
scientific data centers 11
scientific lab 365
SDGs *see* Sustainable Development Goals
SECOP *see* Electronic Public Procurement System
Selbst, A. D. 247
selection bias 272
self-employment 39
semantic space models 26
sensitivity analysis 27
sentiment analysis 86
service accountability 128–30
Services Producer Price Index (SPPI) 65
several evidentiary bases 3
SHAP *see* SHapley Additive exPlanations
shaping resources 347–8, 360
SHapley Additive exPlanations (SHAP) 159, 275
shell companies 291
Sherpa (search engine) 334, 343

Shin, D. 249
simulation in AI systems 180–81, 361
Singapore
    data-driven government in 169
    strategies or initiatives for government data 169
Singapore Green Plan (2030) 103
Singapore Power (SP) 105
Singh, U. 243
SINOBAS network 152
SIP *see* Social Investment Package
SLE *see* Super Low Energy
SLO *see* social licence to operate
Slobogin, Christopher 323
smart cities 240, 241, 269
smart contracts 205
"smart homes" environments 366
"SMART OR" 83–4
smartphones and apps 96
Smith, H. J. 333
SMOTE *see* synthetic minority oversampling technique
SNT *see* National Transparency System
social capital 11, 346–7
    cognitive 351–2, 356
    community-level 361
    data centers 204, 346, 352–4
        cognitive and relational social capital relationship 354, 357
        cognitive and structural social capital relationship 357–8
        structural and relational social capital relationship 358–9
    perspective to open community sustainability 348–52
    relational 350–51, 356–7
    structural 349–50, 355
    to sustainability resources 359–60
    sustainable open communities 347–8
    theoretical approach to 352
social investment as analytical perspective 16–17
Social Investment Package (SIP) 16
social labs 368
social licence 66
social licence to operate (SLO) 66–7
social media
    data as potential solution 17–18
    monitoring 8, 141
        implementation in public administrations 144–9
        potential models in public sector 149–54
    in public sector 142–4
    platforms 214
social norms 350
Social Tension Indicator 71

social welfare 326–7
societal challenges 202
societal harms 10
society demanding innovation 61
sociological surveys 143
SODA *see* Strategic Options Development and Analysis
Soft Operational Research (Soft OR) 5, 7, 75
　advantages of combining with Big Data 83–7
　cognitive biases in training datasets 82
　criticism of Big Data 81–2
　dealing with qualitative "truths" 82
　emergence of 76–7
　interactions between difficult emotions 82
　lack of ability to account for values 82
　problems with application to policy problems 80–81
　problems with Big Data application to policy analysis 81
Soft OR *see* Soft Operational Research
Soft Systems Methodology (SSM) 78
Sorensen, K. H. 102
South Korean AI Ethics Guidelines 270
SP *see* Singapore Power
Spain, data government ecosystems in 171
specific life course transition and policies 19
SPEI-Codi in Mexico 205
SPI in Colombia 205
sponsorship 269
SPPI *see* Services Producer Price Index
SSM *see* Soft Systems Methodology
STA *see* State Taxation Administration
Standaert, W. 126
standards-based accountability 308
Stansbury, J. 184
State Taxation Administration (STA) 132
statistical capacity 4
statistical information, demand for 72
Statistics Netherlands 65–6, 70
STM *see* Structural Topic Model
Strategic Choice Approach 78, 79
strategic integration of digital technologies and AI 9–10
Strategic Options Development and Analysis (SODA) 78
stratified sampling 273
Straub, Vincent J. 8
Strøm, K. 46
structural imbalances in property rights 9
structural power dynamics 215
structural social capital 349–50, 355
　cognitive social capital, relationship with 357–8
　relational social capital, relationship with 358–9

Structural Topic Model (STM) 20, 23
Styrin, E. 164
subject access report 311
Super Low Energy (SLE) 103
supply chain platforms 125, 130
surveillance capitalism 240, 255, 317
Susanto, H. 241
Sustainable Development Goals (SDGs) 226
sustainable open communities 346–8
synthetic minority oversampling technique (SMOTE) 273
systems for detecting deviations by public servants, of Union General-Comptroller 214

tabula rasa 106
Taddeo, M. 247
Taeihagh, A. 272
targeted record swapping 62
Tavella, E. 78
term-topic matrix 20
text-as-data methods 55
text-based ML models 70
Tilson, D. 136
tipsters 309
Tiwana, A. 126
Tõnurist, P. 371
topic
　coherence measure 26
　model 22–3
　topic-document matrix 20
　Topic filter in WoS 244
traceability 308
Transfer365 in El Salvador 205
transformative data regimes 10–11
transparency 130–31, 149, 222, 276, 295, 298
　in AI 234
　data science research views 275
　demand for 72
　digital governance research views 272–3
　government information 295
　open data 283
　principle of 227
　public algorithms in Colombia 227–32
　transparency-as-a-right 273
　"transparency rush" 41
　see also proactive algorithmic transparency
Transparency Watch Platform and Apps 336
"Trustworthy AI Strategy" 270
Twitters Streaming API 18

unemployment 15, 37
United Kingdom (UK)
　in cost of living crisis 109
　Data Ethics Framework 302
　e-petition platform 113–14

originators of legislation in 51
United States of America (USA)
　e-petition in 120
　　Lobbying Disclosure Act (1995) 45
　　National Science Foundation 346
　　strategies/initiatives for government data 170
unsupervised approach 14–15, 19–20
unsupervised classification algorithm 113
urban development 99
Urbanite project (2021) 186
usability gaps 288–9
use gaps 289
user content 334
user data 142, 334
user innovation 367
'Users' Information Privacy Concerns' model (IUIPC model) 334
Ushahidi open-source software 336, 343

VAEs *see* variational autoencoders
Valderrama, M. 224, 234
Valle-Cruz, David 8, 146
van der Aalst, W. 1–2
Vandewal, Eveline 6
van Noordt, C. 240
van 't Boveneind, Koen 6
Van Twist, A. 269
van Veenstra, A. F. 372
Vargas Leal, J. 222
variational autoencoders (VAEs) 273
Verhulst, S. G. 4
Victor system of the Federal Supreme Court 214
Vidgen, B. 113, 115
Villodre, Julián 8
Vinnova agency 373
Violence Risk Appraisal Guide (VRAG) 322
virtual audits 96
virtual buildings/digital twin cities 96
Virtual Gothenburg Lab 373
visibility of transparency 229, 233
Visser, S. S. 185
Vlados, C. 158
volume, velocity, variety and veracity (4 Vs) 79
VOSviewer software 243
VRAG *see* Violence Risk Appraisal Guide
vTaiwan platform 189–90
Vydra, Simon 6, 380, 382

Waag 186
Wachter, S. 247, 249
Wang, X. 243
Waples, Gregory 299
WAR *see* wins above replacement

Ward, J. H.
　D hierarchical classification 115
　technique 113
Warin, P. 182–3
"Watson–Machine Learning" system 232
Weather Amateurs 152
web
　search and analytics 97
　web-scraping techniques 67
　Web 2.0 79
　Web 3.0 70
Web of Sciences (WoS) 240
　categories and percentage of records and article citations 246
　citations and articles per year in 245
　published articles in 244
Welch, Eric 11, 381
Wen, C. H. R. 242
Wesselink, A. 3
Westwood, S. 45
whistleblower
　protection 10, 309
　report on cases of abuse 295
White, L. 83, 84
wicked problems 76, 86
Widder, D. G. 182
Wilkinson, C. 184
Willems, J. 240
Williamson, B. 371
willingness to experiment with experimental approaches 370
wins above replacement (WAR) 318
Winter, J. S. 239
Wirtz, B. W. 254
wisdom of the crowds 152
Wong, Janis 8
Woodard, C. J. 126
Woolgar, Steve 366
WoS *see* Web of Sciences
Wukich, C. 146–7
Wu, X. 4

XAI *see* Explainable Artificial Intelligence

Yang, L. 247
Yasseri, T. 113, 115
Yearworth, M. 83, 84
Yoo, Y. 126
Yu, H. 283

Zhu, L. 254
Zhurenkov, D. 241
Zuboff, S. 247